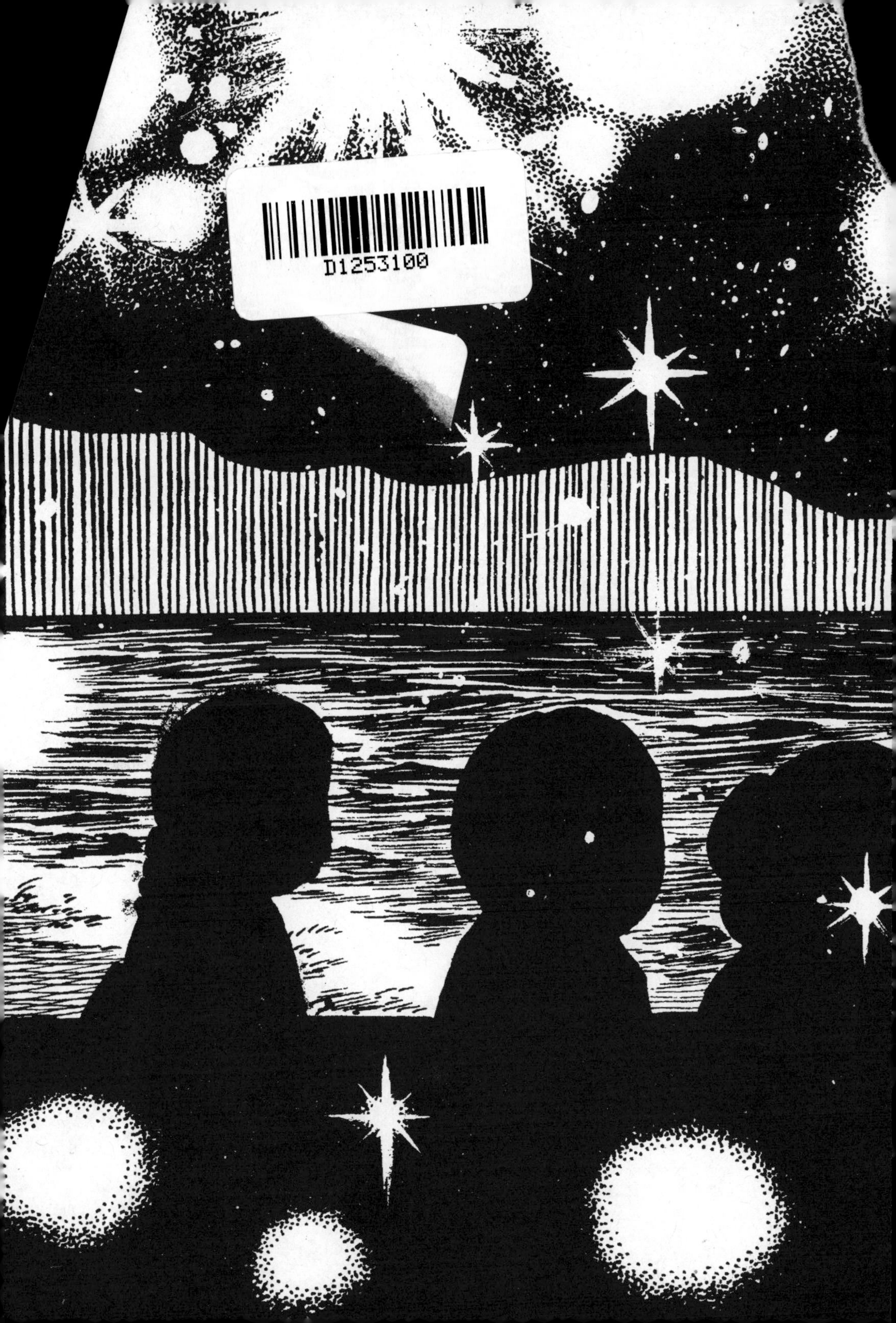

THIS BOOK
IS A GIFT FROM
THE
SMALL PRESS EXPO
WWW.SPXPO.COM / SPX.TUMBLR.COM
ART BY KALI CIESEMIER

ALSO BY SHIGERU MIZUKI

Onward Towards Our Noble Deaths (2011)

Story and art copyright © 2012 Shigeru Mizuki/Mizuki Productions. Afterword copyright © 2012 Kimie Imura. Translation copyright © 2012 Jocelyne Allen. This edition copyright © 2012 Drawn & Quarterly. All rights reserved. No part of this book (except small portions for review purposes) may be reproduced in any form without written permission from Shigeru Mizuki/ Mizuki Productions or Drawn & Quarterly. Originally published as *NonNonBa to Ore* in 1977.

Font design: Kevin Huizenga. Production assistance: Dana Centeno, Robin Clugston, Dani Farmer, Clara Johansson, Marie-Jade Menni, and Shannon Tien. Drawn & Quarterly acknowledges the financial contribution of the Government of Canada through the Canada Book Fund for our publishing activities and for support of this edition. Drawn & Quarterly also gratefully acknowledges Presspop Inc. and Maki Hakui for their invaluable assistance with the publication of this book.

www.drawnandquarterly.com.

Drawn & Quarterly, Post Office Box 48056, Montréal, Quebec, Canada H2V 4S8.

First softcover edition: April 2012. Printed in Canada. 10 9 8 7 6 5 4 3 2 1. Library and Archives Canada Cataloguing in Publication; Mizuki, Shigeru, 1922–; *NonNonBa* / Shigeru Mizuki. ISBN 978-1-77046-072-0; 1. *Yokai* (Japanese folklore)—Comic books, strips, etc. I. Title. PN6790.J33M5913 2012   741.5'952   C2011-907514-8.

Distributed in the United States by Farrar, Straus & Giroux, 18 West 18th Street, New York, NY 10011; Orders: 888.330.8477. Distributed in Canada by Raincoast Books, 2440 Viking Way, Richmond, BC V6V 1N2; Orders: 800.663.5714. Distributed in the United Kingdom by Publishers Group UK, 8 The Arena, Mollison Avenue, Enfield, Middlesex EN3 7NL; Orders: 0208.804.0400.

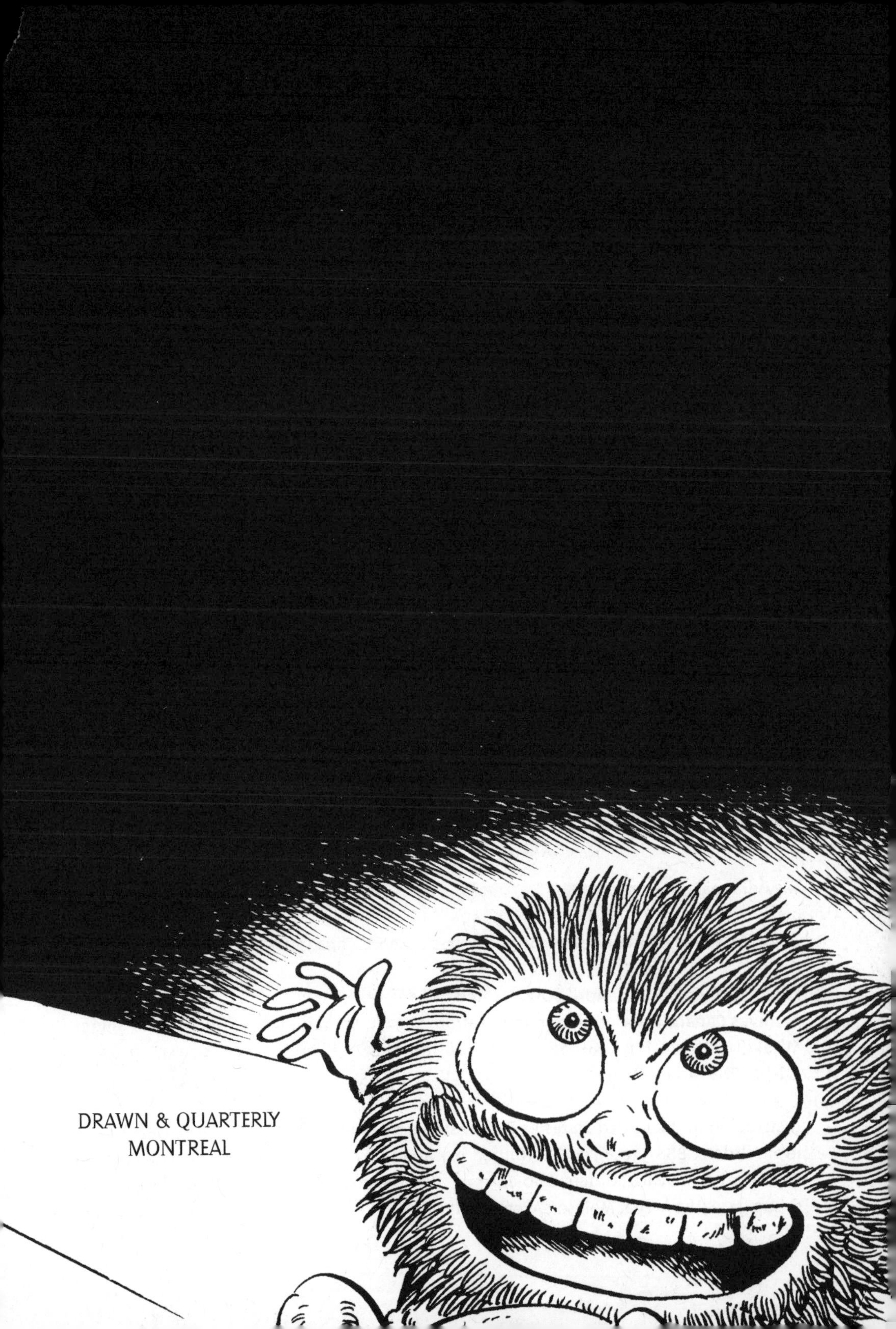

DRAWN & QUARTERLY
MONTREAL

Shigeru Mizuki

NONNONBA

TRANSLATION BY
JOCELYNE ALLEN

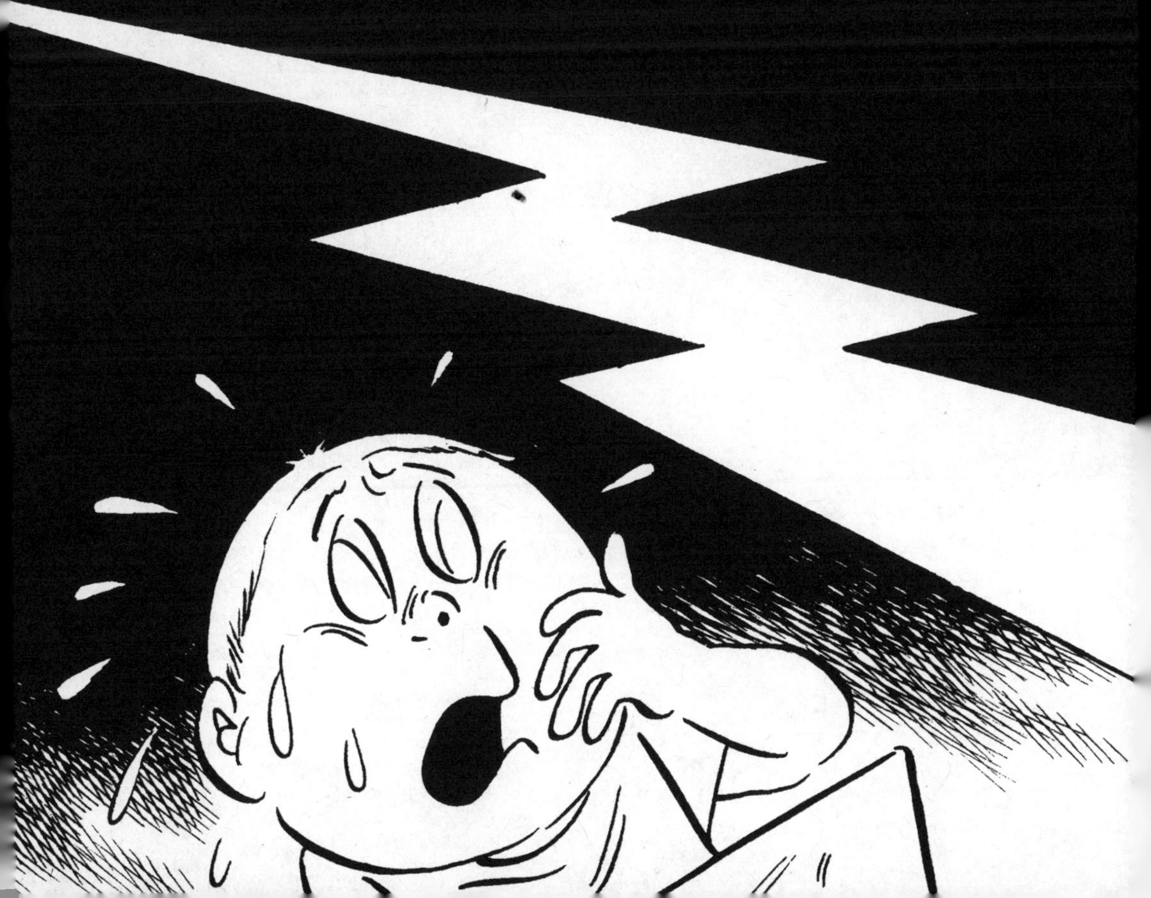

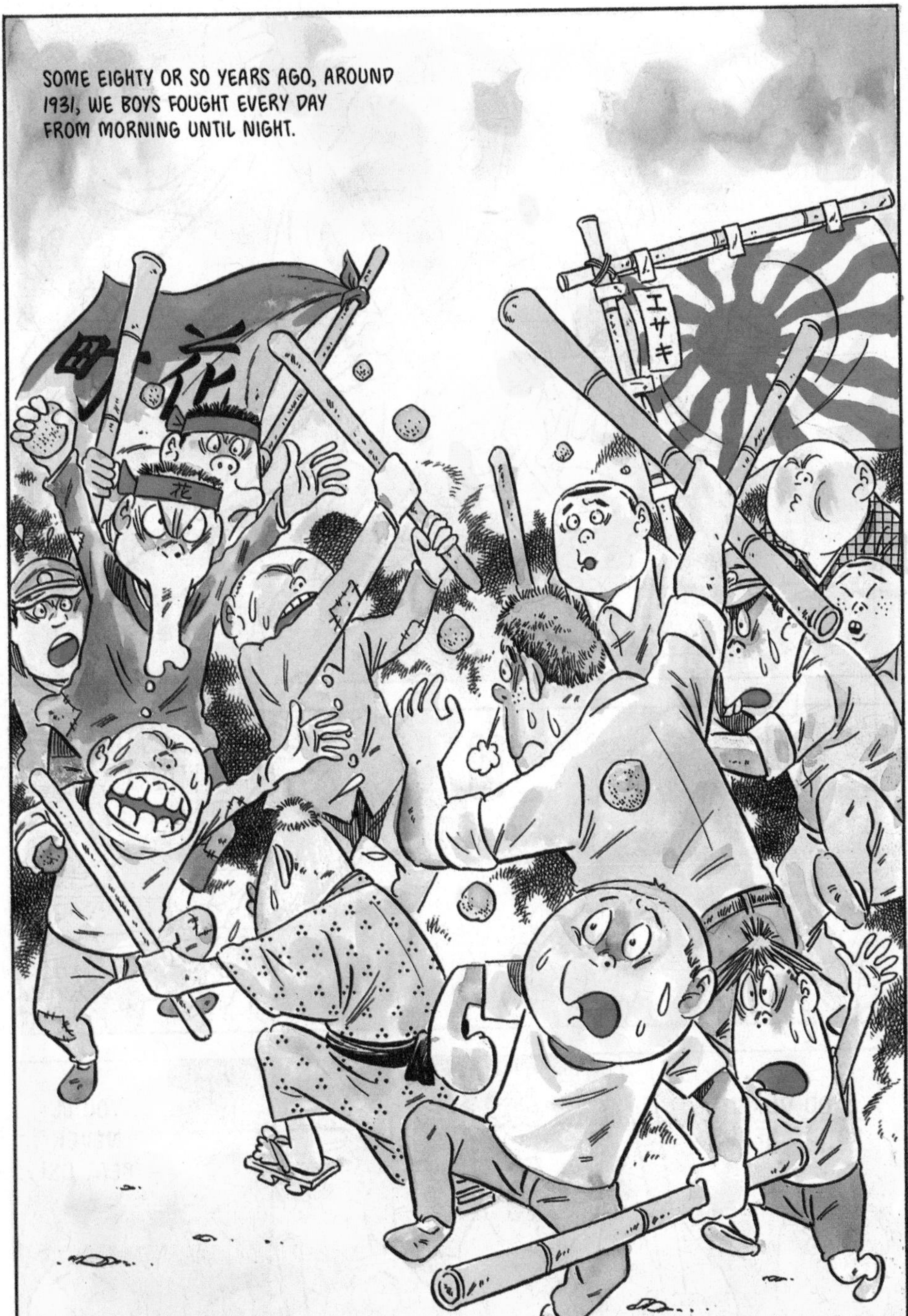
SOME EIGHTY OR SO YEARS AGO, AROUND 1931, WE BOYS FOUGHT EVERY DAY FROM MORNING UNTIL NIGHT.
花町
花
エサキ

FLAGS (RIGHT TO LEFT): HANAMACHI; ESAKI. BANDANA: HANA. (ALL NAMES OF NEIGHBORHOODS.)

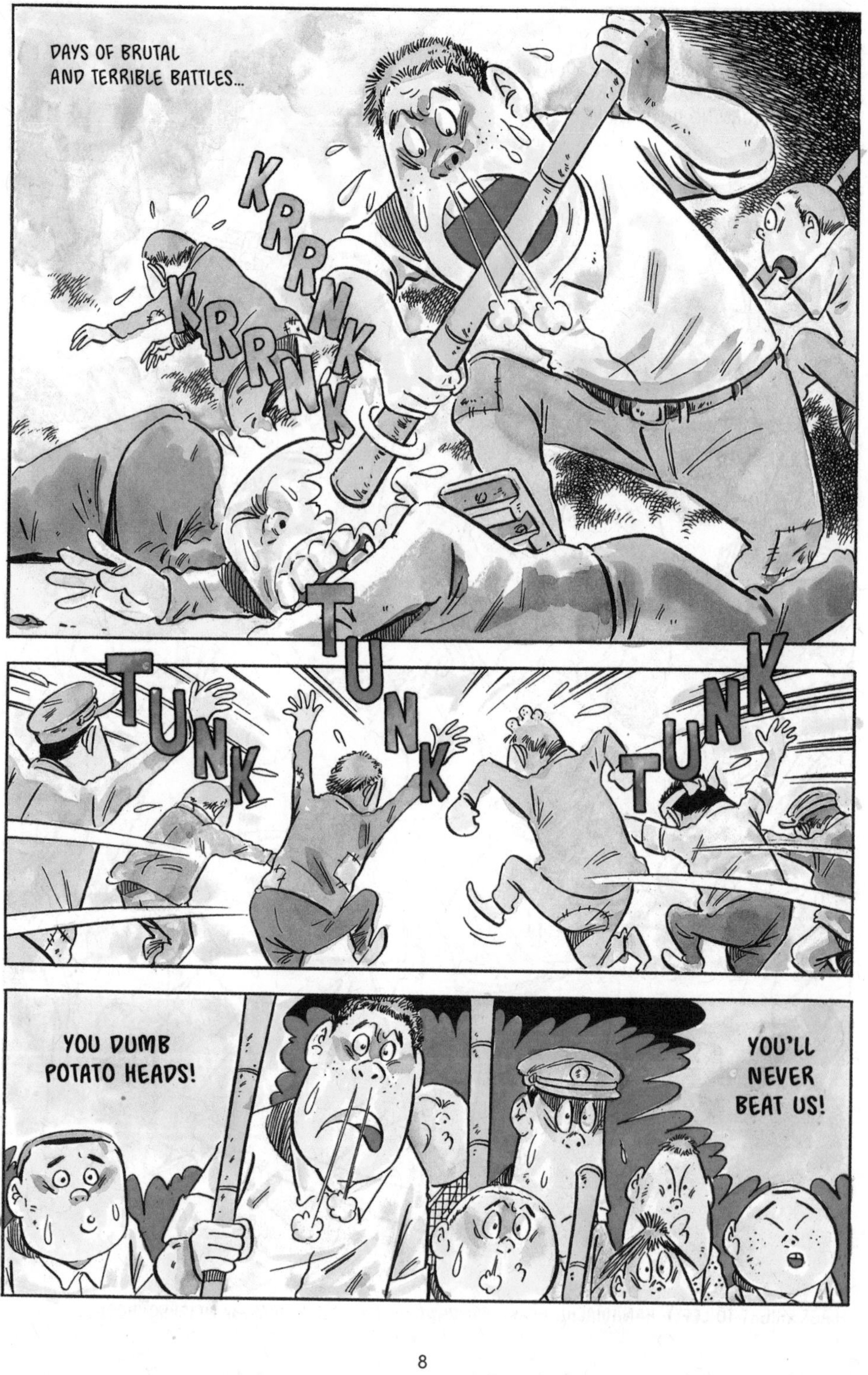
DAYS OF BRUTAL AND TERRIBLE BATTLES...
KRRNK
KRRNK
TUNK
TUNK
TUNK
YOU'LL NEVER BEAT US!
YOU DUMB POTATO HEADS!

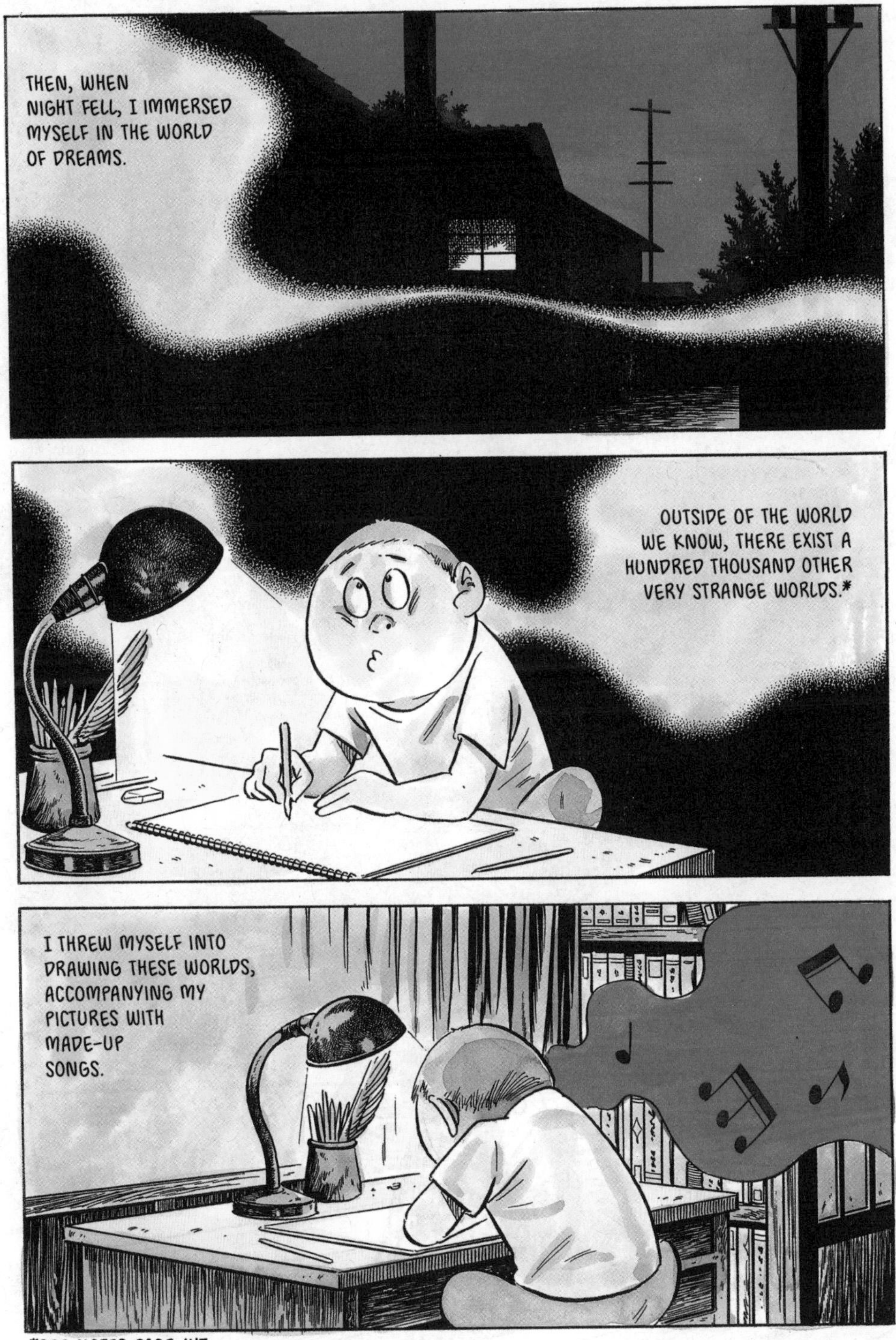
THEN, WHEN NIGHT FELL, I IMMERSED MYSELF IN THE WORLD OF DREAMS.
OUTSIDE OF THE WORLD WE KNOW, THERE EXIST A HUNDRED THOUSAND OTHER VERY STRANGE WORLDS.*
I THREW MYSELF INTO DRAWING THESE WORLDS, ACCOMPANYING MY PICTURES WITH MADE-UP SONGS.

*SEE NOTES PAGE 417.

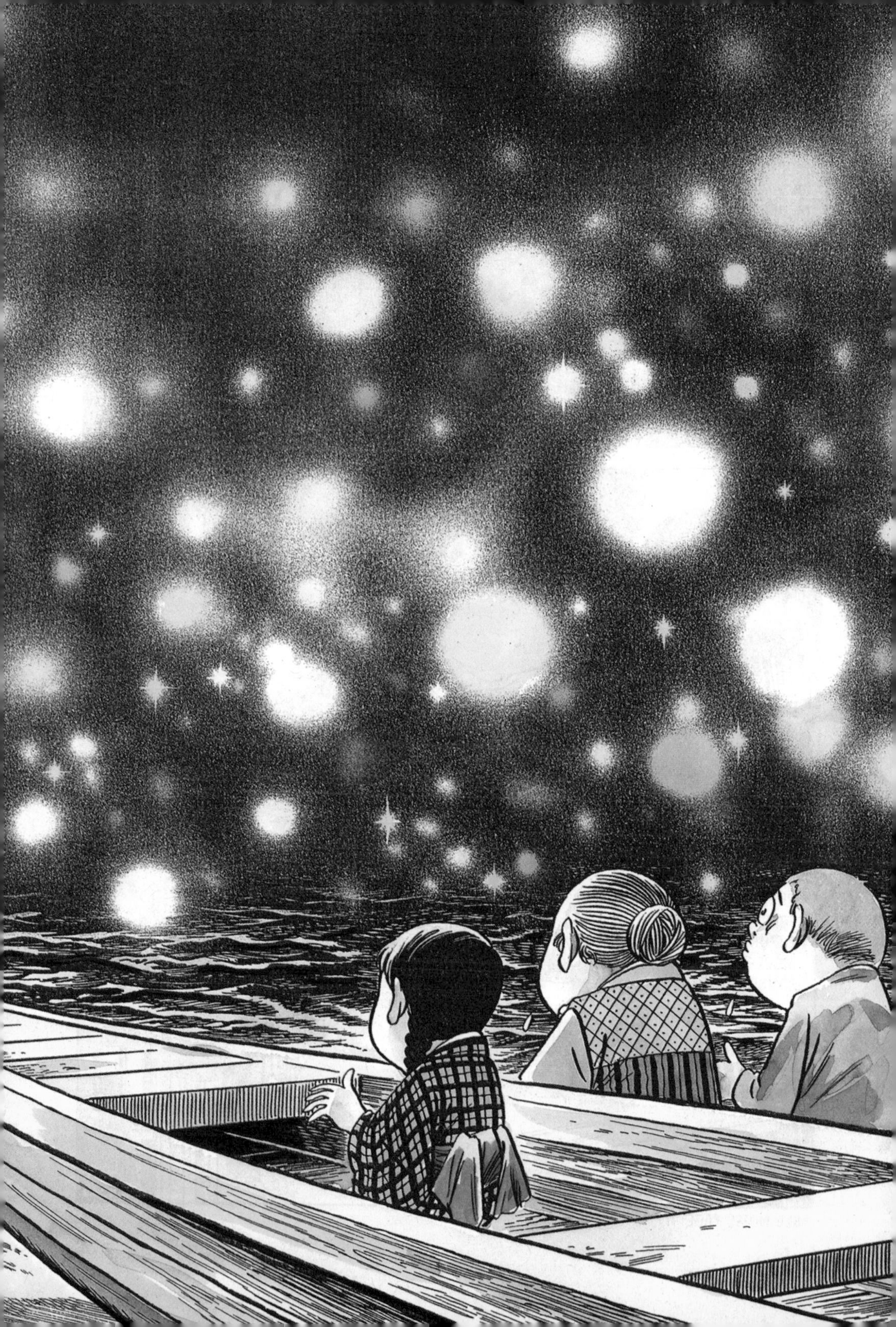

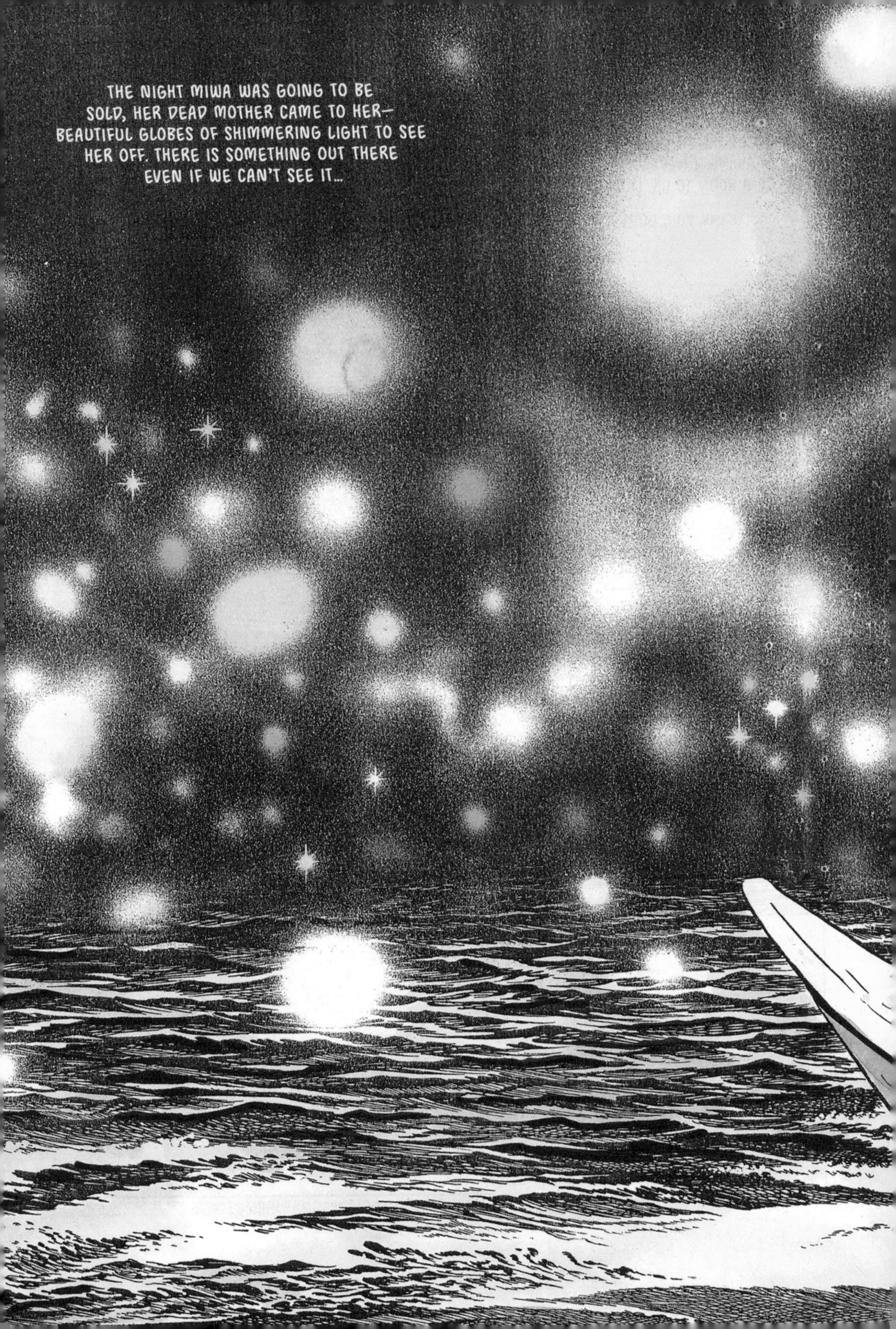
THE NIGHT MIWA WAS GOING TO BE SOLD, HER DEAD MOTHER CAME TO HER— BEAUTIFUL GLOBES OF SHIMMERING LIGHT TO SEE HER OFF. THERE IS SOMETHING OUT THERE EVEN IF WE CAN'T SEE IT...

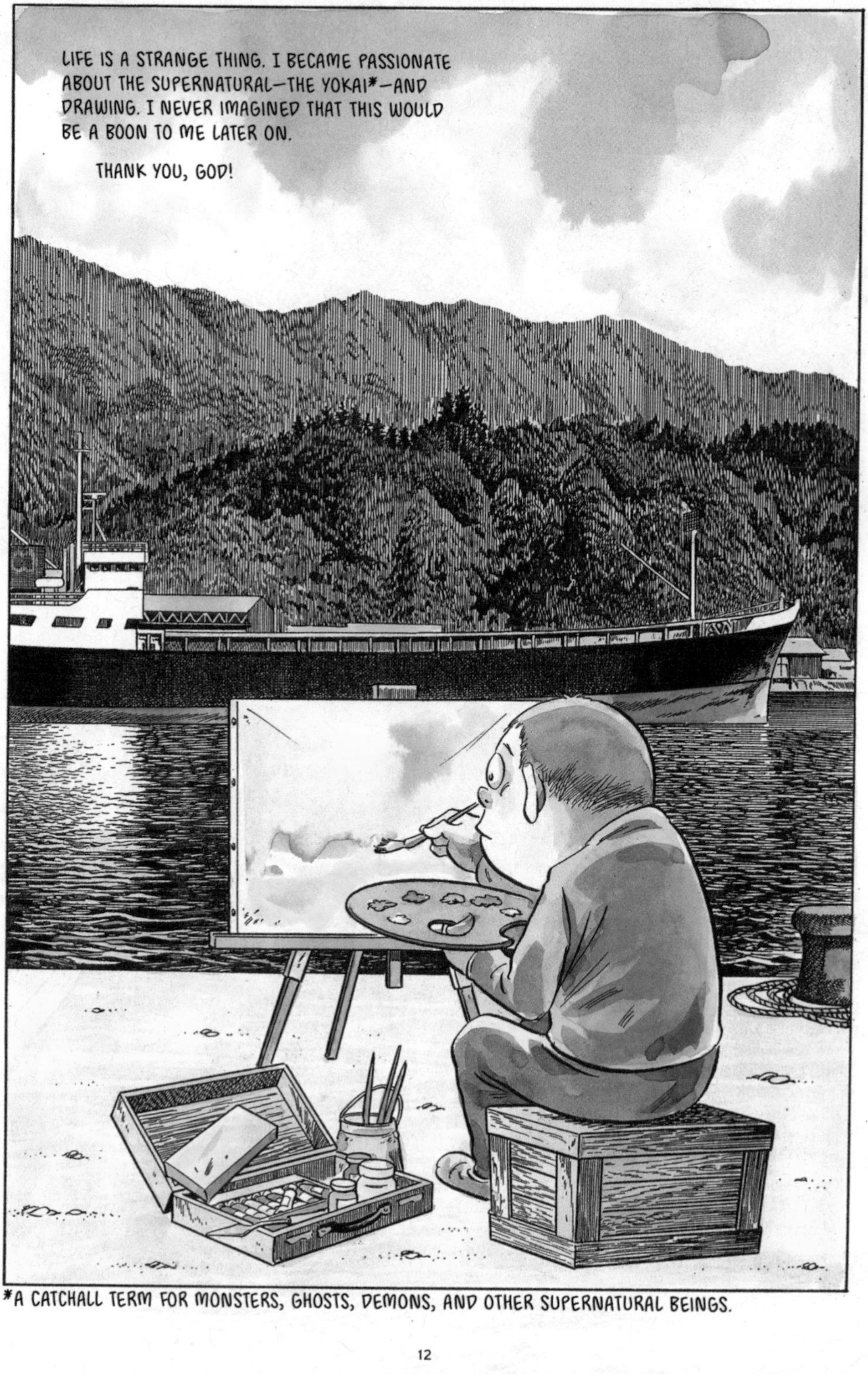
LIFE IS A STRANGE THING. I BECAME PASSIONATE ABOUT THE SUPERNATURAL—THE YOKAI*—AND DRAWING. I NEVER IMAGINED THAT THIS WOULD BE A BOON TO ME LATER ON.
THANK YOU, GOD!

*A CATCHALL TERM FOR MONSTERS, GHOSTS, DEMONS, AND OTHER SUPERNATURAL BEINGS.

NONNONBA AND HER HUSBAND

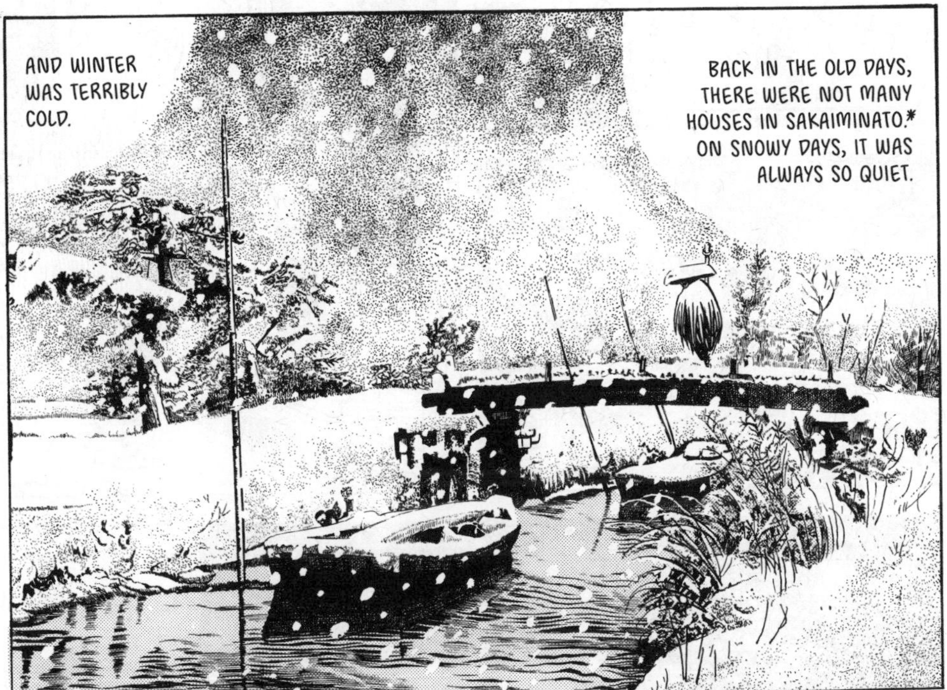
BACK IN THE OLD DAYS, THERE WERE NOT MANY HOUSES IN SAKAIMINATO.* ON SNOWY DAYS, IT WAS ALWAYS SO QUIET.
AND WINTER WAS TERRIBLY COLD.

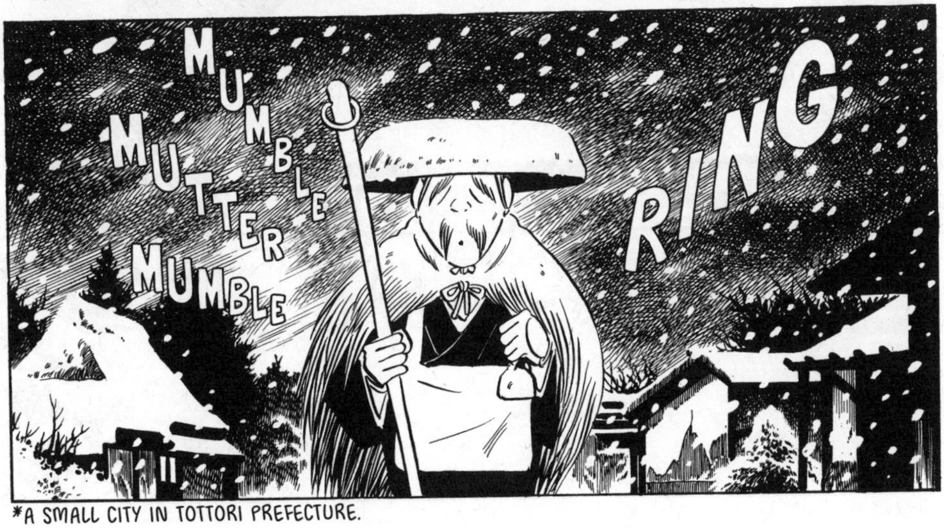
RING
MUMBLE
MUTTER
MUMBLE

*A SMALL CITY IN TOTTORI PREFECTURE.

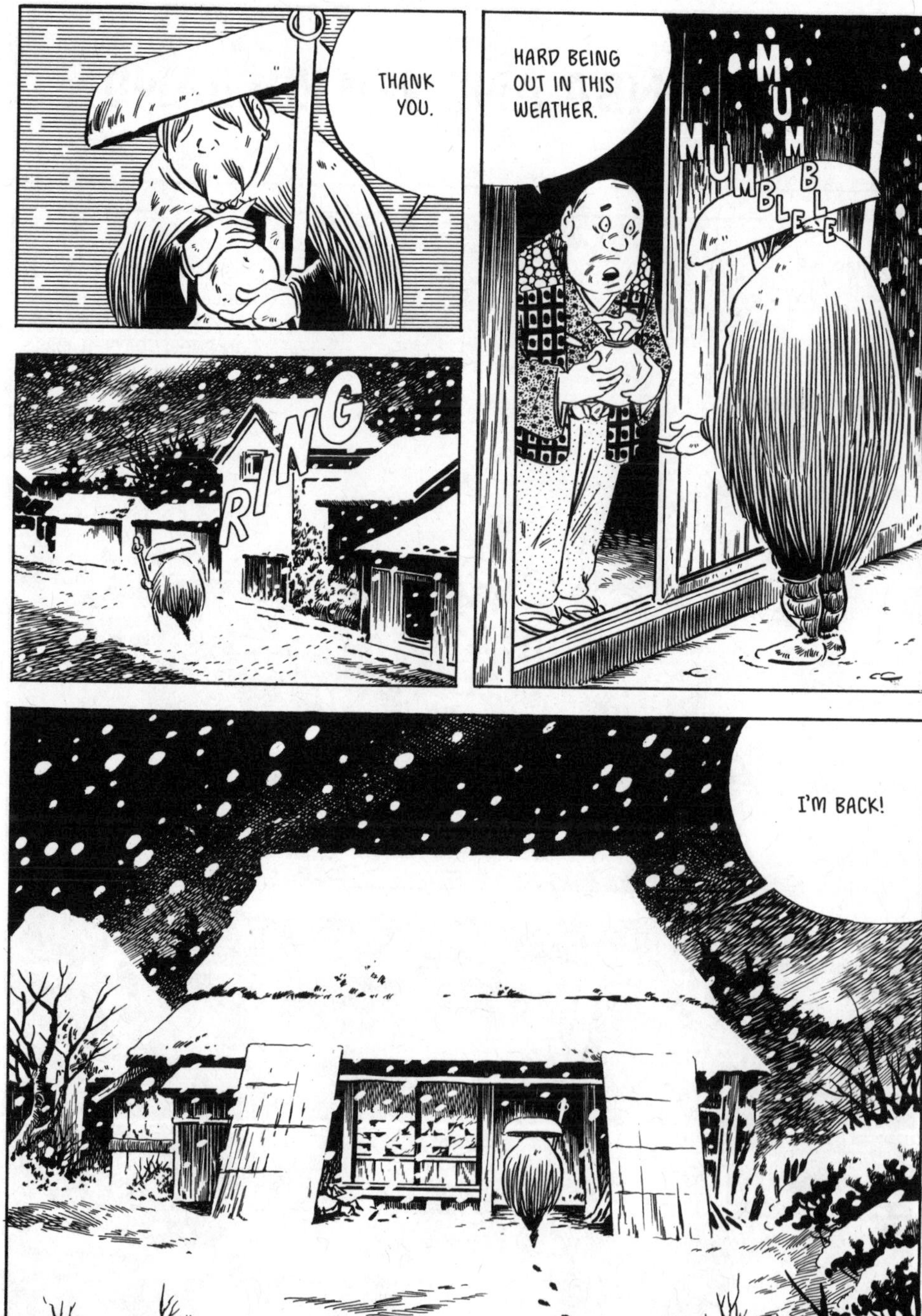
HARD BEING OUT IN THIS WEATHER.
MUMBLE MUMBLE
THANK YOU.
RING
I'M BACK!

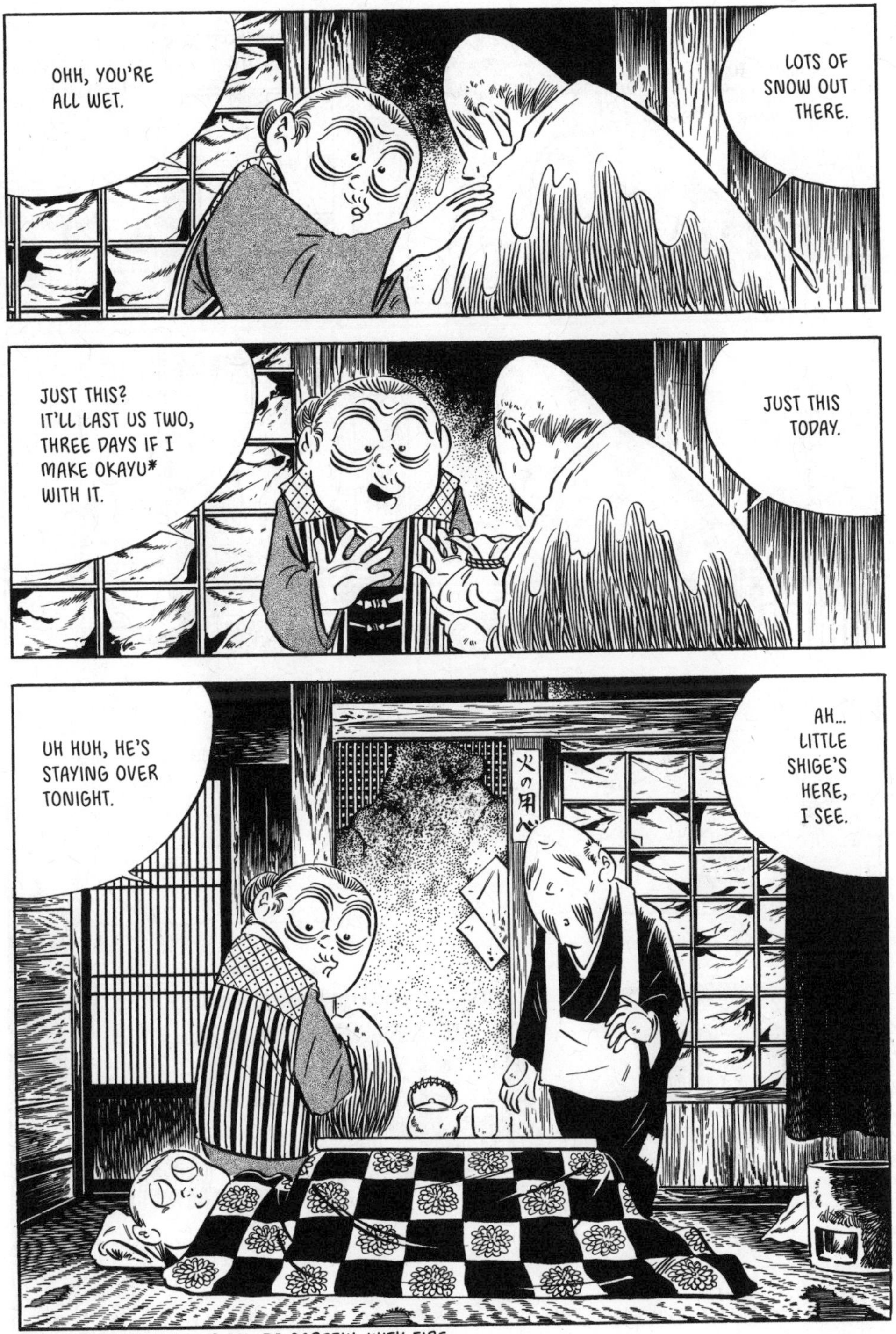
LOTS OF SNOW OUT THERE.
OHH, YOU'RE ALL WET.
JUST THIS TODAY.
JUST THIS? IT'LL LAST US TWO, THREE DAYS IF I MAKE OKAYU* WITH IT.
AH... LITTLE SHIGE'S HERE, I SEE.
UH HUH, HE'S STAYING OVER TONIGHT.
火の用心

*SEE NOTES PAGE 417. SIGN: BE CAREFUL WITH FIRE.

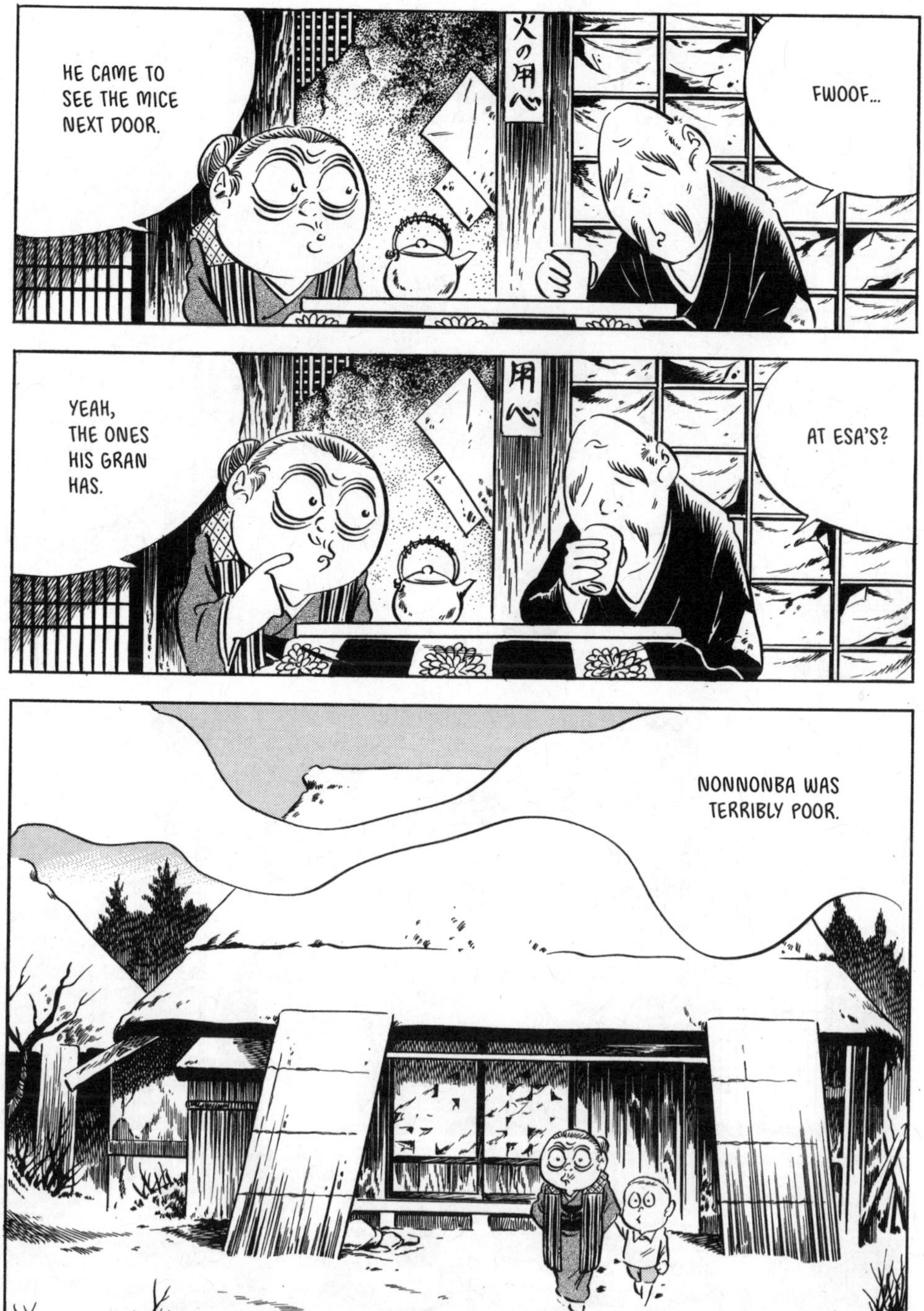
FWOOF...
火の用心
HE CAME TO SEE THE MICE NEXT DOOR.
AT ESA'S?
用心
YEAH, THE ONES HIS GRAN HAS.
NONNONBA WAS TERRIBLY POOR.

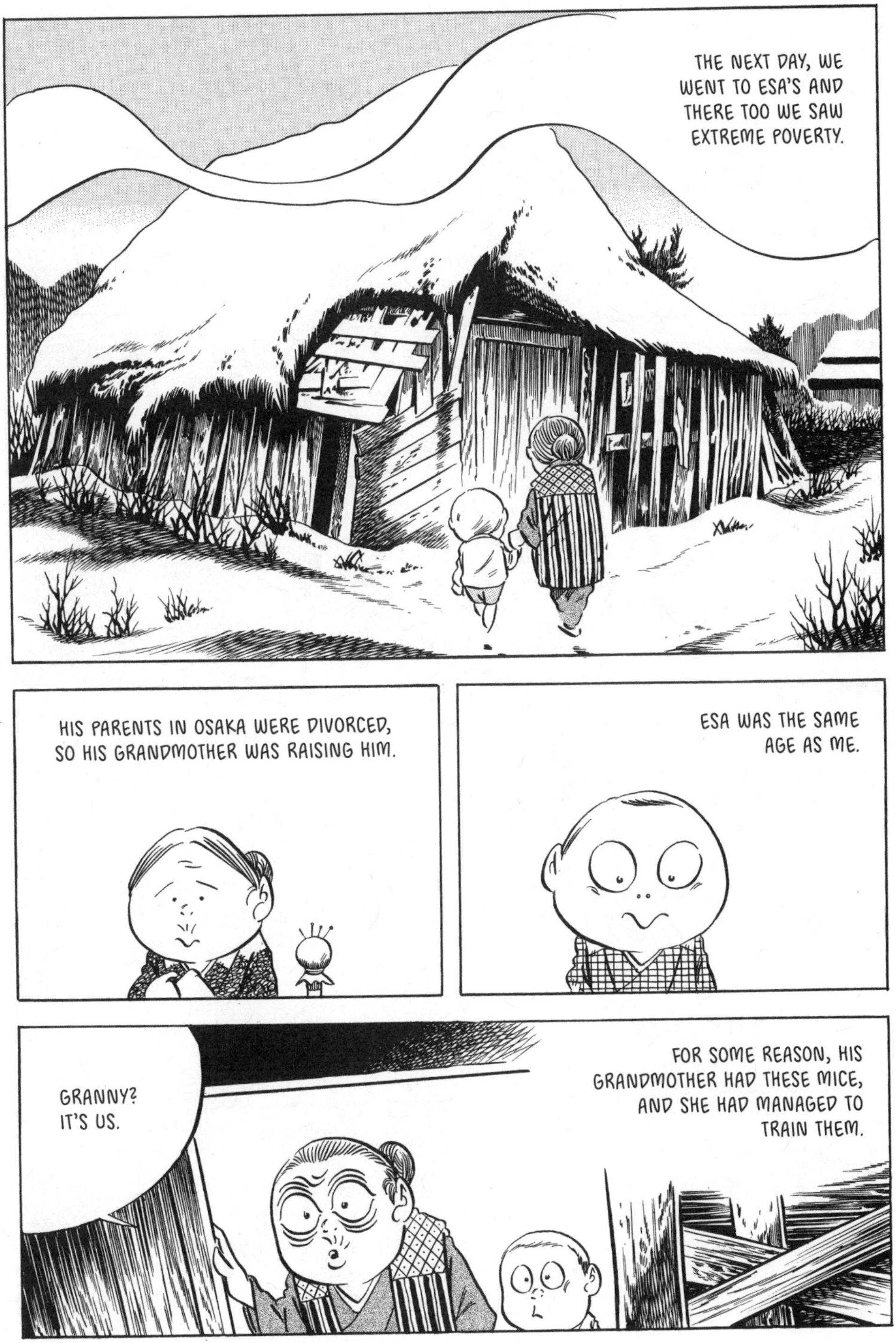
THE NEXT DAY, WE WENT TO ESA'S AND THERE TOO WE SAW EXTREME POVERTY.
ESA WAS THE SAME AGE AS ME.
HIS PARENTS IN OSAKA WERE DIVORCED, SO HIS GRANDMOTHER WAS RAISING HIM.
FOR SOME REASON, HIS GRANDMOTHER HAD THESE MICE, AND SHE HAD MANAGED TO TRAIN THEM.
GRANNY? IT'S US.

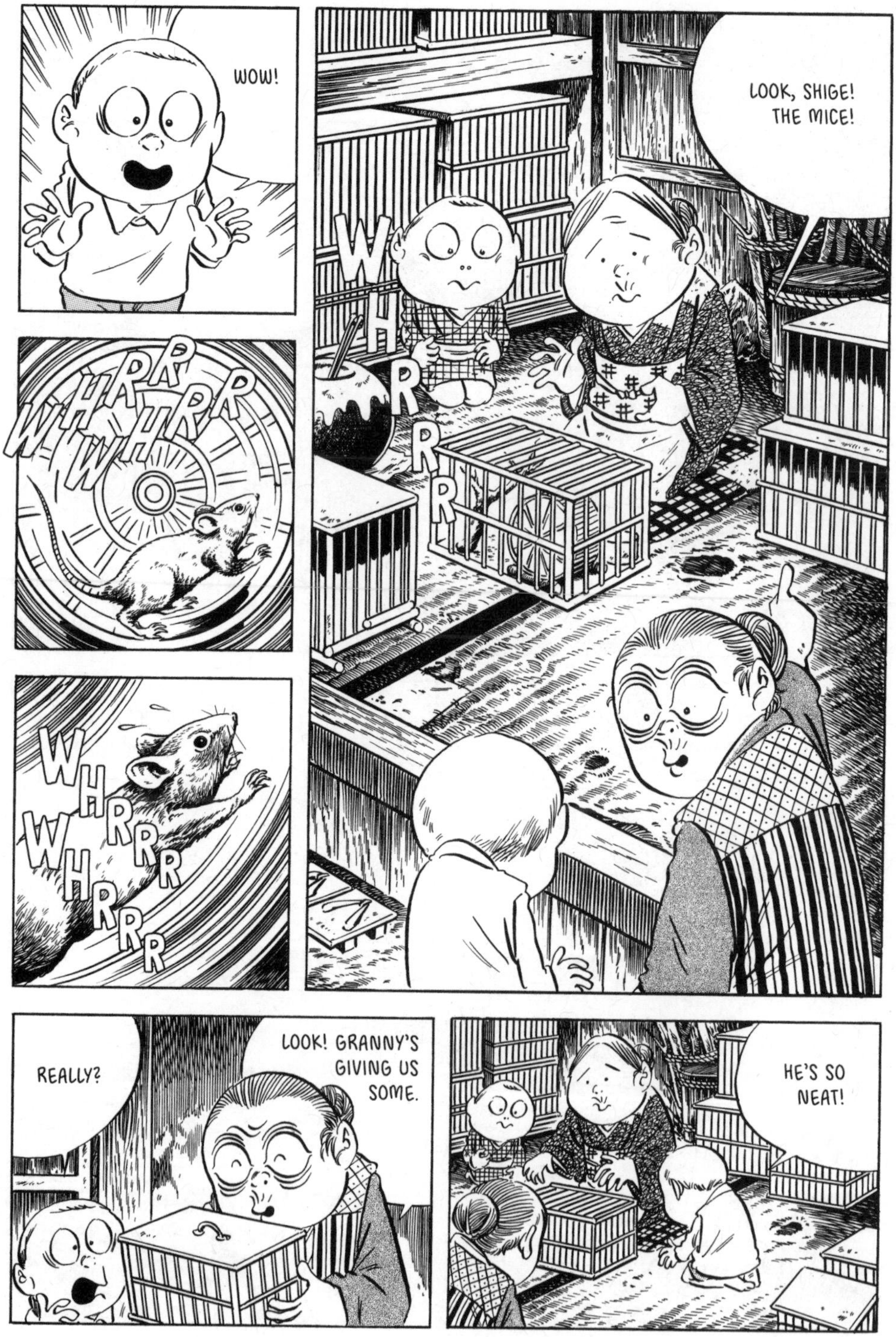
LOOK, SHIGE! THE MICE!
WHRRRR
WOW!
WHRRR WHRRR
WHRRRR WHRRRR
HE'S SO NEAT!
LOOK! GRANNY'S GIVING US SOME.
REALLY?

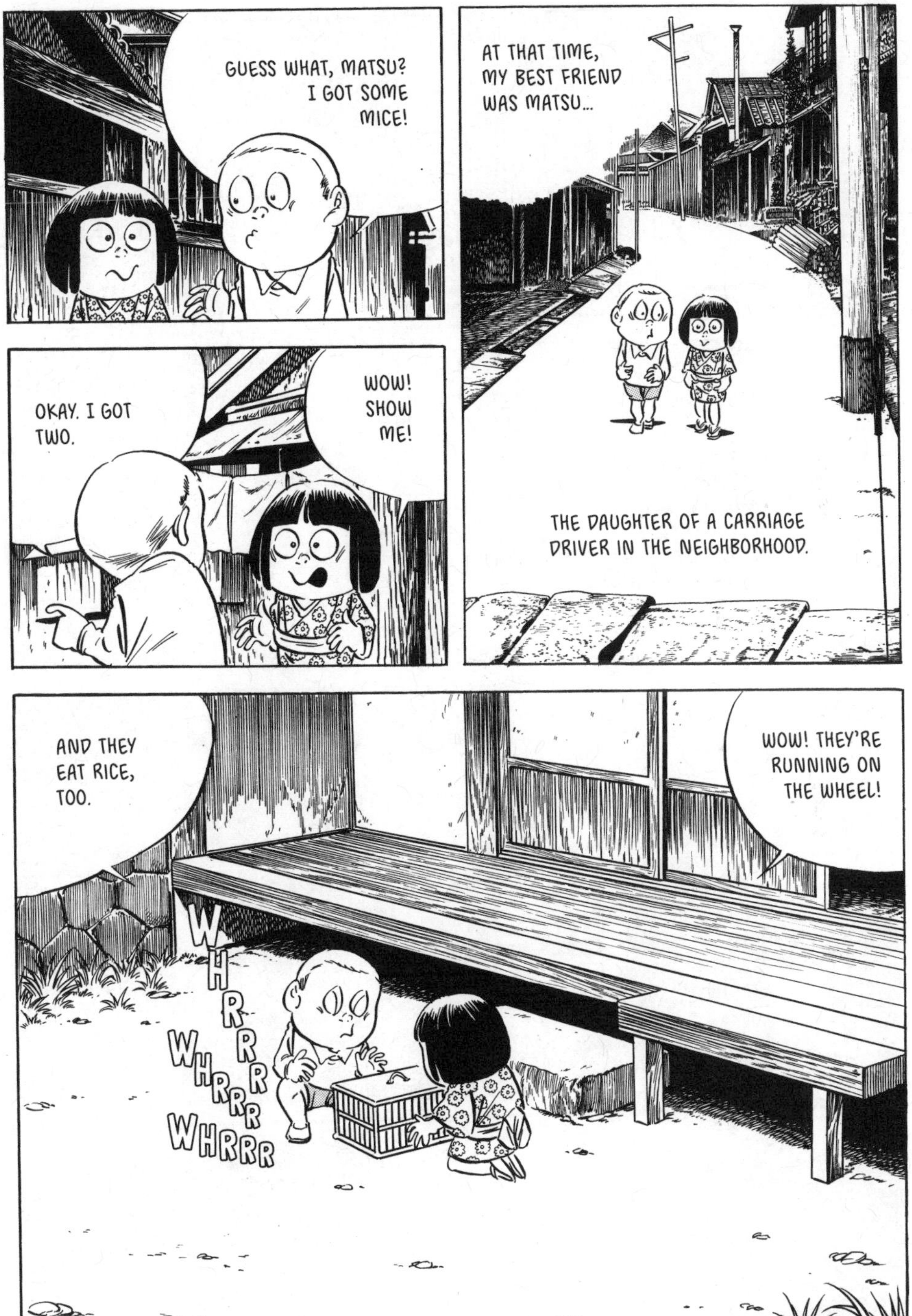
AT THAT TIME, MY BEST FRIEND WAS MATSU...
THE DAUGHTER OF A CARRIAGE DRIVER IN THE NEIGHBORHOOD.
GUESS WHAT, MATSU? I GOT SOME MICE!
WOW! SHOW ME!
OKAY. I GOT TWO.
WOW! THEY'RE RUNNING ON THE WHEEL!
AND THEY EAT RICE, TOO.
WHRRRR
WHRRRR
WHRRRR

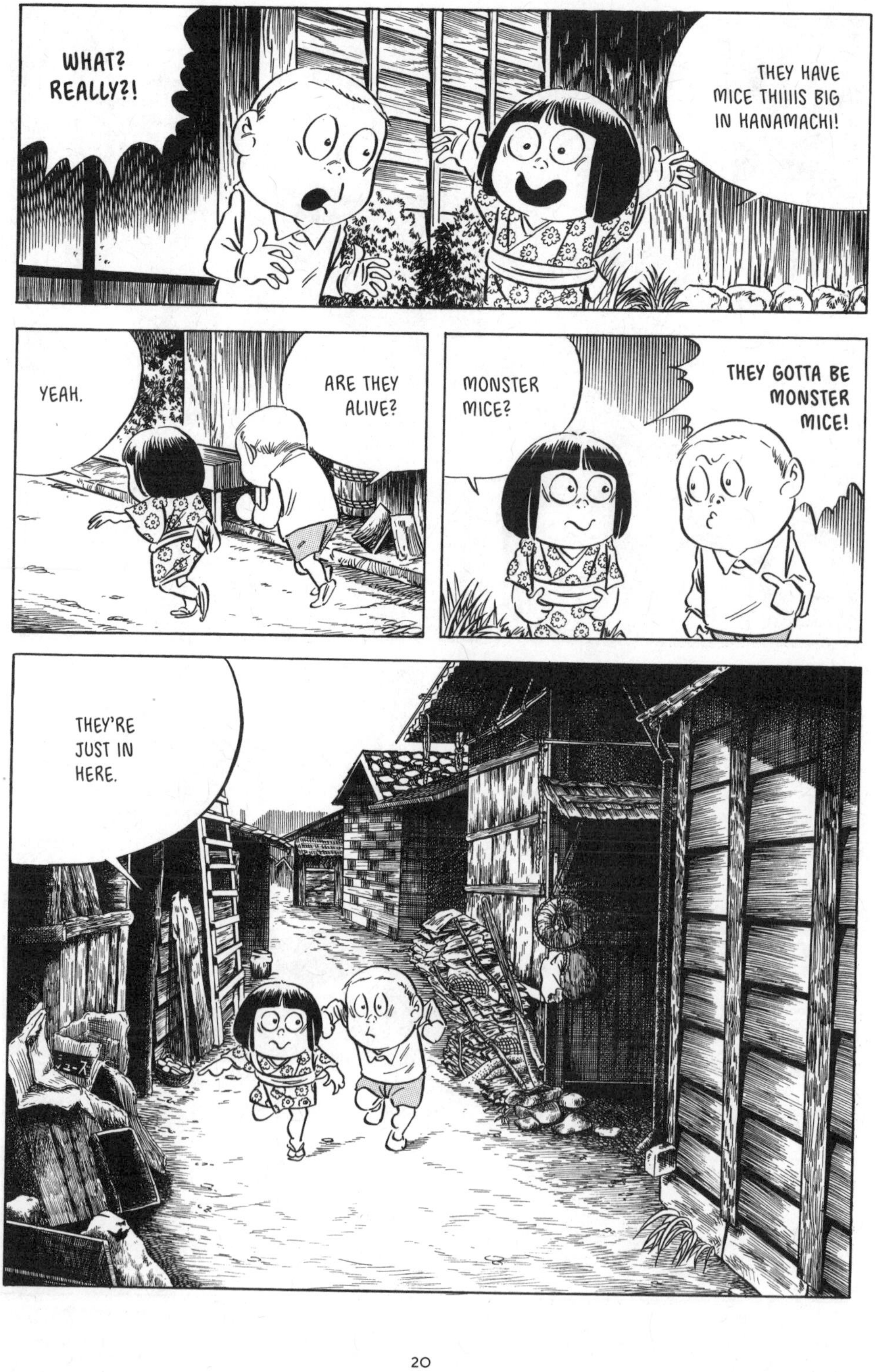
THEY HAVE MICE THIIIIS BIG IN HANAMACHI!
WHAT? REALLY?!
THEY GOTTA BE MONSTER MICE!
MONSTER MICE?
ARE THEY ALIVE?
YEAH.
THEY'RE JUST IN HERE.

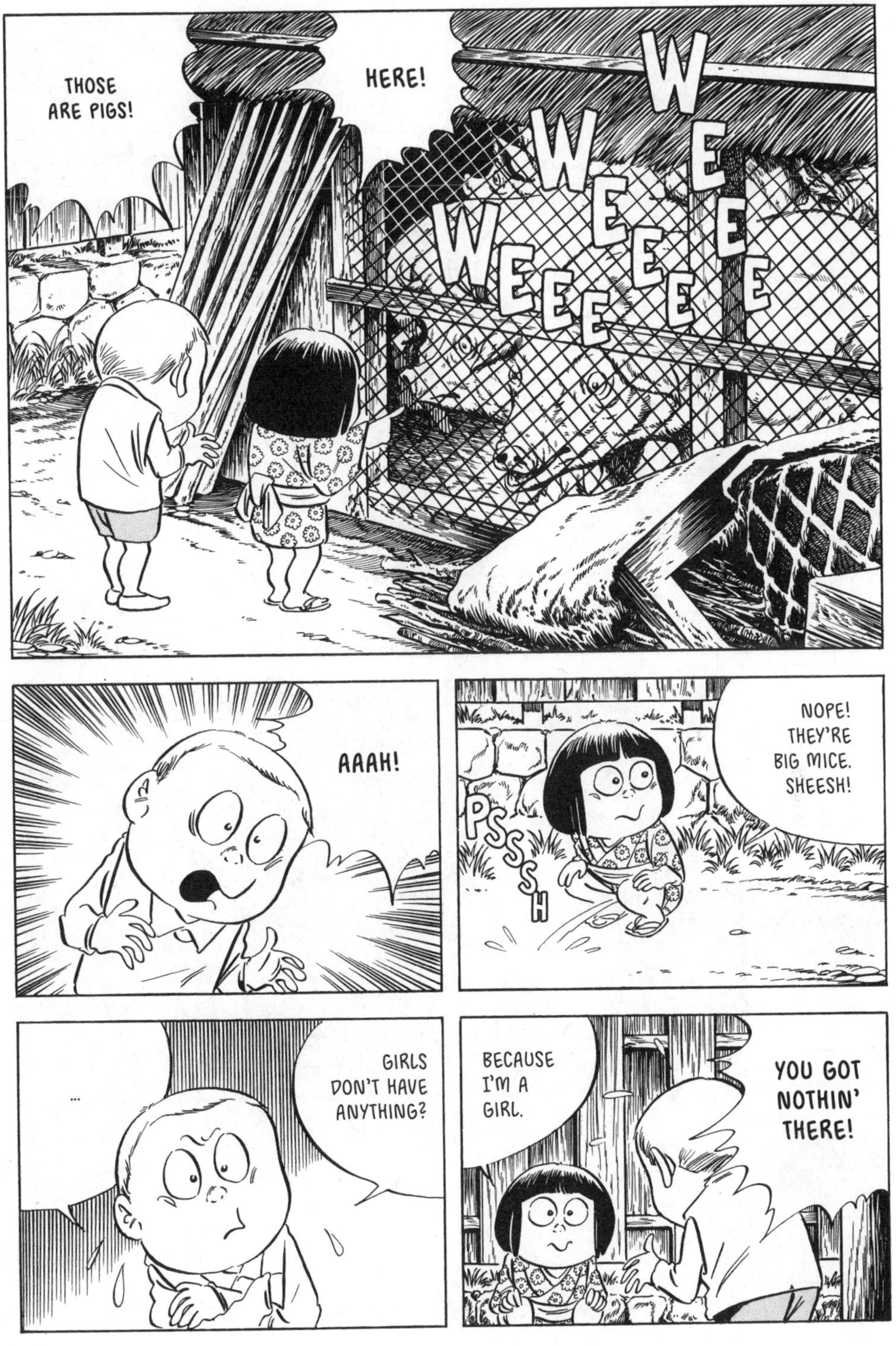
WEEEE
WEEEE
WEEEEE
HERE!
THOSE ARE PIGS!
NOPE! THEY'RE BIG MICE. SHEESH!
PSSSSH
AAAH!
YOU GOT NOTHIN' THERE!
BECAUSE I'M A GIRL.
GIRLS DON'T HAVE ANYTHING?
...

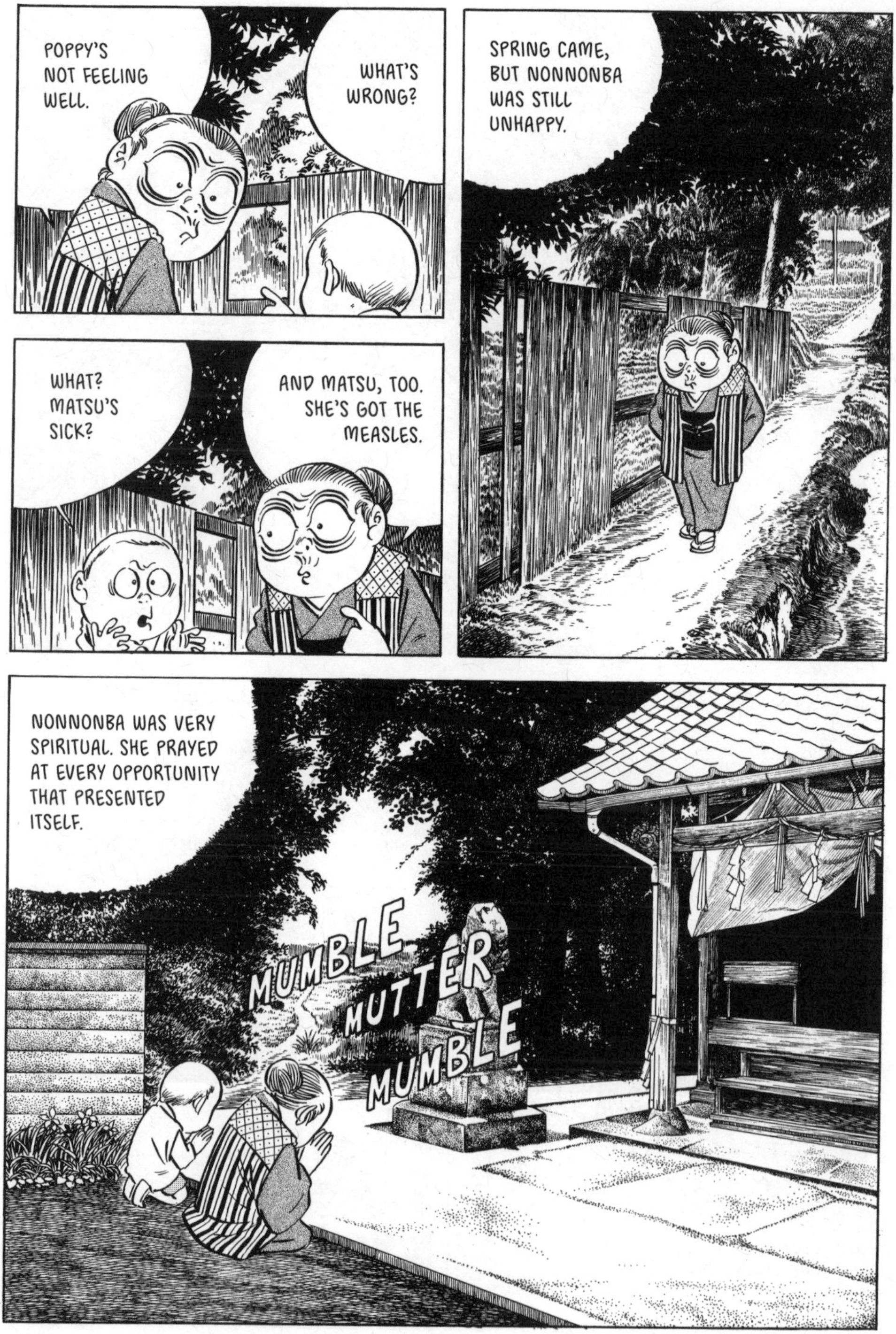
SPRING CAME, BUT NONNONBA WAS STILL UNHAPPY.
WHAT'S WRONG?
POPPY'S NOT FEELING WELL.
AND MATSU, TOO. SHE'S GOT THE MEASLES.
WHAT? MATSU'S SICK?
NONNONBA WAS VERY SPIRITUAL. SHE PRAYED AT EVERY OPPORTUNITY THAT PRESENTED ITSELF.
MUMBLE
MUTTER
MUMBLE
MUMBLE

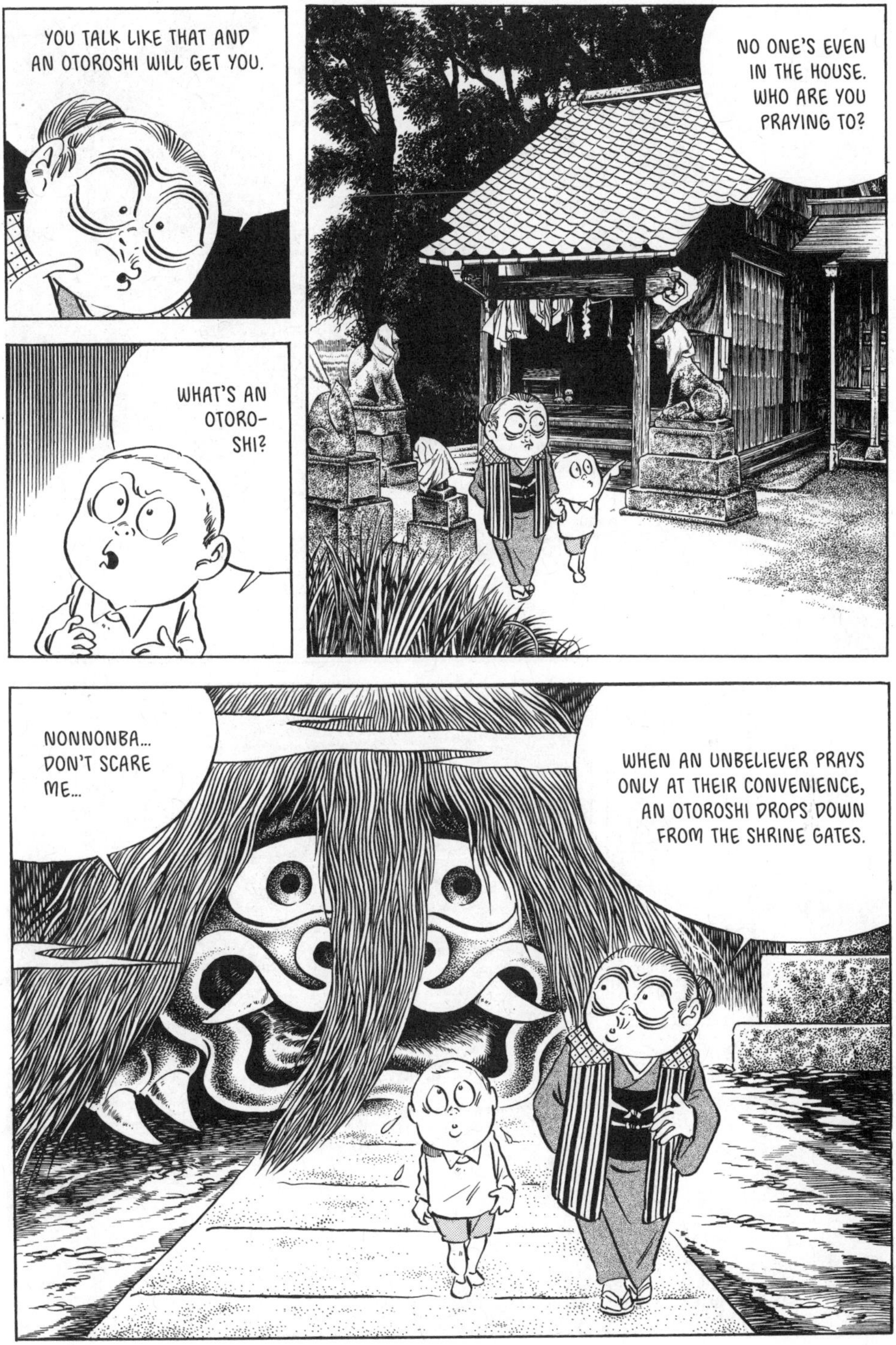
NO ONE'S EVEN IN THE HOUSE. WHO ARE YOU PRAYING TO?
YOU TALK LIKE THAT AND AN OTOROSHI WILL GET YOU.
WHAT'S AN OTORO-SHI?
WHEN AN UNBELIEVER PRAYS ONLY AT THEIR CONVENIENCE, AN OTOROSHI DROPS DOWN FROM THE SHRINE GATES.
NONNONBA... DON'T SCARE ME...

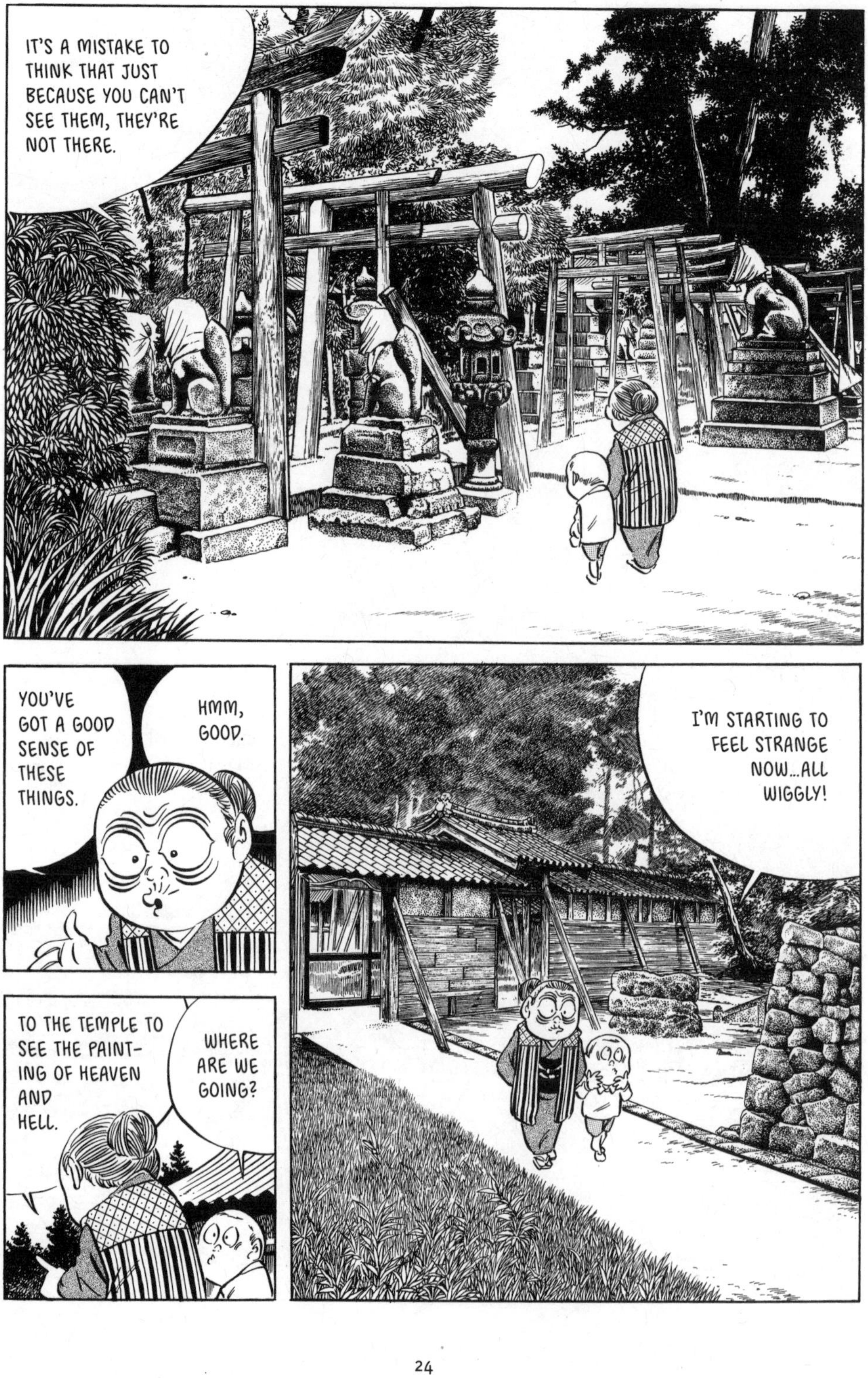
IT'S A MISTAKE TO THINK THAT JUST BECAUSE YOU CAN'T SEE THEM, THEY'RE NOT THERE.
I'M STARTING TO FEEL STRANGE NOW...ALL WIGGLY!
HMM, GOOD.
YOU'VE GOT A GOOD SENSE OF THESE THINGS.
WHERE ARE WE GOING?
TO THE TEMPLE TO SEE THE PAINTING OF HEAVEN AND HELL.

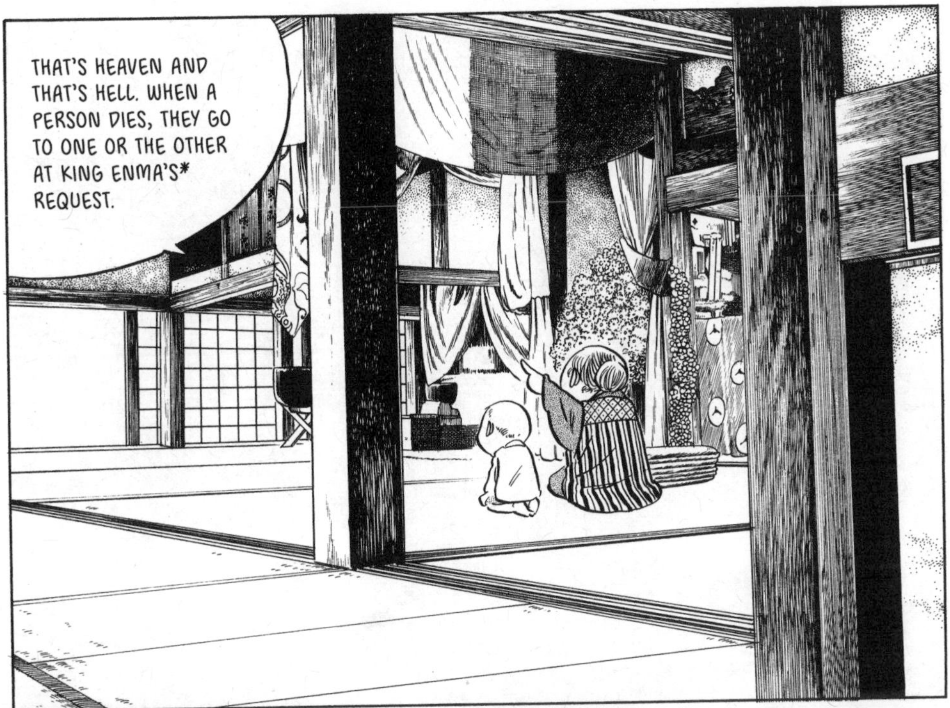
THAT'S HEAVEN AND THAT'S HELL. WHEN A PERSON DIES, THEY GO TO ONE OR THE OTHER AT KING ENMA'S* REQUEST.

*KING ENMA IS THE LORD OF DEATH IN JAPANESE BUDDHIST TRADITION.

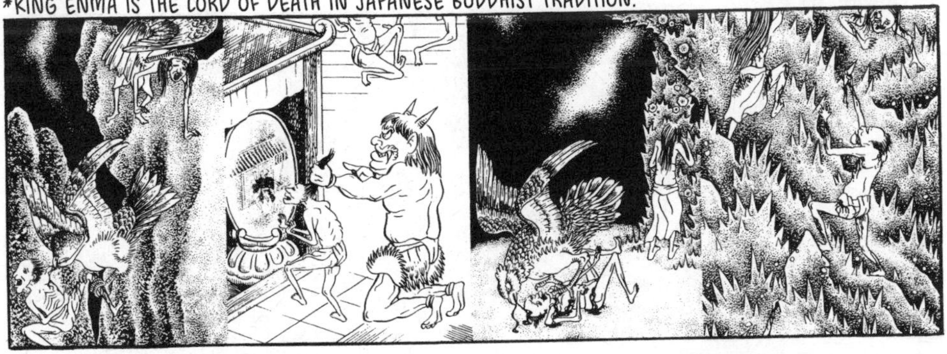

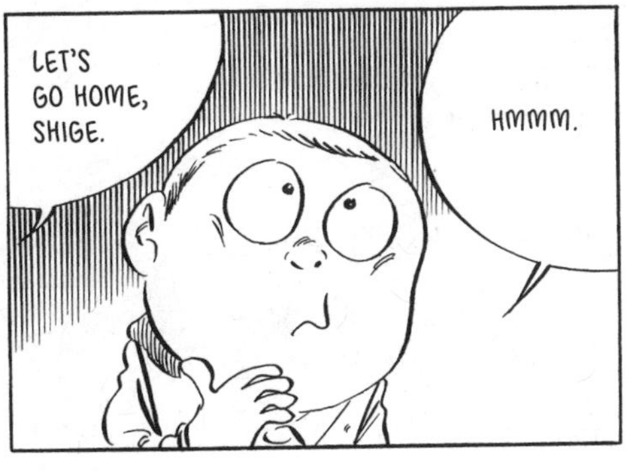
HMMM.
LET'S GO HOME, SHIGE.

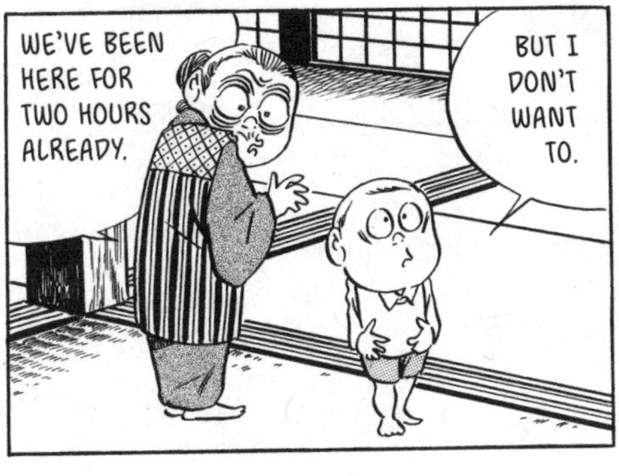
BUT I DON'T WANT TO.
WE'VE BEEN HERE FOR TWO HOURS ALREADY.

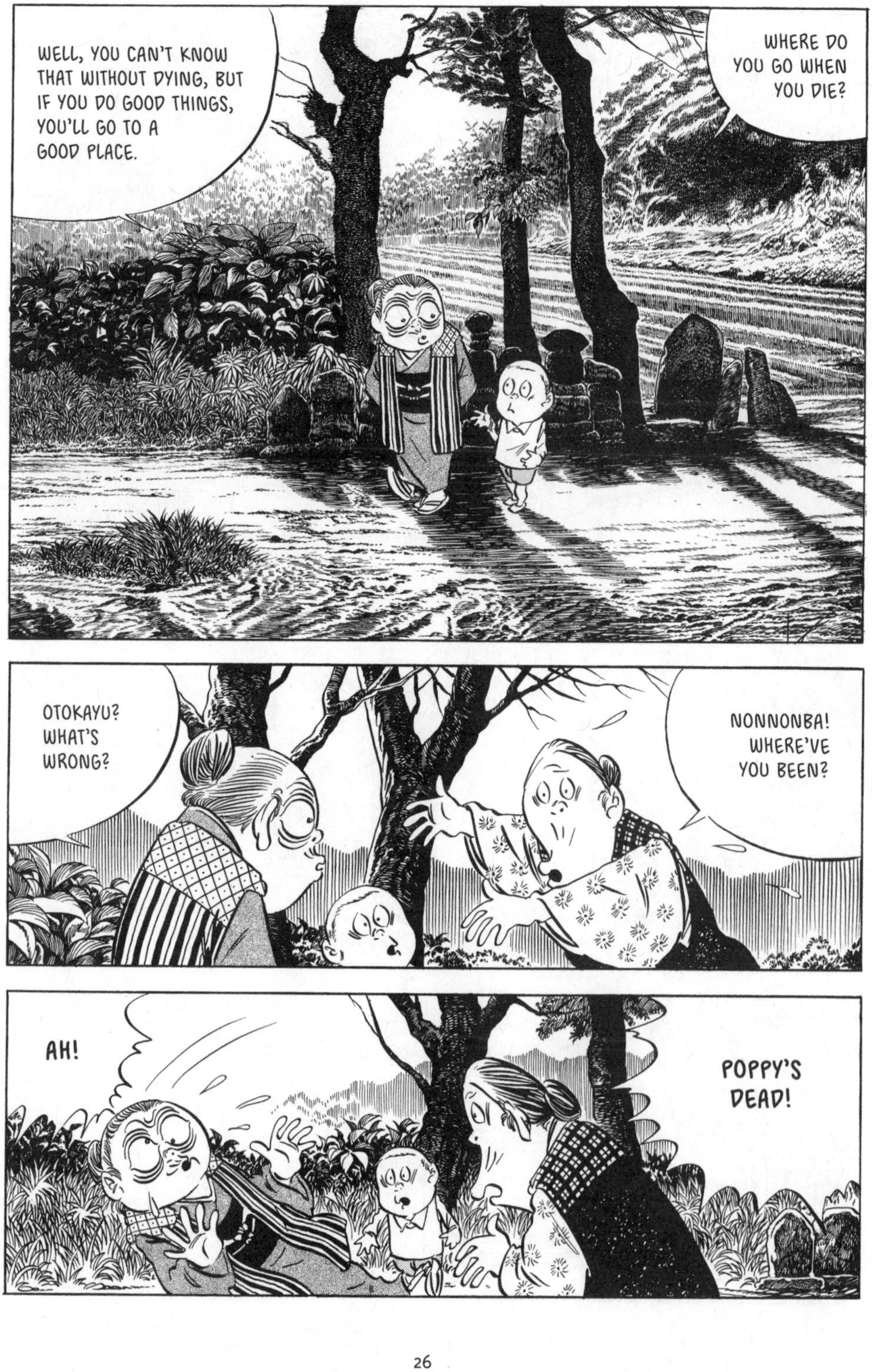
WHERE DO YOU GO WHEN YOU DIE?
WELL, YOU CAN'T KNOW THAT WITHOUT DYING, BUT IF YOU DO GOOD THINGS, YOU'LL GO TO A GOOD PLACE.
NONNONBA! WHERE'VE YOU BEEN?
OTOKAYU? WHAT'S WRONG?
POPPY'S DEAD!
AH!

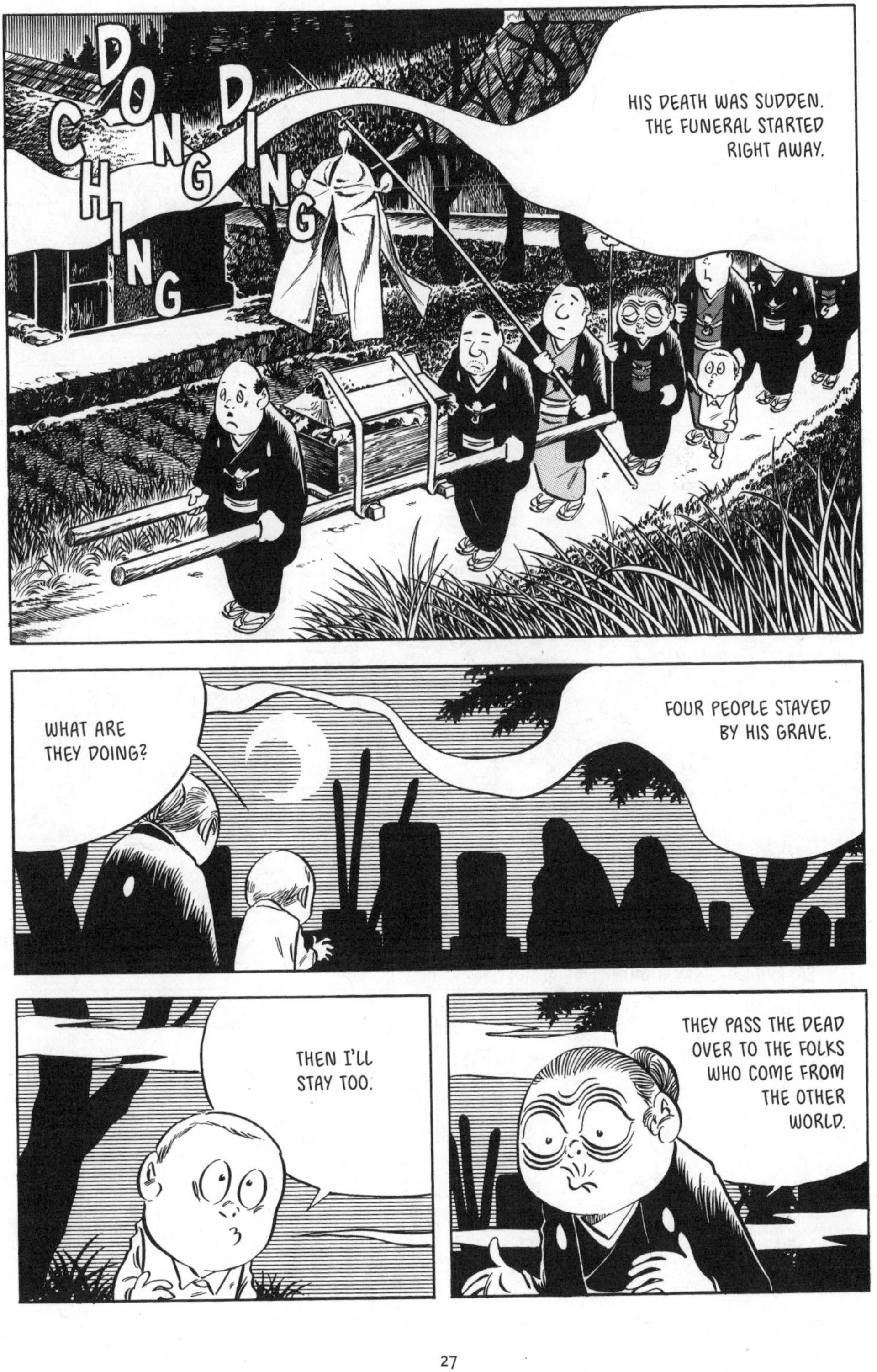
HIS DEATH WAS SUDDEN. THE FUNERAL STARTED RIGHT AWAY.
DING
DONG
CHING
FOUR PEOPLE STAYED BY HIS GRAVE.
WHAT ARE THEY DOING?
THEY PASS THE DEAD OVER TO THE FOLKS WHO COME FROM THE OTHER WORLD.
THEN I'LL STAY TOO.

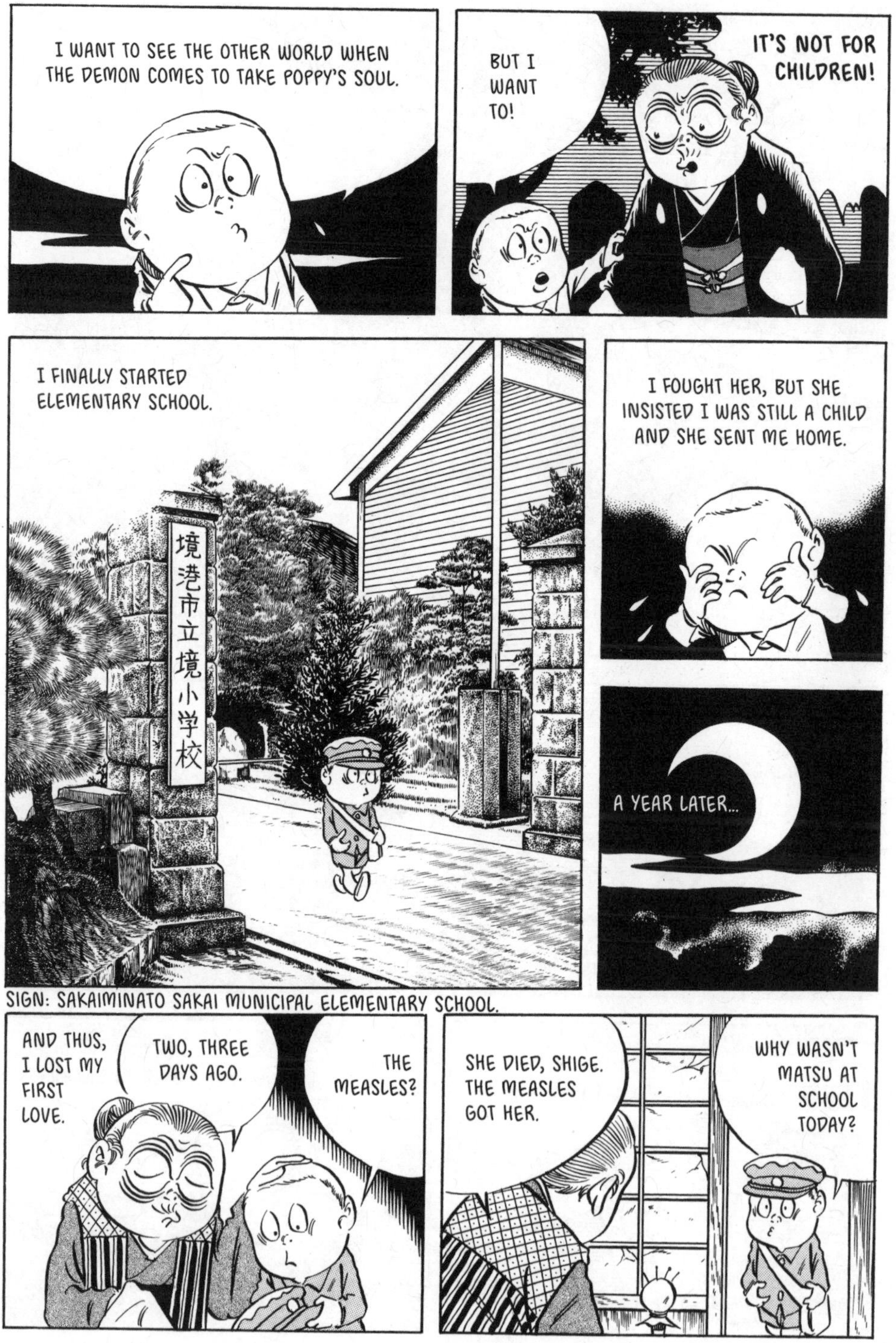

IT'S NOT FOR CHILDREN!
BUT I WANT TO!
I WANT TO SEE THE OTHER WORLD WHEN THE DEMON COMES TO TAKE POPPY'S SOUL.
I FOUGHT HER, BUT SHE INSISTED I WAS STILL A CHILD AND SHE SENT ME HOME.
A YEAR LATER...
I FINALLY STARTED ELEMENTARY SCHOOL.
境港市立境小学校
SIGN: SAKAIMINATO SAKAI MUNICIPAL ELEMENTARY SCHOOL.
WHY WASN'T MATSU AT SCHOOL TODAY?
SHE DIED, SHIGE. THE MEASLES GOT HER.
THE MEASLES?
TWO, THREE DAYS AGO.
AND THUS, I LOST MY FIRST LOVE.

NONNONBA COMES TO LIVE WITH US

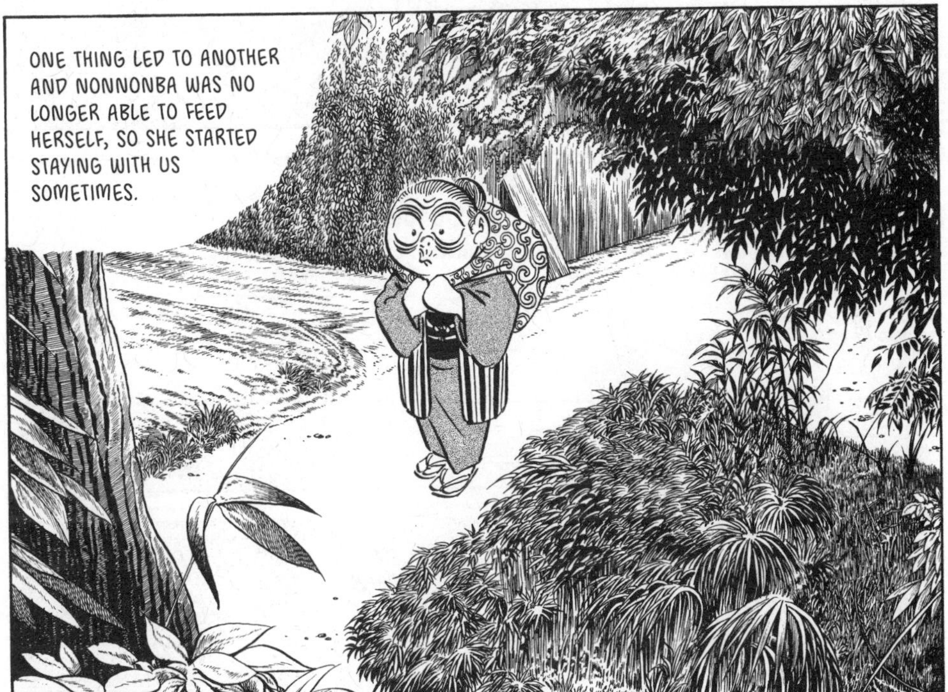
ONE THING LED TO ANOTHER AND NONNONBA WAS NO LONGER ABLE TO FEED HERSELF, SO SHE STARTED STAYING WITH US SOMETIMES.

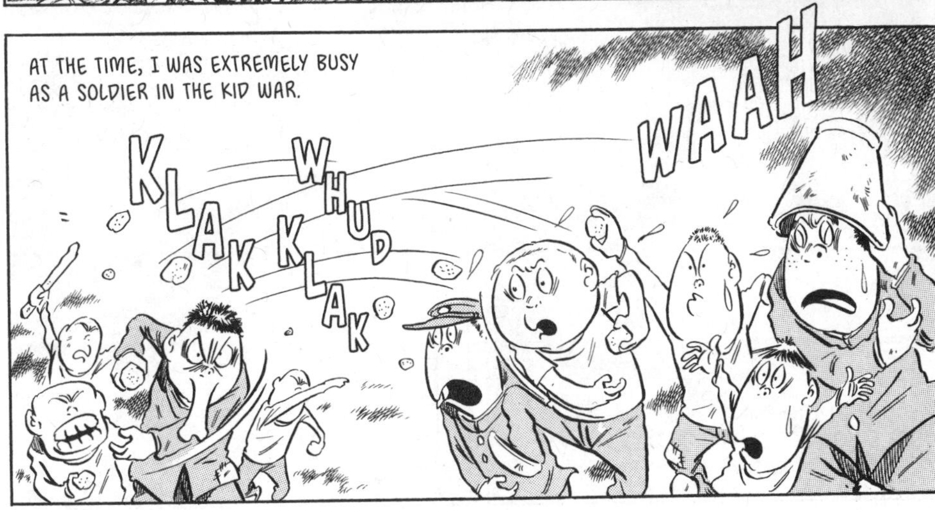
WAAH
AT THE TIME, I WAS EXTREMELY BUSY AS A SOLDIER IN THE KID WAR.
WHUD
KLAK
KLAK
KLAK

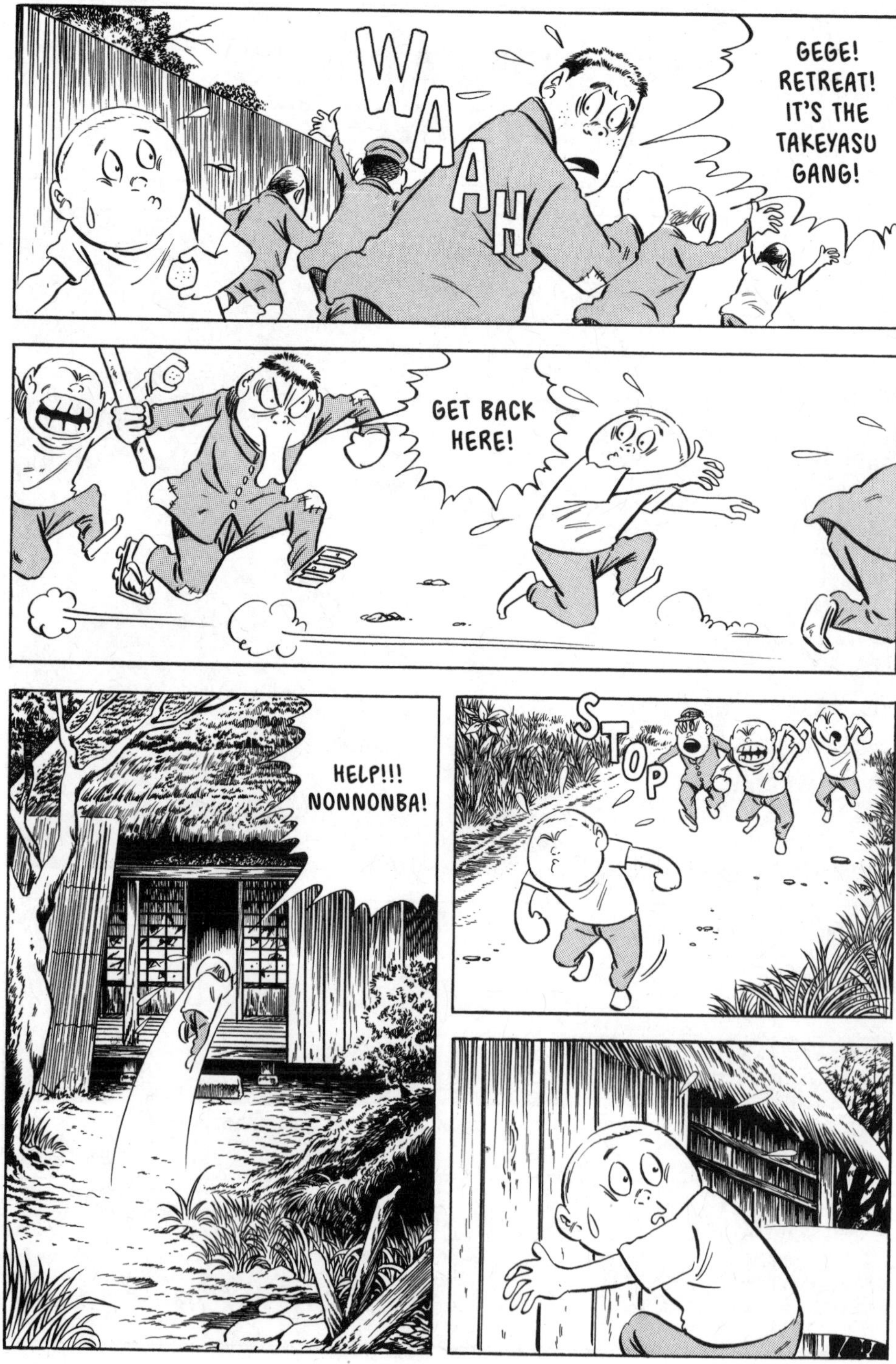
GEGE! RETREAT! IT'S THE TAKEYASU GANG!
WAAAH
GET BACK HERE!
STOP
HELP!!! NONNONBA!

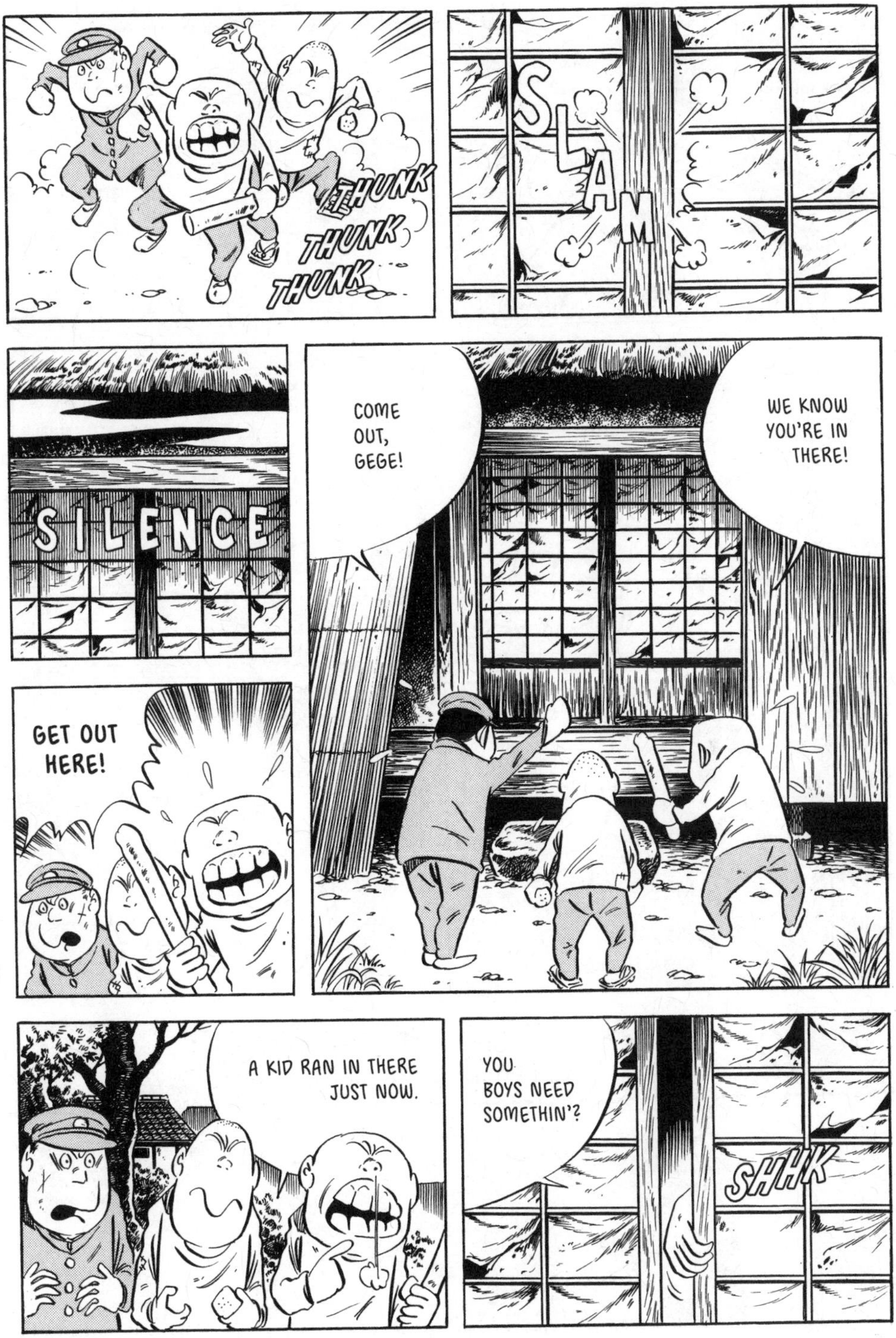
SLAM
THUNK
THUNK
THUNK
WE KNOW YOU'RE IN THERE!
COME OUT, GEGE!
SILENCE
GET OUT HERE!
YOU BOYS NEED SOMETHIN'?
SHHK
A KID RAN IN THERE JUST NOW.

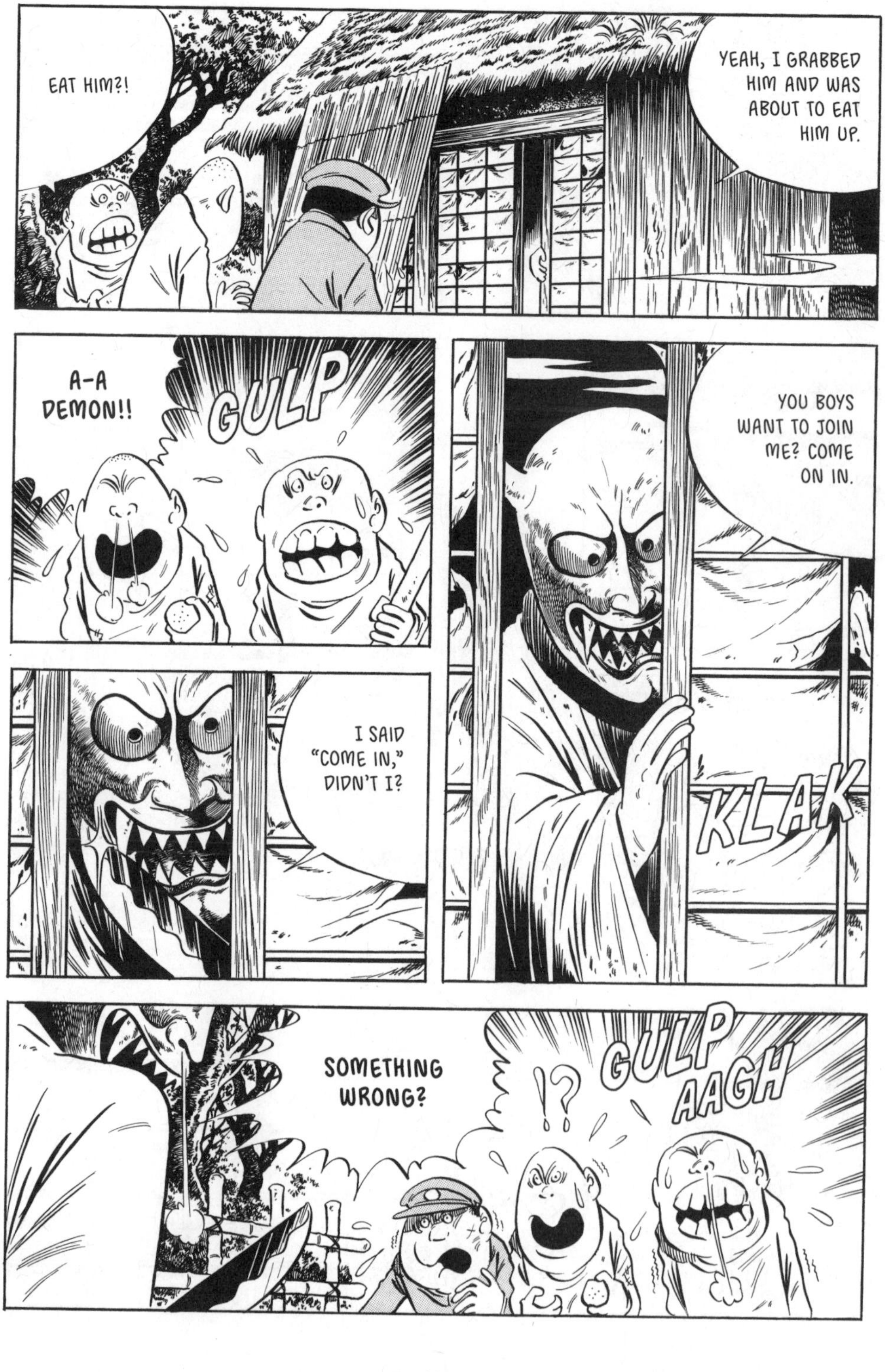
YEAH, I GRABBED HIM AND WAS ABOUT TO EAT HIM UP.
EAT HIM?!
YOU BOYS WANT TO JOIN ME? COME ON IN.
KLAK
GULP
A-A DEMON!!
I SAID "COME IN," DIDN'T I?
GULP
AAGH
!?
SOMETHING WRONG?

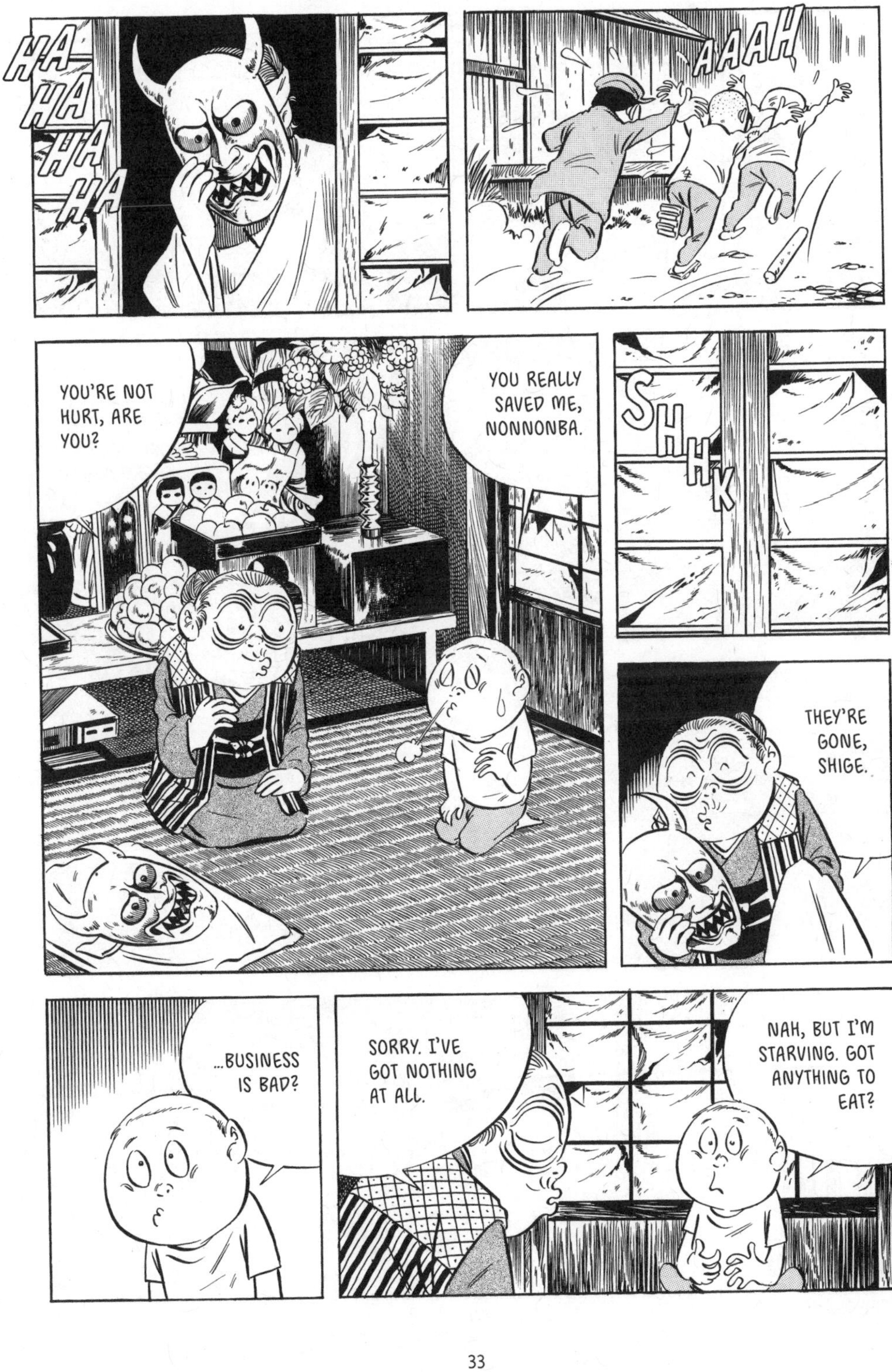
AAAH
HA HA HA HA
SHHHK
THEY'RE GONE, SHIGE.
YOU REALLY SAVED ME, NONNONBA.
YOU'RE NOT HURT, ARE YOU?
NAH, BUT I'M STARVING. GOT ANYTHING TO EAT?
SORRY. I'VE GOT NOTHING AT ALL.
...BUSINESS IS BAD?

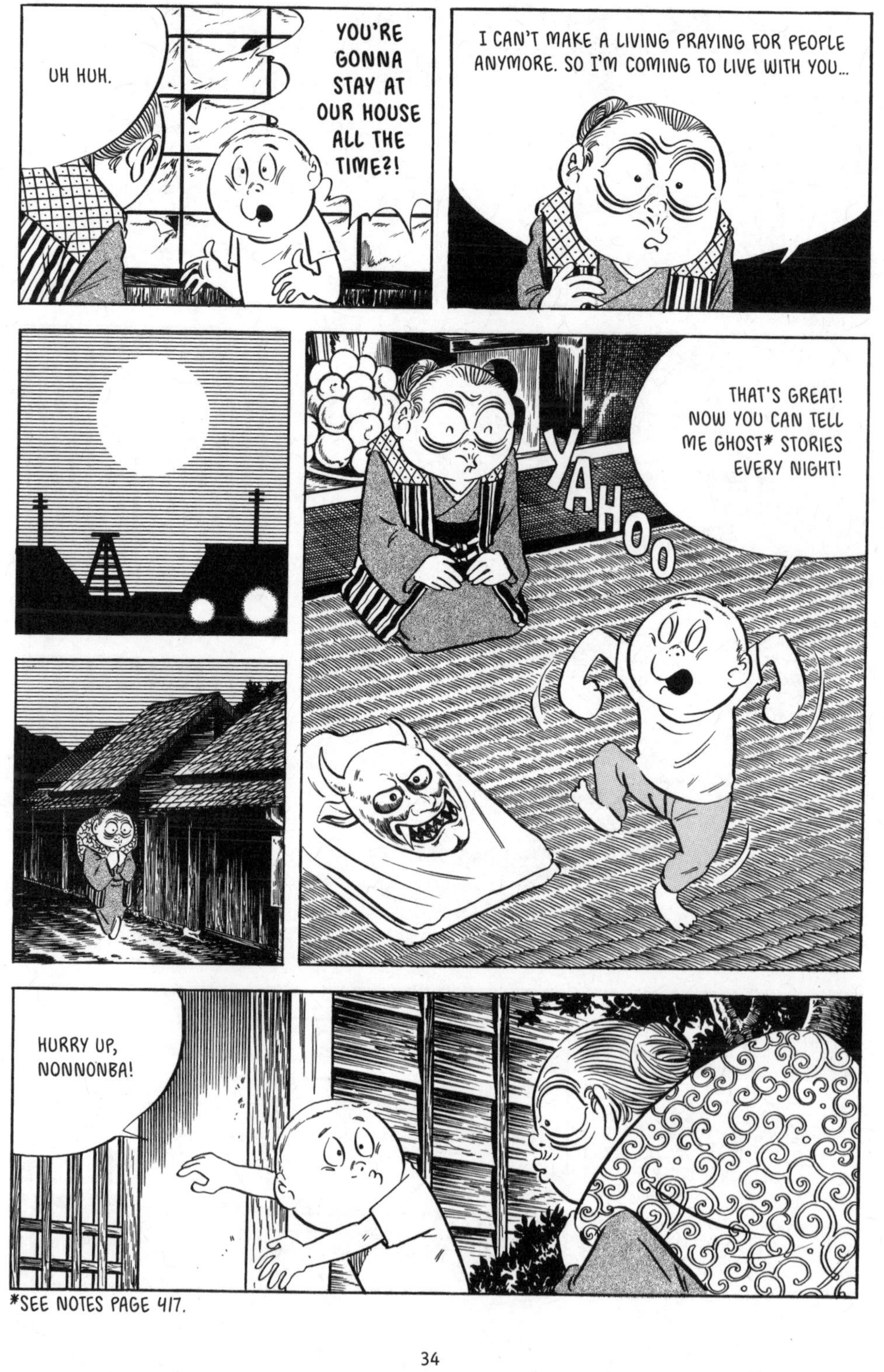
I CAN'T MAKE A LIVING PRAYING FOR PEOPLE ANYMORE. SO I'M COMING TO LIVE WITH YOU...
YOU'RE GONNA STAY AT OUR HOUSE ALL THE TIME?!
UH HUH.
THAT'S GREAT! NOW YOU CAN TELL ME GHOST* STORIES EVERY NIGHT!
YAHOO
HURRY UP, NONNONBA!

*SEE NOTES PAGE 417.

MOM! NONNON-BA'S HERE!
OH, COME ON IN!
MRS. MURAKI, I CANNOT THANK YOU ENOUGH FOR OPENING YOUR HOME TO ME.
YOU'RE ALWAYS WELCOME. WE CAN'T REALLY PAY YOU A PROPER WAGE, SO WE'LL TRY NOT TO ASK TOO MUCH OF YOU.
YOU SAY THAT, BUT YOU'LL WORK HER LIKE A SLAVE.
DID YOU SAY SOMETHING?
NOTHING!
WELL THEN, I KNOW YOU JUST GOT HERE, BUT WOULD YOU MIND HEATING THE WATER FOR THE BATH?
NOT AT ALL.

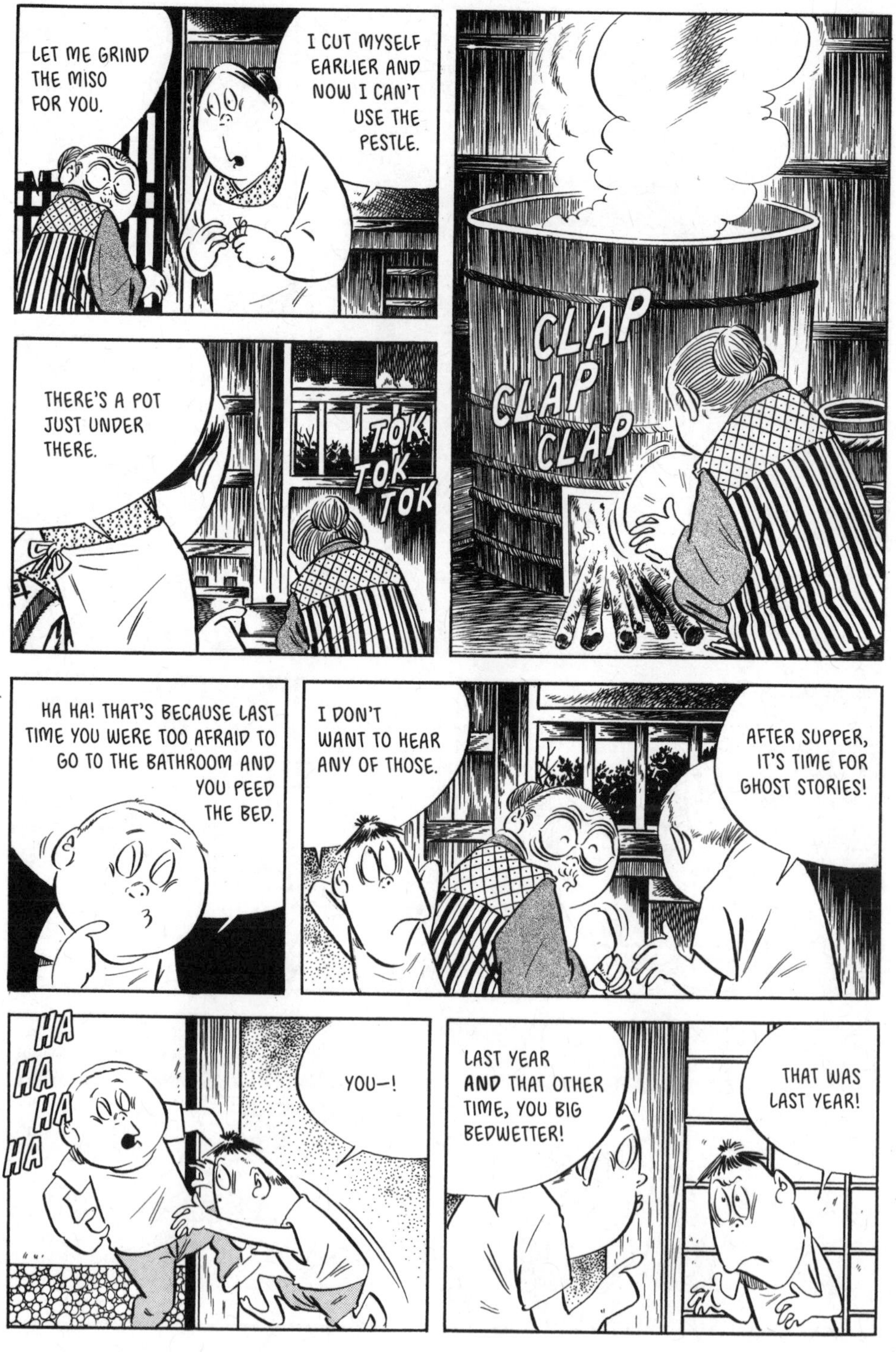
CLAP
CLAP
CLAP
I CUT MYSELF EARLIER AND NOW I CAN'T USE THE PESTLE.
LET ME GRIND THE MISO FOR YOU.
THERE'S A POT JUST UNDER THERE.
TOK
TOK
TOK
AFTER SUPPER, IT'S TIME FOR GHOST STORIES!
I DON'T WANT TO HEAR ANY OF THOSE.
HA HA! THAT'S BECAUSE LAST TIME YOU WERE TOO AFRAID TO GO TO THE BATHROOM AND YOU PEED THE BED.
THAT WAS LAST YEAR!
LAST YEAR **AND** THAT OTHER TIME, YOU BIG BEDWETTER!
YOU—!
HA
HA
HA
HA

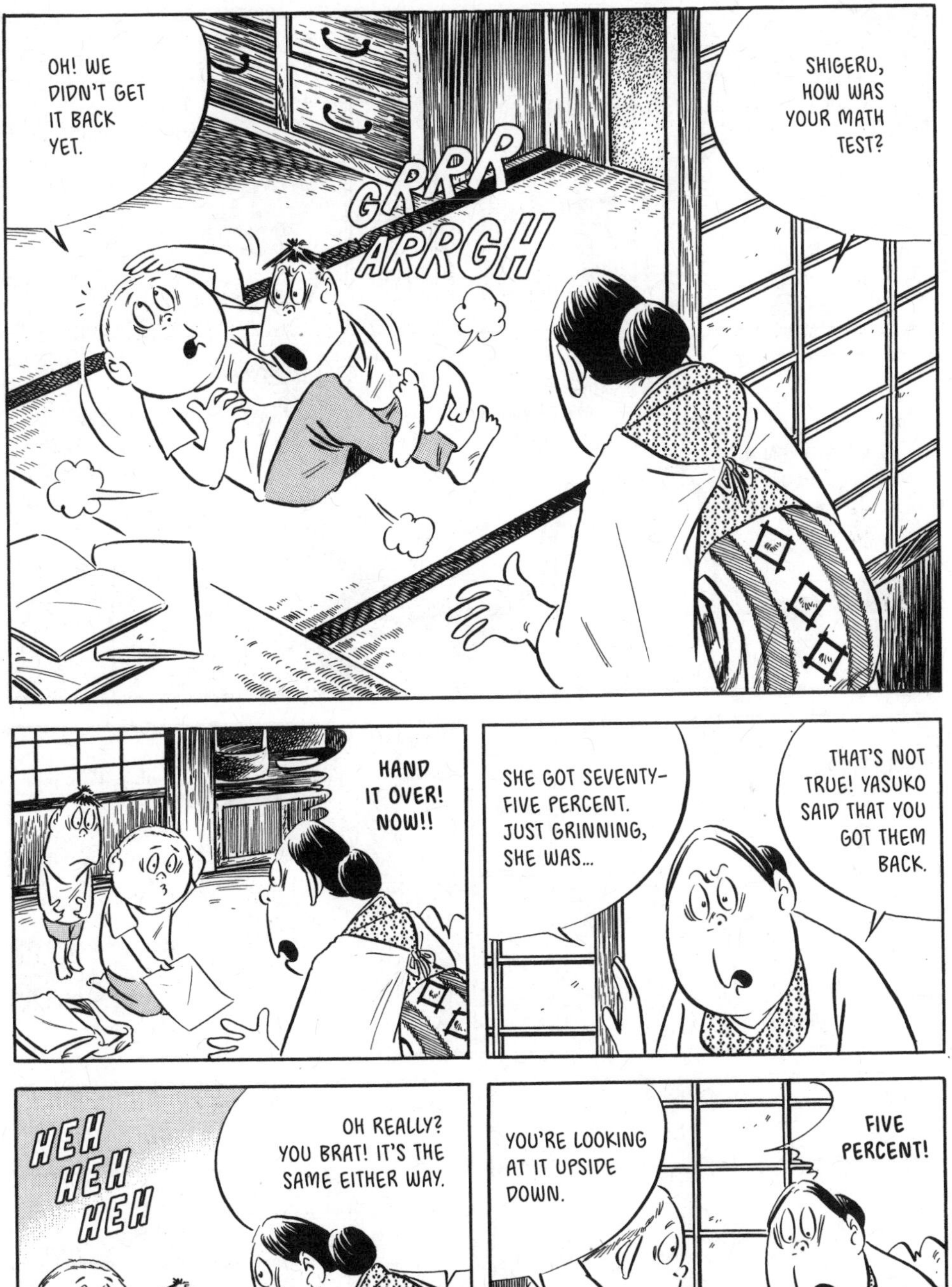
SHIGERU, HOW WAS YOUR MATH TEST?
OH! WE DIDN'T GET IT BACK YET.
GRRR ARRGH
THAT'S NOT TRUE! YASUKO SAID THAT YOU GOT THEM BACK.
SHE GOT SEVENTY-FIVE PERCENT. JUST GRINNING, SHE WAS...
HAND IT OVER! NOW!!
FIVE PERCENT!
YOU'RE LOOKING AT IT UPSIDE DOWN.
OH REALLY? YOU BRAT! IT'S THE SAME EITHER WAY.
HEH HEH HEH

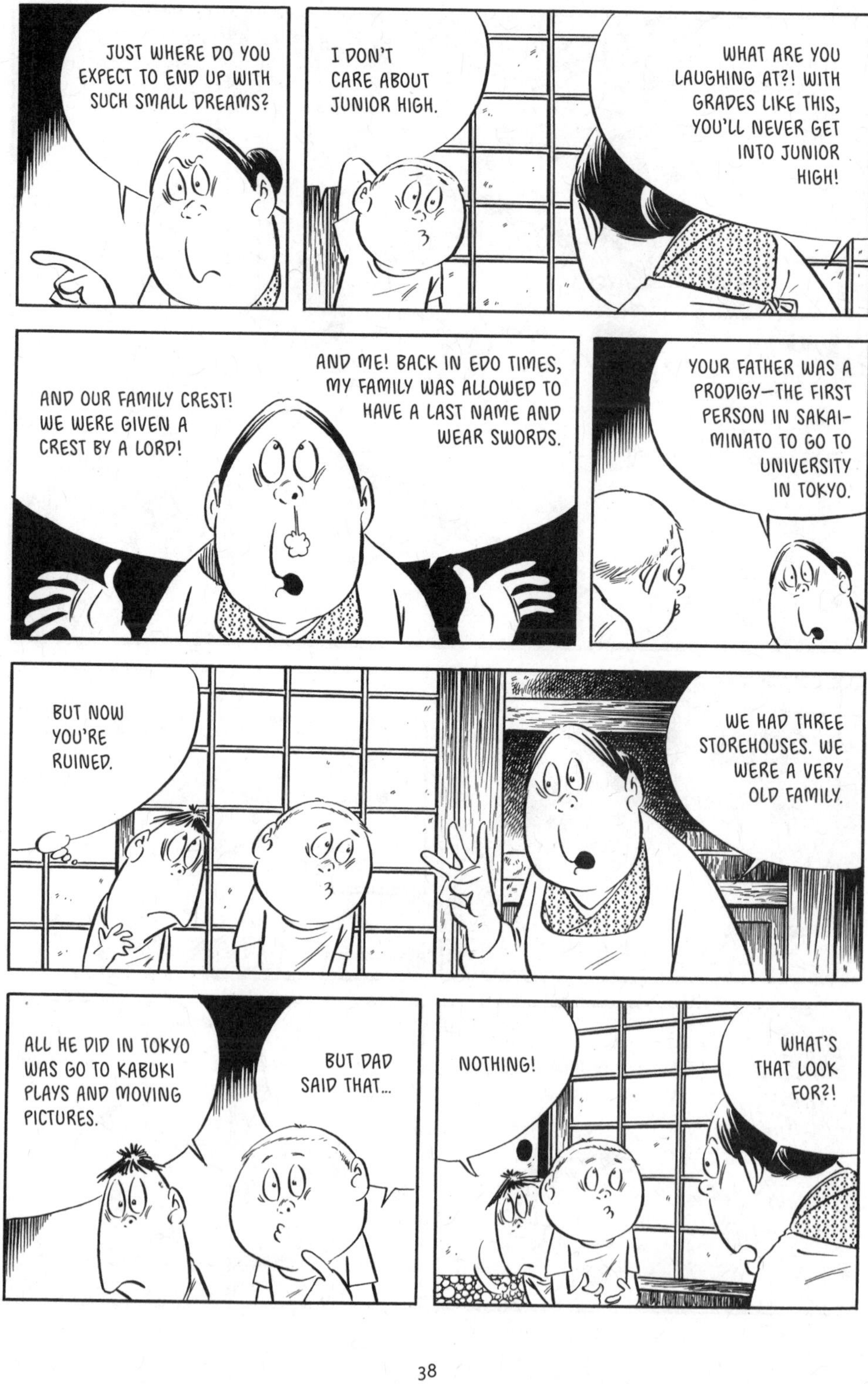
WHAT ARE YOU LAUGHING AT?! WITH GRADES LIKE THIS, YOU'LL NEVER GET INTO JUNIOR HIGH!
I DON'T CARE ABOUT JUNIOR HIGH.
JUST WHERE DO YOU EXPECT TO END UP WITH SUCH SMALL DREAMS?
YOUR FATHER WAS A PRODIGY—THE FIRST PERSON IN SAKAI-MINATO TO GO TO UNIVERSITY IN TOKYO.
AND ME! BACK IN EDO TIMES, MY FAMILY WAS ALLOWED TO HAVE A LAST NAME AND WEAR SWORDS.
AND OUR FAMILY CREST! WE WERE GIVEN A CREST BY A LORD!
WE HAD THREE STOREHOUSES. WE WERE A VERY OLD FAMILY.
BUT NOW YOU'RE RUINED.
WHAT'S THAT LOOK FOR?!
NOTHING!
BUT DAD SAID THAT...
ALL HE DID IN TOKYO WAS GO TO KABUKI PLAYS AND MOVING PICTURES.

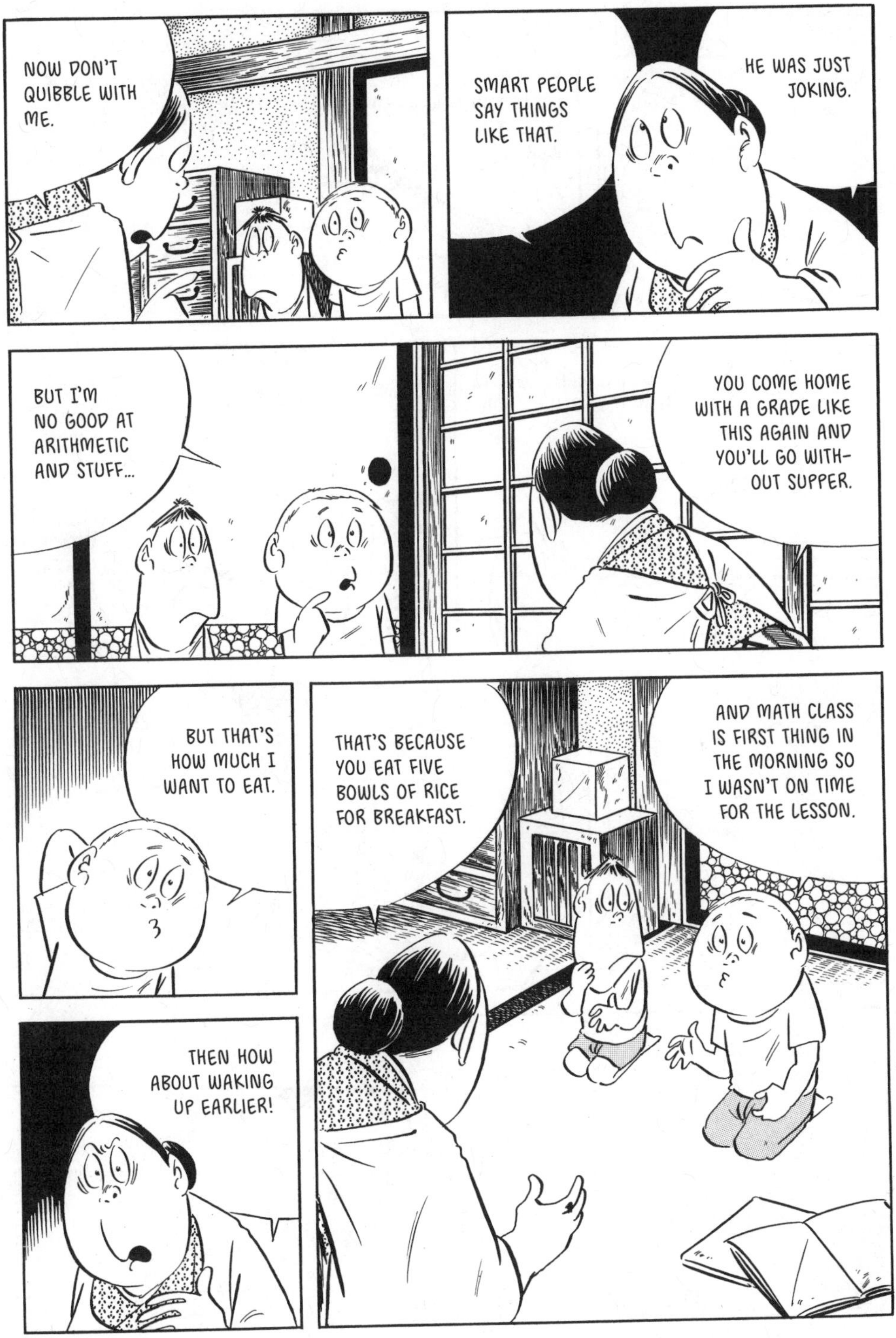
HE WAS JUST JOKING.
SMART PEOPLE SAY THINGS LIKE THAT.
NOW DON'T QUIBBLE WITH ME.
YOU COME HOME WITH A GRADE LIKE THIS AGAIN AND YOU'LL GO WITH-OUT SUPPER.
BUT I'M NO GOOD AT ARITHMETIC AND STUFF...
AND MATH CLASS IS FIRST THING IN THE MORNING SO I WASN'T ON TIME FOR THE LESSON.
THAT'S BECAUSE YOU EAT FIVE BOWLS OF RICE FOR BREAKFAST.
BUT THAT'S HOW MUCH I WANT TO EAT.
THEN HOW ABOUT WAKING UP EARLIER!

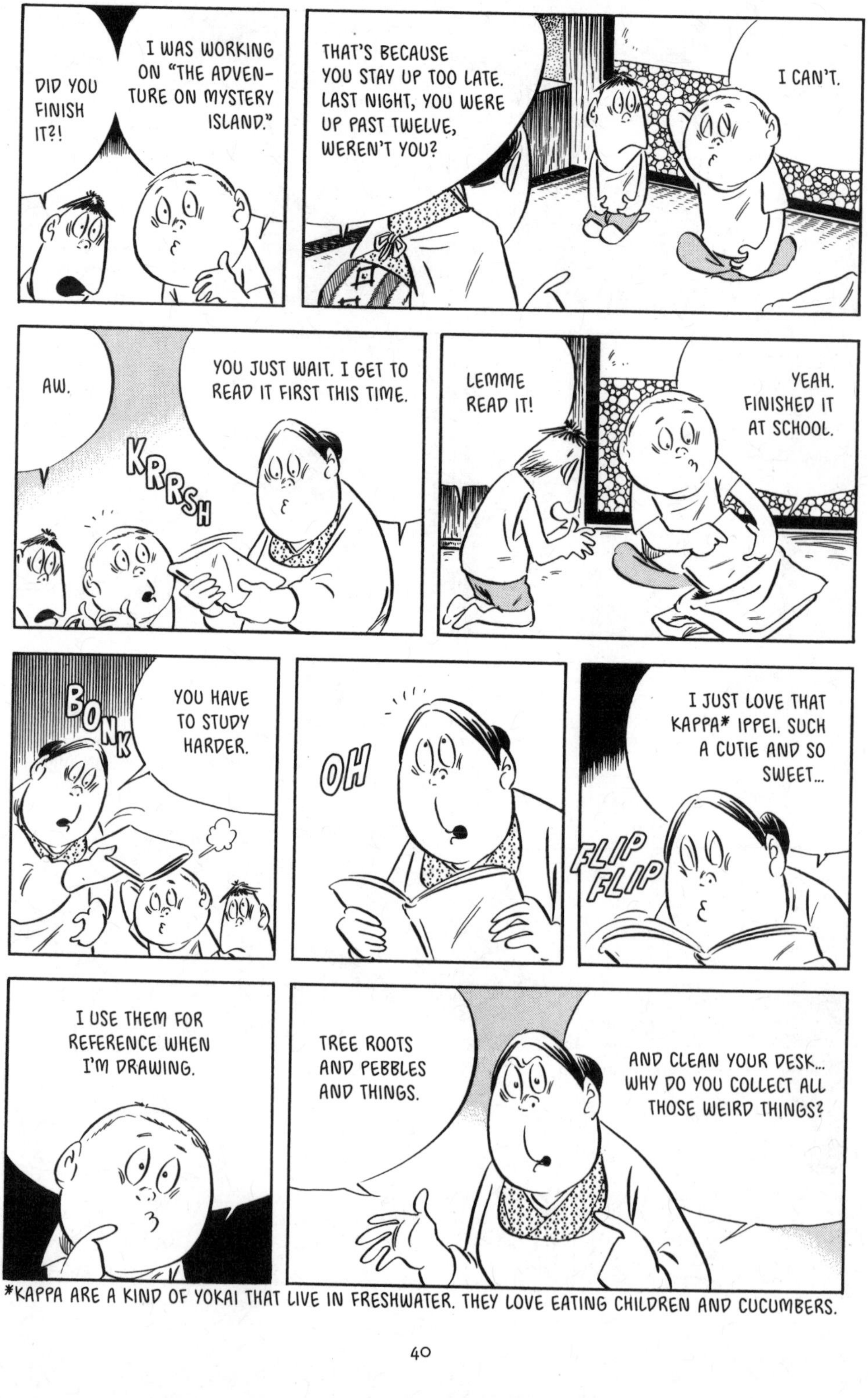
I CAN'T.
THAT'S BECAUSE YOU STAY UP TOO LATE. LAST NIGHT, YOU WERE UP PAST TWELVE, WEREN'T YOU?
I WAS WORKING ON "THE ADVENTURE ON MYSTERY ISLAND."
DID YOU FINISH IT?!
YEAH. FINISHED IT AT SCHOOL.
LEMME READ IT!
YOU JUST WAIT. I GET TO READ IT FIRST THIS TIME.
KRRSH
AW.
I JUST LOVE THAT KAPPA* IPPEI. SUCH A CUTIE AND SO SWEET...
FLIP FLIP
OH
YOU HAVE TO STUDY HARDER.
BONK
AND CLEAN YOUR DESK... WHY DO YOU COLLECT ALL THOSE WEIRD THINGS?
TREE ROOTS AND PEBBLES AND THINGS.
I USE THEM FOR REFERENCE WHEN I'M DRAWING.

*KAPPA ARE A KIND OF YOKAI THAT LIVE IN FRESHWATER. THEY LOVE EATING CHILDREN AND CUCUMBERS.

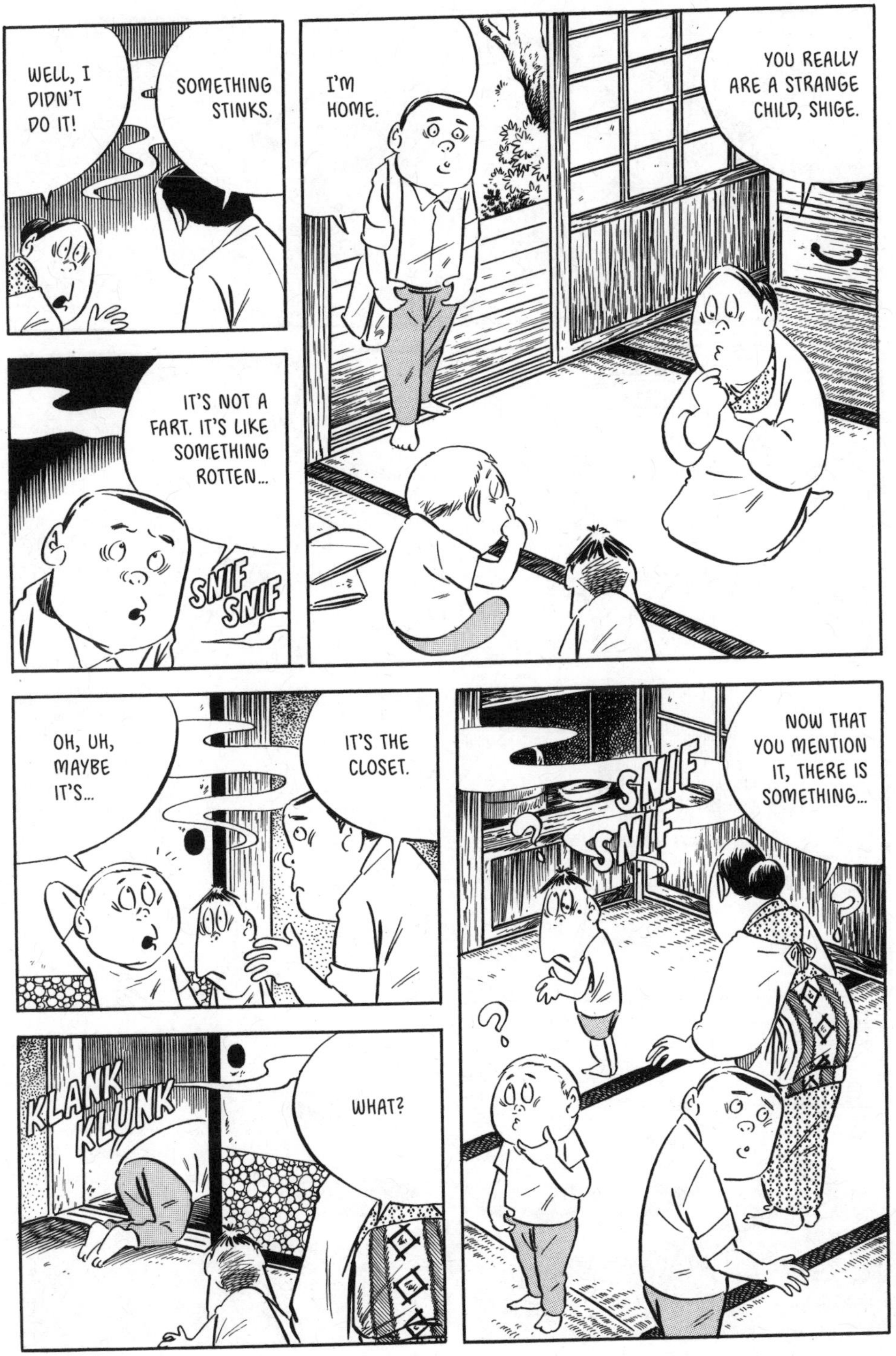
YOU REALLY ARE A STRANGE CHILD, SHIGE.
I'M HOME.
SOMETHING STINKS.
WELL, I DIDN'T DO IT!
IT'S NOT A FART. IT'S LIKE SOMETHING ROTTEN...
SNIF SNIF
NOW THAT YOU MENTION IT, THERE IS SOMETHING...
SNIF SNIF
IT'S THE CLOSET.
OH, UH, MAYBE IT'S...
WHAT?
KLANK KLUNK

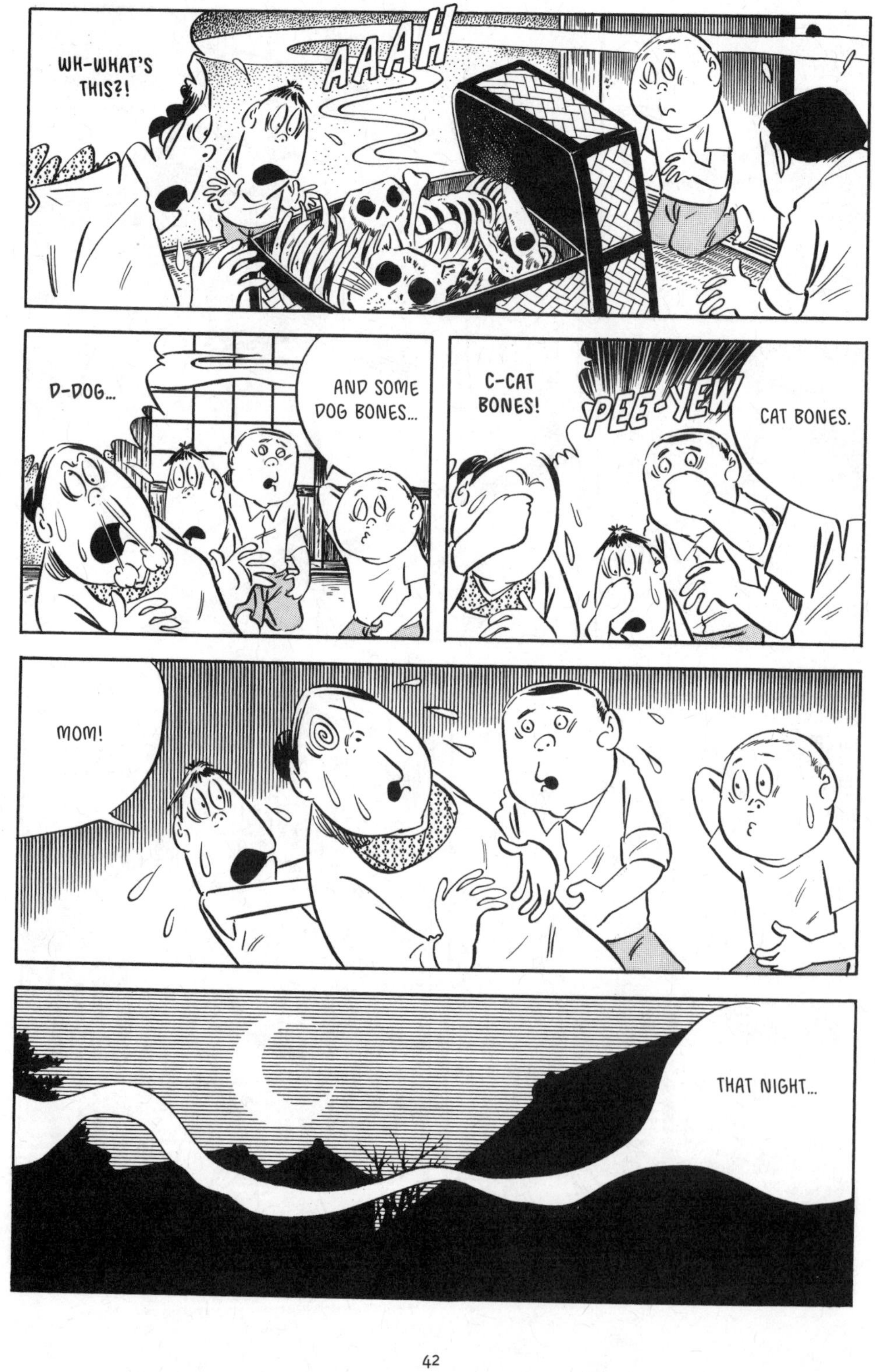
AAAH
WH-WHAT'S THIS?!
CAT BONES.
PEE-YEW
C-CAT BONES!
AND SOME DOG BONES...
D-DOG...
MOM!
THAT NIGHT...

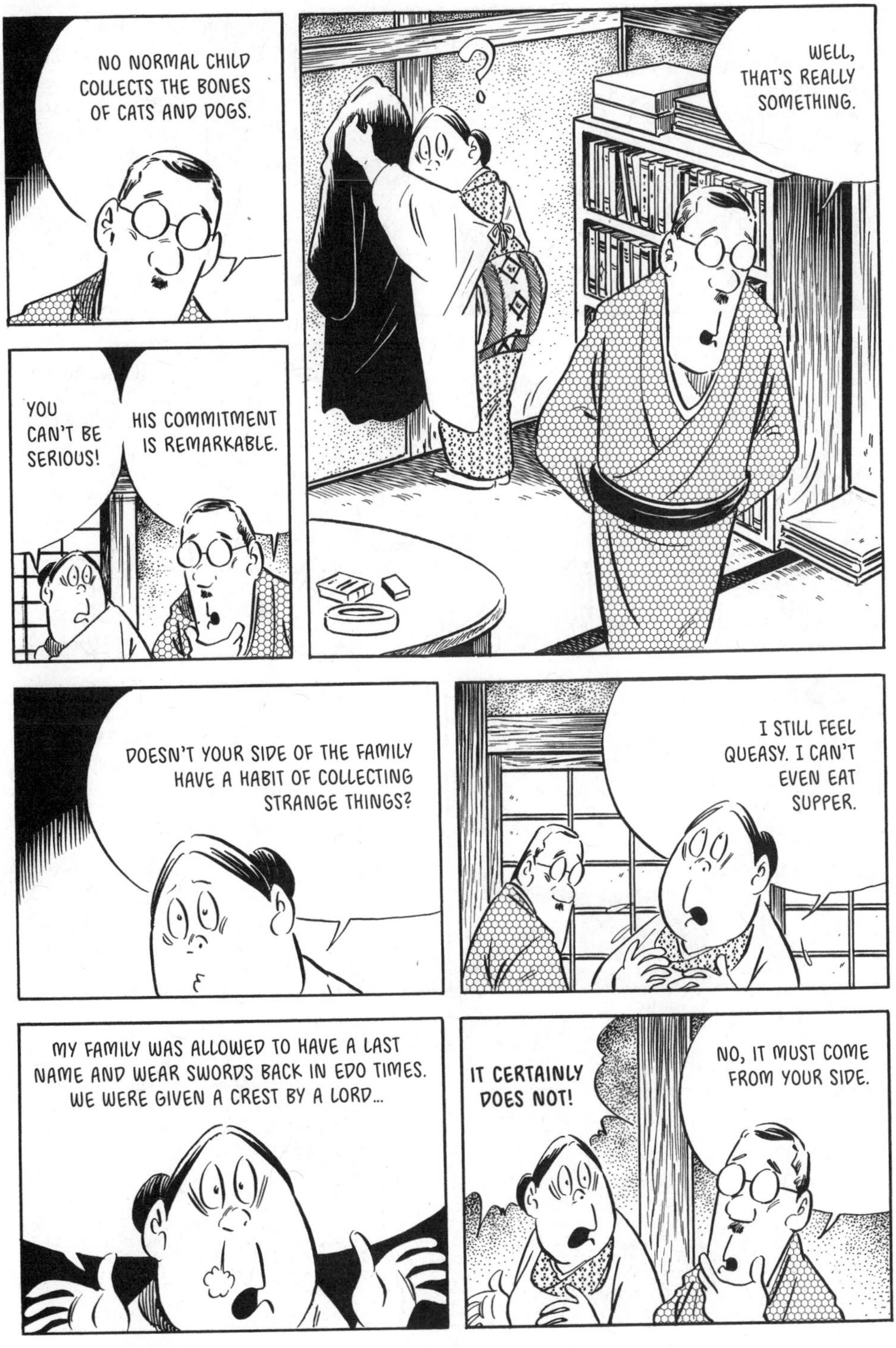
WELL, THAT'S REALLY SOMETHING.
NO NORMAL CHILD COLLECTS THE BONES OF CATS AND DOGS.
HIS COMMITMENT IS REMARKABLE.
YOU CAN'T BE SERIOUS!
I STILL FEEL QUEASY. I CAN'T EVEN EAT SUPPER.
DOESN'T YOUR SIDE OF THE FAMILY HAVE A HABIT OF COLLECTING STRANGE THINGS?
NO, IT MUST COME FROM YOUR SIDE.
IT CERTAINLY DOES NOT!
MY FAMILY WAS ALLOWED TO HAVE A LAST NAME AND WEAR SWORDS BACK IN EDO TIMES. WE WERE GIVEN A CREST BY A LORD...

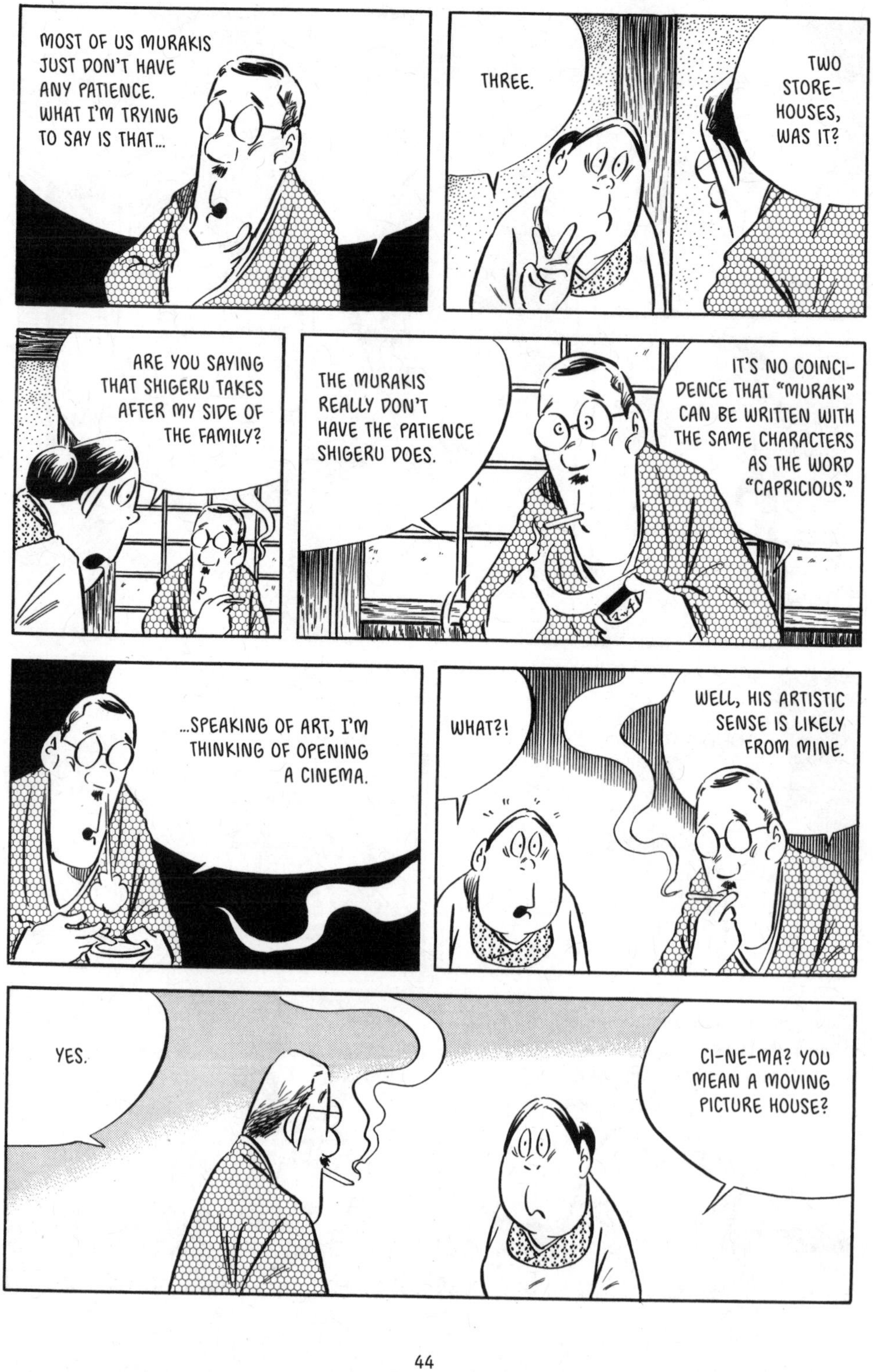
TWO STORE-HOUSES, WAS IT?
THREE.
MOST OF US MURAKIS JUST DON'T HAVE ANY PATIENCE. WHAT I'M TRYING TO SAY IS THAT...
IT'S NO COINCIDENCE THAT "MURAKI" CAN BE WRITTEN WITH THE SAME CHARACTERS AS THE WORD "CAPRICIOUS."
THE MURAKIS REALLY DON'T HAVE THE PATIENCE SHIGERU DOES.
ARE YOU SAYING THAT SHIGERU TAKES AFTER MY SIDE OF THE FAMILY?
WELL, HIS ARTISTIC SENSE IS LIKELY FROM MINE.
WHAT?!
...SPEAKING OF ART, I'M THINKING OF OPENING A CINEMA.
CI-NE-MA? YOU MEAN A MOVING PICTURE HOUSE?
YES.

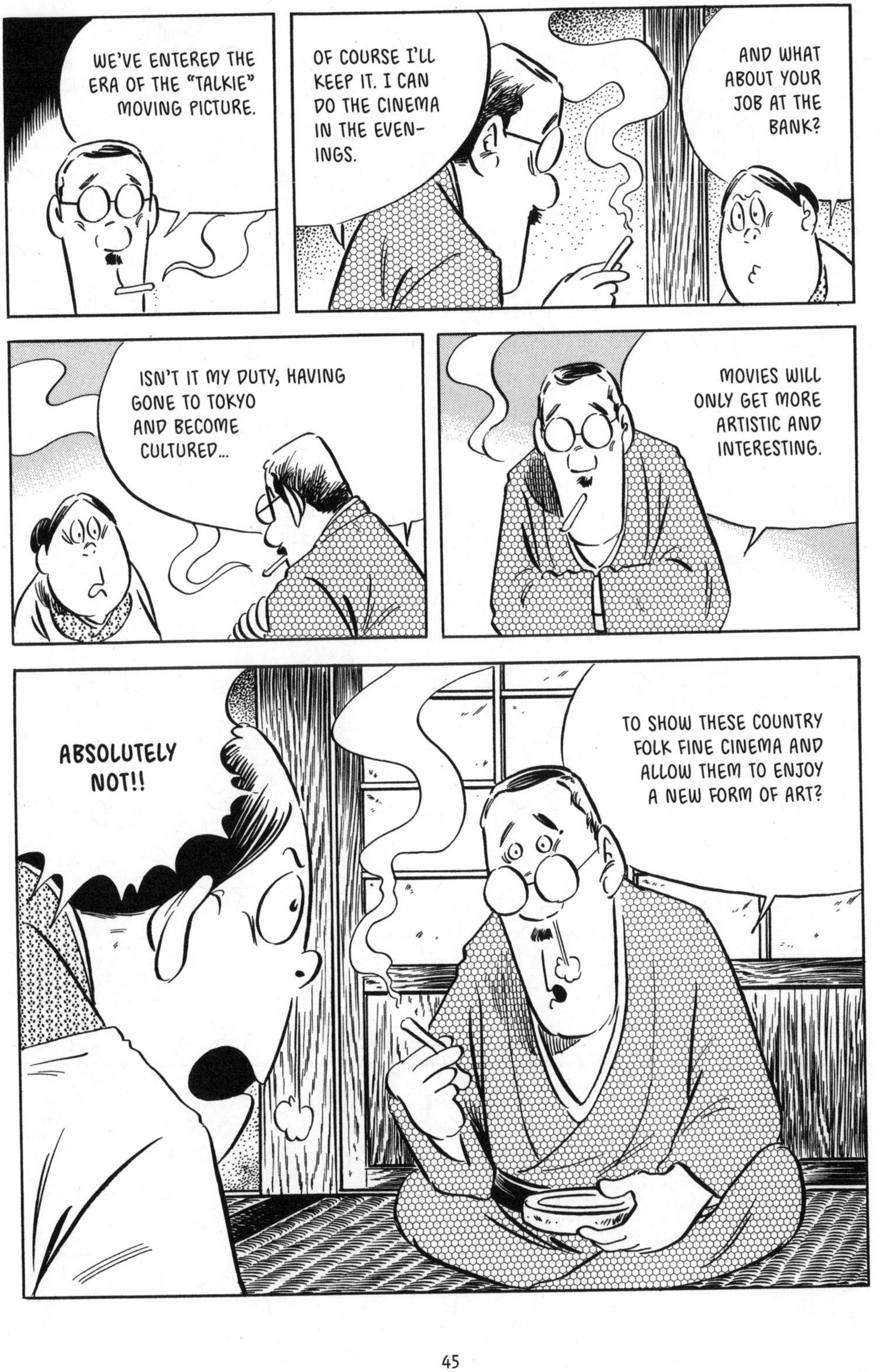
AND WHAT ABOUT YOUR JOB AT THE BANK?
OF COURSE I'LL KEEP IT. I CAN DO THE CINEMA IN THE EVEN-INGS.
WE'VE ENTERED THE ERA OF THE "TALKIE" MOVING PICTURE.
MOVIES WILL ONLY GET MORE ARTISTIC AND INTERESTING.
ISN'T IT MY DUTY, HAVING GONE TO TOKYO AND BECOME CULTURED...
TO SHOW THESE COUNTRY FOLK FINE CINEMA AND ALLOW THEM TO ENJOY A NEW FORM OF ART?
ABSOLUTELY NOT!!

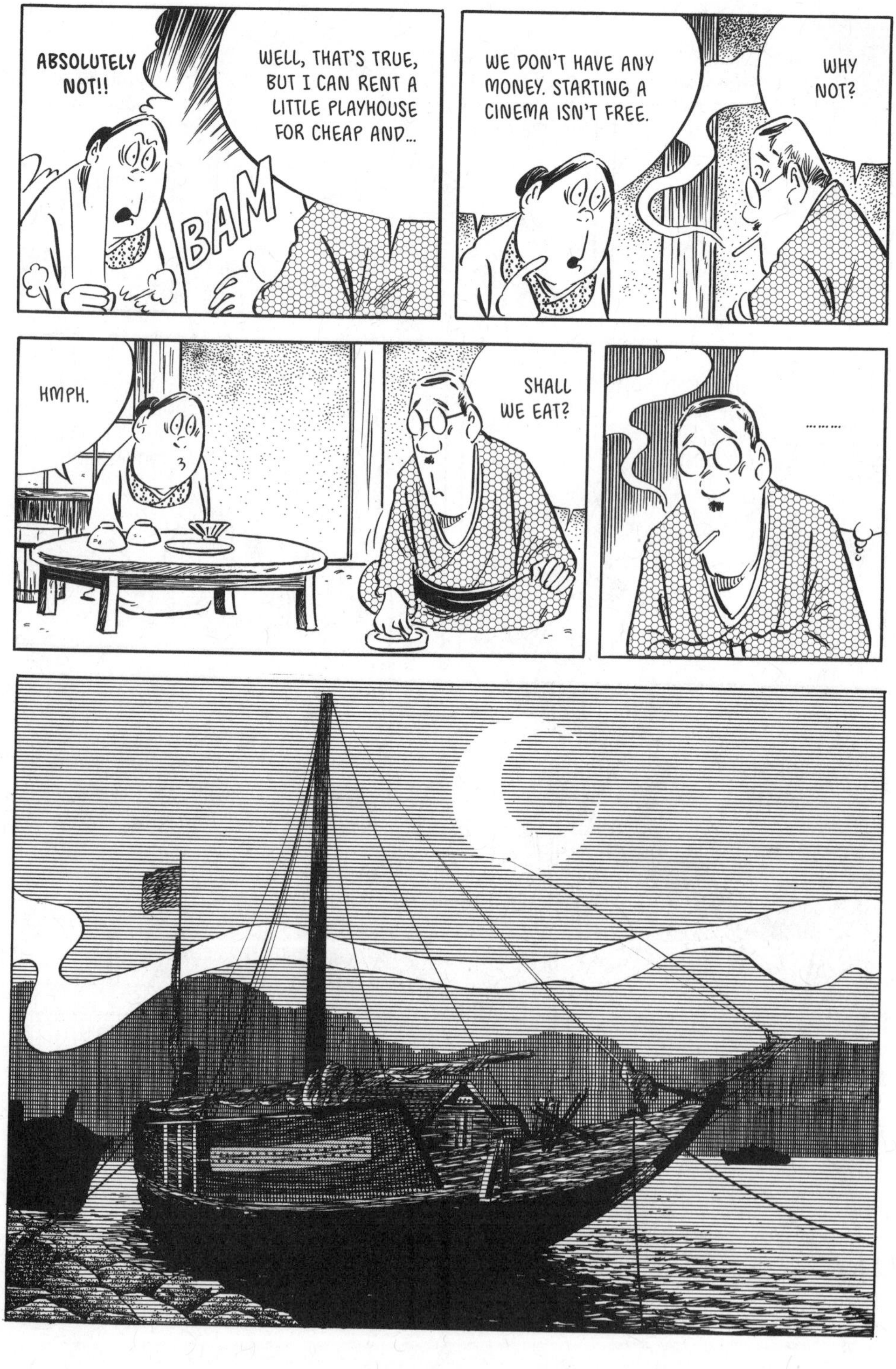
WHY NOT?
WE DON'T HAVE ANY MONEY. STARTING A CINEMA ISN'T FREE.
WELL, THAT'S TRUE, BUT I CAN RENT A LITTLE PLAYHOUSE FOR CHEAP AND...
ABSOLUTELY NOT!!
BAM
....
SHALL WE EAT?
HMPH.

MR. STICKY, PLEASE, AFTER YOU

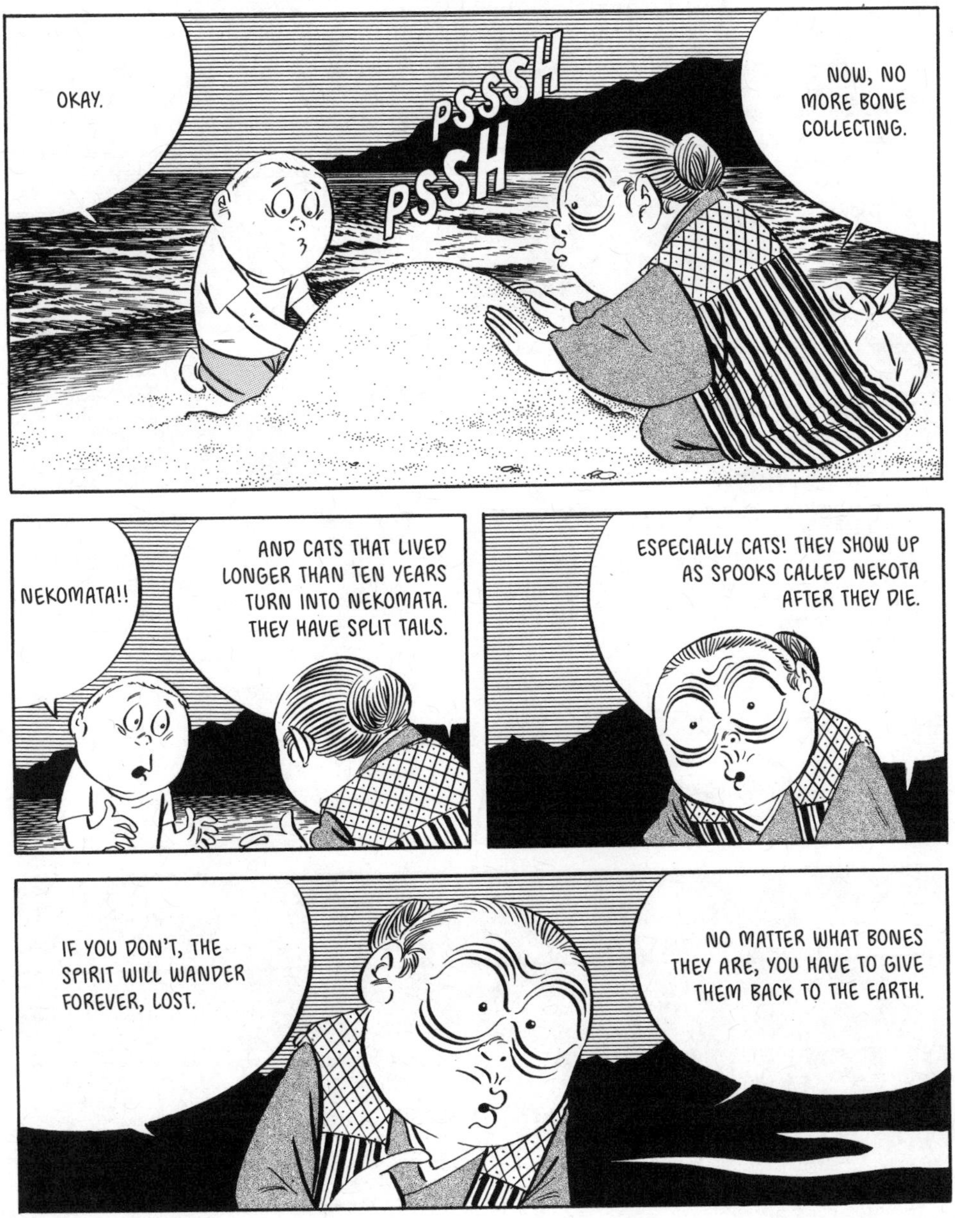
NOW, NO MORE BONE COLLECTING.
PSSSH
PSSH
OKAY.
ESPECIALLY CATS! THEY SHOW UP AS SPOOKS CALLED NEKOTA AFTER THEY DIE.
AND CATS THAT LIVED LONGER THAN TEN YEARS TURN INTO NEKOMATA. THEY HAVE SPLIT TAILS.
NEKOMATA!!
NO MATTER WHAT BONES THEY ARE, YOU HAVE TO GIVE THEM BACK TO THE EARTH.
IF YOU DON'T, THE SPIRIT WILL WANDER FOREVER, LOST.

OKAY.
GLUG GLUG GLUG
GULP GULP
ARE THERE YOKAI IN THE OCEAN TOO?
FWOOO
OF COURSE.
THERE'S UMIBOZU, UMIZATO, TOMOKAZUKI, MIZUCHI... PLENTY OF STRANGE THINGS.*
IS THERE ONE THAT CAN MAKE MY GRADES BETTER?
NO SUCH THING AS THAT.
HA HA HA
PSSH PSSH

*SEE NOTES PAGE 417.

KLAK KLEK
KLAK KLEK
NO-NONNONBA! S-SOMETHING'S BEHIND US.
KLAK KLEK
MMM, MR. STICKY'S* GOTTEN HIMSELF STUCK TO US.
YOU CAN HEAR HIS GETA SANDALS.
KLAK KLEK
L-LET'S RUN!
KLAK KLEK
YOU CAN RUN, OR YOU CAN STEP ASIDE AND SAY, "MR. STICKY, PLEASE, AFTER YOU."
KLAK KLEK

*SEE NOTES PAGE 417.

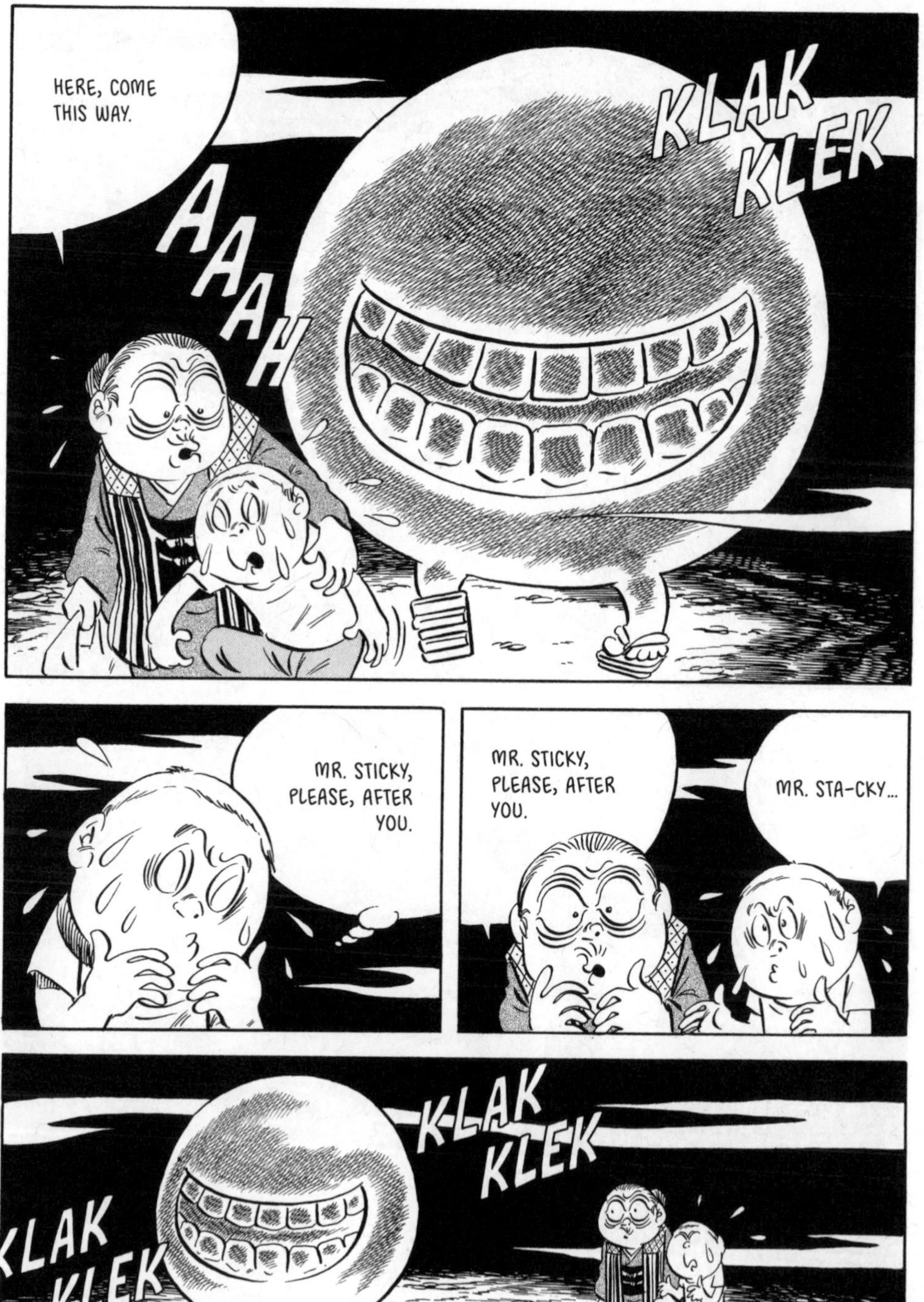
KLAK KLEK
HERE, COME THIS WAY.
AAAAH
MR. STA-CKY...
MR. STICKY, PLEASE, AFTER YOU.
MR. STICKY, PLEASE, AFTER YOU.
KLAK KLEK
KLAK KLEK

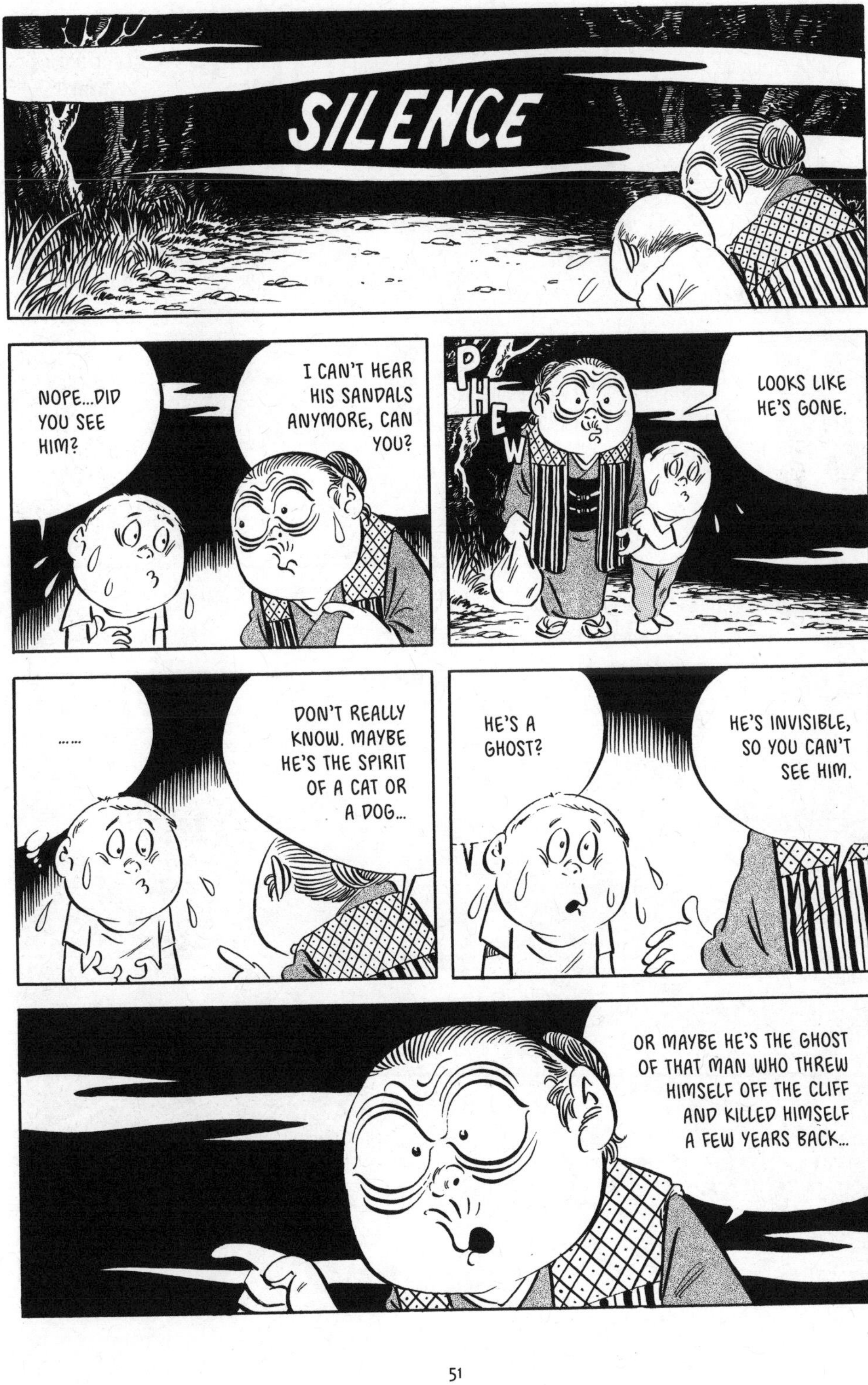
SILENCE
PHEW
LOOKS LIKE HE'S GONE.
I CAN'T HEAR HIS SANDALS ANYMORE, CAN YOU?
NOPE...DID YOU SEE HIM?
HE'S INVISIBLE, SO YOU CAN'T SEE HIM.
HE'S A GHOST?
DON'T REALLY KNOW. MAYBE HE'S THE SPIRIT OF A CAT OR A DOG...
……
OR MAYBE HE'S THE GHOST OF THAT MAN WHO THREW HIMSELF OFF THE CLIFF AND KILLED HIMSELF A FEW YEARS BACK...

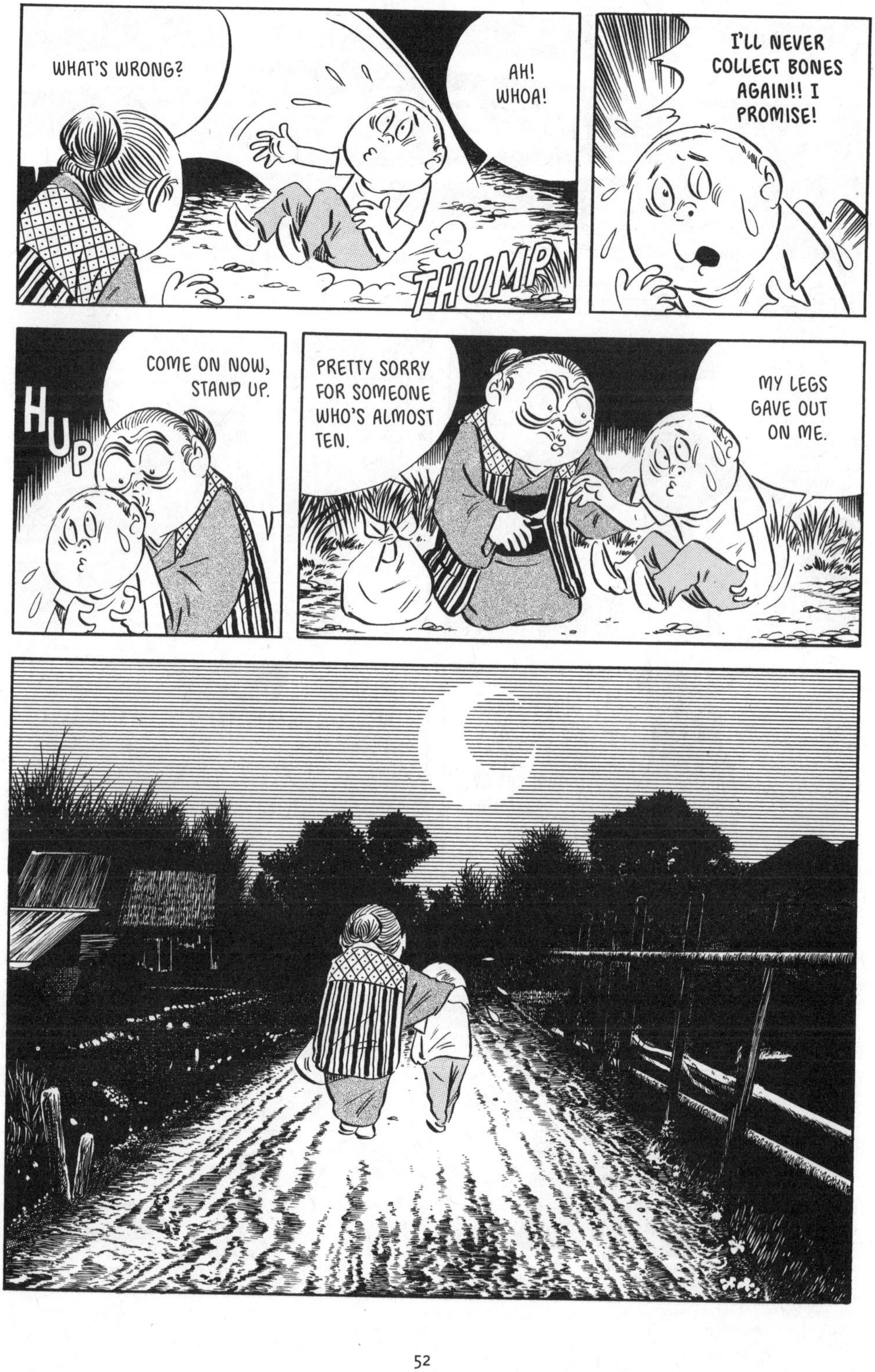
I'LL NEVER COLLECT BONES AGAIN!! I PROMISE!
AH! WHOA!
WHAT'S WRONG?
THUMP
MY LEGS GAVE OUT ON ME.
PRETTY SORRY FOR SOMEONE WHO'S ALMOST TEN.
COME ON NOW, STAND UP.
HUP

THE WART

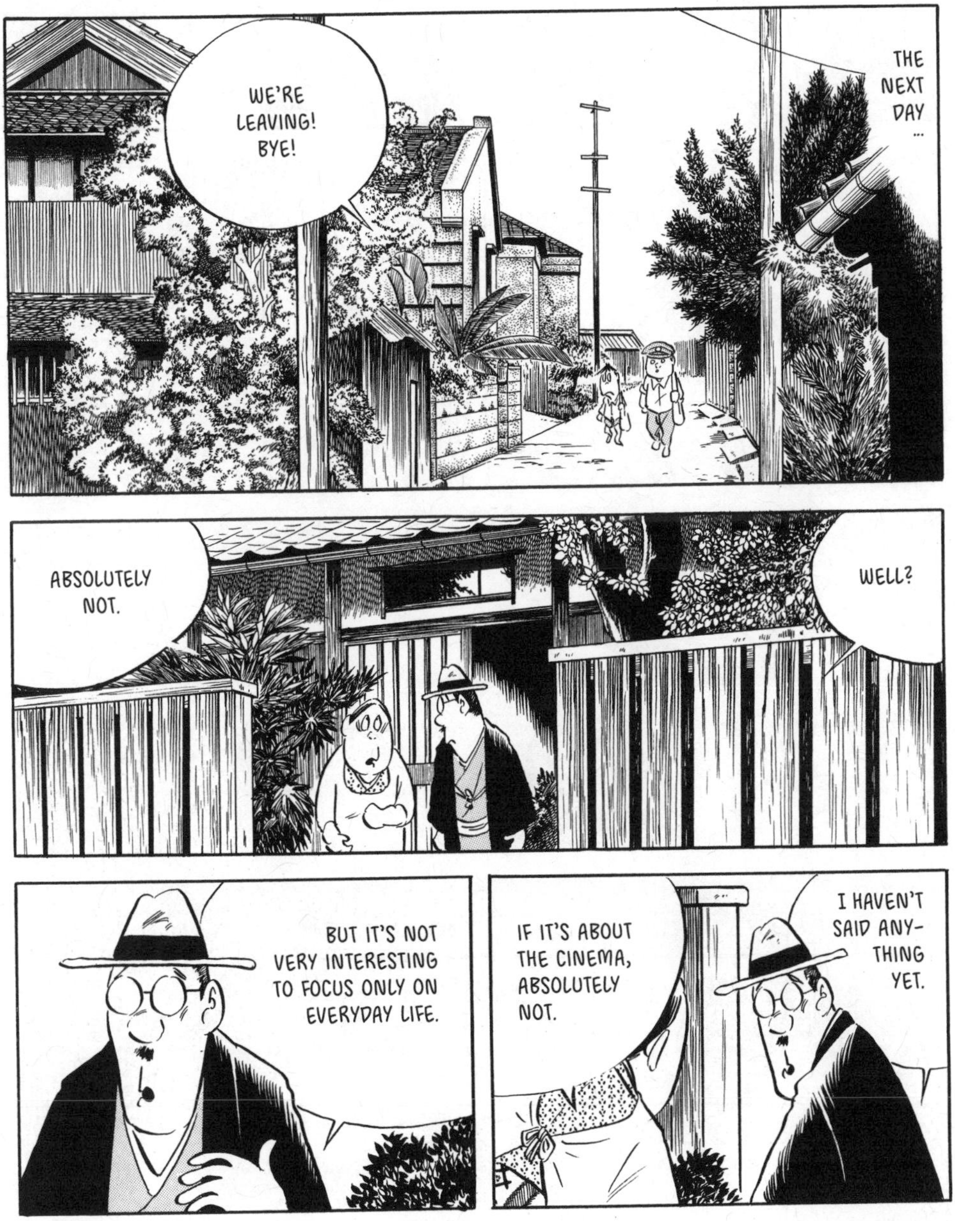
THE NEXT DAY ...
WE'RE LEAVING! BYE!
WELL?
ABSOLUTELY NOT.
I HAVEN'T SAID ANY-THING YET.
IF IT'S ABOUT THE CINEMA, ABSOLUTELY NOT.
BUT IT'S NOT VERY INTERESTING TO FOCUS ONLY ON EVERYDAY LIFE.

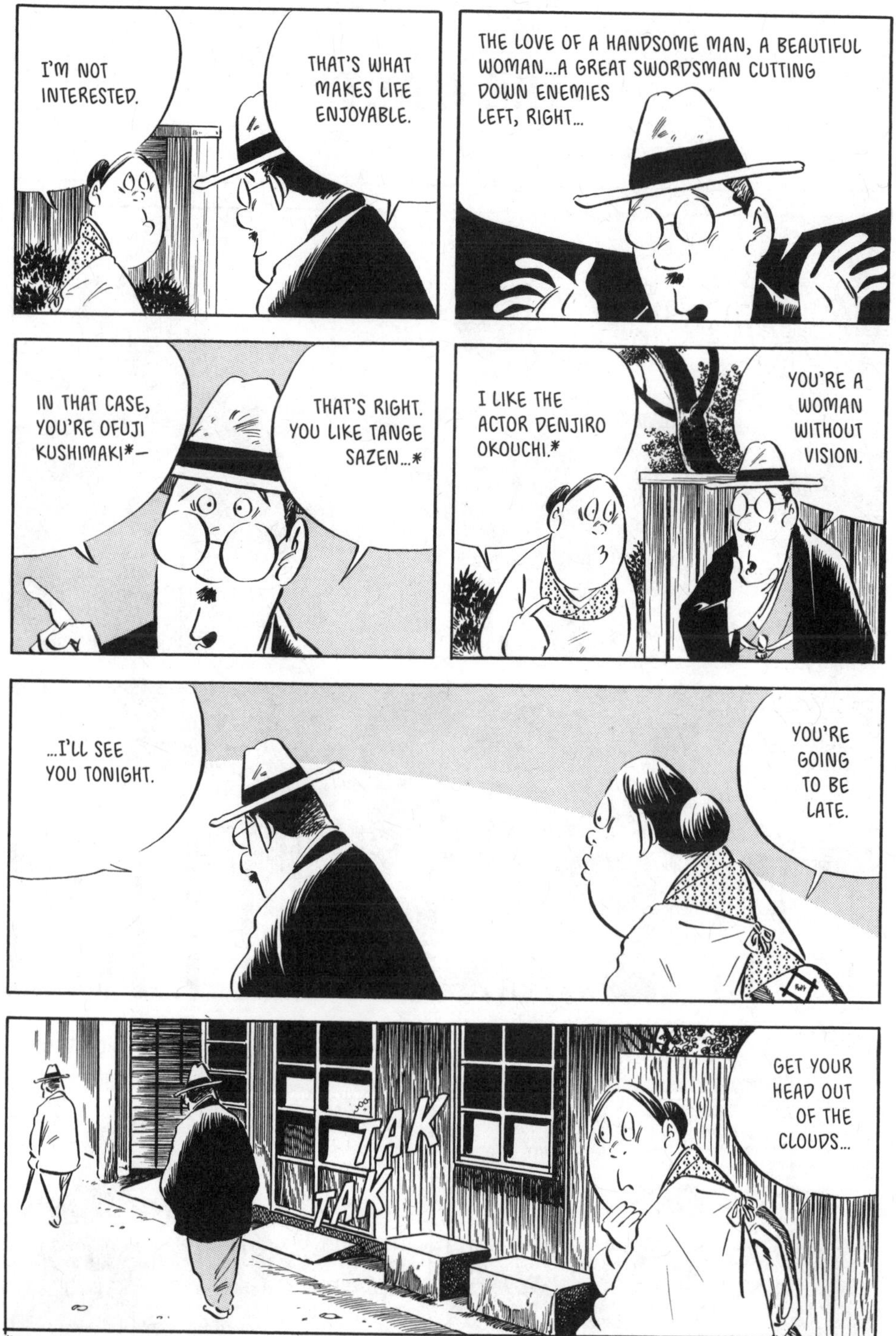
THE LOVE OF A HANDSOME MAN, A BEAUTIFUL WOMAN...A GREAT SWORDSMAN CUTTING DOWN ENEMIES LEFT, RIGHT...
THAT'S WHAT MAKES LIFE ENJOYABLE.
I'M NOT INTERESTED.
YOU'RE A WOMAN WITHOUT VISION.
I LIKE THE ACTOR DENJIRO OKOUCHI.*
THAT'S RIGHT. YOU LIKE TANGE SAZEN...*
IN THAT CASE, YOU'RE OFUJI KUSHIMAKI*—
YOU'RE GOING TO BE LATE.
...I'LL SEE YOU TONIGHT.
GET YOUR HEAD OUT OF THE CLOUDS...
TAK
TAK

*SEE NOTES PAGE 417.

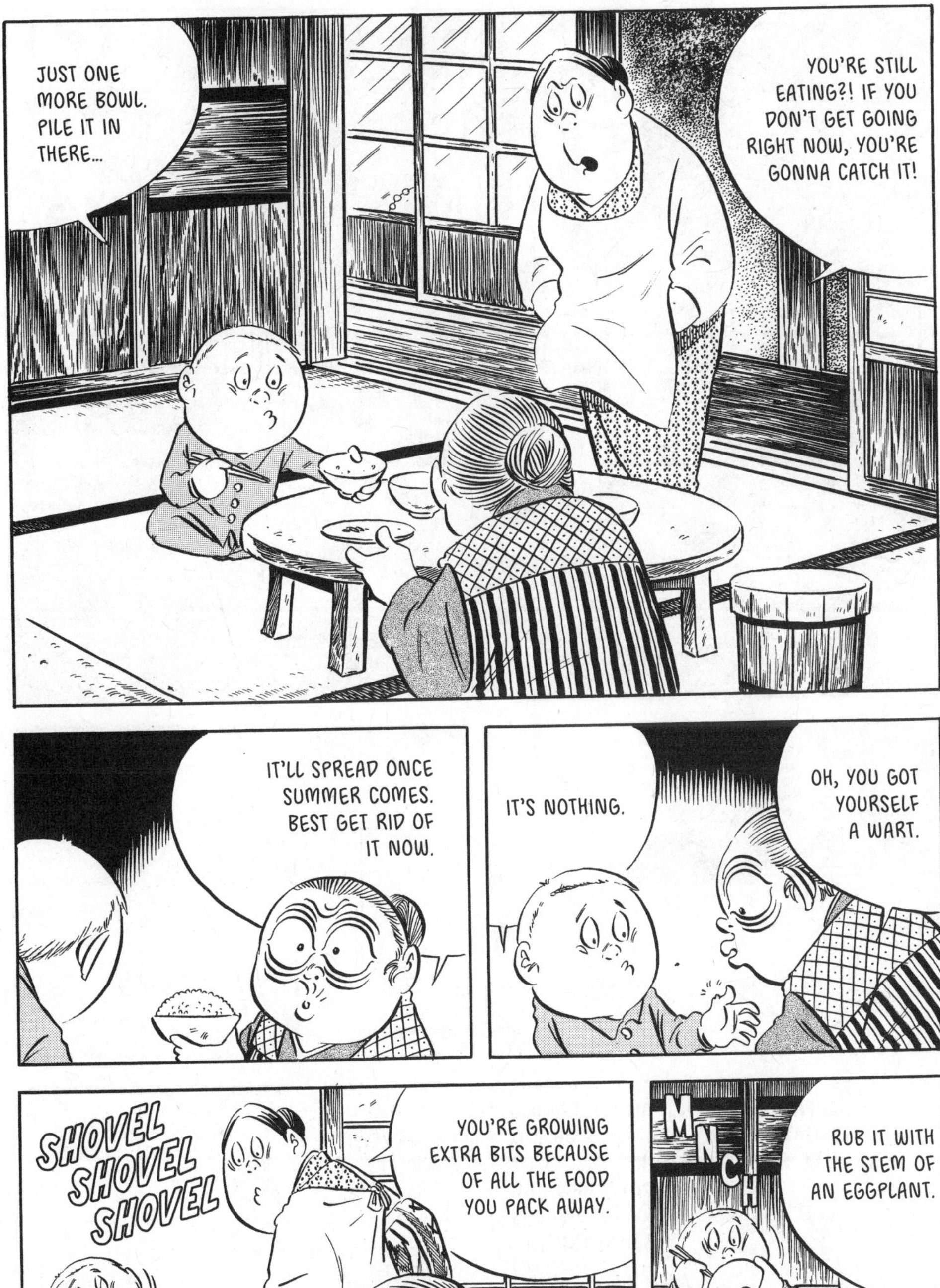
YOU'RE STILL EATING?! IF YOU DON'T GET GOING RIGHT NOW, YOU'RE GONNA CATCH IT!
JUST ONE MORE BOWL. PILE IT IN THERE...
OH, YOU GOT YOURSELF A WART.
IT'S NOTHING.
IT'LL SPREAD ONCE SUMMER COMES. BEST GET RID OF IT NOW.
MNCH
RUB IT WITH THE STEM OF AN EGGPLANT.
YOU'RE GROWING EXTRA BITS BECAUSE OF ALL THE FOOD YOU PACK AWAY.
SHOVEL SHOVEL SHOVEL

SNEAK
MURAKI!!
YEAH?
NOT "YEAH"! WHY ARE YOU NEVER ON TIME?
JAPAN IS ISOLATED AND OUTSHONE INTERNATIONALLY.* WHAT KIND OF SON OF THE EMPIRE ARE YOU SHOWING UP LATE EVERY DAY WHEN OUR VERY SURVIVAL IS BEING THREATENED!!

*SEE NOTES PAGE 417.

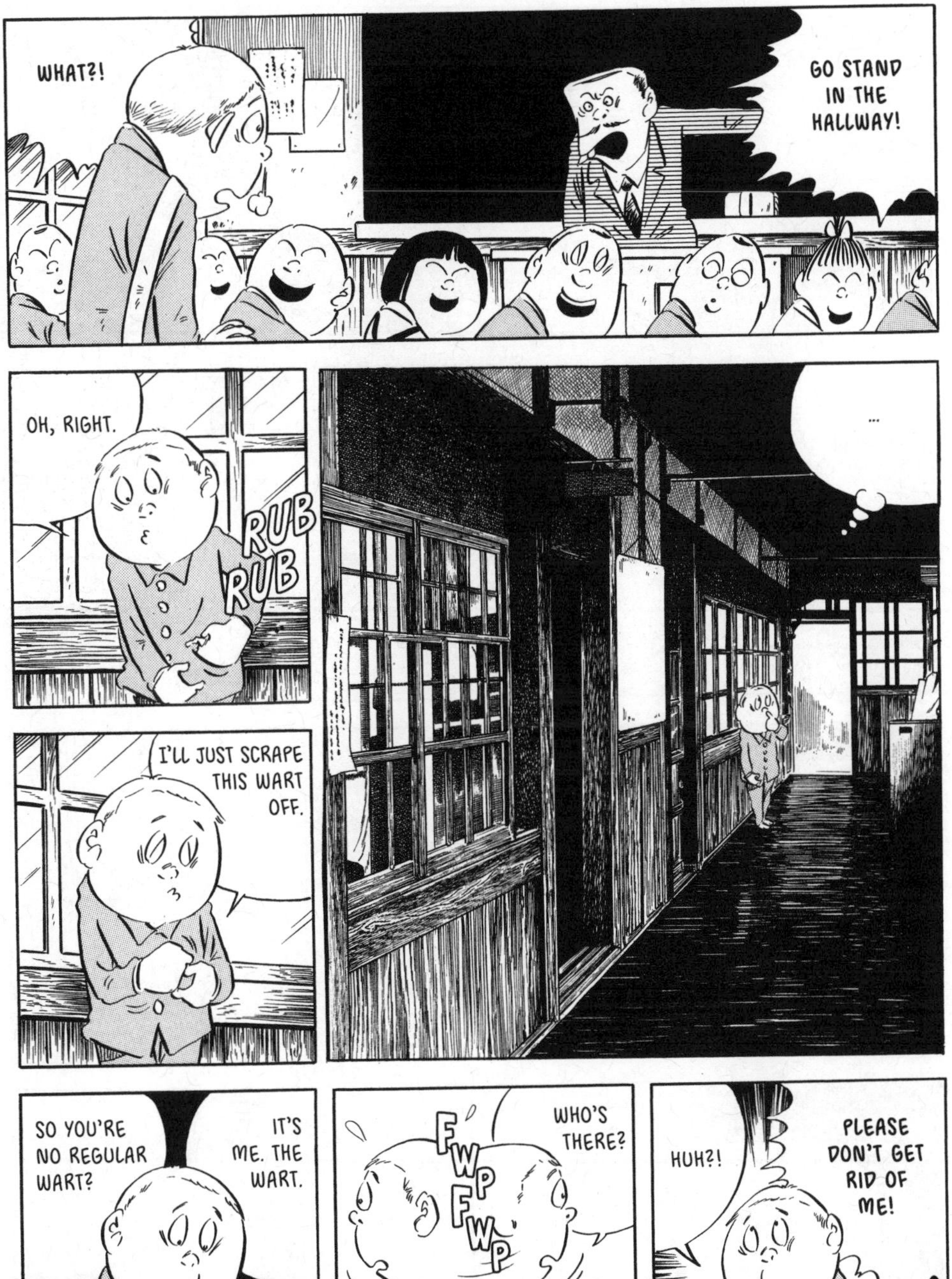
GO STAND IN THE HALLWAY!
WHAT?!
...
OH, RIGHT.
RUB RUB
I'LL JUST SCRAPE THIS WART OFF.
PLEASE DON'T GET RID OF ME!
HUH?!
WHO'S THERE?
FWP FWP
IT'S ME. THE WART.
SO YOU'RE NO REGULAR WART?

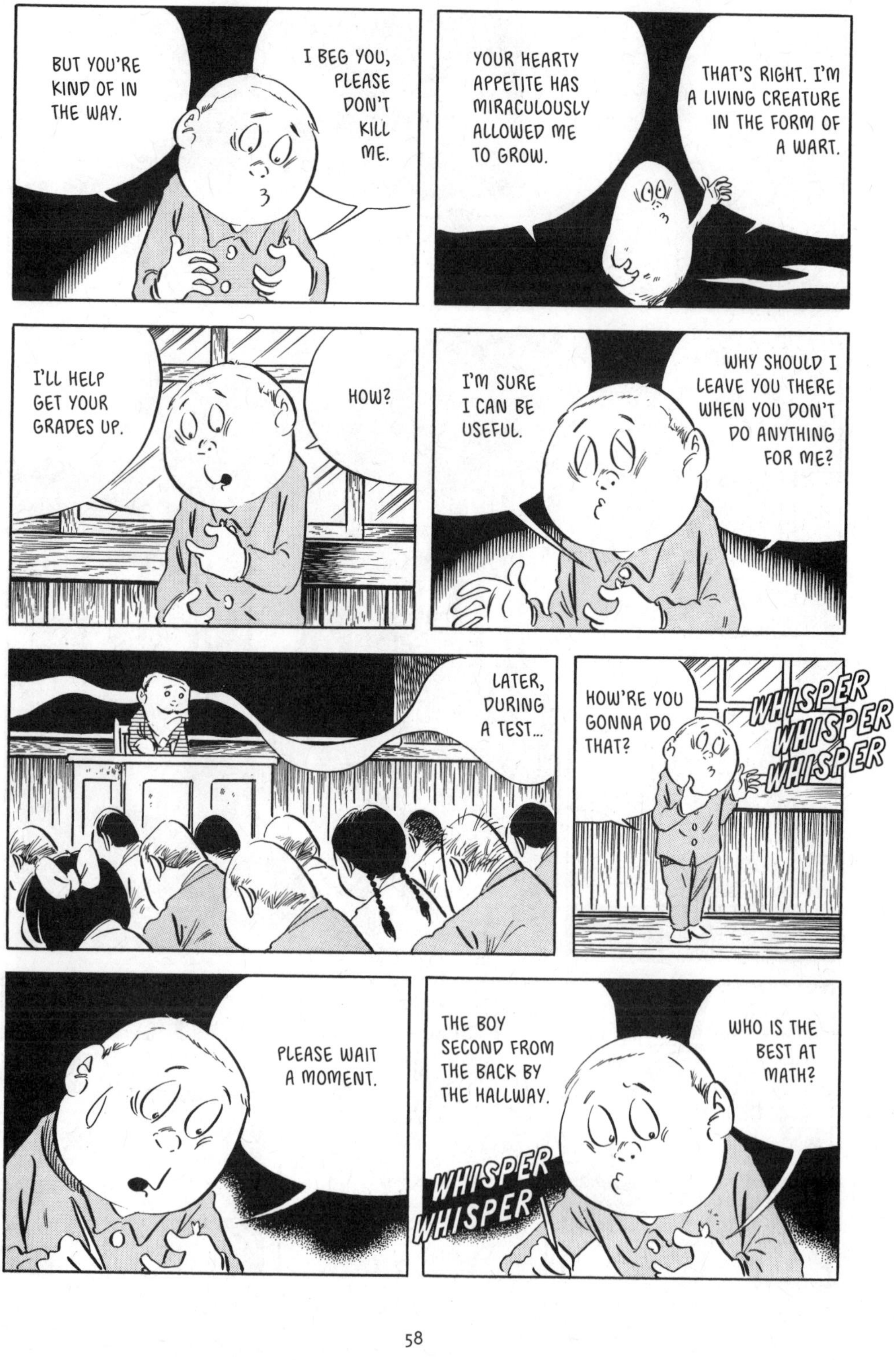
THAT'S RIGHT. I'M A LIVING CREATURE IN THE FORM OF A WART.
YOUR HEARTY APPETITE HAS MIRACULOUSLY ALLOWED ME TO GROW.
I BEG YOU, PLEASE DON'T KILL ME.
BUT YOU'RE KIND OF IN THE WAY.
WHY SHOULD I LEAVE YOU THERE WHEN YOU DON'T DO ANYTHING FOR ME?
I'M SURE I CAN BE USEFUL.
HOW?
I'LL HELP GET YOUR GRADES UP.
WHISPER WHISPER WHISPER
HOW'RE YOU GONNA DO THAT?
LATER, DURING A TEST...
WHO IS THE BEST AT MATH?
THE BOY SECOND FROM THE BACK BY THE HALLWAY.
WHISPER WHISPER
PLEASE WAIT A MOMENT.

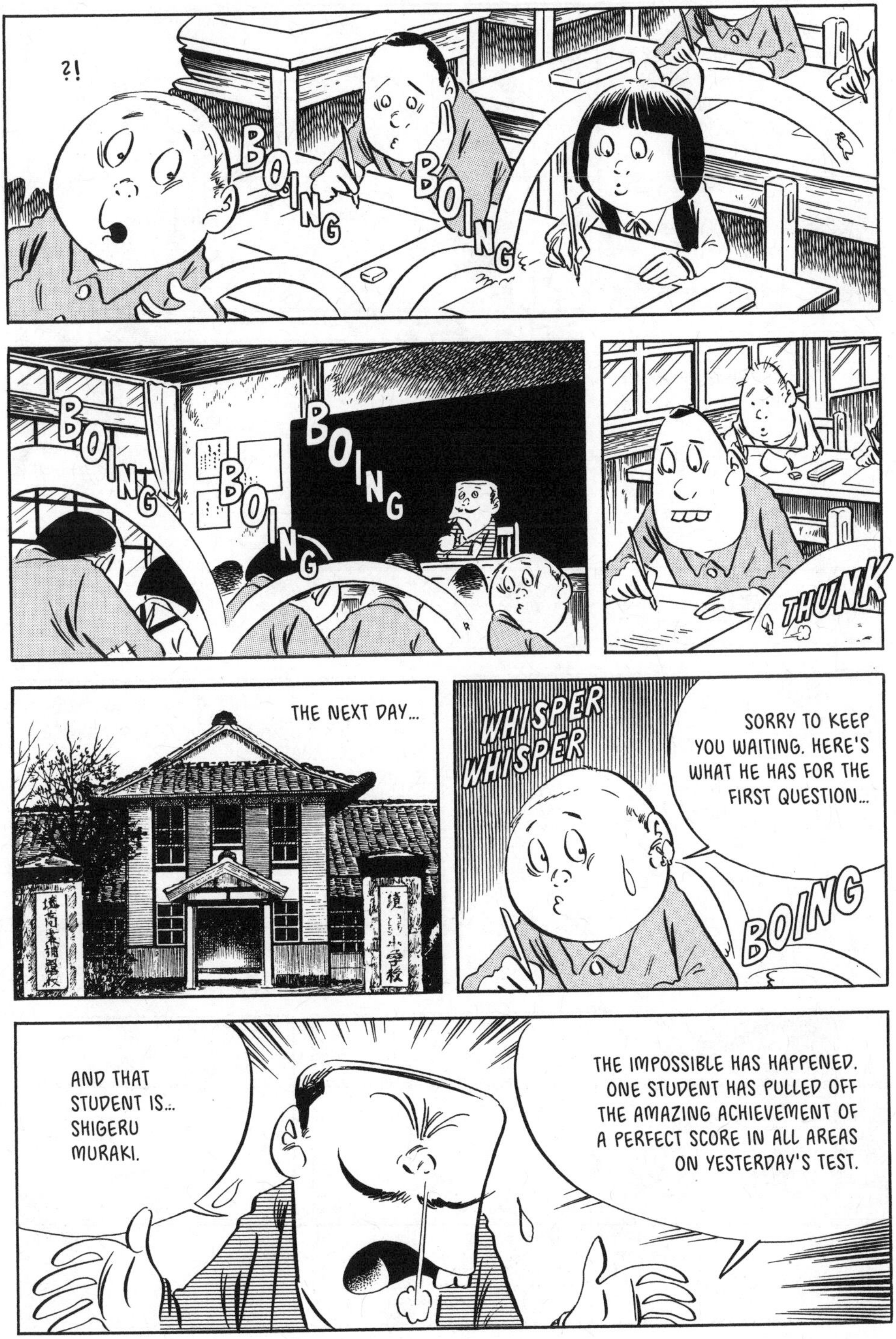
?!
BOING
BOING
THUNK
BOING
BOING
BOING
WHISPER
WHISPER
SORRY TO KEEP YOU WAITING. HERE'S WHAT HE HAS FOR THE FIRST QUESTION...
BOING
THE NEXT DAY...
THE IMPOSSIBLE HAS HAPPENED. ONE STUDENT HAS PULLED OFF THE AMAZING ACHIEVEMENT OF A PERFECT SCORE IN ALL AREAS ON YESTERDAY'S TEST.
AND THAT STUDENT IS... SHIGERU MURAKI.

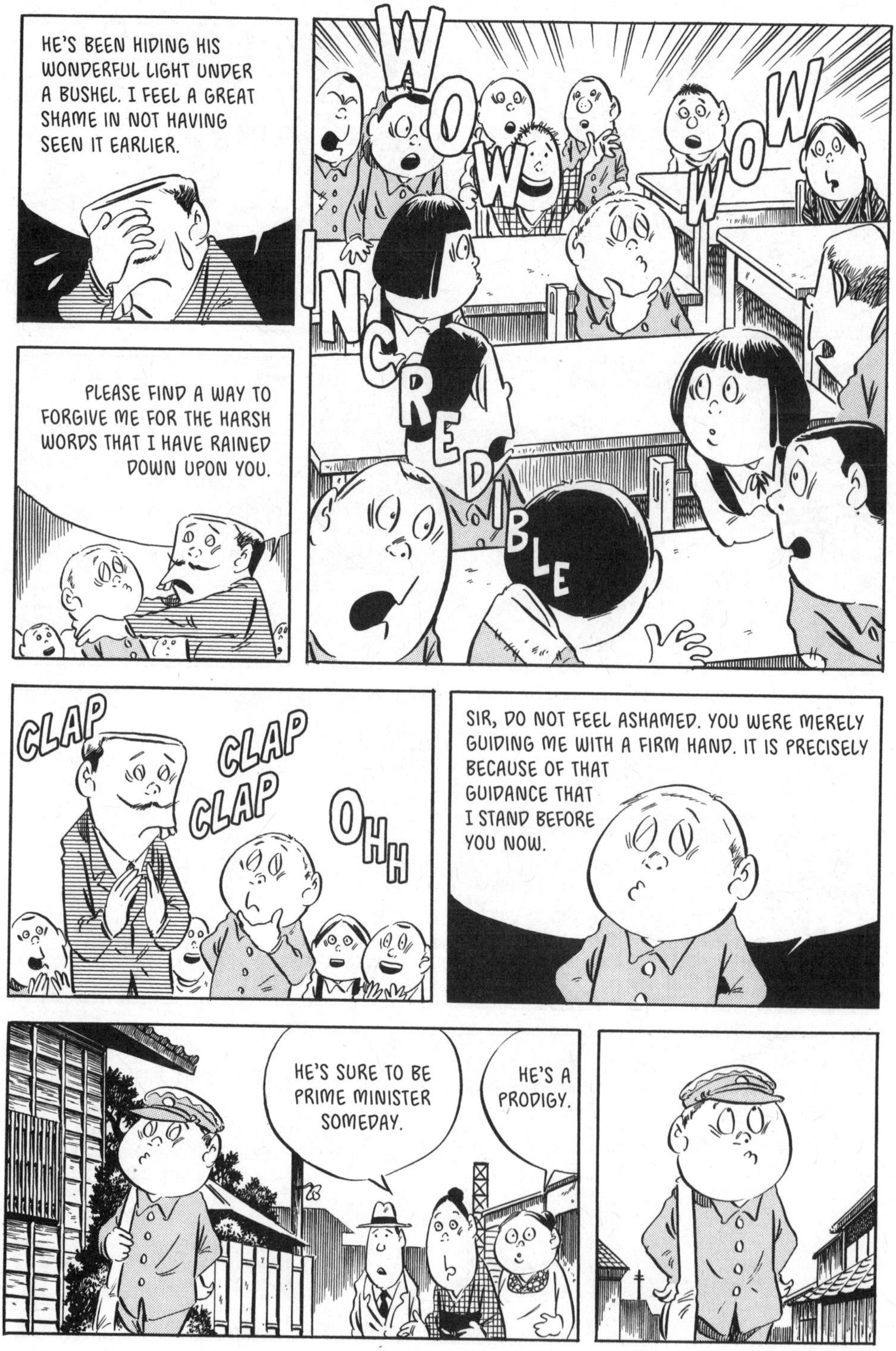
WOW
WOW
WOW
INCREDIBLE
HE'S BEEN HIDING HIS WONDERFUL LIGHT UNDER A BUSHEL. I FEEL A GREAT SHAME IN NOT HAVING SEEN IT EARLIER.
PLEASE FIND A WAY TO FORGIVE ME FOR THE HARSH WORDS THAT I HAVE RAINED DOWN UPON YOU.
SIR, DO NOT FEEL ASHAMED. YOU WERE MERELY GUIDING ME WITH A FIRM HAND. IT IS PRECISELY BECAUSE OF THAT GUIDANCE THAT I STAND BEFORE YOU NOW.
OHH
CLAP
CLAP
CLAP
HE'S A PRODIGY.
HE'S SURE TO BE PRIME MINISTER SOMEDAY.

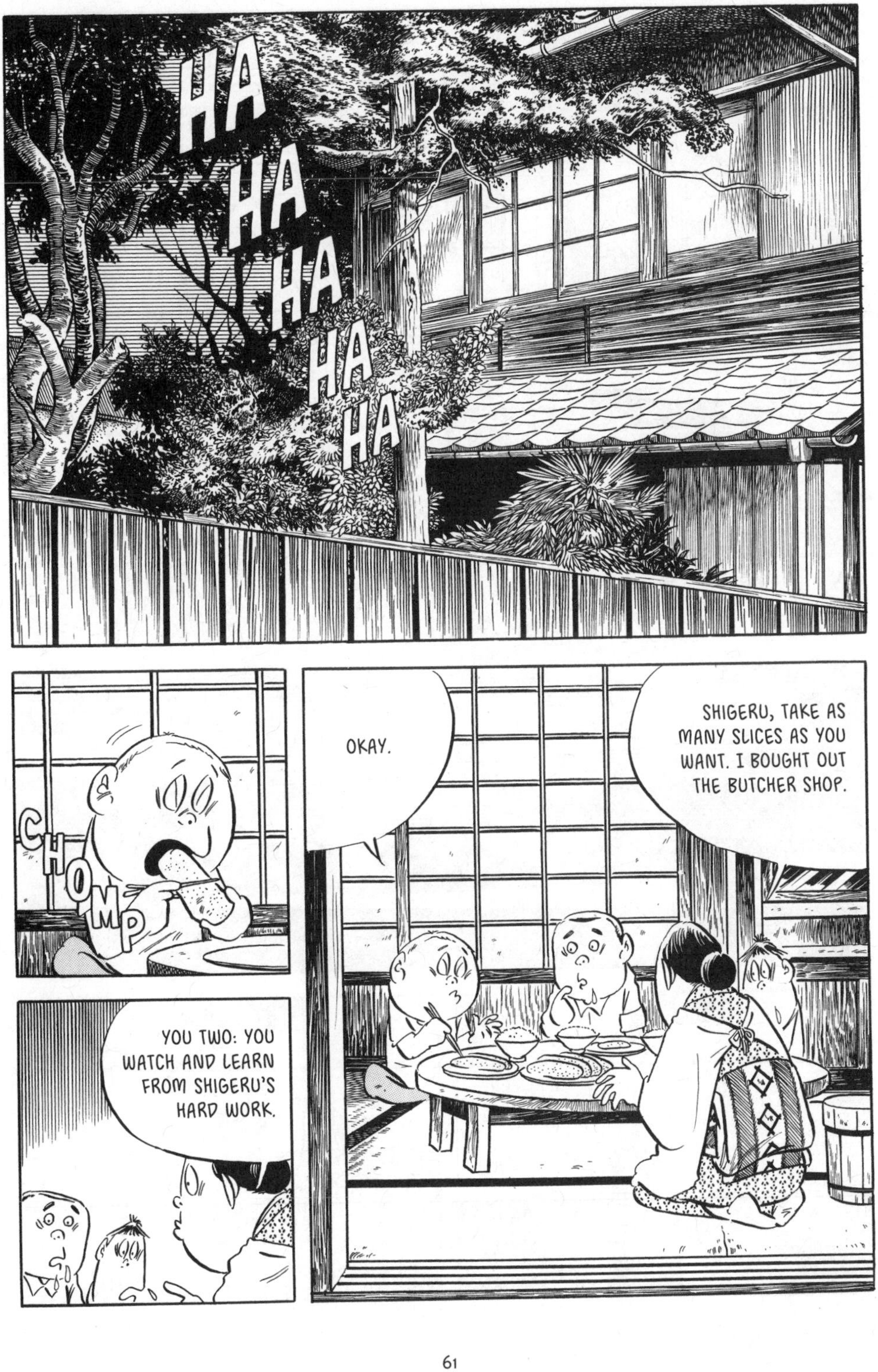
HA HA HA HA HA HA
SHIGERU, TAKE AS MANY SLICES AS YOU WANT. I BOUGHT OUT THE BUTCHER SHOP.
OKAY.
CHOMP
YOU TWO: YOU WATCH AND LEARN FROM SHIGERU'S HARD WORK.

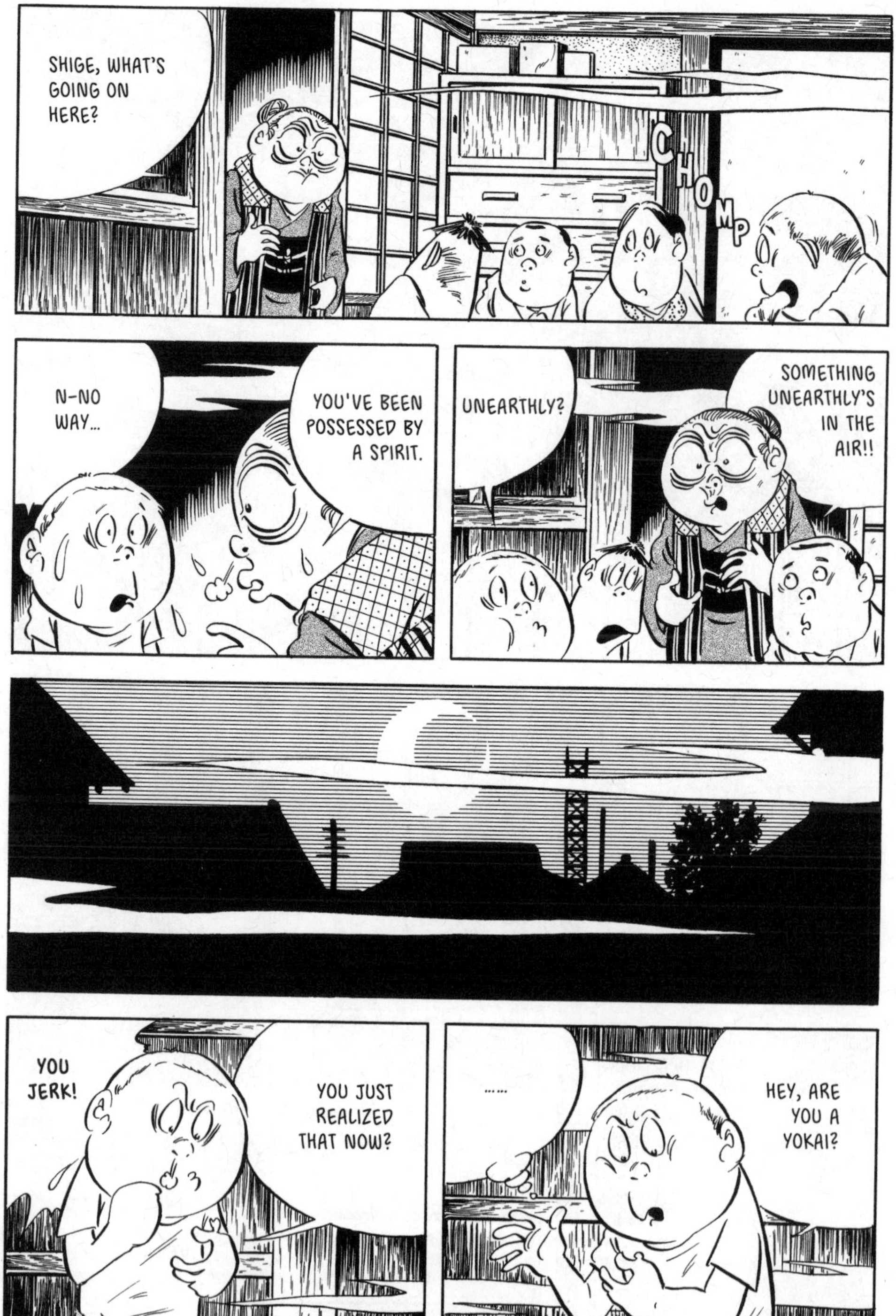
SHIGE, WHAT'S GOING ON HERE?
CHOMP
SOMETHING UNEARTHLY'S IN THE AIR!!
UNEARTHLY?
YOU'VE BEEN POSSESSED BY A SPIRIT.
N-NO WAY...
HEY, ARE YOU A YOKAI?
......
YOU JUST REALIZED THAT NOW?
YOU JERK!

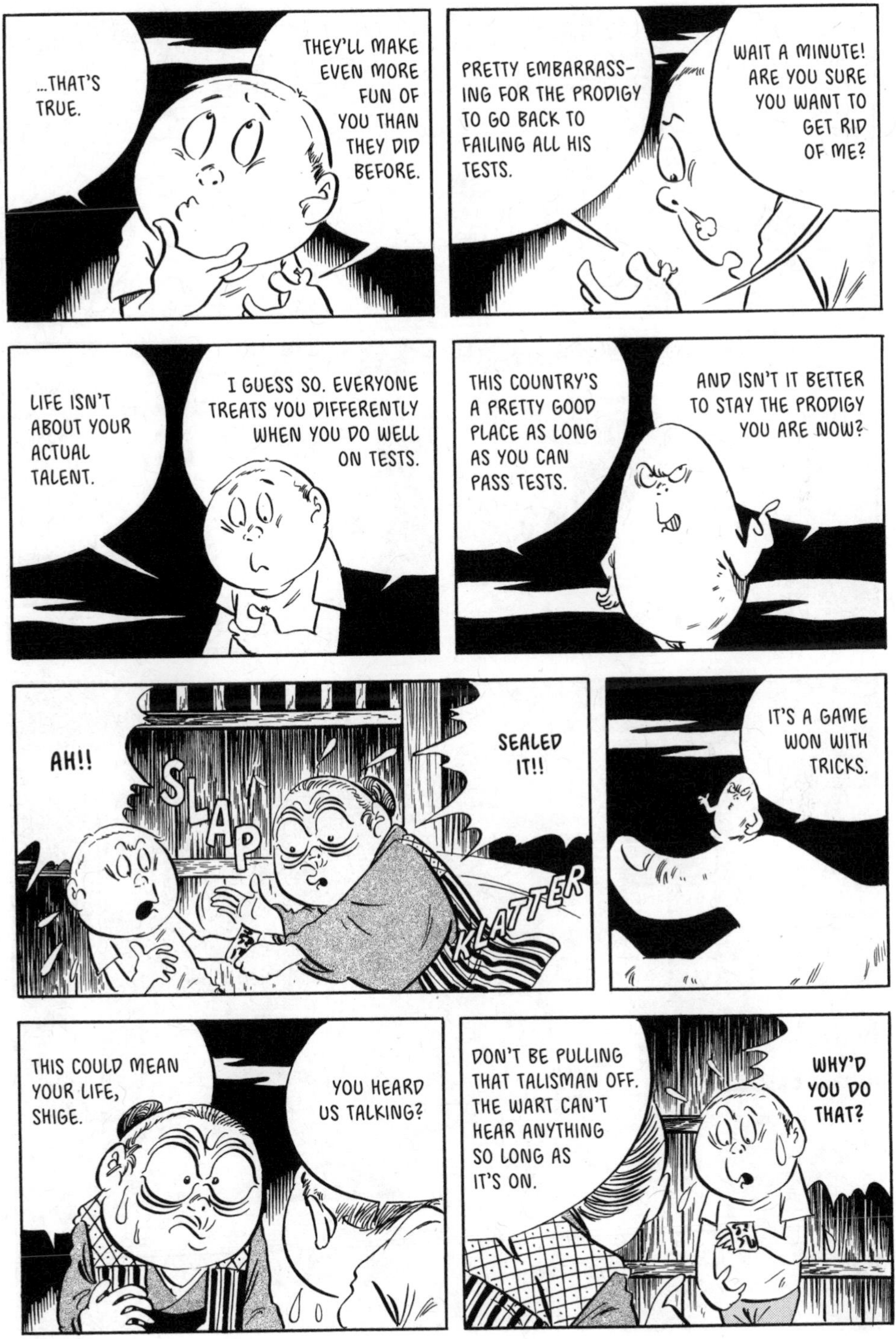
WAIT A MINUTE! ARE YOU SURE YOU WANT TO GET RID OF ME?
PRETTY EMBARRASSING FOR THE PRODIGY TO GO BACK TO FAILING ALL HIS TESTS.
THEY'LL MAKE EVEN MORE FUN OF YOU THAN THEY DID BEFORE.
...THAT'S TRUE.
AND ISN'T IT BETTER TO STAY THE PRODIGY YOU ARE NOW?
THIS COUNTRY'S A PRETTY GOOD PLACE AS LONG AS YOU CAN PASS TESTS.
I GUESS SO. EVERYONE TREATS YOU DIFFERENTLY WHEN YOU DO WELL ON TESTS.
LIFE ISN'T ABOUT YOUR ACTUAL TALENT.
IT'S A GAME WON WITH TRICKS.
SEALED IT!!
SLAP
KLATTER
AH!!
WHY'D YOU DO THAT?
DON'T BE PULLING THAT TALISMAN OFF. THE WART CAN'T HEAR ANYTHING SO LONG AS IT'S ON.
YOU HEARD US TALKING?
THIS COULD MEAN YOUR LIFE, SHIGE.

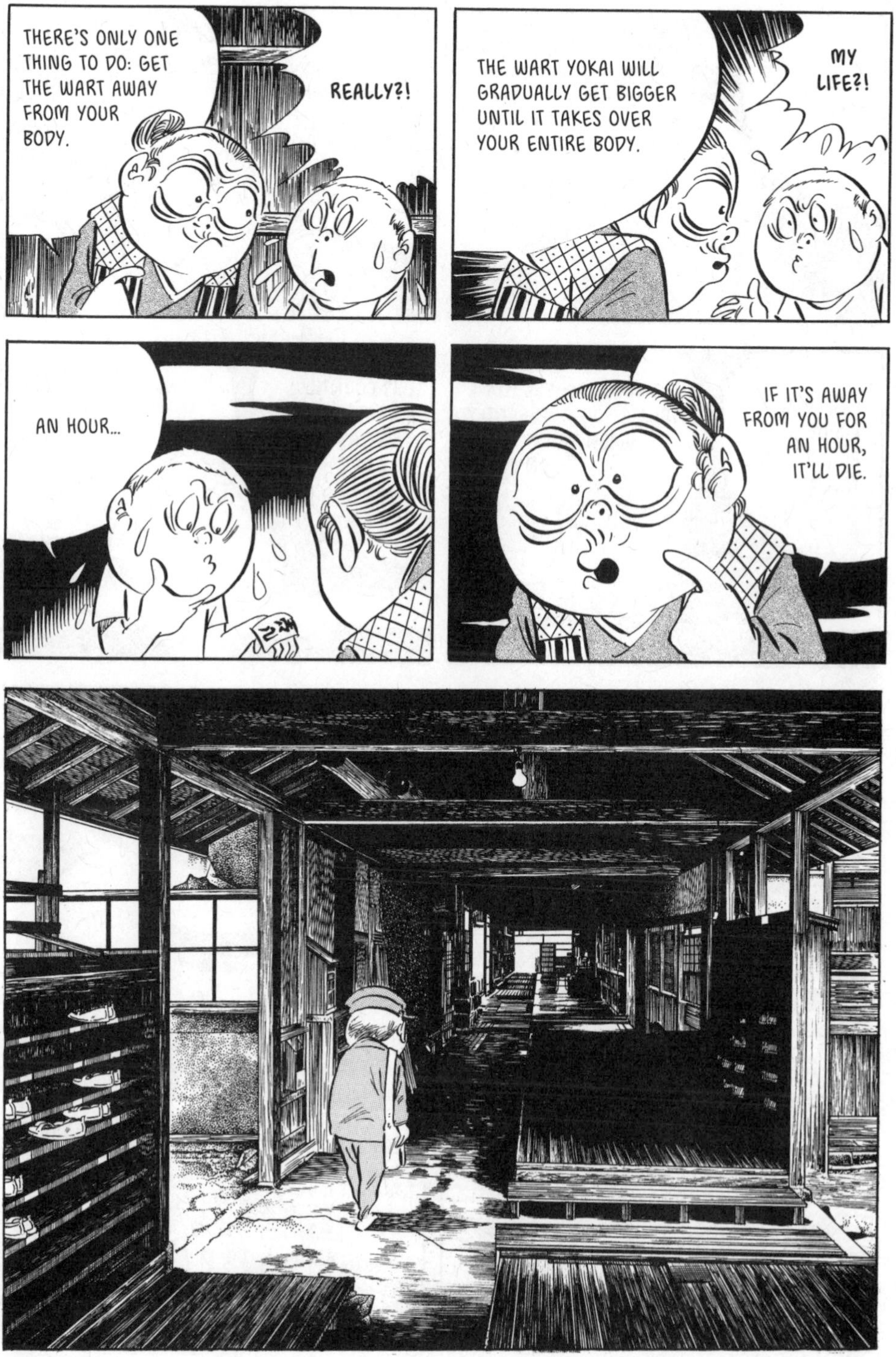
THE WART YOKAI WILL GRADUALLY GET BIGGER UNTIL IT TAKES OVER YOUR ENTIRE BODY.
MY LIFE?!
THERE'S ONLY ONE THING TO DO: GET THE WART AWAY FROM YOUR BODY.
REALLY?!
IF IT'S AWAY FROM YOU FOR AN HOUR, IT'LL DIE.
AN HOUR...

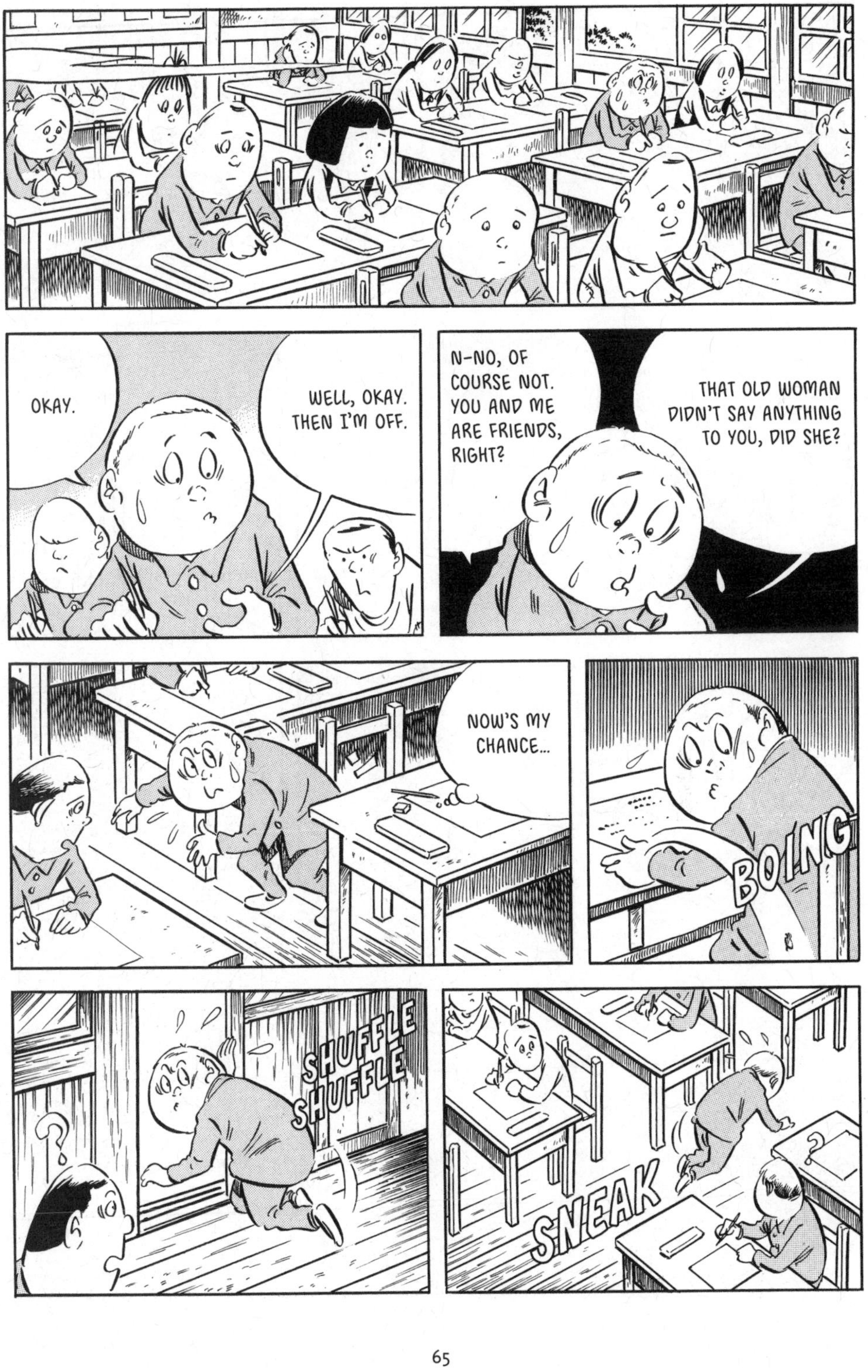
THAT OLD WOMAN DIDN'T SAY ANYTHING TO YOU, DID SHE?
N-NO, OF COURSE NOT. YOU AND ME ARE FRIENDS, RIGHT?
WELL, OKAY. THEN I'M OFF.
OKAY.
BOING
NOW'S MY CHANCE...
SNEAK
SHUFFLE SHUFFLE

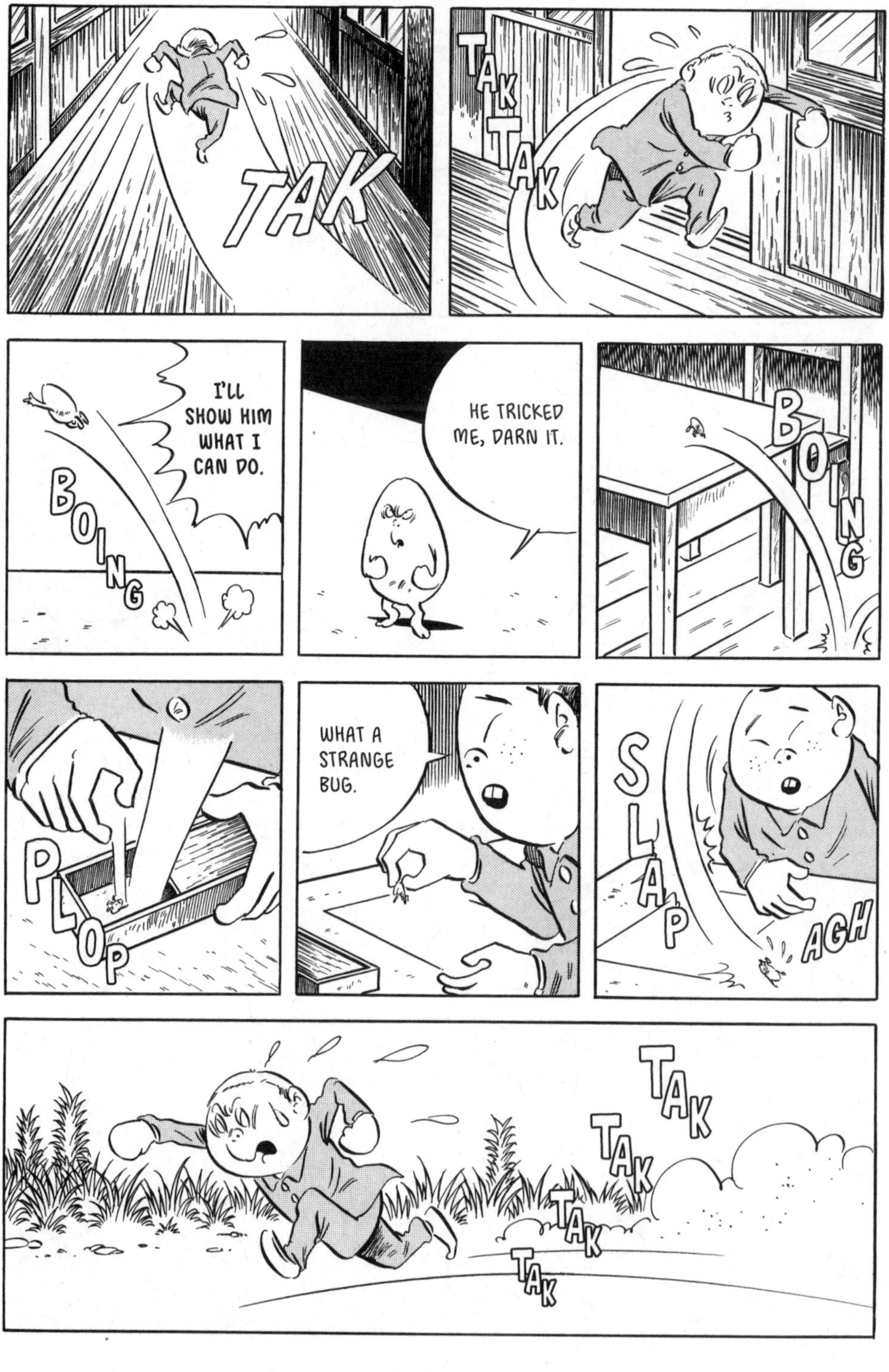
TAK
TAK
TAK
TAK
BOING
HE TRICKED ME, DARN IT.
I'LL SHOW HIM WHAT I CAN DO.
BOING
SLAP
AGH
WHAT A STRANGE BUG.
PLOP
TAK
TAK
TAK
TAK

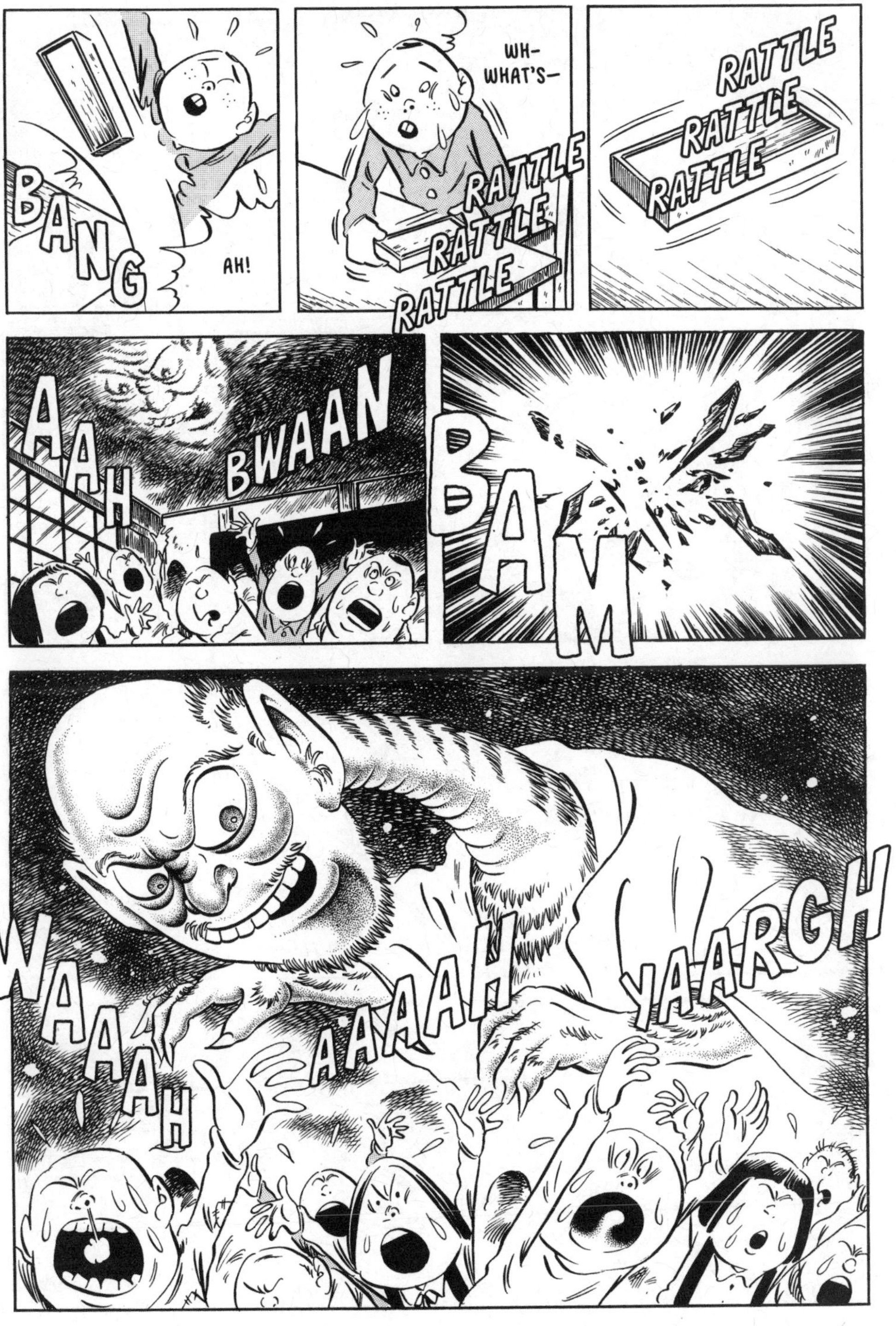
RATTLE
RATTLE
RATTLE
WH-
WHAT'S—
RATTLE
RATTLE
RATTLE
BANG
AH!
BAM
BWAAN
AAH
YAARGH
AAAAAH
WAAAAH

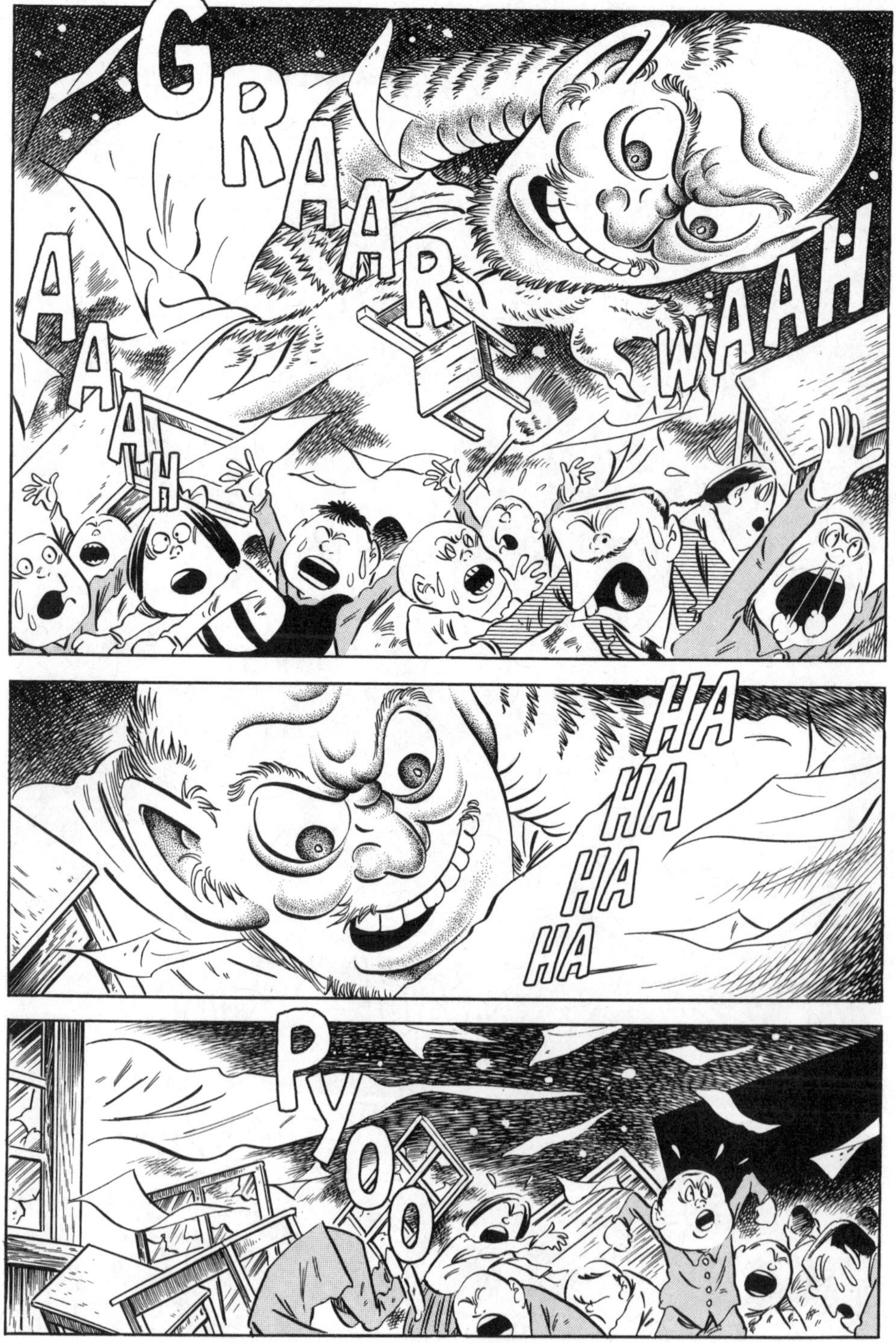
GRAARR
WAAH
AAAAH
HA HA HA HA
PYOOO

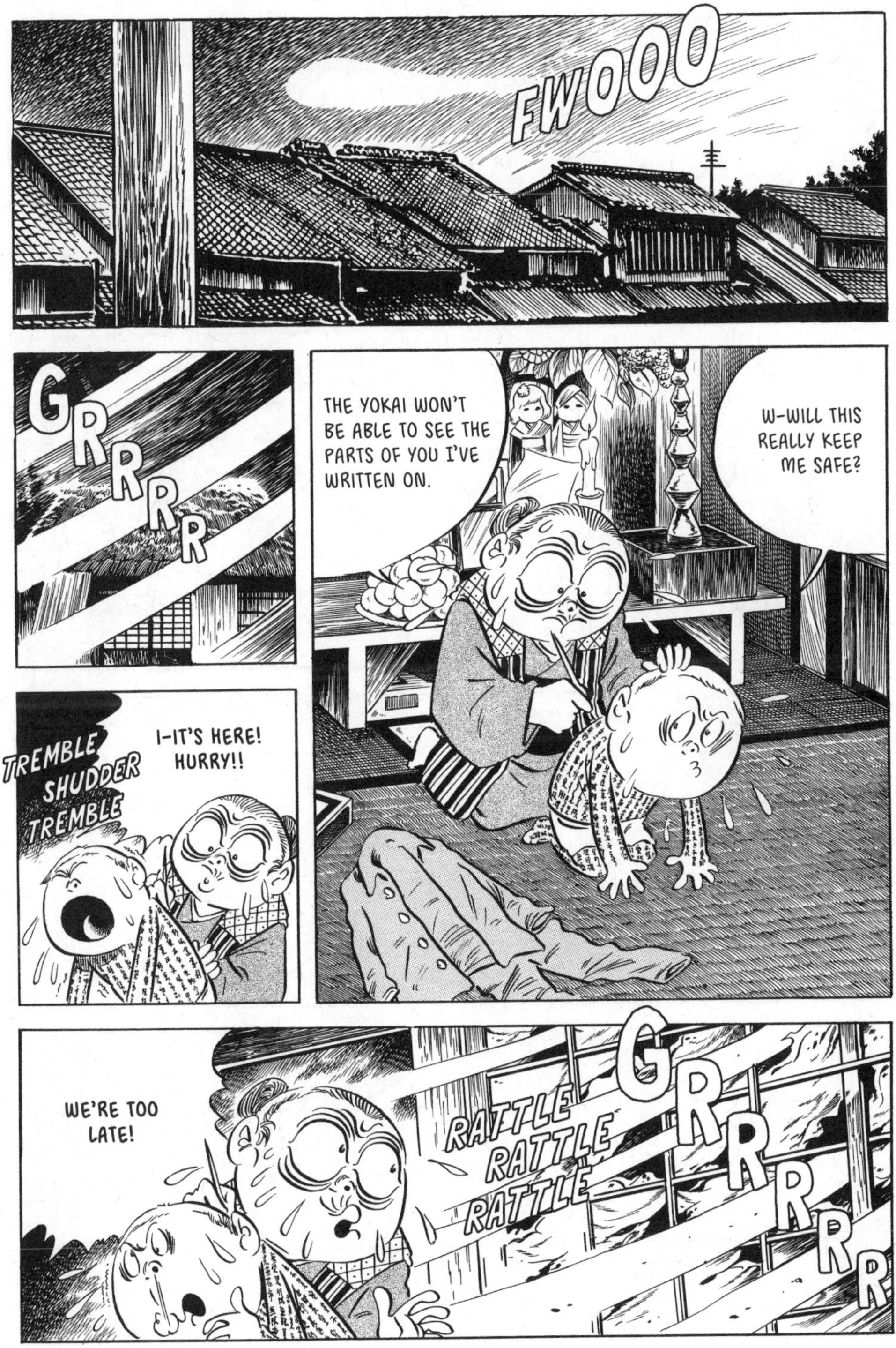
FWOOO
W-WILL THIS REALLY KEEP ME SAFE?
THE YOKAI WON'T BE ABLE TO SEE THE PARTS OF YOU I'VE WRITTEN ON.
GRRRRR
I-IT'S HERE! HURRY!!
TREMBLE SHUDDER TREMBLE
GRRRRRR
RATTLE RATTLE RATTLE
WE'RE TOO LATE!

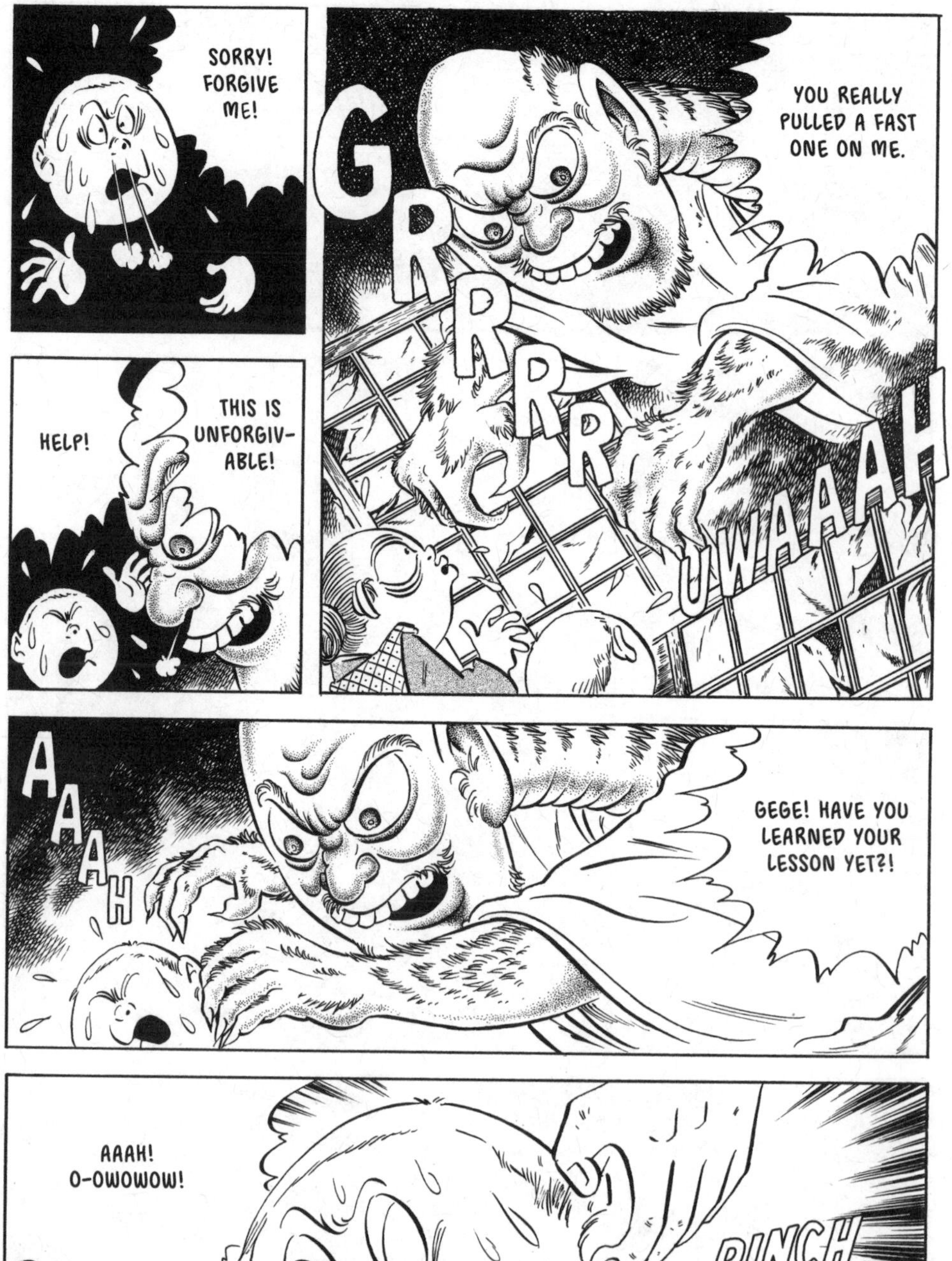
GRRRRR
YOU REALLY PULLED A FAST ONE ON ME.
UWAAAAH
SORRY! FORGIVE ME!
THIS IS UNFORGIV-ABLE!
HELP!
GEGE! HAVE YOU LEARNED YOUR LESSON YET?!
AAAH
PINCH
AAAH! O-OWOWOW!

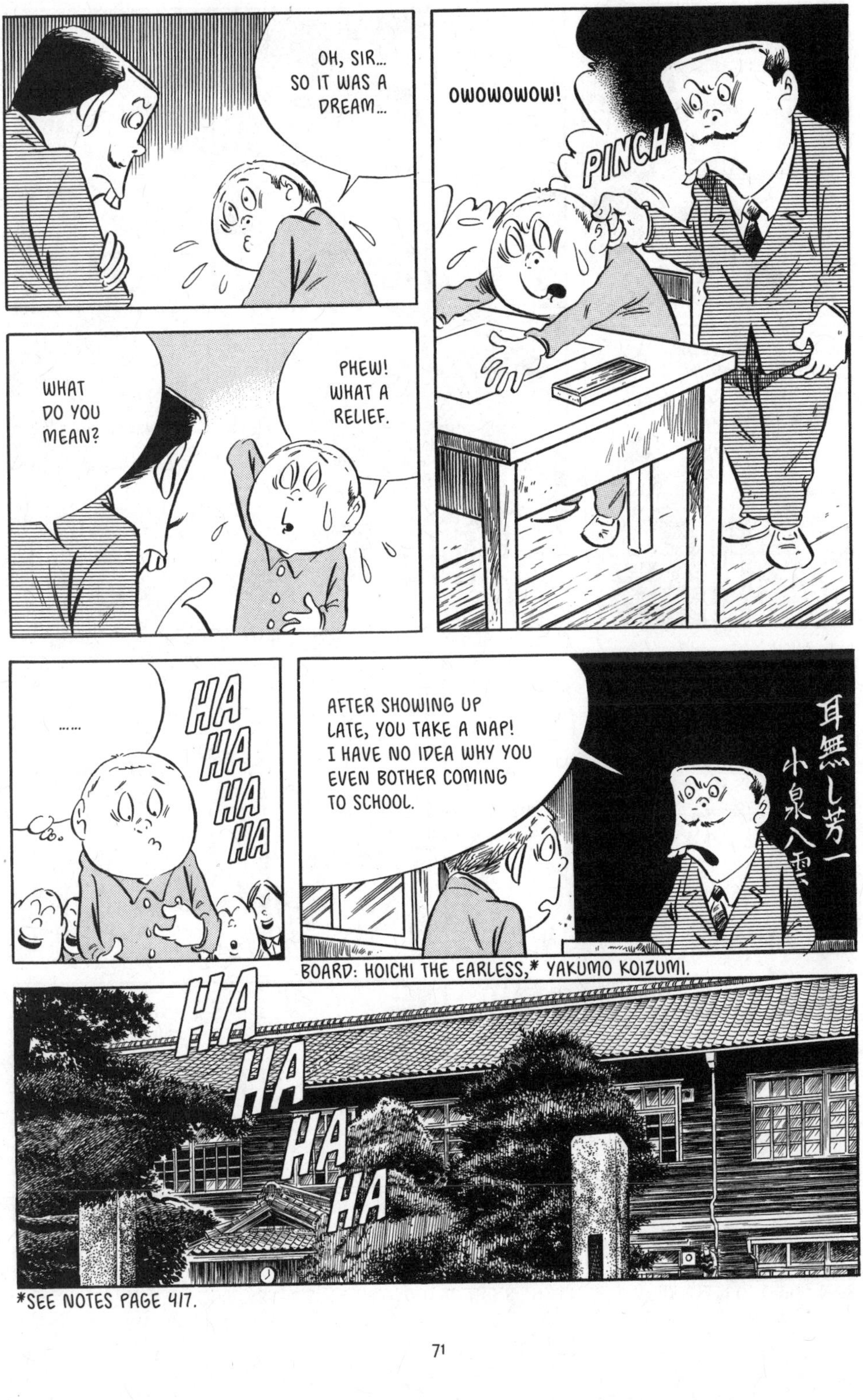
OWOWOWOW!
PINCH
OH, SIR... SO IT WAS A DREAM...
PHEW! WHAT A RELIEF.
WHAT DO YOU MEAN?
AFTER SHOWING UP LATE, YOU TAKE A NAP! I HAVE NO IDEA WHY YOU EVEN BOTHER COMING TO SCHOOL.
耳無し芳一
小泉八雲
BOARD: HOICHI THE EARLESS,* YAKUMO KOIZUMI.
HA HA HA HA
......
HA HA HA HA

*SEE NOTES PAGE 417.

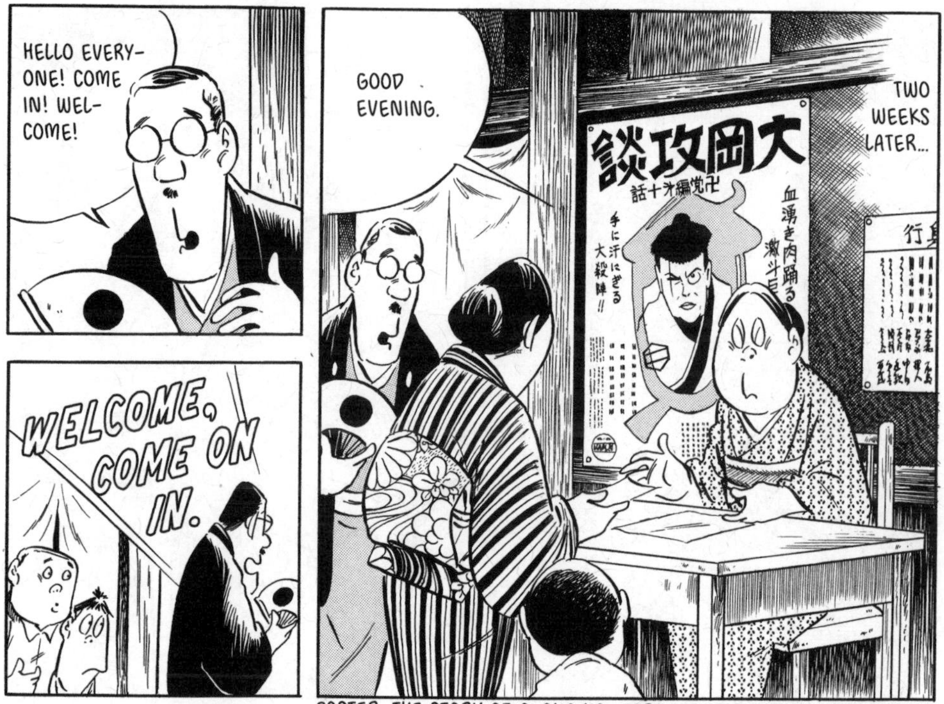
TWO WEEKS LATER...
GOOD EVENING.
HELLO EVERY-ONE! COME IN! WEL-COME!
WELCOME, COME ON IN.
POSTER: THE STORY OF O-OKA KO, PART TEN: THE MANJI FACTION.

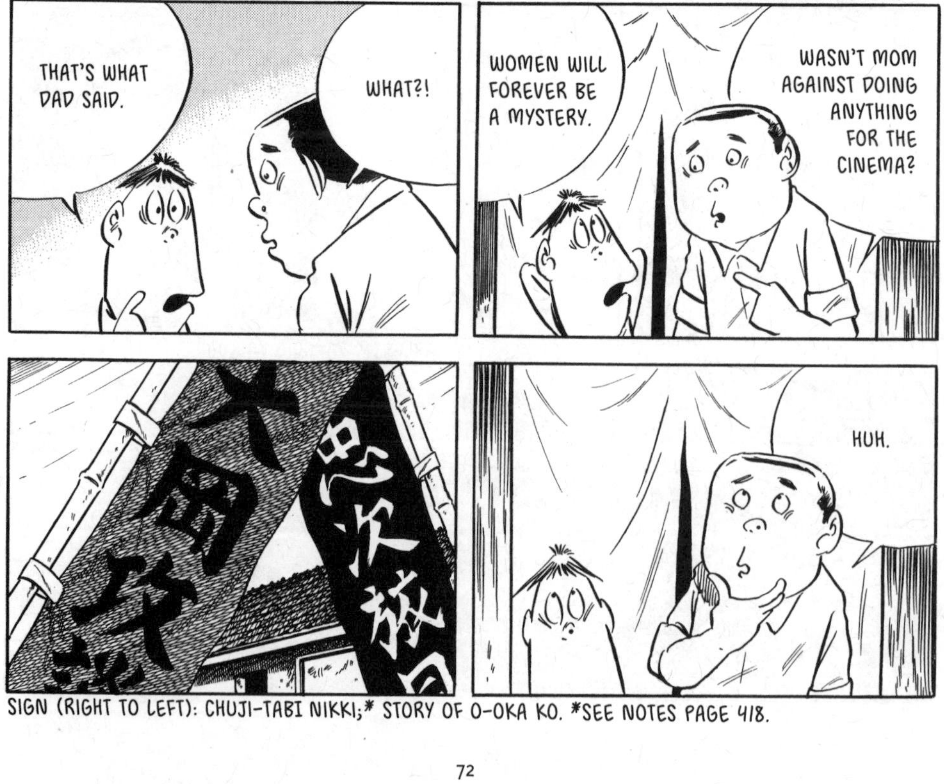
WASN'T MOM AGAINST DOING ANYTHING FOR THE CINEMA?
WOMEN WILL FOREVER BE A MYSTERY.
WHAT?!
THAT'S WHAT DAD SAID.
HUH.
SIGN (RIGHT TO LEFT): CHUJI-TABI NIKKI;* STORY OF O-OKA KO. *SEE NOTES PAGE 418.

WHO WILL BE TAKEN?

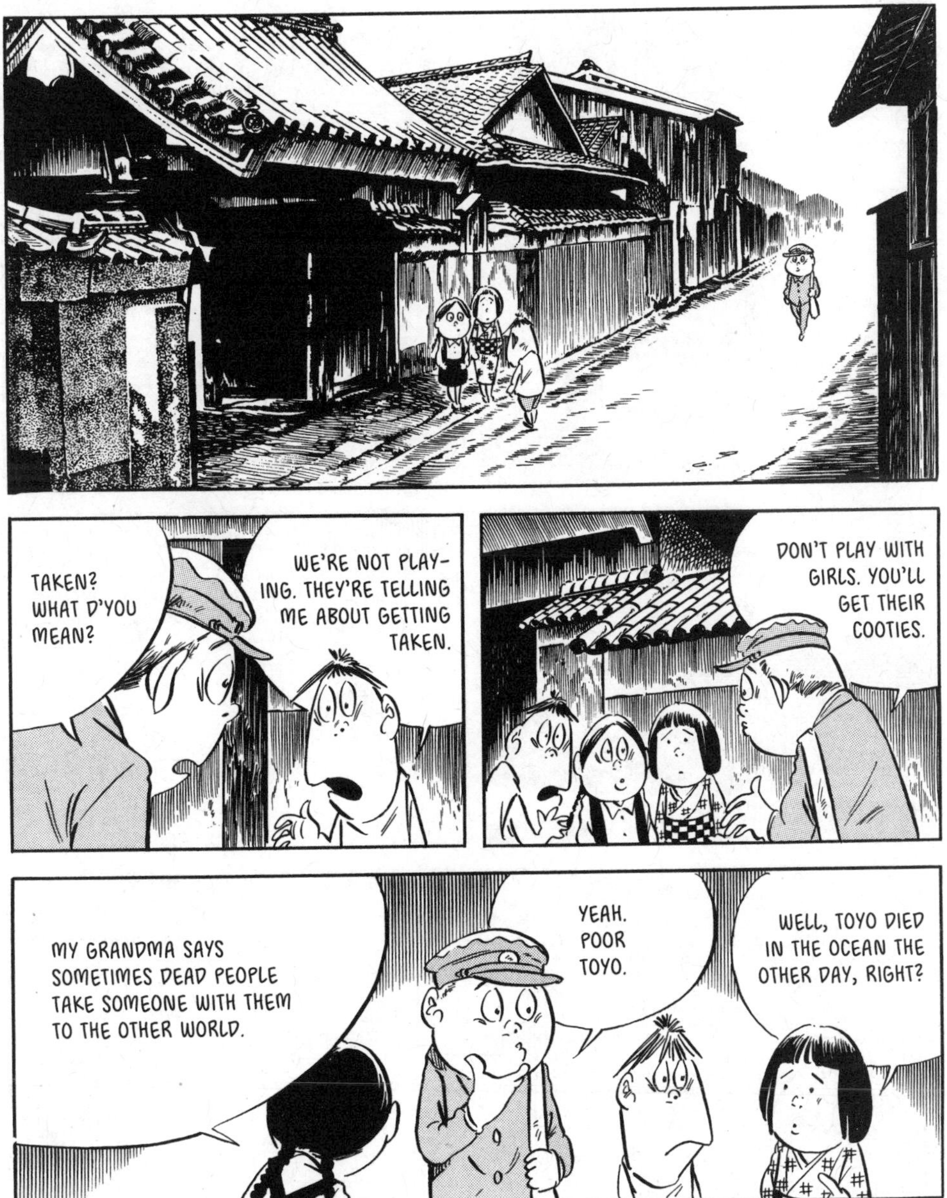
DON'T PLAY WITH GIRLS. YOU'LL GET THEIR COOTIES.
WE'RE NOT PLAY-ING. THEY'RE TELLING ME ABOUT GETTING TAKEN.
TAKEN? WHAT D'YOU MEAN?
WELL, TOYO DIED IN THE OCEAN THE OTHER DAY, RIGHT?
YEAH. POOR TOYO.
MY GRANDMA SAYS SOMETIMES DEAD PEOPLE TAKE SOMEONE WITH THEM TO THE OTHER WORLD.

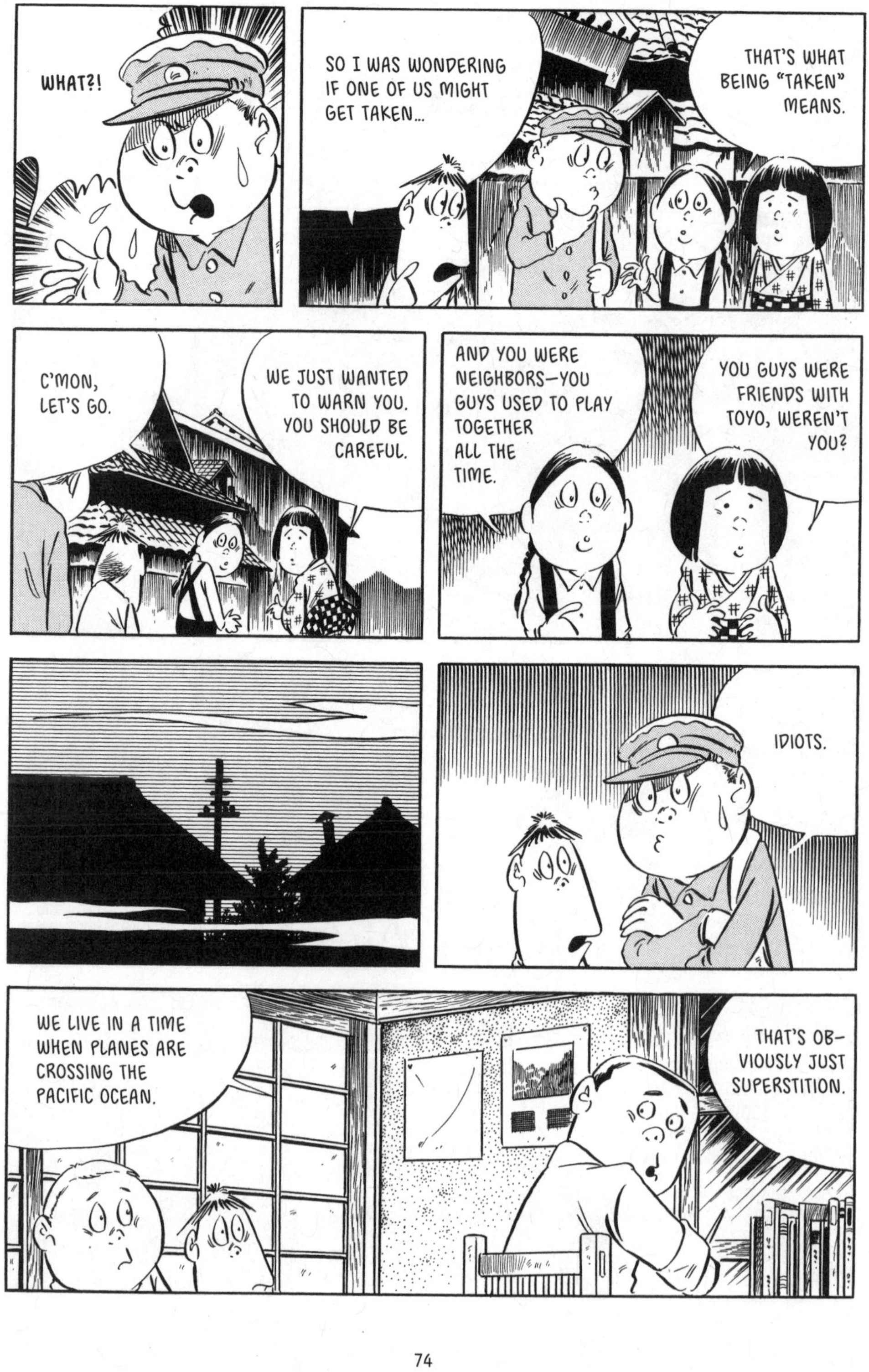
THAT'S WHAT BEING "TAKEN" MEANS.
SO I WAS WONDERING IF ONE OF US MIGHT GET TAKEN...
WHAT?!
YOU GUYS WERE FRIENDS WITH TOYO, WEREN'T YOU?
AND YOU WERE NEIGHBORS—YOU GUYS USED TO PLAY TOGETHER ALL THE TIME.
WE JUST WANTED TO WARN YOU. YOU SHOULD BE CAREFUL.
C'MON, LET'S GO.
IDIOTS.
THAT'S OBVIOUSLY JUST SUPERSTITION.
WE LIVE IN A TIME WHEN PLANES ARE CROSSING THE PACIFIC OCEAN.

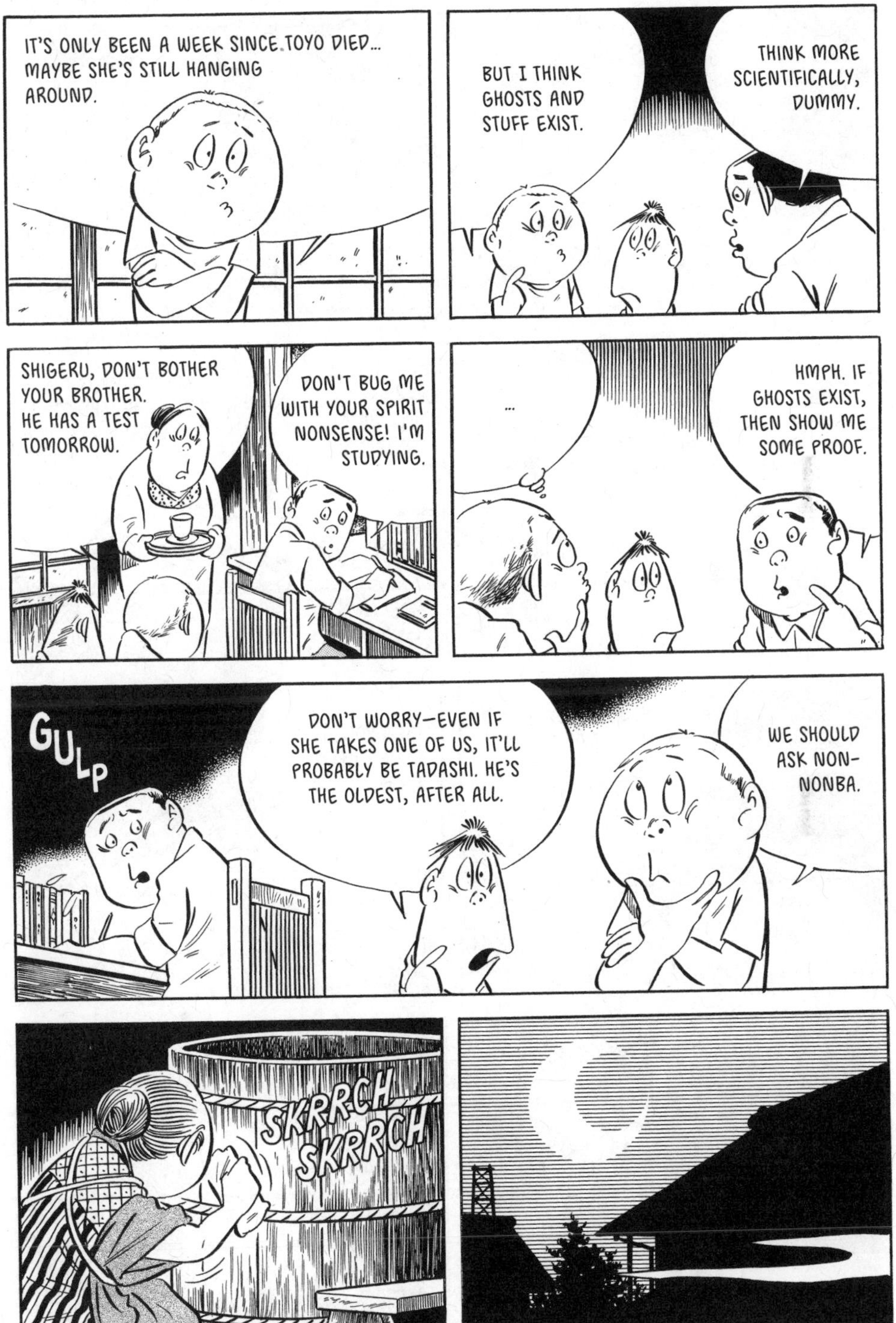
THINK MORE SCIENTIFICALLY, DUMMY.
BUT I THINK GHOSTS AND STUFF EXIST.
IT'S ONLY BEEN A WEEK SINCE TOYO DIED... MAYBE SHE'S STILL HANGING AROUND.
HMPH. IF GHOSTS EXIST, THEN SHOW ME SOME PROOF.
...
DON'T BUG ME WITH YOUR SPIRIT NONSENSE! I'M STUDYING.
SHIGERU, DON'T BOTHER YOUR BROTHER. HE HAS A TEST TOMORROW.
WE SHOULD ASK NON-NONBA.
DON'T WORRY—EVEN IF SHE TAKES ONE OF US, IT'LL PROBABLY BE TADASHI. HE'S THE OLDEST, AFTER ALL.
GULP
SKRRCH SKRRCH

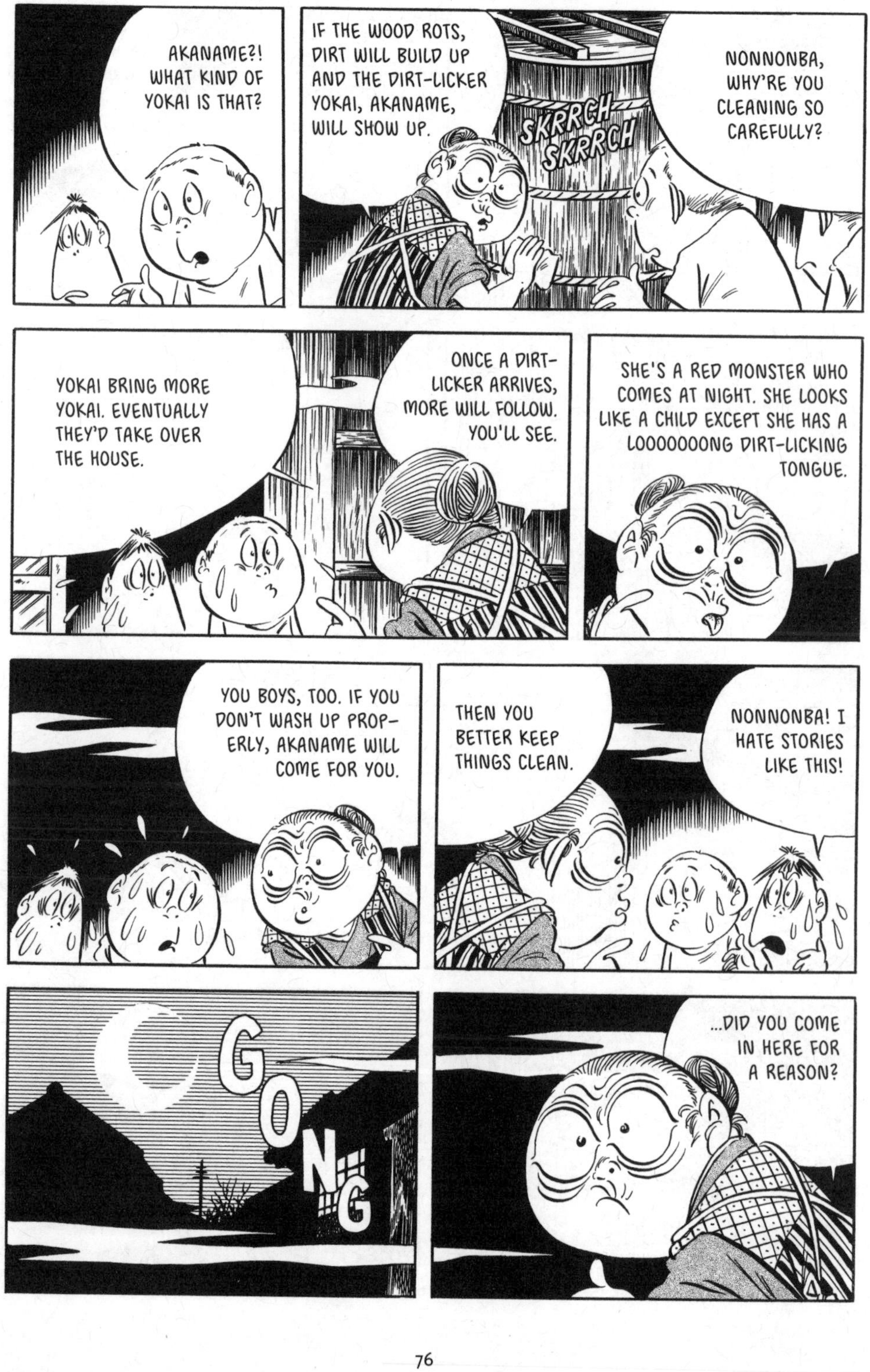
NONNONBA, WHY'RE YOU CLEANING SO CAREFULLY?
SKRRCH SKRRCH
IF THE WOOD ROTS, DIRT WILL BUILD UP AND THE DIRT-LICKER YOKAI, AKANAME, WILL SHOW UP.
AKANAME?! WHAT KIND OF YOKAI IS THAT?
SHE'S A RED MONSTER WHO COMES AT NIGHT. SHE LOOKS LIKE A CHILD EXCEPT SHE HAS A LOOOOOOONG DIRT-LICKING TONGUE.
ONCE A DIRT-LICKER ARRIVES, MORE WILL FOLLOW. YOU'LL SEE.
YOKAI BRING MORE YOKAI. EVENTUALLY THEY'D TAKE OVER THE HOUSE.
NONNONBA! I HATE STORIES LIKE THIS!
THEN YOU BETTER KEEP THINGS CLEAN.
YOU BOYS, TOO. IF YOU DON'T WASH UP PROP-ERLY, AKANAME WILL COME FOR YOU.
...DID YOU COME IN HERE FOR A REASON?
GONG

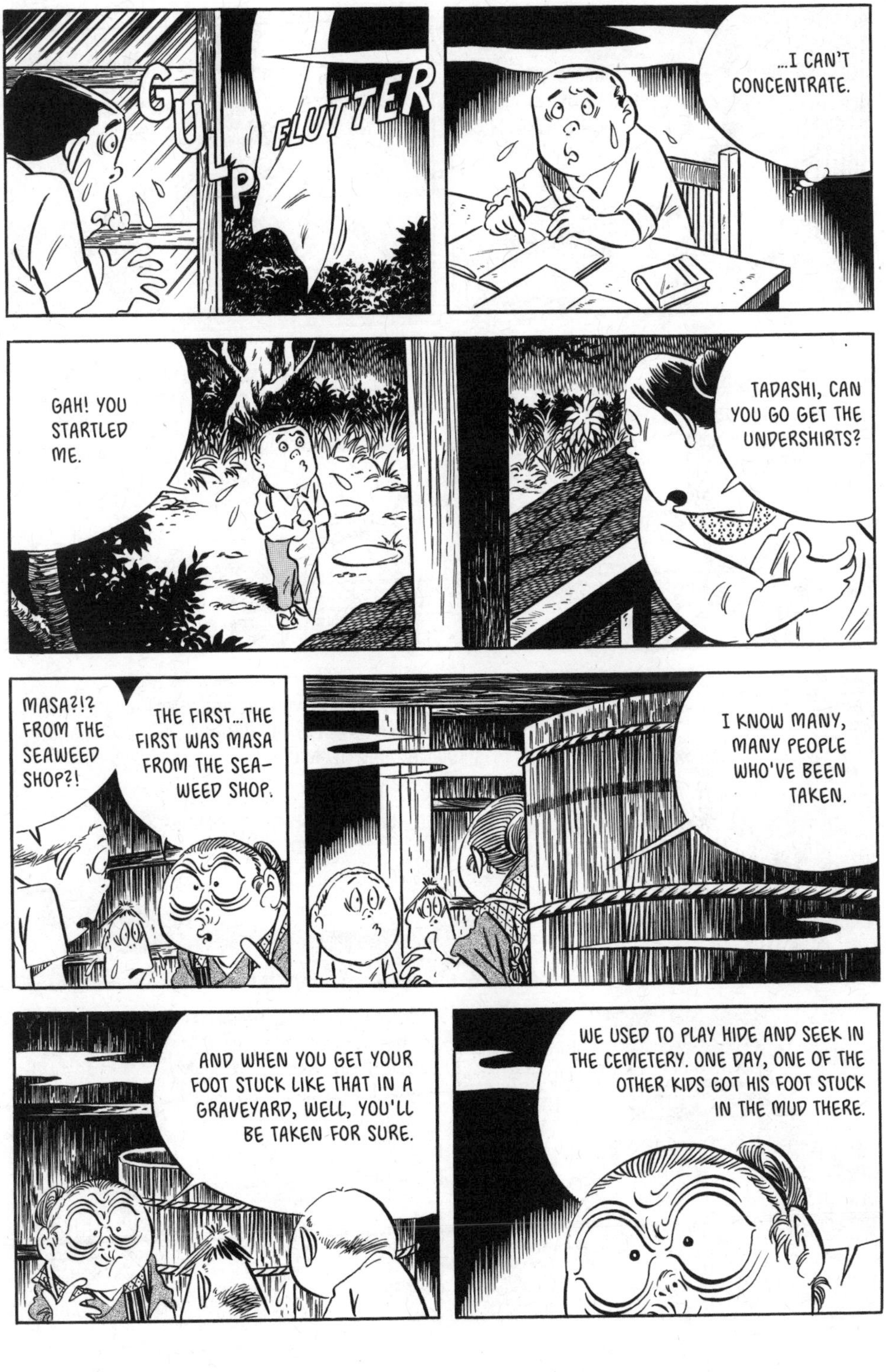
...I CAN'T CONCENTRATE.
GULP
FLUTTER
TADASHI, CAN YOU GO GET THE UNDERSHIRTS?
GAH! YOU STARTLED ME.
I KNOW MANY, MANY PEOPLE WHO'VE BEEN TAKEN.
THE FIRST...THE FIRST WAS MASA FROM THE SEA-WEED SHOP.
MASA?!? FROM THE SEAWEED SHOP?!
WE USED TO PLAY HIDE AND SEEK IN THE CEMETERY. ONE DAY, ONE OF THE OTHER KIDS GOT HIS FOOT STUCK IN THE MUD THERE.
AND WHEN YOU GET YOUR FOOT STUCK LIKE THAT IN A GRAVEYARD, WELL, YOU'LL BE TAKEN FOR SURE.

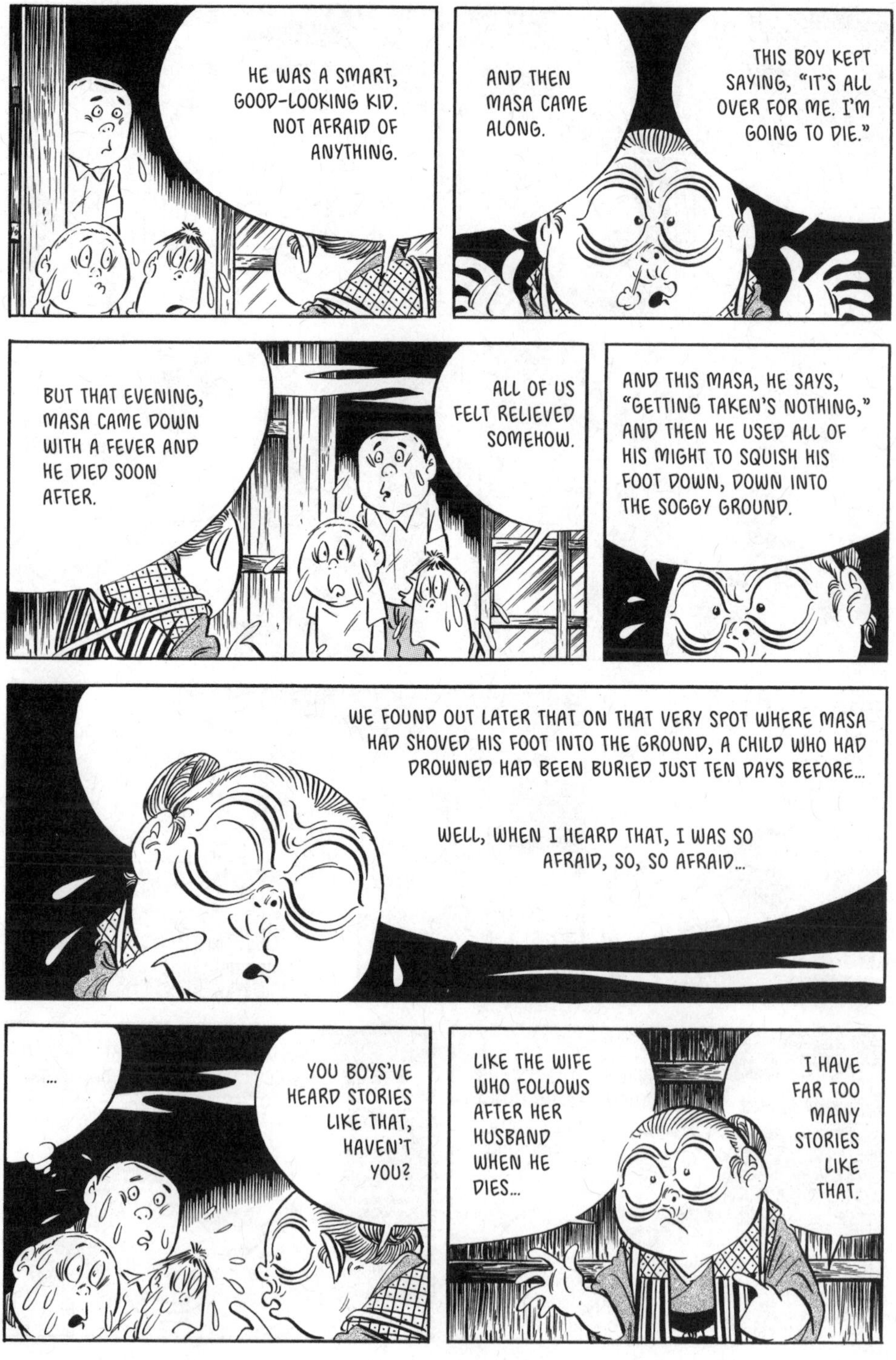
THIS BOY KEPT SAYING, "IT'S ALL OVER FOR ME. I'M GOING TO DIE."
AND THEN MASA CAME ALONG.
HE WAS A SMART, GOOD-LOOKING KID. NOT AFRAID OF ANYTHING.
AND THIS MASA, HE SAYS, "GETTING TAKEN'S NOTHING," AND THEN HE USED ALL OF HIS MIGHT TO SQUISH HIS FOOT DOWN, DOWN INTO THE SOGGY GROUND.
ALL OF US FELT RELIEVED SOMEHOW.
BUT THAT EVENING, MASA CAME DOWN WITH A FEVER AND HE DIED SOON AFTER.
WE FOUND OUT LATER THAT ON THAT VERY SPOT WHERE MASA HAD SHOVED HIS FOOT INTO THE GROUND, A CHILD WHO HAD DROWNED HAD BEEN BURIED JUST TEN DAYS BEFORE...
WELL, WHEN I HEARD THAT, I WAS SO AFRAID, SO, SO AFRAID...
I HAVE FAR TOO MANY STORIES LIKE THAT.
LIKE THE WIFE WHO FOLLOWS AFTER HER HUSBAND WHEN HE DIES...
YOU BOYS'VE HEARD STORIES LIKE THAT, HAVEN'T YOU?
...

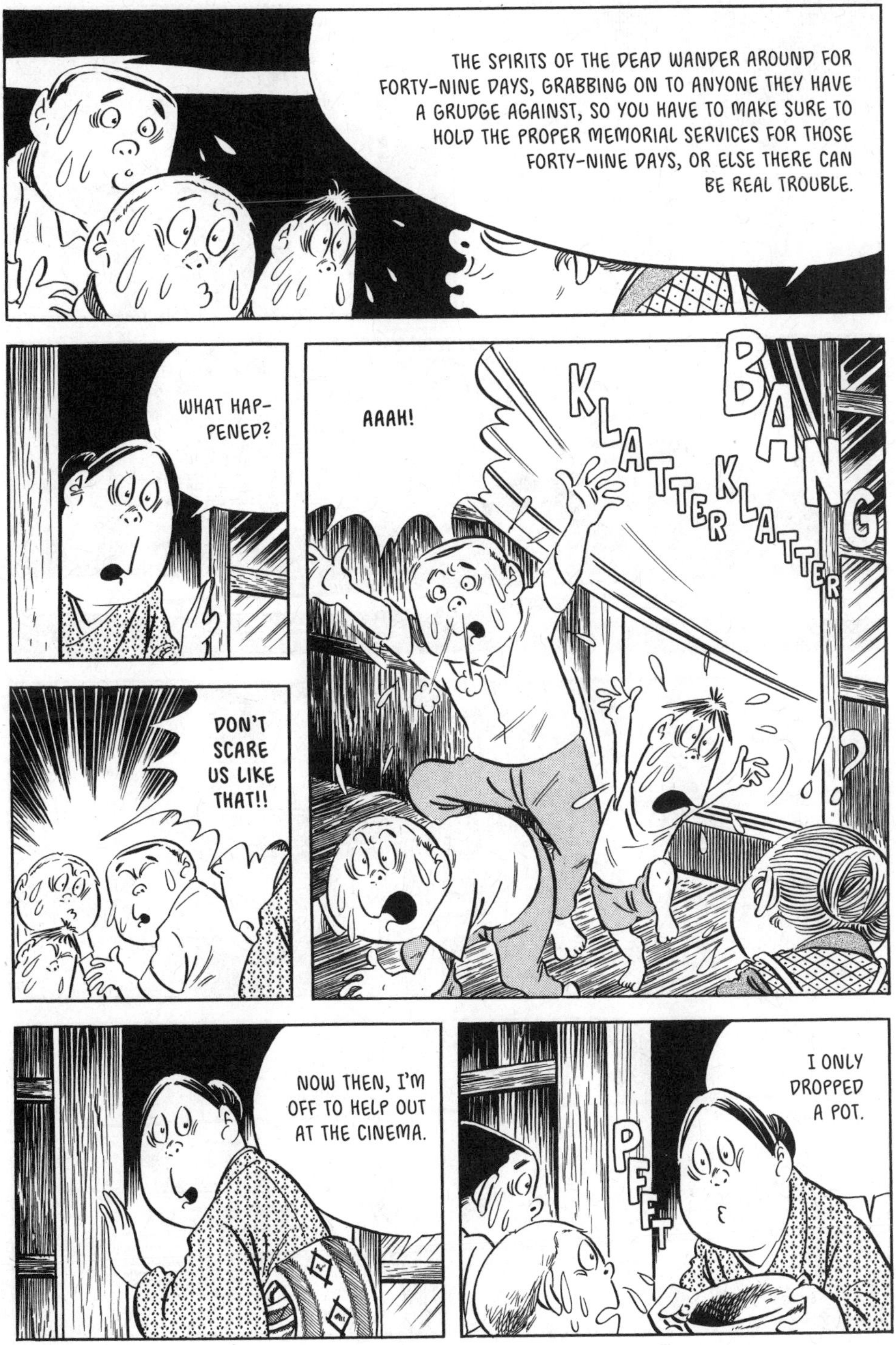
THE SPIRITS OF THE DEAD WANDER AROUND FOR FORTY-NINE DAYS, GRABBING ON TO ANYONE THEY HAVE A GRUDGE AGAINST, SO YOU HAVE TO MAKE SURE TO HOLD THE PROPER MEMORIAL SERVICES FOR THOSE FORTY-NINE DAYS, OR ELSE THERE CAN BE REAL TROUBLE.
BANG
KLATTER KLATTER
AAAH!
!?
WHAT HAP-PENED?
DON'T SCARE US LIKE THAT!!
I ONLY DROPPED A POT.
PFFT
NOW THEN, I'M OFF TO HELP OUT AT THE CINEMA.

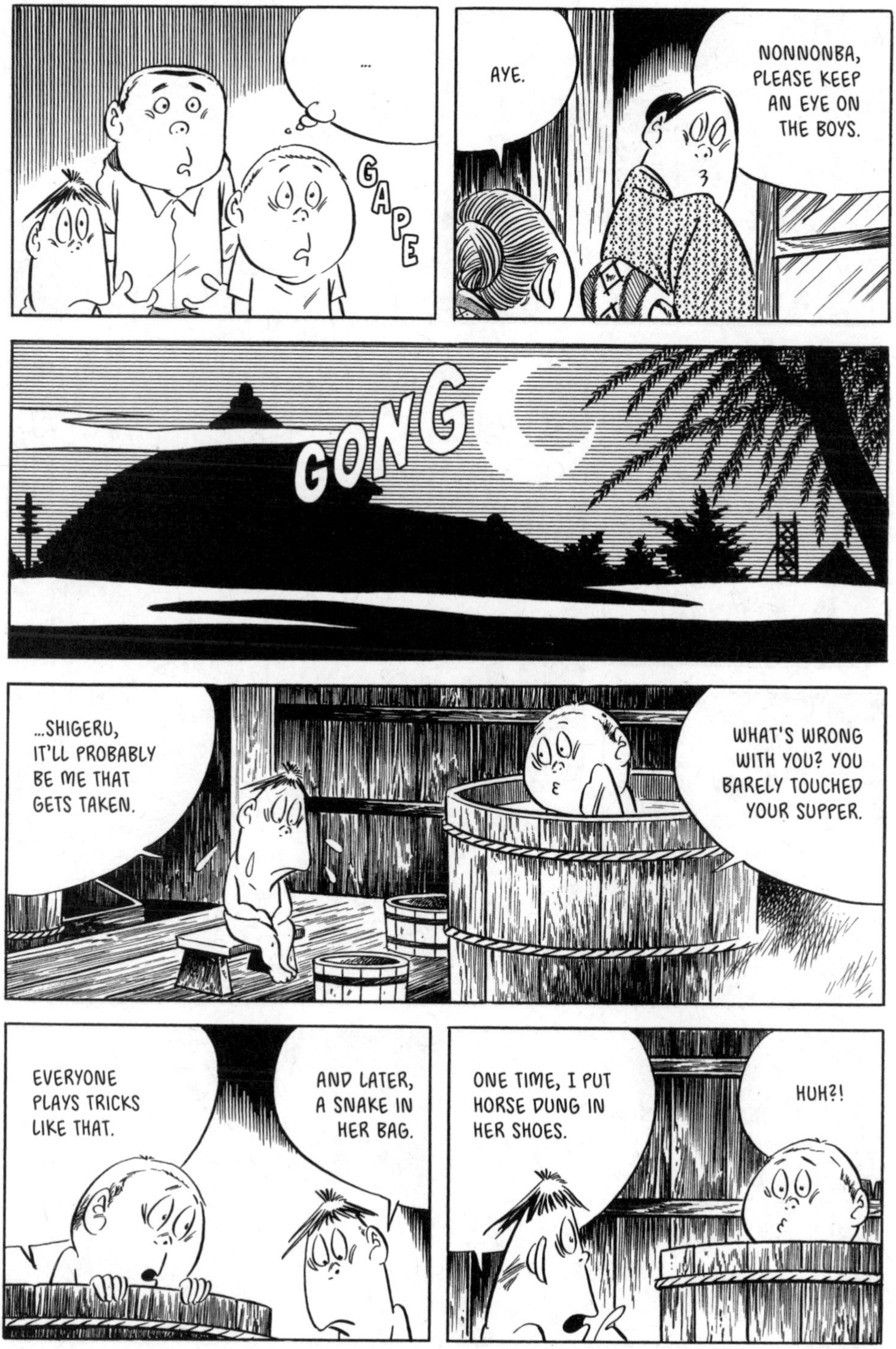
NONNONBA, PLEASE KEEP AN EYE ON THE BOYS.
AYE.
...
GAPE
GONG
WHAT'S WRONG WITH YOU? YOU BARELY TOUCHED YOUR SUPPER.
...SHIGERU, IT'LL PROBABLY BE ME THAT GETS TAKEN.
HUH?!
ONE TIME, I PUT HORSE DUNG IN HER SHOES.
AND LATER, A SNAKE IN HER BAG.
EVERYONE PLAYS TRICKS LIKE THAT.

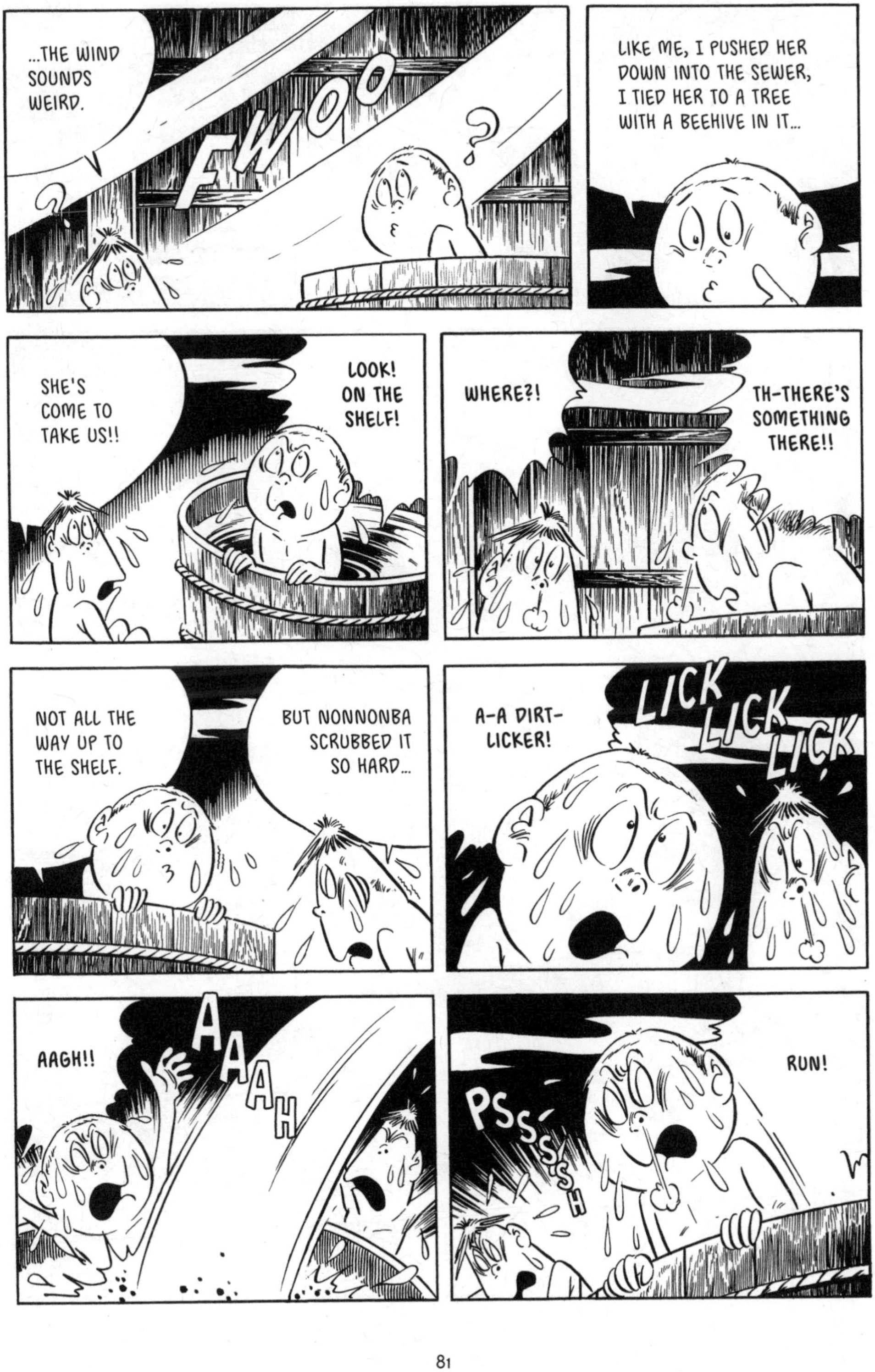
LIKE ME, I PUSHED HER DOWN INTO THE SEWER, I TIED HER TO A TREE WITH A BEEHIVE IN IT...
FWOO
...THE WIND SOUNDS WEIRD.
TH-THERE'S SOMETHING THERE!!
WHERE?!
LOOK! ON THE SHELF!
SHE'S COME TO TAKE US!!
LICK LICK LICK
A-A DIRT-LICKER!
BUT NONNONBA SCRUBBED IT SO HARD...
NOT ALL THE WAY UP TO THE SHELF.
RUN!
PSSSSSH
AAAAH
AAGH!!

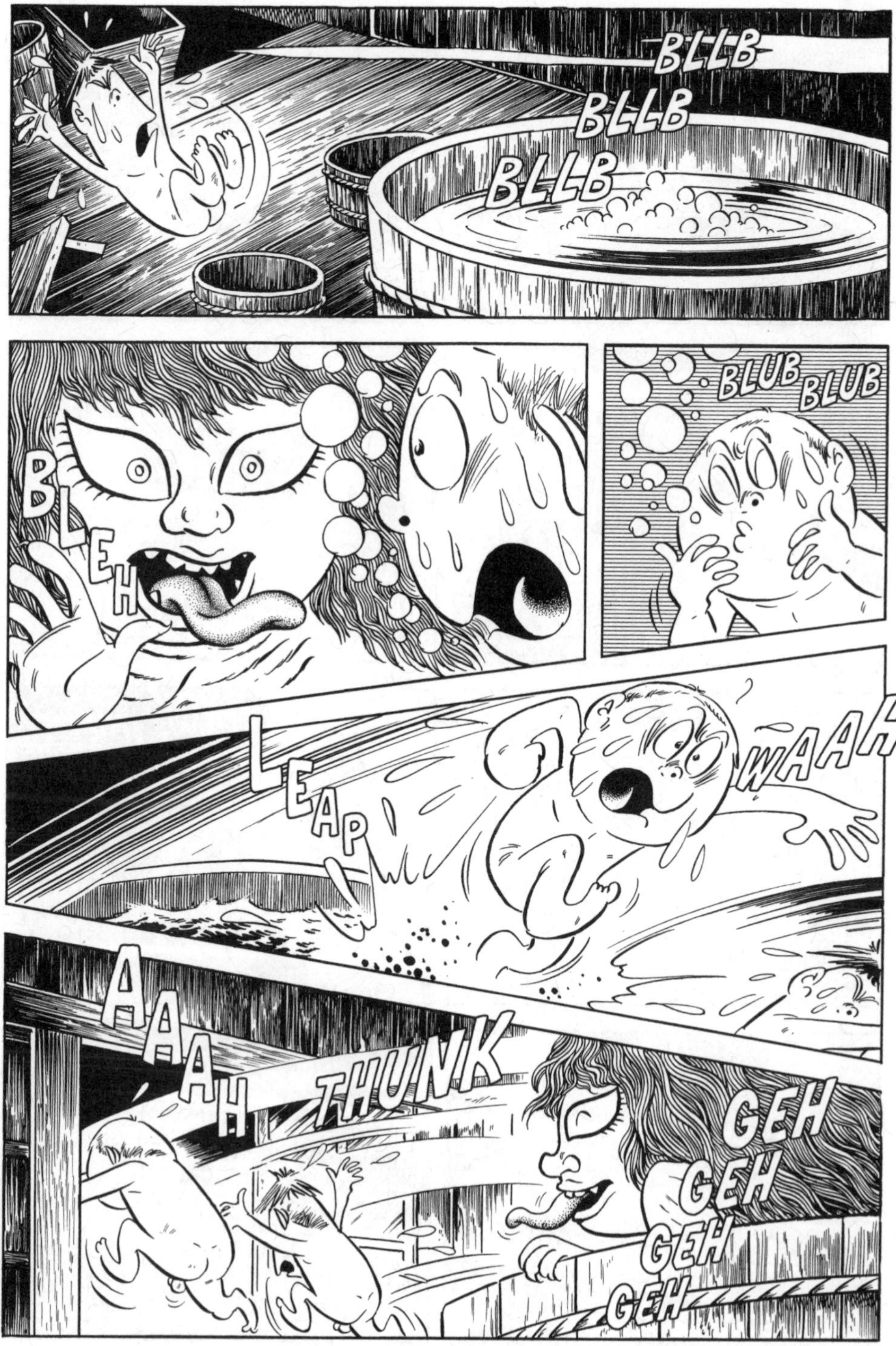
BLLB
BLLB
BLLB
BLUB BLUB
BLEH
WAAH
LEAP
GEH
GEH
GEH
GEH
THUNK
AAAH

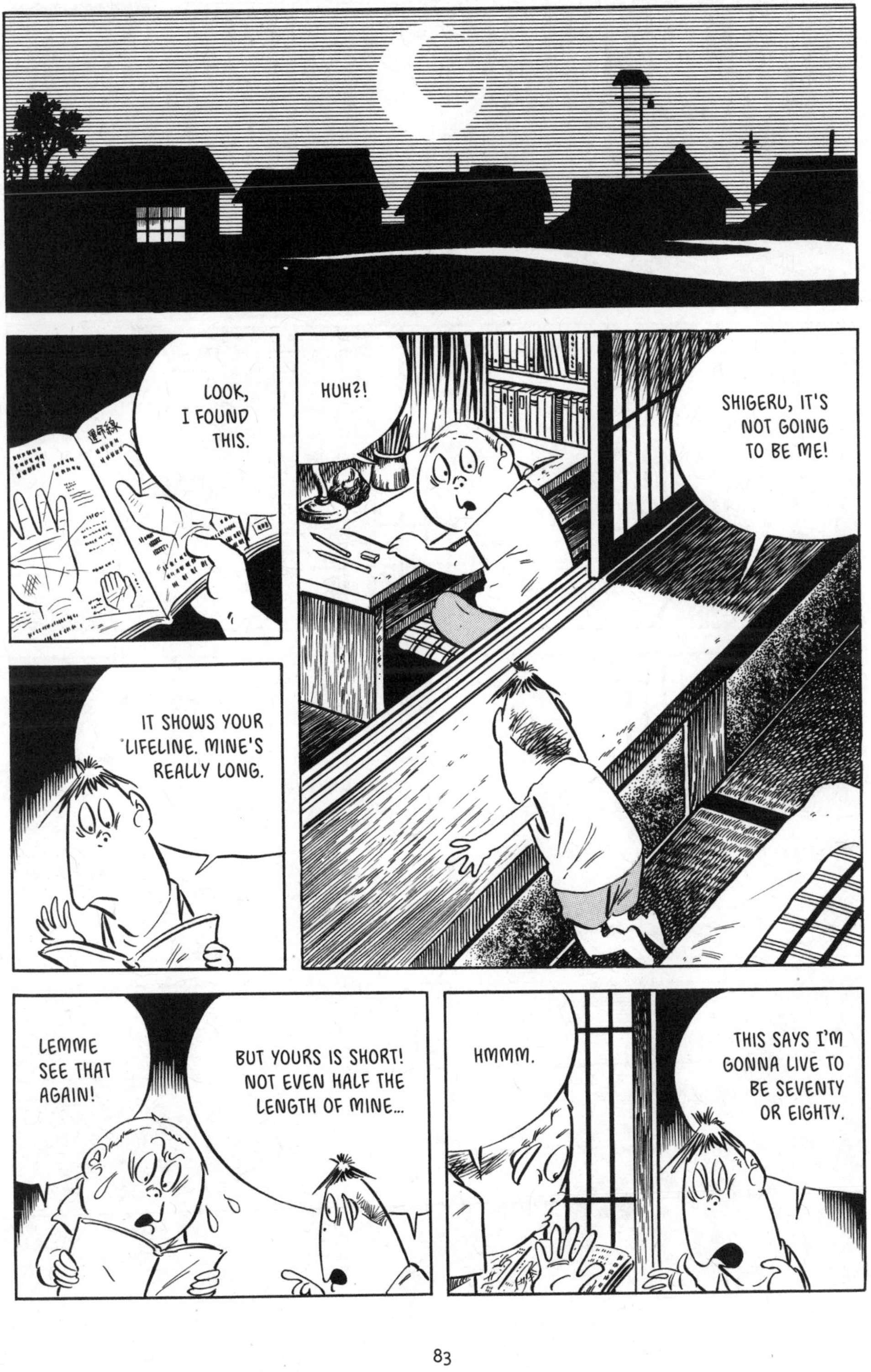
SHIGERU, IT'S NOT GOING TO BE ME!
HUH?!
LOOK, I FOUND THIS.
IT SHOWS YOUR LIFELINE. MINE'S REALLY LONG.
THIS SAYS I'M GONNA LIVE TO BE SEVENTY OR EIGHTY.
HMMM.
BUT YOURS IS SHORT! NOT EVEN HALF THE LENGTH OF MINE...
LEMME SEE THAT AGAIN!

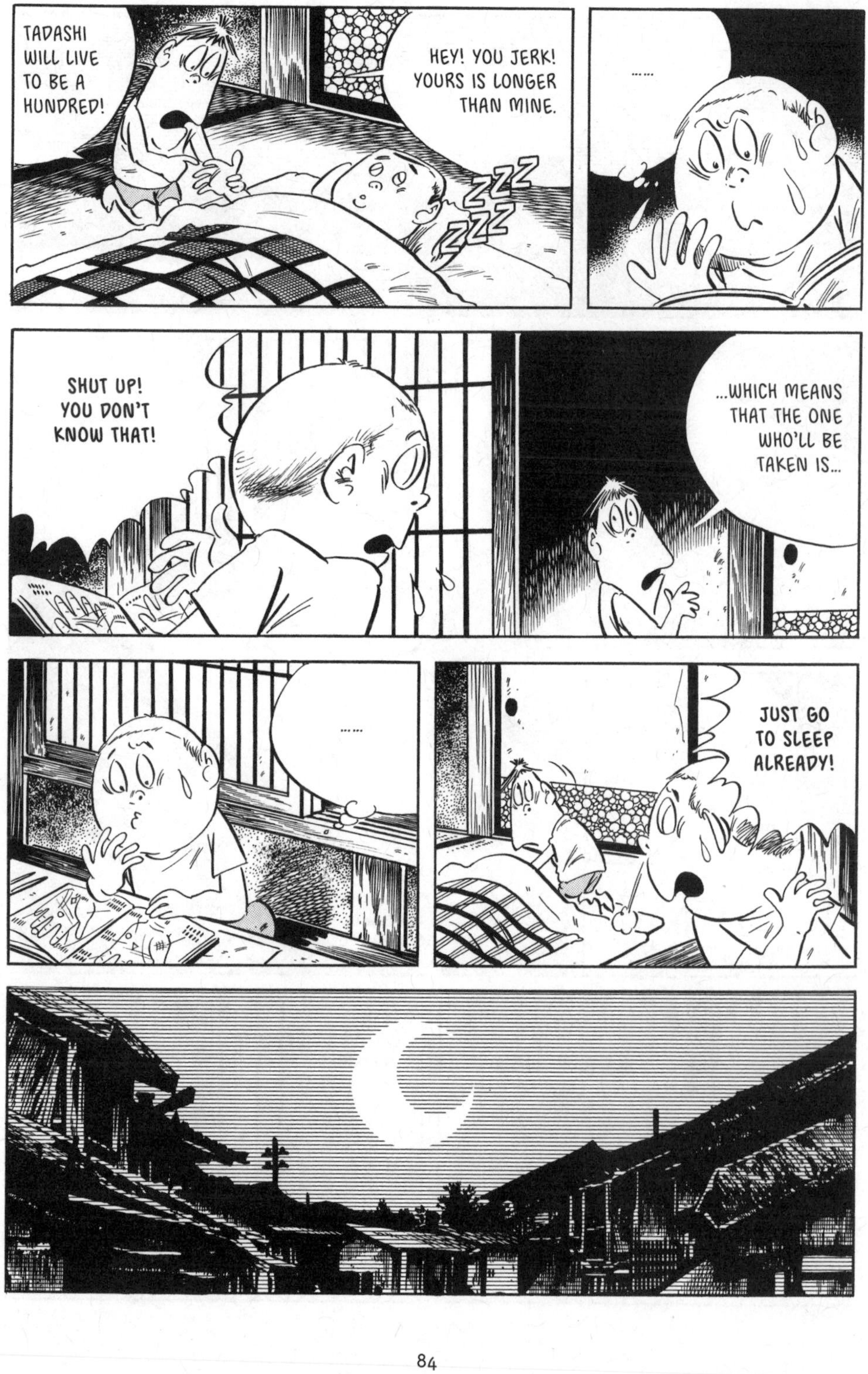
……
HEY! YOU JERK! YOURS IS LONGER THAN MINE.
TADASHI WILL LIVE TO BE A HUNDRED!
...WHICH MEANS THAT THE ONE WHO'LL BE TAKEN IS...
SHUT UP! YOU DON'T KNOW THAT!
JUST GO TO SLEEP ALREADY!
……

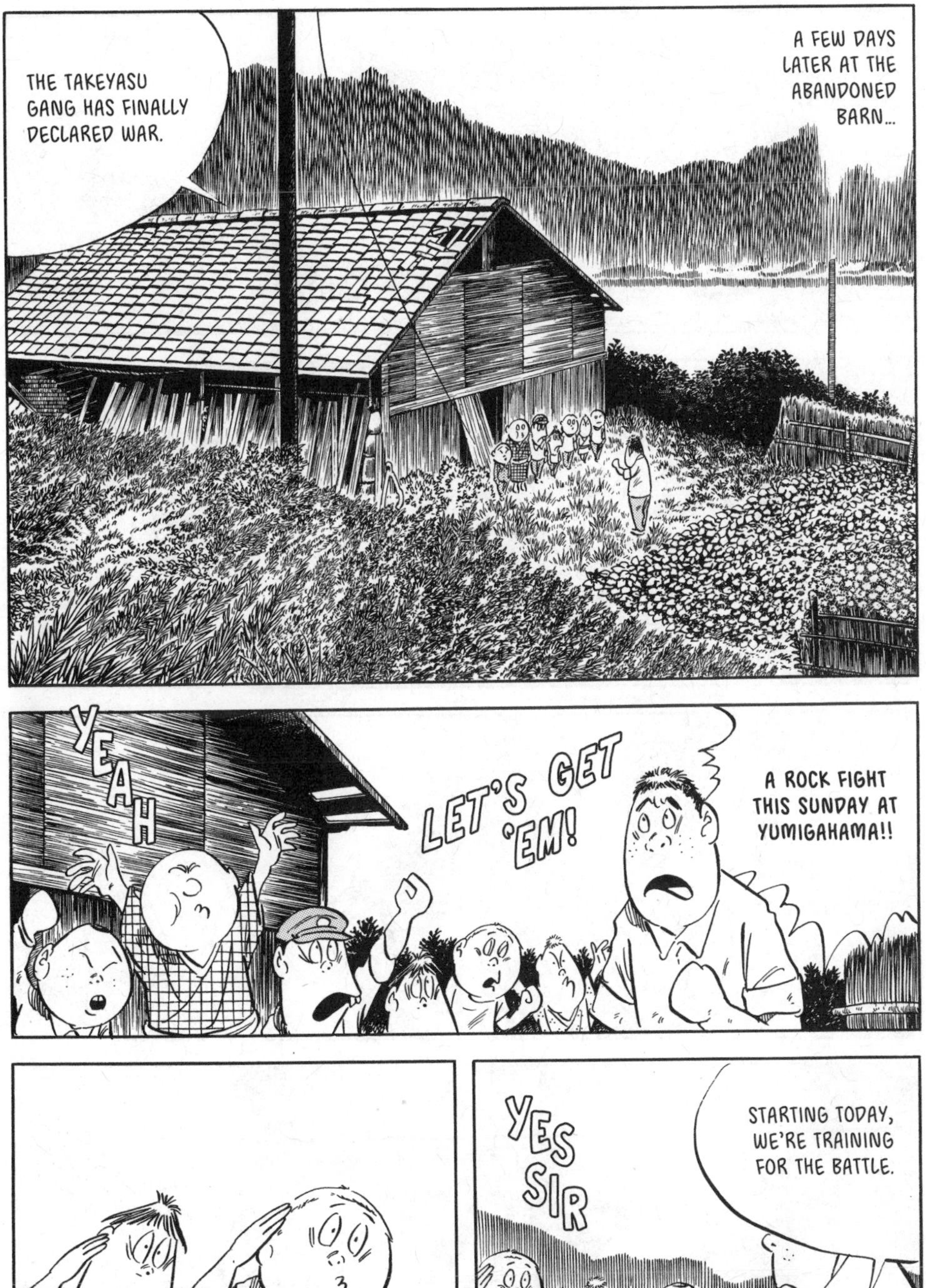
A FEW DAYS LATER AT THE ABANDONED BARN...
THE TAKEYASU GANG HAS FINALLY DECLARED WAR.
A ROCK FIGHT THIS SUNDAY AT YUMIGAHAMA!!
LET'S GET 'EM!
YEAH
STARTING TODAY, WE'RE TRAINING FOR THE BATTLE.
YES SIR

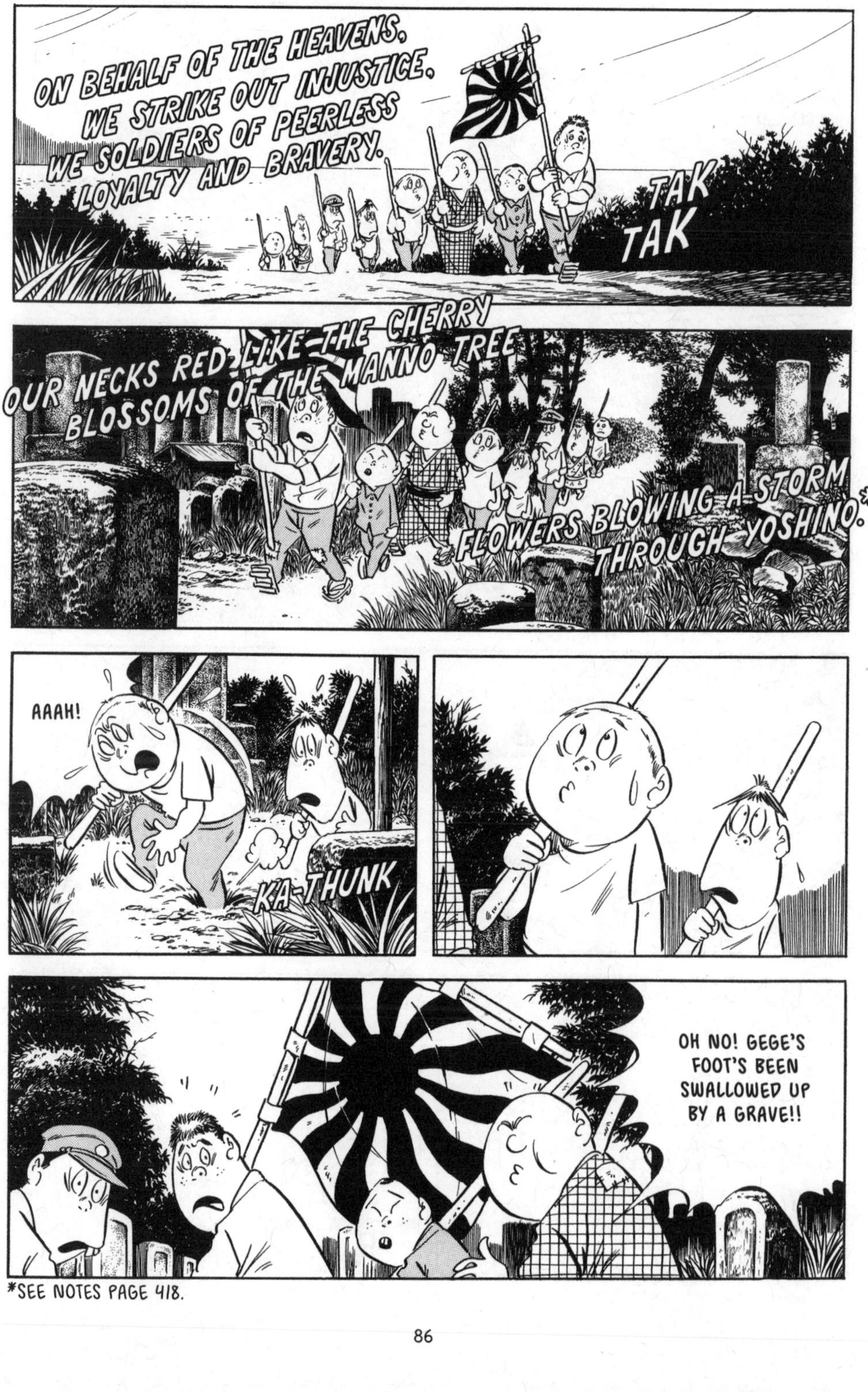
ON BEHALF OF THE HEAVENS, WE STRIKE OUT INJUSTICE, WE SOLDIERS OF PEERLESS LOYALTY AND BRAVERY.
TAK TAK
OUR NECKS RED LIKE THE CHERRY BLOSSOMS OF THE MANNO TREE
FLOWERS BLOWING A STORM THROUGH YOSHINO.*
AAAH!
KA-THUNK
OH NO! GEGE'S FOOT'S BEEN SWALLOWED UP BY A GRAVE!!

*SEE NOTES PAGE 418.

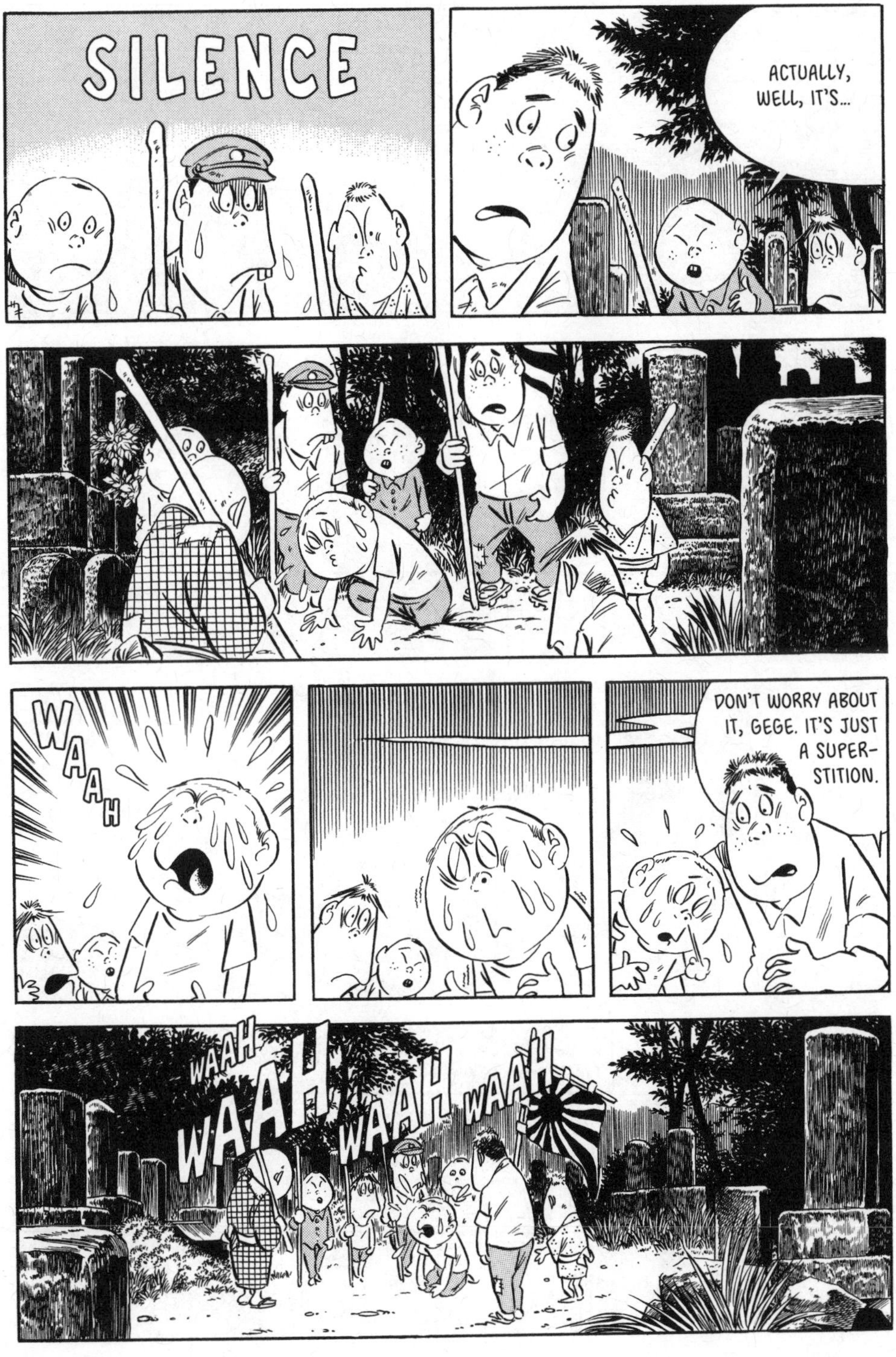
ACTUALLY, WELL, IT'S...
SILENCE
DON'T WORRY ABOUT IT, GEGE. IT'S JUST A SUPER-STITION.
WAAAH
WAAH
WAAH
WAAH
WAAH
WAAH

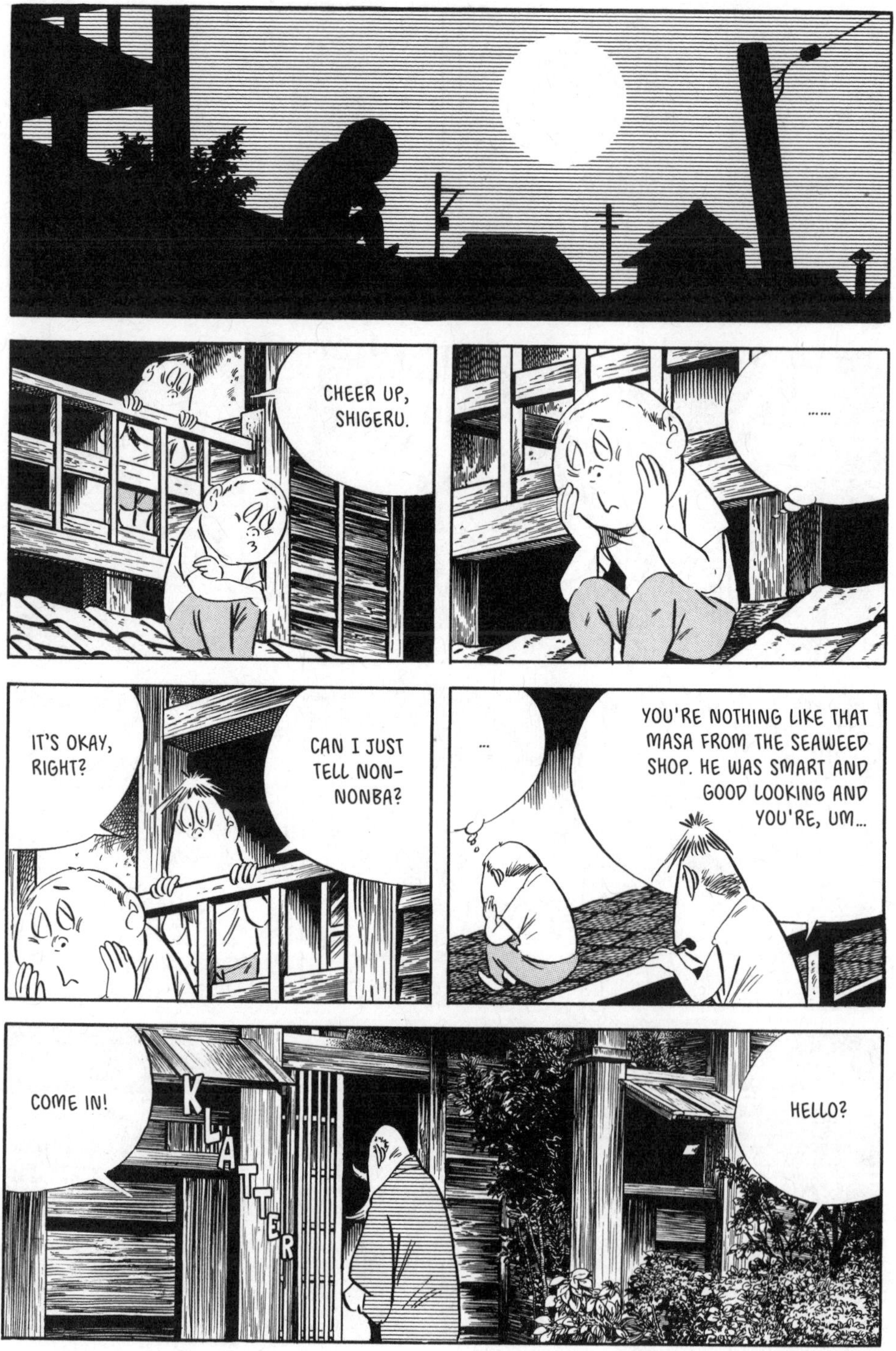
……
CHEER UP, SHIGERU.
YOU'RE NOTHING LIKE THAT MASA FROM THE SEAWEED SHOP. HE WAS SMART AND GOOD LOOKING AND YOU'RE, UM…
…
CAN I JUST TELL NON-NONBA?
IT'S OKAY, RIGHT?
HELLO?
KLATTER
COME IN!

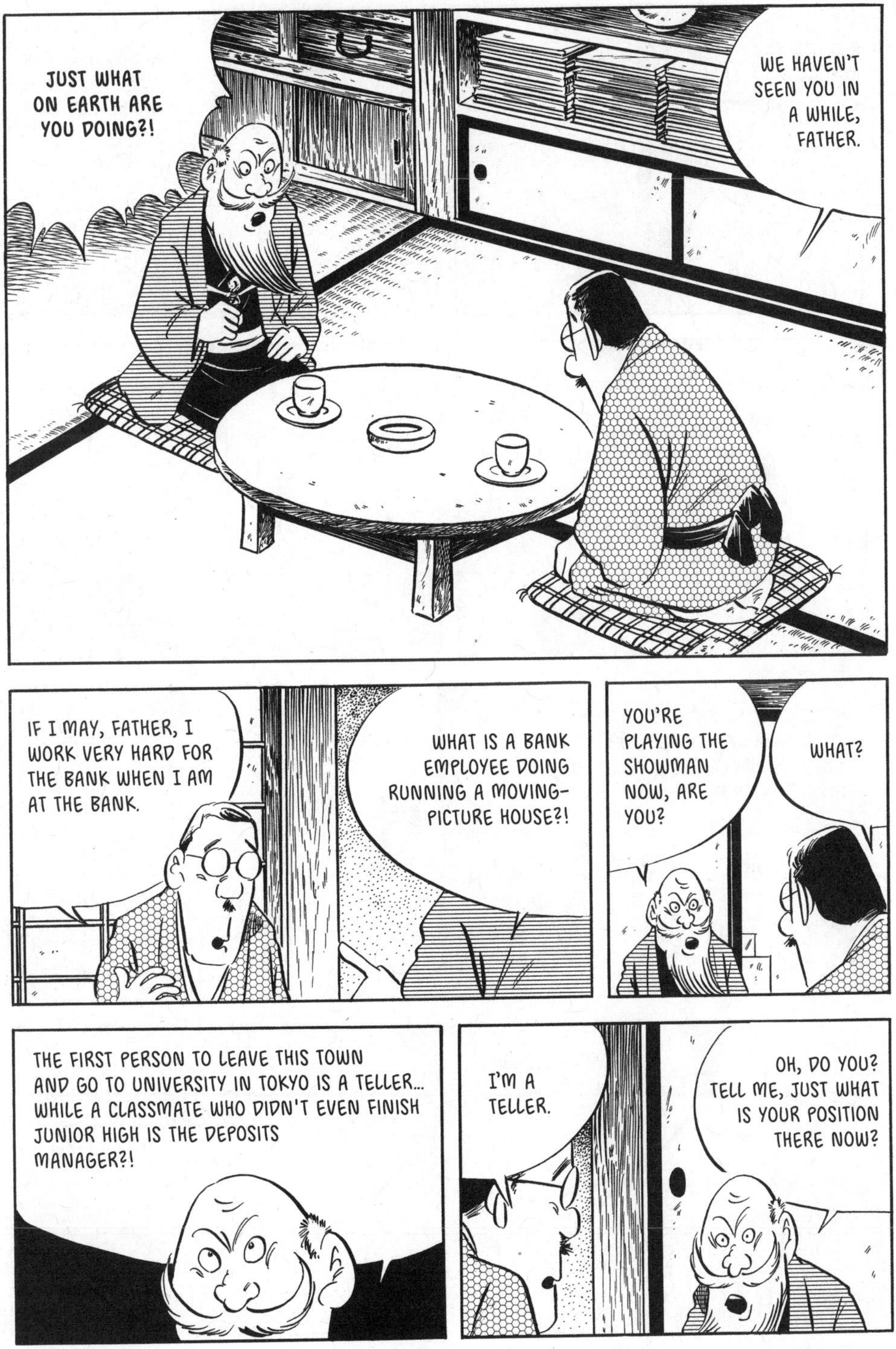
WE HAVEN'T SEEN YOU IN A WHILE, FATHER.
JUST WHAT ON EARTH ARE YOU DOING?!
WHAT?
YOU'RE PLAYING THE SHOWMAN NOW, ARE YOU?
WHAT IS A BANK EMPLOYEE DOING RUNNING A MOVING-PICTURE HOUSE?!
IF I MAY, FATHER, I WORK VERY HARD FOR THE BANK WHEN I AM AT THE BANK.
OH, DO YOU? TELL ME, JUST WHAT IS YOUR POSITION THERE NOW?
I'M A TELLER.
THE FIRST PERSON TO LEAVE THIS TOWN AND GO TO UNIVERSITY IN TOKYO IS A TELLER... WHILE A CLASSMATE WHO DIDN'T EVEN FINISH JUNIOR HIGH IS THE DEPOSITS MANAGER?!

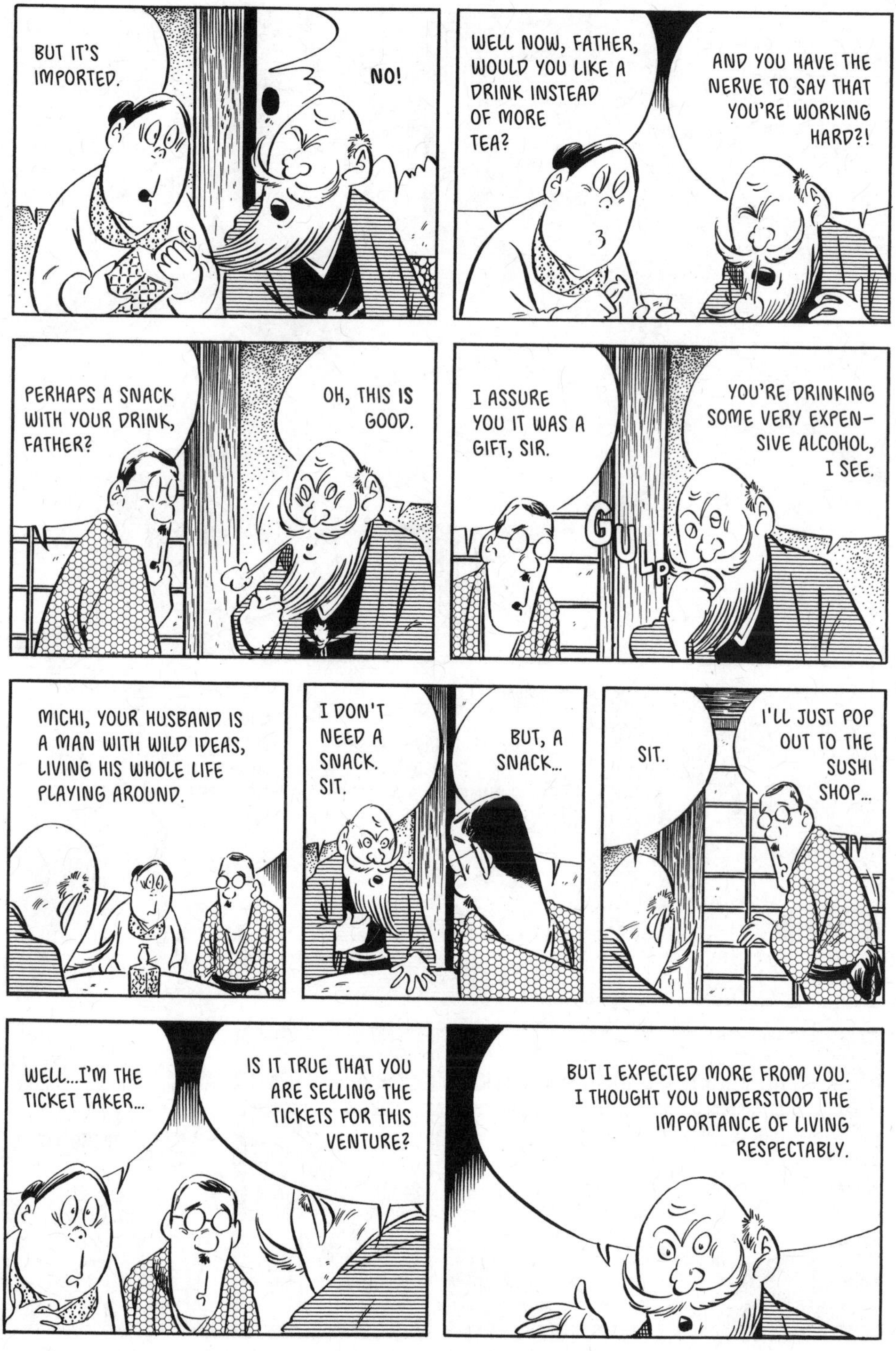
AND YOU HAVE THE NERVE TO SAY THAT YOU'RE WORKING HARD?!
WELL NOW, FATHER, WOULD YOU LIKE A DRINK INSTEAD OF MORE TEA?
NO!
BUT IT'S IMPORTED.
YOU'RE DRINKING SOME VERY EXPEN-SIVE ALCOHOL, I SEE.
I ASSURE YOU IT WAS A GIFT, SIR.
GULP
OH, THIS IS GOOD.
PERHAPS A SNACK WITH YOUR DRINK, FATHER?
I'LL JUST POP OUT TO THE SUSHI SHOP...
SIT.
BUT, A SNACK...
I DON'T NEED A SNACK. SIT.
MICHI, YOUR HUSBAND IS A MAN WITH WILD IDEAS, LIVING HIS WHOLE LIFE PLAYING AROUND.
BUT I EXPECTED MORE FROM YOU. I THOUGHT YOU UNDERSTOOD THE IMPORTANCE OF LIVING RESPECTABLY.
IS IT TRUE THAT YOU ARE SELLING THE TICKETS FOR THIS VENTURE?
WELL...I'M THE TICKET TAKER...

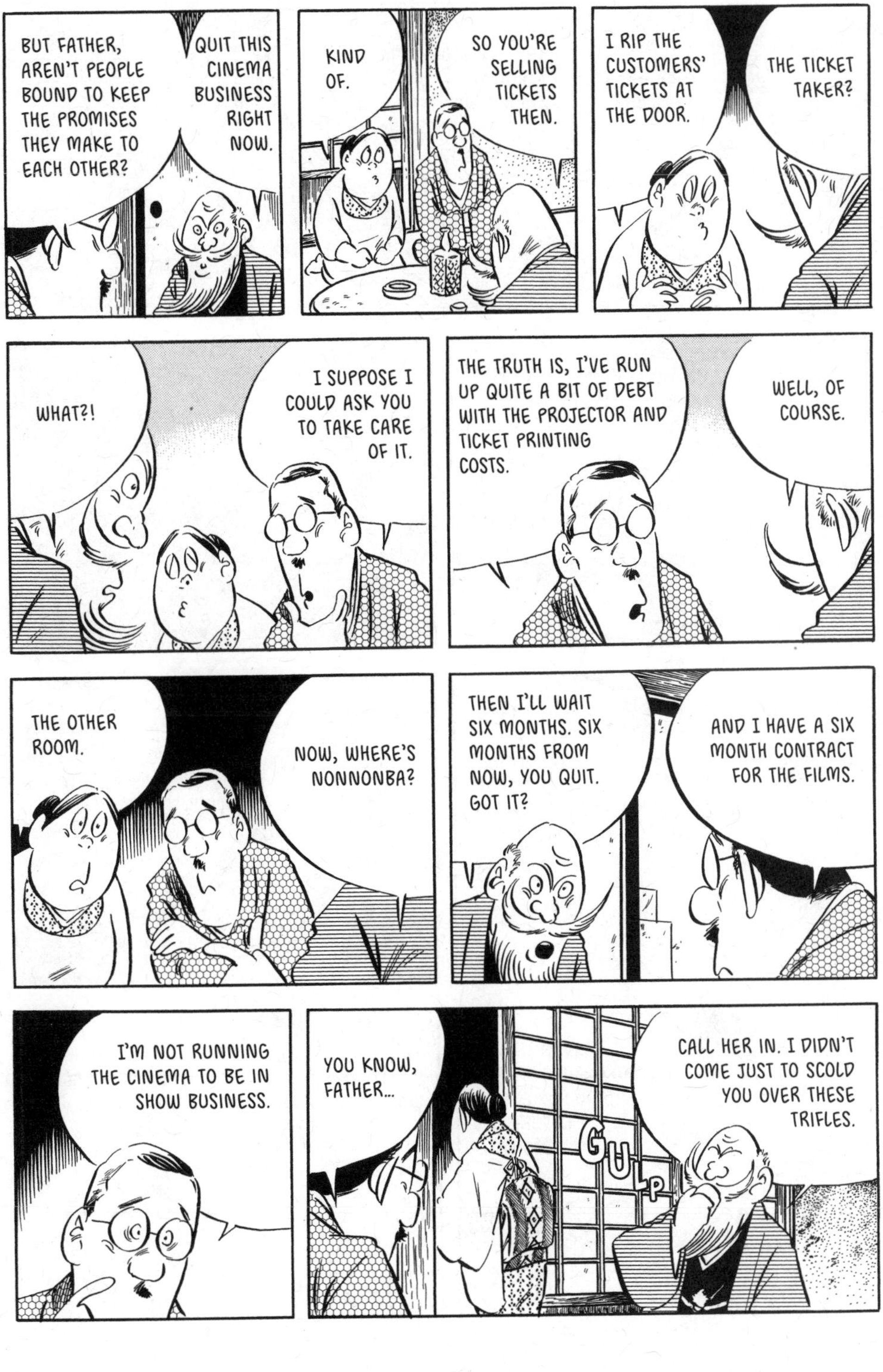
THE TICKET TAKER?
I RIP THE CUSTOMERS' TICKETS AT THE DOOR.
SO YOU'RE SELLING TICKETS THEN.
KIND OF.
QUIT THIS CINEMA BUSINESS RIGHT NOW.
BUT FATHER, AREN'T PEOPLE BOUND TO KEEP THE PROMISES THEY MAKE TO EACH OTHER?
WELL, OF COURSE.
THE TRUTH IS, I'VE RUN UP QUITE A BIT OF DEBT WITH THE PROJECTOR AND TICKET PRINTING COSTS.
I SUPPOSE I COULD ASK YOU TO TAKE CARE OF IT.
WHAT?!
AND I HAVE A SIX MONTH CONTRACT FOR THE FILMS.
THEN I'LL WAIT SIX MONTHS. SIX MONTHS FROM NOW, YOU QUIT. GOT IT?
NOW, WHERE'S NONNONBA?
THE OTHER ROOM.
CALL HER IN. I DIDN'T COME JUST TO SCOLD YOU OVER THESE TRIFLES.
GULP
YOU KNOW, FATHER...
I'M NOT RUNNING THE CINEMA TO BE IN SHOW BUSINESS.

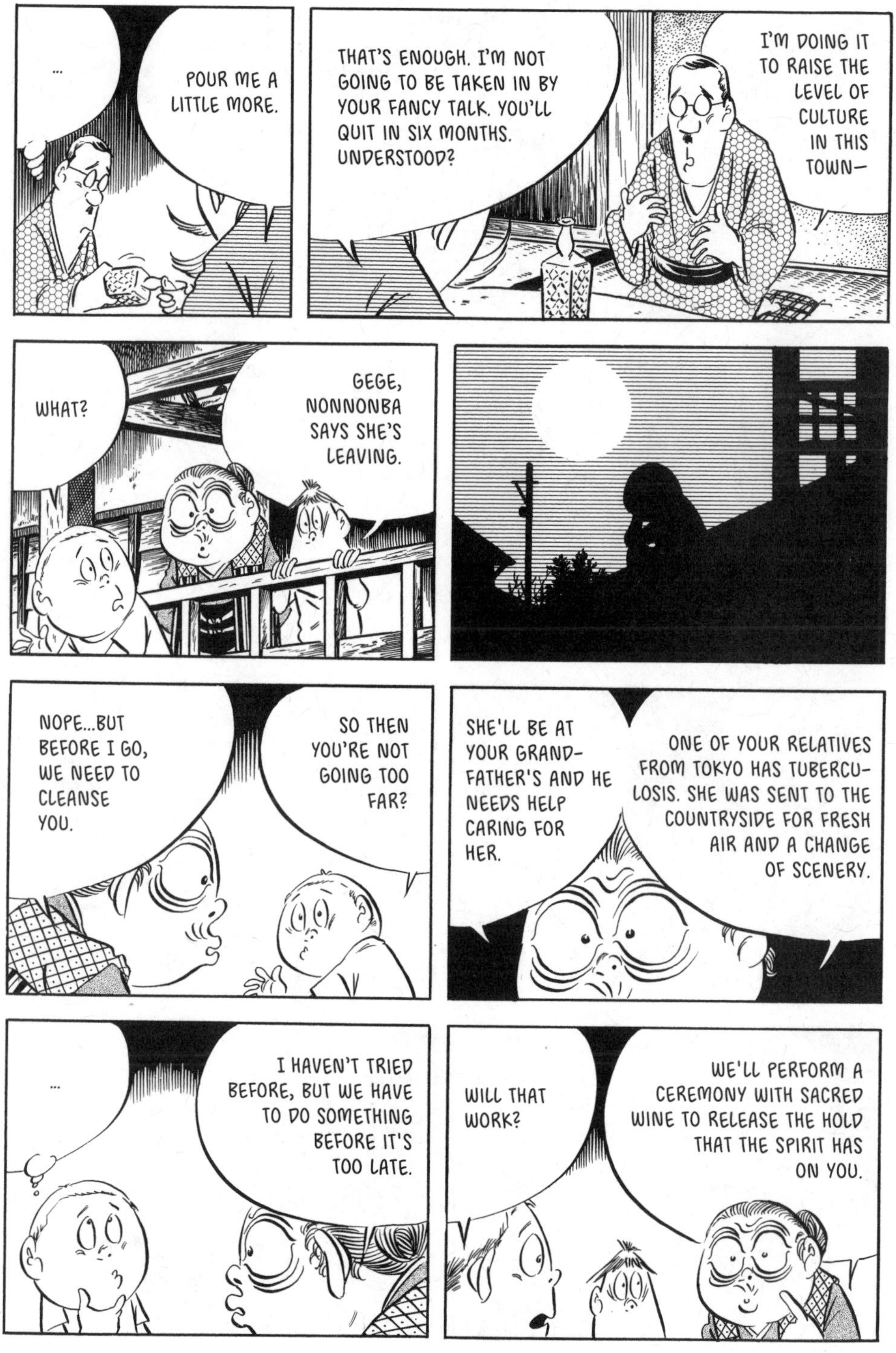
I'M DOING IT TO RAISE THE LEVEL OF CULTURE IN THIS TOWN—
THAT'S ENOUGH. I'M NOT GOING TO BE TAKEN IN BY YOUR FANCY TALK. YOU'LL QUIT IN SIX MONTHS. UNDERSTOOD?
POUR ME A LITTLE MORE.
...
GEGE, NONNONBA SAYS SHE'S LEAVING.
WHAT?
ONE OF YOUR RELATIVES FROM TOKYO HAS TUBERCULOSIS. SHE WAS SENT TO THE COUNTRYSIDE FOR FRESH AIR AND A CHANGE OF SCENERY.
SHE'LL BE AT YOUR GRANDFATHER'S AND HE NEEDS HELP CARING FOR HER.
SO THEN YOU'RE NOT GOING TOO FAR?
NOPE...BUT BEFORE I GO, WE NEED TO CLEANSE YOU.
WE'LL PERFORM A CEREMONY WITH SACRED WINE TO RELEASE THE HOLD THAT THE SPIRIT HAS ON YOU.
WILL THAT WORK?
I HAVEN'T TRIED BEFORE, BUT WE HAVE TO DO SOMETHING BEFORE IT'S TOO LATE.
...

CHIGUSA

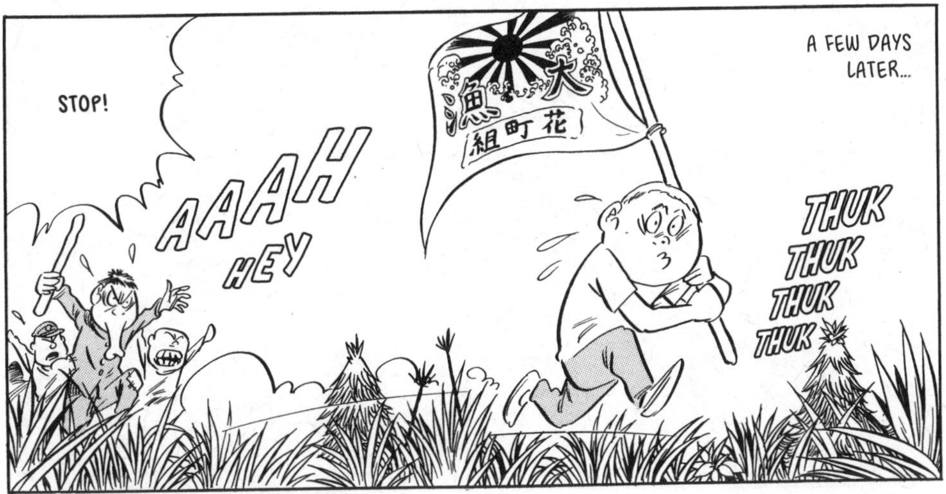
A FEW DAYS LATER...
THUK
THUK
THUK
THUK
大漁
花町組
STOP!
AAAH
HEY

SIGN: GOOD CATCH* HANAMACHI GANG.

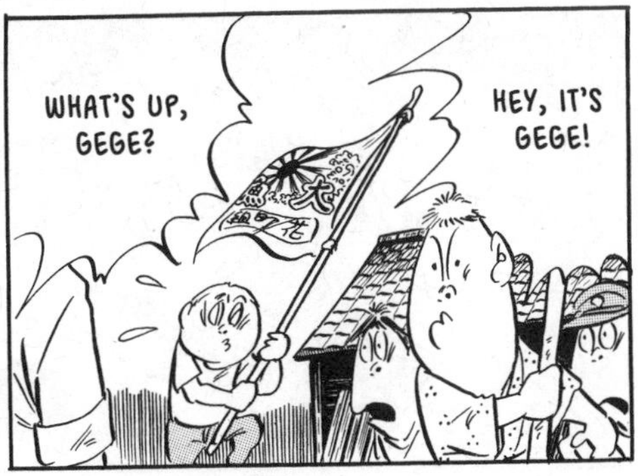
HEY, IT'S GEGE!
WHAT'S UP, GEGE?

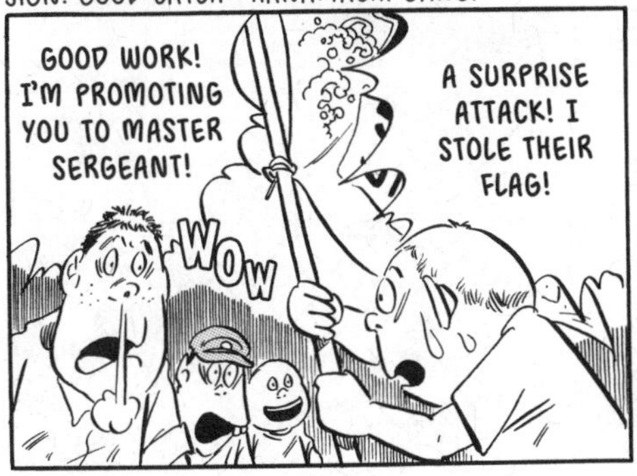
A SURPRISE ATTACK! I STOLE THEIR FLAG!
GOOD WORK! I'M PROMOTING YOU TO MASTER SERGEANT!
WOW

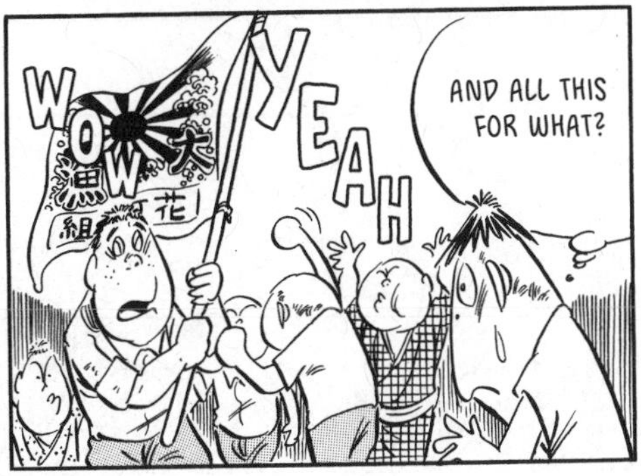
AND ALL THIS FOR WHAT?
YEAH
WOW

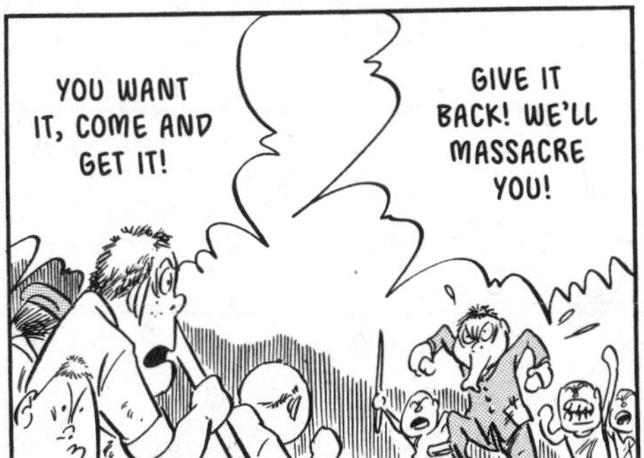
GIVE IT BACK! WE'LL MASSACRE YOU!
YOU WANT IT, COME AND GET IT!

*SEE NOTES PAGE 418.

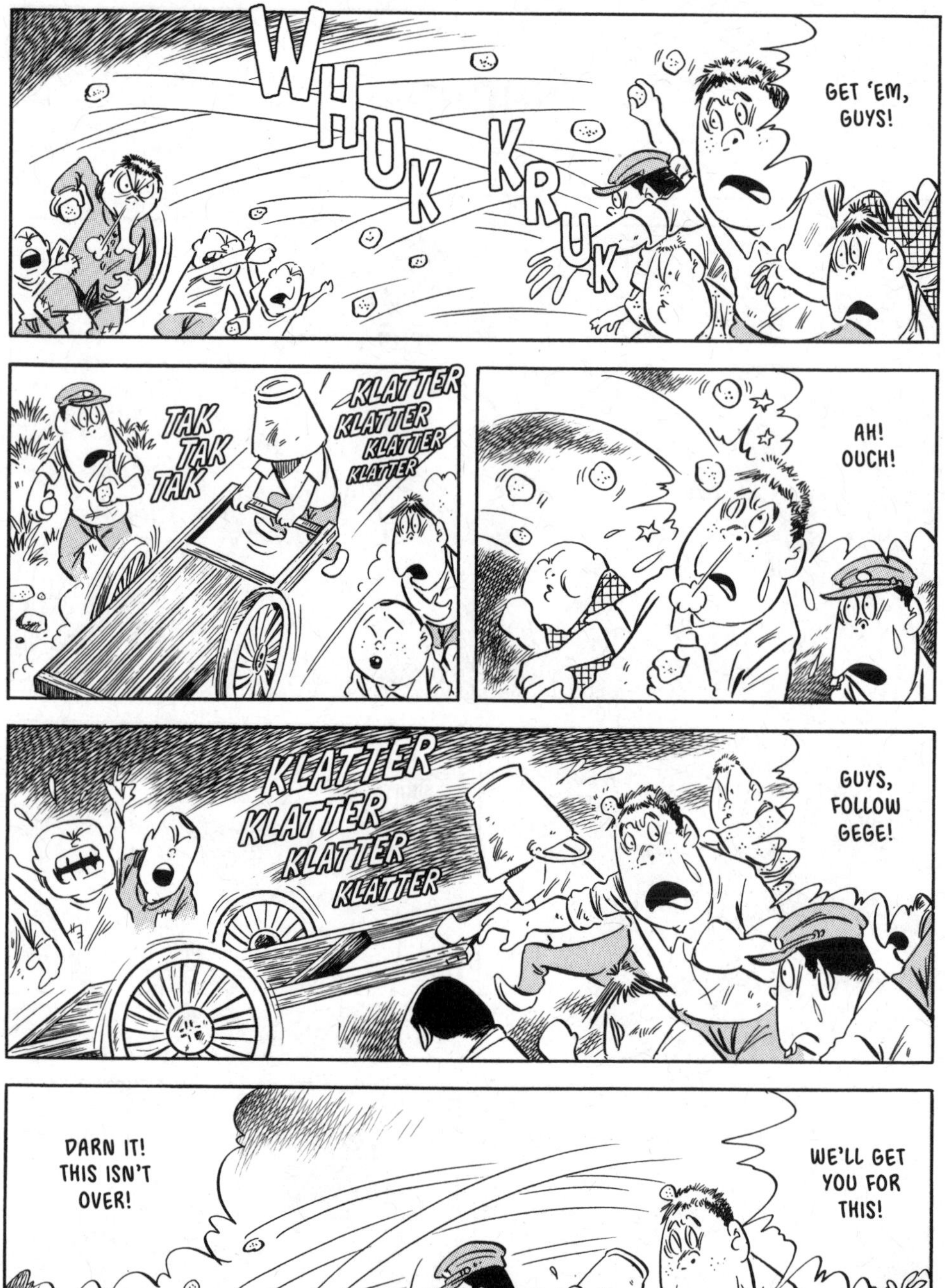
GET 'EM, GUYS!
WHUK
KRUK
AH! OUCH!
KLATTER KLATTER KLATTER KLATTER
TAK TAK TAK
GUYS, FOLLOW GEGE!
KLATTER KLATTER KLATTER KLATTER
WE'LL GET YOU FOR THIS!
DARN IT! THIS ISN'T OVER!

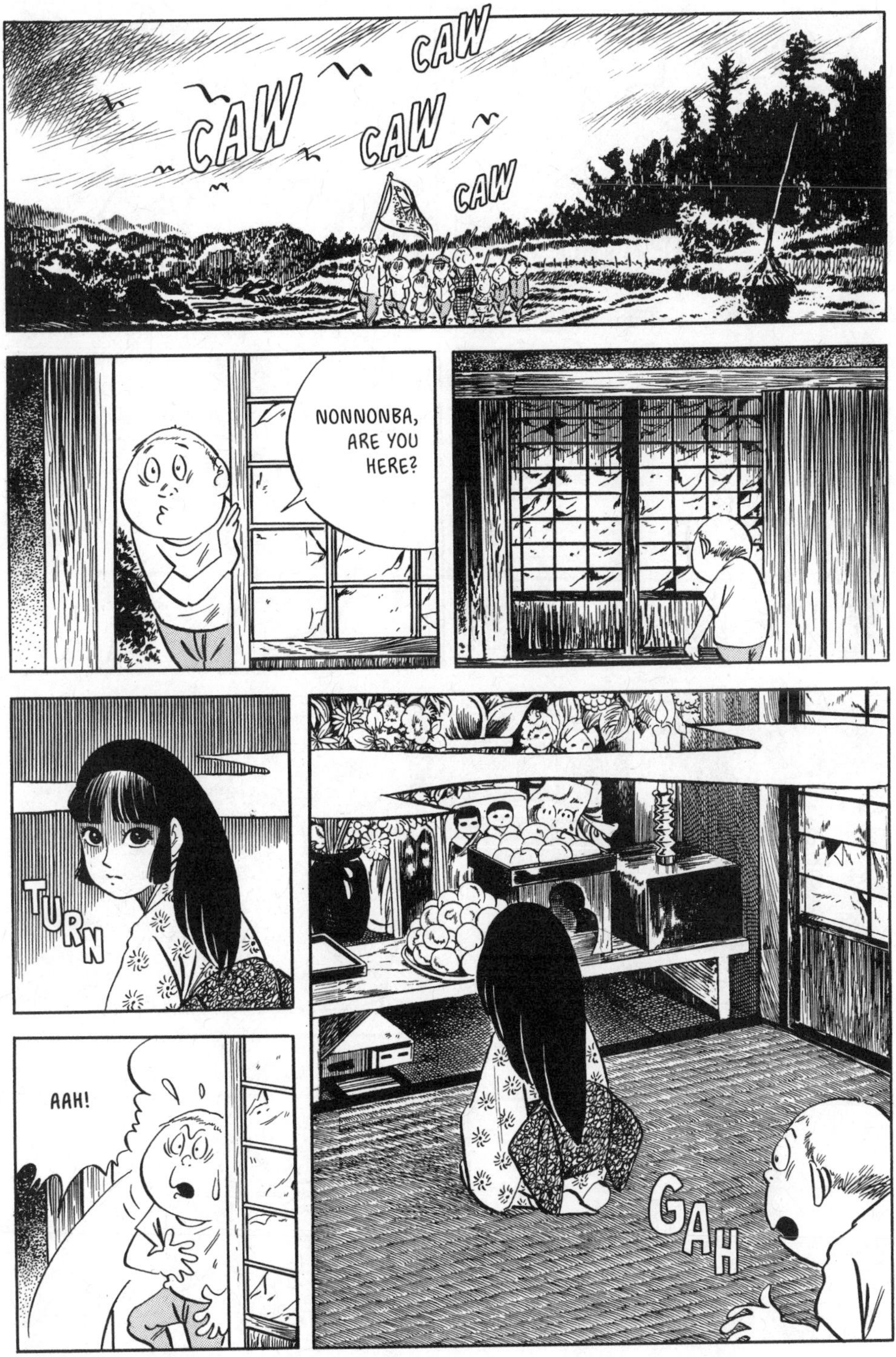
CAW
CAW
CAW
CAW
NONNONBA, ARE YOU HERE?
GAH
TURN
AAH!

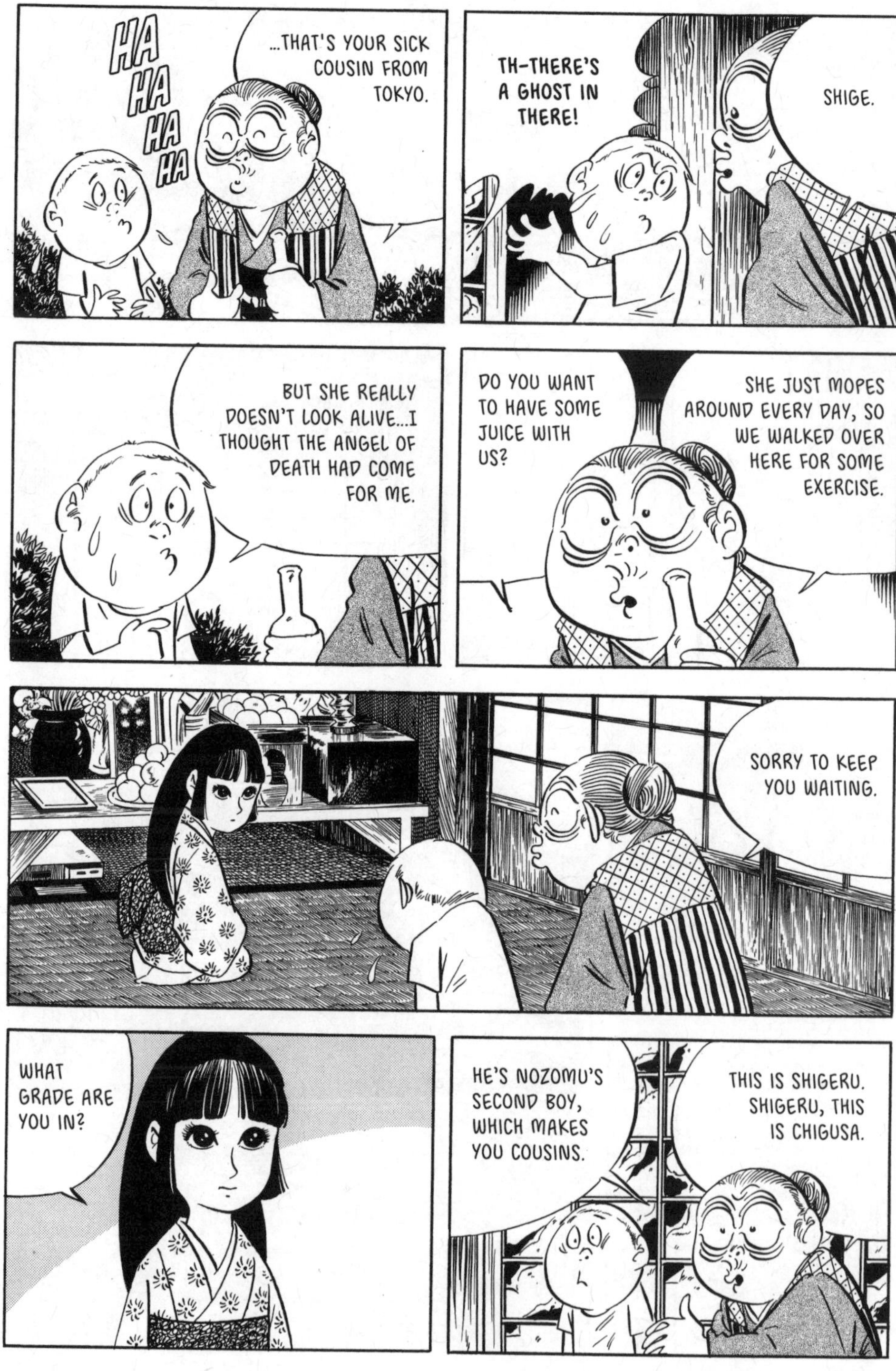
SHIGE.
TH-THERE'S A GHOST IN THERE!
...THAT'S YOUR SICK COUSIN FROM TOKYO.
HA HA HA HA
SHE JUST MOPES AROUND EVERY DAY, SO WE WALKED OVER HERE FOR SOME EXERCISE.
DO YOU WANT TO HAVE SOME JUICE WITH US?
BUT SHE REALLY DOESN'T LOOK ALIVE...I THOUGHT THE ANGEL OF DEATH HAD COME FOR ME.
SORRY TO KEEP YOU WAITING.
THIS IS SHIGERU. SHIGERU, THIS IS CHIGUSA.
HE'S NOZOMU'S SECOND BOY, WHICH MAKES YOU COUSINS.
WHAT GRADE ARE YOU IN?

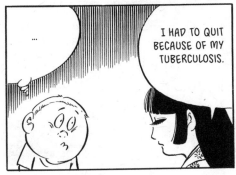

FOURTH GRADE.
I WAS IN GRADE ONE AT A GIRLS' SCHOOL...
I HAD TO QUIT BECAUSE OF MY TUBERCULOSIS.
...
THERE ARE NO CUPS. THIS WILL HAVE TO DO.
OKAY.
WHEN YOU FIRST SAW ME, YOU THOUGHT I WAS A GHOST, RIGHT?
N-NO...
DID TOO. IT'S OKAY. I'LL BE A GHOST SOON ENOUGH ANYWAY.
MISS, THAT'S...
THEY ABANDONED ME. EVEN THOUGH THERE'S A HOSPITAL NEAR TOKYO, THEY SENT ME ALL THE WAY OUT HERE TO THE COUNTRY.
NO ONE WANTS TO BE ANYWHERE NEAR ME.
YOU, GRAN, YOU'RE JUST BEING PAID TO BE HERE.
SO WHAT?
WHAT?

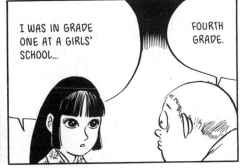

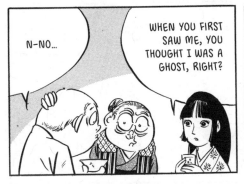

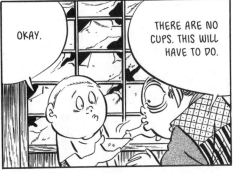

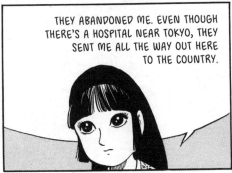

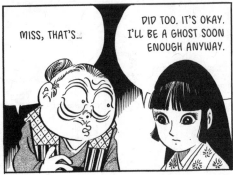

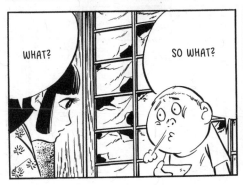

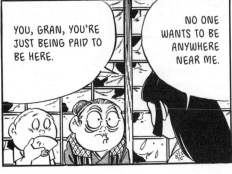

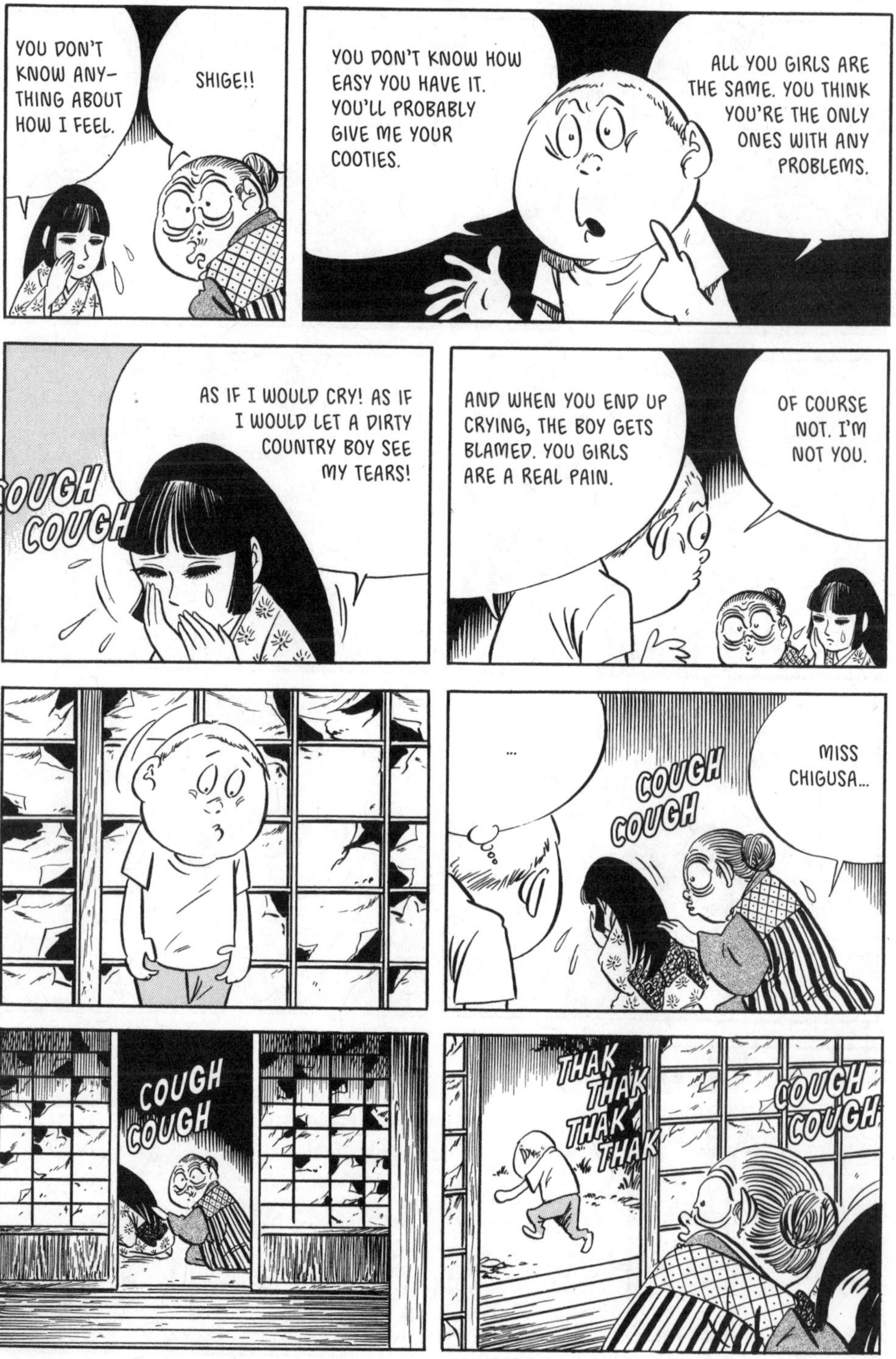
ALL YOU GIRLS ARE THE SAME. YOU THINK YOU'RE THE ONLY ONES WITH ANY PROBLEMS.
YOU DON'T KNOW HOW EASY YOU HAVE IT. YOU'LL PROBABLY GIVE ME YOUR COOTIES.
SHIGE!!
YOU DON'T KNOW ANY-THING ABOUT HOW I FEEL.
OF COURSE NOT. I'M NOT YOU.
AND WHEN YOU END UP CRYING, THE BOY GETS BLAMED. YOU GIRLS ARE A REAL PAIN.
AS IF I WOULD CRY! AS IF I WOULD LET A DIRTY COUNTRY BOY SEE MY TEARS!
COUGH COUGH
MISS CHIGUSA...
COUGH COUGH
...
COUGH COUGH
THAK THAK THAK THAK
COUGH COUGH

IS IT A ROCK?

HEY!

DIG DEEPER. THE HOLE HAS TO BE SO DEEP THAT ONCE TAKEYASU AND HIS GANG FALL IN, THEY WON'T BE ABLE TO CLIMB OUT.

THAT'S A JIZO* STATUE!

A STATUE!

*SEE NOTES PAGE 418.

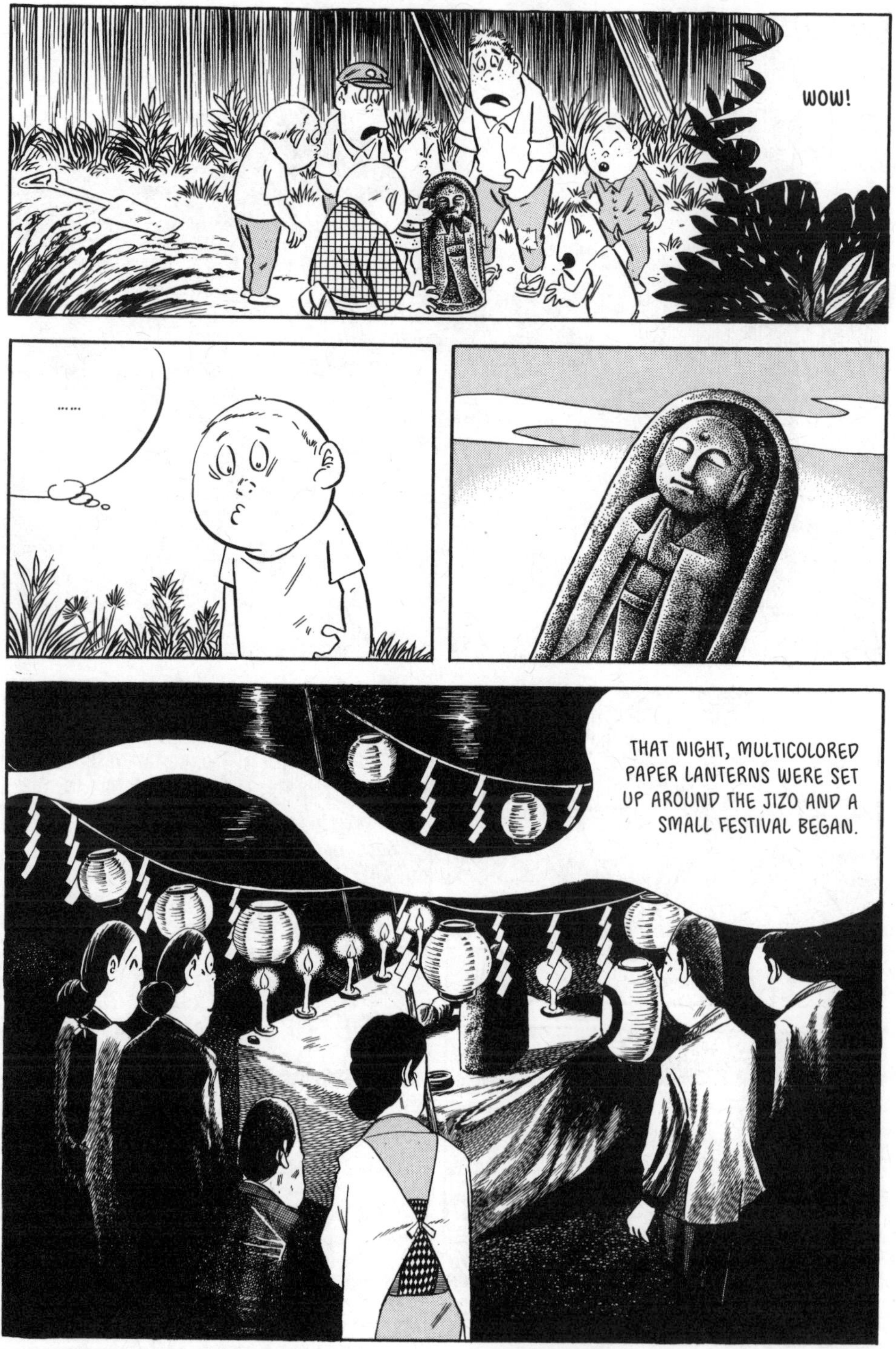
WOW!
……
THAT NIGHT, MULTICOLORED PAPER LANTERNS WERE SET UP AROUND THE JIZO AND A SMALL FESTIVAL BEGAN.

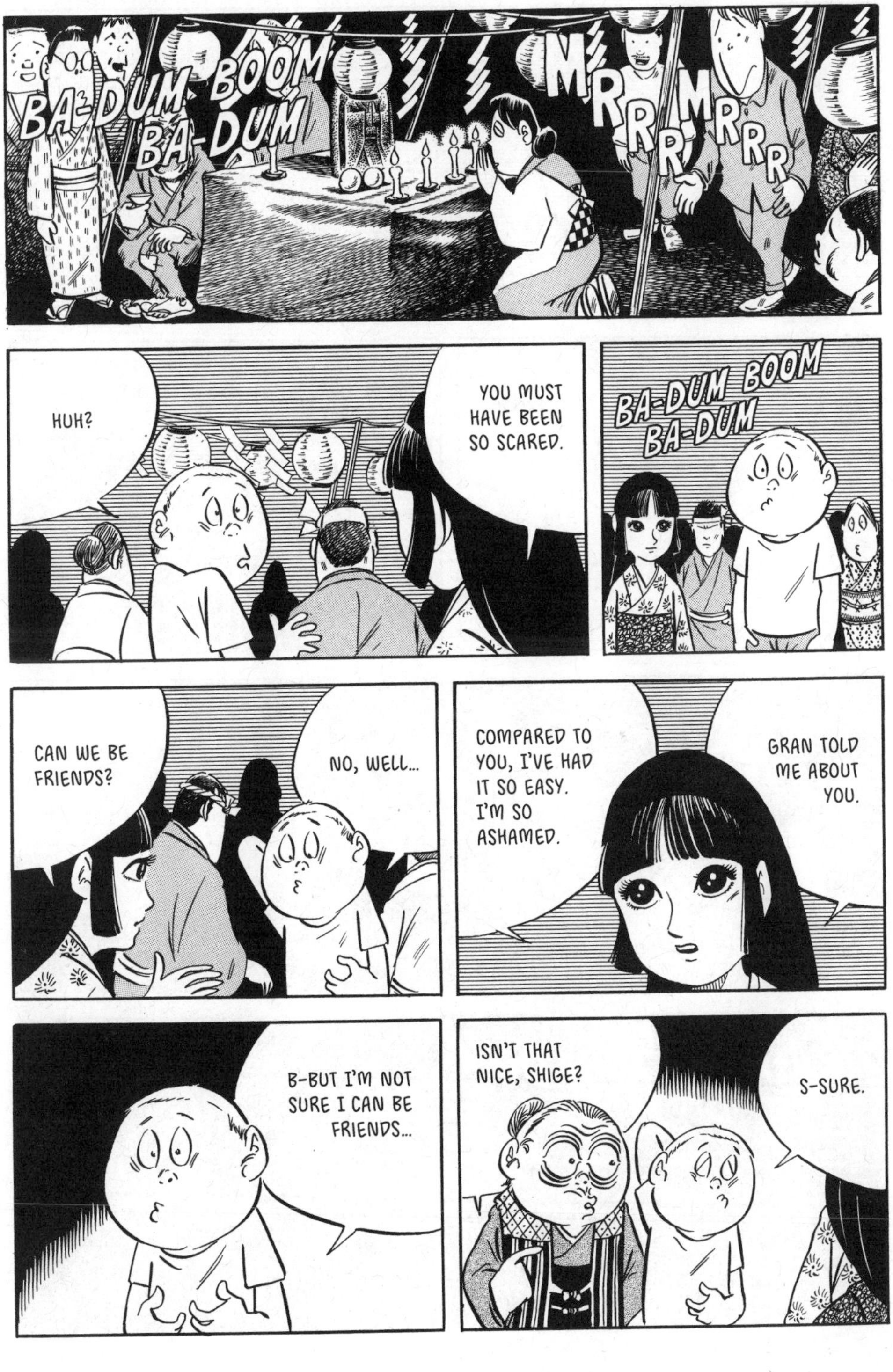
MRRRMRRRR
BA-DUM BOOM BA-DUM
BA-DUM BOOM BA-DUM
YOU MUST HAVE BEEN SO SCARED.
HUH?
GRAN TOLD ME ABOUT YOU.
COMPARED TO YOU, I'VE HAD IT SO EASY. I'M SO ASHAMED.
NO, WELL...
CAN WE BE FRIENDS?
S-SURE.
ISN'T THAT NICE, SHIGE?
B-BUT I'M NOT SURE I CAN BE FRIENDS...

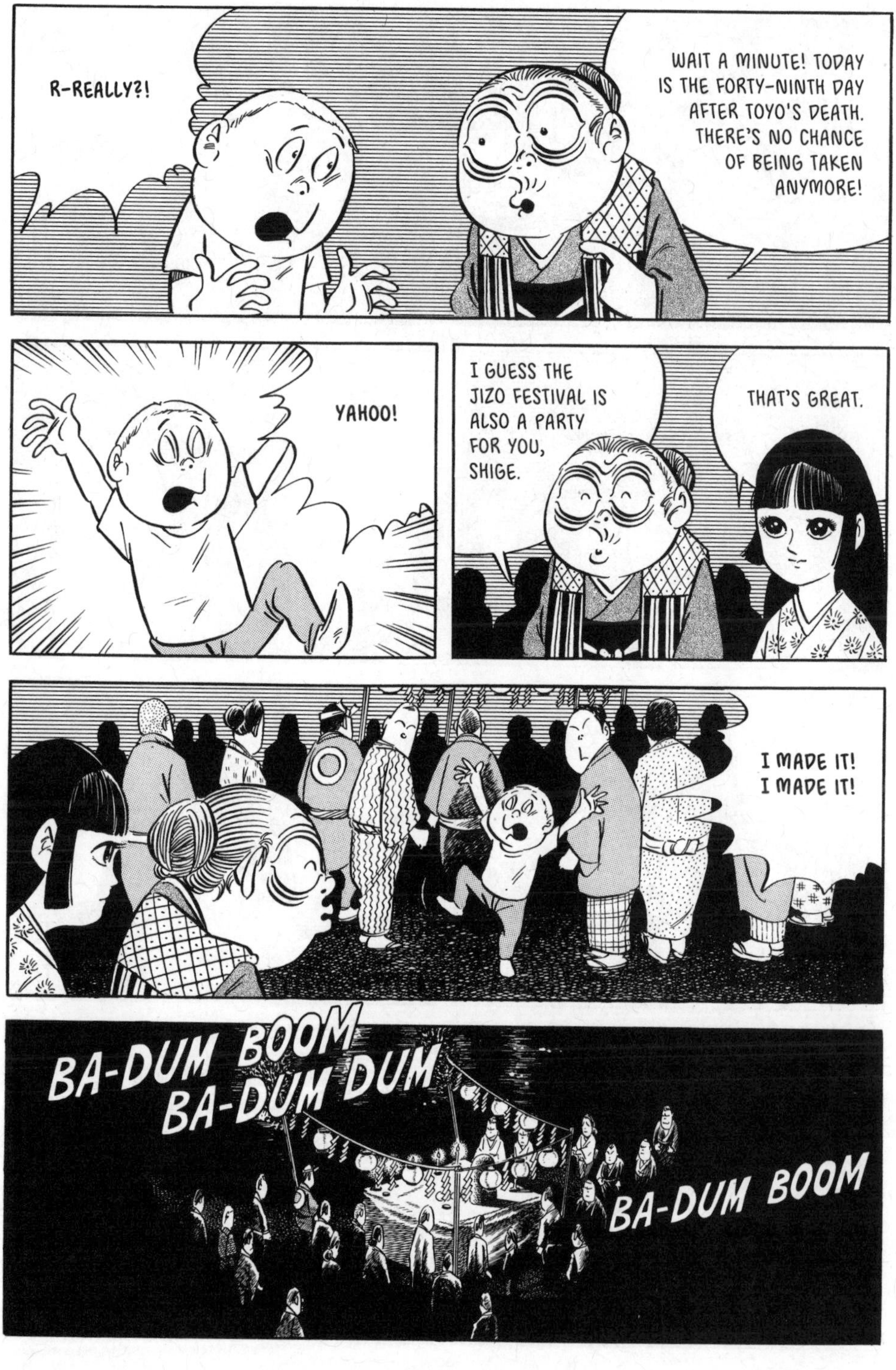

WAIT A MINUTE! TODAY IS THE FORTY-NINTH DAY AFTER TOYO'S DEATH. THERE'S NO CHANCE OF BEING TAKEN ANYMORE!
R-REALLY?!
THAT'S GREAT.
I GUESS THE JIZO FESTIVAL IS ALSO A PARTY FOR YOU, SHIGE.
YAHOO!
I MADE IT! I MADE IT!
BA-DUM BOOM
BA-DUM DUM
BA-DUM BOOM

BANK ROBBERY

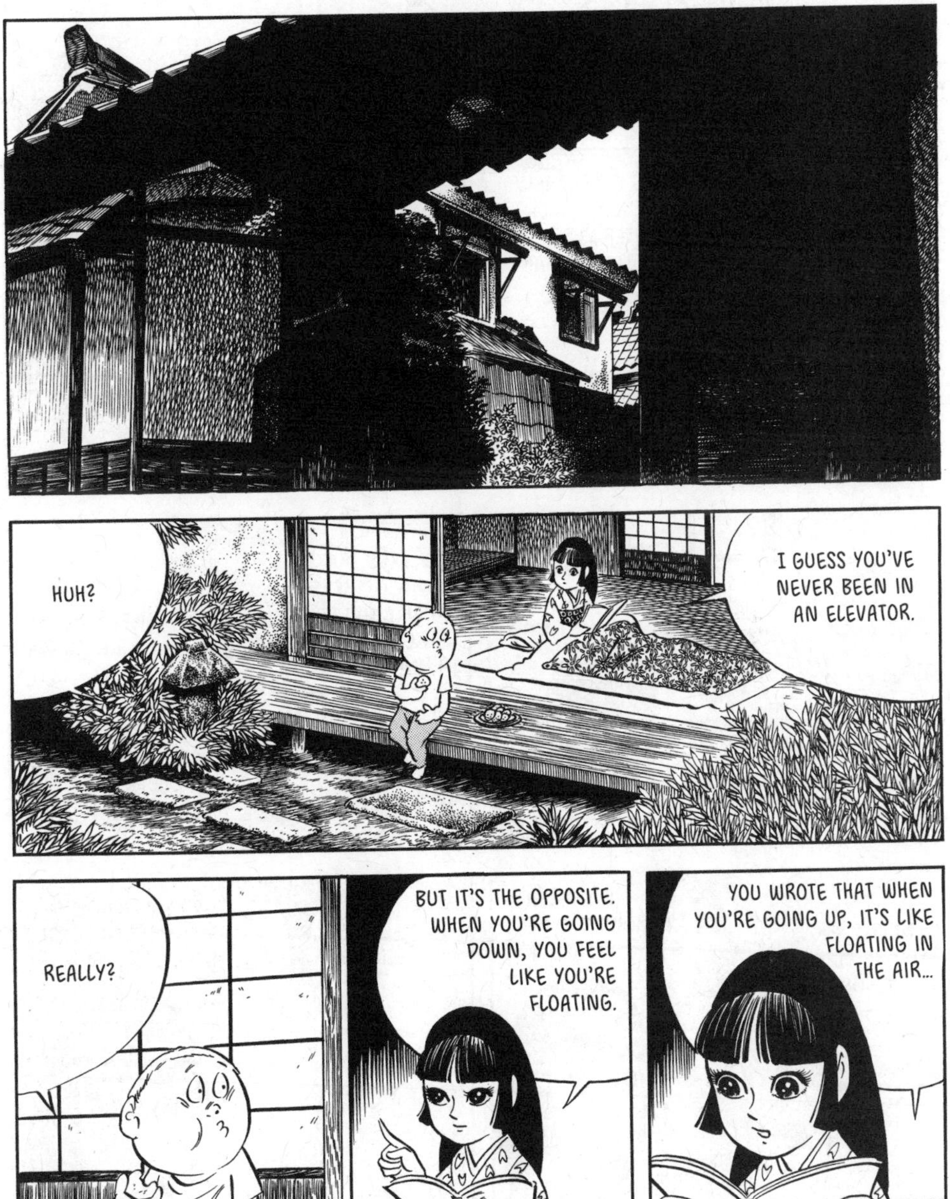
I GUESS YOU'VE NEVER BEEN IN AN ELEVATOR.
HUH?
YOU WROTE THAT WHEN YOU'RE GOING UP, IT'S LIKE FLOATING IN THE AIR...
BUT IT'S THE OPPOSITE. WHEN YOU'RE GOING DOWN, YOU FEEL LIKE YOU'RE FLOATING.
REALLY?

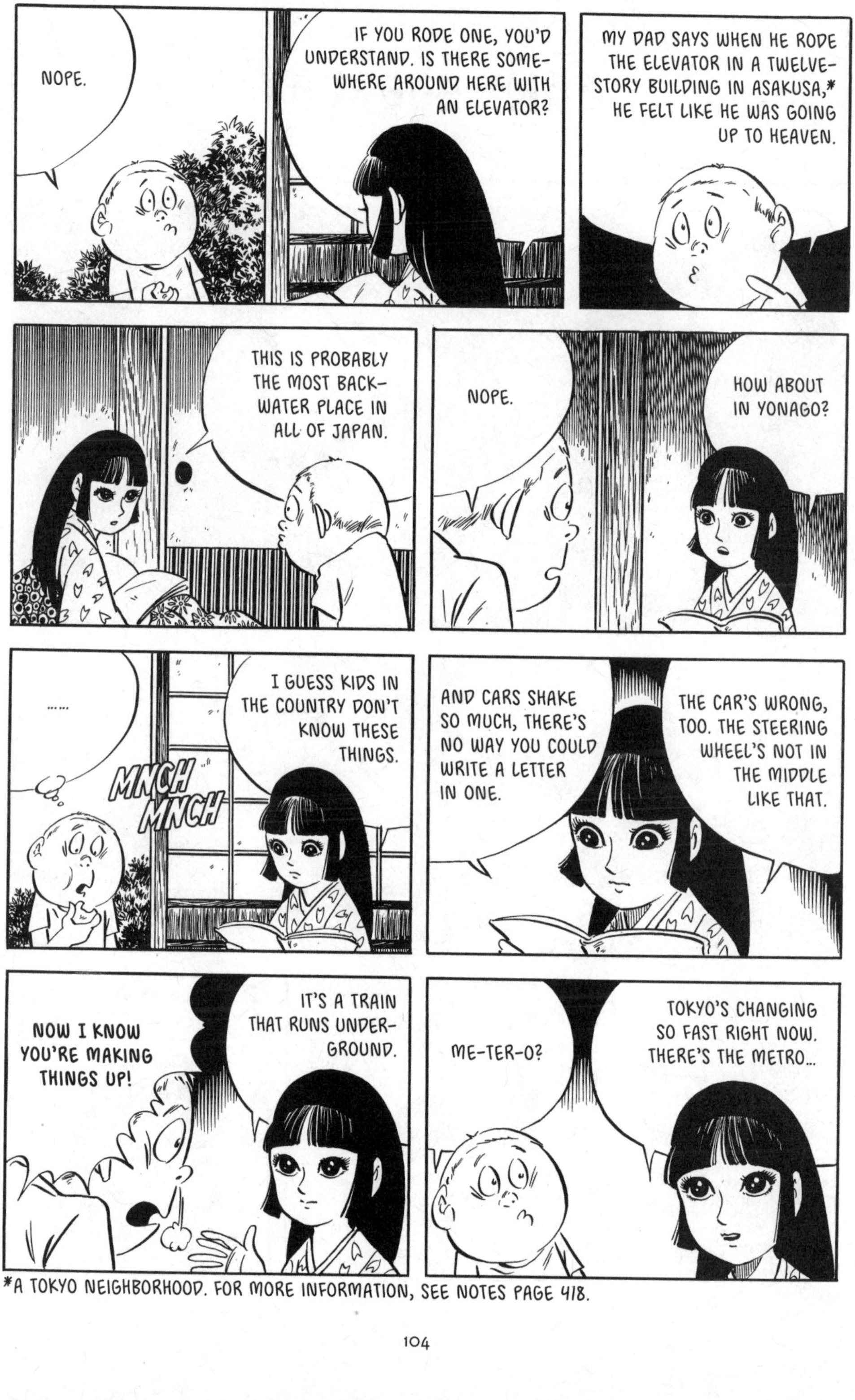
MY DAD SAYS WHEN HE RODE THE ELEVATOR IN A TWELVE-STORY BUILDING IN ASAKUSA,* HE FELT LIKE HE WAS GOING UP TO HEAVEN.
IF YOU RODE ONE, YOU'D UNDERSTAND. IS THERE SOMEWHERE AROUND HERE WITH AN ELEVATOR?
NOPE.
HOW ABOUT IN YONAGO?
NOPE.
THIS IS PROBABLY THE MOST BACKWATER PLACE IN ALL OF JAPAN.
THE CAR'S WRONG, TOO. THE STEERING WHEEL'S NOT IN THE MIDDLE LIKE THAT.
AND CARS SHAKE SO MUCH, THERE'S NO WAY YOU COULD WRITE A LETTER IN ONE.
I GUESS KIDS IN THE COUNTRY DON'T KNOW THESE THINGS.
MNCH MNCH
……
TOKYO'S CHANGING SO FAST RIGHT NOW. THERE'S THE METRO...
ME-TER-O?
IT'S A TRAIN THAT RUNS UNDERGROUND.
NOW I KNOW YOU'RE MAKING THINGS UP!

*A TOKYO NEIGHBORHOOD. FOR MORE INFORMATION, SEE NOTES PAGE 418.

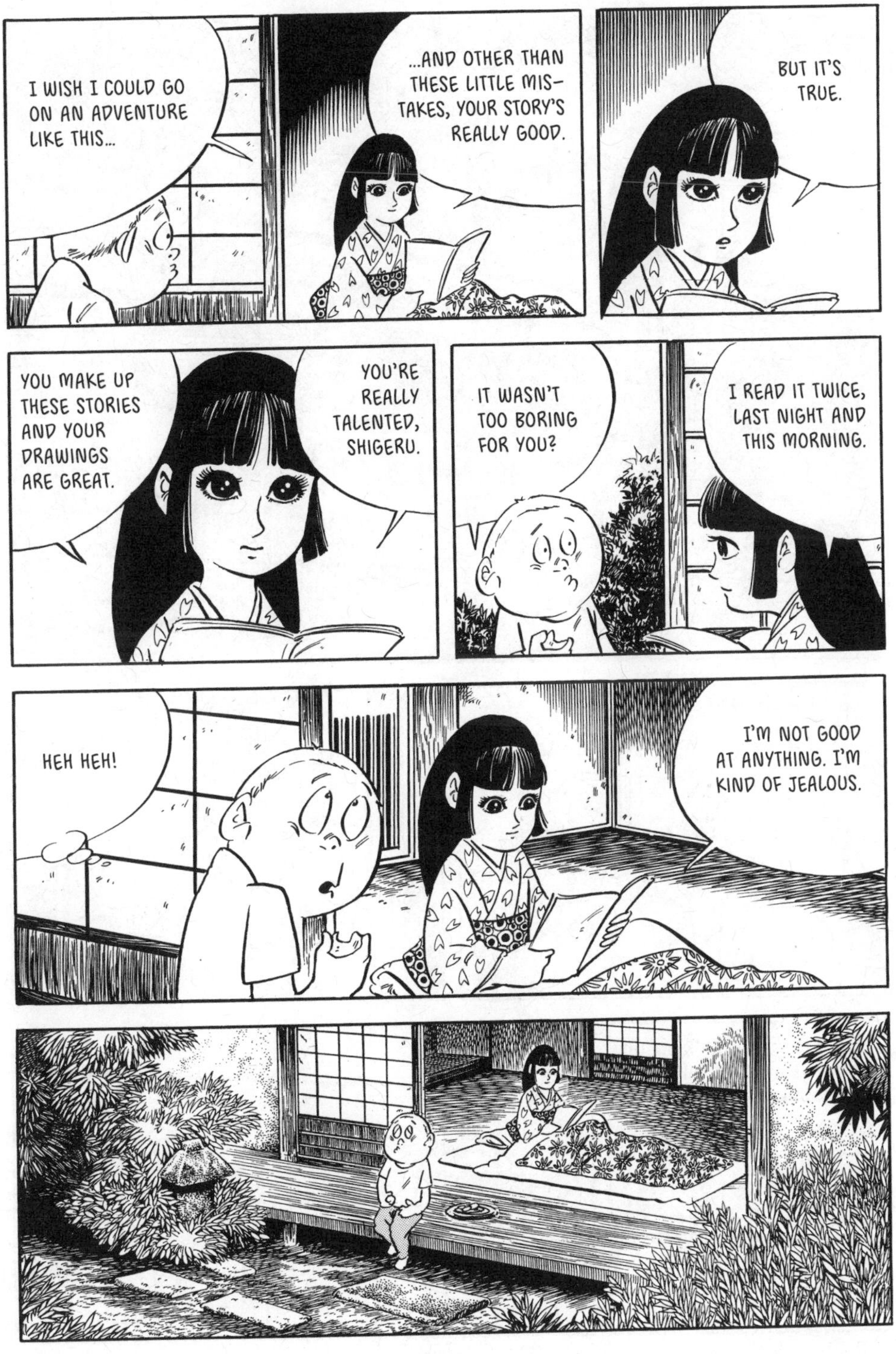
I WISH I COULD GO ON AN ADVENTURE LIKE THIS...
...AND OTHER THAN THESE LITTLE MIS-TAKES, YOUR STORY'S REALLY GOOD.
BUT IT'S TRUE.
YOU MAKE UP THESE STORIES AND YOUR DRAWINGS ARE GREAT.
YOU'RE REALLY TALENTED, SHIGERU.
IT WASN'T TOO BORING FOR YOU?
I READ IT TWICE, LAST NIGHT AND THIS MORNING.
HEH HEH!
I'M NOT GOOD AT ANYTHING. I'M KIND OF JEALOUS.

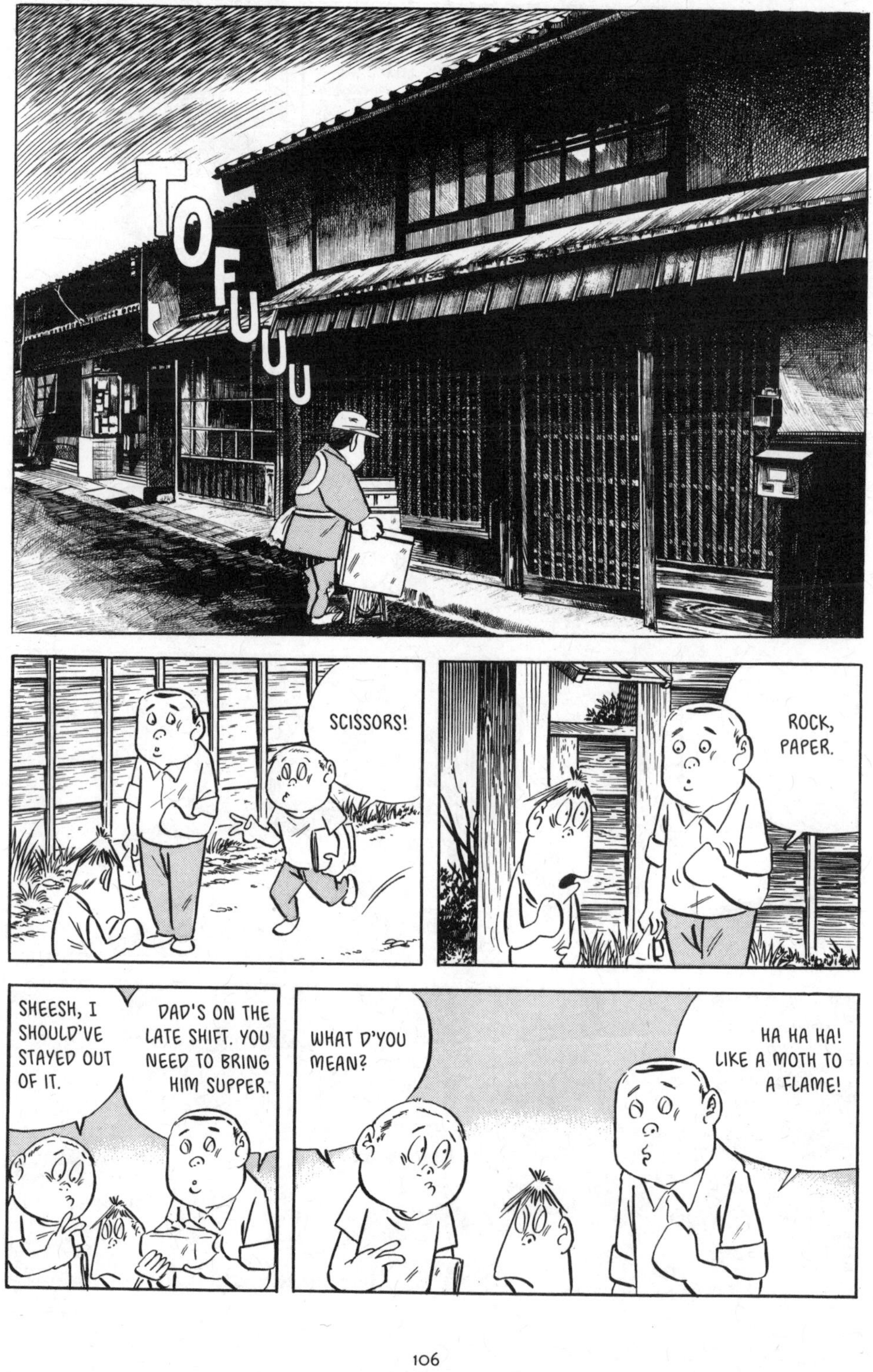
TOFUUU
ROCK, PAPER.
SCISSORS!
HA HA HA! LIKE A MOTH TO A FLAME!
WHAT D'YOU MEAN?
DAD'S ON THE LATE SHIFT. YOU NEED TO BRING HIM SUPPER.
SHEESH, I SHOULD'VE STAYED OUT OF IT.

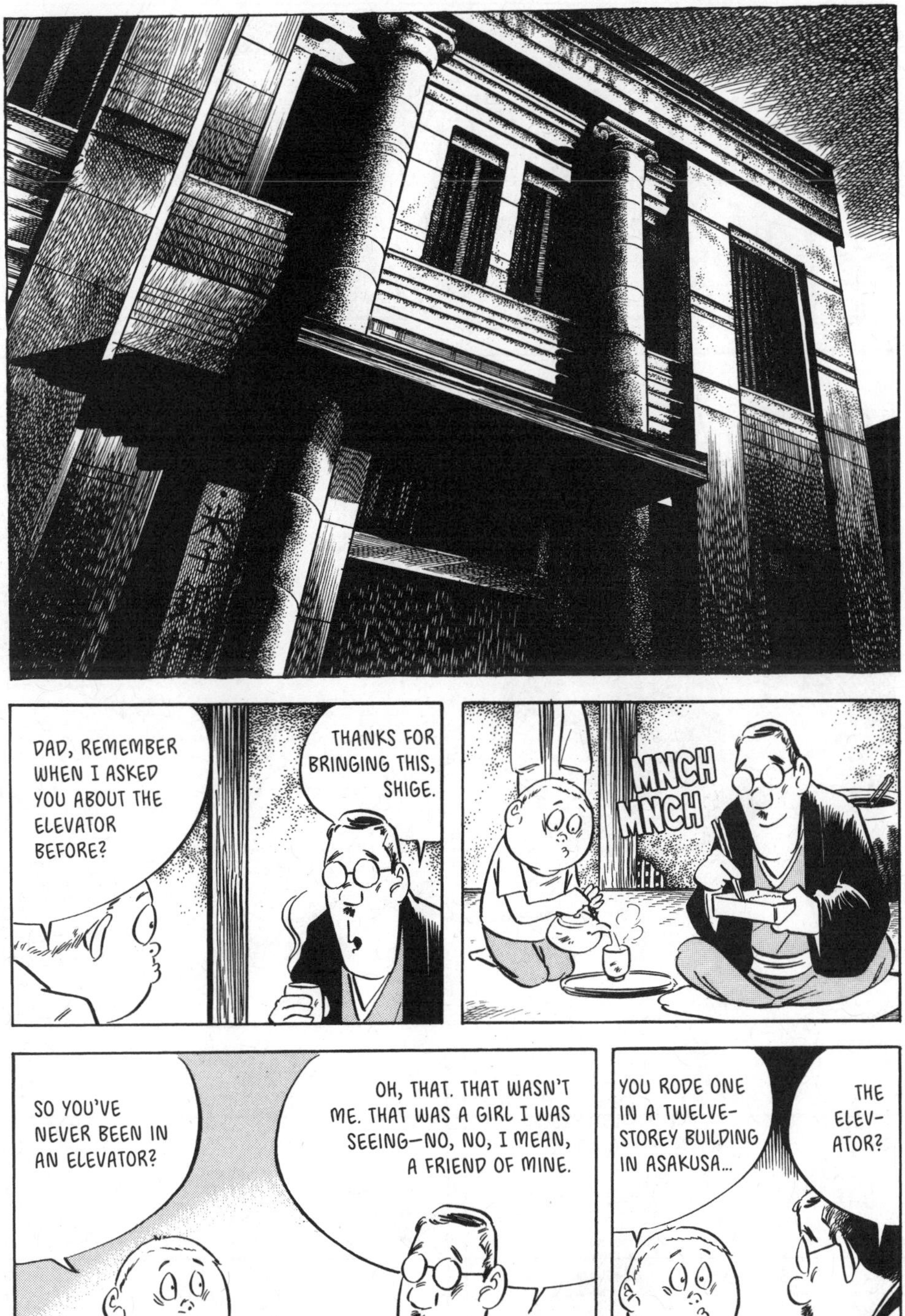
MNCH
MNCH
THANKS FOR BRINGING THIS, SHIGE.
DAD, REMEMBER WHEN I ASKED YOU ABOUT THE ELEVATOR BEFORE?
THE ELEV-ATOR?
YOU RODE ONE IN A TWELVE-STOREY BUILDING IN ASAKUSA...
OH, THAT. THAT WASN'T ME. THAT WAS A GIRL I WAS SEEING—NO, NO, I MEAN, A FRIEND OF MINE.
SO YOU'VE NEVER BEEN IN AN ELEVATOR?

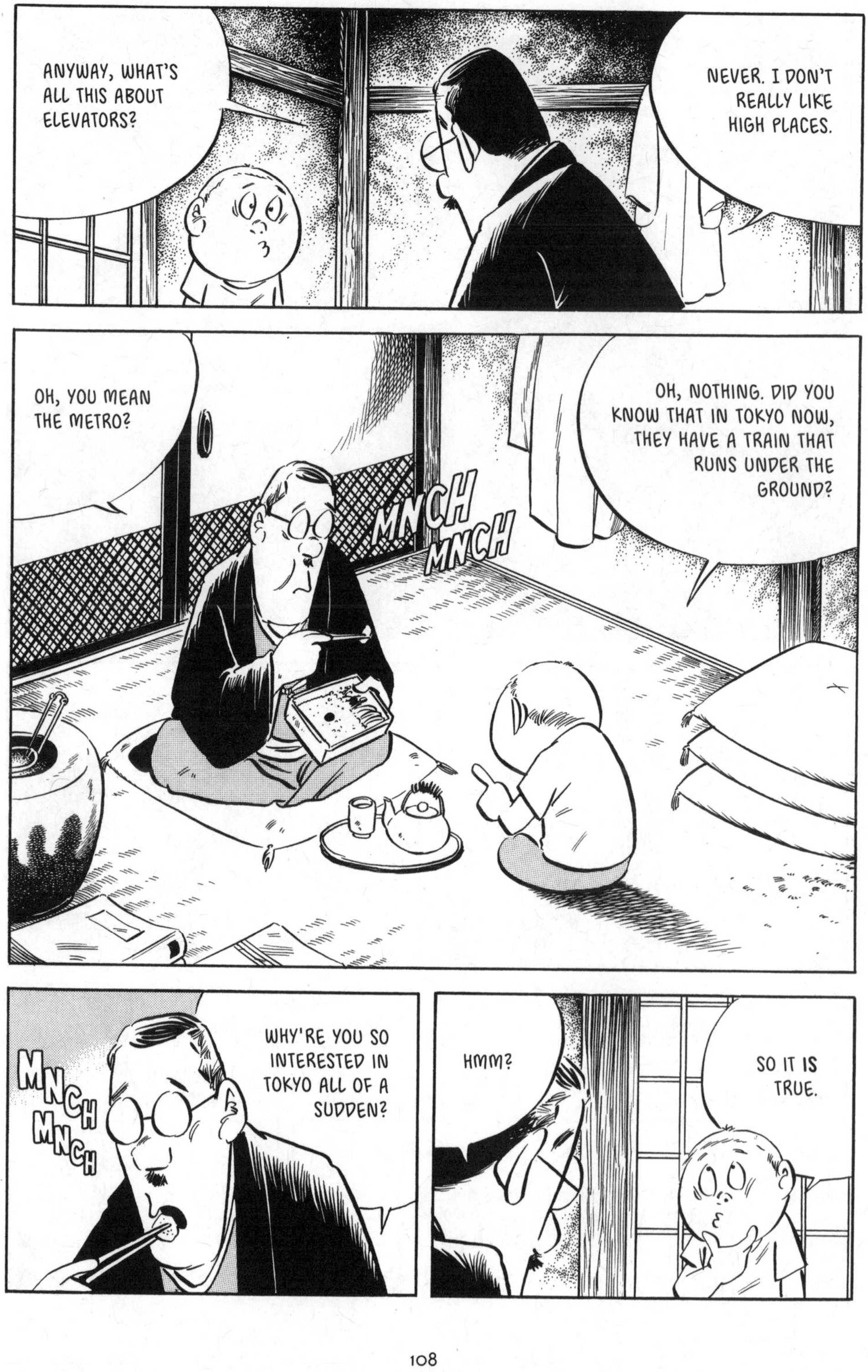
NEVER. I DON'T REALLY LIKE HIGH PLACES.
ANYWAY, WHAT'S ALL THIS ABOUT ELEVATORS?
OH, NOTHING. DID YOU KNOW THAT IN TOKYO NOW, THEY HAVE A TRAIN THAT RUNS UNDER THE GROUND?
MNCH MNCH
OH, YOU MEAN THE METRO?
SO IT IS TRUE.
HMM?
WHY'RE YOU SO INTERESTED IN TOKYO ALL OF A SUDDEN?
MNCH MNCH

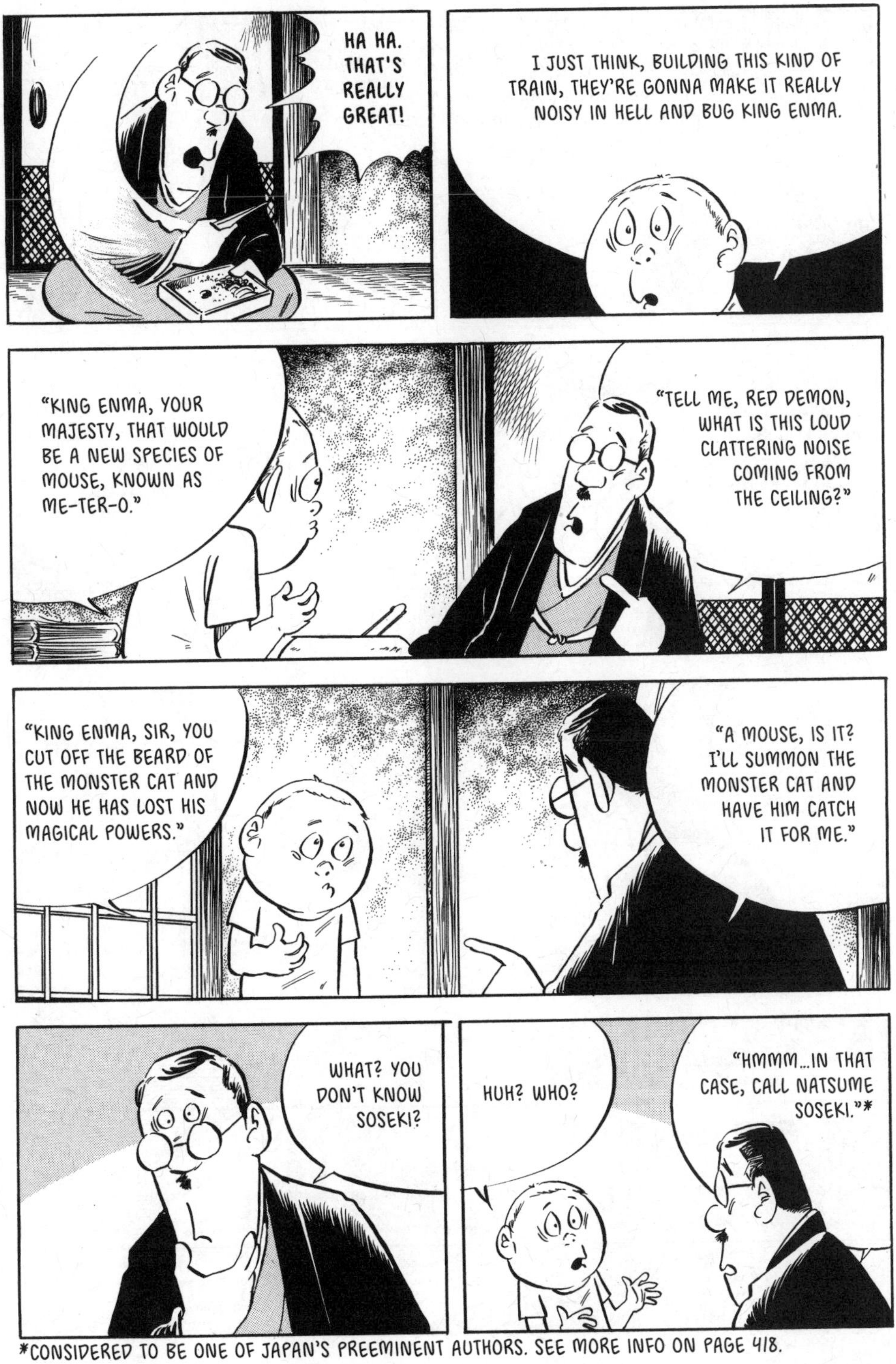
I JUST THINK, BUILDING THIS KIND OF TRAIN, THEY'RE GONNA MAKE IT REALLY NOISY IN HELL AND BUG KING ENMA.
HA HA. THAT'S REALLY GREAT!
"TELL ME, RED DEMON, WHAT IS THIS LOUD CLATTERING NOISE COMING FROM THE CEILING?"
"KING ENMA, YOUR MAJESTY, THAT WOULD BE A NEW SPECIES OF MOUSE, KNOWN AS ME-TER-O."
"A MOUSE, IS IT? I'LL SUMMON THE MONSTER CAT AND HAVE HIM CATCH IT FOR ME."
"KING ENMA, SIR, YOU CUT OFF THE BEARD OF THE MONSTER CAT AND NOW HE HAS LOST HIS MAGICAL POWERS."
"HMMM...IN THAT CASE, CALL NATSUME SOSEKI."*
HUH? WHO?
WHAT? YOU DON'T KNOW SOSEKI?

*CONSIDERED TO BE ONE OF JAPAN'S PREEMINENT AUTHORS. SEE MORE INFO ON PAGE 418.

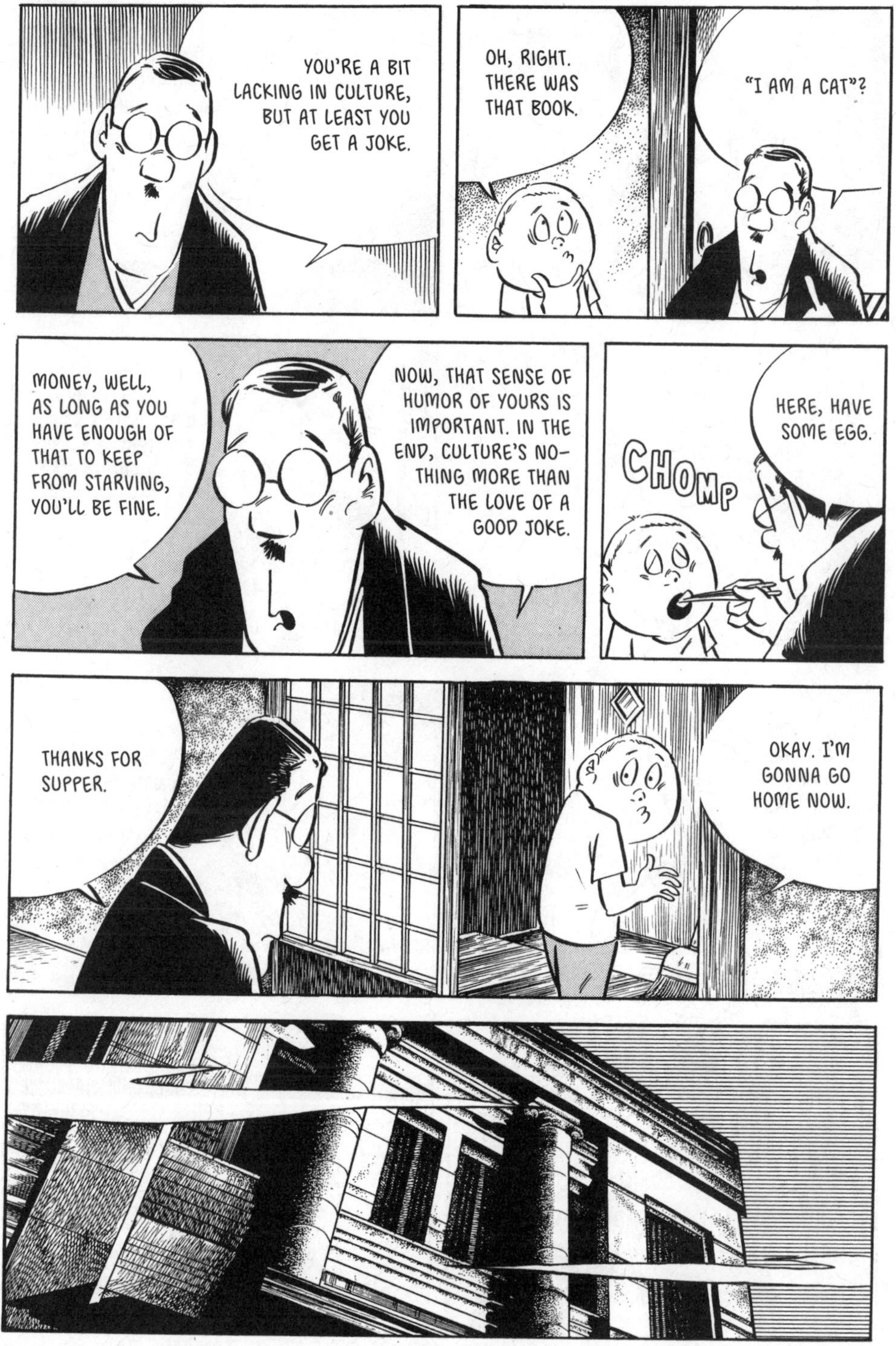
"I AM A CAT"?
OH, RIGHT. THERE WAS THAT BOOK.
YOU'RE A BIT LACKING IN CULTURE, BUT AT LEAST YOU GET A JOKE.
HERE, HAVE SOME EGG.
CHOMP
NOW, THAT SENSE OF HUMOR OF YOURS IS IMPORTANT. IN THE END, CULTURE'S NOTHING MORE THAN THE LOVE OF A GOOD JOKE.
MONEY, WELL, AS LONG AS YOU HAVE ENOUGH OF THAT TO KEEP FROM STARVING, YOU'LL BE FINE.
OKAY. I'M GONNA GO HOME NOW.
THANKS FOR SUPPER.

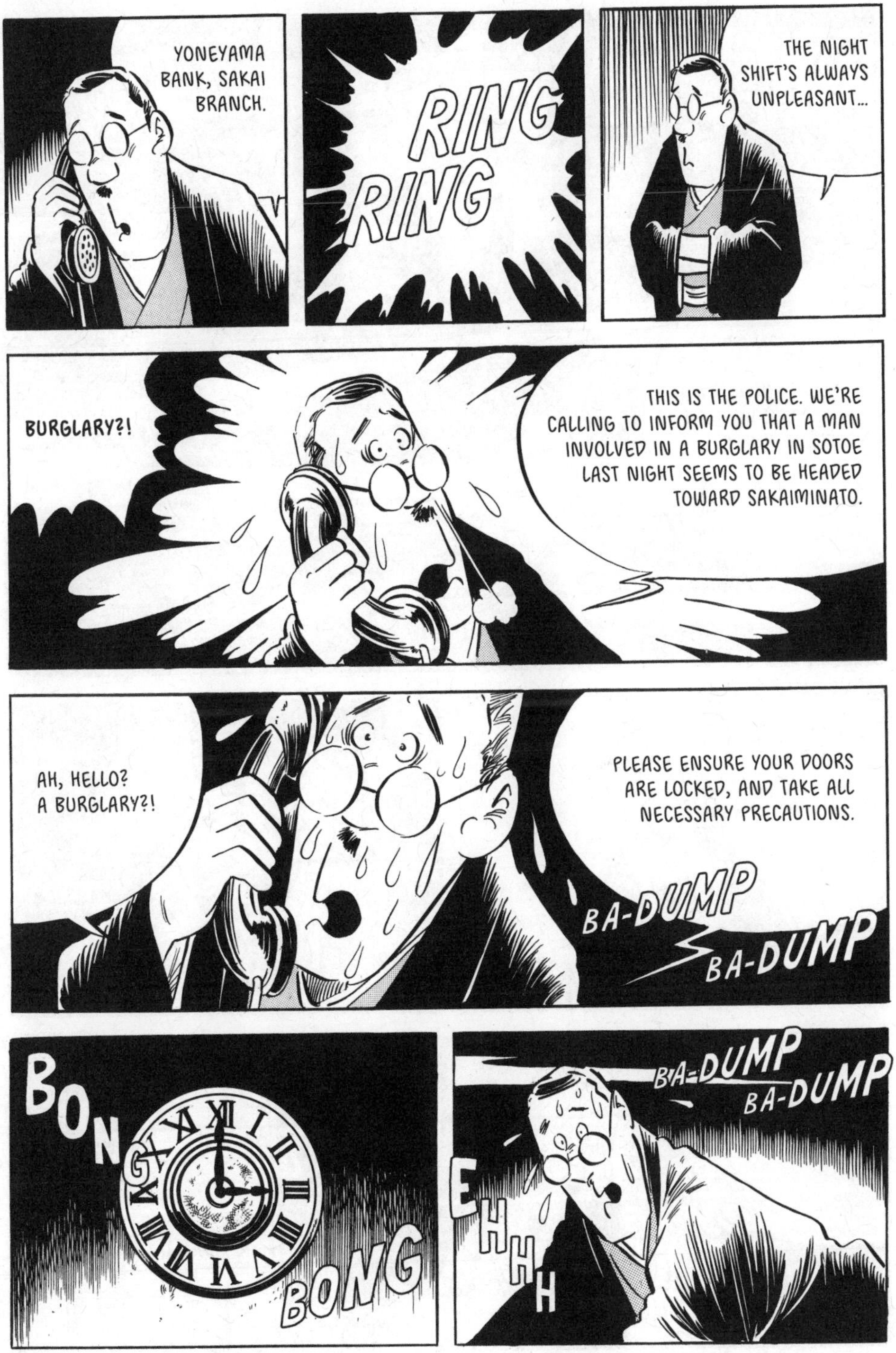
THE NIGHT SHIFT'S ALWAYS UNPLEASANT...
RING RING
YONEYAMA BANK, SAKAI BRANCH.
THIS IS THE POLICE. WE'RE CALLING TO INFORM YOU THAT A MAN INVOLVED IN A BURGLARY IN SOTOE LAST NIGHT SEEMS TO BE HEADED TOWARD SAKAIMINATO.
BURGLARY?!
PLEASE ENSURE YOUR DOORS ARE LOCKED, AND TAKE ALL NECESSARY PRECAUTIONS.
AH, HELLO? A BURGLARY?!
BA-DUMP BA-DUMP
BA-DUMP BA-DUMP
EHHHH
BONG BONG

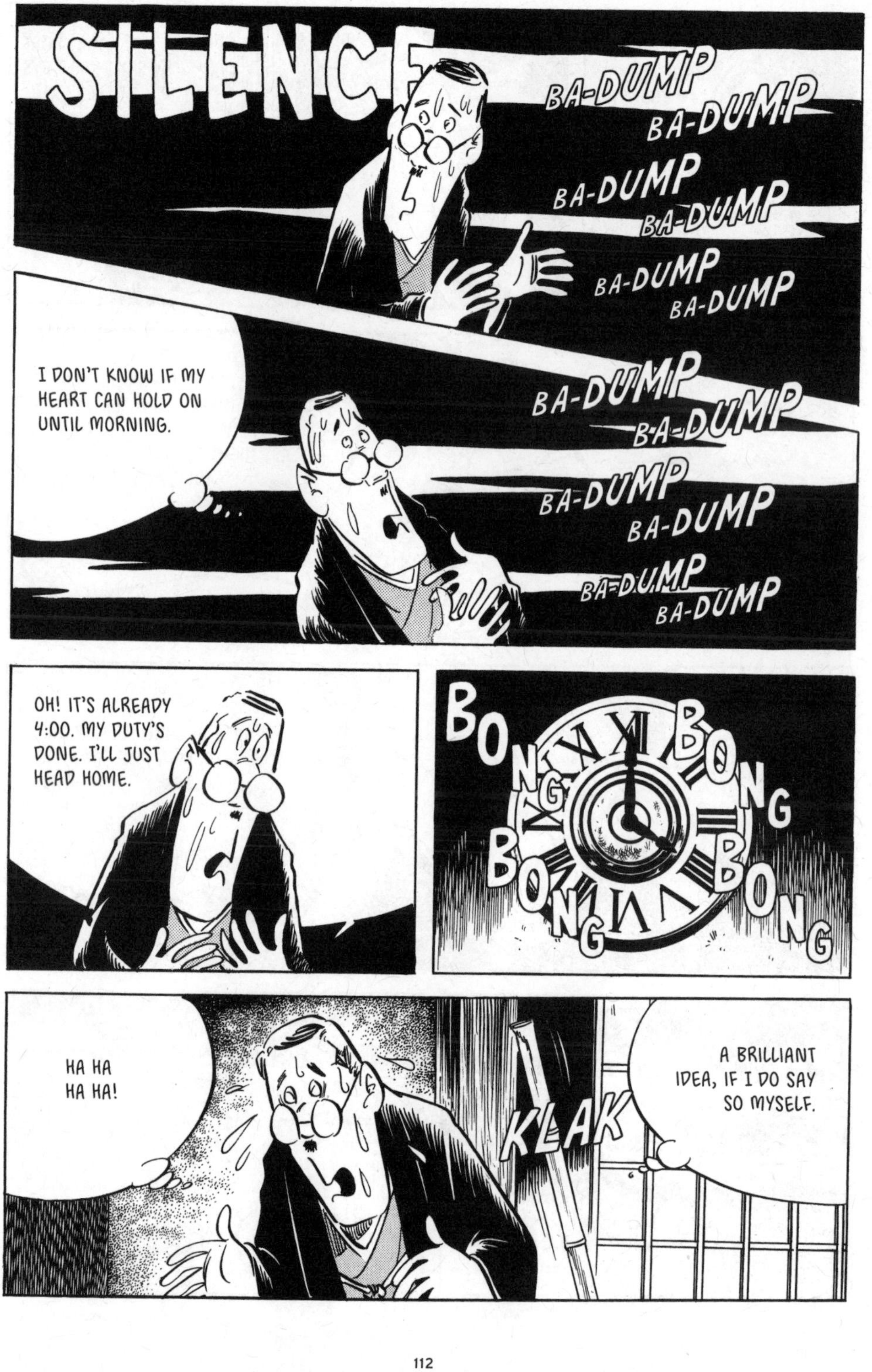
SILENCE
BA-DUMP
BA-DUMP
BA-DUMP
BA-DUMP
BA-DUMP
BA-DUMP
I DON'T KNOW IF MY HEART CAN HOLD ON UNTIL MORNING.
BA-DUMP
BA-DUMP
BA-DUMP
BA-DUMP
BA-DUMP
BA-DUMP
BONG
BONG
BONG
BONG
BONG
BONG
OH! IT'S ALREADY 4:00. MY DUTY'S DONE. I'LL JUST HEAD HOME.
A BRILLIANT IDEA, IF I DO SAY SO MYSELF.
KLAK
HA HA HA HA!

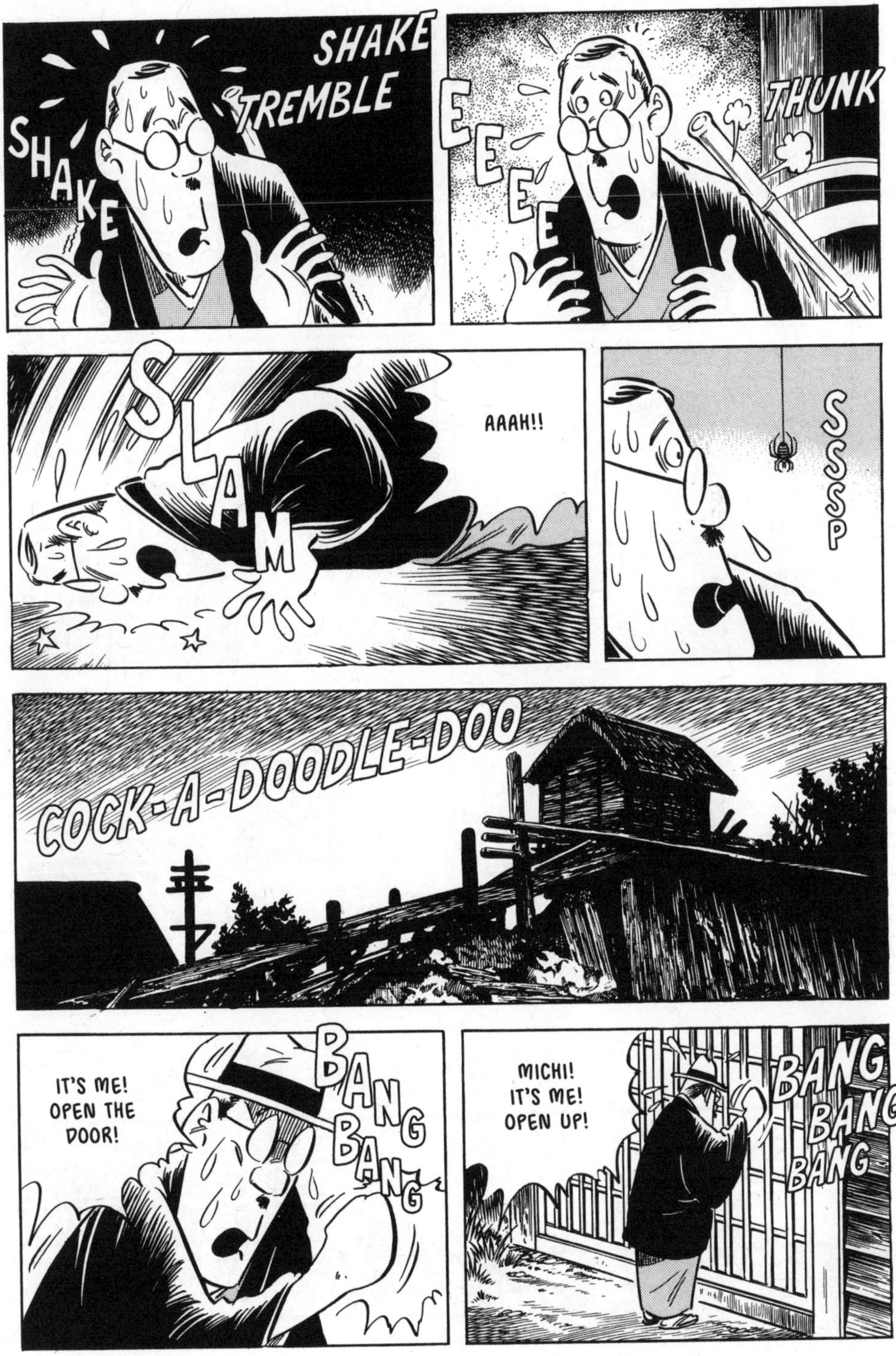
EEEEE
THUNK
SHAKE
TREMBLE
SHAKE
SSSSP
SLAM
AAAH!!
COCK-A-DOODLE-DOO
MICHI! IT'S ME! OPEN UP!
BANG BANG BANG
IT'S ME! OPEN THE DOOR!
BANG BANG BANG

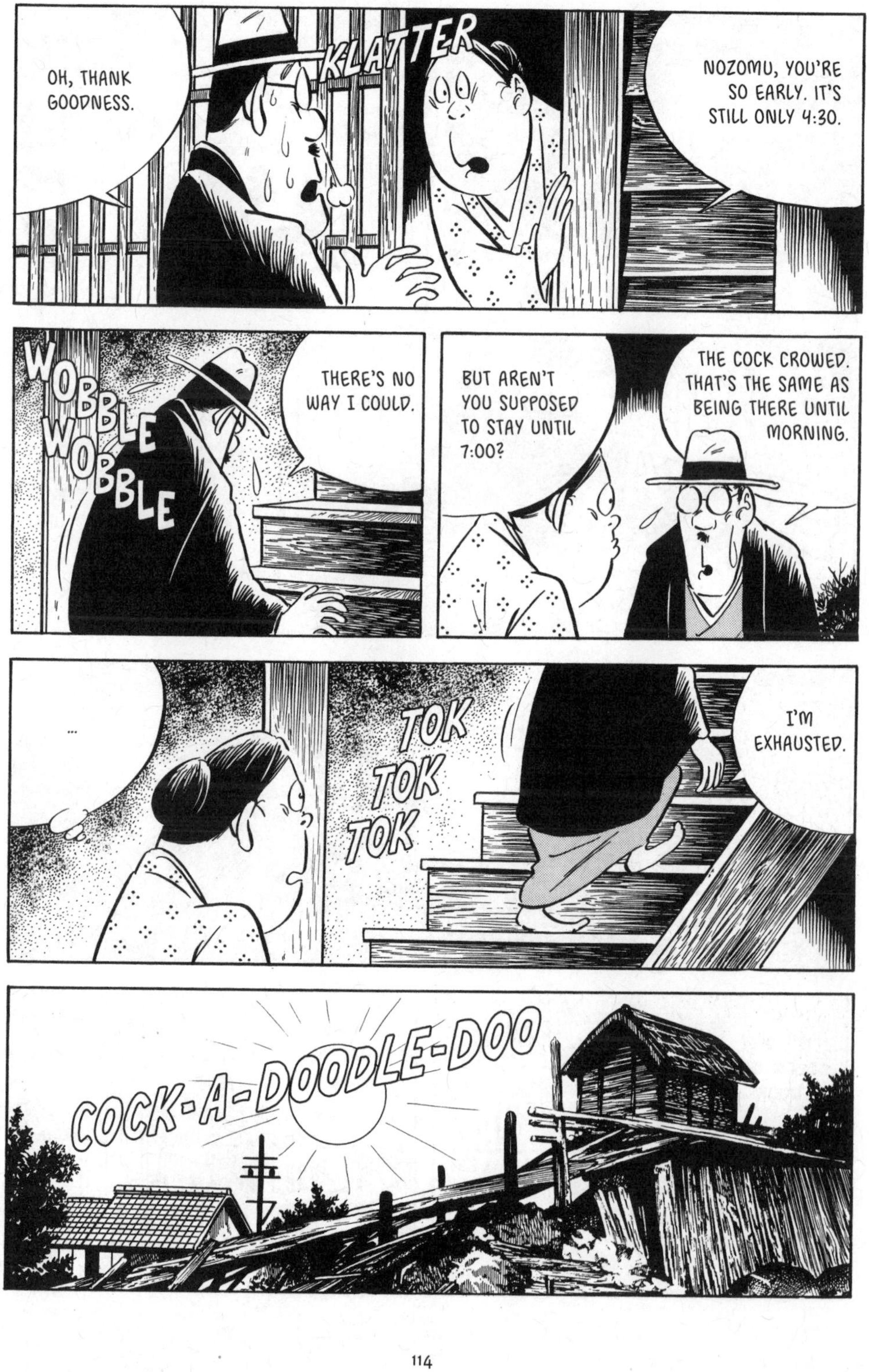
OH, THANK GOODNESS.
KLATTER
NOZOMU, YOU'RE SO EARLY. IT'S STILL ONLY 4:30.
WOBBLE WOBBLE
THERE'S NO WAY I COULD.
BUT AREN'T YOU SUPPOSED TO STAY UNTIL 7:00?
THE COCK CROWED. THAT'S THE SAME AS BEING THERE UNTIL MORNING.
...
TOK TOK TOK
I'M EXHAUSTED.
COCK-A-DOODLE-DOO

SLIPPERY LAD

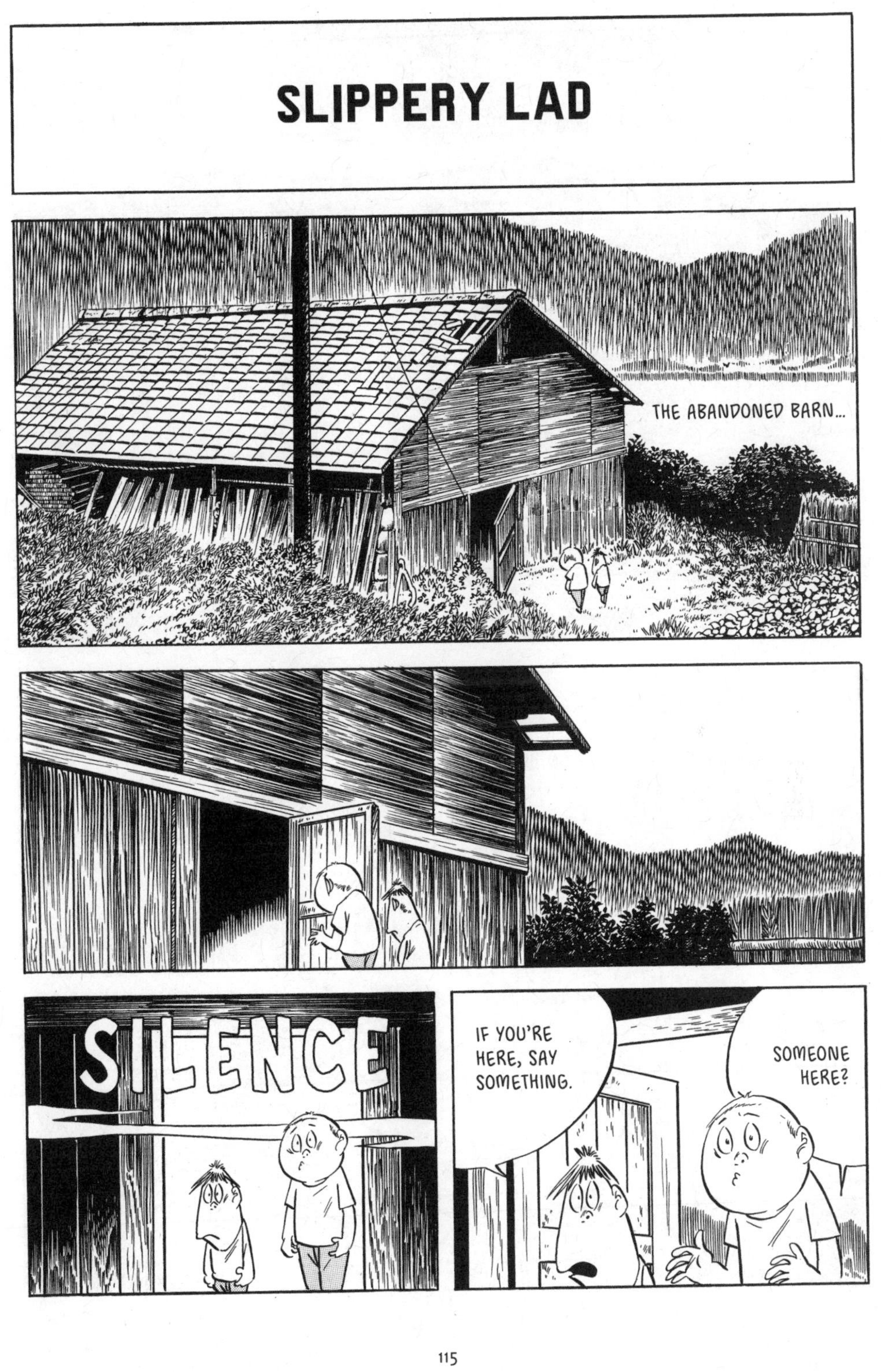

THE ABANDONED BARN...
SOMEONE HERE?
IF YOU'RE HERE, SAY SOMETHING.
SILENCE

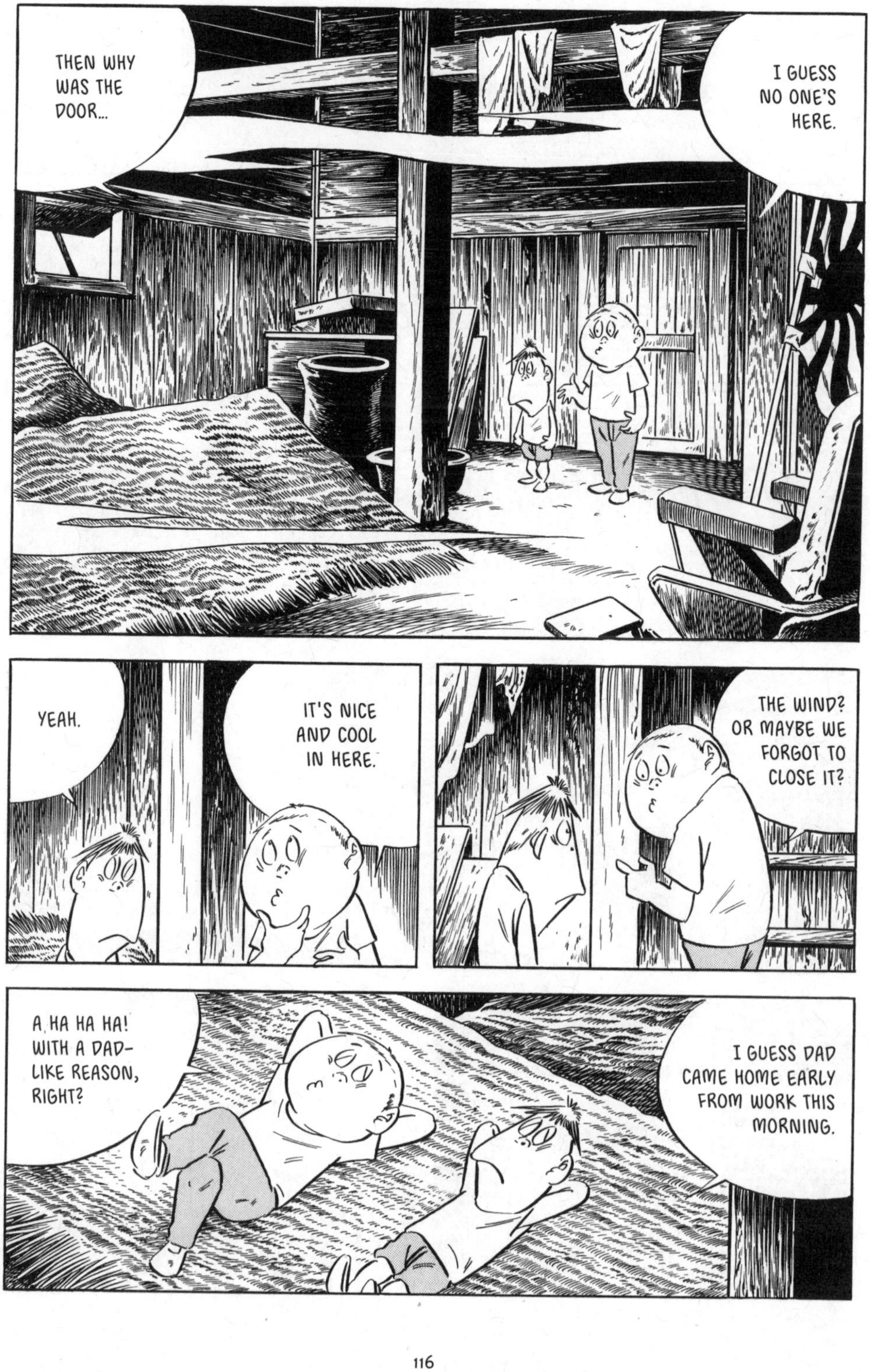
I GUESS NO ONE'S HERE.
THEN WHY WAS THE DOOR...
THE WIND? OR MAYBE WE FORGOT TO CLOSE IT?
IT'S NICE AND COOL IN HERE.
YEAH.
I GUESS DAD CAME HOME EARLY FROM WORK THIS MORNING.
A HA HA HA! WITH A DAD-LIKE REASON, RIGHT?

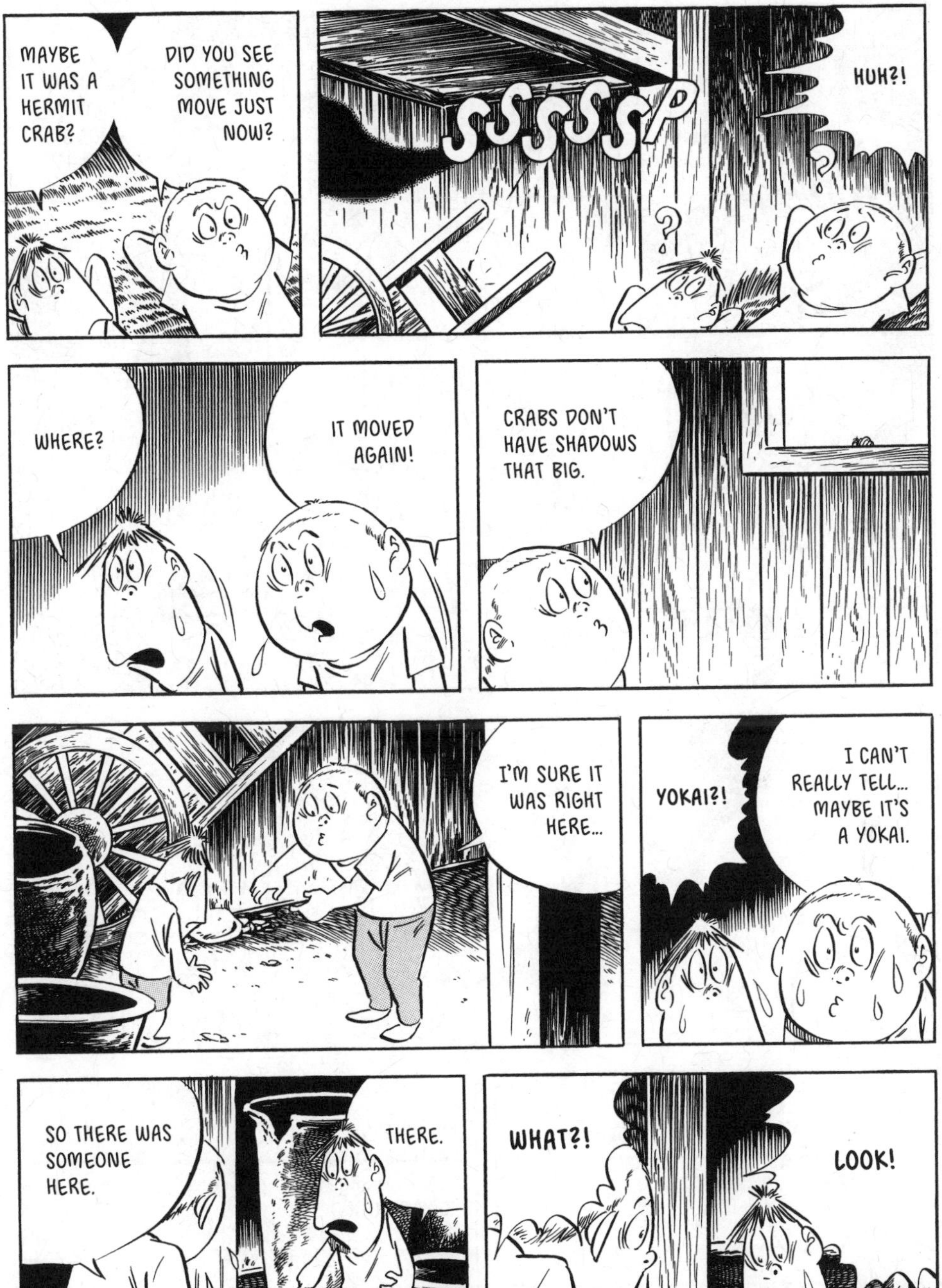
HUH?!
SSSSSP
DID YOU SEE SOMETHING MOVE JUST NOW?
MAYBE IT WAS A HERMIT CRAB?
CRABS DON'T HAVE SHADOWS THAT BIG.
IT MOVED AGAIN!
WHERE?
I CAN'T REALLY TELL... MAYBE IT'S A YOKAI.
YOKAI?!
I'M SURE IT WAS RIGHT HERE...
LOOK!
WHAT?!
THERE.
SO THERE WAS SOMEONE HERE.

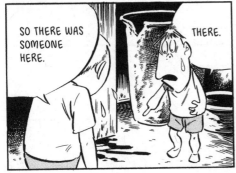

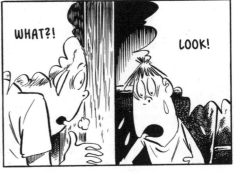

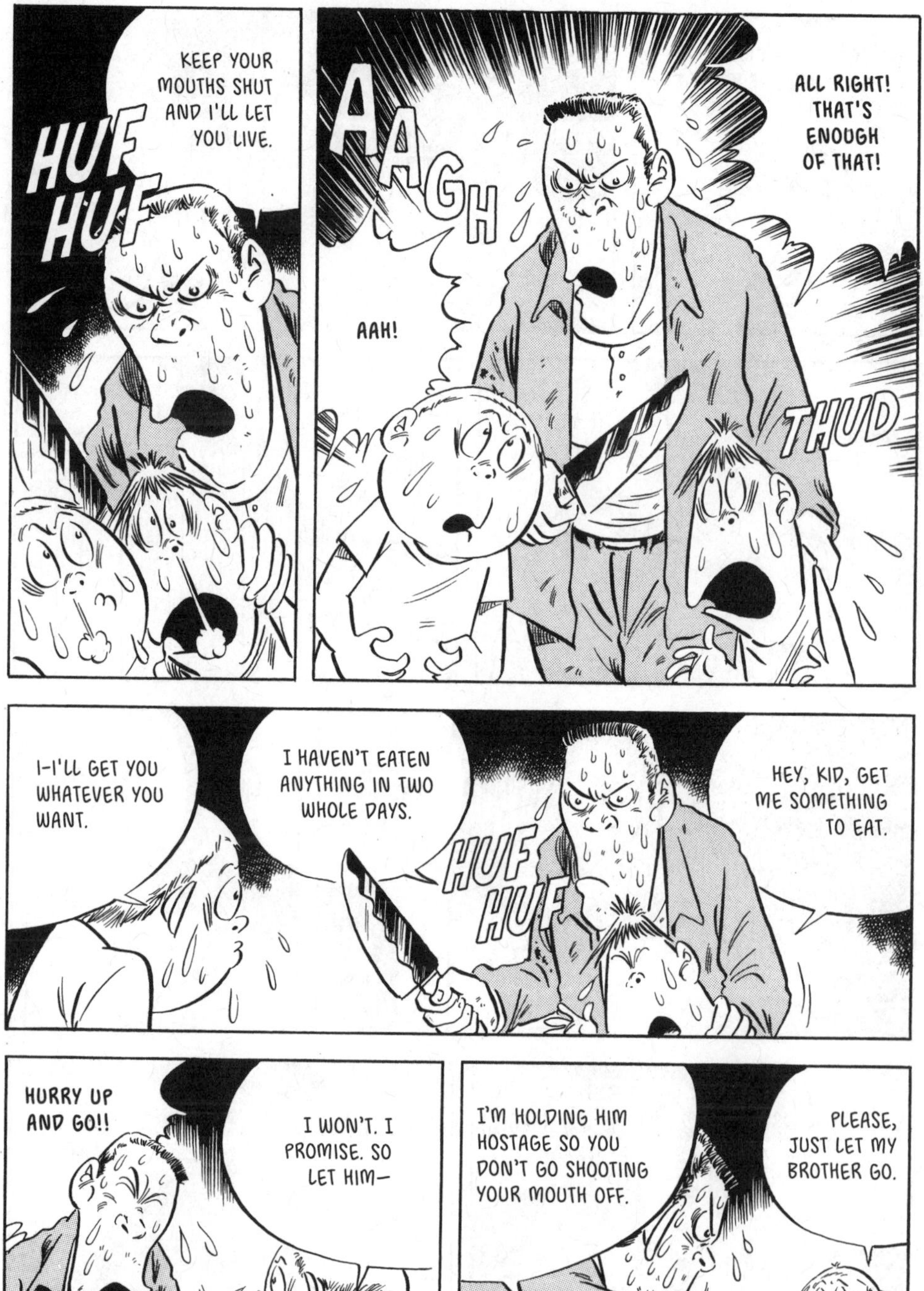
ALL RIGHT! THAT'S ENOUGH OF THAT!
AAGH
AAH!
THUD
KEEP YOUR MOUTHS SHUT AND I'LL LET YOU LIVE.
HUF HUF
HEY, KID, GET ME SOMETHING TO EAT.
HUF HUF
I HAVEN'T EATEN ANYTHING IN TWO WHOLE DAYS.
I-I'LL GET YOU WHATEVER YOU WANT.
PLEASE, JUST LET MY BROTHER GO.
I'M HOLDING HIM HOSTAGE SO YOU DON'T GO SHOOTING YOUR MOUTH OFF.
I WON'T. I PROMISE. SO LET HIM—
HURRY UP AND GO!!

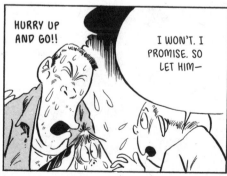

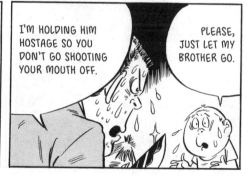

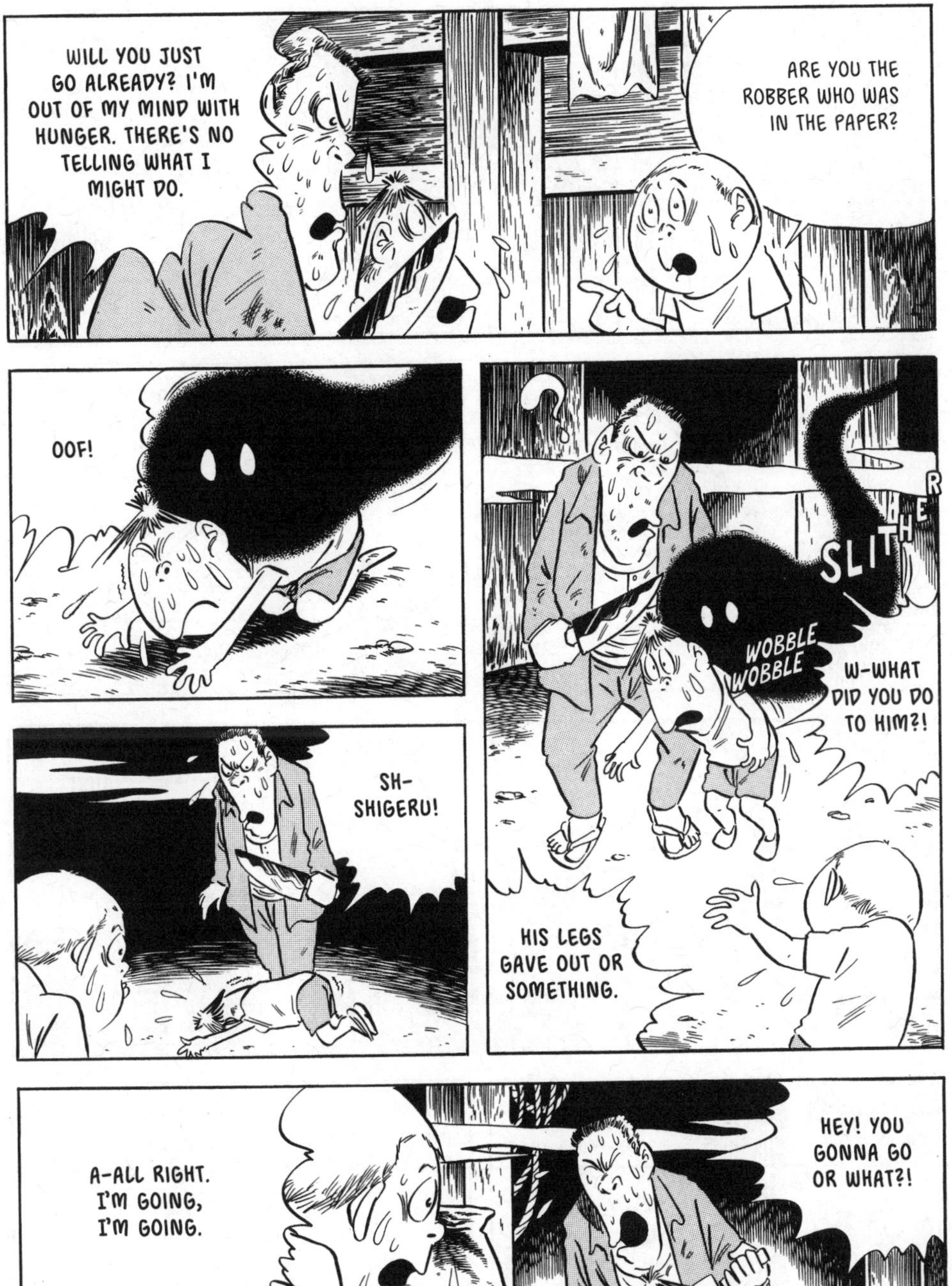
ARE YOU THE ROBBER WHO WAS IN THE PAPER?
WILL YOU JUST GO ALREADY? I'M OUT OF MY MIND WITH HUNGER. THERE'S NO TELLING WHAT I MIGHT DO.
SLITHER
WOBBLE WOBBLE
W-WHAT DID YOU DO TO HIM?!
HIS LEGS GAVE OUT OR SOMETHING.
OOF!
SH-SHIGERU!
HEY! YOU GONNA GO OR WHAT?!
A-ALL RIGHT. I'M GOING, I'M GOING.

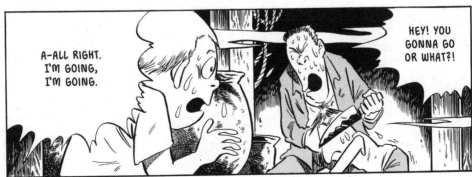

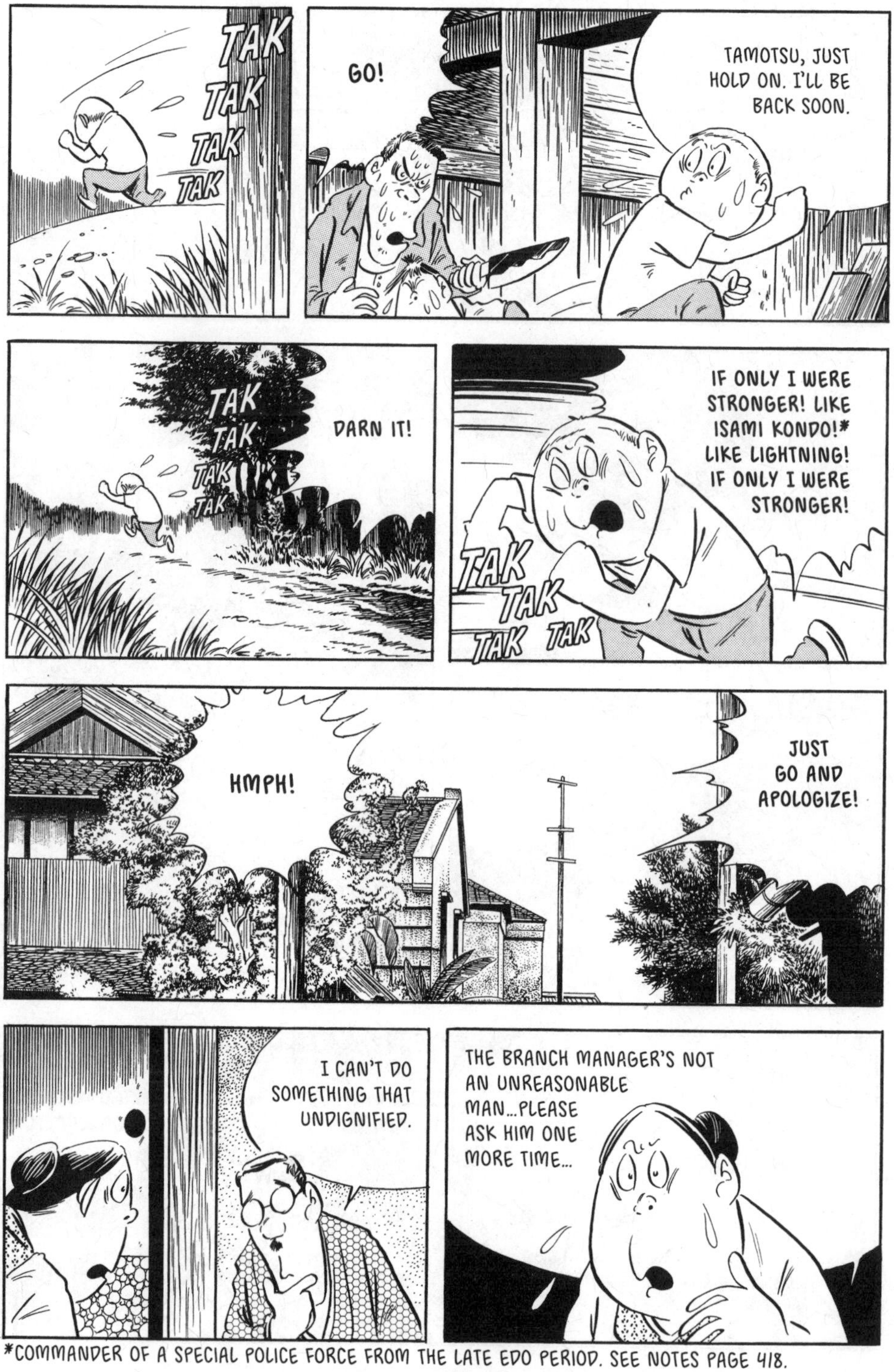
TAMOTSU, JUST HOLD ON. I'LL BE BACK SOON.
GO!
TAK TAK TAK TAK
IF ONLY I WERE STRONGER! LIKE ISAMI KONDO!* LIKE LIGHTNING! IF ONLY I WERE STRONGER!
TAK TAK TAK TAK
DARN IT!
TAK TAK TAK TAK
JUST GO AND APOLOGIZE!
HMPH!
THE BRANCH MANAGER'S NOT AN UNREASONABLE MAN...PLEASE ASK HIM ONE MORE TIME...
I CAN'T DO SOMETHING THAT UNDIGNIFIED.

*COMMANDER OF A SPECIAL POLICE FORCE FROM THE LATE EDO PERIOD. SEE NOTES PAGE 418.

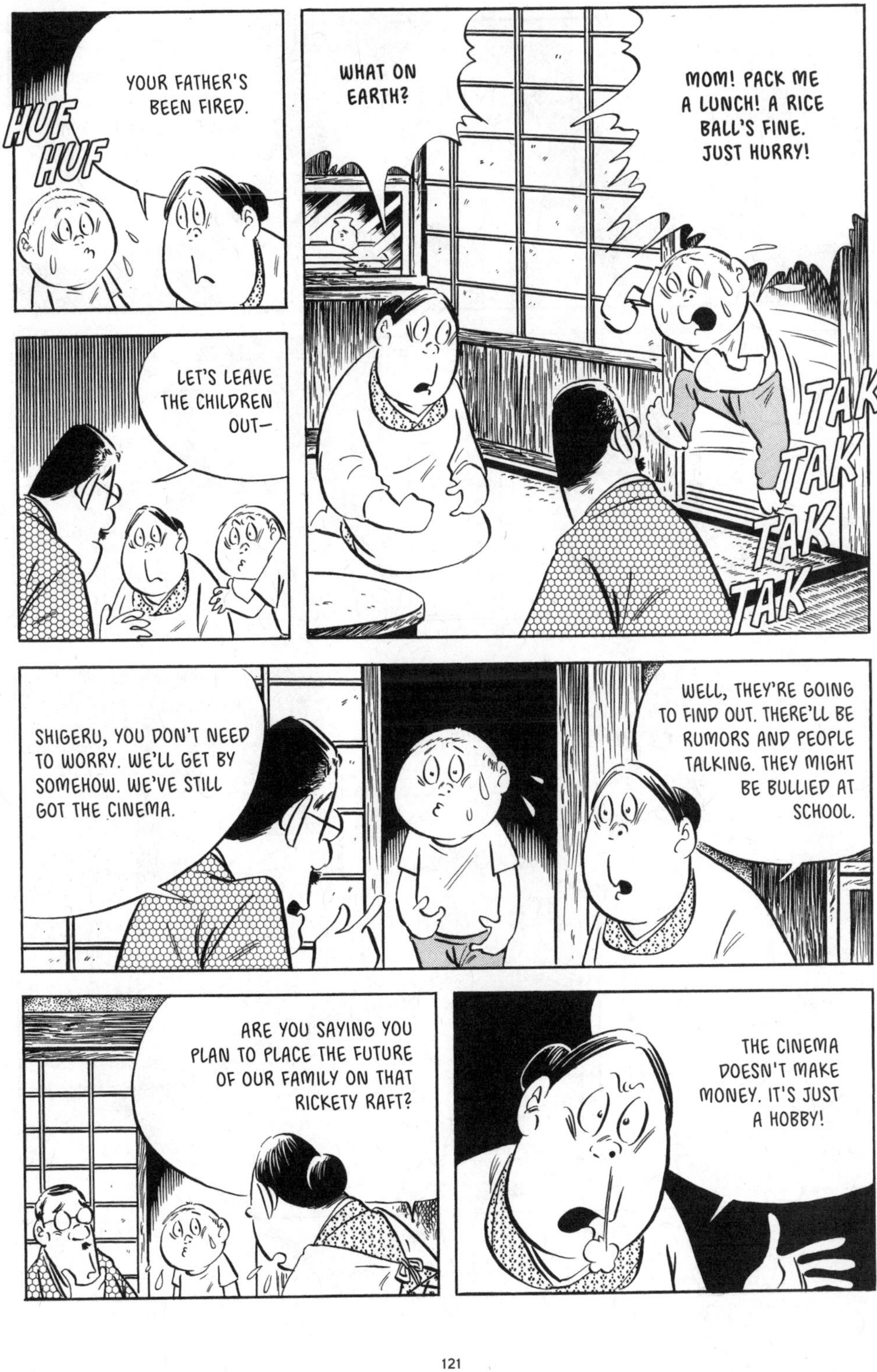
MOM! PACK ME A LUNCH! A RICE BALL'S FINE. JUST HURRY!
WHAT ON EARTH?
TAK TAK TAK TAK
HUF HUF
YOUR FATHER'S BEEN FIRED.
LET'S LEAVE THE CHILDREN OUT—
WELL, THEY'RE GOING TO FIND OUT. THERE'LL BE RUMORS AND PEOPLE TALKING. THEY MIGHT BE BULLIED AT SCHOOL.
SHIGERU, YOU DON'T NEED TO WORRY. WE'LL GET BY SOMEHOW. WE'VE STILL GOT THE CINEMA.
THE CINEMA DOESN'T MAKE MONEY. IT'S JUST A HOBBY!
ARE YOU SAYING YOU PLAN TO PLACE THE FUTURE OF OUR FAMILY ON THAT RICKETY RAFT?

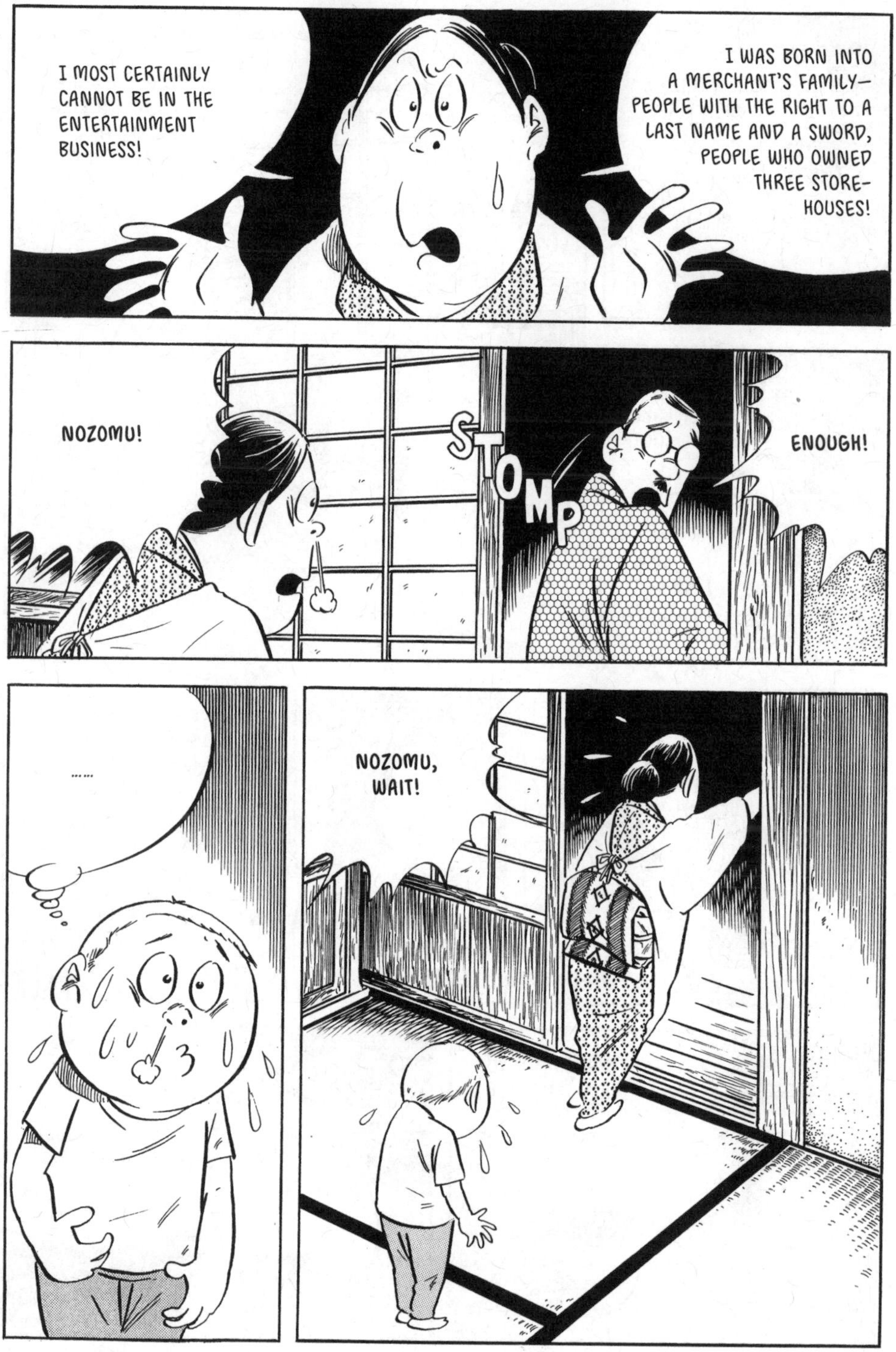
I WAS BORN INTO A MERCHANT'S FAMILY— PEOPLE WITH THE RIGHT TO A LAST NAME AND A SWORD, PEOPLE WHO OWNED THREE STORE-HOUSES!
I MOST CERTAINLY CANNOT BE IN THE ENTERTAINMENT BUSINESS!
ENOUGH!
STOMP
NOZOMU!
NOZOMU, WAIT!
……

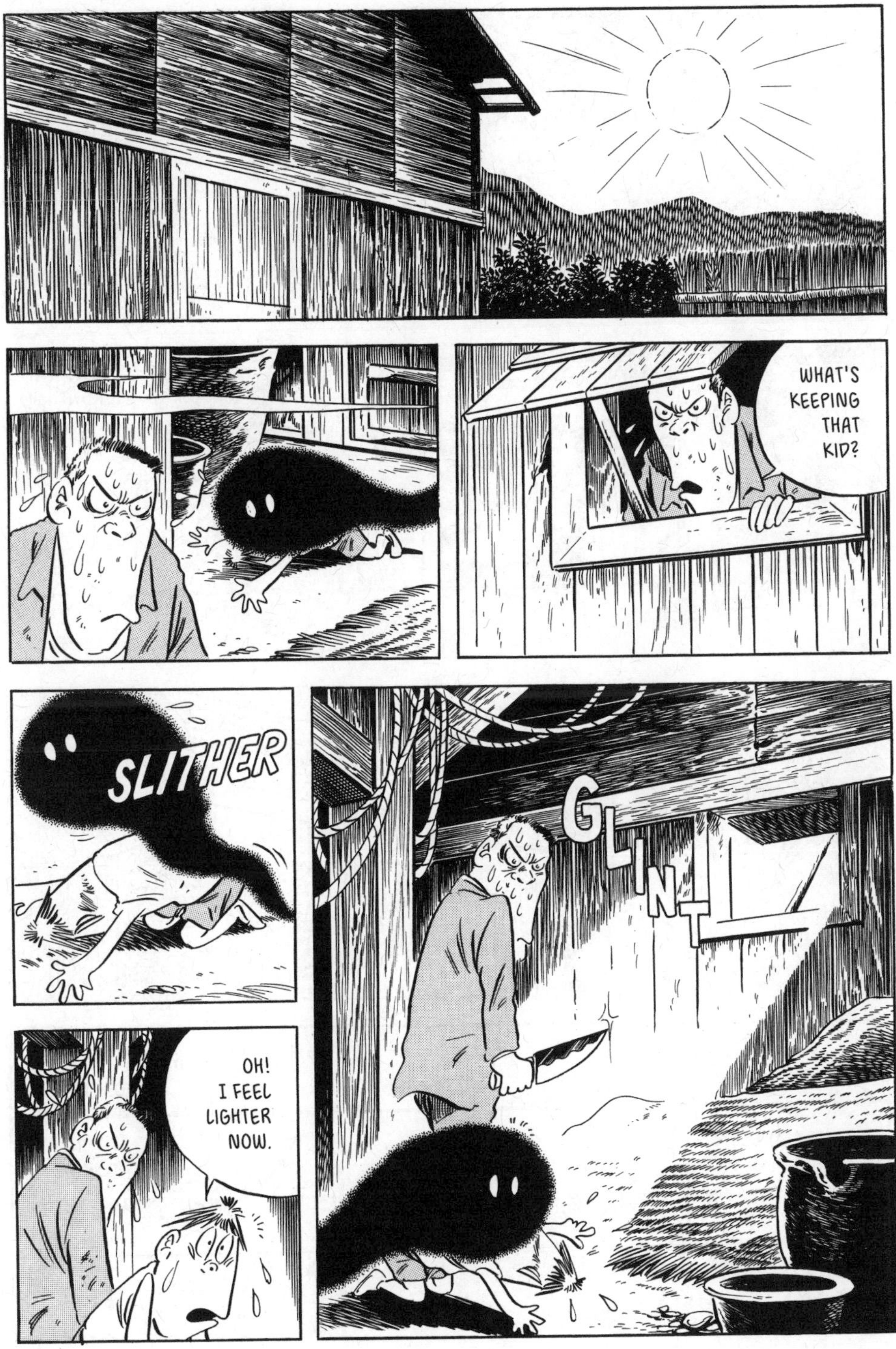
WHAT'S KEEPING THAT KID?
GLINT
SLITHER
OH! I FEEL LIGHTER NOW.

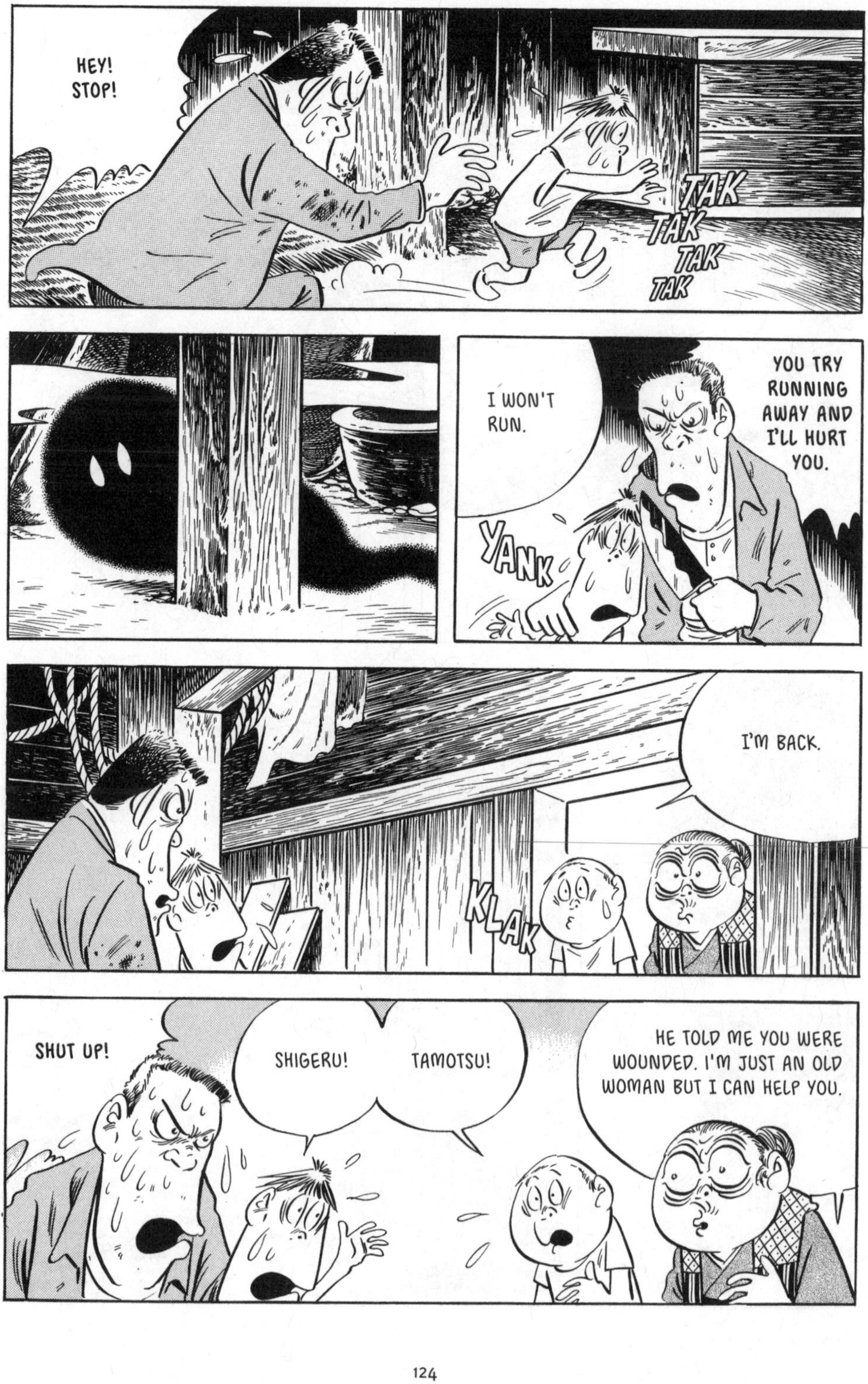
HEY! STOP!
TAK
TAK
TAK
TAK
YOU TRY RUNNING AWAY AND I'LL HURT YOU.
I WON'T RUN.
YANK
I'M BACK.
KLAK
HE TOLD ME YOU WERE WOUNDED. I'M JUST AN OLD WOMAN BUT I CAN HELP YOU.
TAMOTSU!
SHIGERU!
SHUT UP!

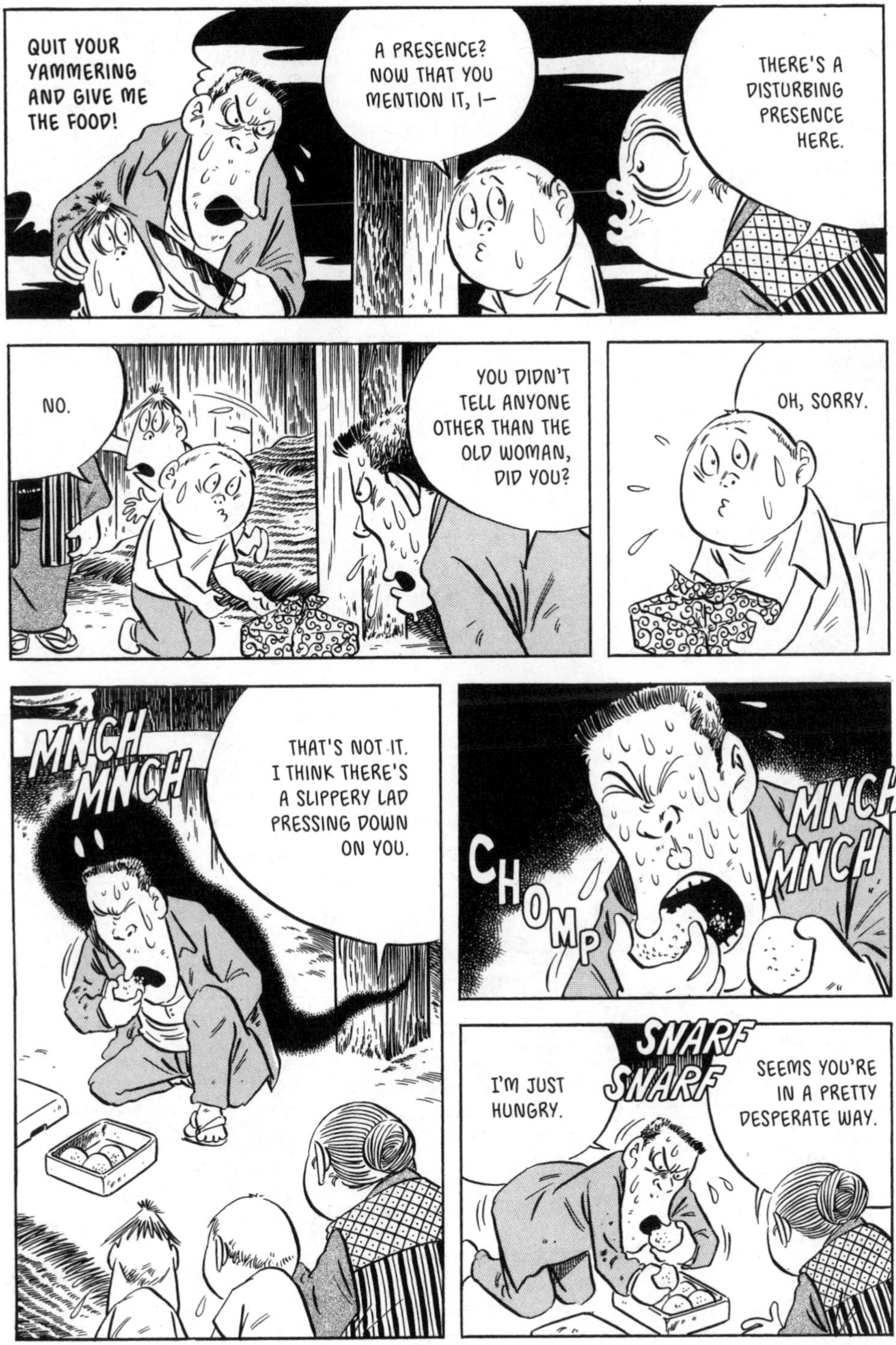
THERE'S A DISTURBING PRESENCE HERE.
A PRESENCE? NOW THAT YOU MENTION IT, I—
QUIT YOUR YAMMERING AND GIVE ME THE FOOD!
OH, SORRY.
YOU DIDN'T TELL ANYONE OTHER THAN THE OLD WOMAN, DID YOU?
NO.
MNCH MNCH
CHOMP
SEEMS YOU'RE IN A PRETTY DESPERATE WAY.
SNARF SNARF
I'M JUST HUNGRY.
THAT'S NOT IT. I THINK THERE'S A SLIPPERY LAD PRESSING DOWN ON YOU.
MNCH MNCH

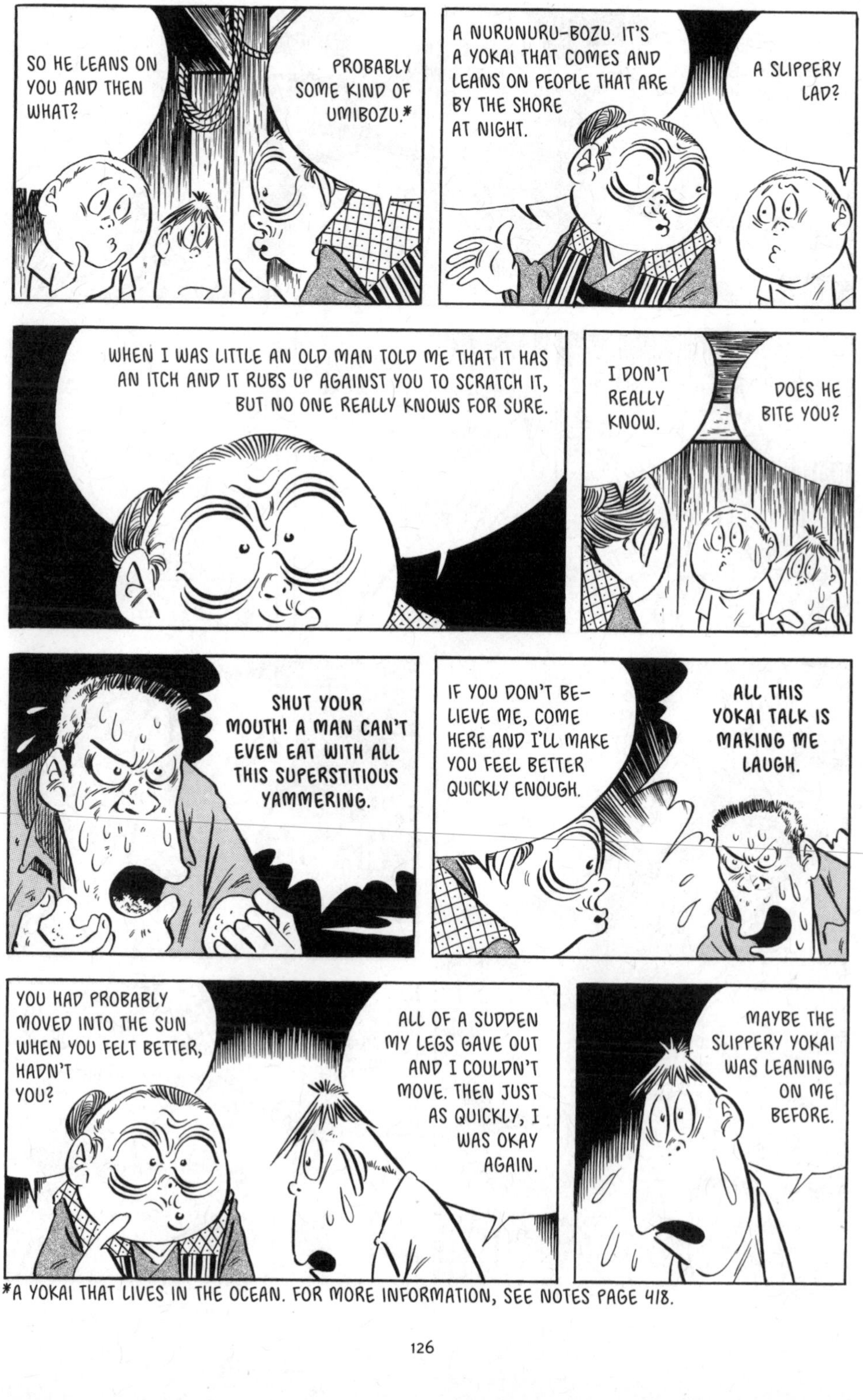
A SLIPPERY LAD?
A NURUNURU-BOZU. IT'S A YOKAI THAT COMES AND LEANS ON PEOPLE THAT ARE BY THE SHORE AT NIGHT.
PROBABLY SOME KIND OF UMIBOZU.*
SO HE LEANS ON YOU AND THEN WHAT?
DOES HE BITE YOU?
I DON'T REALLY KNOW.
WHEN I WAS LITTLE AN OLD MAN TOLD ME THAT IT HAS AN ITCH AND IT RUBS UP AGAINST YOU TO SCRATCH IT, BUT NO ONE REALLY KNOWS FOR SURE.
ALL THIS YOKAI TALK IS MAKING ME LAUGH.
IF YOU DON'T BE-LIEVE ME, COME HERE AND I'LL MAKE YOU FEEL BETTER QUICKLY ENOUGH.
SHUT YOUR MOUTH! A MAN CAN'T EVEN EAT WITH ALL THIS SUPERSTITIOUS YAMMERING.
MAYBE THE SLIPPERY YOKAI WAS LEANING ON ME BEFORE.
ALL OF A SUDDEN MY LEGS GAVE OUT AND I COULDN'T MOVE. THEN JUST AS QUICKLY, I WAS OKAY AGAIN.
YOU HAD PROBABLY MOVED INTO THE SUN WHEN YOU FELT BETTER, HADN'T YOU?

*A YOKAI THAT LIVES IN THE OCEAN. FOR MORE INFORMATION, SEE NOTES PAGE 418.

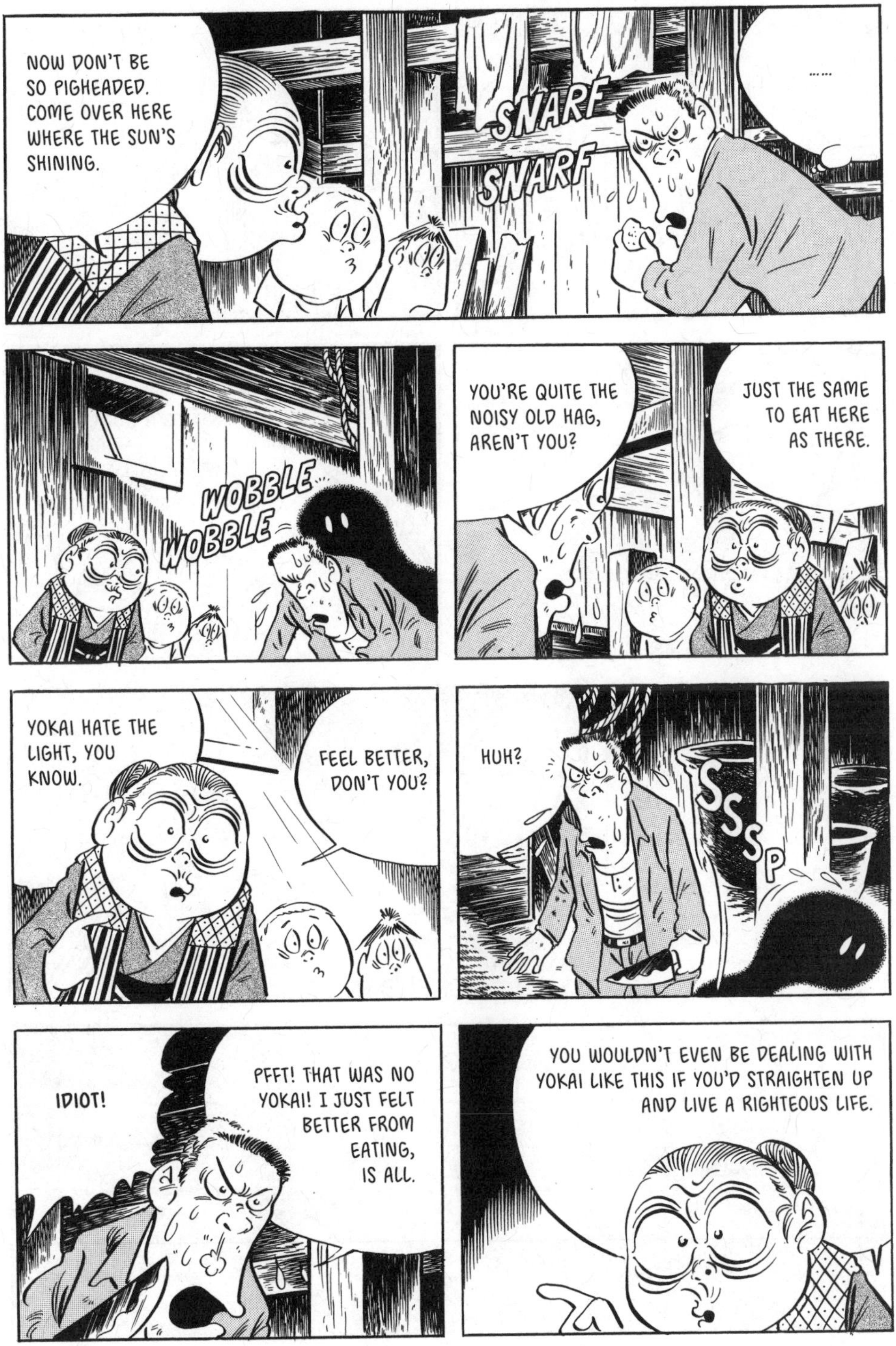
……
NOW DON'T BE SO PIGHEADED. COME OVER HERE WHERE THE SUN'S SHINING.
SNARF
SNARF
JUST THE SAME TO EAT HERE AS THERE.
YOU'RE QUITE THE NOISY OLD HAG, AREN'T YOU?
WOBBLE
WOBBLE
HUH?
SSSP
FEEL BETTER, DON'T YOU?
YOKAI HATE THE LIGHT, YOU KNOW.
YOU WOULDN'T EVEN BE DEALING WITH YOKAI LIKE THIS IF YOU'D STRAIGHTEN UP AND LIVE A RIGHTEOUS LIFE.
PFFT! THAT WAS NO YOKAI! I JUST FELT BETTER FROM EATING, IS ALL.
IDIOT!

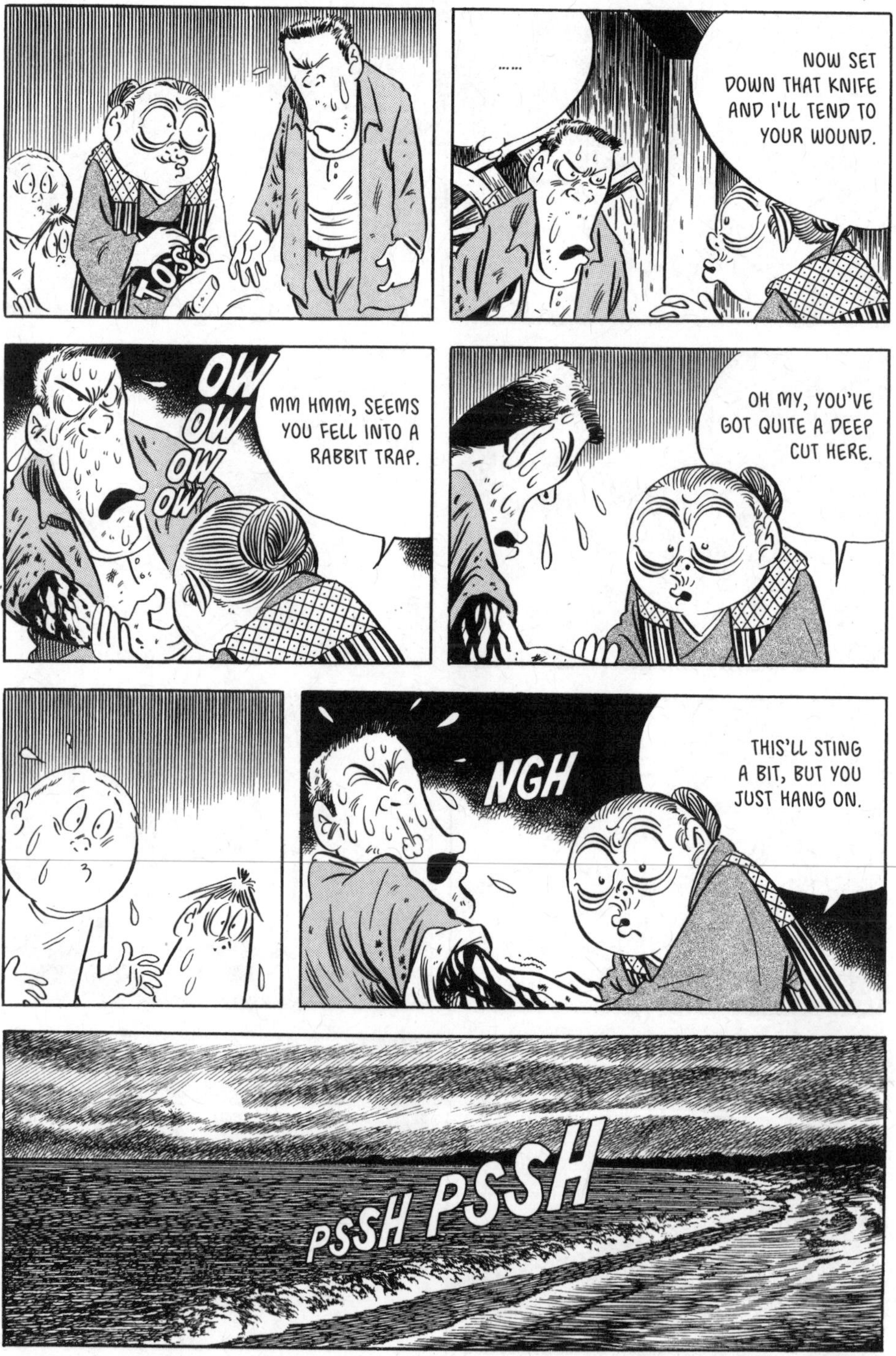
NOW SET DOWN THAT KNIFE AND I'LL TEND TO YOUR WOUND.
……
TOSS
OH MY, YOU'VE GOT QUITE A DEEP CUT HERE.
MM HMM, SEEMS YOU FELL INTO A RABBIT TRAP.
OW OW OW OW
THIS'LL STING A BIT, BUT YOU JUST HANG ON.
NGH
PSSH PSSH

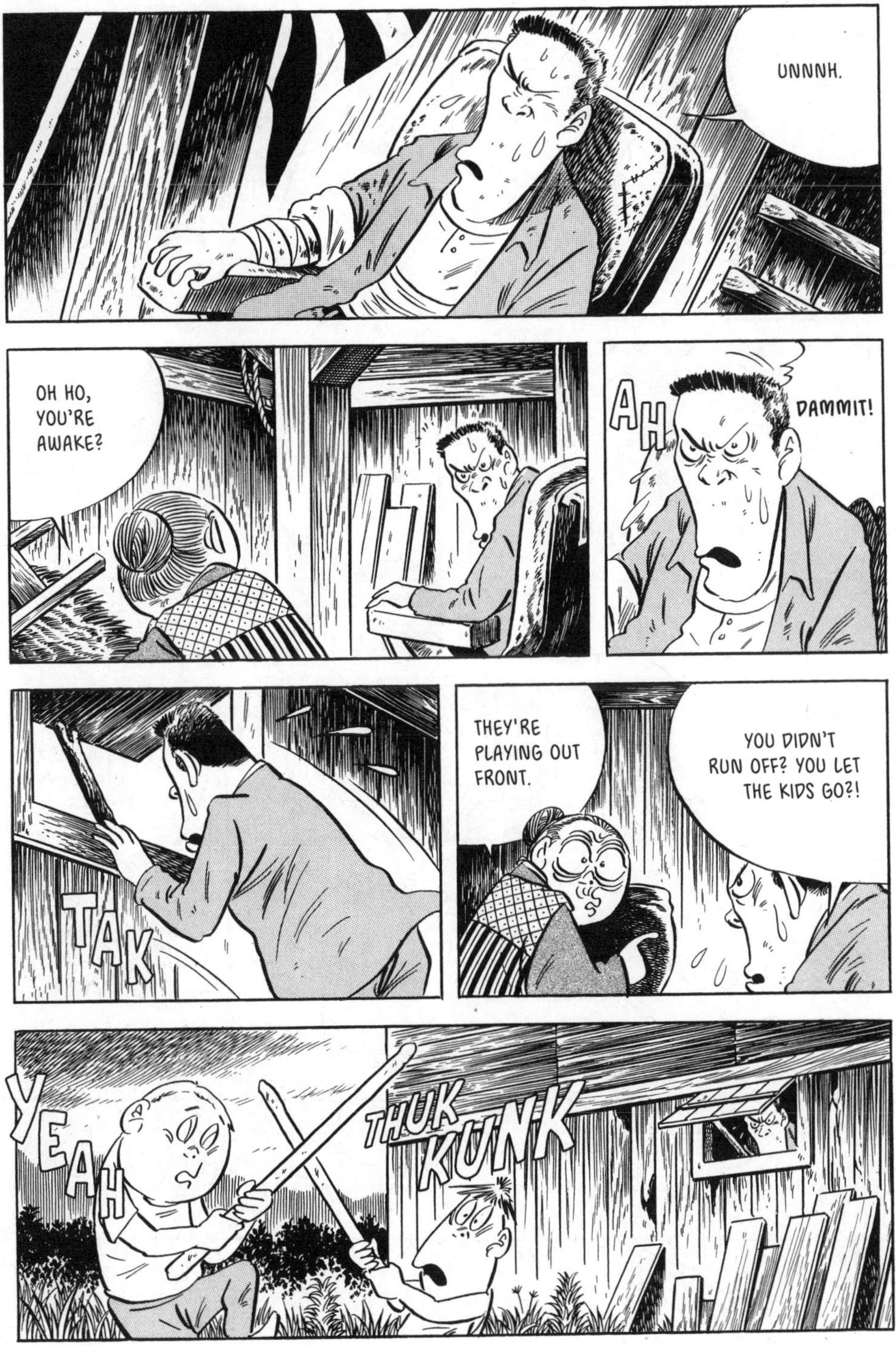
UNNNH.
AH
DAMMIT!
OH HO, YOU'RE AWAKE?
YOU DIDN'T RUN OFF? YOU LET THE KIDS GO?!
THEY'RE PLAYING OUT FRONT.
TAK
THUK
KUNK
YEAH

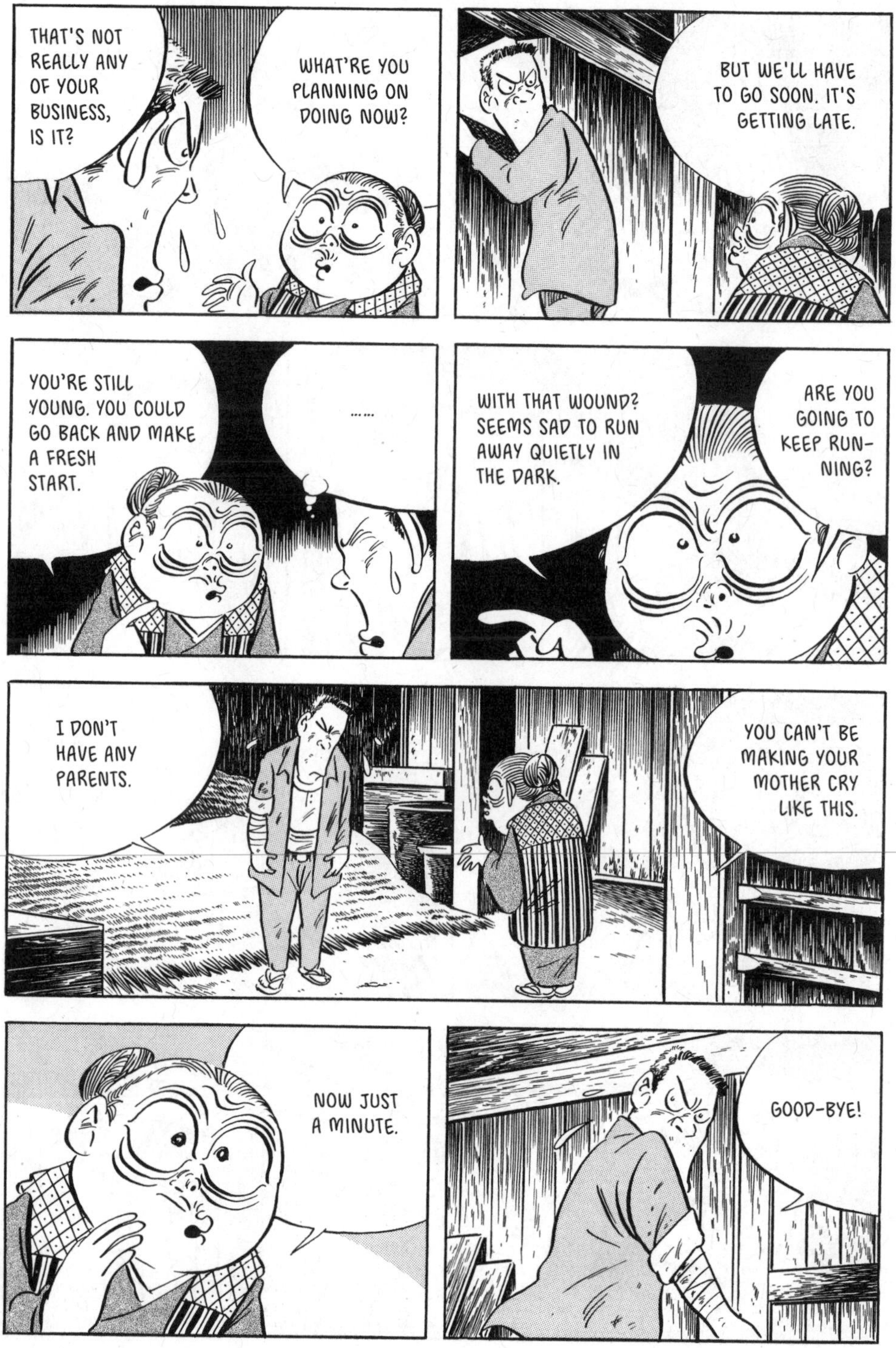
BUT WE'LL HAVE TO GO SOON. IT'S GETTING LATE.
WHAT'RE YOU PLANNING ON DOING NOW?
THAT'S NOT REALLY ANY OF YOUR BUSINESS, IS IT?
ARE YOU GOING TO KEEP RUN-NING?
WITH THAT WOUND? SEEMS SAD TO RUN AWAY QUIETLY IN THE DARK.
……
YOU'RE STILL YOUNG. YOU COULD GO BACK AND MAKE A FRESH START.
YOU CAN'T BE MAKING YOUR MOTHER CRY LIKE THIS.
I DON'T HAVE ANY PARENTS.
GOOD-BYE!
NOW JUST A MINUTE.

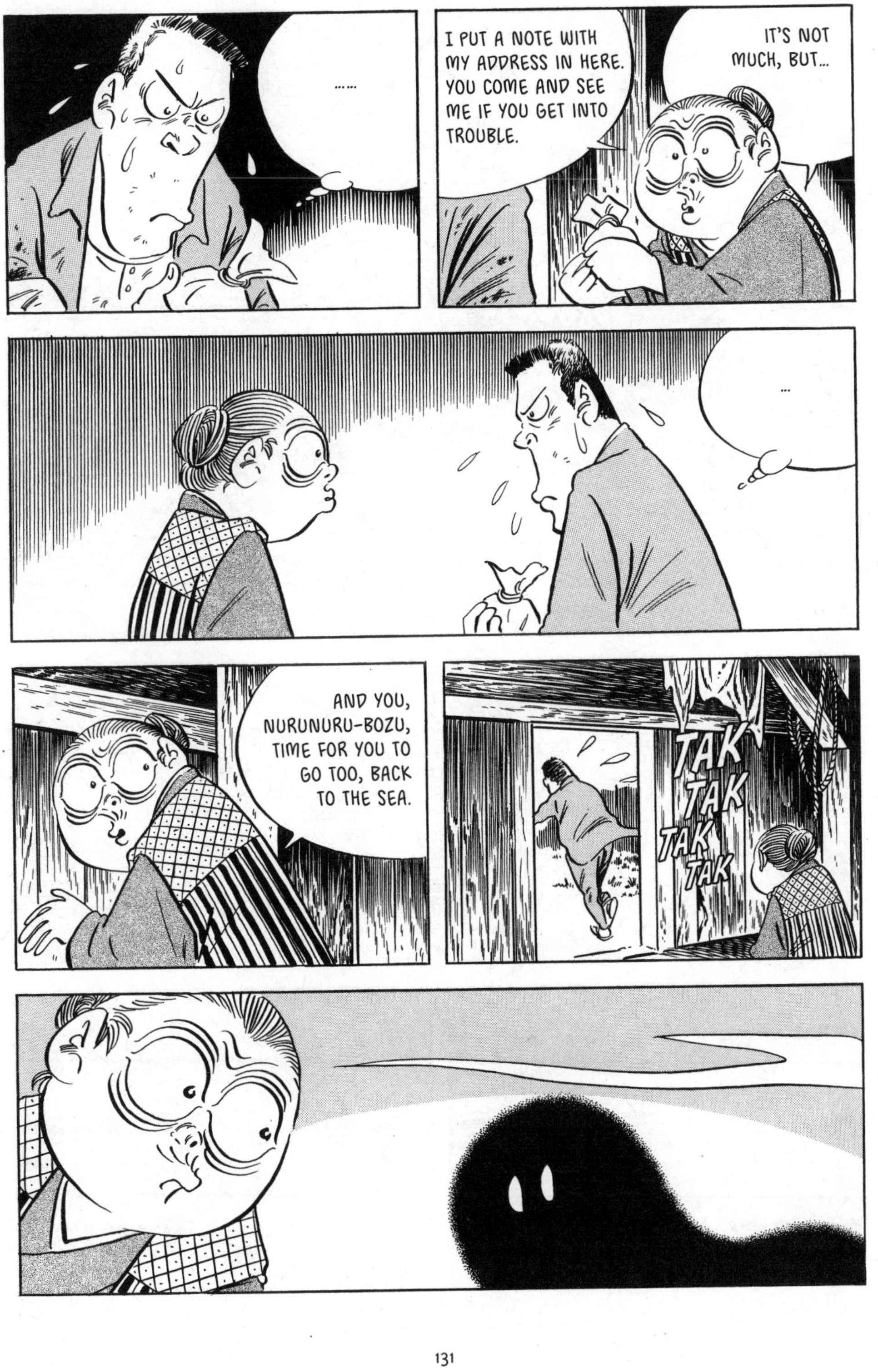
IT'S NOT MUCH, BUT...
I PUT A NOTE WITH MY ADDRESS IN HERE. YOU COME AND SEE ME IF YOU GET INTO TROUBLE.
......
...
TAK TAK TAK TAK
AND YOU, NURUNURU-BOZU, TIME FOR YOU TO GO TOO, BACK TO THE SEA.

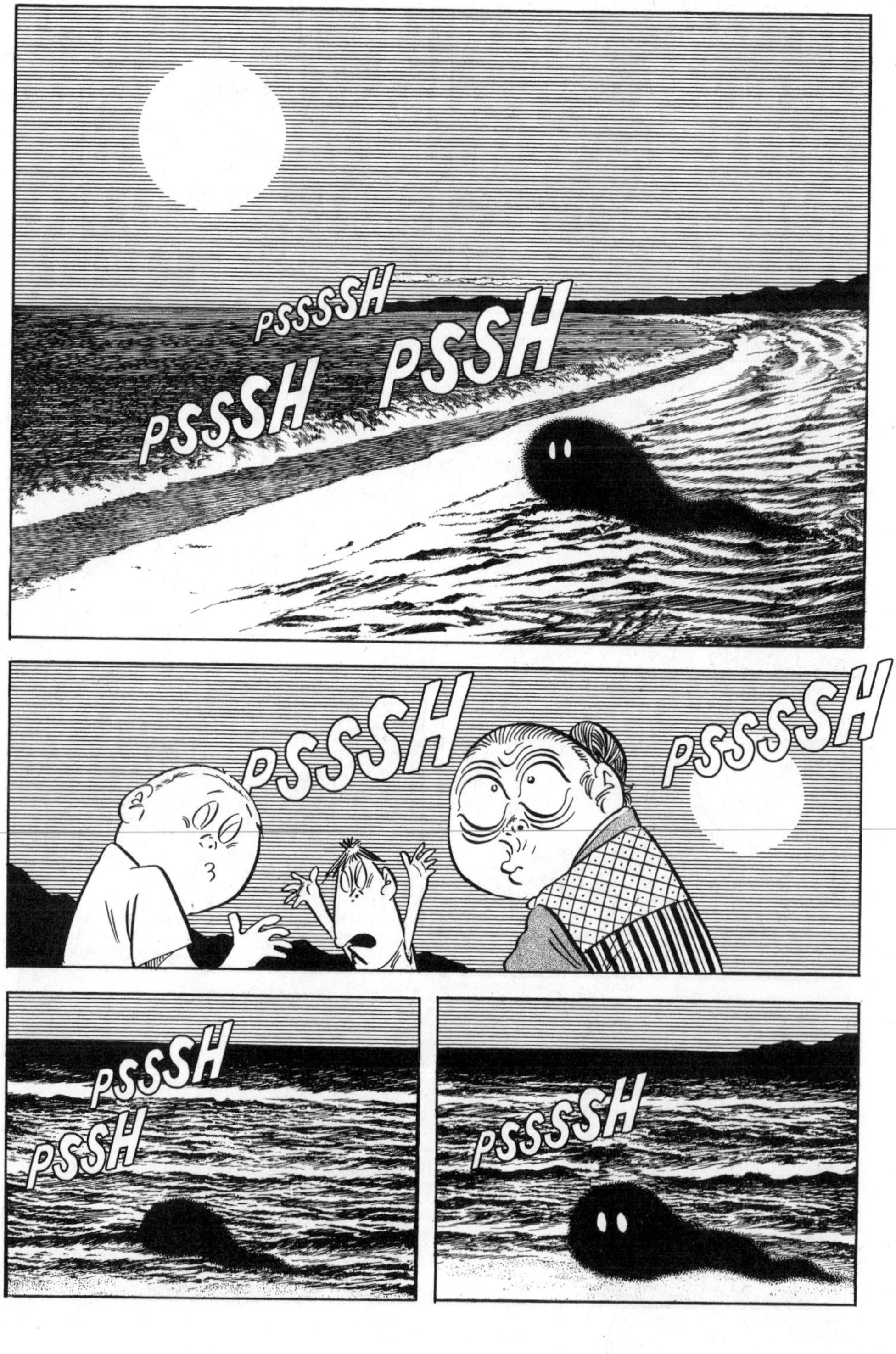
PSSSSH
PSSH
PSSSH
PSSSSH
PSSSH
PSSSSH
PSSSH
PSSH

BEAN COUNTER

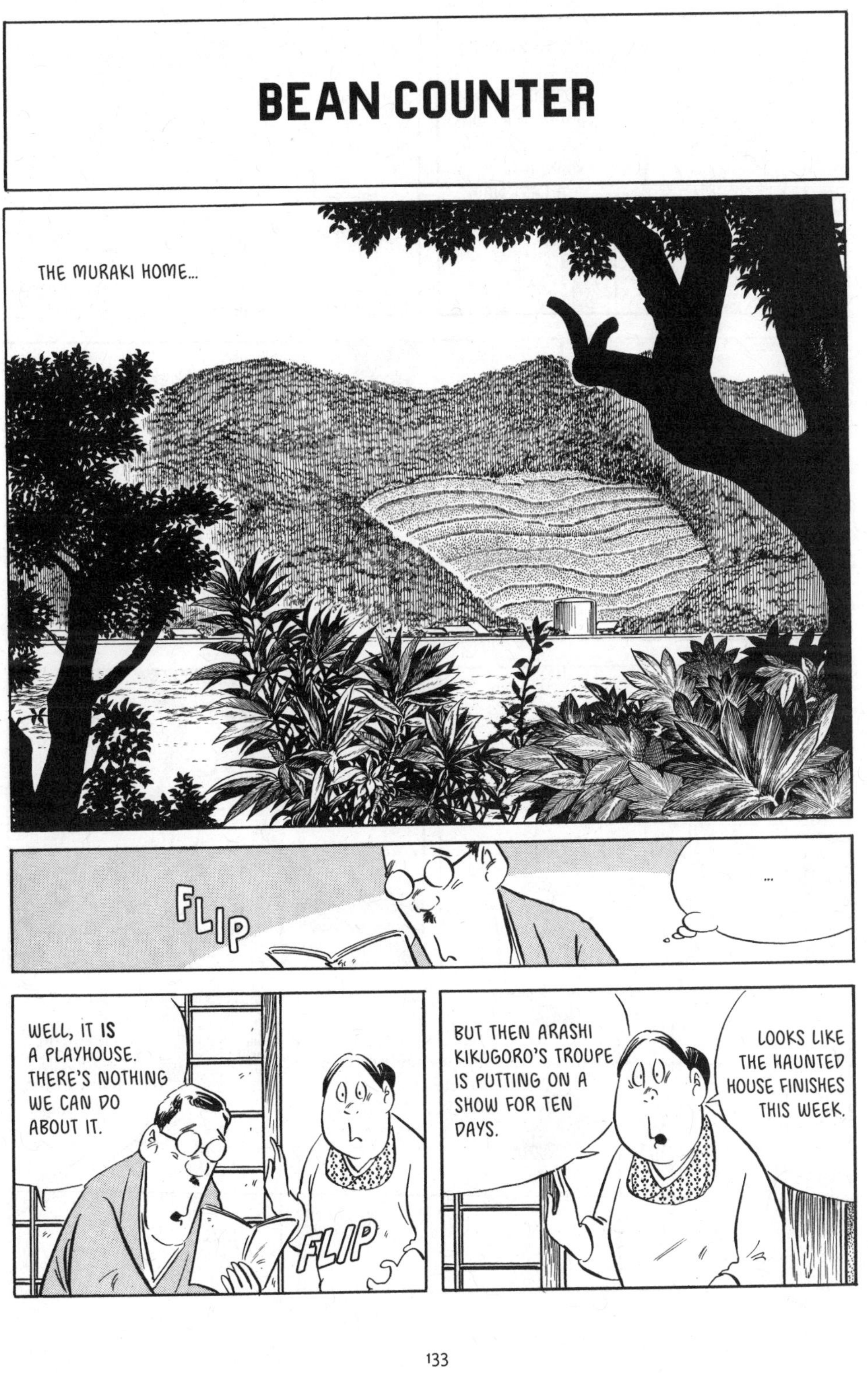

THE MURAKI HOME...
...
FLIP
LOOKS LIKE THE HAUNTED HOUSE FINISHES THIS WEEK.
BUT THEN ARASHI KIKUGORO'S TROUPE IS PUTTING ON A SHOW FOR TEN DAYS.
WELL, IT IS A PLAYHOUSE. THERE'S NOTHING WE CAN DO ABOUT IT.
FLIP

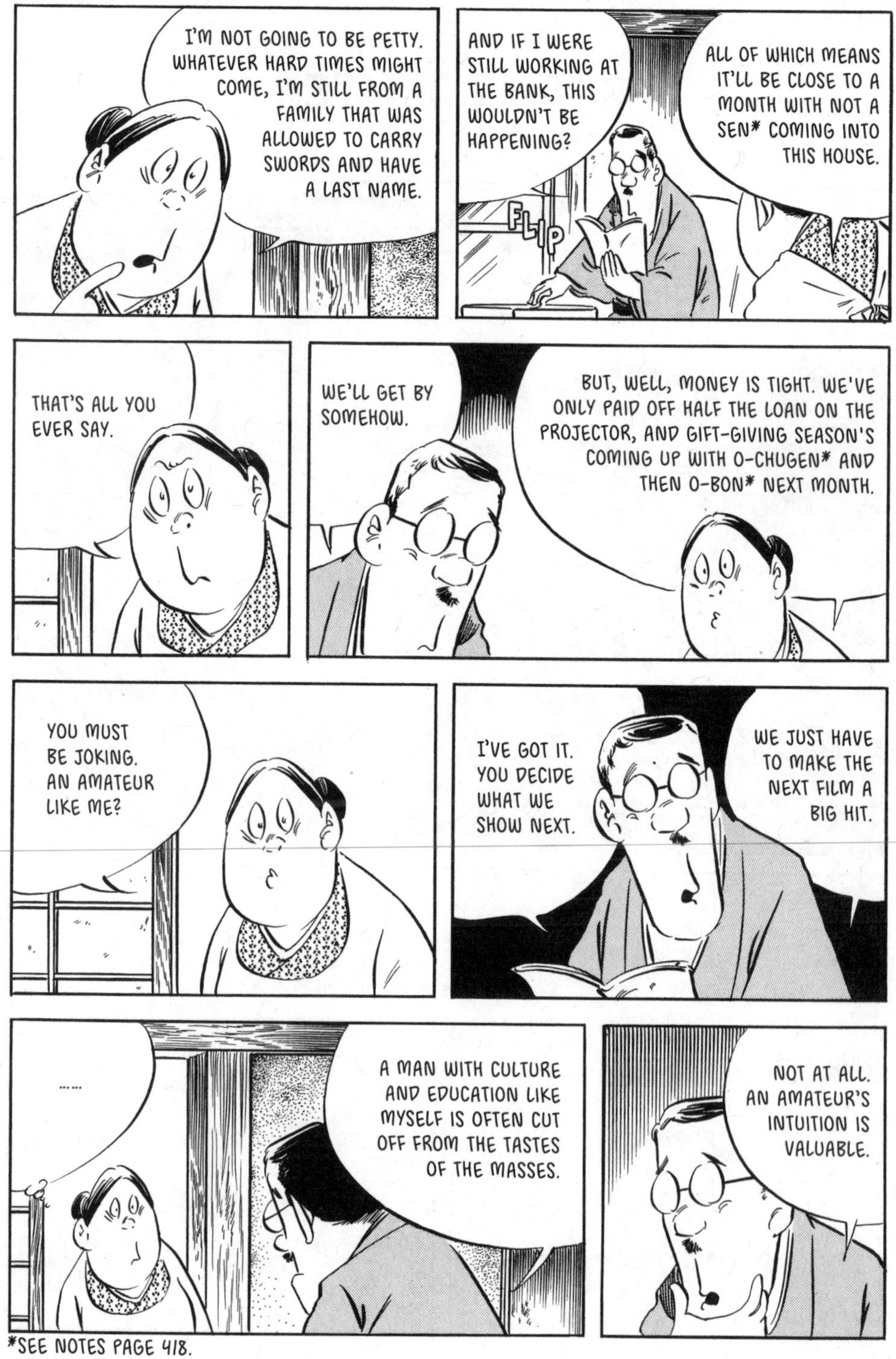
ALL OF WHICH MEANS IT'LL BE CLOSE TO A MONTH WITH NOT A SEN* COMING INTO THIS HOUSE.
AND IF I WERE STILL WORKING AT THE BANK, THIS WOULDN'T BE HAPPENING?
FLIP
I'M NOT GOING TO BE PETTY. WHATEVER HARD TIMES MIGHT COME, I'M STILL FROM A FAMILY THAT WAS ALLOWED TO CARRY SWORDS AND HAVE A LAST NAME.
BUT, WELL, MONEY IS TIGHT. WE'VE ONLY PAID OFF HALF THE LOAN ON THE PROJECTOR, AND GIFT-GIVING SEASON'S COMING UP WITH O-CHUGEN* AND THEN O-BON* NEXT MONTH.
WE'LL GET BY SOMEHOW.
THAT'S ALL YOU EVER SAY.
WE JUST HAVE TO MAKE THE NEXT FILM A BIG HIT.
I'VE GOT IT. YOU DECIDE WHAT WE SHOW NEXT.
YOU MUST BE JOKING. AN AMATEUR LIKE ME?
NOT AT ALL. AN AMATEUR'S INTUITION IS VALUABLE.
A MAN WITH CULTURE AND EDUCATION LIKE MYSELF IS OFTEN CUT OFF FROM THE TASTES OF THE MASSES.
……

*SEE NOTES PAGE 418.

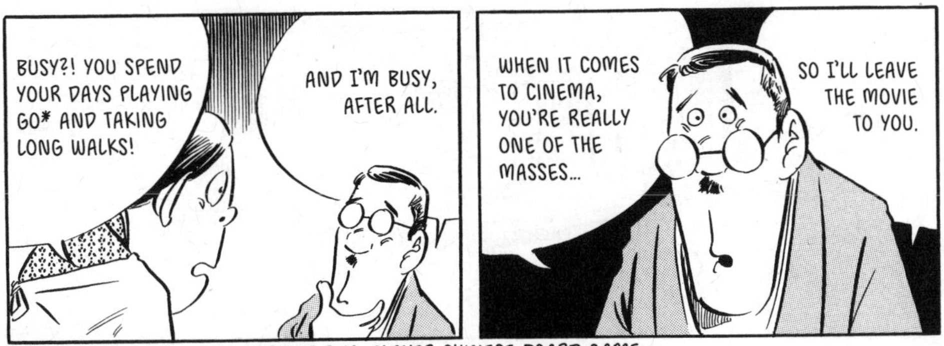
WHEN IT COMES TO CINEMA, YOU'RE REALLY ONE OF THE MASSES...
SO I'LL LEAVE THE MOVIE TO YOU.
AND I'M BUSY, AFTER ALL.
BUSY?! YOU SPEND YOUR DAYS PLAYING GO* AND TAKING LONG WALKS!

*A SIMPLE YET STRATEGIC ANCIENT TWO-PLAYER CHINESE BOARD GAME.

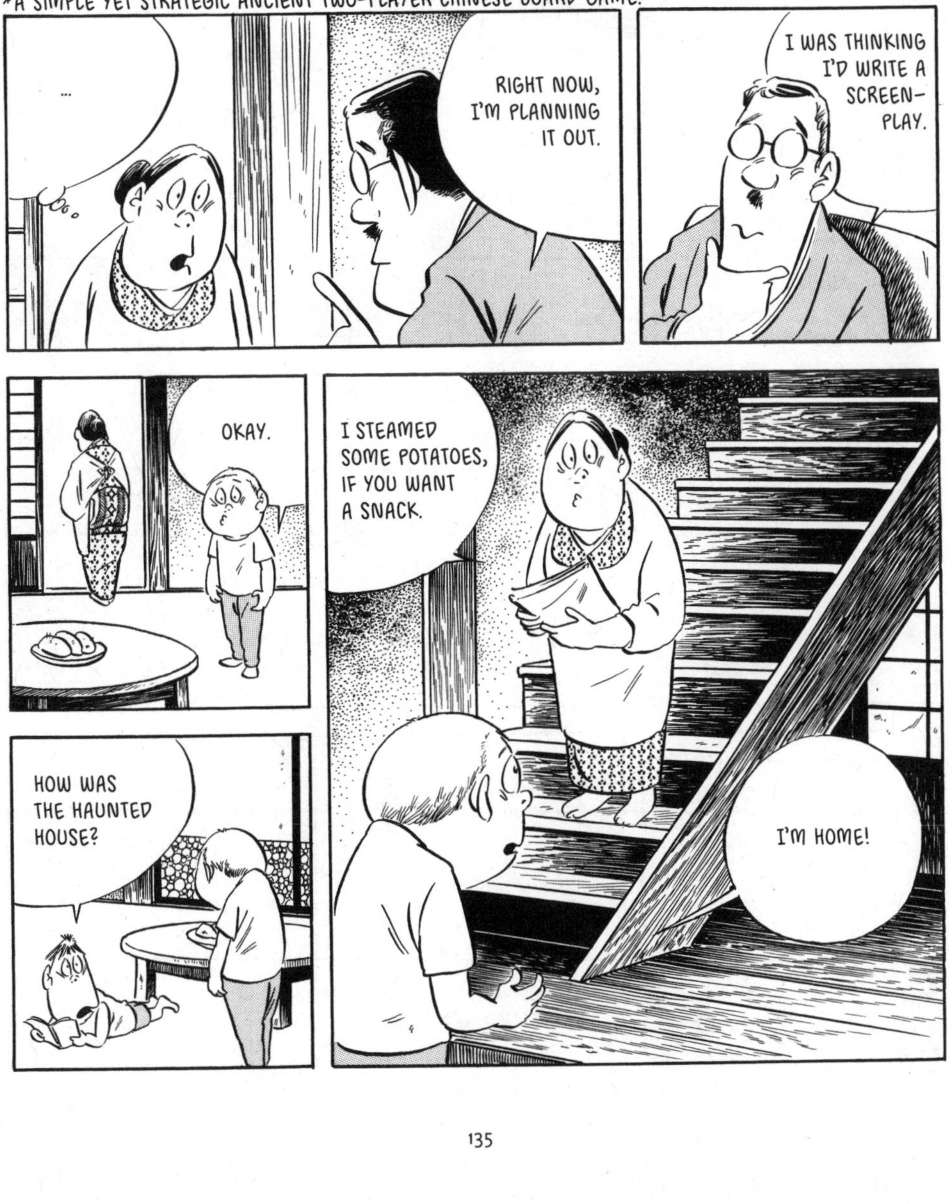
I WAS THINKING I'D WRITE A SCREEN-PLAY.
RIGHT NOW, I'M PLANNING IT OUT.
...
I'M HOME!
I STEAMED SOME POTATOES, IF YOU WANT A SNACK.
OKAY.
HOW WAS THE HAUNTED HOUSE?

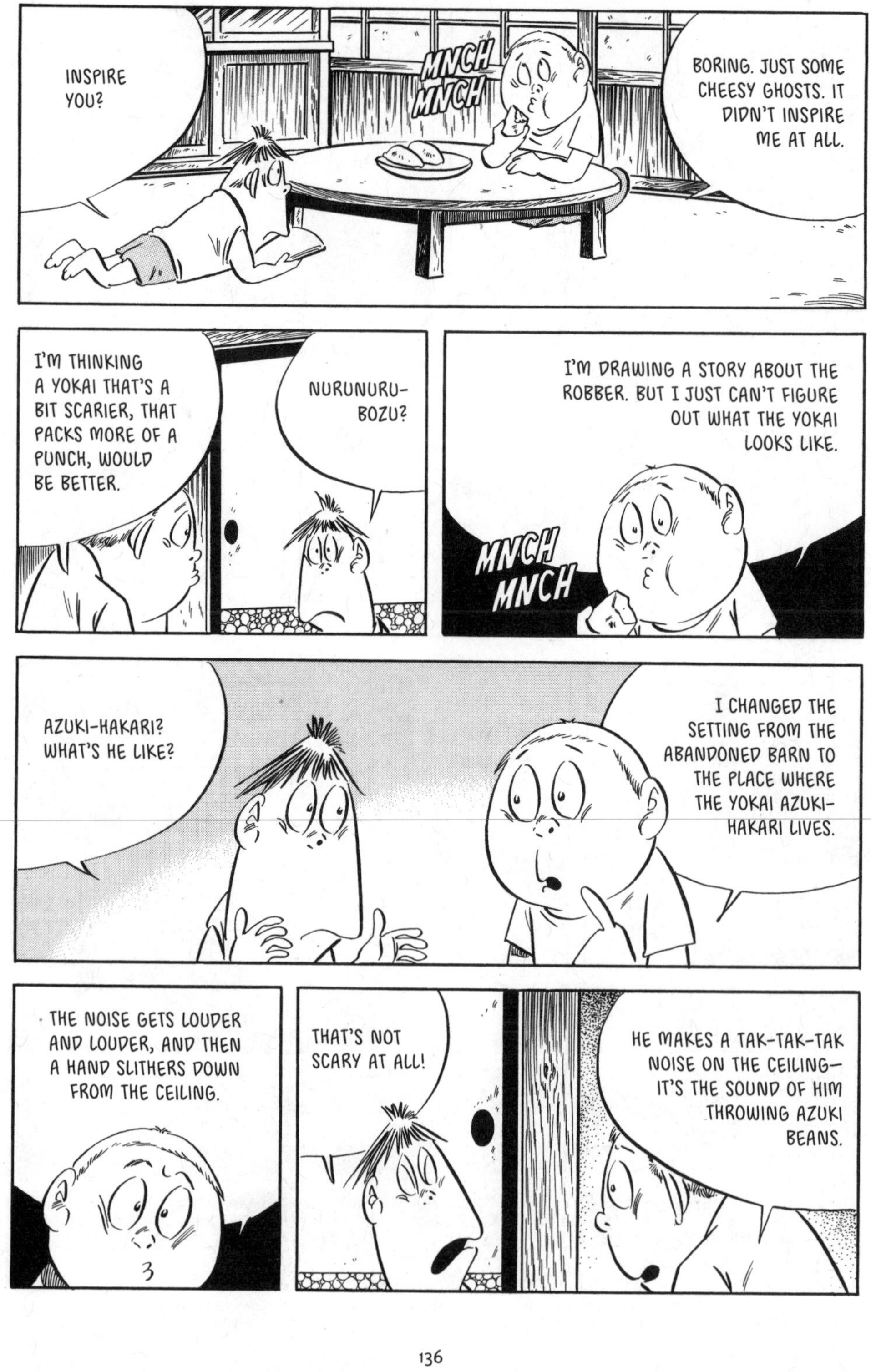
BORING. JUST SOME CHEESY GHOSTS. IT DIDN'T INSPIRE ME AT ALL.
MNCH MNCH
INSPIRE YOU?
I'M DRAWING A STORY ABOUT THE ROBBER. BUT I JUST CAN'T FIGURE OUT WHAT THE YOKAI LOOKS LIKE.
MNCH MNCH
NURUNURU-BOZU?
I'M THINKING A YOKAI THAT'S A BIT SCARIER, THAT PACKS MORE OF A PUNCH, WOULD BE BETTER.
I CHANGED THE SETTING FROM THE ABANDONED BARN TO THE PLACE WHERE THE YOKAI AZUKI-HAKARI LIVES.
AZUKI-HAKARI? WHAT'S HE LIKE?
HE MAKES A TAK-TAK-TAK NOISE ON THE CEILING—IT'S THE SOUND OF HIM THROWING AZUKI BEANS.
THAT'S NOT SCARY AT ALL!
THE NOISE GETS LOUDER AND LOUDER, AND THEN A HAND SLITHERS DOWN FROM THE CEILING.

THEN HE THROWS AROUND POTS AND LIDS, AND THEN FINALLY, HE DROPS SAND AND ROCKS ON YOU AND BURIES YOU ALIVE.
TH-THAT'S PRETTY SCARY.
BUT I CAN'T FIGURE OUT WHAT THIS AZUKI-HAKARI LOOKS LIKE.
SO I WENT TO THE HAUNTED HOUSE, THINKING IT MIGHT GIVE ME SOME IDEAS.
TOTAL WASTE OF FIFTEEN SEN.*
MNCH
MNCH
MNCH
MNCH
AZUKI-HAKARI, HUH?
PSSH
PSSSH

*FIFTEEN SEN WAS THE EQUIVALENT OF ABOUT A NICKEL IN TERMS OF SPENDING POWER.

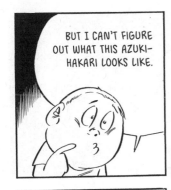

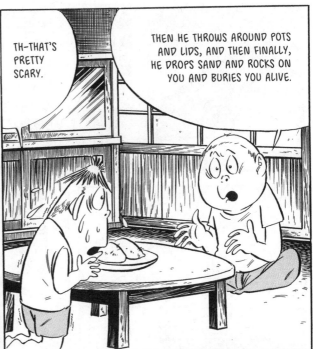

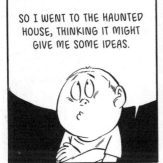

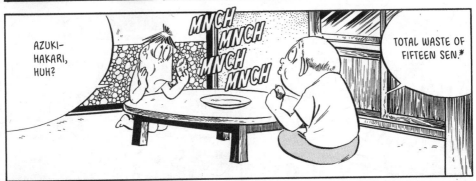

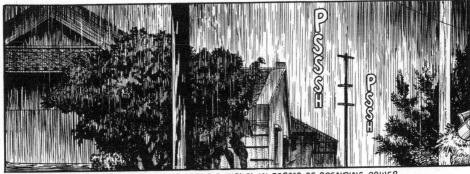

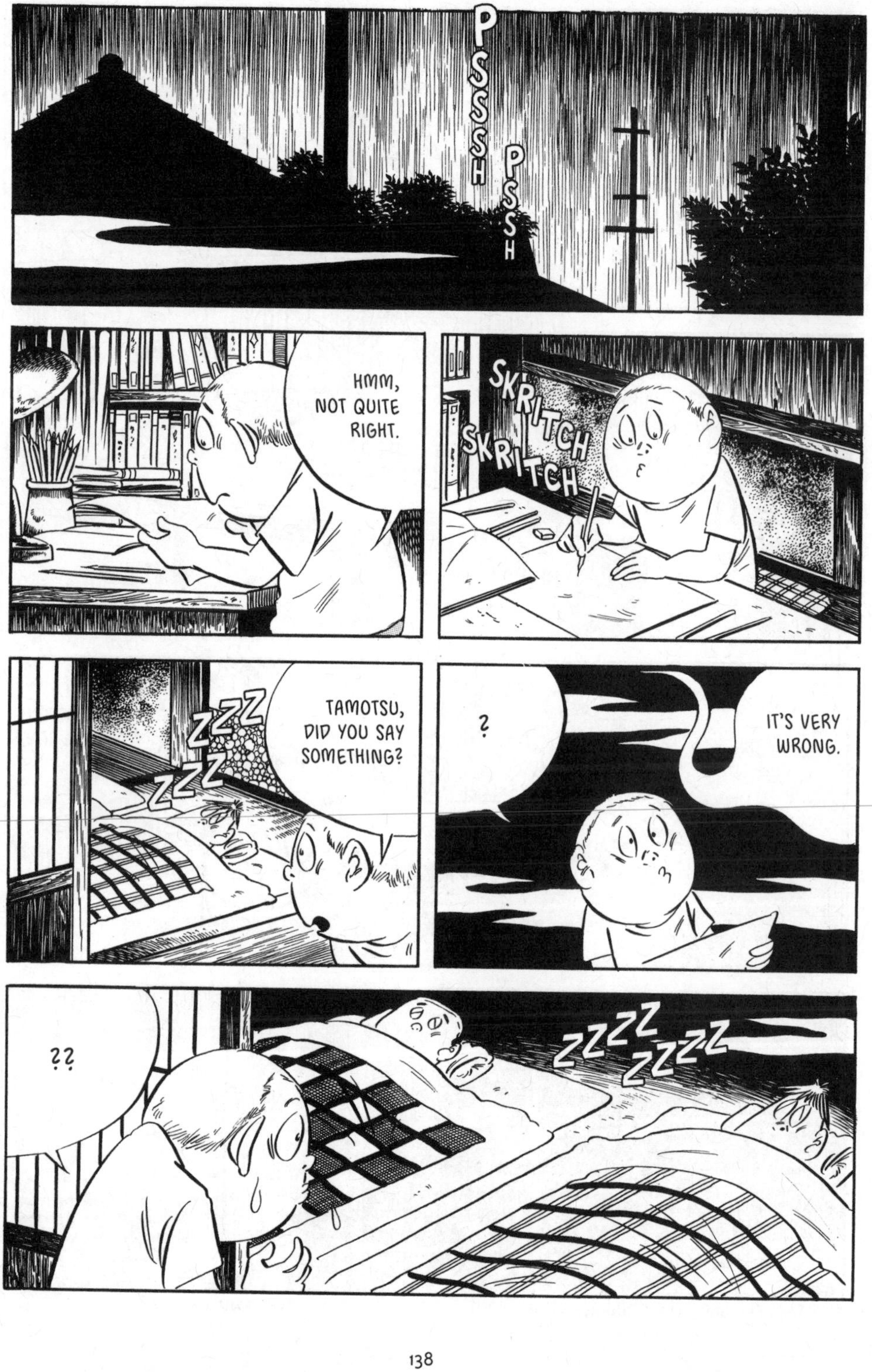
PSSSH
PSSH
SKRITCH
SKRITCH
HMM, NOT QUITE RIGHT.
IT'S VERY WRONG.
?
TAMOTSU, DID YOU SAY SOMETHING?
ZZZ
ZZZ
ZZZZ
ZZZZ
??

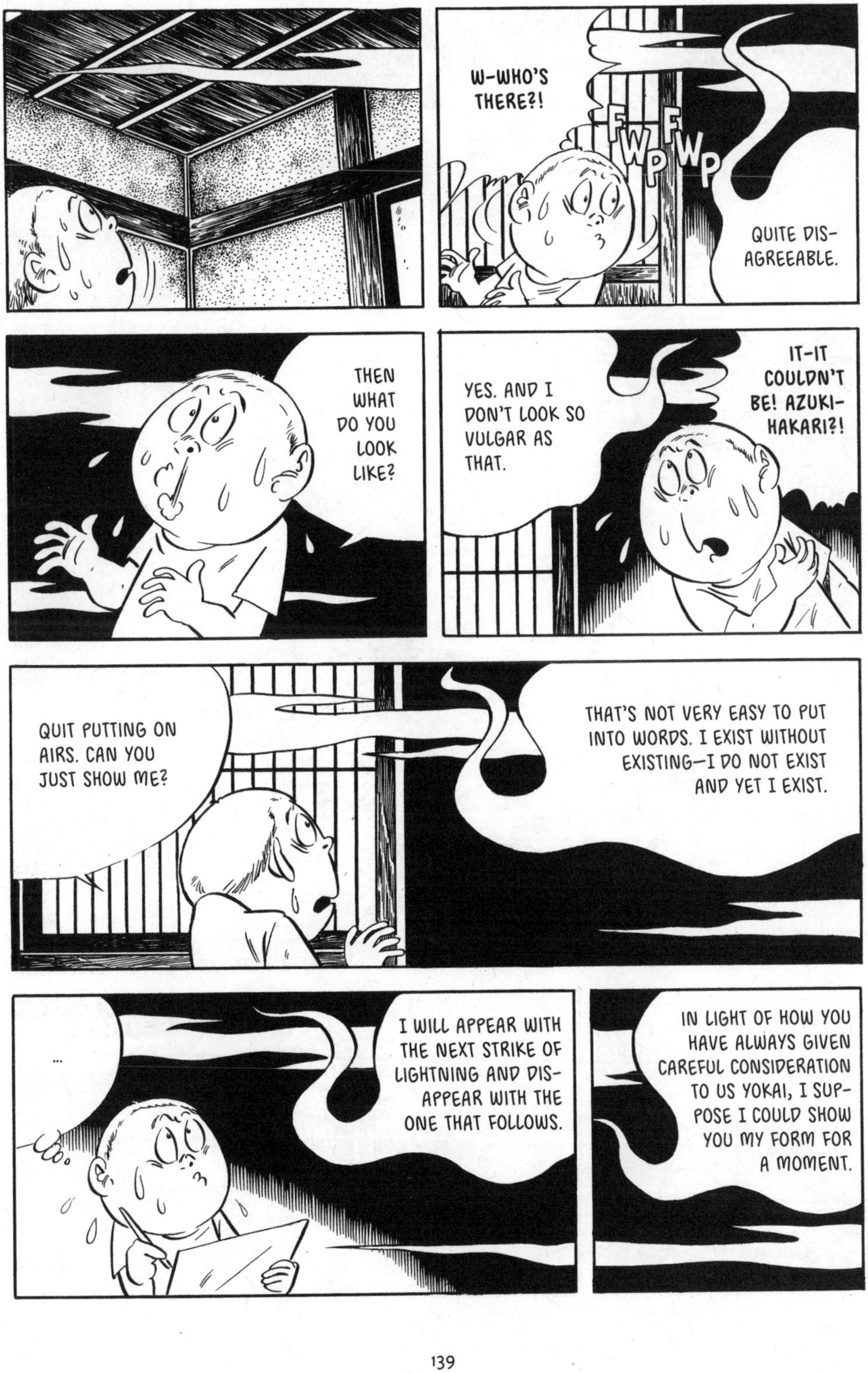
W-WHO'S THERE?!
FWP FWP
QUITE DIS-AGREEABLE.
IT-IT COULDN'T BE! AZUKI-HAKARI?!
YES. AND I DON'T LOOK SO VULGAR AS THAT.
THEN WHAT DO YOU LOOK LIKE?
THAT'S NOT VERY EASY TO PUT INTO WORDS. I EXIST WITHOUT EXISTING—I DO NOT EXIST AND YET I EXIST.
QUIT PUTTING ON AIRS. CAN YOU JUST SHOW ME?
IN LIGHT OF HOW YOU HAVE ALWAYS GIVEN CAREFUL CONSIDERATION TO US YOKAI, I SUPPOSE I COULD SHOW YOU MY FORM FOR A MOMENT.
I WILL APPEAR WITH THE NEXT STRIKE OF LIGHTNING AND DISAPPEAR WITH THE ONE THAT FOLLOWS.
...

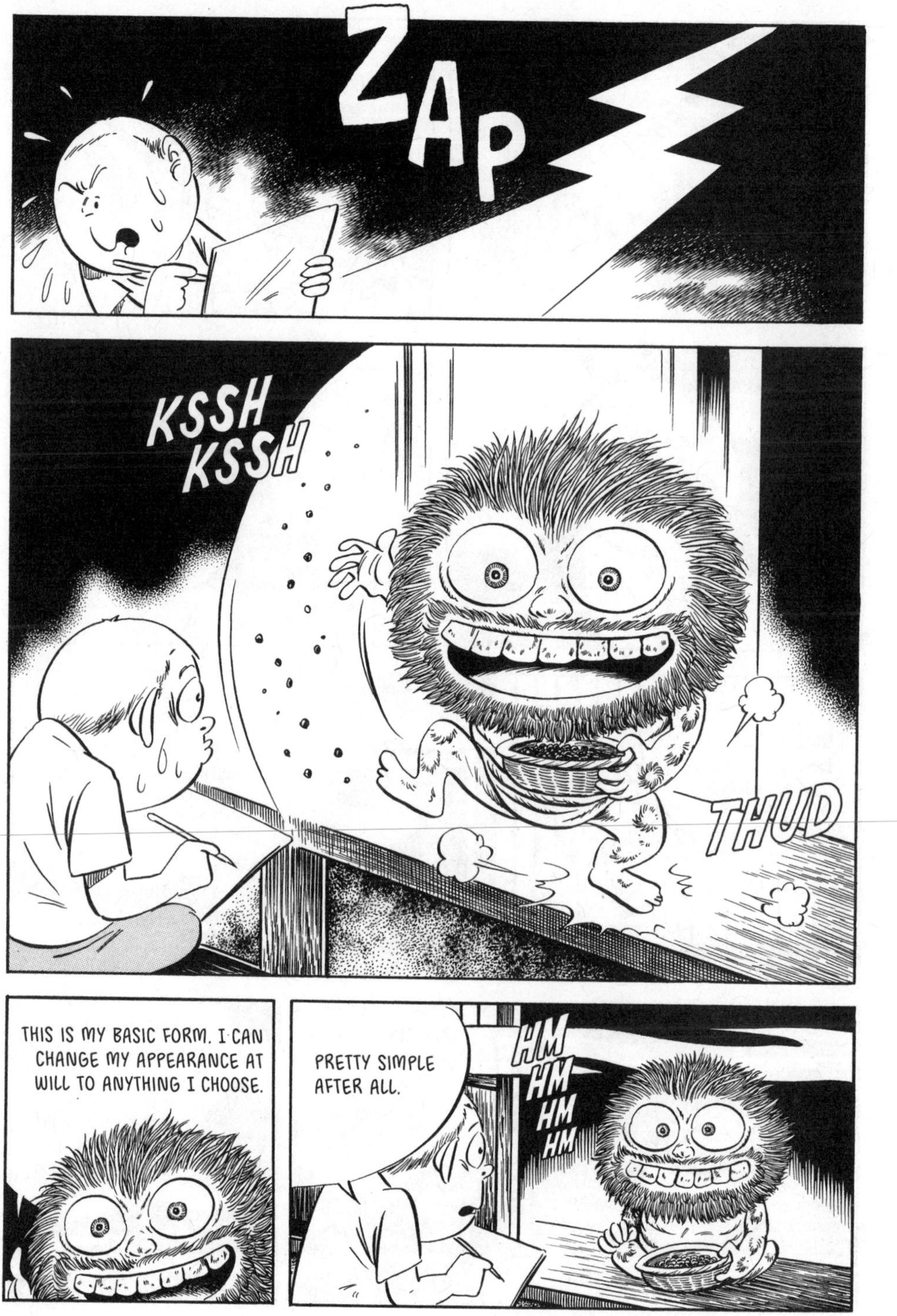
ZAP
KSSH KSSH
THUD
HM HM HM HM
PRETTY SIMPLE AFTER ALL.
THIS IS MY BASIC FORM. I CAN CHANGE MY APPEARANCE AT WILL TO ANYTHING I CHOOSE.

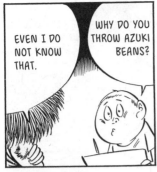

SHOW ME HOW YOU THROW THE BEANS.
MOVEMENT IN THE STILLNESS, STILL IN THE MOVEMENT.
KLATTER
KLATTER
KLATTER
KLATTER
WHY DO YOU THROW AZUKI BEANS?
EVEN I DO NOT KNOW THAT.
IT IS WHAT I'M DESTINED TO DO.
IS IT FUN TO SCARE PEOPLE?
IT'S NOT PARTICULARLY FUN, BUT IT IS MY ROLE TO PLAY.
WHY WERE YOU BORN INTO THE MURAKI FAMILY?
HUH?
WHY DO YOU DRAW STORIES THAT NO ONE HAS ASKED FOR? IT IS THE SAME THING.
ALL THINGS ARE DETERMINED BY FATE.

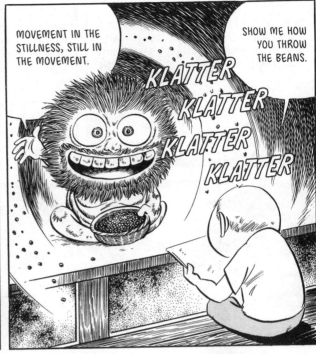

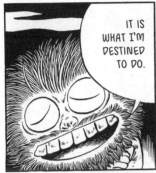

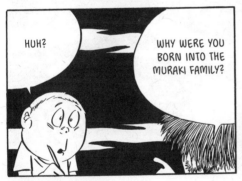

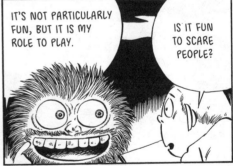

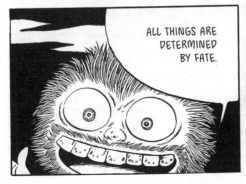

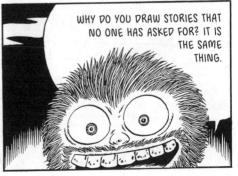

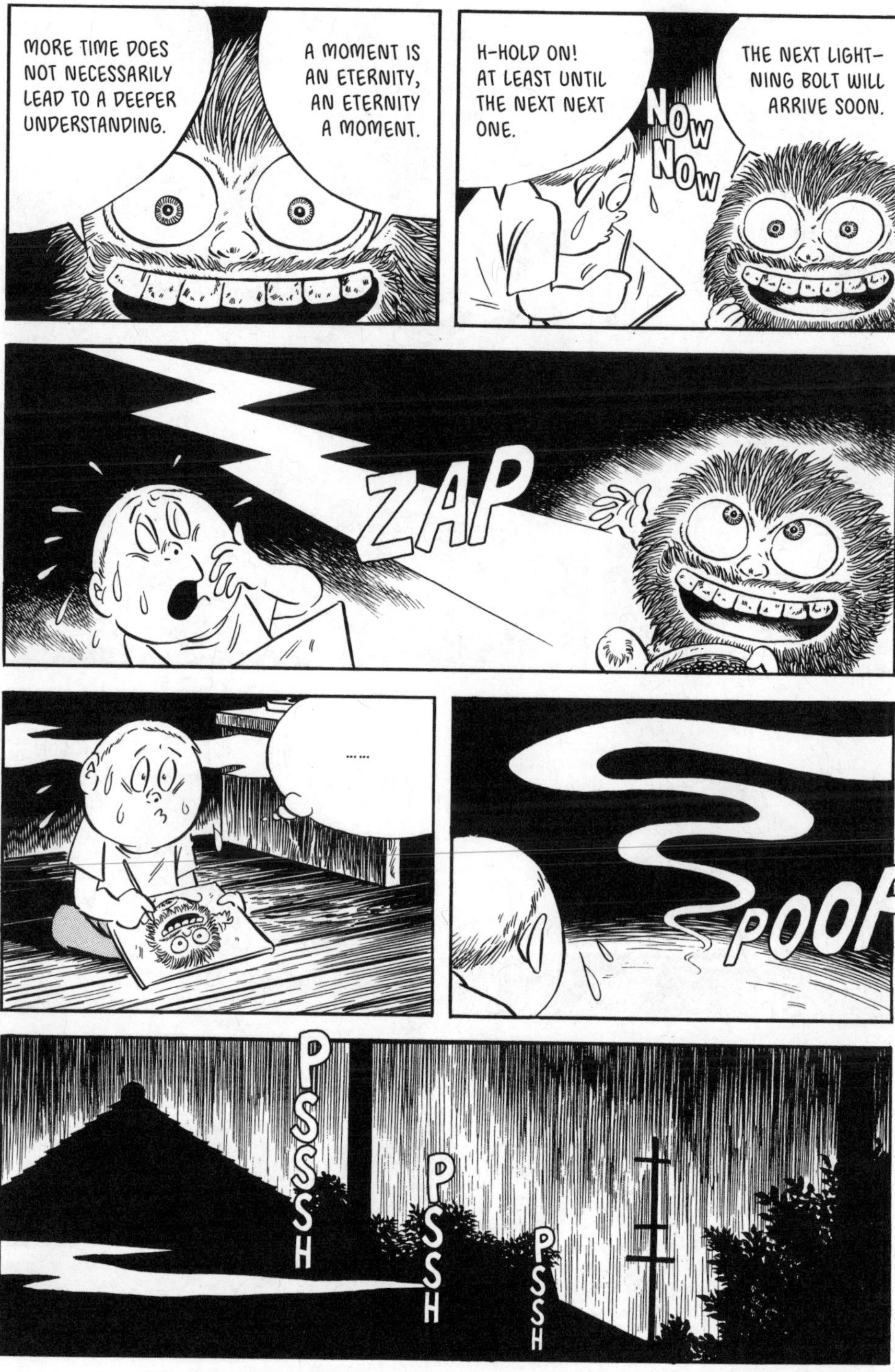
THE NEXT LIGHT-
NING BOLT WILL
ARRIVE SOON.
NOW NOW
H-HOLD ON!
AT LEAST UNTIL
THE NEXT NEXT
ONE.
A MOMENT IS
AN ETERNITY,
AN ETERNITY
A MOMENT.
MORE TIME DOES
NOT NECESSARILY
LEAD TO A DEEPER
UNDERSTANDING.
ZAP
POOF
…… ……
PSSH
PSSH
PSSH

DOUGHNUTS

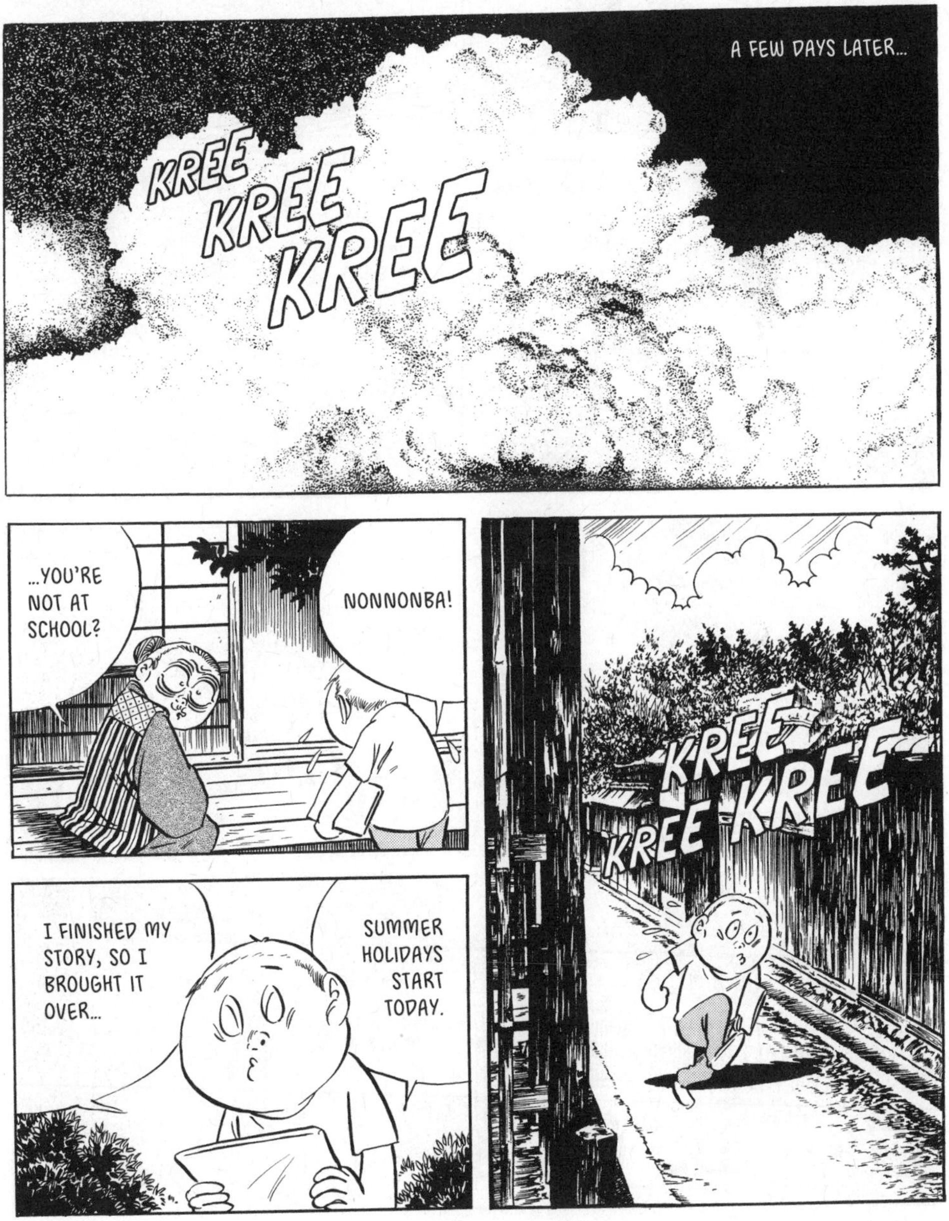
A FEW DAYS LATER...
KREE KREE KREE
KREE KREE KREE
NONNONBA!
...YOU'RE NOT AT SCHOOL?
SUMMER HOLIDAYS START TODAY.
I FINISHED MY STORY, SO I BROUGHT IT OVER...

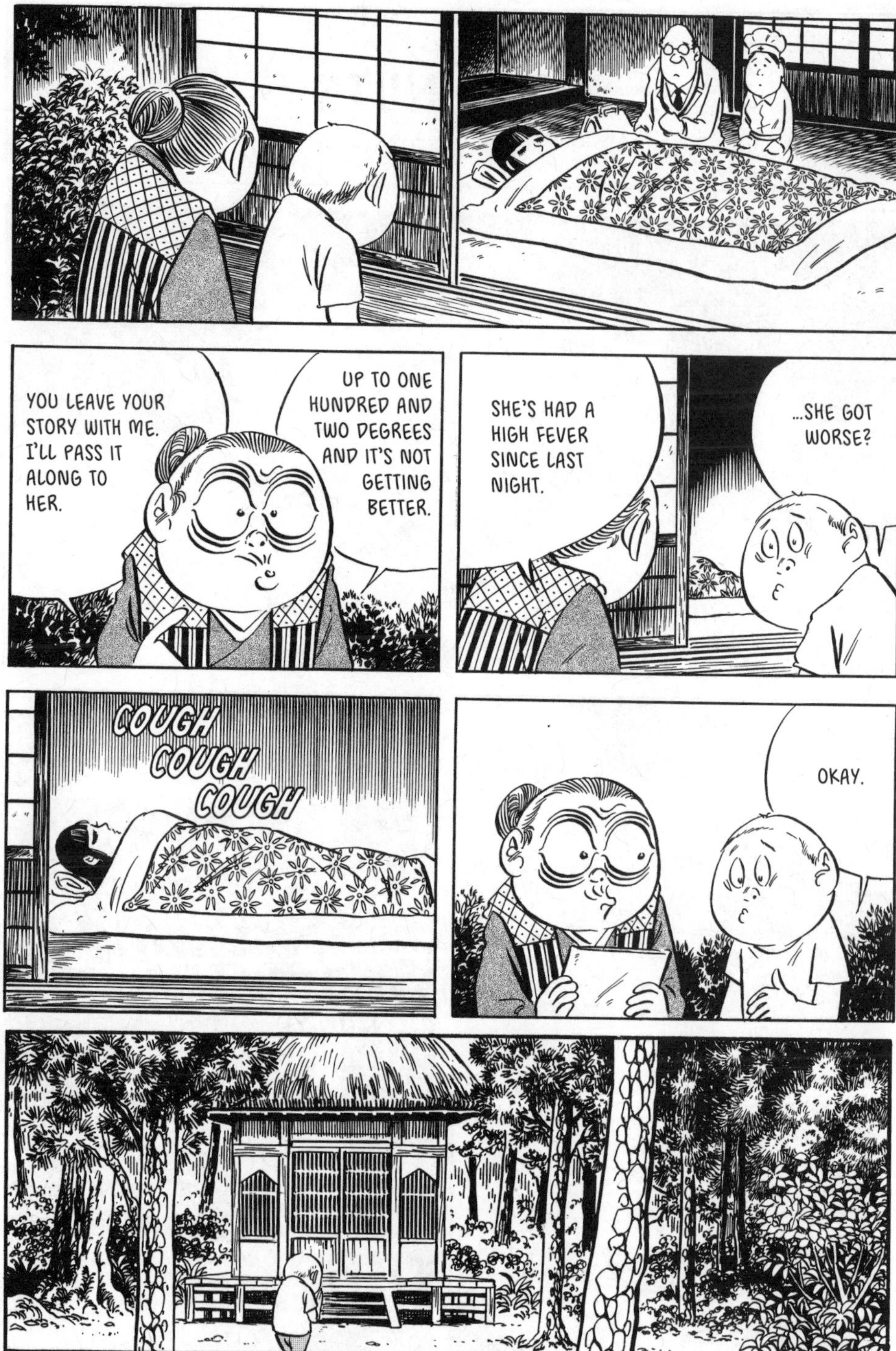
...SHE GOT WORSE?
SHE'S HAD A HIGH FEVER SINCE LAST NIGHT.
UP TO ONE HUNDRED AND TWO DEGREES AND IT'S NOT GETTING BETTER.
YOU LEAVE YOUR STORY WITH ME. I'LL PASS IT ALONG TO HER.
OKAY.
COUGH COUGH COUGH

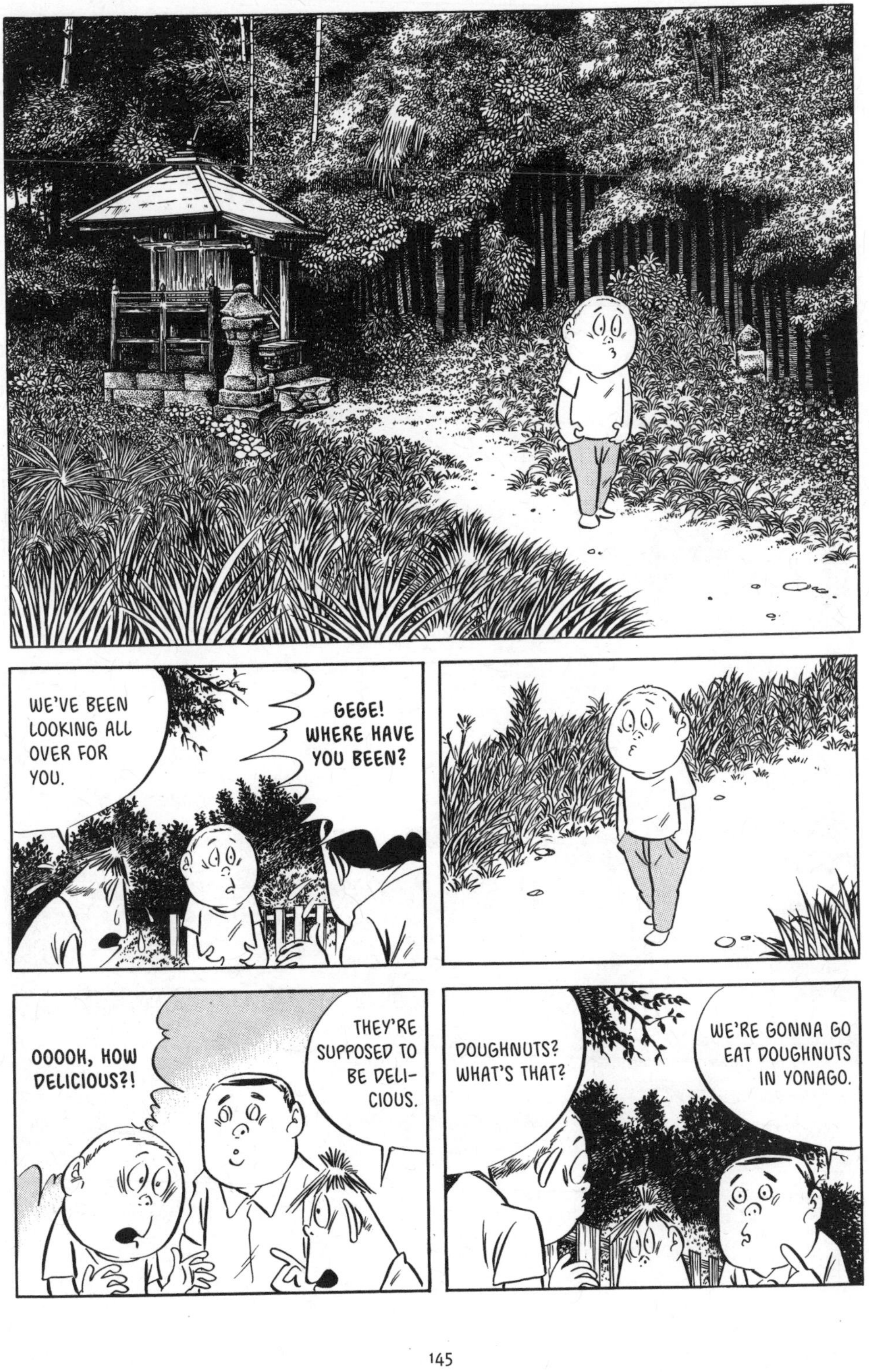
GEGE! WHERE HAVE YOU BEEN?
WE'VE BEEN LOOKING ALL OVER FOR YOU.
WE'RE GONNA GO EAT DOUGHNUTS IN YONAGO.
DOUGHNUTS? WHAT'S THAT?
THEY'RE SUPPOSED TO BE DELI- CIOUS.
OOOOH, HOW DELICIOUS?!

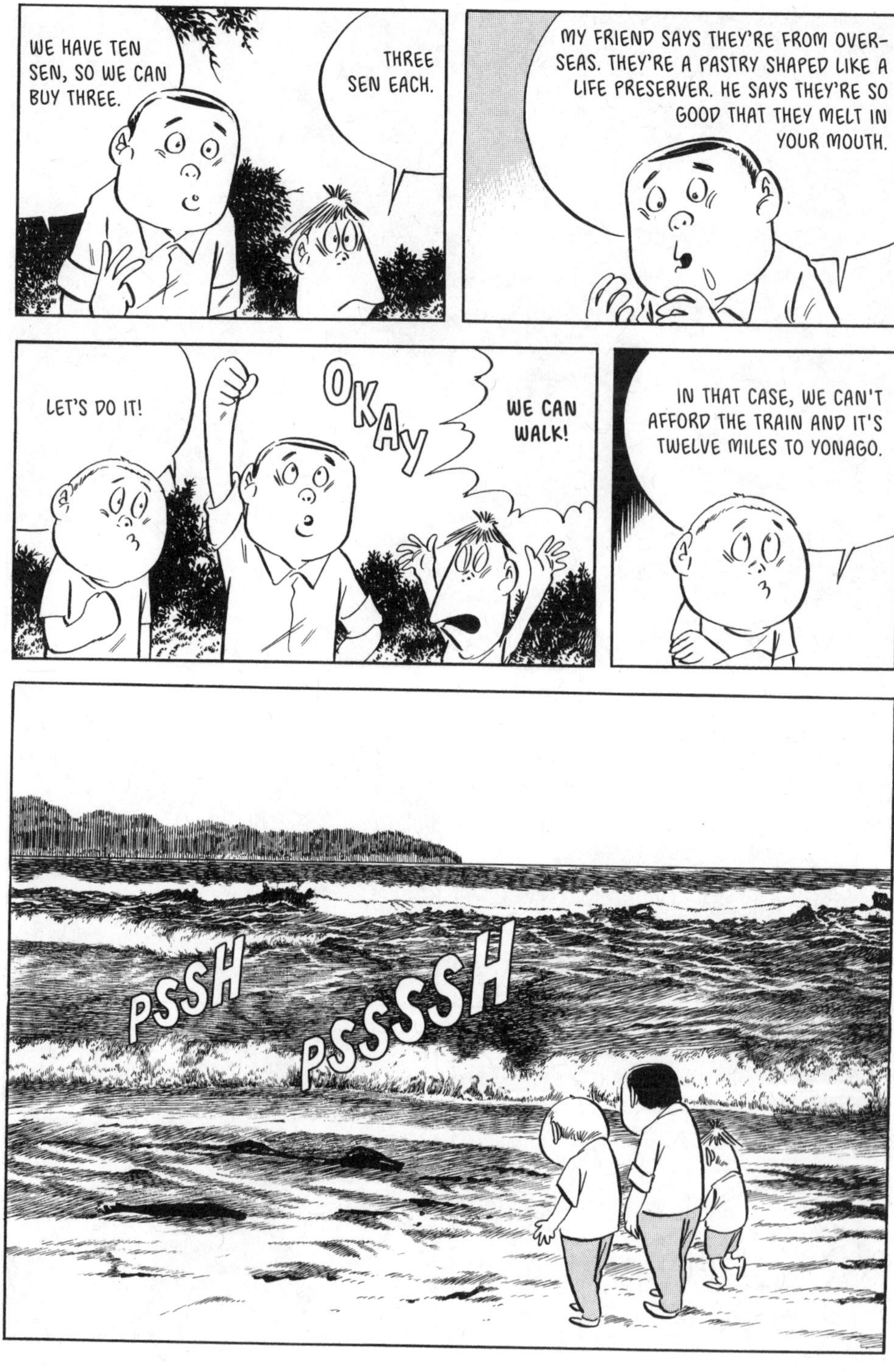
MY FRIEND SAYS THEY'RE FROM OVERSEAS. THEY'RE A PASTRY SHAPED LIKE A LIFE PRESERVER. HE SAYS THEY'RE SO GOOD THAT THEY MELT IN YOUR MOUTH.
THREE SEN EACH.
WE HAVE TEN SEN, SO WE CAN BUY THREE.
IN THAT CASE, WE CAN'T AFFORD THE TRAIN AND IT'S TWELVE MILES TO YONAGO.
WE CAN WALK!
OKAY
LET'S DO IT!
PSSSSH
PSSH

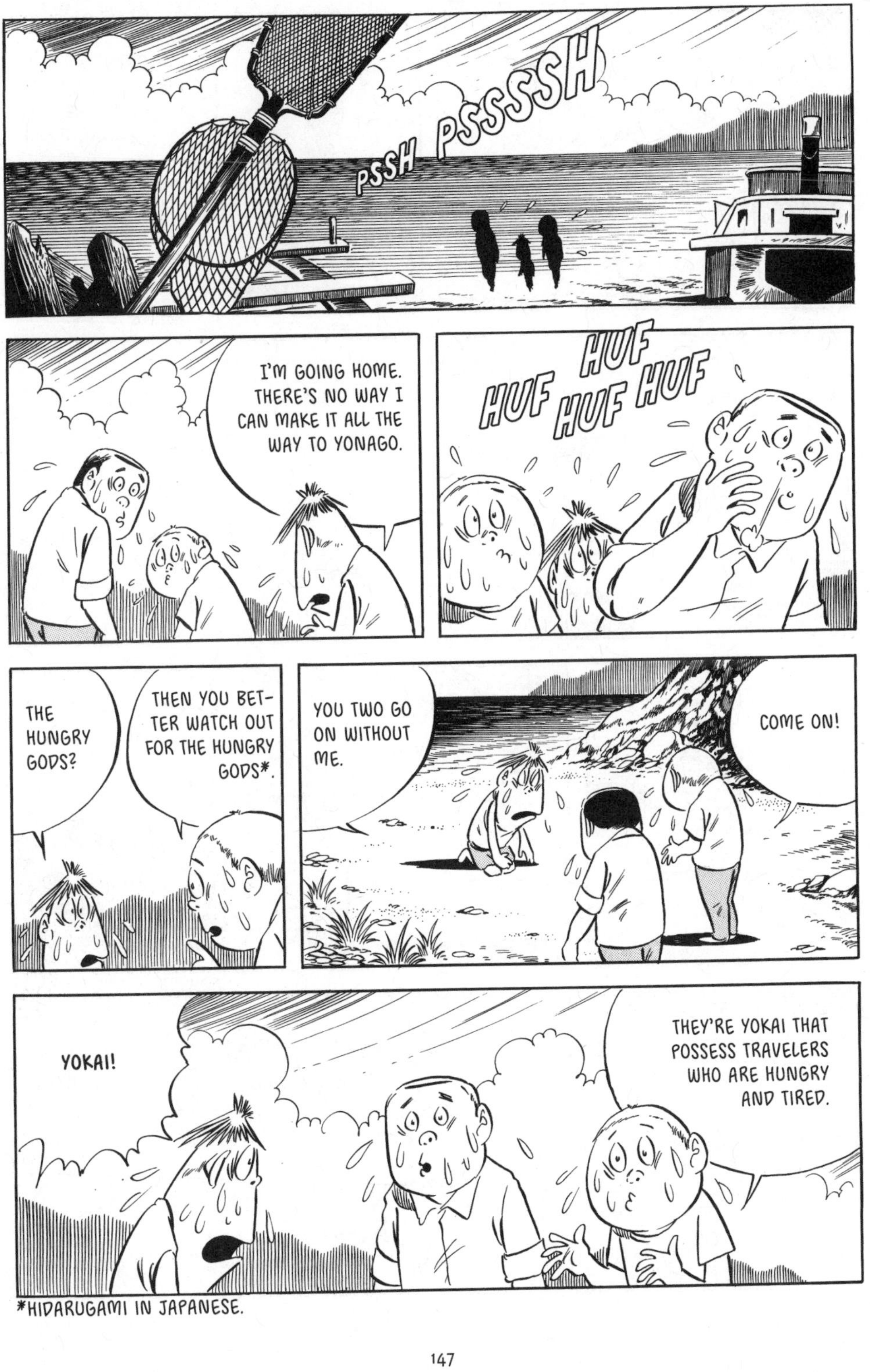
PSSH PSSSSSH
HUF HUF HUF HUF
I'M GOING HOME. THERE'S NO WAY I CAN MAKE IT ALL THE WAY TO YONAGO.
COME ON!
YOU TWO GO ON WITHOUT ME.
THEN YOU BETTER WATCH OUT FOR THE HUNGRY GODS*.
THE HUNGRY GODS?
THEY'RE YOKAI THAT POSSESS TRAVELERS WHO ARE HUNGRY AND TIRED.
YOKAI!

*HIDARUGAMI IN JAPANESE.

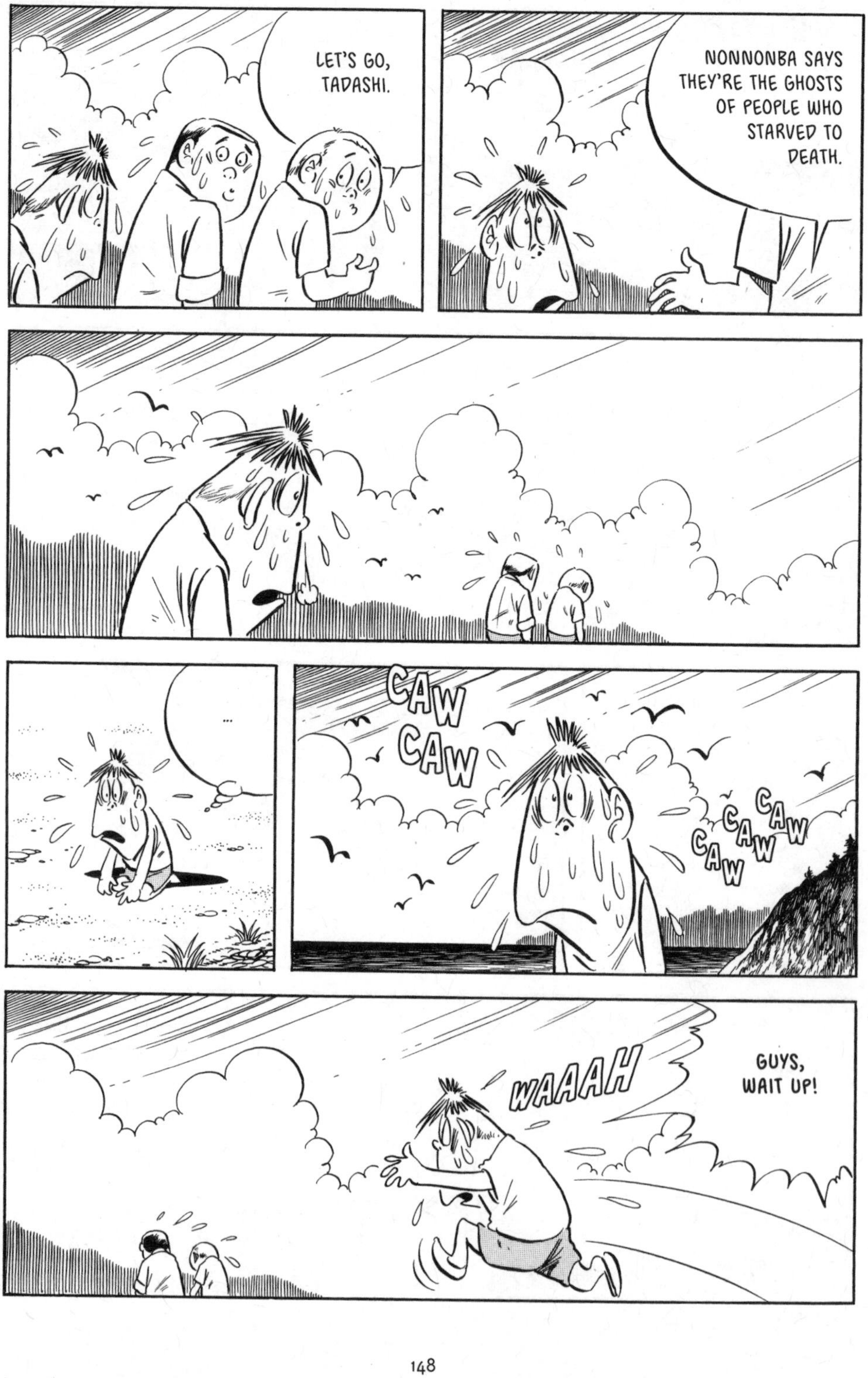
NONNONBA SAYS THEY'RE THE GHOSTS OF PEOPLE WHO STARVED TO DEATH.
LET'S GO, TADASHI.
CAW CAW CAW
CAW CAW
...
GUYS, WAIT UP!
WAAAH

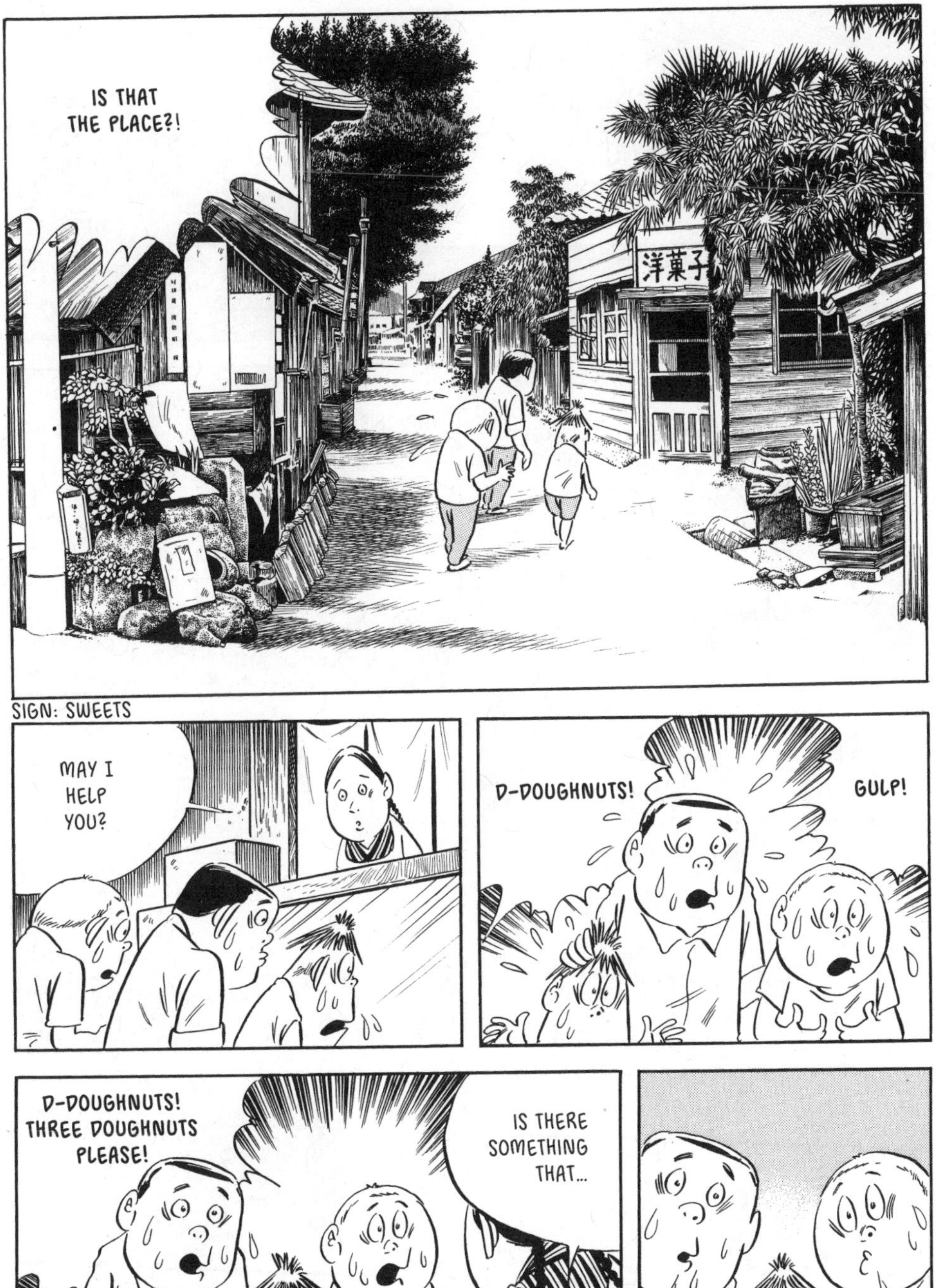
IS THAT THE PLACE?!
洋菓子
SIGN: SWEETS
GULP!
D-DOUGHNUTS!
MAY I HELP YOU?
IS THERE SOMETHING THAT...
D-DOUGHNUTS! THREE DOUGHNUTS PLEASE!

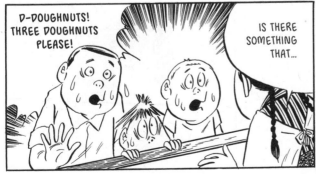

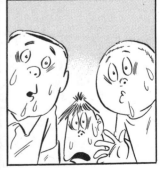

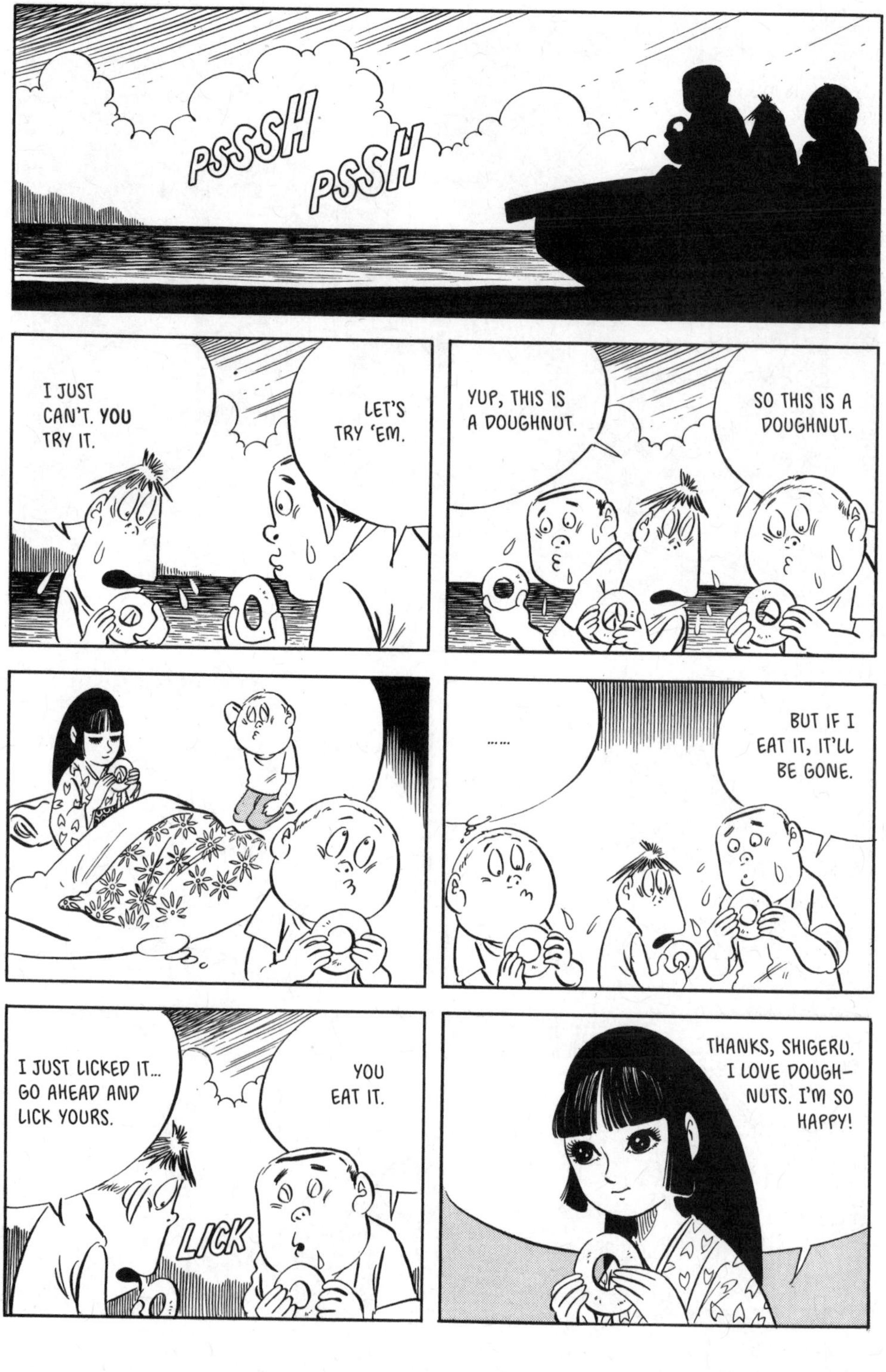
PSSSH
PSSH
SO THIS IS A DOUGHNUT.
YUP, THIS IS A DOUGHNUT.
LET'S TRY 'EM.
I JUST CAN'T. YOU TRY IT.
BUT IF I EAT IT, IT'LL BE GONE.
……
THANKS, SHIGERU. I LOVE DOUGH-NUTS. I'M SO HAPPY!
YOU EAT IT.
I JUST LICKED IT... GO AHEAD AND LICK YOURS.
LICK

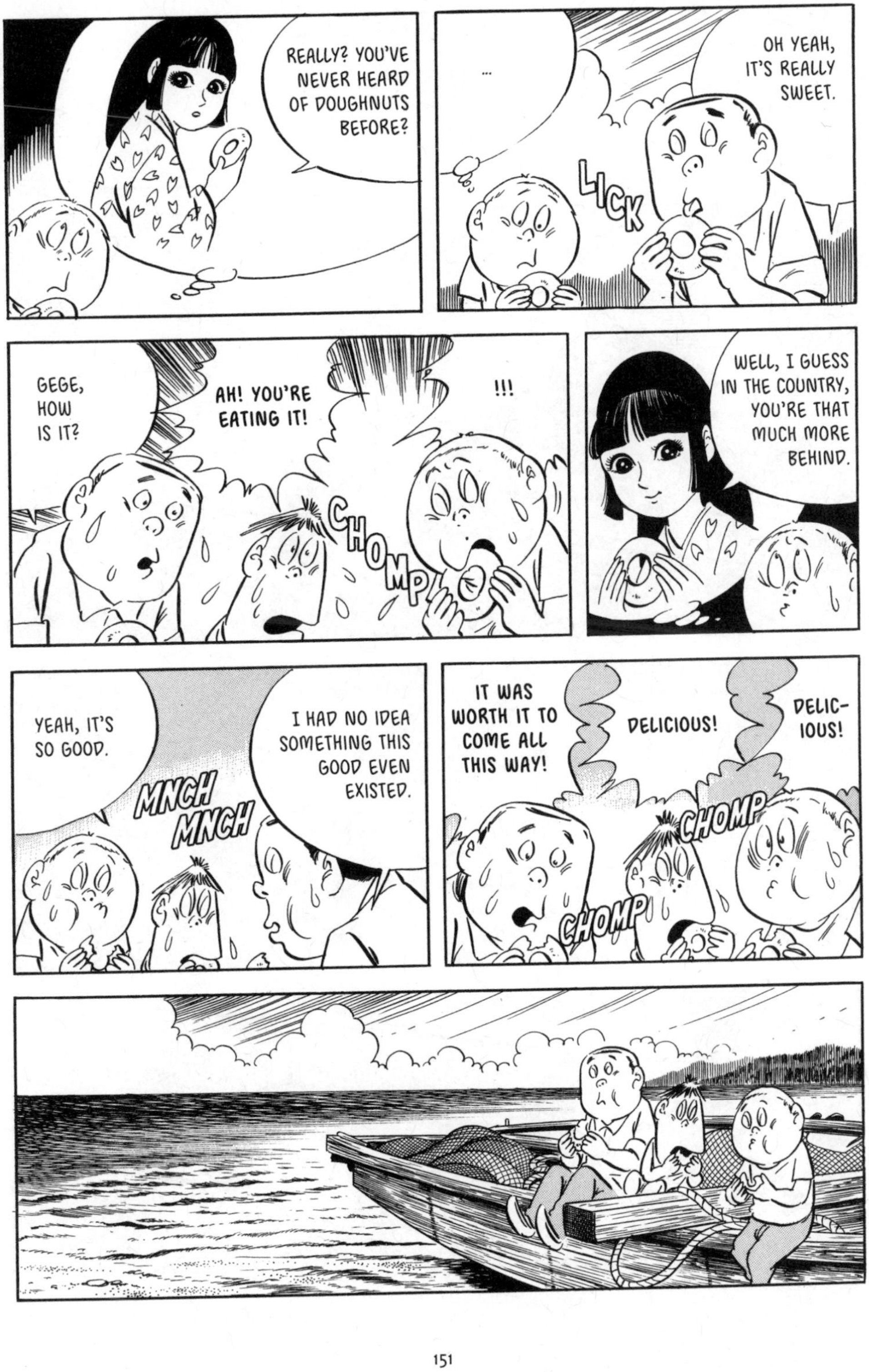
OH YEAH, IT'S REALLY SWEET.
...
LICK
REALLY? YOU'VE NEVER HEARD OF DOUGHNUTS BEFORE?
WELL, I GUESS IN THE COUNTRY, YOU'RE THAT MUCH MORE BEHIND.
!!!
AH! YOU'RE EATING IT!
GEGE, HOW IS IT?
CHOMP
DELIC-IOUS!
DELICIOUS!
IT WAS WORTH IT TO COME ALL THIS WAY!
CHOMP
CHOMP
I HAD NO IDEA SOMETHING THIS GOOD EVEN EXISTED.
YEAH, IT'S SO GOOD.
MNCH MNCH

FOX

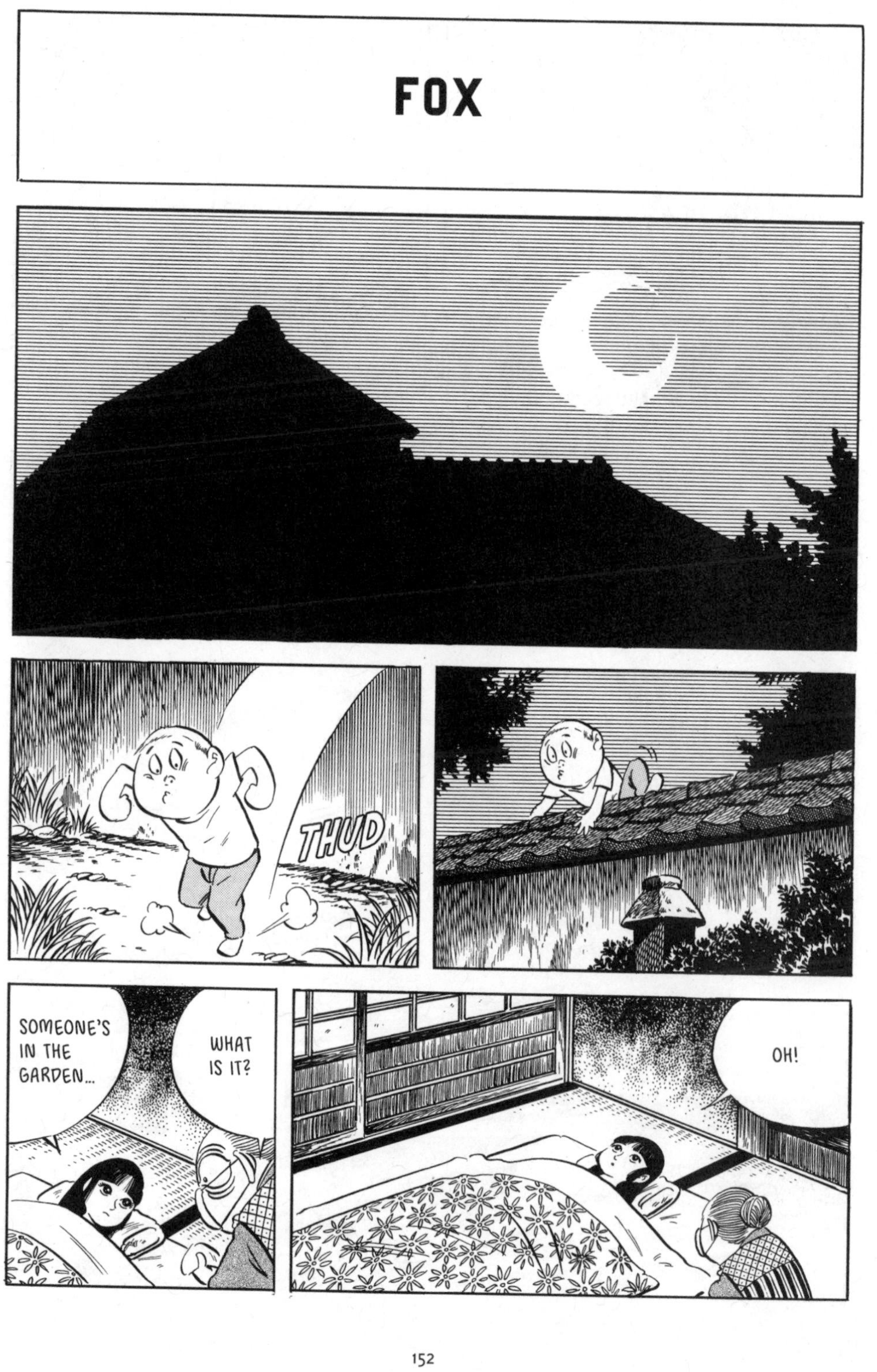
THUD
OH!
WHAT IS IT?
SOMEONE'S IN THE GARDEN...

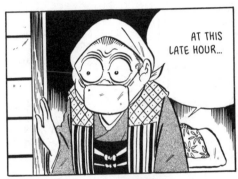

THE BUGS GOT QUIET ALL OF A SUDDEN...I HOPE IT'S SHIGERU.
IT HAS TO BE.
AT THIS LATE HOUR...
OH! IT REALLY IS SHIGERU.
WHAT'S GOING ON, NONNONBA?
WHY THE MASK? DID SOMETHING HAPPEN?
I THINK IT'S DEPRES-SING, BUT THE DOCTOR TOLD ME TO WEAR IT.
DID YOU COME BECAUSE YOU'RE WORRIED?
CHIGUSA'S TEMPERATURE BROKE JUST AFTER LUNCH.
GOOD.
SHIGERU, SORRY TO MAKE YOU WORRY.
NAH...GUESS I'LL BE OFF THEN.
WHAT, YOU'RE LEAVING ALREADY?
IT **IS** QUITE LATE.
JUST FIVE MINUTES?

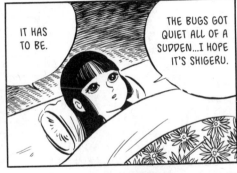

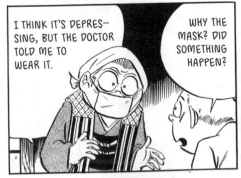

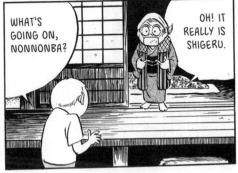

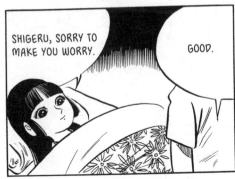

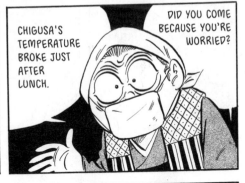

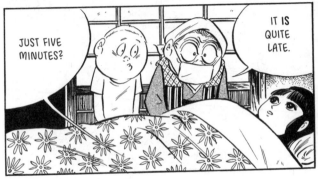

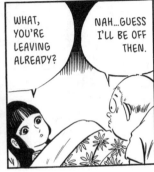

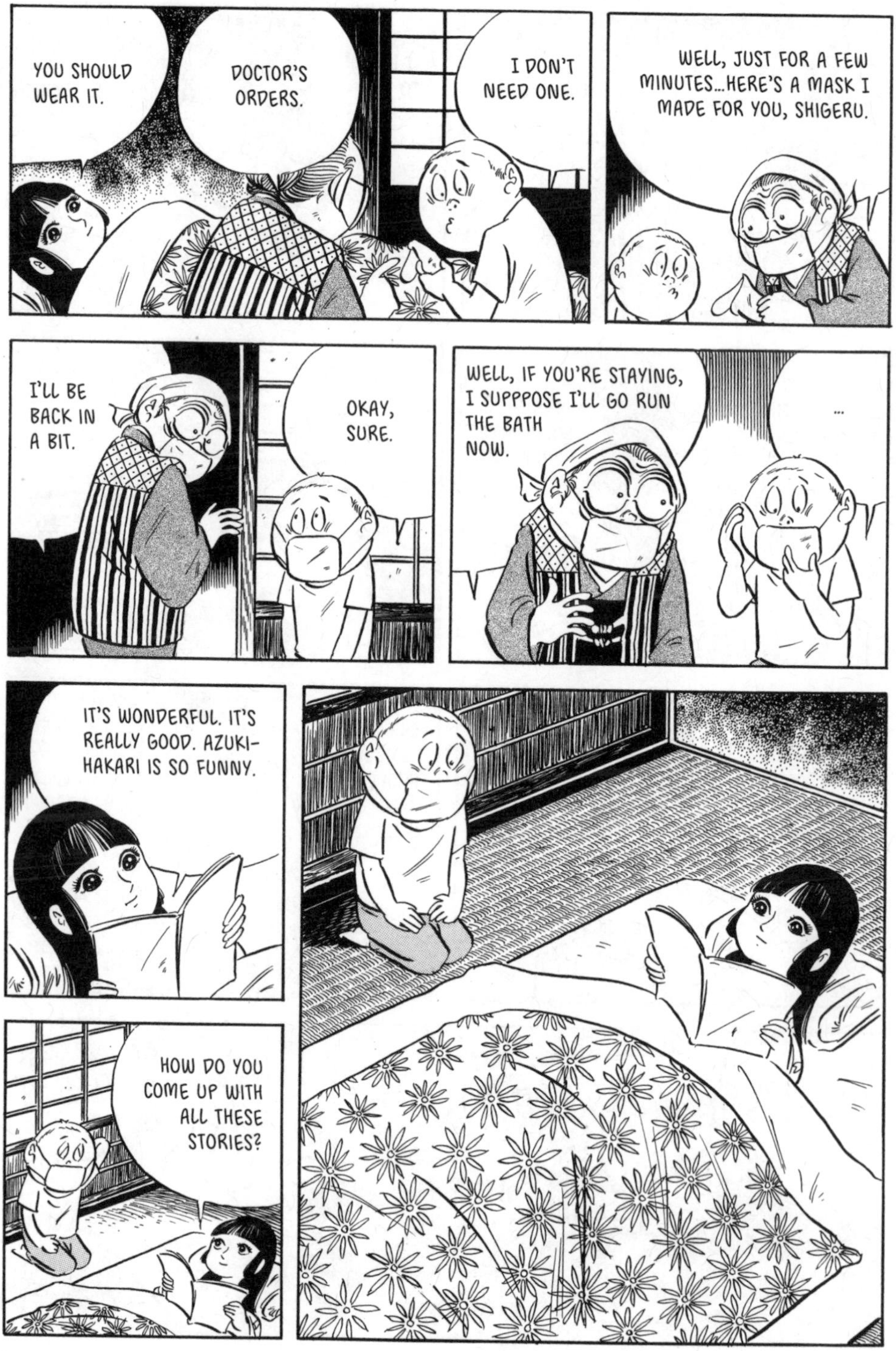
WELL, JUST FOR A FEW MINUTES...HERE'S A MASK I MADE FOR YOU, SHIGERU.
I DON'T NEED ONE.
DOCTOR'S ORDERS.
YOU SHOULD WEAR IT.
...
WELL, IF YOU'RE STAYING, I SUPPPOSE I'LL GO RUN THE BATH NOW.
OKAY, SURE.
I'LL BE BACK IN A BIT.
IT'S WONDERFUL. IT'S REALLY GOOD. AZUKI-HAKARI IS SO FUNNY.
HOW DO YOU COME UP WITH ALL THESE STORIES?

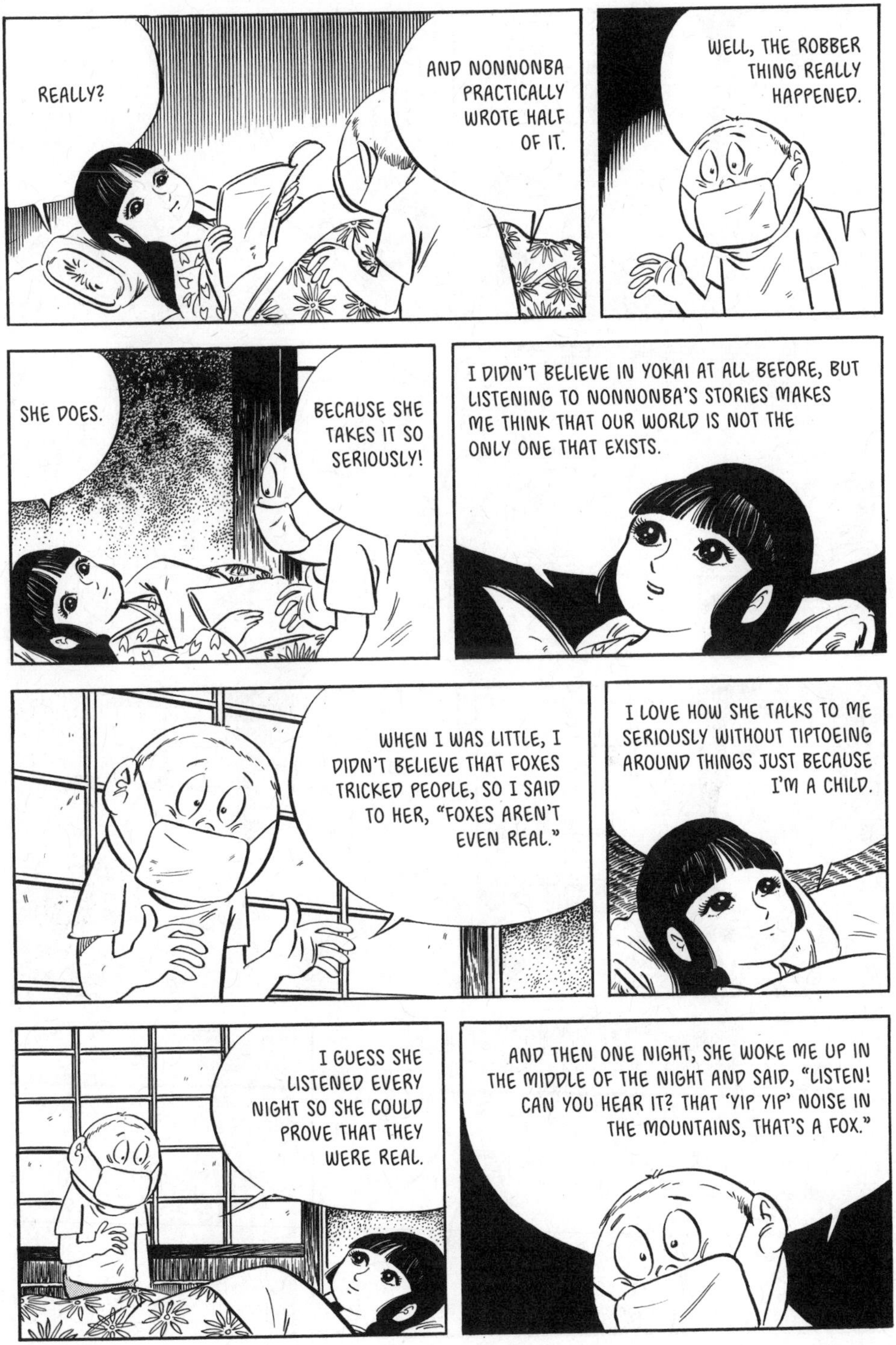
WELL, THE ROBBER THING REALLY HAPPENED.
AND NONNONBA PRACTICALLY WROTE HALF OF IT.
REALLY?
I DIDN'T BELIEVE IN YOKAI AT ALL BEFORE, BUT LISTENING TO NONNONBA'S STORIES MAKES ME THINK THAT OUR WORLD IS NOT THE ONLY ONE THAT EXISTS.
BECAUSE SHE TAKES IT SO SERIOUSLY!
SHE DOES.
I LOVE HOW SHE TALKS TO ME SERIOUSLY WITHOUT TIPTOEING AROUND THINGS JUST BECAUSE I'M A CHILD.
WHEN I WAS LITTLE, I DIDN'T BELIEVE THAT FOXES TRICKED PEOPLE, SO I SAID TO HER, "FOXES AREN'T EVEN REAL."
AND THEN ONE NIGHT, SHE WOKE ME UP IN THE MIDDLE OF THE NIGHT AND SAID, "LISTEN! CAN YOU HEAR IT? THAT 'YIP YIP' NOISE IN THE MOUNTAINS, THAT'S A FOX."
I GUESS SHE LISTENED EVERY NIGHT SO SHE COULD PROVE THAT THEY WERE REAL.

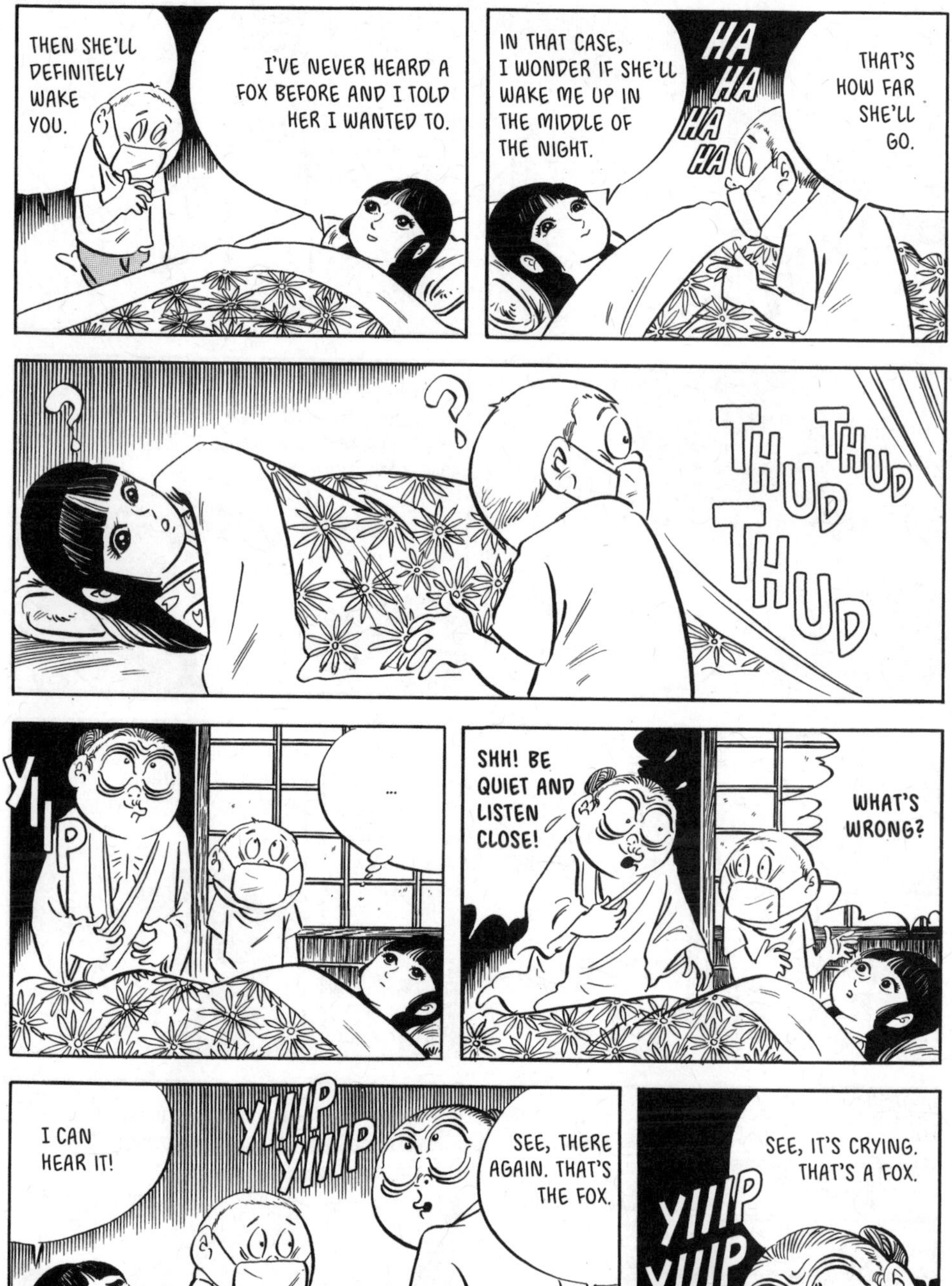
THAT'S HOW FAR SHE'LL GO.
HA HA HA HA
IN THAT CASE, I WONDER IF SHE'LL WAKE ME UP IN THE MIDDLE OF THE NIGHT.
I'VE NEVER HEARD A FOX BEFORE AND I TOLD HER I WANTED TO.
THEN SHE'LL DEFINITELY WAKE YOU.
THUD THUD
THUD
THUD
WHAT'S WRONG?
SHH! BE QUIET AND LISTEN CLOSE!
...
YIIP
SEE, IT'S CRYING. THAT'S A FOX.
YIIIP YIIIP
SEE, THERE AGAIN. THAT'S THE FOX.
YIIIP YIIIP
I CAN HEAR IT!

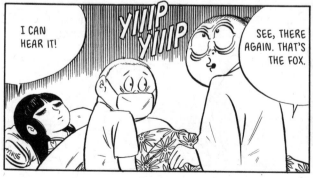

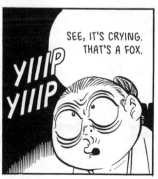

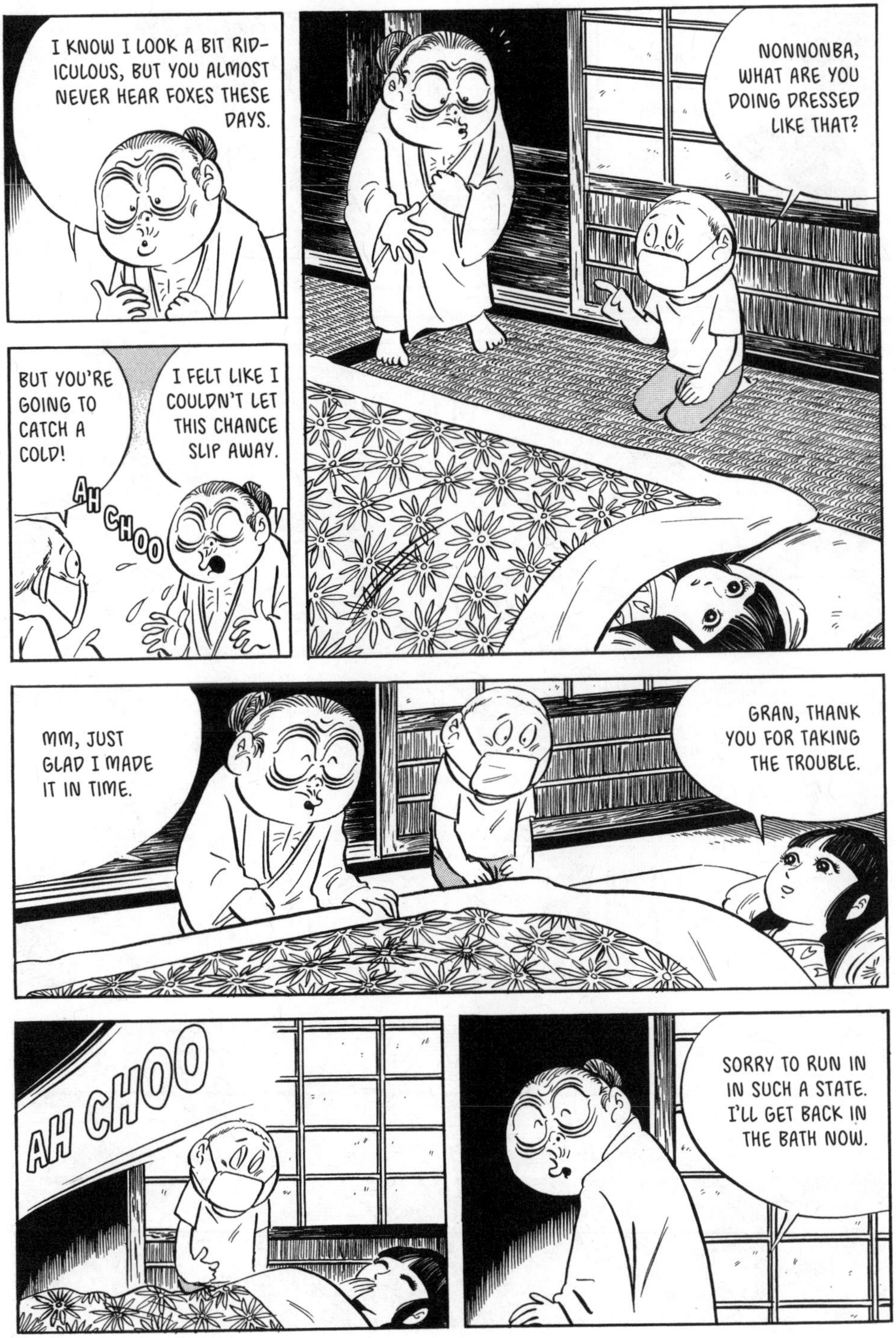
NONNONBA, WHAT ARE YOU DOING DRESSED LIKE THAT?
I KNOW I LOOK A BIT RIDICULOUS, BUT YOU ALMOST NEVER HEAR FOXES THESE DAYS.
I FELT LIKE I COULDN'T LET THIS CHANCE SLIP AWAY.
BUT YOU'RE GOING TO CATCH A COLD!
AH CHOO
GRAN, THANK YOU FOR TAKING THE TROUBLE.
MM, JUST GLAD I MADE IT IN TIME.
SORRY TO RUN IN IN SUCH A STATE. I'LL GET BACK IN THE BATH NOW.
AH CHOO

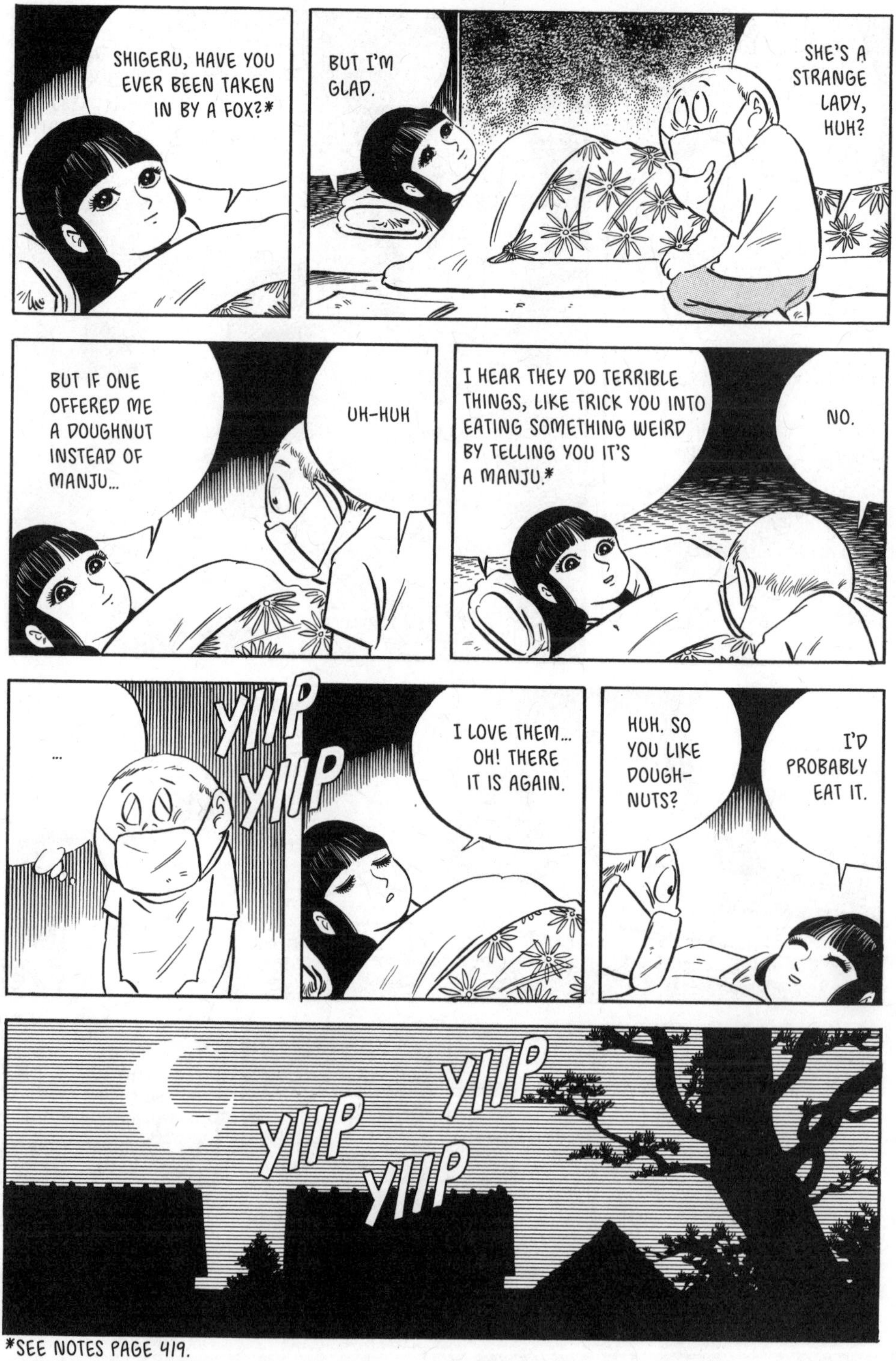
SHE'S A STRANGE LADY, HUH?
BUT I'M GLAD.
SHIGERU, HAVE YOU EVER BEEN TAKEN IN BY A FOX?*
NO.
I HEAR THEY DO TERRIBLE THINGS, LIKE TRICK YOU INTO EATING SOMETHING WEIRD BY TELLING YOU IT'S A MANJU.*
UH-HUH
BUT IF ONE OFFERED ME A DOUGHNUT INSTEAD OF MANJU...
I'D PROBABLY EAT IT.
HUH. SO YOU LIKE DOUGHNUTS?
I LOVE THEM... OH! THERE IT IS AGAIN.
YIIP
YIIP
...
YIIP
YIIP
YIIP
YIIP

*SEE NOTES PAGE 419.

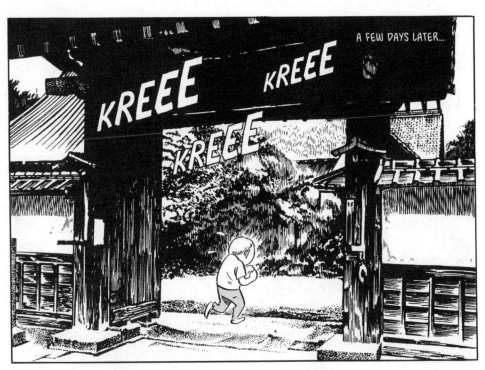

A FEW DAYS LATER...
KREEE
KREEE
KREEE
NONNONBA. I GOT THIS DOUGHNUT. CAN YOU GIVE IT TO CHIGUSA?
A DOUGH-NUT?
YOU DIDN'T KNOW, HUH? DOUGHNUTS ARE HER FAVORITE.
NOT SURE IF SHE'S IN ANY CONDITION TO EAT ONE NOW.
SHE'S LOST CONSCIOUS-NESS...
WHAT?!
DOES SHE HAVE ANOTHER FEVER?
YES, AND SHE WAS COUGHING UP BLOOD.

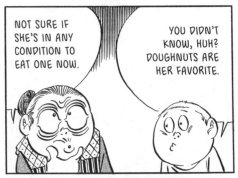

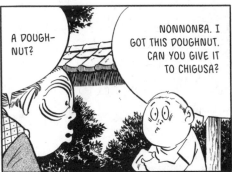

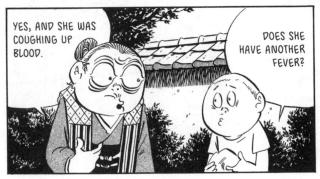

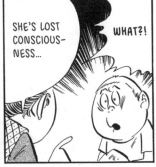

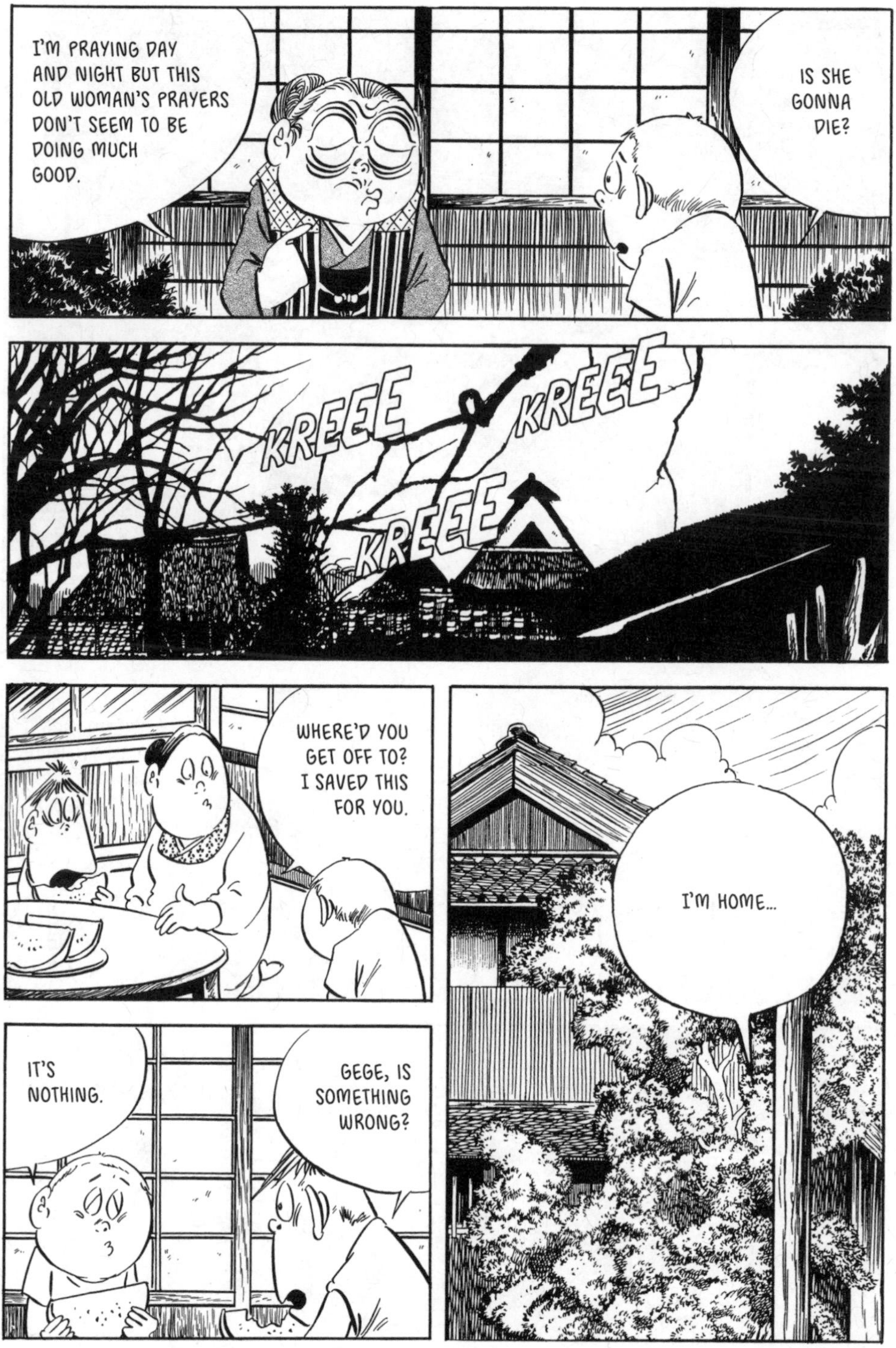
IS SHE GONNA DIE?
I'M PRAYING DAY AND NIGHT BUT THIS OLD WOMAN'S PRAYERS DON'T SEEM TO BE DOING MUCH GOOD.
KREEE
KREEE
KREEE
I'M HOME...
WHERE'D YOU GET OFF TO? I SAVED THIS FOR YOU.
GEGE, IS SOMETHING WRONG?
IT'S NOTHING.

WHY'RE YOU CLEANING AZUKI BEANS, MOM?

SLRP MNCH

SLRP MNCH MNCH MNCH

SLRP MNCH

I'M MAKING SEKIHAN* TO GIVE PEOPLE IN THE NEIGHBORHOOD TO CELEBRATE THE CINEMA'S BIG HIT.

I'M BUSY TOO!

BUSY!

IF YOU'VE GOT NOTHING TO DO, YOU CAN—

!?

BWAAN

PFF.

*RICE STEAMED WITH AZUKI BEANS. FOR MORE INFORMATION, SEE NOTES PAGE 419.

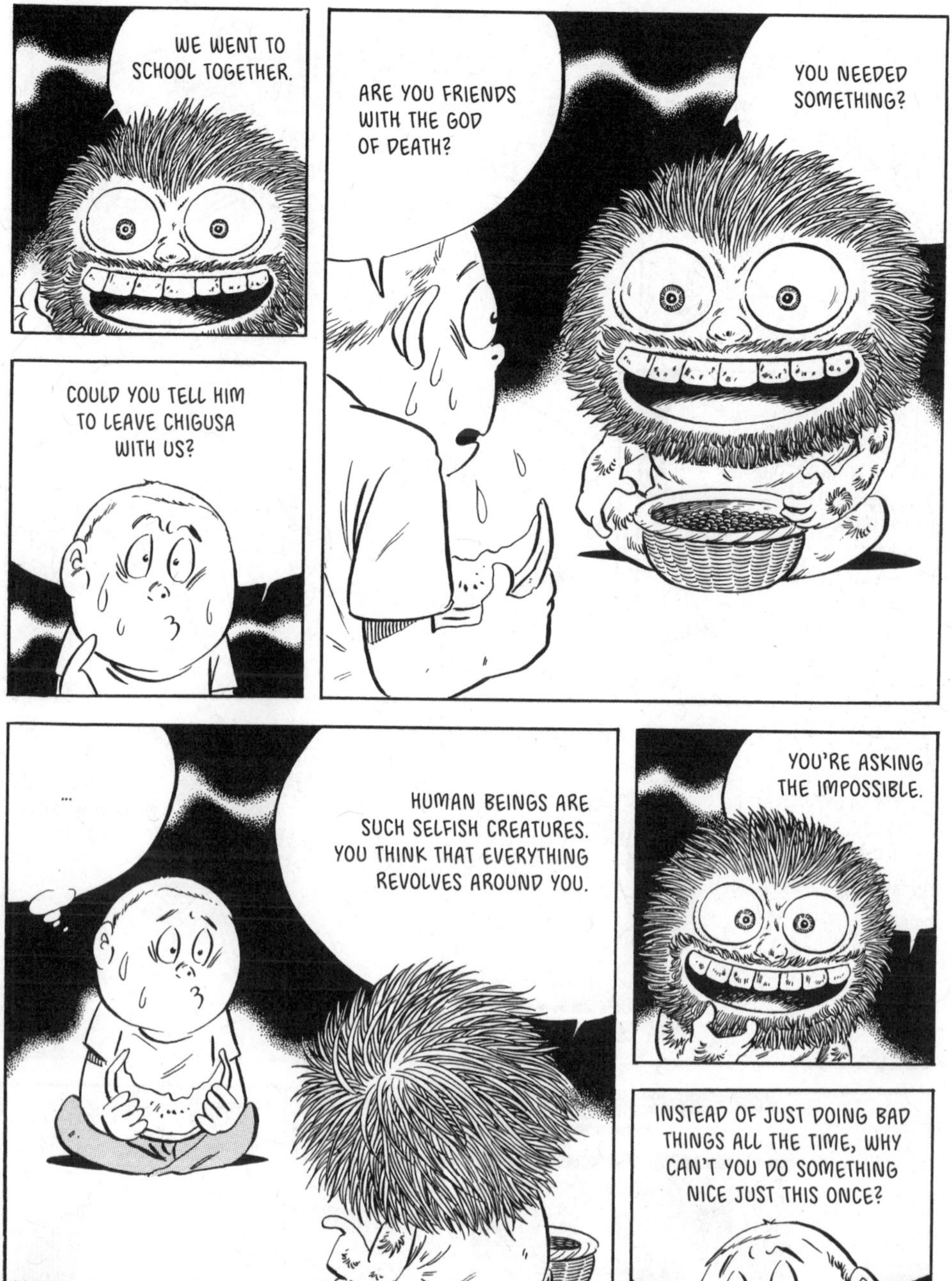
YOU NEEDED SOMETHING?
ARE YOU FRIENDS WITH THE GOD OF DEATH?
WE WENT TO SCHOOL TOGETHER.
COULD YOU TELL HIM TO LEAVE CHIGUSA WITH US?
YOU'RE ASKING THE IMPOSSIBLE.
INSTEAD OF JUST DOING BAD THINGS ALL THE TIME, WHY CAN'T YOU DO SOMETHING NICE JUST THIS ONCE?
HUMAN BEINGS ARE SUCH SELFISH CREATURES. YOU THINK THAT EVERYTHING REVOLVES AROUND YOU.
...

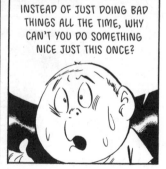

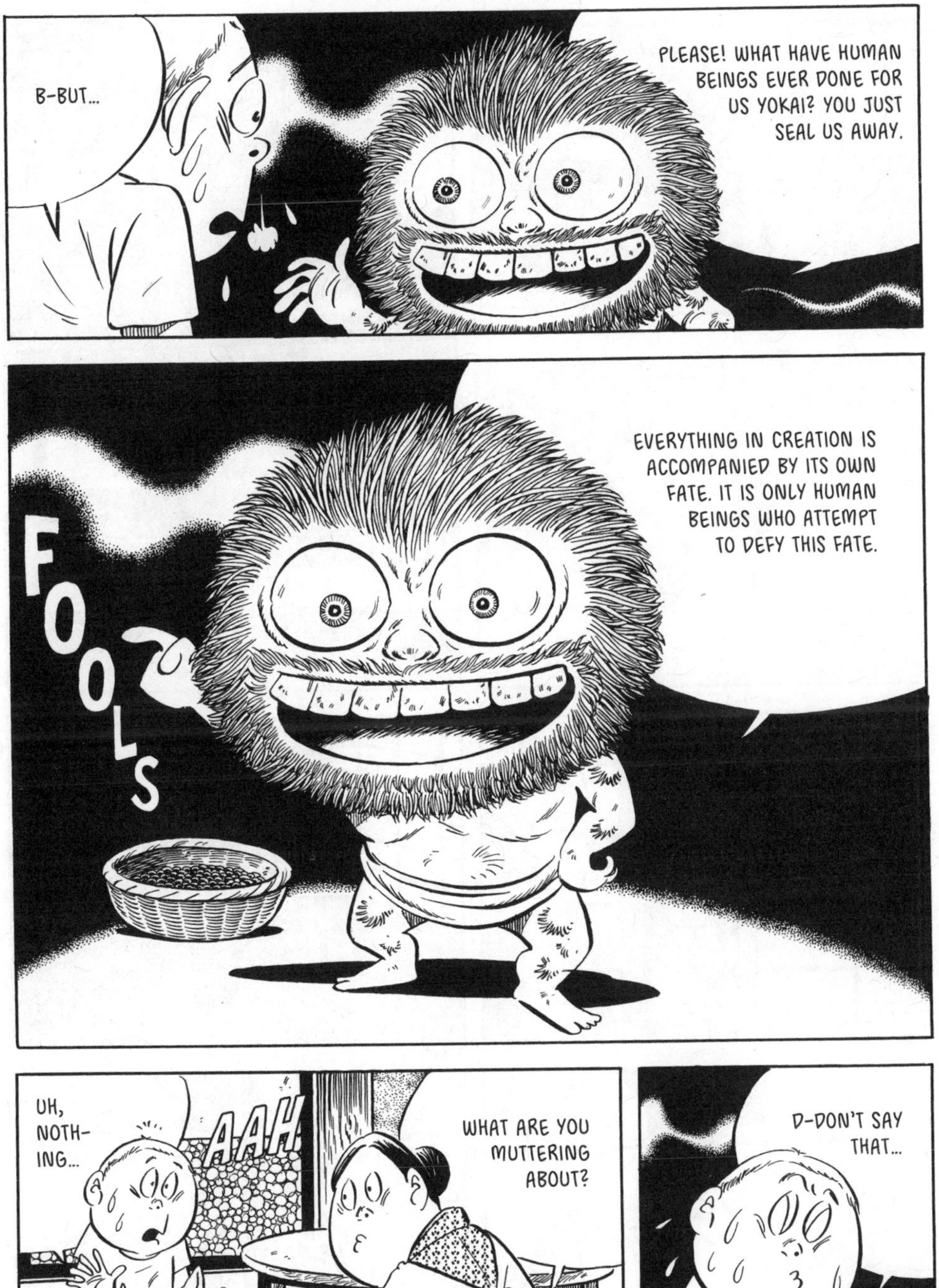
PLEASE! WHAT HAVE HUMAN BEINGS EVER DONE FOR US YOKAI? YOU JUST SEAL US AWAY.
B-BUT...
EVERYTHING IN CREATION IS ACCOMPANIED BY ITS OWN FATE. IT IS ONLY HUMAN BEINGS WHO ATTEMPT TO DEFY THIS FATE.
FOOLS
D-DON'T SAY THAT...
WHAT ARE YOU MUTTERING ABOUT?
AAH
UH, NOTHING...

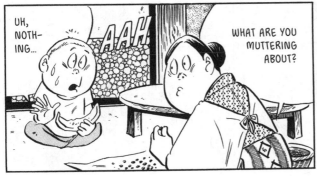

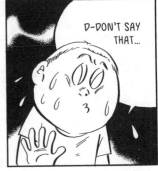

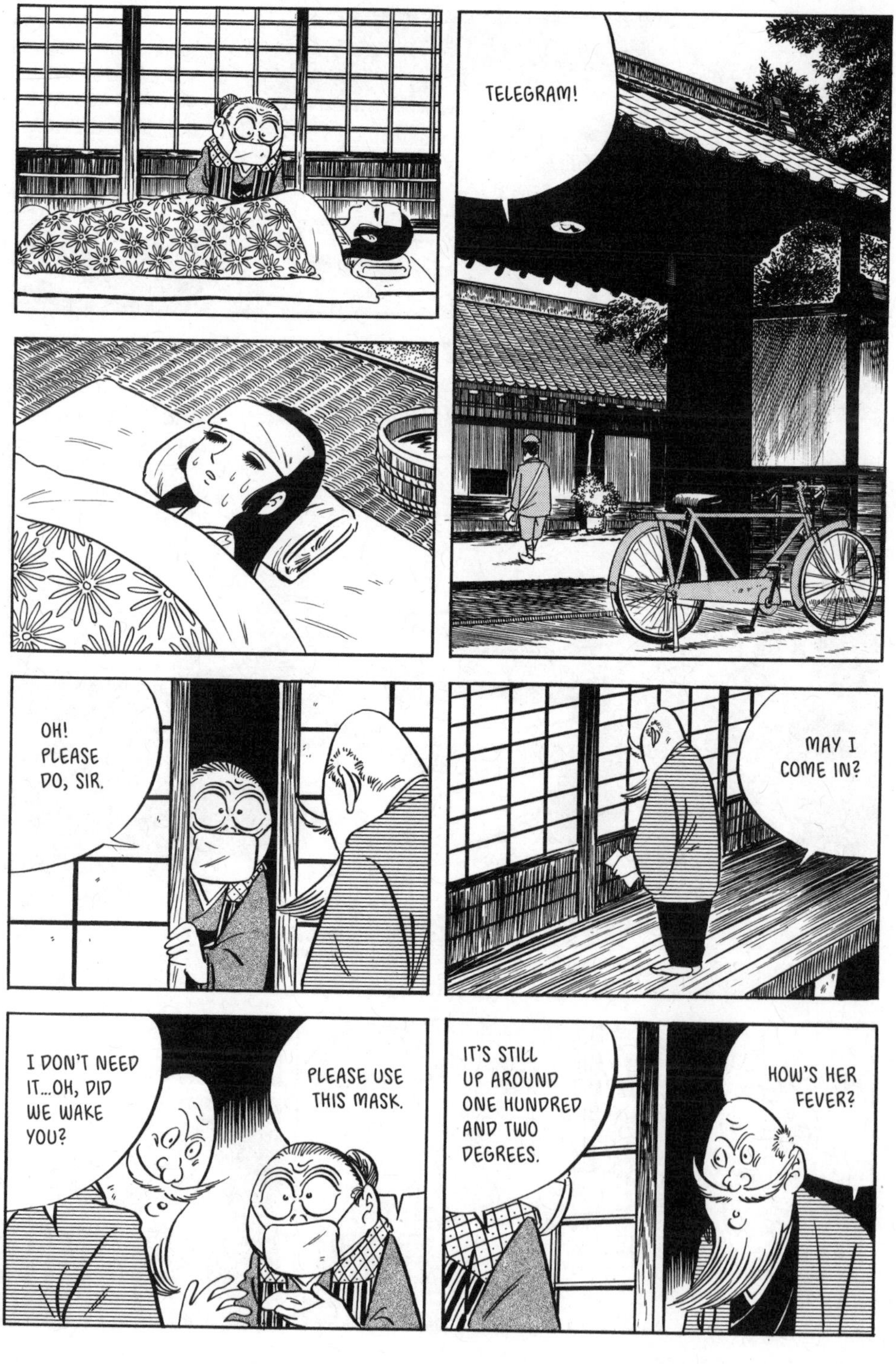
TELEGRAM!
MAY I COME IN?
OH! PLEASE DO, SIR.
HOW'S HER FEVER?
IT'S STILL UP AROUND ONE HUNDRED AND TWO DEGREES.
PLEASE USE THIS MASK.
I DON'T NEED IT...OH, DID WE WAKE YOU?

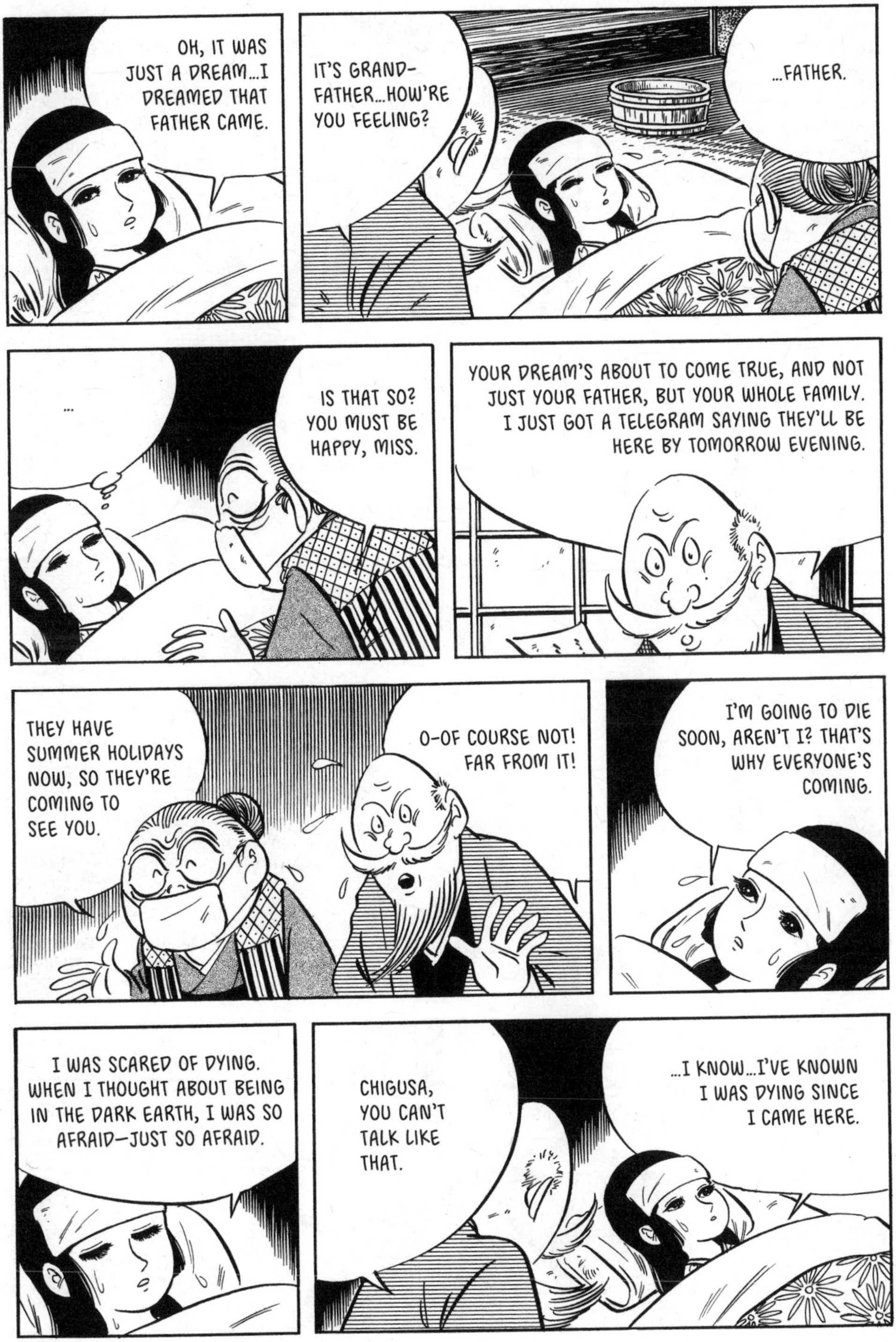
...FATHER.
IT'S GRAND-FATHER...HOW'RE YOU FEELING?
OH, IT WAS JUST A DREAM...I DREAMED THAT FATHER CAME.
YOUR DREAM'S ABOUT TO COME TRUE, AND NOT JUST YOUR FATHER, BUT YOUR WHOLE FAMILY. I JUST GOT A TELEGRAM SAYING THEY'LL BE HERE BY TOMORROW EVENING.
IS THAT SO? YOU MUST BE HAPPY, MISS.
...
I'M GOING TO DIE SOON, AREN'T I? THAT'S WHY EVERYONE'S COMING.
O-OF COURSE NOT! FAR FROM IT!
THEY HAVE SUMMER HOLIDAYS NOW, SO THEY'RE COMING TO SEE YOU.
...I KNOW...I'VE KNOWN I WAS DYING SINCE I CAME HERE.
CHIGUSA, YOU CAN'T TALK LIKE THAT.
I WAS SCARED OF DYING. WHEN I THOUGHT ABOUT BEING IN THE DARK EARTH, I WAS SO AFRAID—JUST SO AFRAID.

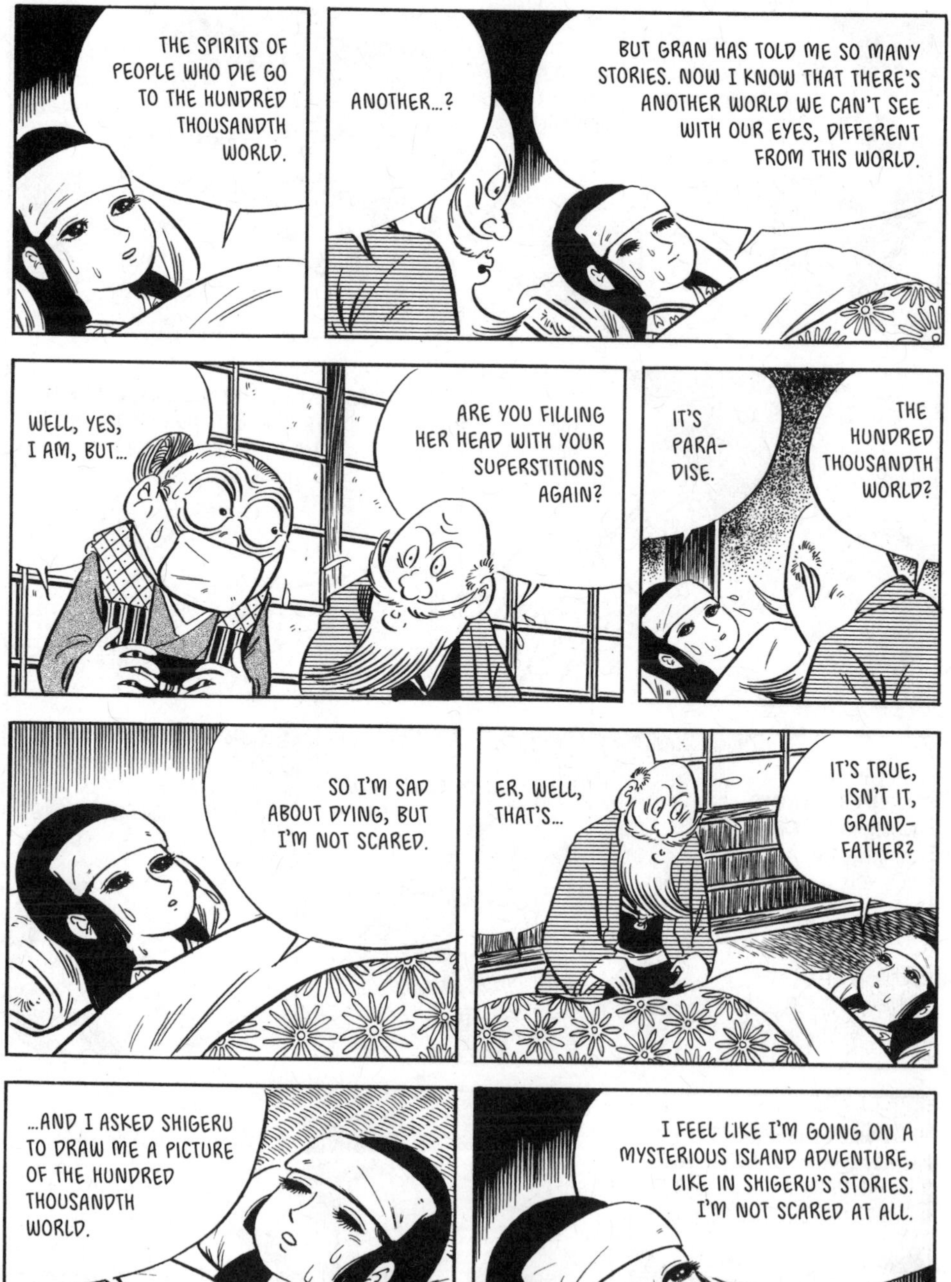
BUT GRAN HAS TOLD ME SO MANY STORIES. NOW I KNOW THAT THERE'S ANOTHER WORLD WE CAN'T SEE WITH OUR EYES, DIFFERENT FROM THIS WORLD.
ANOTHER...?
THE SPIRITS OF PEOPLE WHO DIE GO TO THE HUNDRED THOUSANDTH WORLD.
THE HUNDRED THOUSANDTH WORLD?
IT'S PARA-DISE.
ARE YOU FILLING HER HEAD WITH YOUR SUPERSTITIONS AGAIN?
WELL, YES, I AM, BUT...
IT'S TRUE, ISN'T IT, GRAND-FATHER?
ER, WELL, THAT'S...
SO I'M SAD ABOUT DYING, BUT I'M NOT SCARED.
I FEEL LIKE I'M GOING ON A MYSTERIOUS ISLAND ADVENTURE, LIKE IN SHIGERU'S STORIES. I'M NOT SCARED AT ALL.
...AND I ASKED SHIGERU TO DRAW ME A PICTURE OF THE HUNDRED THOUSANDTH WORLD.

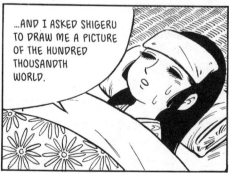

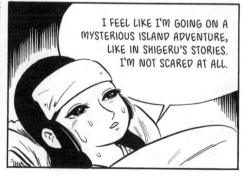

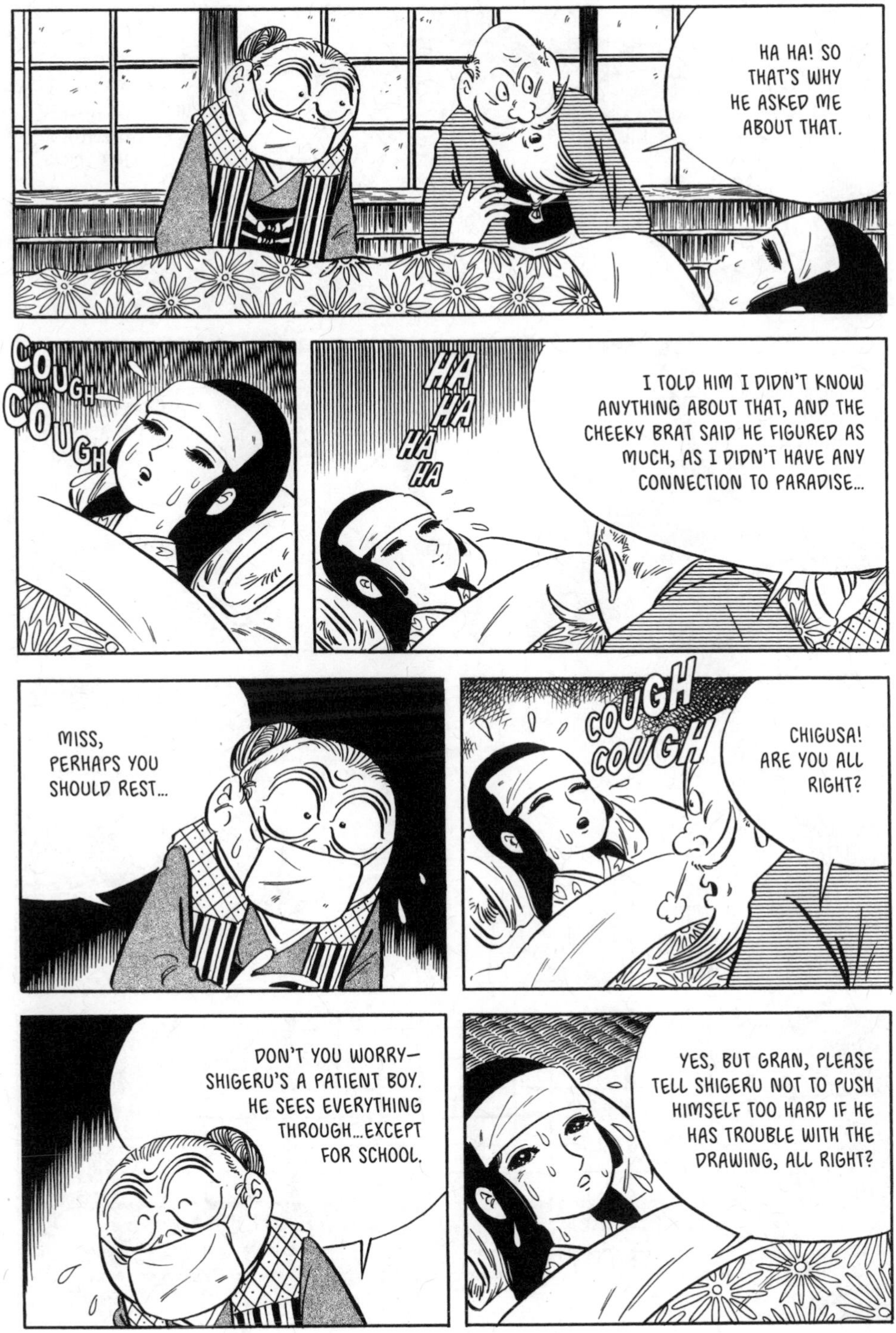

HA HA! SO THAT'S WHY HE ASKED ME ABOUT THAT.
HA HA HA HA
I TOLD HIM I DIDN'T KNOW ANYTHING ABOUT THAT, AND THE CHEEKY BRAT SAID HE FIGURED AS MUCH, AS I DIDN'T HAVE ANY CONNECTION TO PARADISE...
COUGH COUGH
COUGH COUGH
CHIGUSA! ARE YOU ALL RIGHT?
MISS, PERHAPS YOU SHOULD REST...
YES, BUT GRAN, PLEASE TELL SHIGERU NOT TO PUSH HIMSELF TOO HARD IF HE HAS TROUBLE WITH THE DRAWING, ALL RIGHT?
DON'T YOU WORRY—SHIGERU'S A PATIENT BOY. HE SEES EVERYTHING THROUGH...EXCEPT FOR SCHOOL.

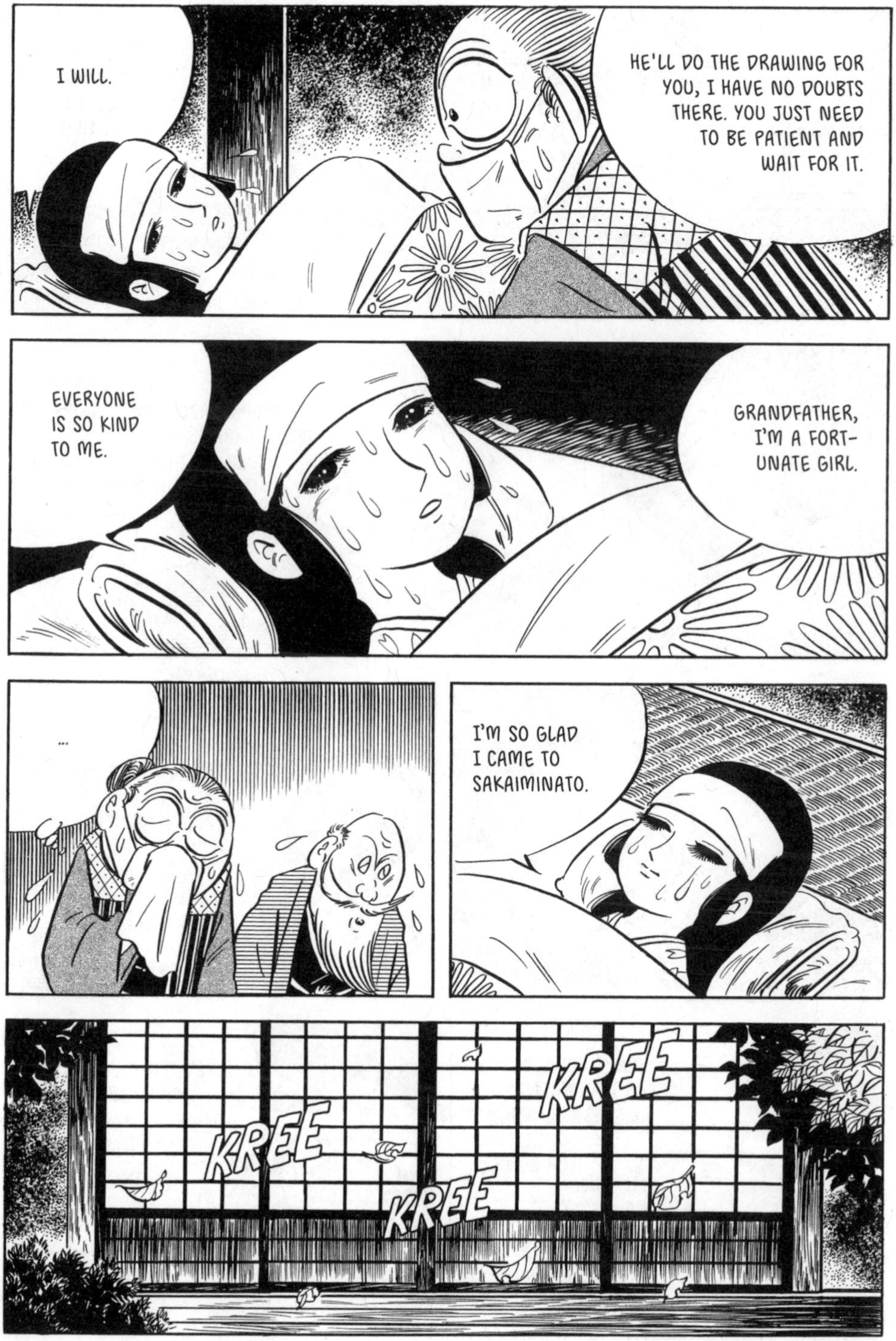
HE'LL DO THE DRAWING FOR YOU, I HAVE NO DOUBTS THERE. YOU JUST NEED TO BE PATIENT AND WAIT FOR IT.
I WILL.
GRANDFATHER, I'M A FORT-UNATE GIRL.
EVERYONE IS SO KIND TO ME.
I'M SO GLAD I CAME TO SAKAIMINATO.
...
KREE
KREE
KREE

THE PROJECTOR IS STOLEN

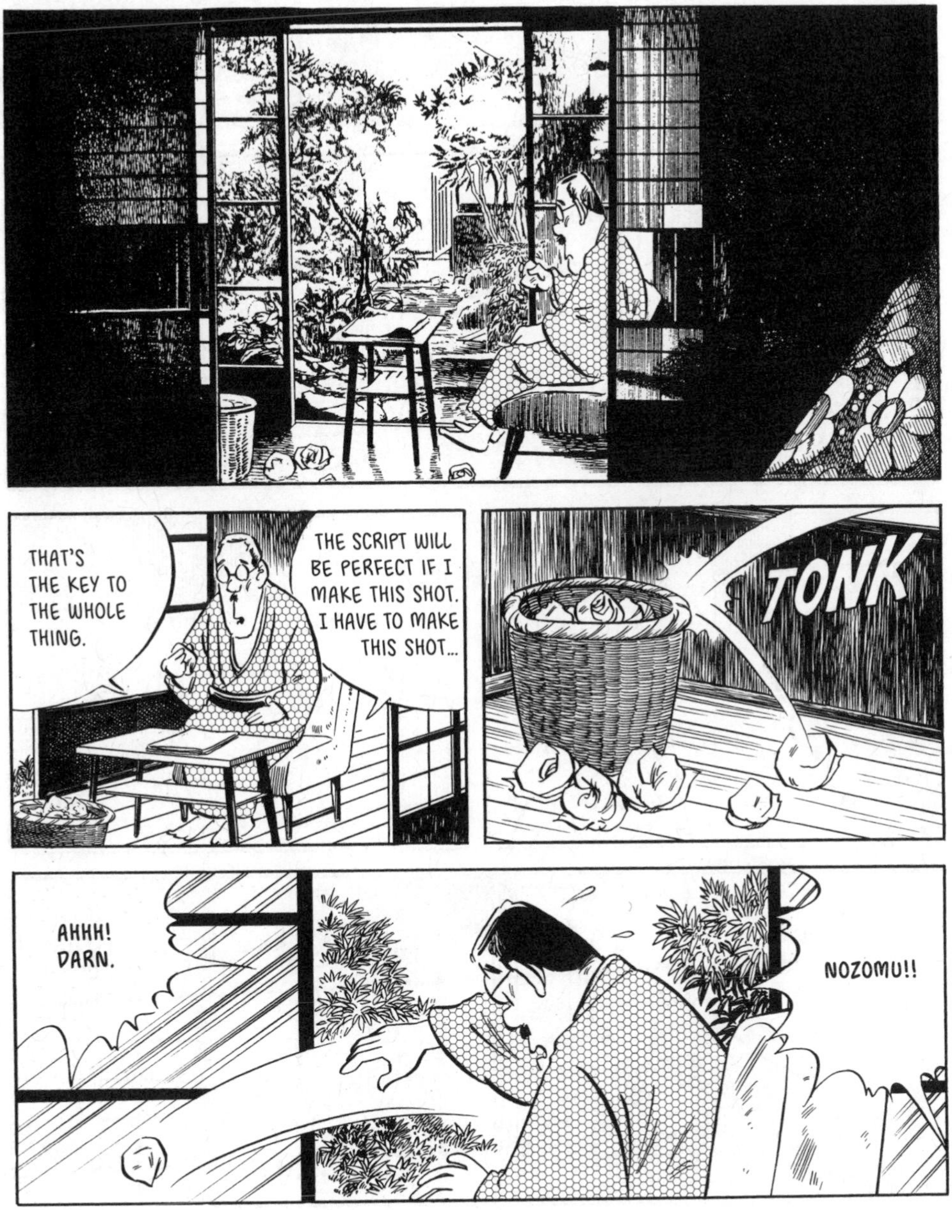
TONK
THE SCRIPT WILL BE PERFECT IF I MAKE THIS SHOT. I HAVE TO MAKE THIS SHOT...
THAT'S THE KEY TO THE WHOLE THING.
NOZOMU!!
AHHH! DARN.

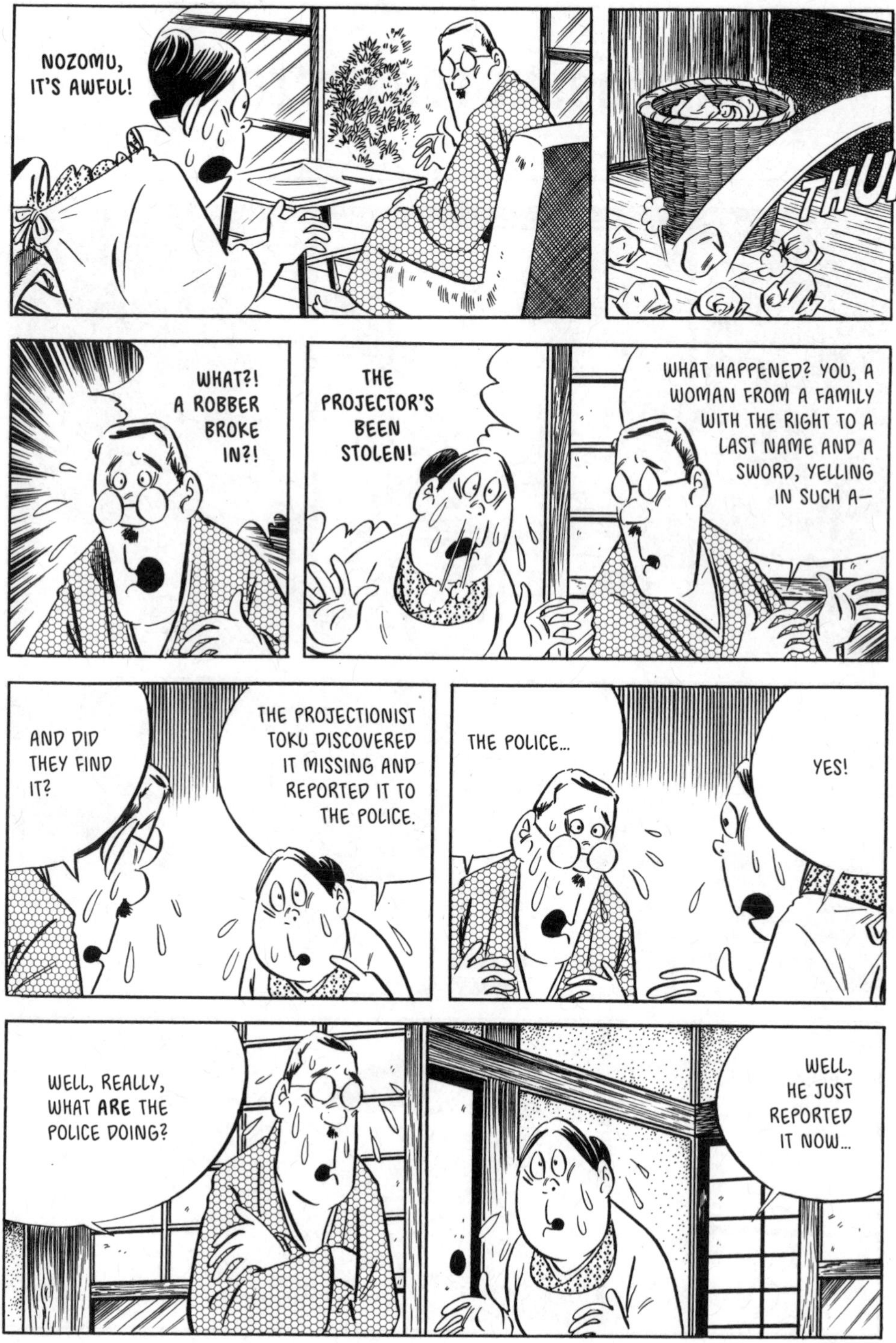
THUK
NOZOMU, IT'S AWFUL!
WHAT HAPPENED? YOU, A WOMAN FROM A FAMILY WITH THE RIGHT TO A LAST NAME AND A SWORD, YELLING IN SUCH A—
THE PROJECTOR'S BEEN STOLEN!
WHAT?! A ROBBER BROKE IN?!
THE POLICE...
YES!
THE PROJECTIONIST TOKU DISCOVERED IT MISSING AND REPORTED IT TO THE POLICE.
AND DID THEY FIND IT?
WELL, HE JUST REPORTED IT NOW...
WELL, REALLY, WHAT **ARE** THE POLICE DOING?

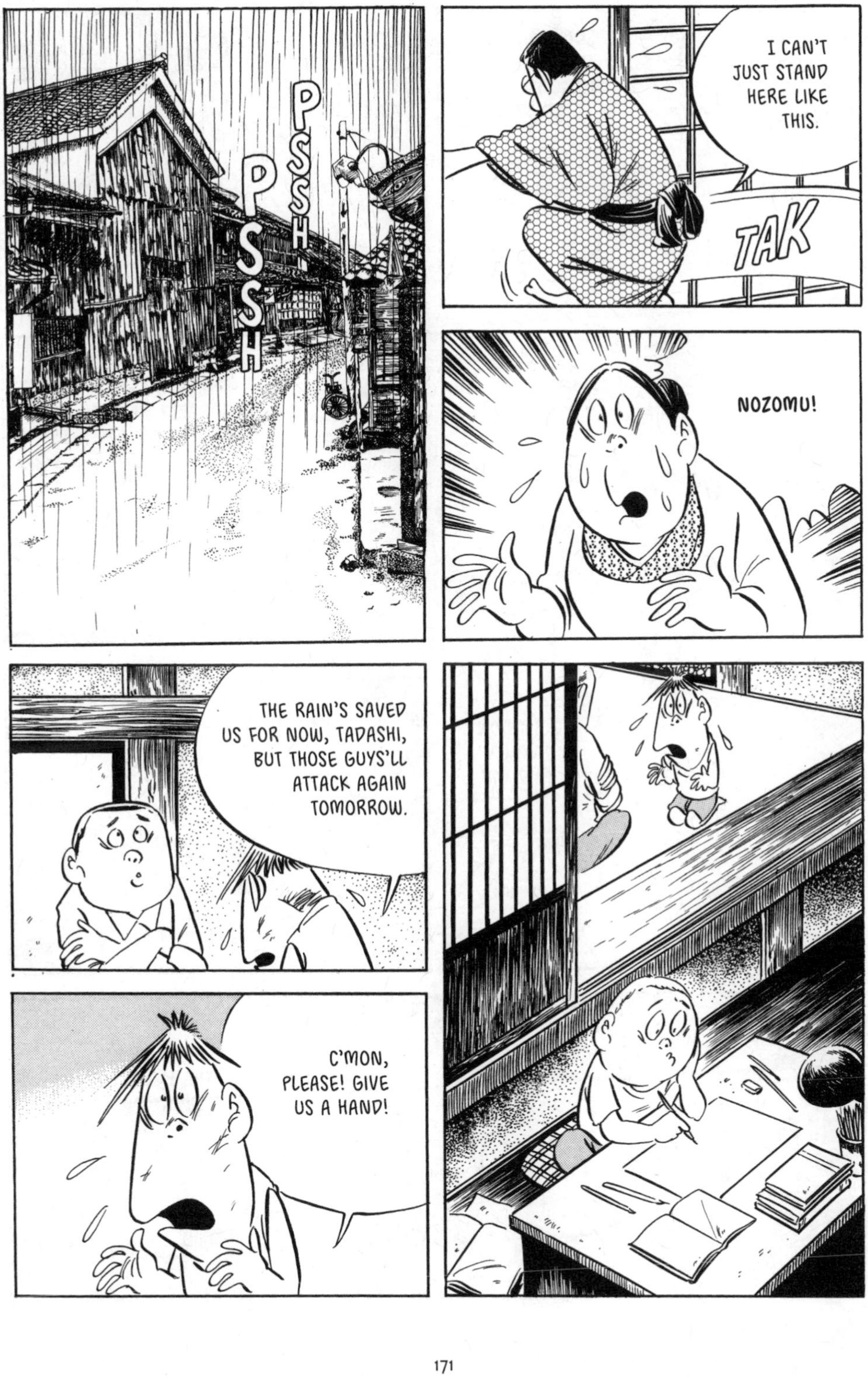
I CAN'T JUST STAND HERE LIKE THIS.
TAK
NOZOMU!
PSSH
PSSH
THE RAIN'S SAVED US FOR NOW, TADASHI, BUT THOSE GUYS'LL ATTACK AGAIN TOMORROW.
C'MON, PLEASE! GIVE US A HAND!

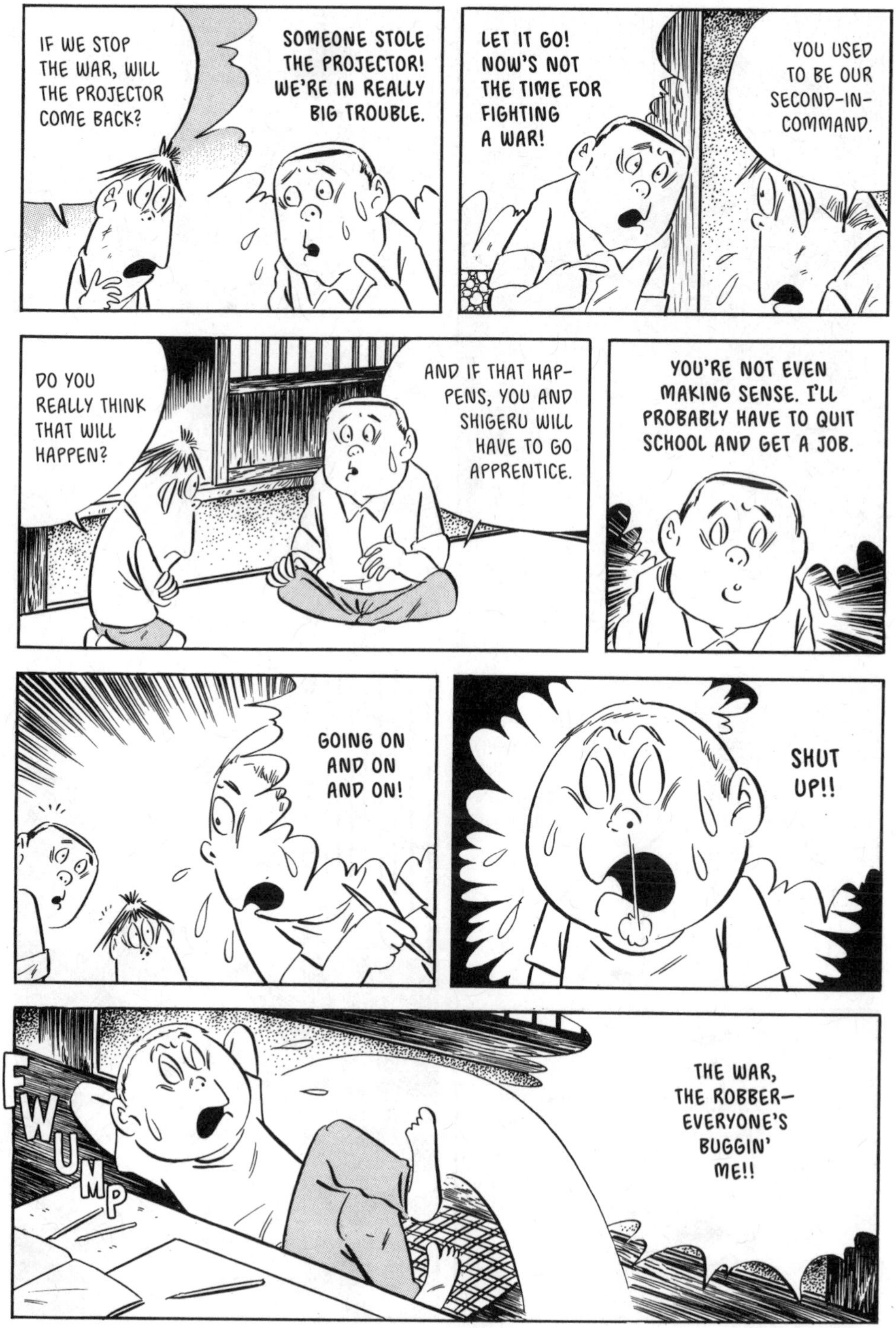
YOU USED TO BE OUR SECOND-IN-COMMAND.
LET IT GO! NOW'S NOT THE TIME FOR FIGHTING A WAR!
SOMEONE STOLE THE PROJECTOR! WE'RE IN REALLY BIG TROUBLE.
IF WE STOP THE WAR, WILL THE PROJECTOR COME BACK?
YOU'RE NOT EVEN MAKING SENSE. I'LL PROBABLY HAVE TO QUIT SCHOOL AND GET A JOB.
AND IF THAT HAP-PENS, YOU AND SHIGERU WILL HAVE TO GO APPRENTICE.
DO YOU REALLY THINK THAT WILL HAPPEN?
SHUT UP!!
GOING ON AND ON AND ON!
THE WAR, THE ROBBER—EVERYONE'S BUGGIN' ME!!
FWUMP

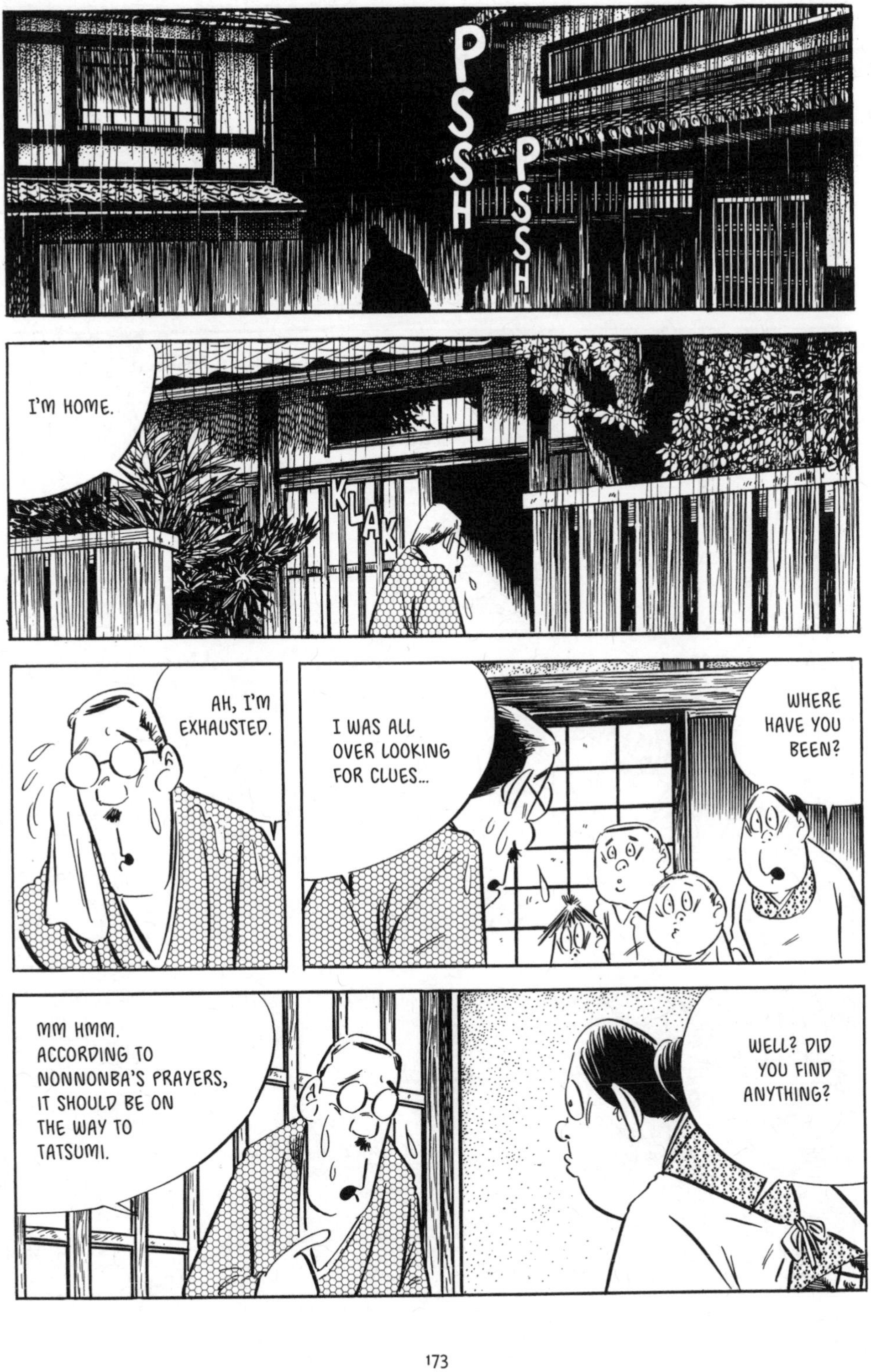
PSSH
PSSH
I'M HOME.
KLAK
WHERE HAVE YOU BEEN?
I WAS ALL OVER LOOKING FOR CLUES...
AH, I'M EXHAUSTED.
WELL? DID YOU FIND ANYTHING?
MM HMM. ACCORDING TO NONNONBA'S PRAYERS, IT SHOULD BE ON THE WAY TO TATSUMI.

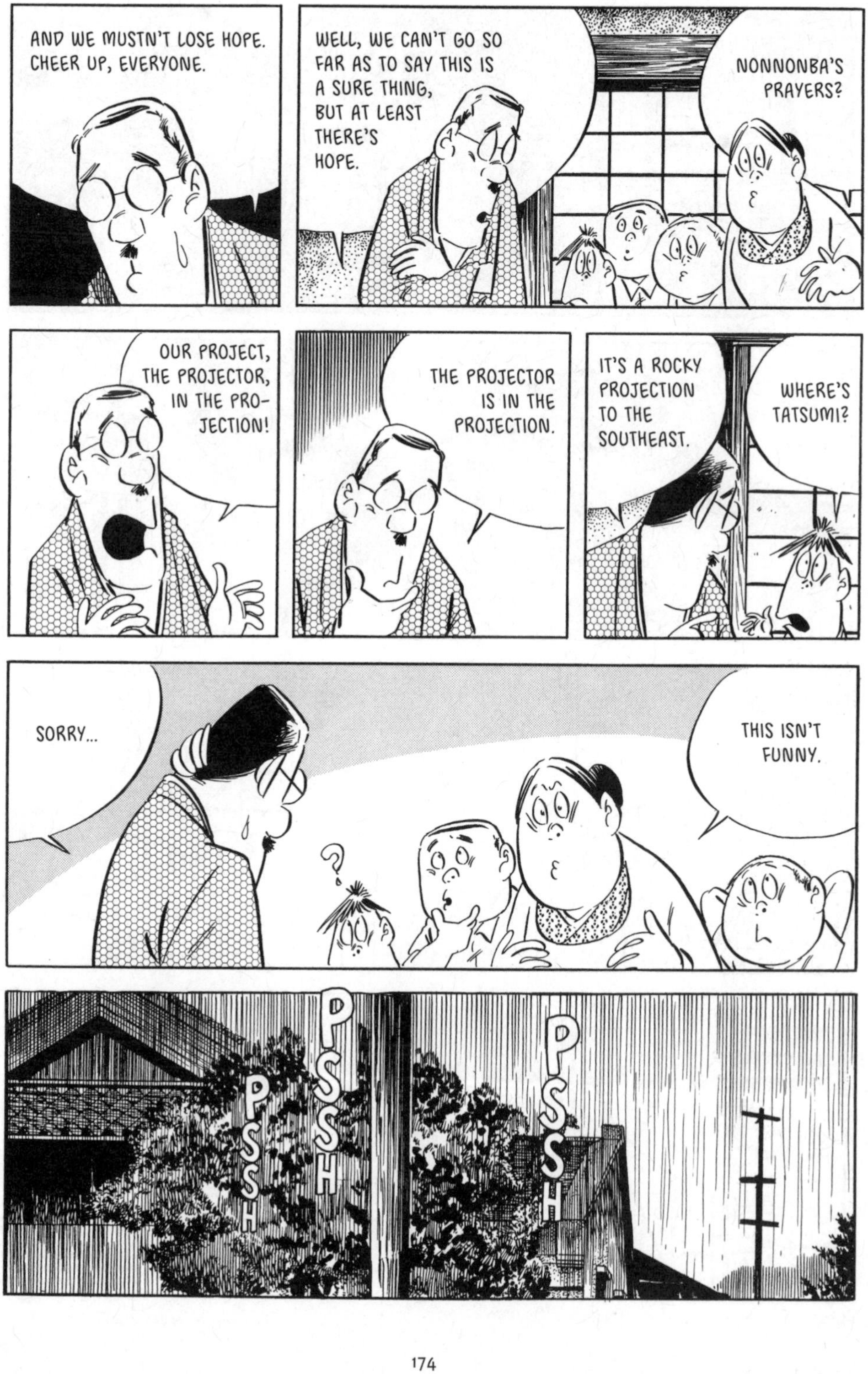
NONNONBA'S PRAYERS?
WELL, WE CAN'T GO SO FAR AS TO SAY THIS IS A SURE THING, BUT AT LEAST THERE'S HOPE.
AND WE MUSTN'T LOSE HOPE. CHEER UP, EVERYONE.
WHERE'S TATSUMI?
IT'S A ROCKY PROJECTION TO THE SOUTHEAST.
THE PROJECTOR IS IN THE PROJECTION.
OUR PROJECT, THE PROJECTOR, IN THE PRO-JECTION!
THIS ISN'T FUNNY.
SORRY...
PSSH
PSSH
PSSH

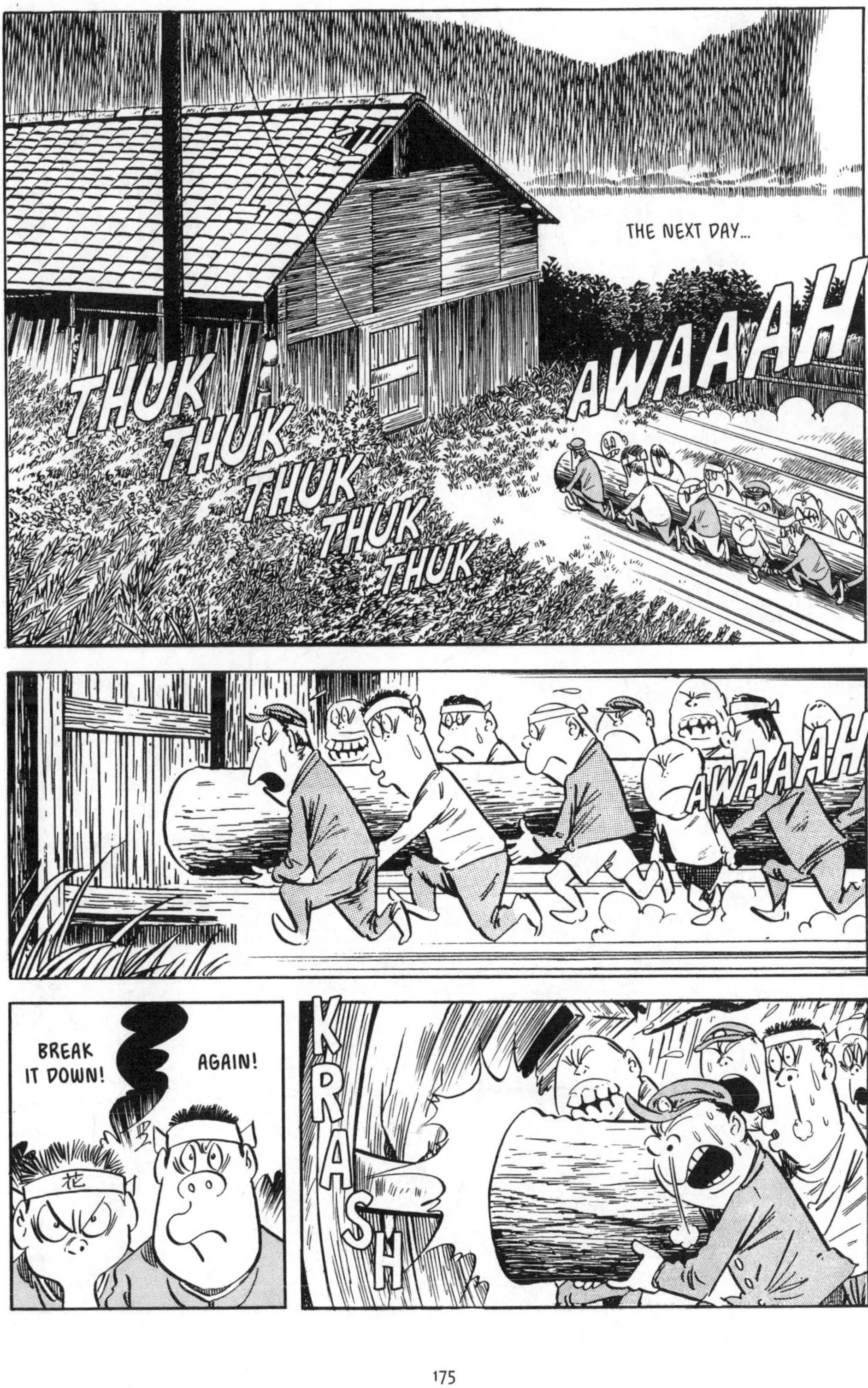
THE NEXT DAY...
AWAAAH
THUK
THUK
THUK
THUK
THUK
AWAAAH
KRASH
AGAIN!
BREAK IT DOWN!

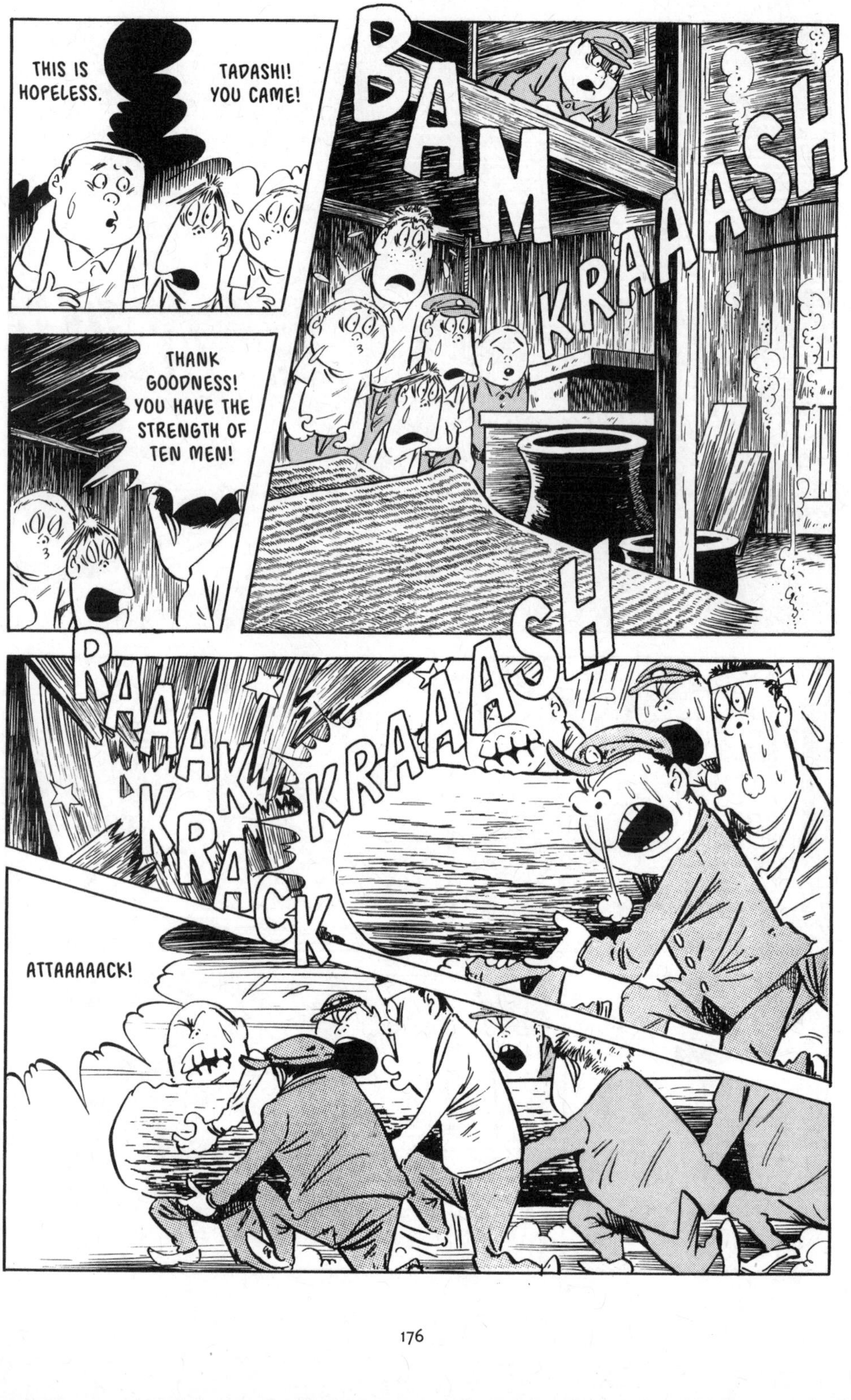
BAM
KRAAASH
TADASHI! YOU CAME!
THIS IS HOPELESS.
THANK GOODNESS! YOU HAVE THE STRENGTH OF TEN MEN!
KRAAAASH
RAAAK
KRACK
ATTAAAAACK!

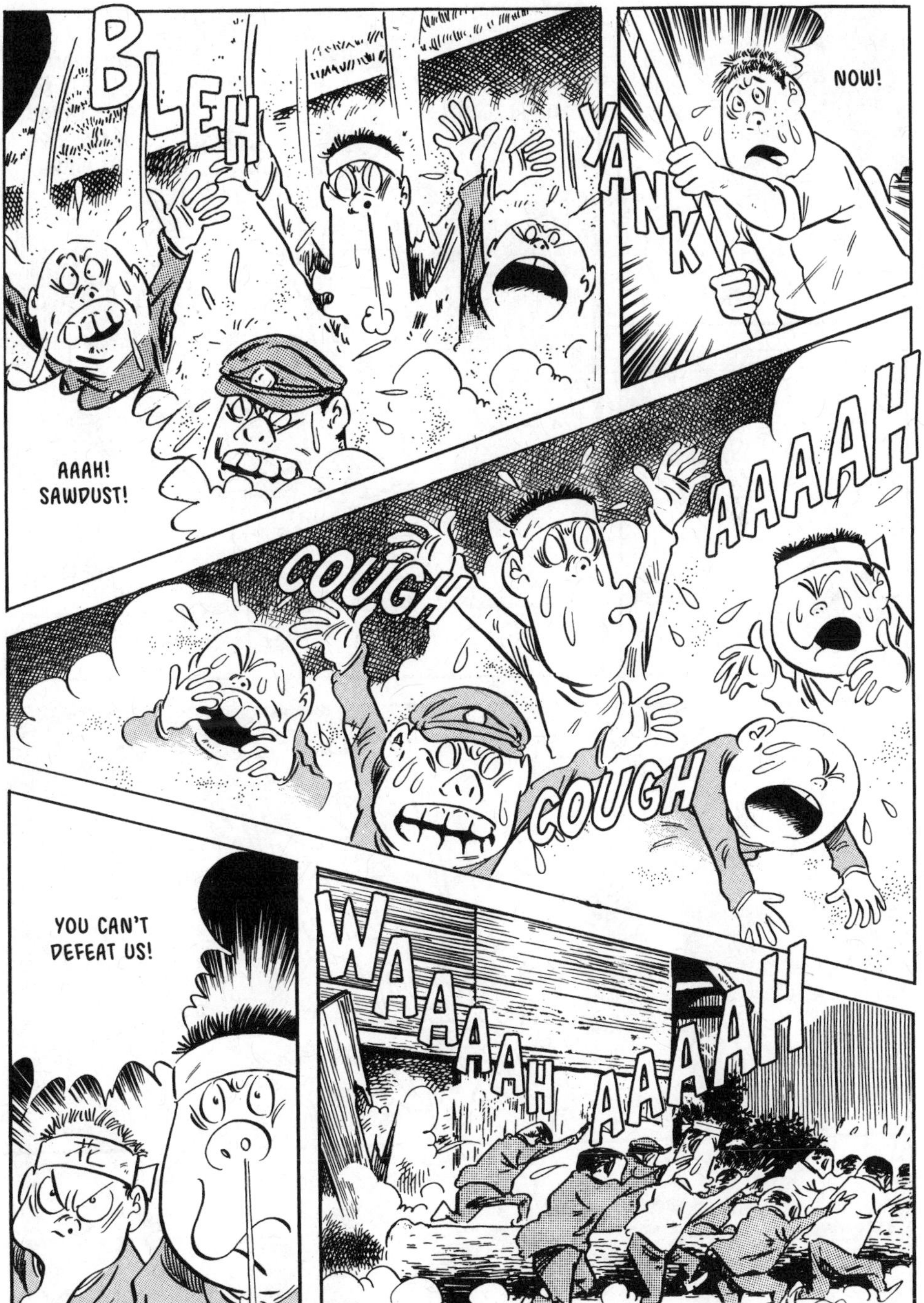
NOW!
YANK
BLEH
AAAH! SAWDUST!
AAAAAH
COUGH
COUGH
WAAAAH
AAAAH
YOU CAN'T DEFEAT US!

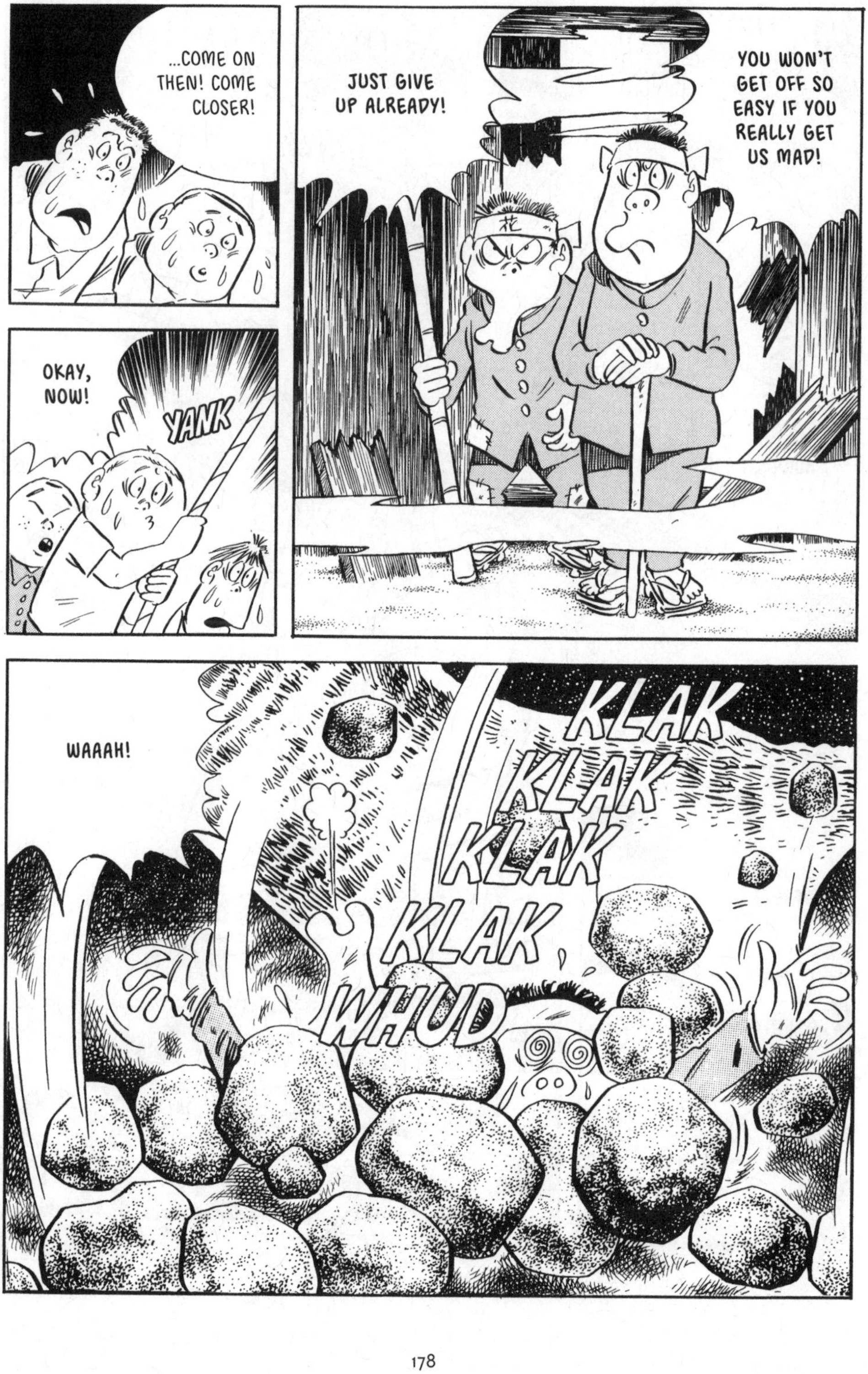
YOU WON'T GET OFF SO EASY IF YOU REALLY GET US MAD!
JUST GIVE UP ALREADY!
...COME ON THEN! COME CLOSER!
OKAY, NOW!
YANK
WAAAH!
KLAK
KLAK
KLAK
KLAK
WHUD

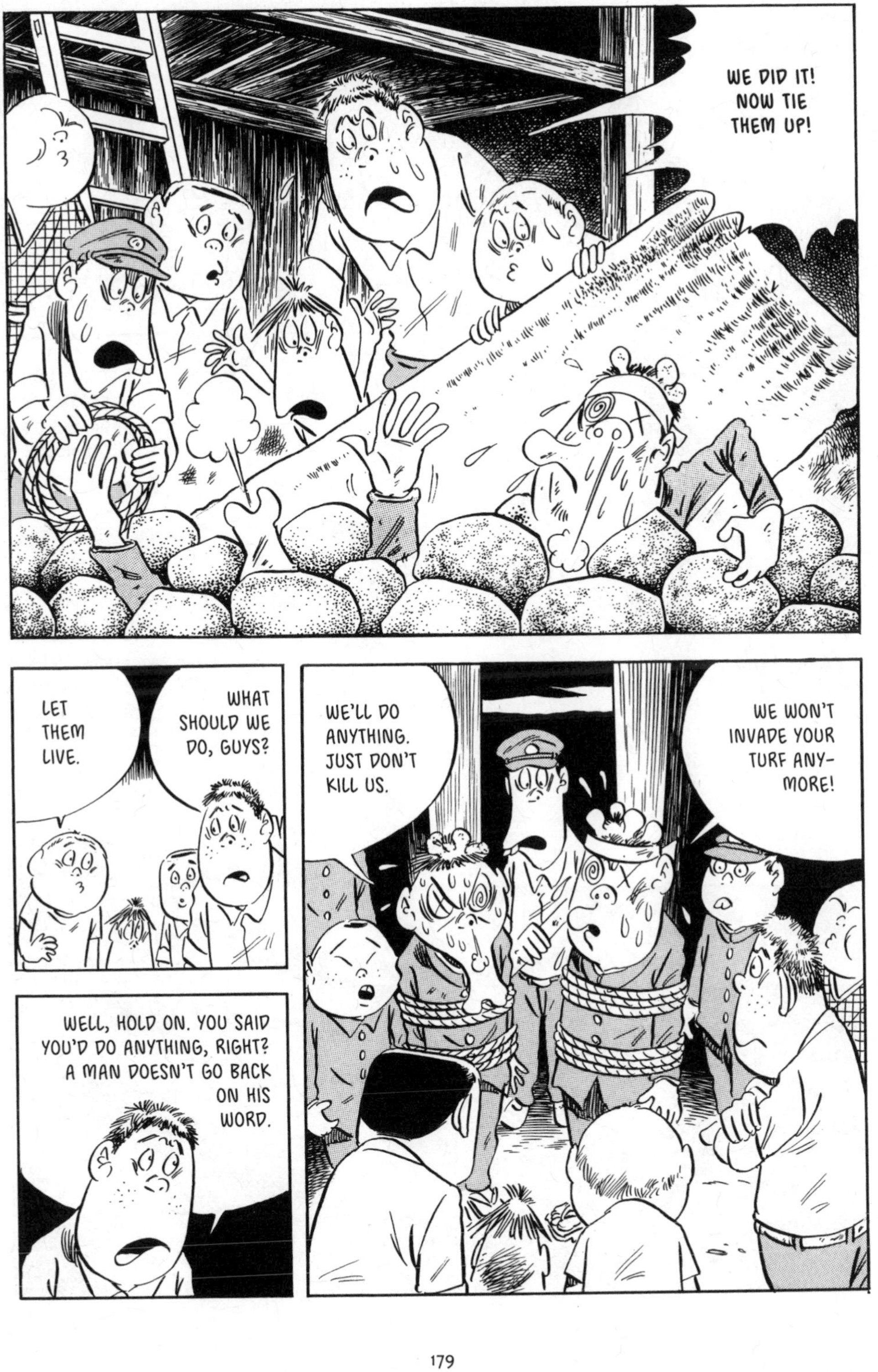
WE DID IT! NOW TIE THEM UP!
WE WON'T INVADE YOUR TURF ANY-MORE!
WE'LL DO ANYTHING. JUST DON'T KILL US.
WHAT SHOULD WE DO, GUYS?
LET THEM LIVE.
WELL, HOLD ON. YOU SAID YOU'D DO ANYTHING, RIGHT? A MAN DOESN'T GO BACK ON HIS WORD.

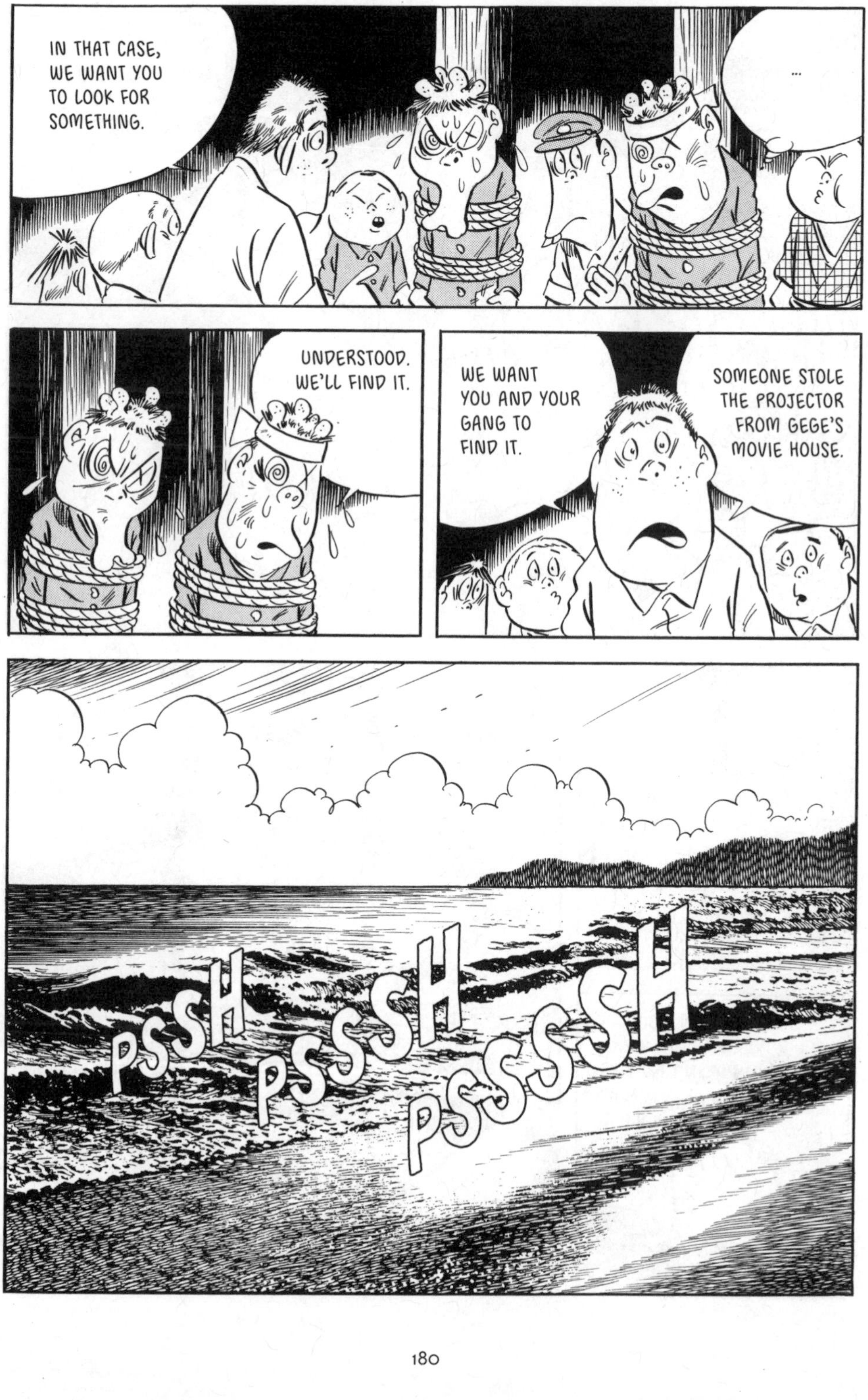
...
IN THAT CASE, WE WANT YOU TO LOOK FOR SOMETHING.
SOMEONE STOLE THE PROJECTOR FROM GEGE'S MOVIE HOUSE.
WE WANT YOU AND YOUR GANG TO FIND IT.
UNDERSTOOD. WE'LL FIND IT.
PSSH
PSSSH
PSSSSH

A HUNDRED THOUSAND WORLDS

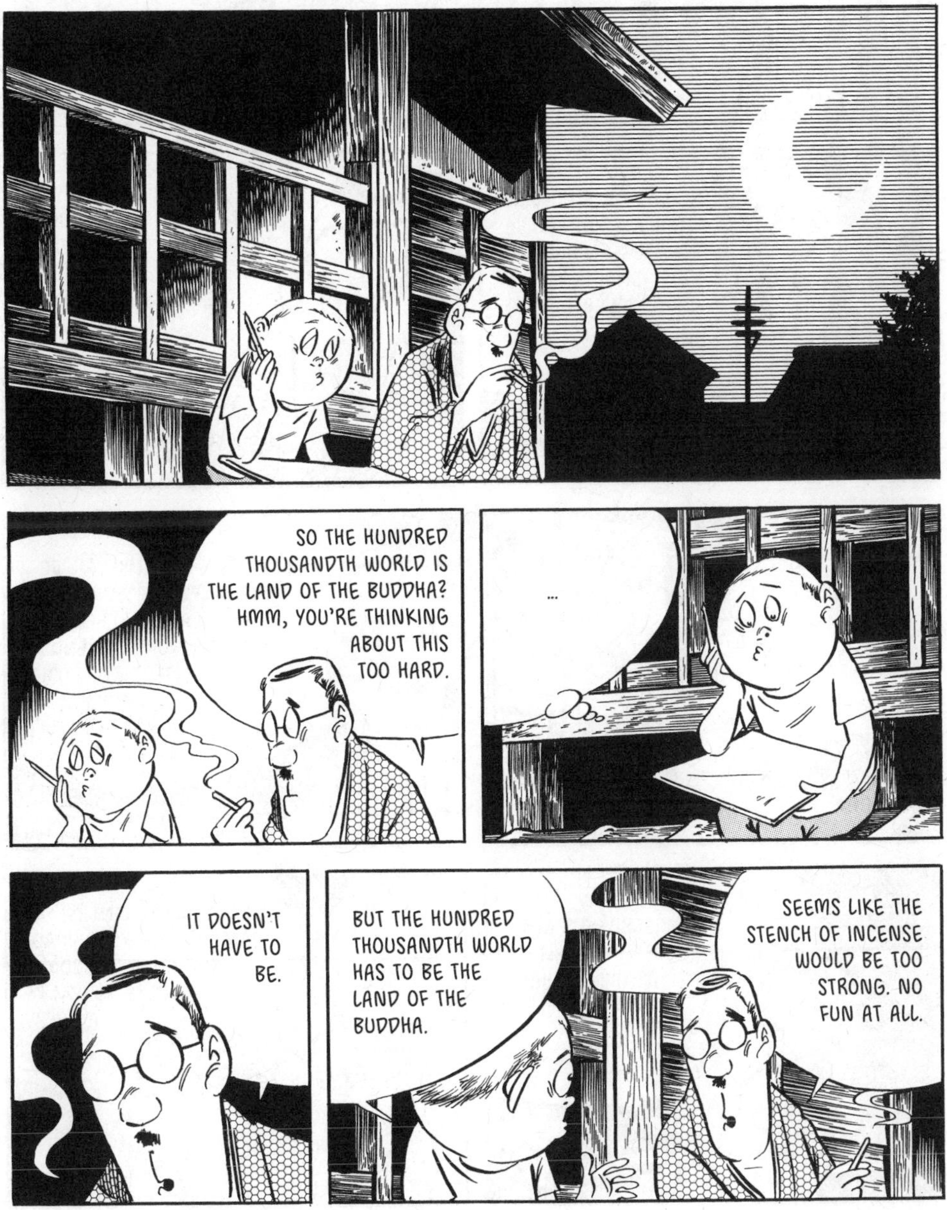
...
SO THE HUNDRED THOUSANDTH WORLD IS THE LAND OF THE BUDDHA? HMM, YOU'RE THINKING ABOUT THIS TOO HARD.
SEEMS LIKE THE STENCH OF INCENSE WOULD BE TOO STRONG. NO FUN AT ALL.
BUT THE HUNDRED THOUSANDTH WORLD HAS TO BE THE LAND OF THE BUDDHA.
IT DOESN'T HAVE TO BE.

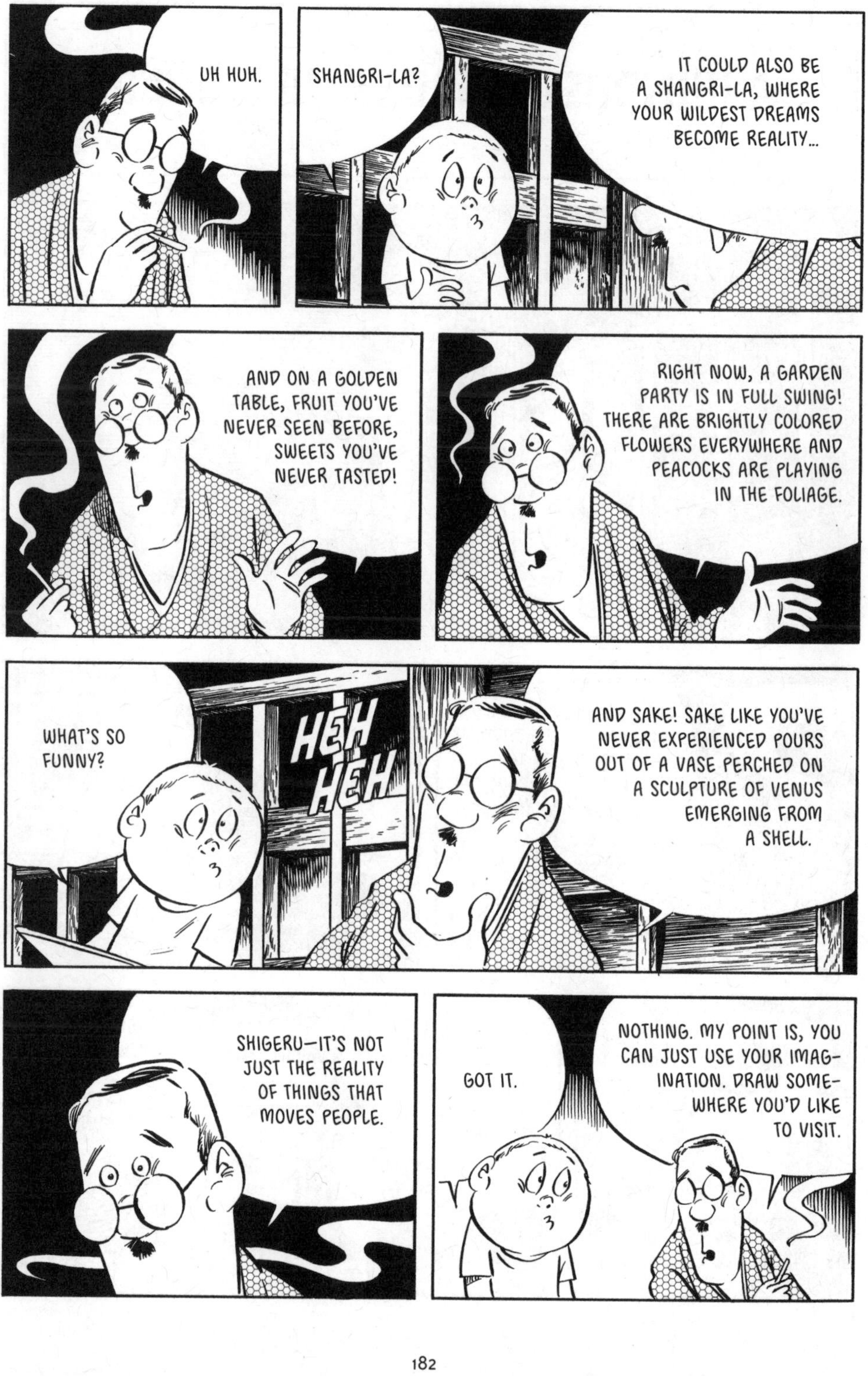
IT COULD ALSO BE A SHANGRI-LA, WHERE YOUR WILDEST DREAMS BECOME REALITY...
SHANGRI-LA?
UH HUH.
RIGHT NOW, A GARDEN PARTY IS IN FULL SWING! THERE ARE BRIGHTLY COLORED FLOWERS EVERYWHERE AND PEACOCKS ARE PLAYING IN THE FOLIAGE.
AND ON A GOLDEN TABLE, FRUIT YOU'VE NEVER SEEN BEFORE, SWEETS YOU'VE NEVER TASTED!
AND SAKE! SAKE LIKE YOU'VE NEVER EXPERIENCED POURS OUT OF A VASE PERCHED ON A SCULPTURE OF VENUS EMERGING FROM A SHELL.
HEH HEH
WHAT'S SO FUNNY?
NOTHING. MY POINT IS, YOU CAN JUST USE YOUR IMAG-INATION. DRAW SOME-WHERE YOU'D LIKE TO VISIT.
GOT IT.
SHIGERU—IT'S NOT JUST THE REALITY OF THINGS THAT MOVES PEOPLE.

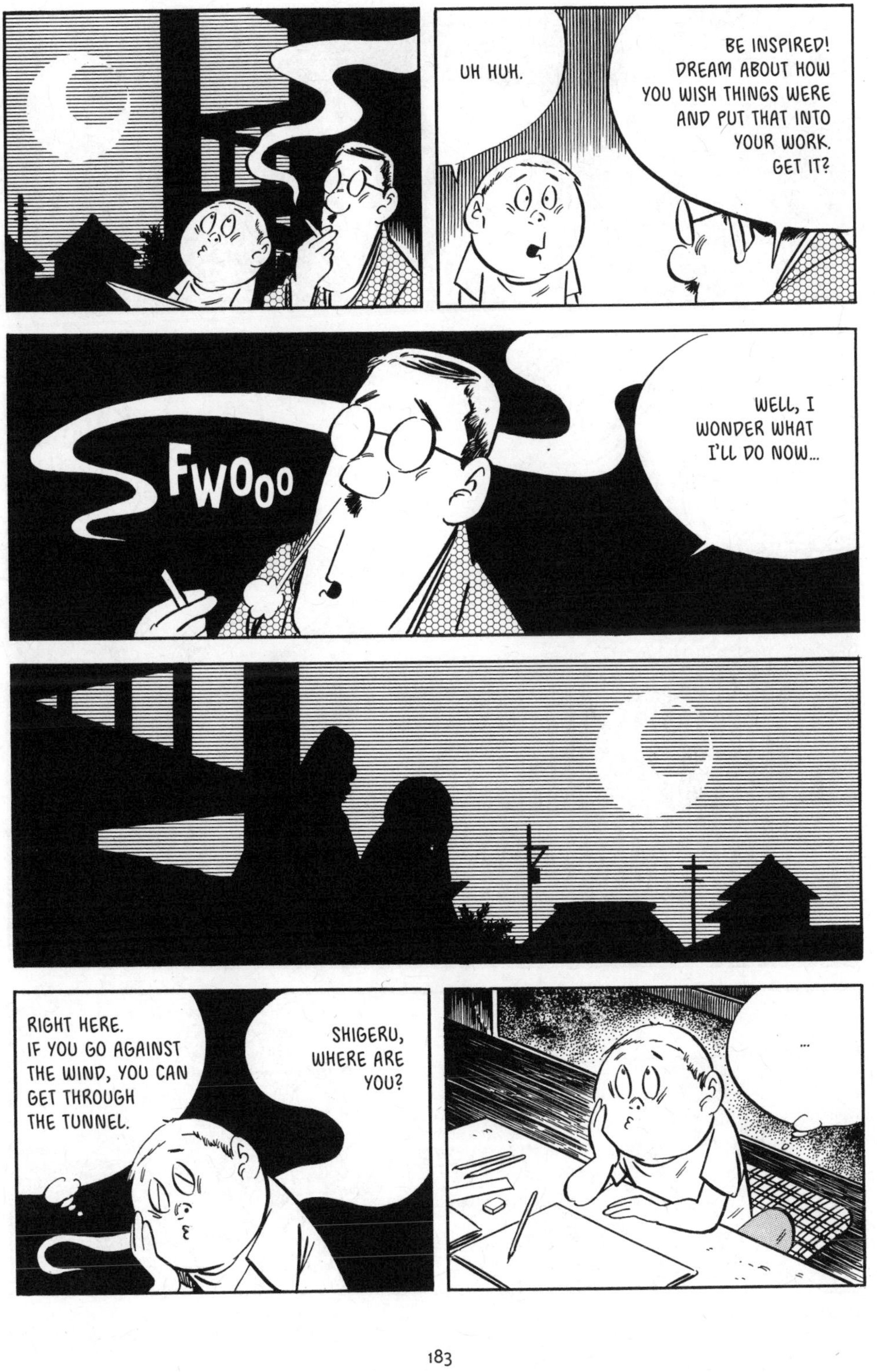
BE INSPIRED! DREAM ABOUT HOW YOU WISH THINGS WERE AND PUT THAT INTO YOUR WORK. GET IT?
UH HUH.
WELL, I WONDER WHAT I'LL DO NOW...
FWOOO
...
SHIGERU, WHERE ARE YOU?
RIGHT HERE. IF YOU GO AGAINST THE WIND, YOU CAN GET THROUGH THE TUNNEL.

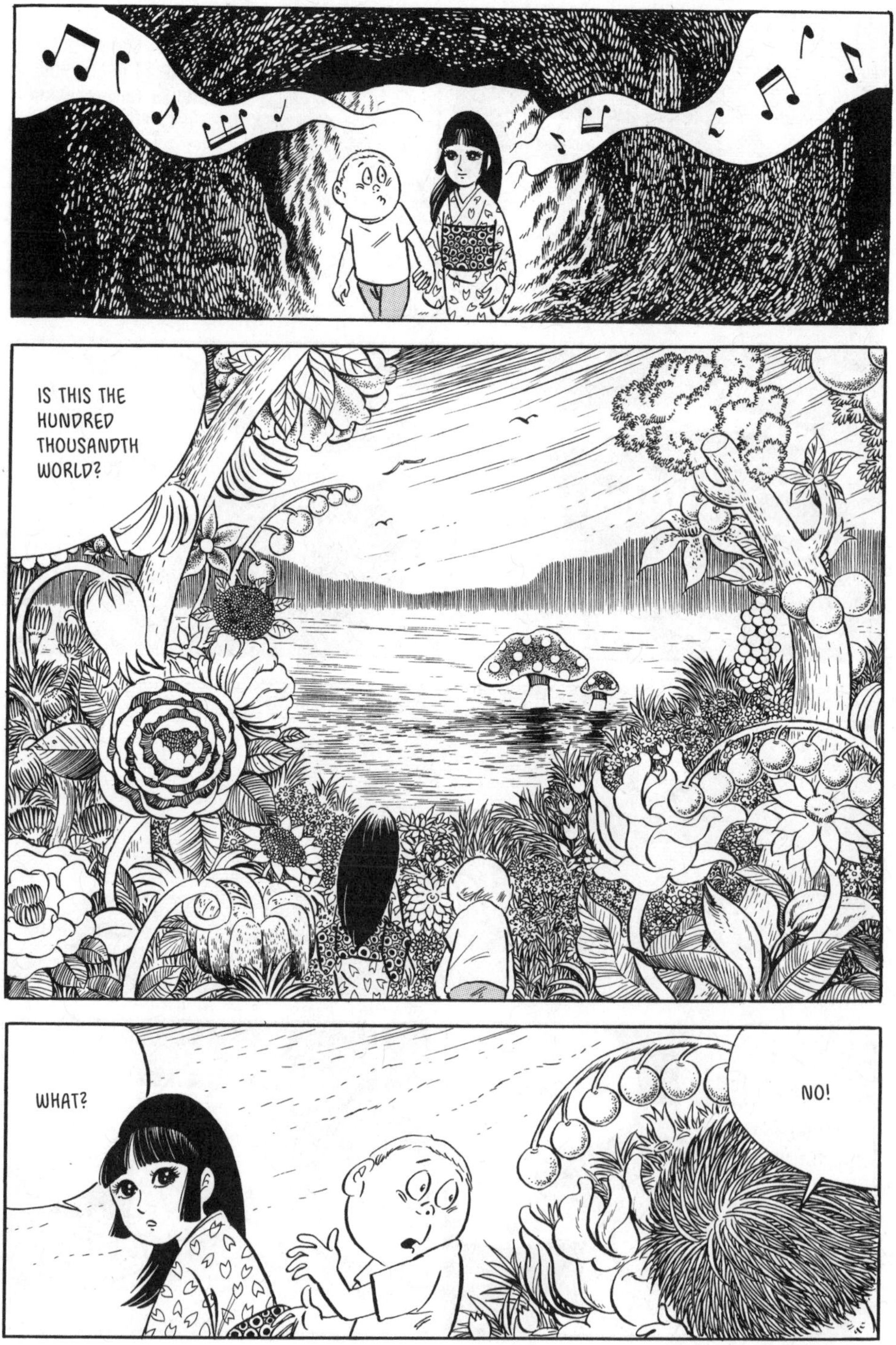
IS THIS THE HUNDRED THOUSANDTH WORLD?
NO!
WHAT?

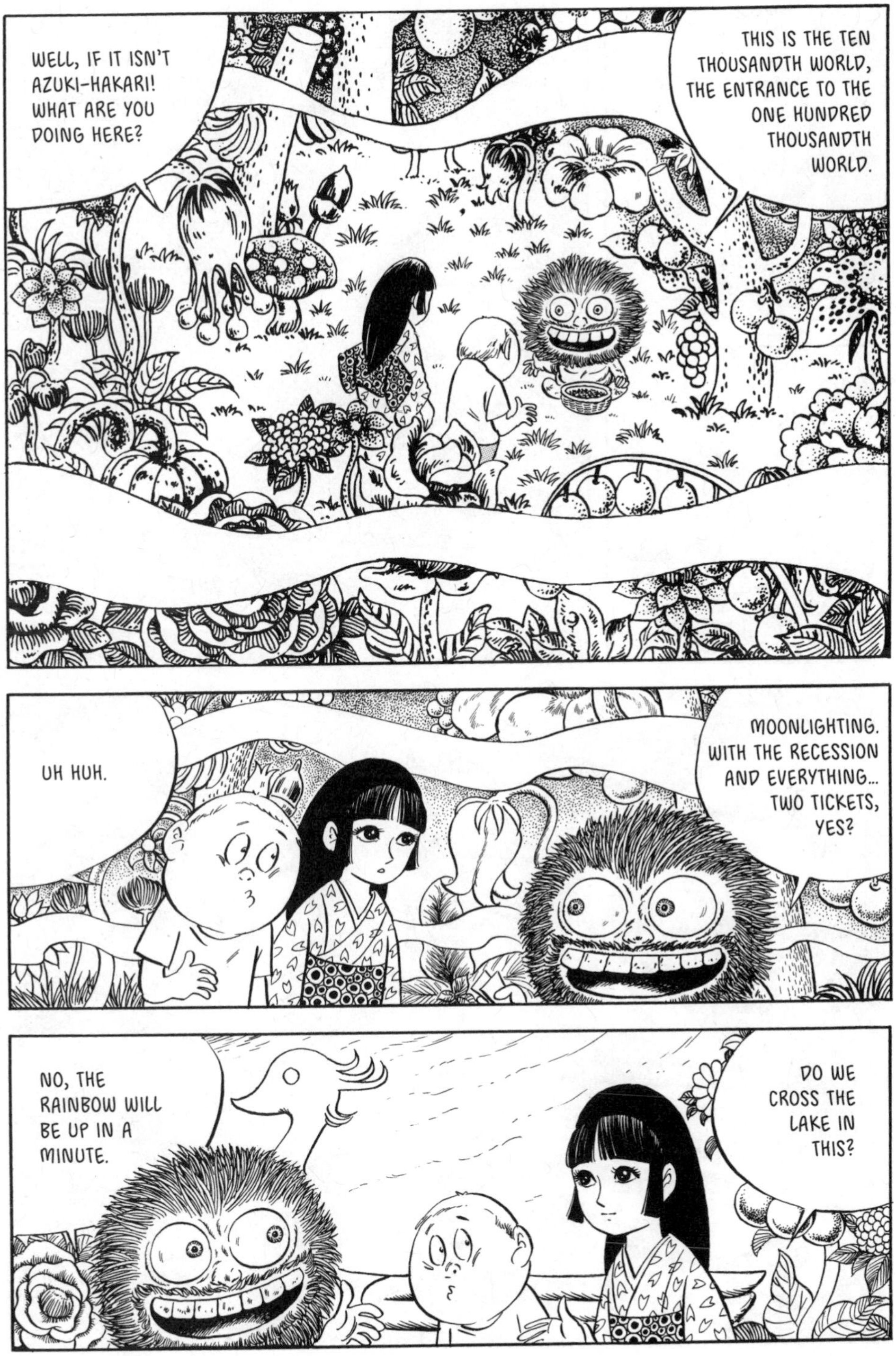
THIS IS THE TEN THOUSANDTH WORLD, THE ENTRANCE TO THE ONE HUNDRED THOUSANDTH WORLD.
WELL, IF IT ISN'T AZUKI-HAKARI! WHAT ARE YOU DOING HERE?
MOONLIGHTING. WITH THE RECESSION AND EVERYTHING... TWO TICKETS, YES?
UH HUH.
DO WE CROSS THE LAKE IN THIS?
NO, THE RAINBOW WILL BE UP IN A MINUTE.

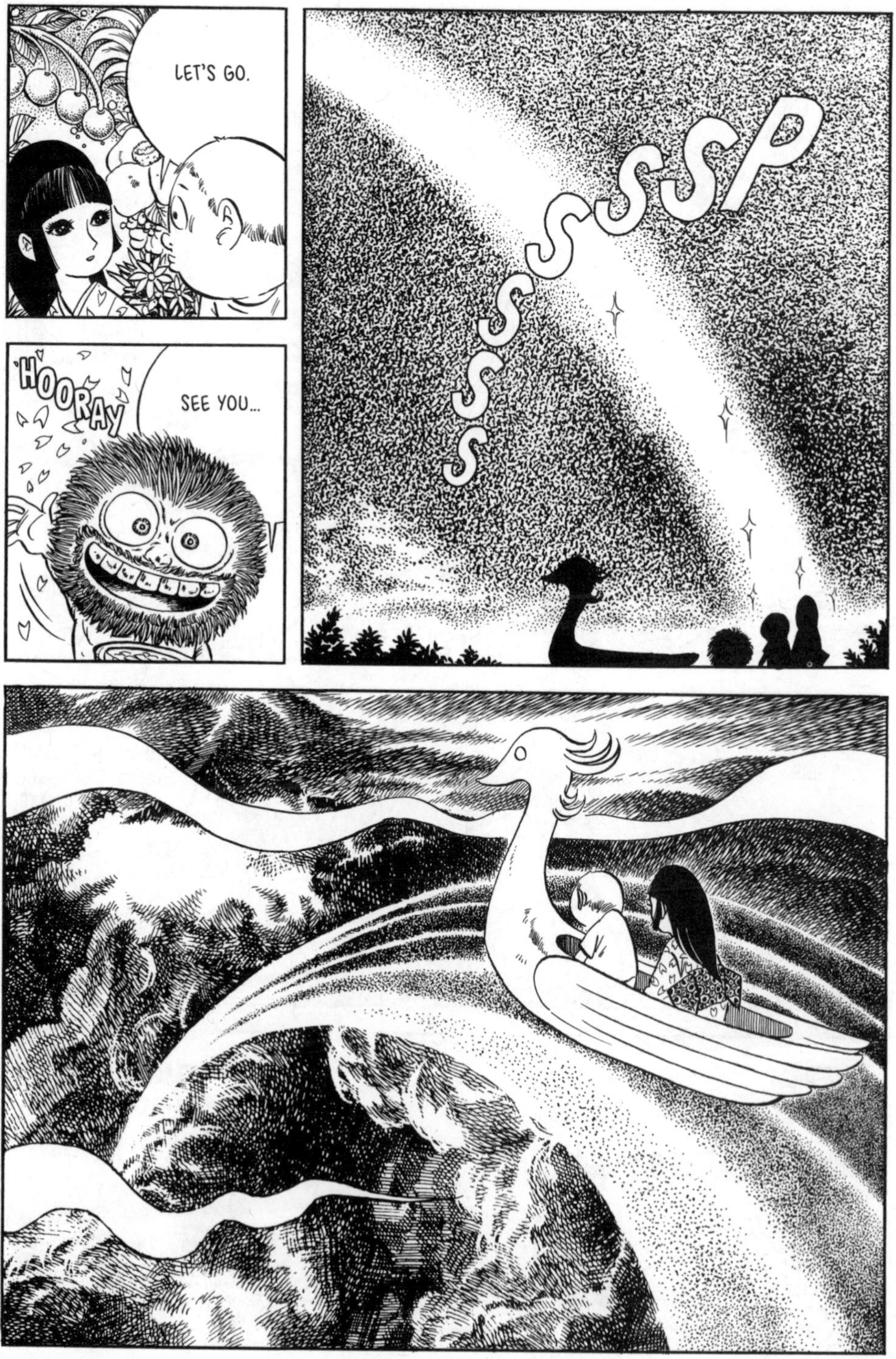
SSSSSSP
LET'S GO.
SEE YOU...
HOORAY

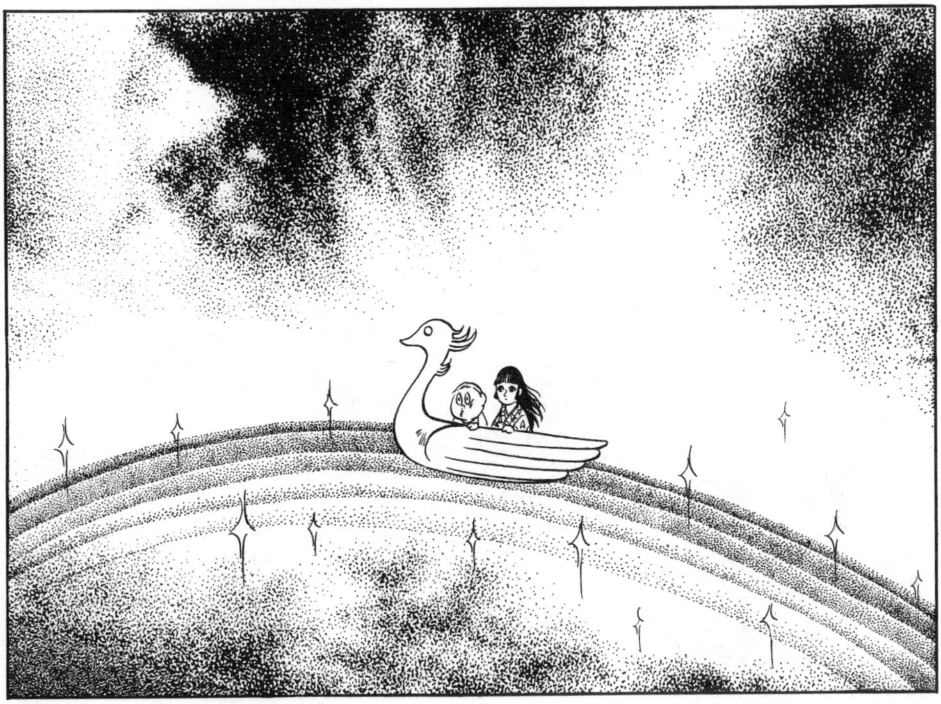
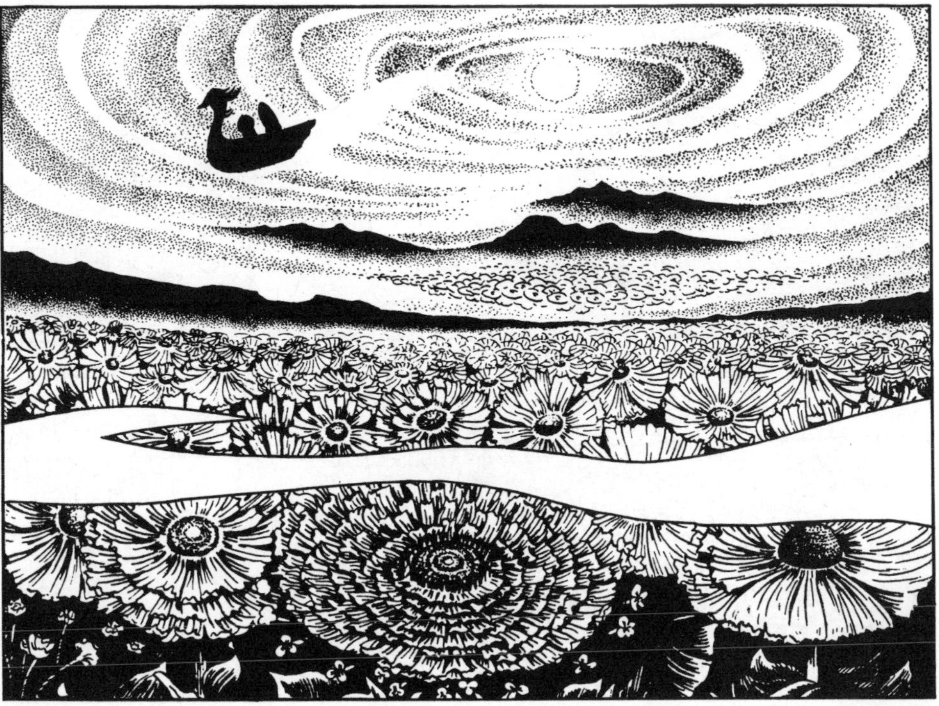

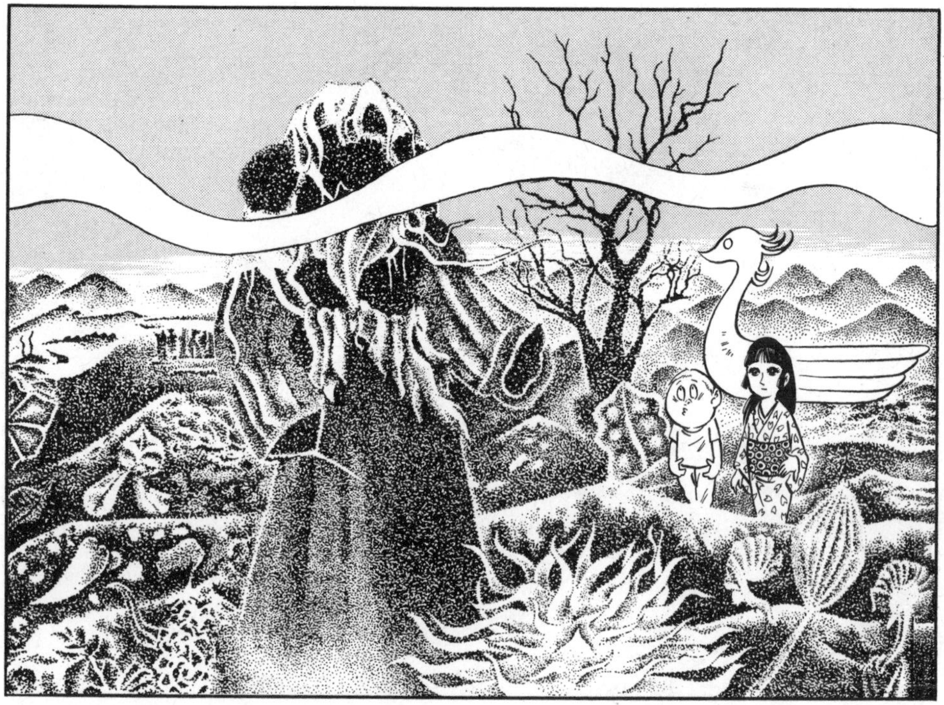

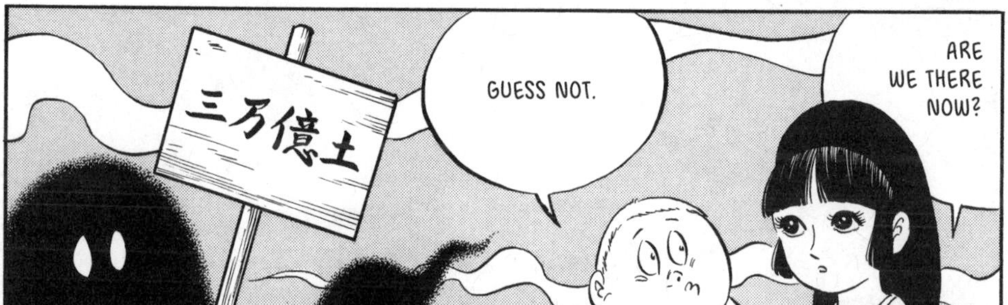
ARE WE THERE NOW?
GUESS NOT.
三万億土

SIGN: THIRTY THOUSANDTH WORLD.

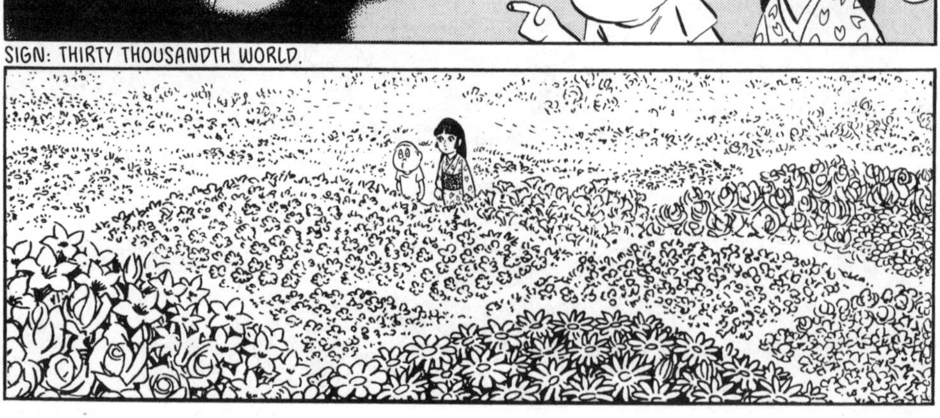

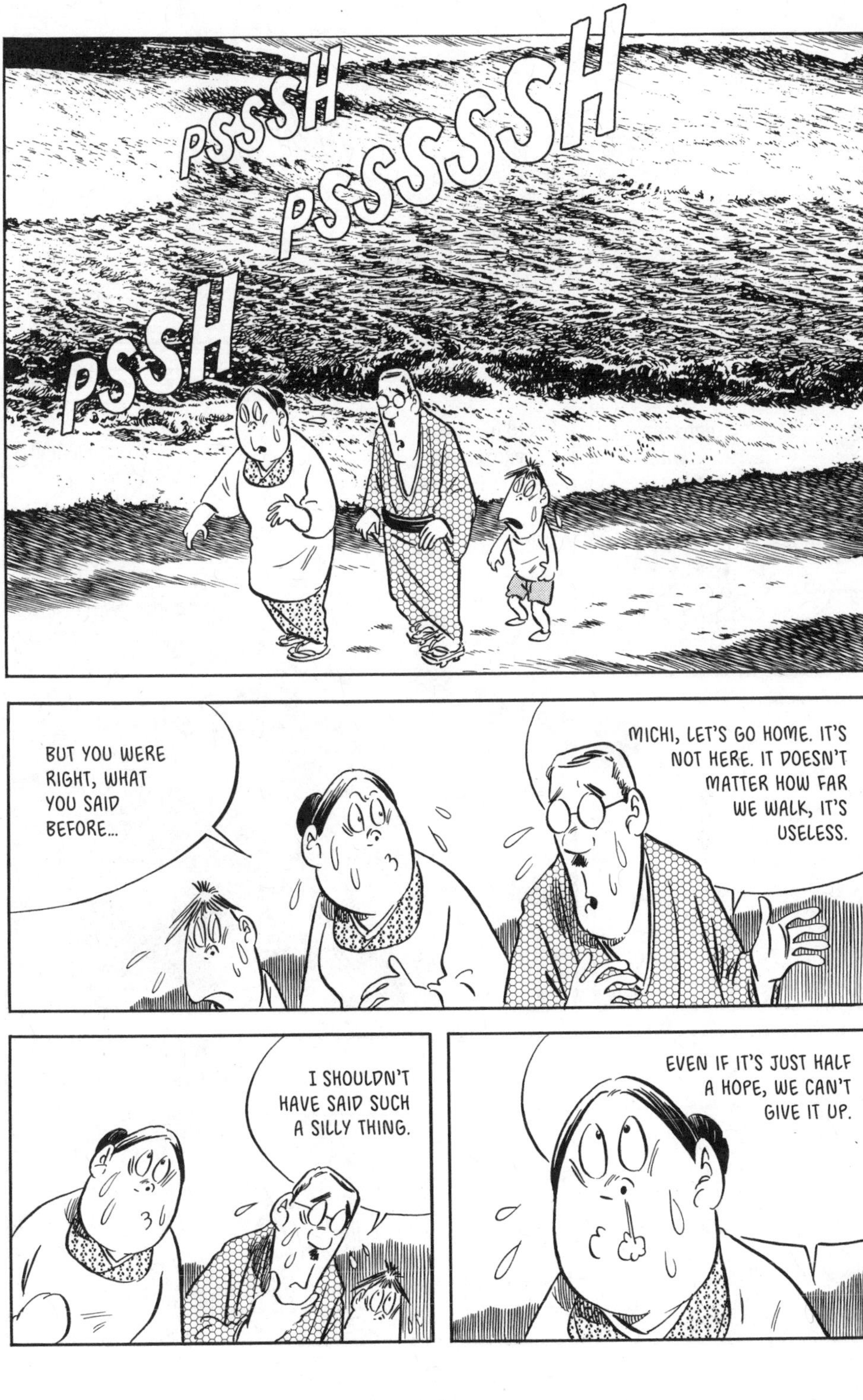
PSSSSSH
PSSSH
PSSH
MICHI, LET'S GO HOME. IT'S NOT HERE. IT DOESN'T MATTER HOW FAR WE WALK, IT'S USELESS.
BUT YOU WERE RIGHT, WHAT YOU SAID BEFORE...
EVEN IF IT'S JUST HALF A HOPE, WE CAN'T GIVE IT UP.
I SHOULDN'T HAVE SAID SUCH A SILLY THING.

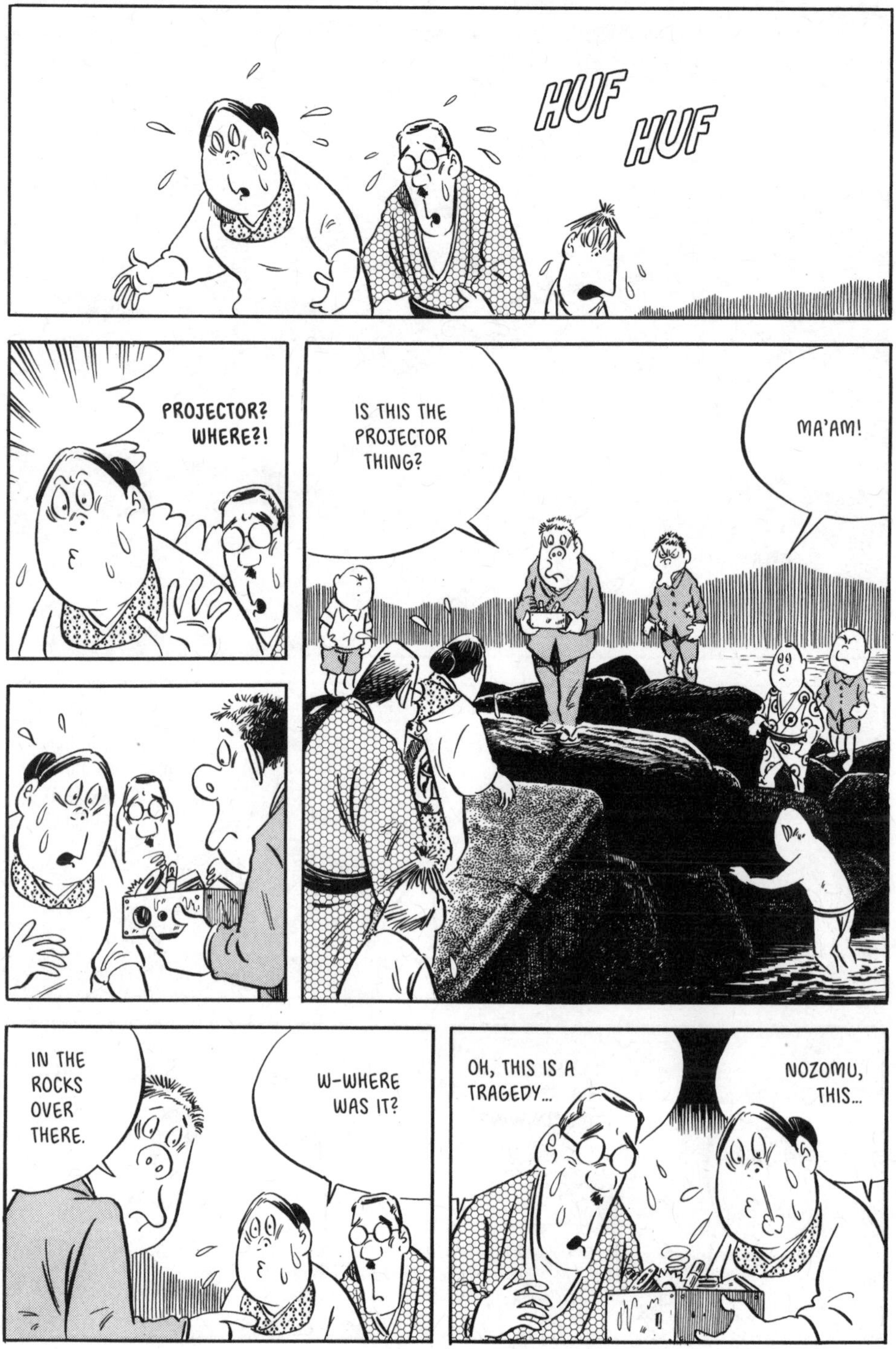
HUF HUF
MA'AM!
IS THIS THE PROJECTOR THING?
PROJECTOR? WHERE?!
NOZOMU, THIS...
OH, THIS IS A TRAGEDY...
W-WHERE WAS IT?
IN THE ROCKS OVER THERE.

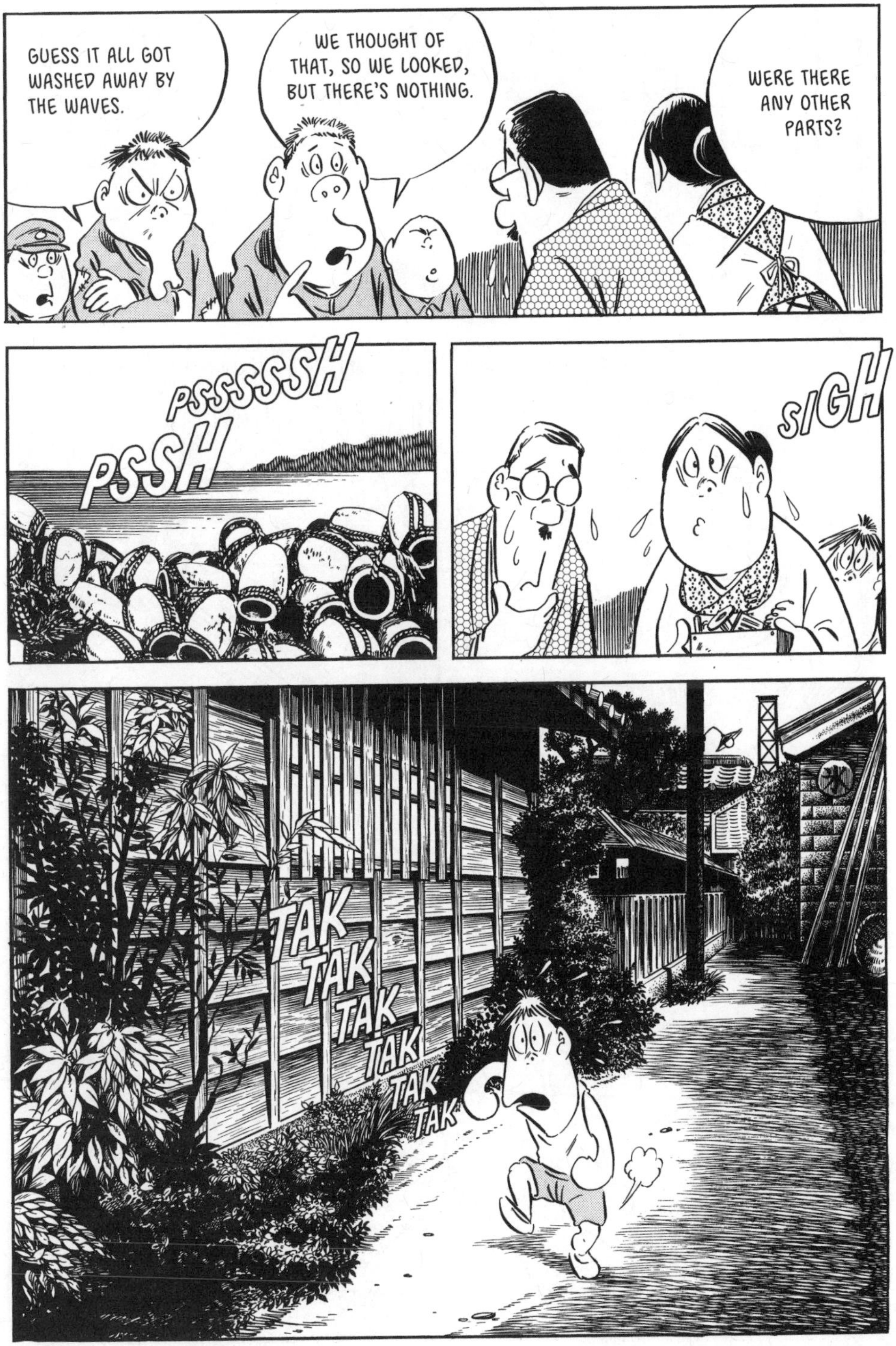
WERE THERE ANY OTHER PARTS?
WE THOUGHT OF THAT, SO WE LOOKED, BUT THERE'S NOTHING.
GUESS IT ALL GOT WASHED AWAY BY THE WAVES.
SIGH
PSSSSSH
PSSH
TAK
TAK
TAK
TAK
TAK
TAK

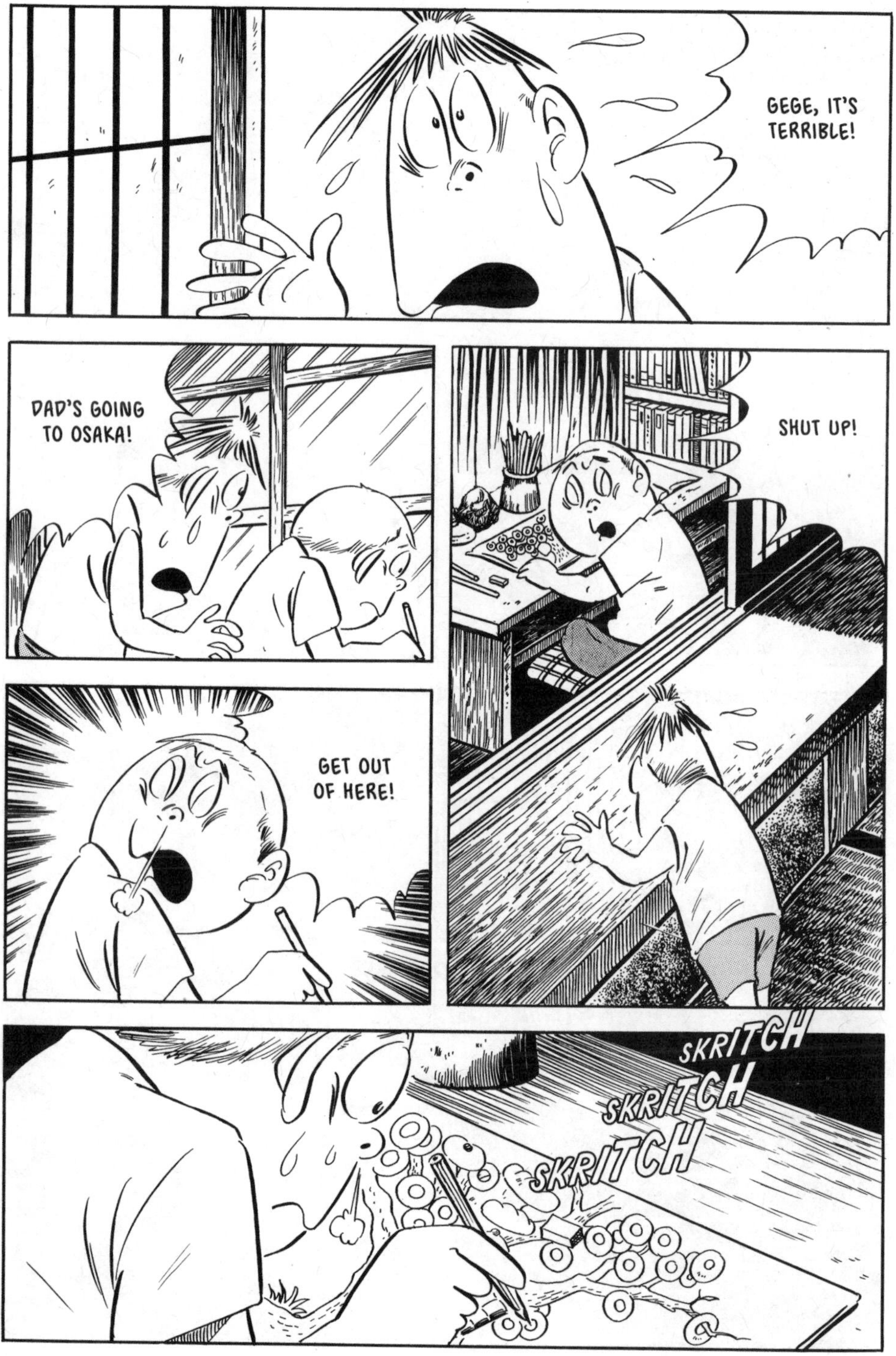
GEGE, IT'S TERRIBLE!
SHUT UP!
DAD'S GOING TO OSAKA!
GET OUT OF HERE!
SKRITCH
SKRITCH
SKRITCH

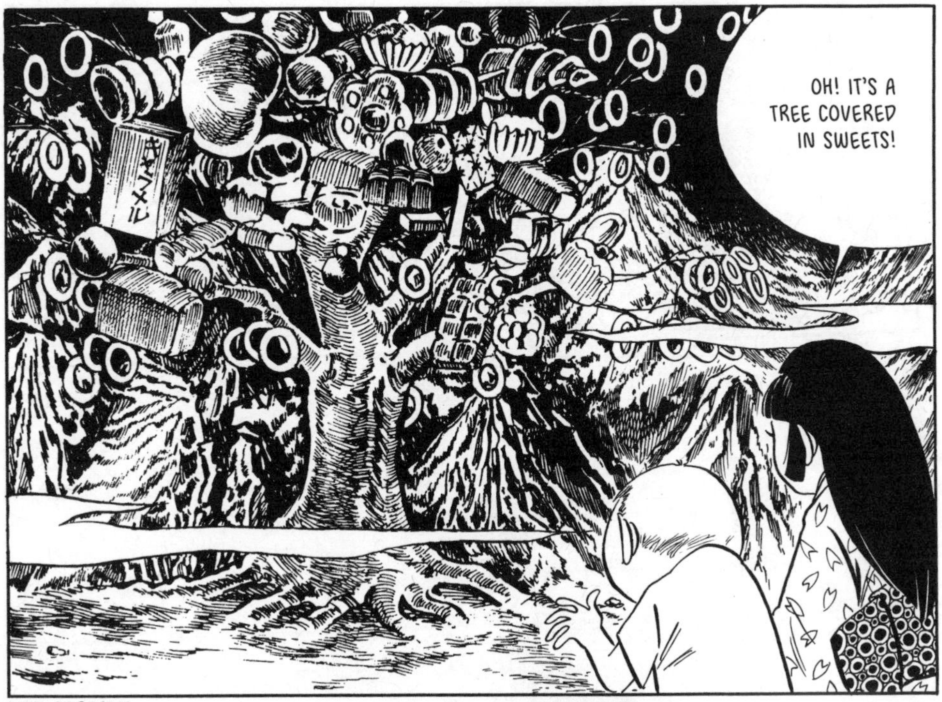
OH! IT'S A TREE COVERED IN SWEETS!

BOX: CARAMEL.

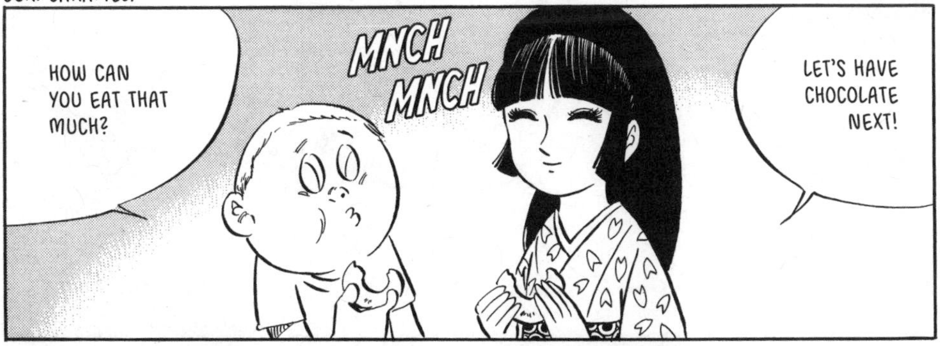
LET'S HAVE CHOCOLATE NEXT!
MNCH MNCH
HOW CAN YOU EAT THAT MUCH?

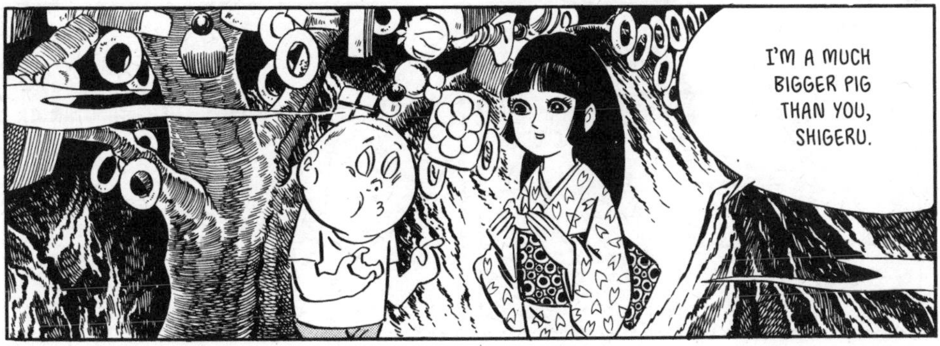
I'M A MUCH BIGGER PIG THAN YOU, SHIGERU.

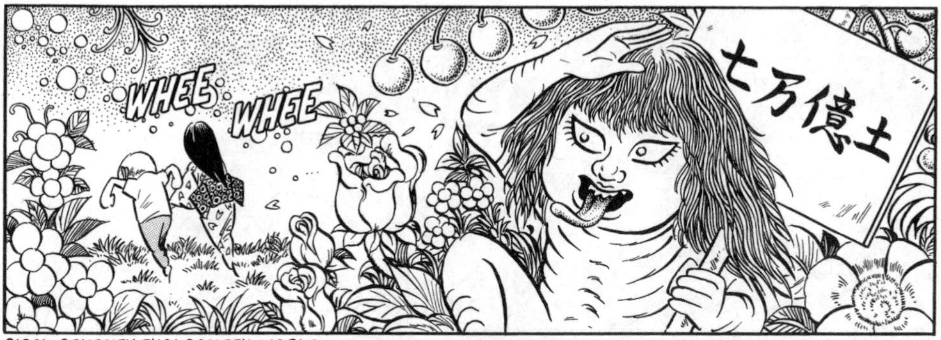
七万億土
WHEE
WHEE

SIGN: SEVENTY THOUSANDTH WORLD.

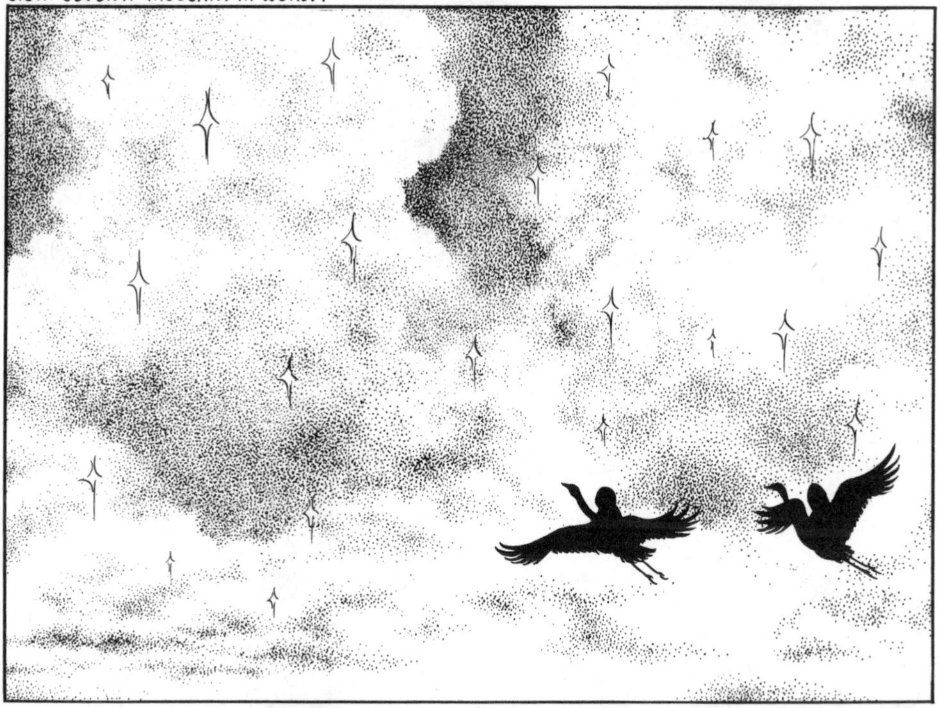

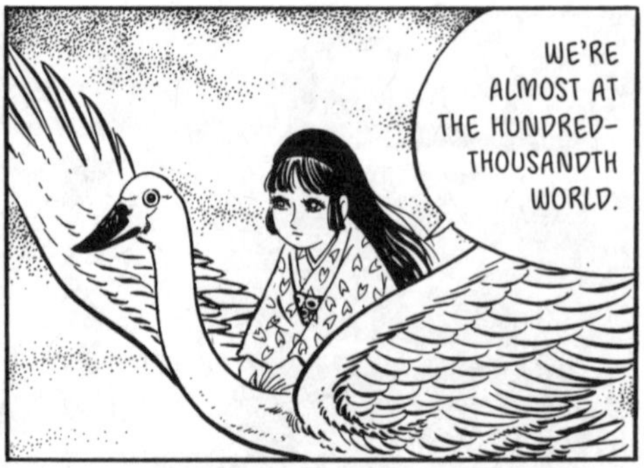
WE'RE ALMOST AT THE HUNDRED-THOUSANDTH WORLD.

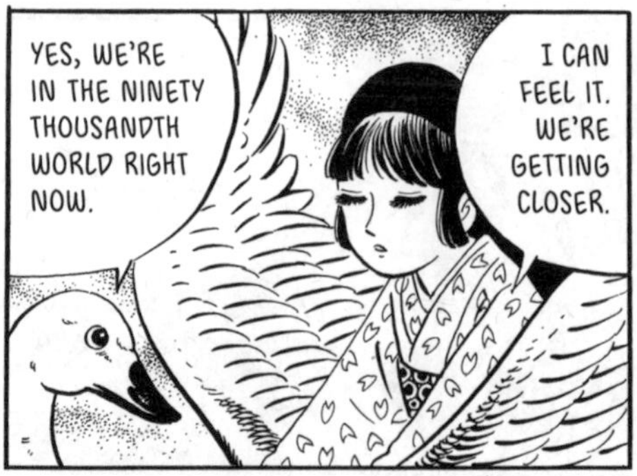
I CAN FEEL IT. WE'RE GETTING CLOSER.
YES, WE'RE IN THE NINETY THOUSANDTH WORLD RIGHT NOW.

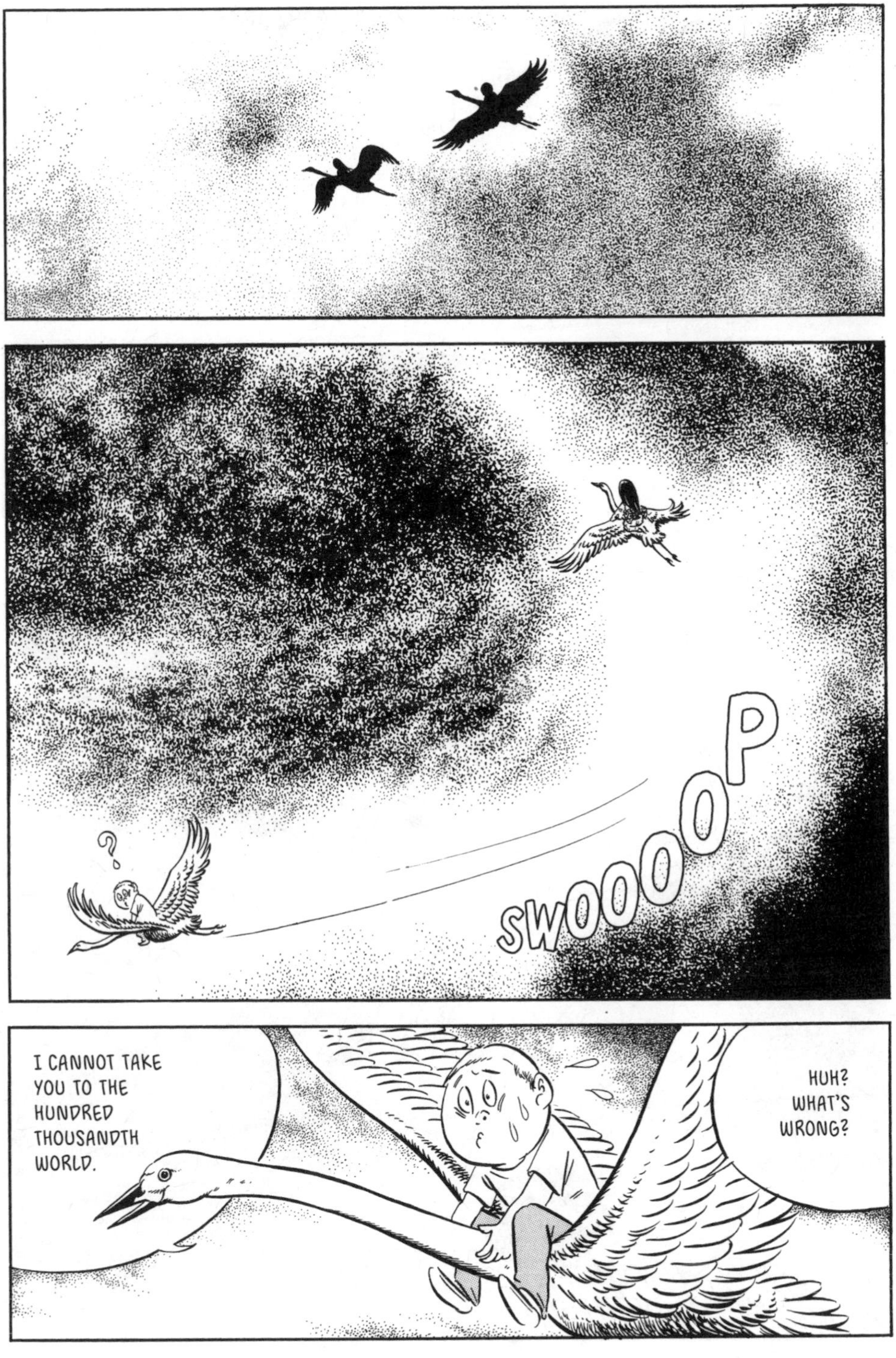
SWOOOOP
HUH? WHAT'S WRONG?
I CANNOT TAKE YOU TO THE HUNDRED THOUSANDTH WORLD.

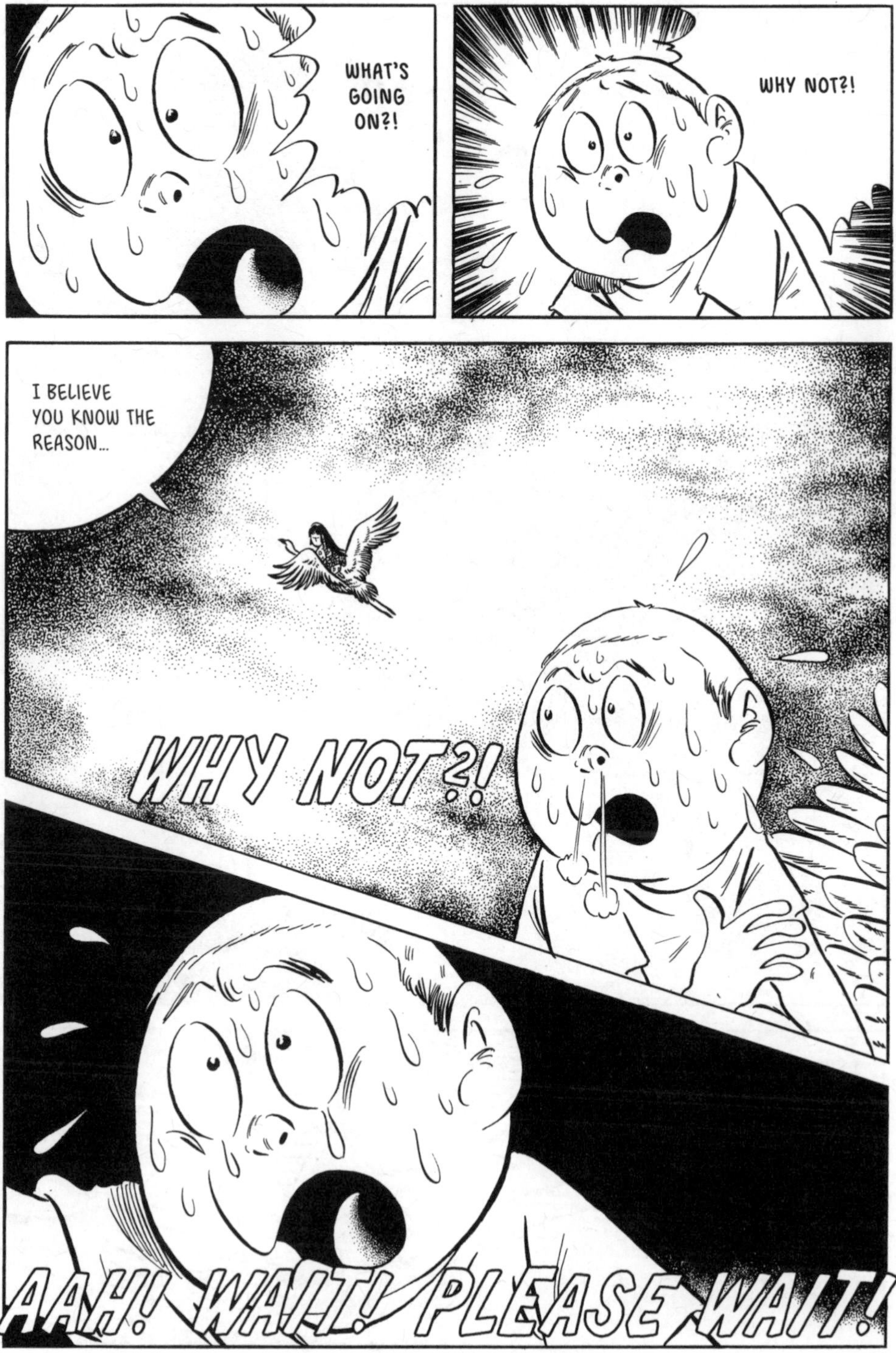
WHY NOT?!
WHAT'S GOING ON?!
I BELIEVE YOU KNOW THE REASON...
WHY NOT?!
AAH! WAIT! PLEASE WAIT!

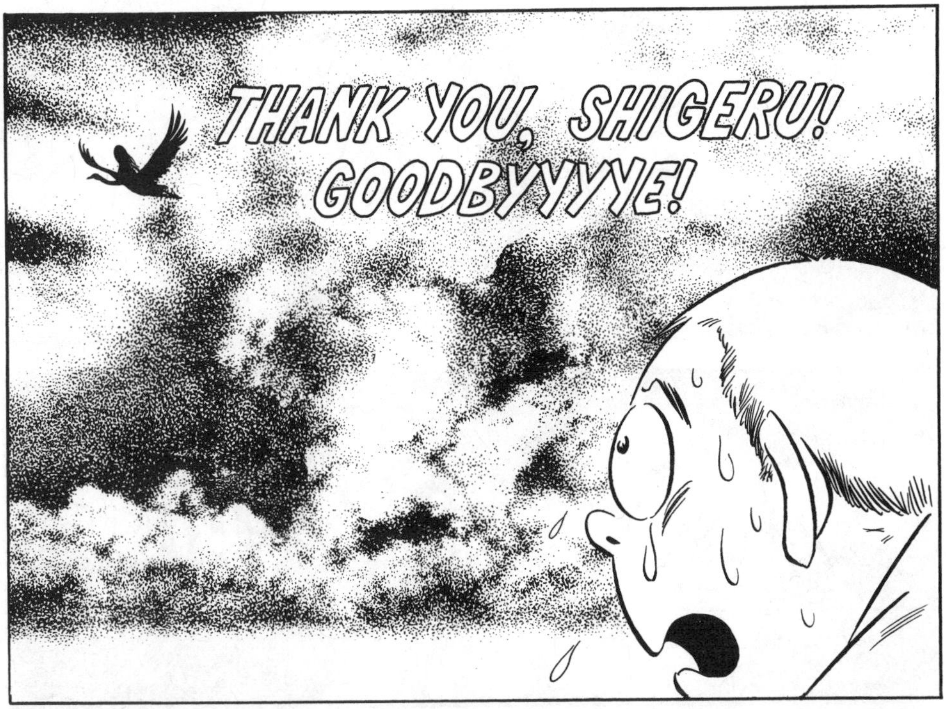
THANK YOU, SHIGERU! GOODBYYYYE!

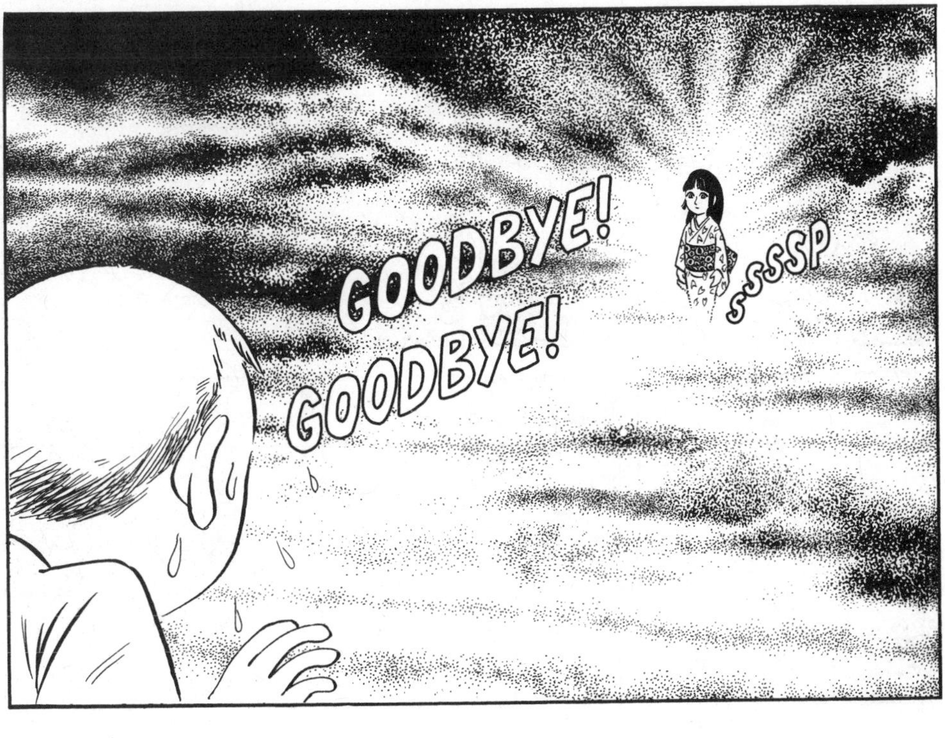
GOODBYE!
GOODBYE!
SSSSP

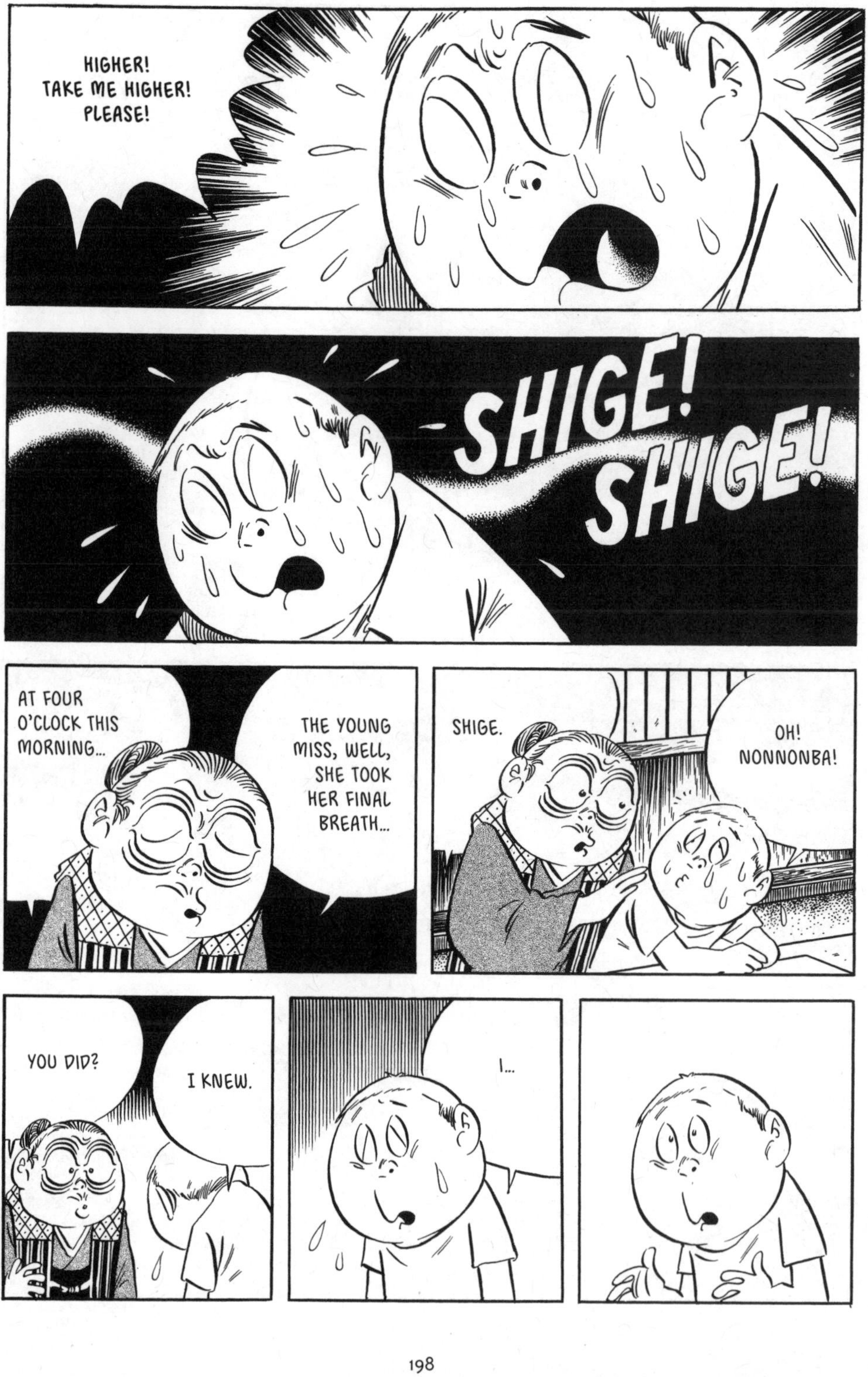
HIGHER! TAKE ME HIGHER! PLEASE!
SHIGE! SHIGE!
OH! NONNONBA!
SHIGE.
AT FOUR O'CLOCK THIS MORNING...
THE YOUNG MISS, WELL, SHE TOOK HER FINAL BREATH...
I...
I KNEW.
YOU DID?

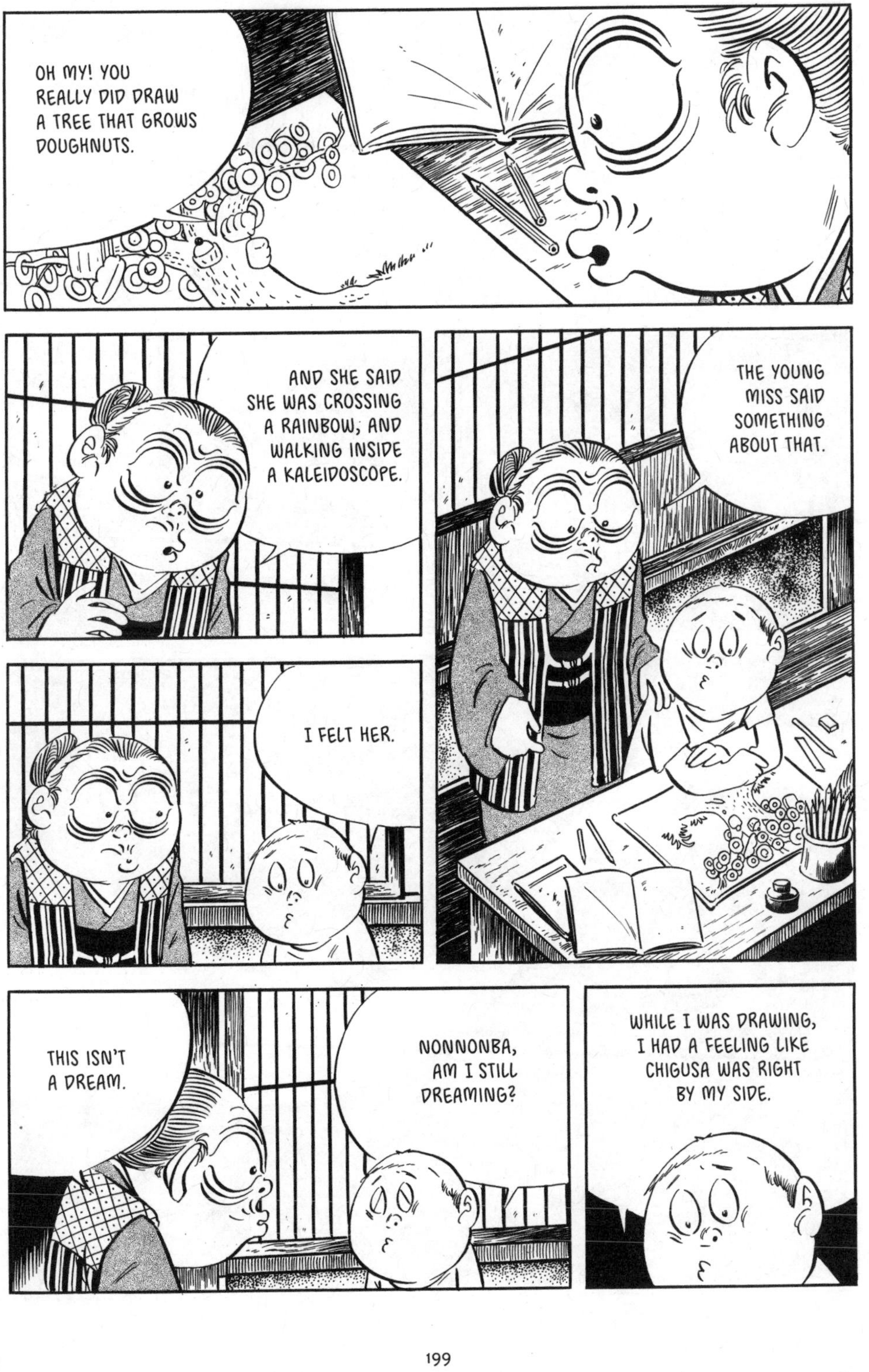
OH MY! YOU REALLY DID DRAW A TREE THAT GROWS DOUGHNUTS.
THE YOUNG MISS SAID SOMETHING ABOUT THAT.
AND SHE SAID SHE WAS CROSSING A RAINBOW, AND WALKING INSIDE A KALEIDOSCOPE.
I FELT HER.
WHILE I WAS DRAWING, I HAD A FEELING LIKE CHIGUSA WAS RIGHT BY MY SIDE.
NONNONBA, AM I STILL DREAMING?
THIS ISN'T A DREAM.

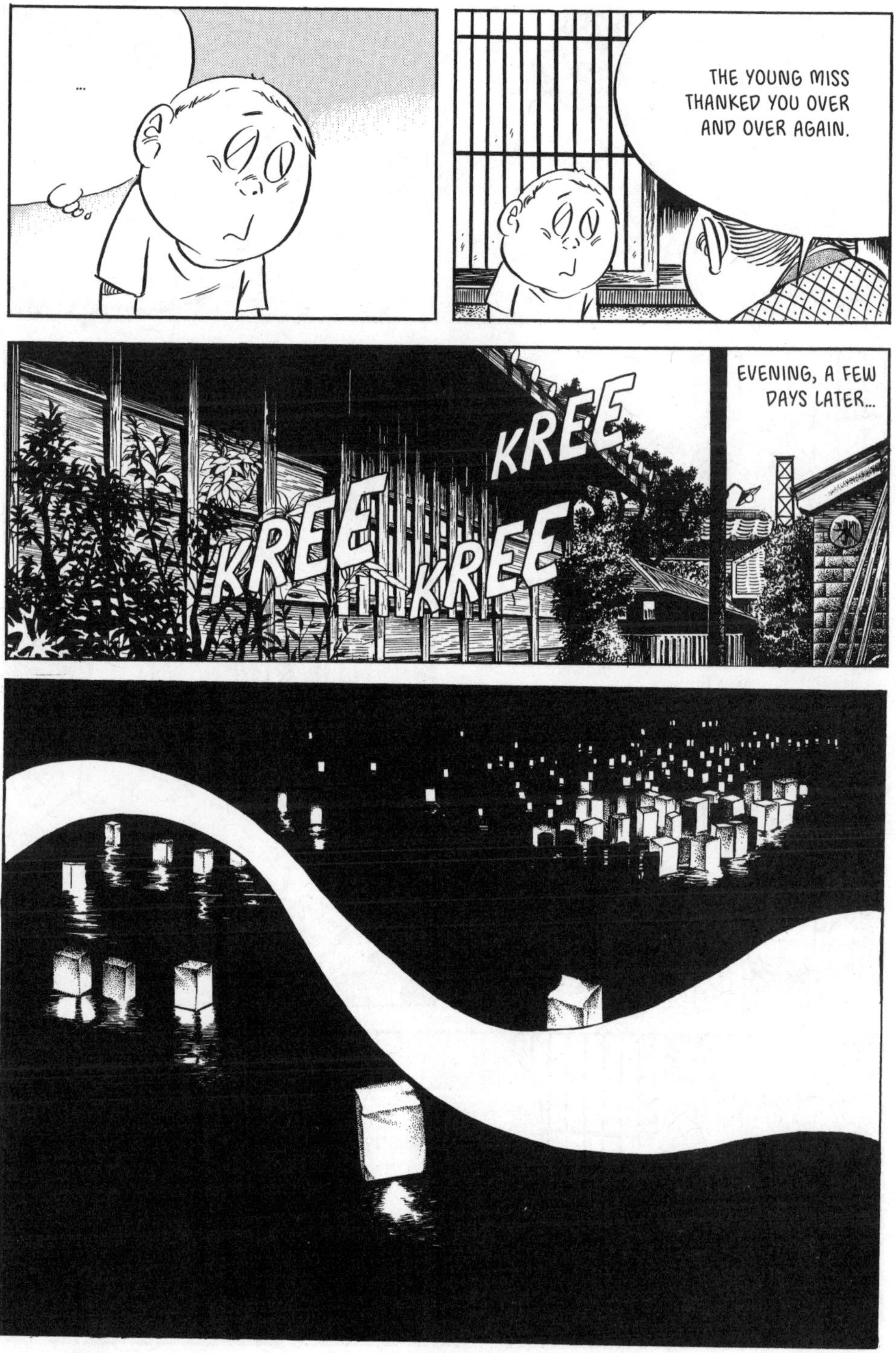
THE YOUNG MISS THANKED YOU OVER AND OVER AGAIN.
...
EVENING, A FEW DAYS LATER...
KREE
KREE
KREE

MEMORIES OF CHIGUSA

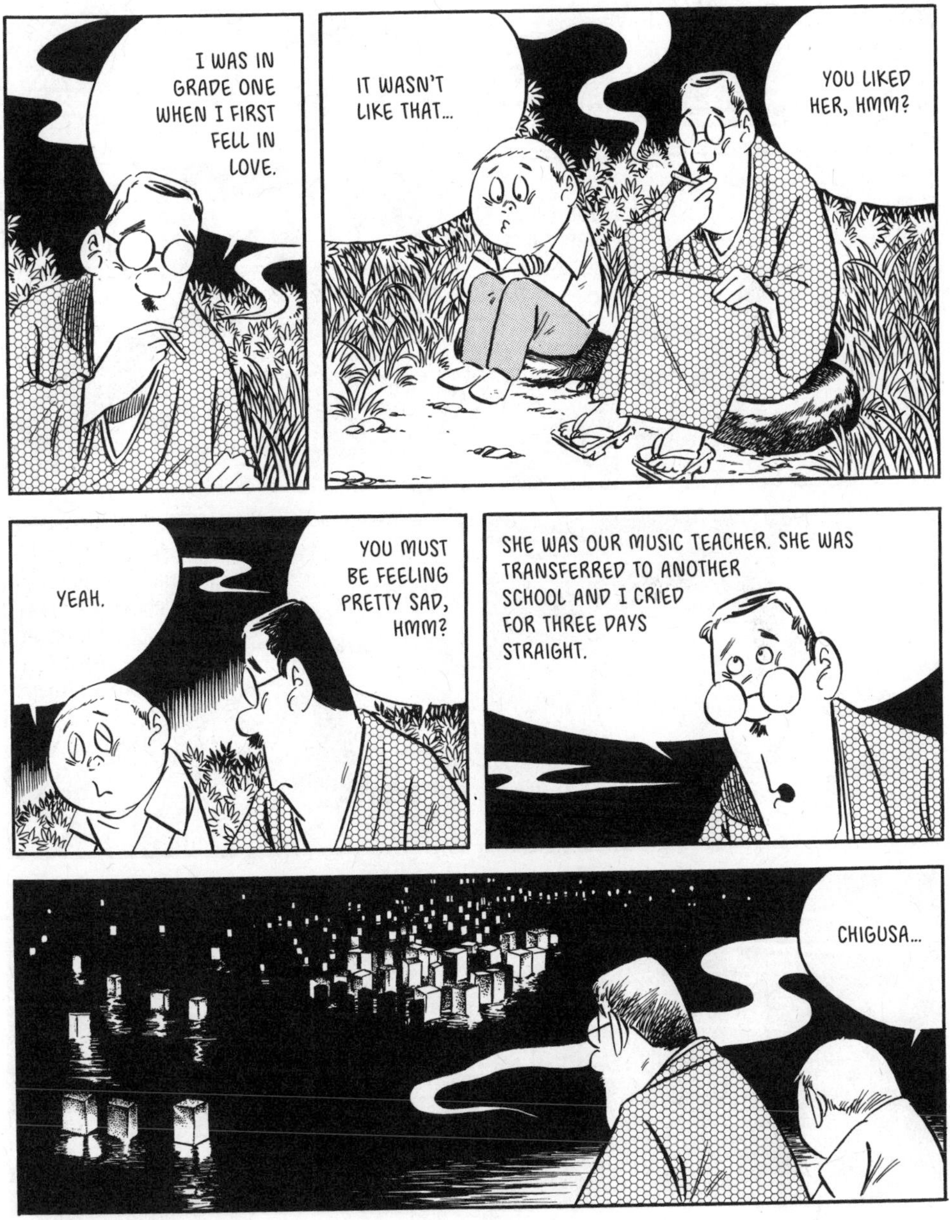
YOU LIKED HER, HMM?
IT WASN'T LIKE THAT...
I WAS IN GRADE ONE WHEN I FIRST FELL IN LOVE.
SHE WAS OUR MUSIC TEACHER. SHE WAS TRANSFERRED TO ANOTHER SCHOOL AND I CRIED FOR THREE DAYS STRAIGHT.
YOU MUST BE FEELING PRETTY SAD, HMM?
YEAH.
CHIGUSA...

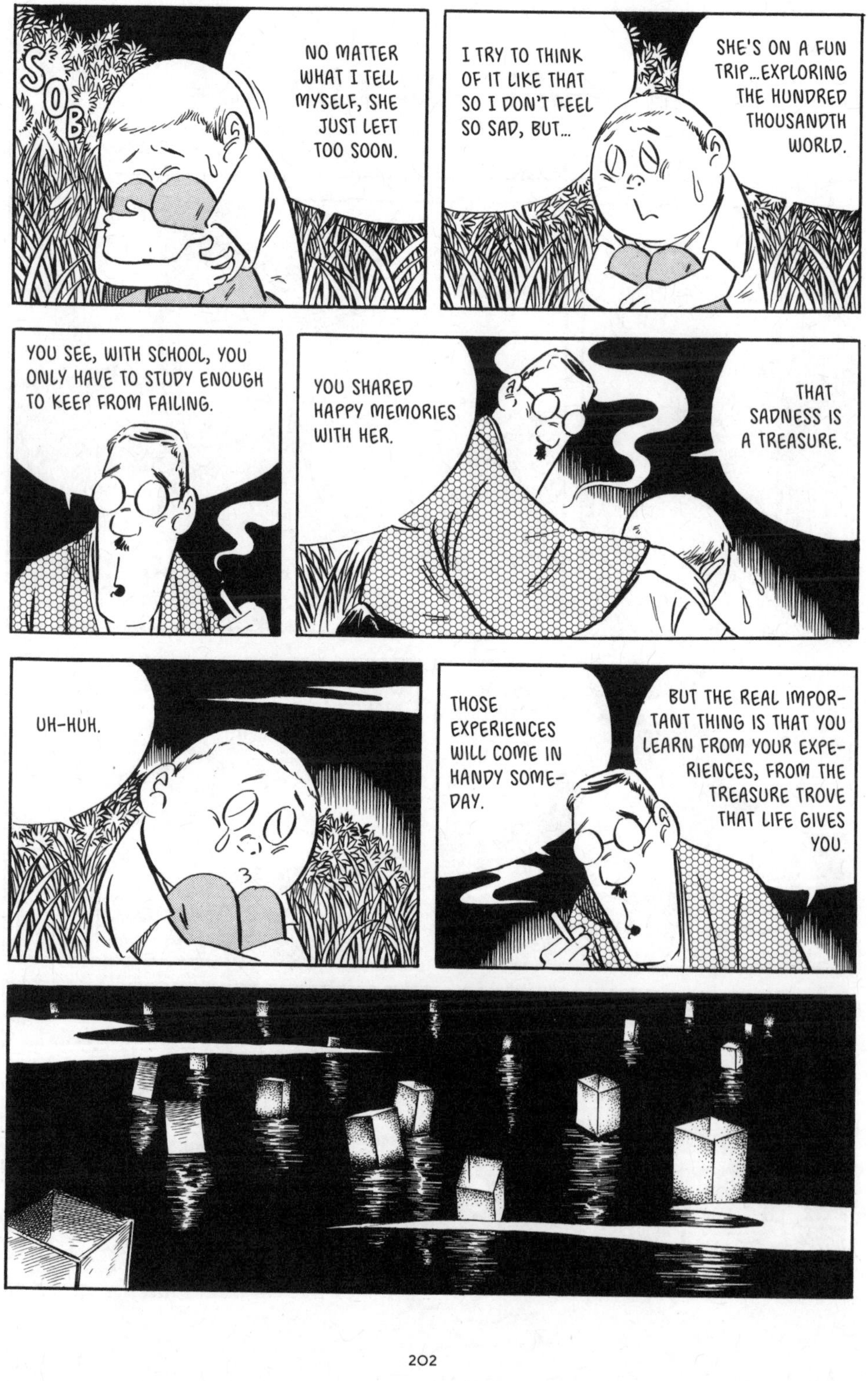
SHE'S ON A FUN TRIP...EXPLORING THE HUNDRED THOUSANDTH WORLD.
I TRY TO THINK OF IT LIKE THAT SO I DON'T FEEL SO SAD, BUT...
NO MATTER WHAT I TELL MYSELF, SHE JUST LEFT TOO SOON.
SOB
THAT SADNESS IS A TREASURE.
YOU SHARED HAPPY MEMORIES WITH HER.
YOU SEE, WITH SCHOOL, YOU ONLY HAVE TO STUDY ENOUGH TO KEEP FROM FAILING.
BUT THE REAL IMPORTANT THING IS THAT YOU LEARN FROM YOUR EXPERIENCES, FROM THE TREASURE TROVE THAT LIFE GIVES YOU.
THOSE EXPERIENCES WILL COME IN HANDY SOMEDAY.
UH-HUH.

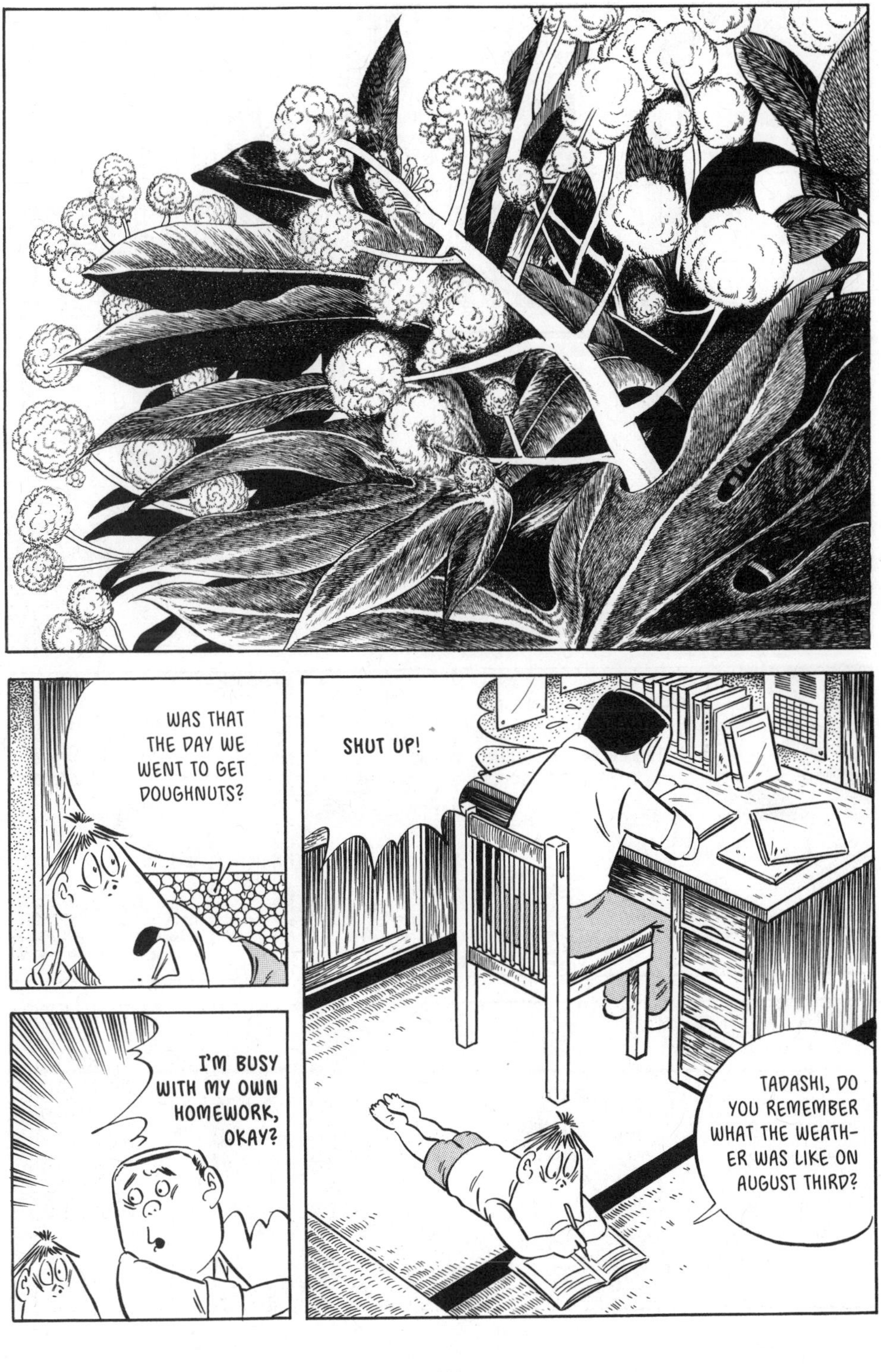
SHUT UP!
TADASHI, DO YOU REMEMBER WHAT THE WEATH-ER WAS LIKE ON AUGUST THIRD?
WAS THAT THE DAY WE WENT TO GET DOUGHNUTS?
I'M BUSY WITH MY OWN HOMEWORK, OKAY?

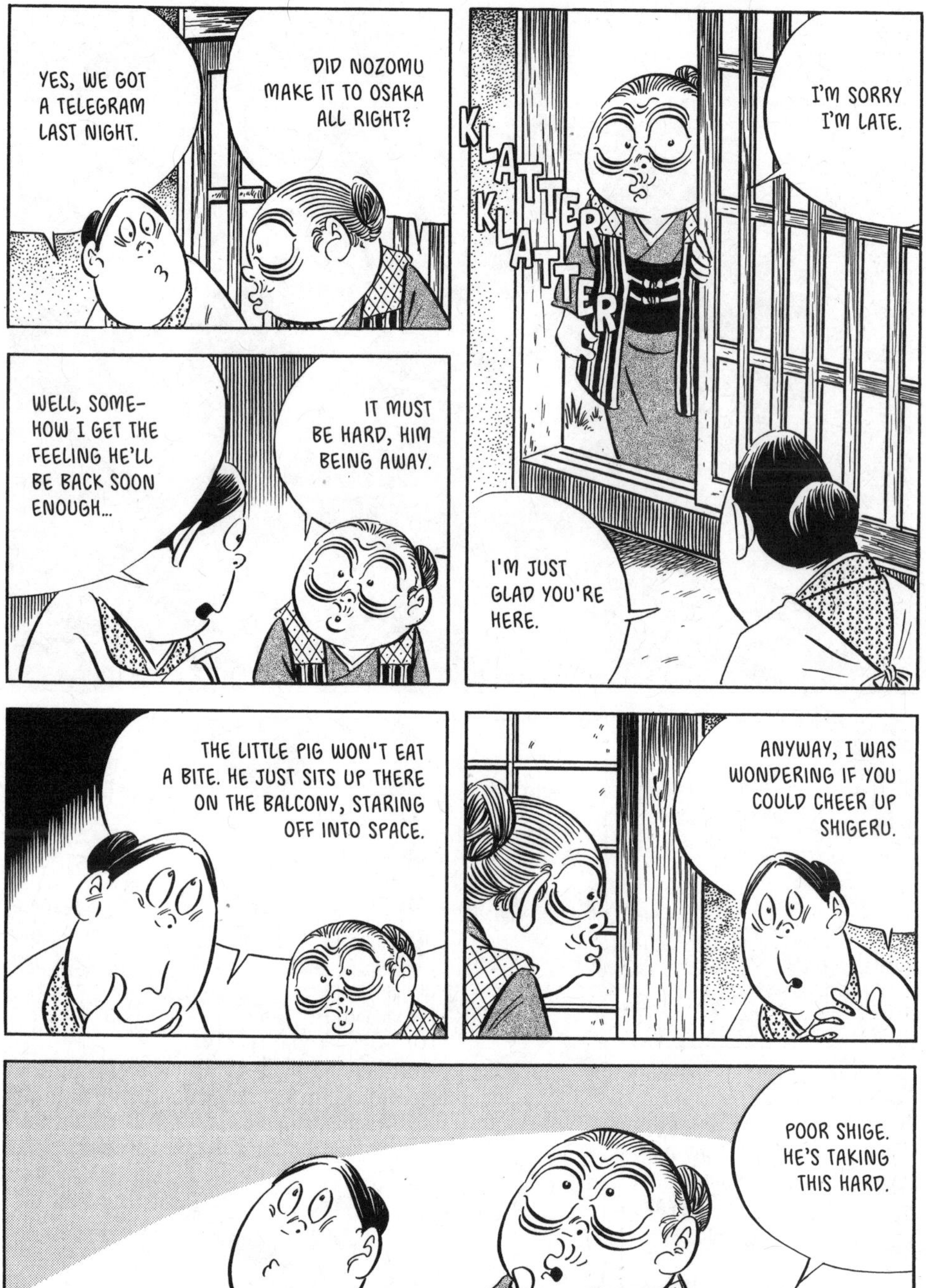
KLATTER KLATTER
I'M SORRY I'M LATE.
I'M JUST GLAD YOU'RE HERE.
DID NOZOMU MAKE IT TO OSAKA ALL RIGHT?
YES, WE GOT A TELEGRAM LAST NIGHT.
IT MUST BE HARD, HIM BEING AWAY.
WELL, SOME-HOW I GET THE FEELING HE'LL BE BACK SOON ENOUGH...
ANYWAY, I WAS WONDERING IF YOU COULD CHEER UP SHIGERU.
THE LITTLE PIG WON'T EAT A BITE. HE JUST SITS UP THERE ON THE BALCONY, STARING OFF INTO SPACE.
POOR SHIGE. HE'S TAKING THIS HARD.

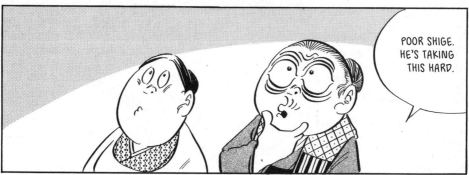

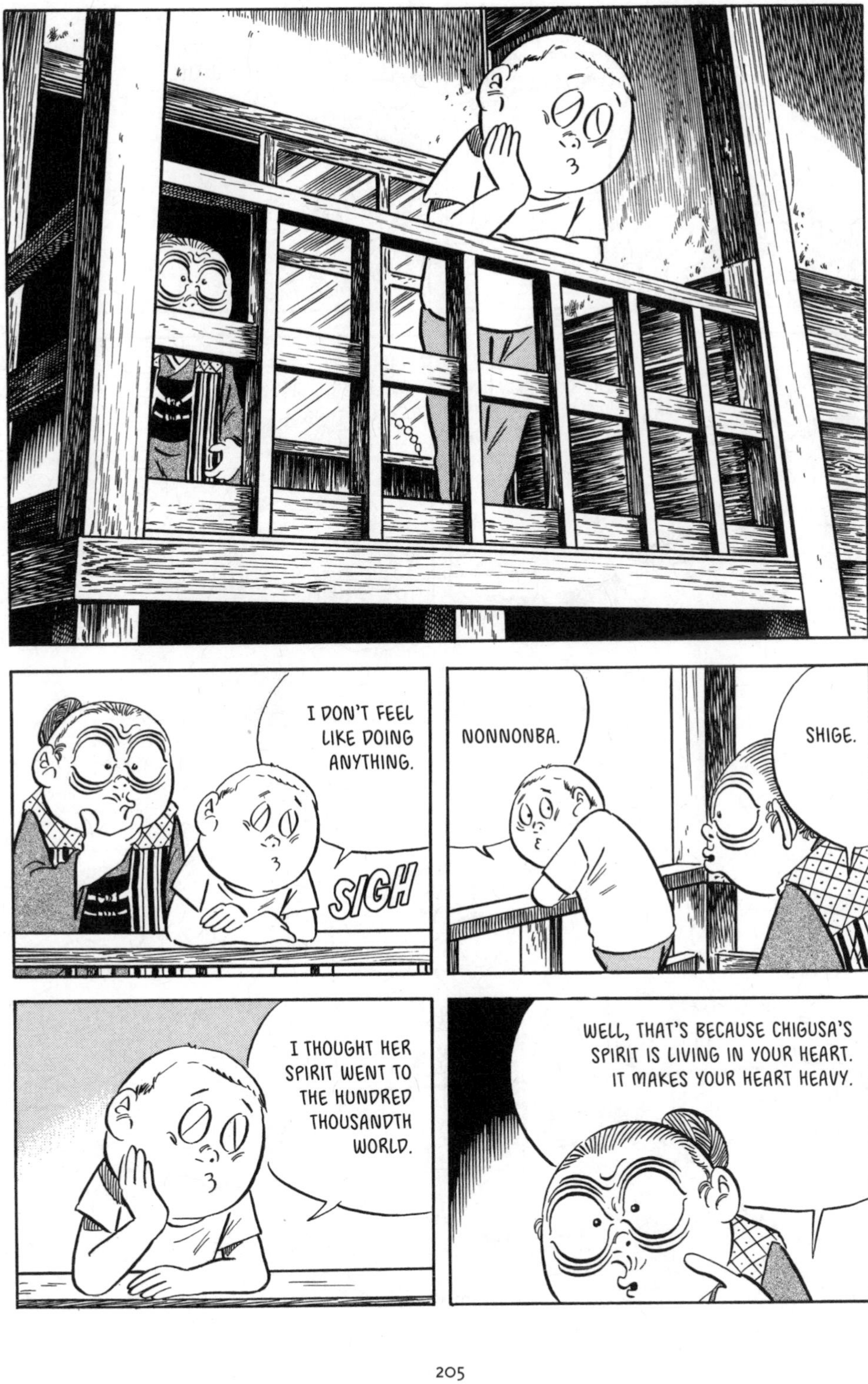
SHIGE.
NONNONBA.
I DON'T FEEL LIKE DOING ANYTHING.
SIGH
WELL, THAT'S BECAUSE CHIGUSA'S SPIRIT IS LIVING IN YOUR HEART. IT MAKES YOUR HEART HEAVY.
I THOUGHT HER SPIRIT WENT TO THE HUNDRED THOUSANDTH WORLD.

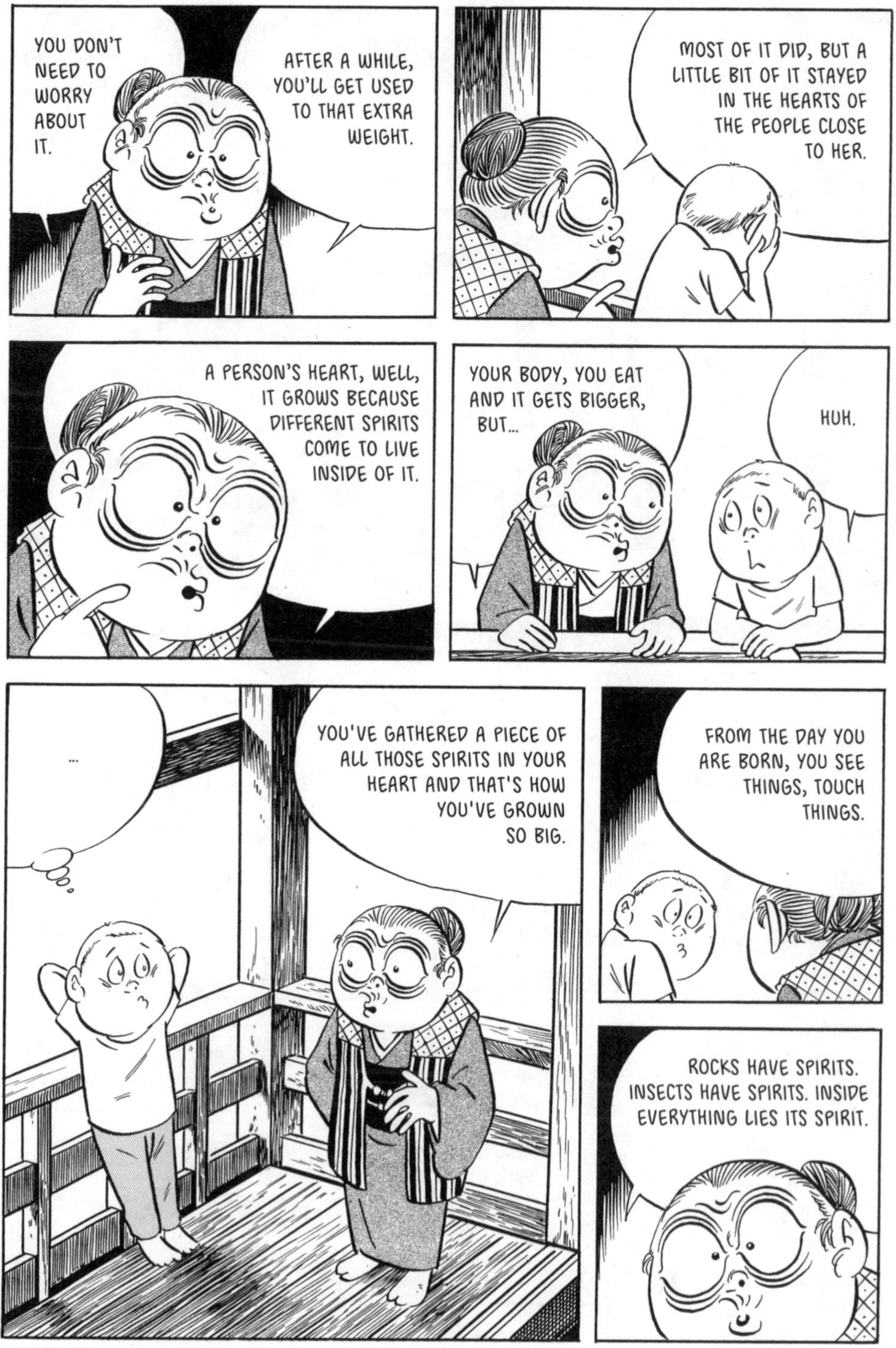
MOST OF IT DID, BUT A LITTLE BIT OF IT STAYED IN THE HEARTS OF THE PEOPLE CLOSE TO HER.
AFTER A WHILE, YOU'LL GET USED TO THAT EXTRA WEIGHT.
YOU DON'T NEED TO WORRY ABOUT IT.
HUH.
YOUR BODY, YOU EAT AND IT GETS BIGGER, BUT...
A PERSON'S HEART, WELL, IT GROWS BECAUSE DIFFERENT SPIRITS COME TO LIVE INSIDE OF IT.
FROM THE DAY YOU ARE BORN, YOU SEE THINGS, TOUCH THINGS.
ROCKS HAVE SPIRITS. INSECTS HAVE SPIRITS. INSIDE EVERYTHING LIES ITS SPIRIT.
YOU'VE GATHERED A PIECE OF ALL THOSE SPIRITS IN YOUR HEART AND THAT'S HOW YOU'VE GROWN SO BIG.
...

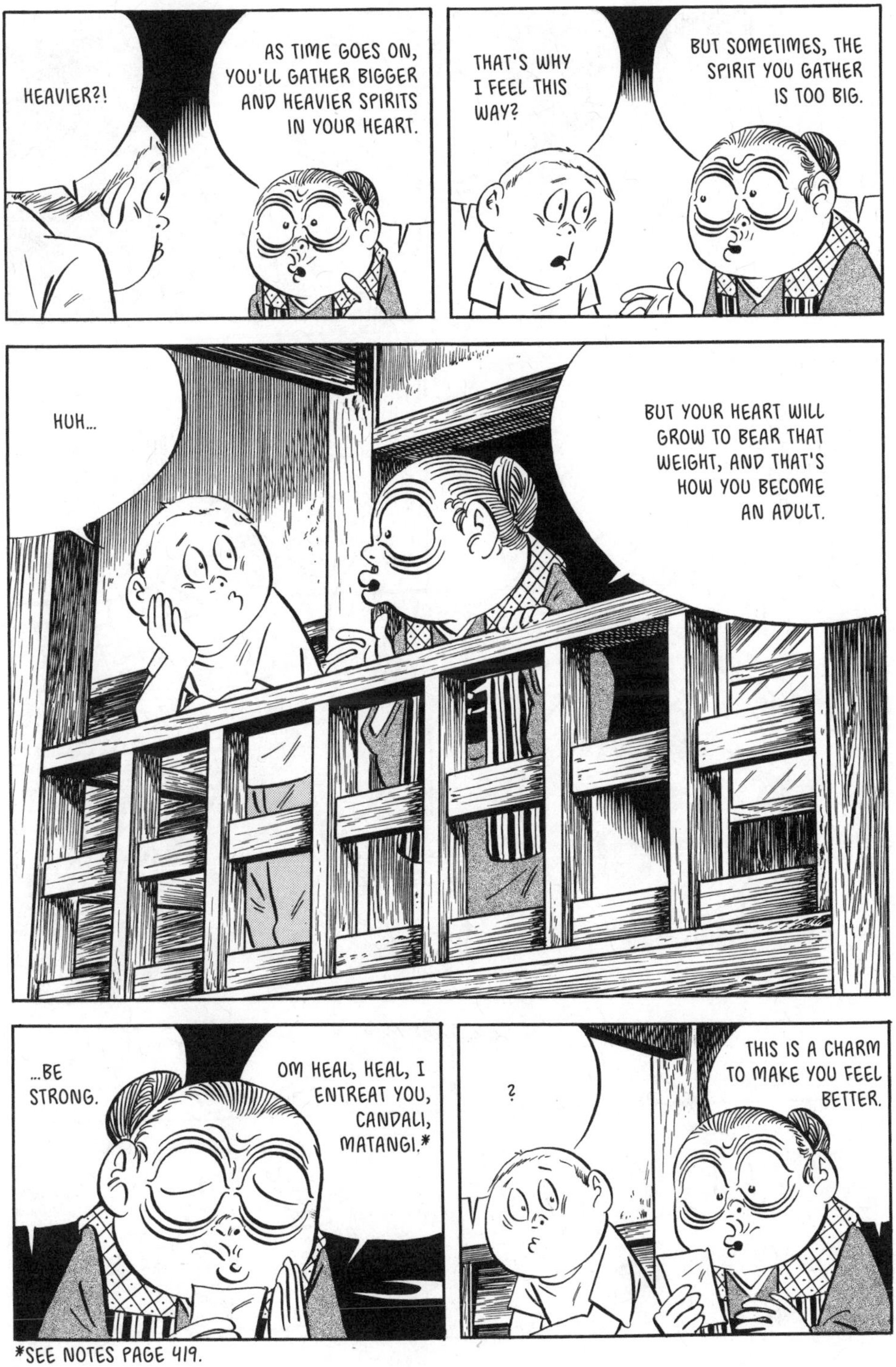
BUT SOMETIMES, THE SPIRIT YOU GATHER IS TOO BIG.
THAT'S WHY I FEEL THIS WAY?
AS TIME GOES ON, YOU'LL GATHER BIGGER AND HEAVIER SPIRITS IN YOUR HEART.
HEAVIER?!
BUT YOUR HEART WILL GROW TO BEAR THAT WEIGHT, AND THAT'S HOW YOU BECOME AN ADULT.
HUH...
THIS IS A CHARM TO MAKE YOU FEEL BETTER.
?
OM HEAL, HEAL, I ENTREAT YOU, CANDALI, MATANGI.*
...BE STRONG.

*SEE NOTES PAGE 419.

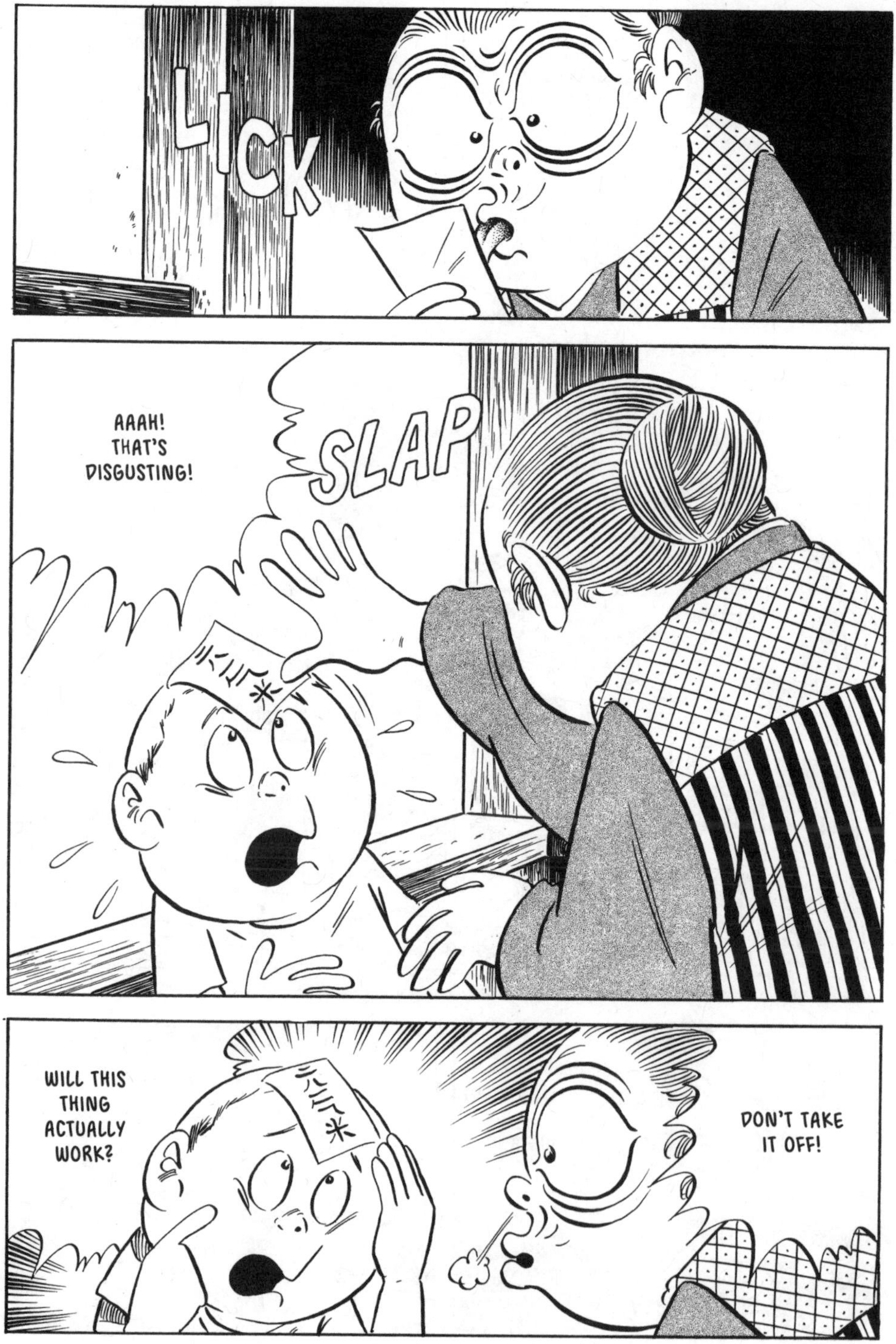
LICK
SLAP
AAAH! THAT'S DISGUSTING!
DON'T TAKE IT OFF!
WILL THIS THING ACTUALLY WORK?

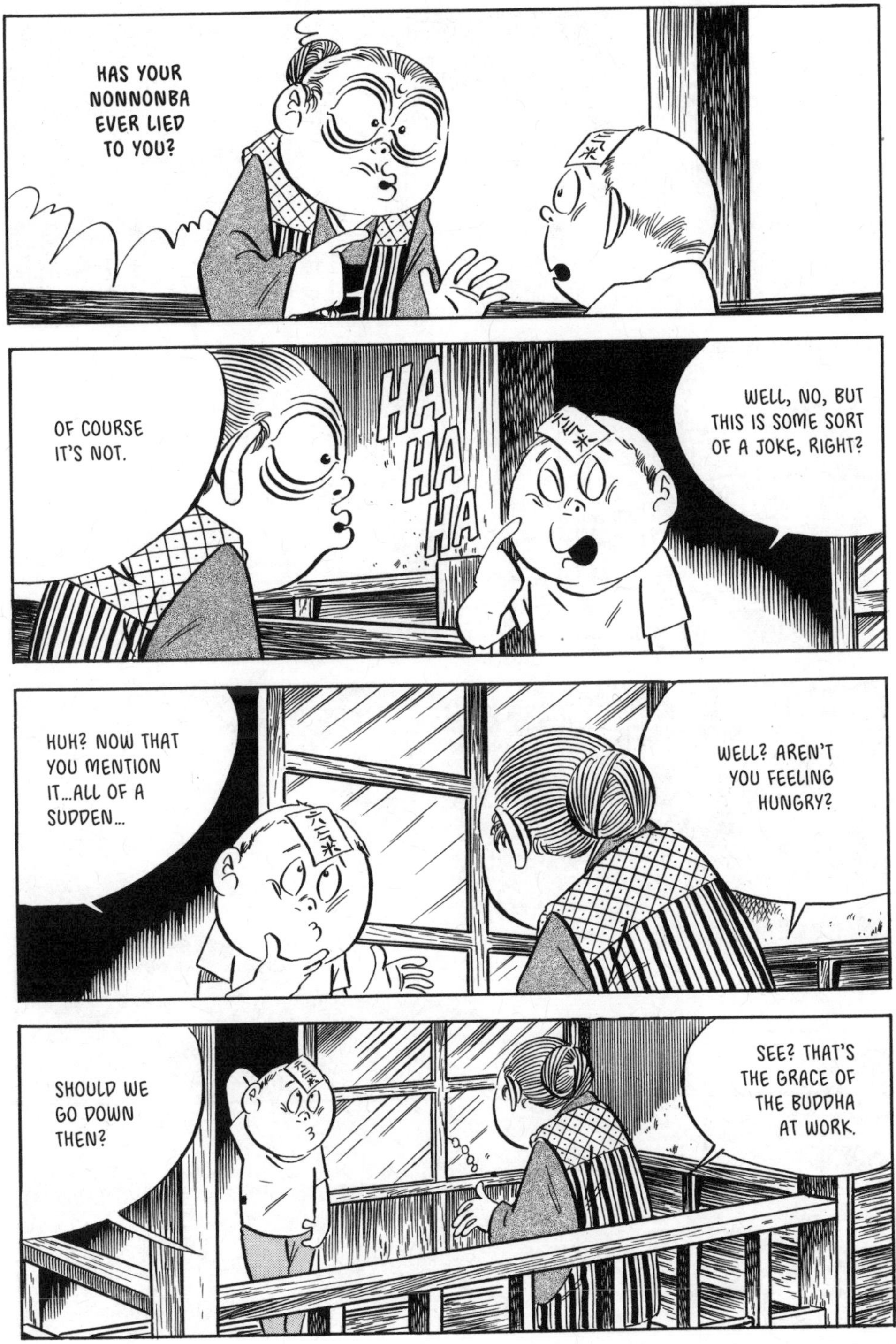
HAS YOUR NONNONBA EVER LIED TO YOU?
WELL, NO, BUT THIS IS SOME SORT OF A JOKE, RIGHT?
HA HA HA
OF COURSE IT'S NOT.
WELL? AREN'T YOU FEELING HUNGRY?
HUH? NOW THAT YOU MENTION IT...ALL OF A SUDDEN...
SEE? THAT'S THE GRACE OF THE BUDDHA AT WORK.
SHOULD WE GO DOWN THEN?

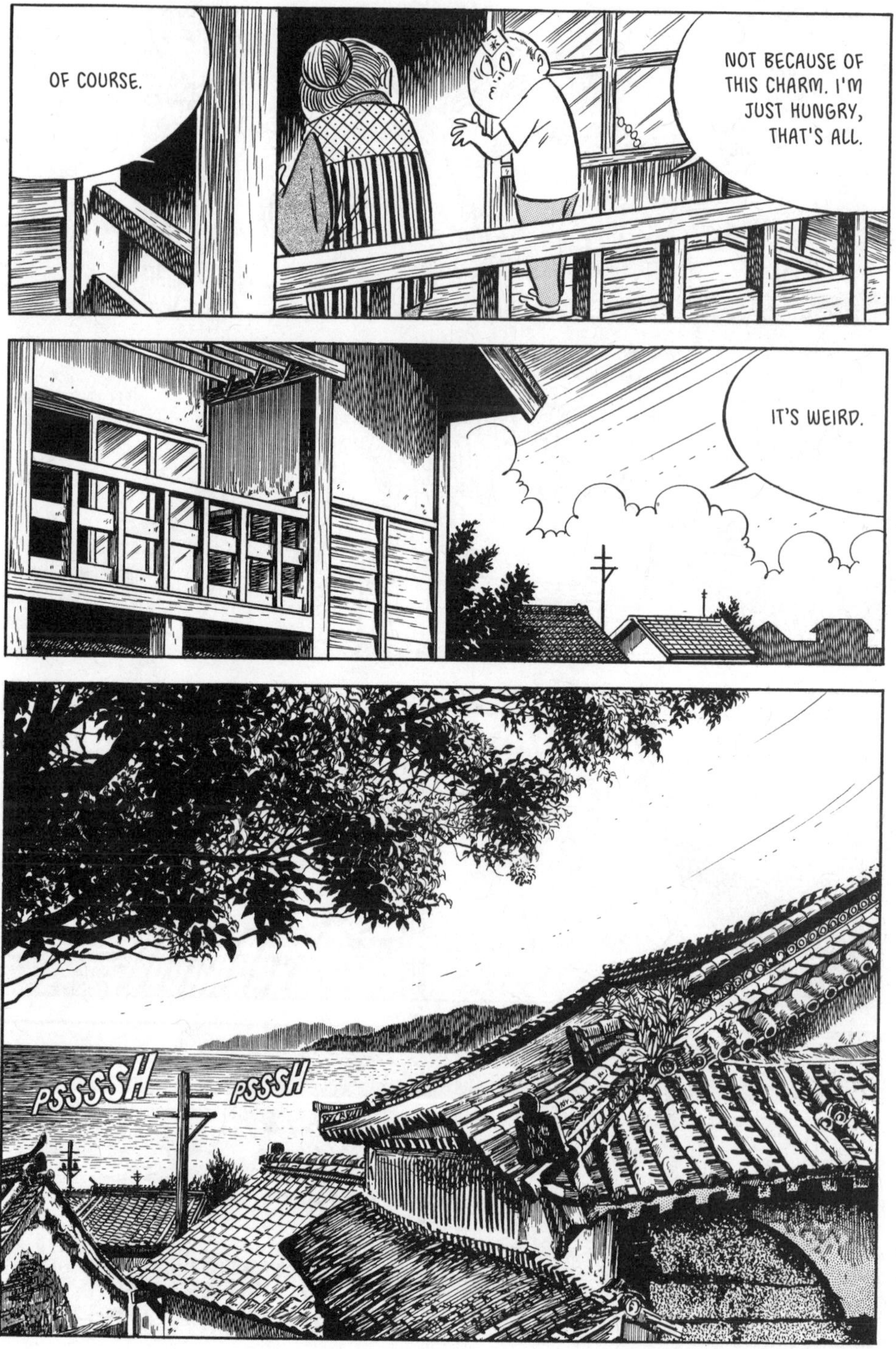
NOT BECAUSE OF THIS CHARM. I'M JUST HUNGRY, THAT'S ALL.
OF COURSE.
IT'S WEIRD.
PSSSH
PSSSSH

THE WALL

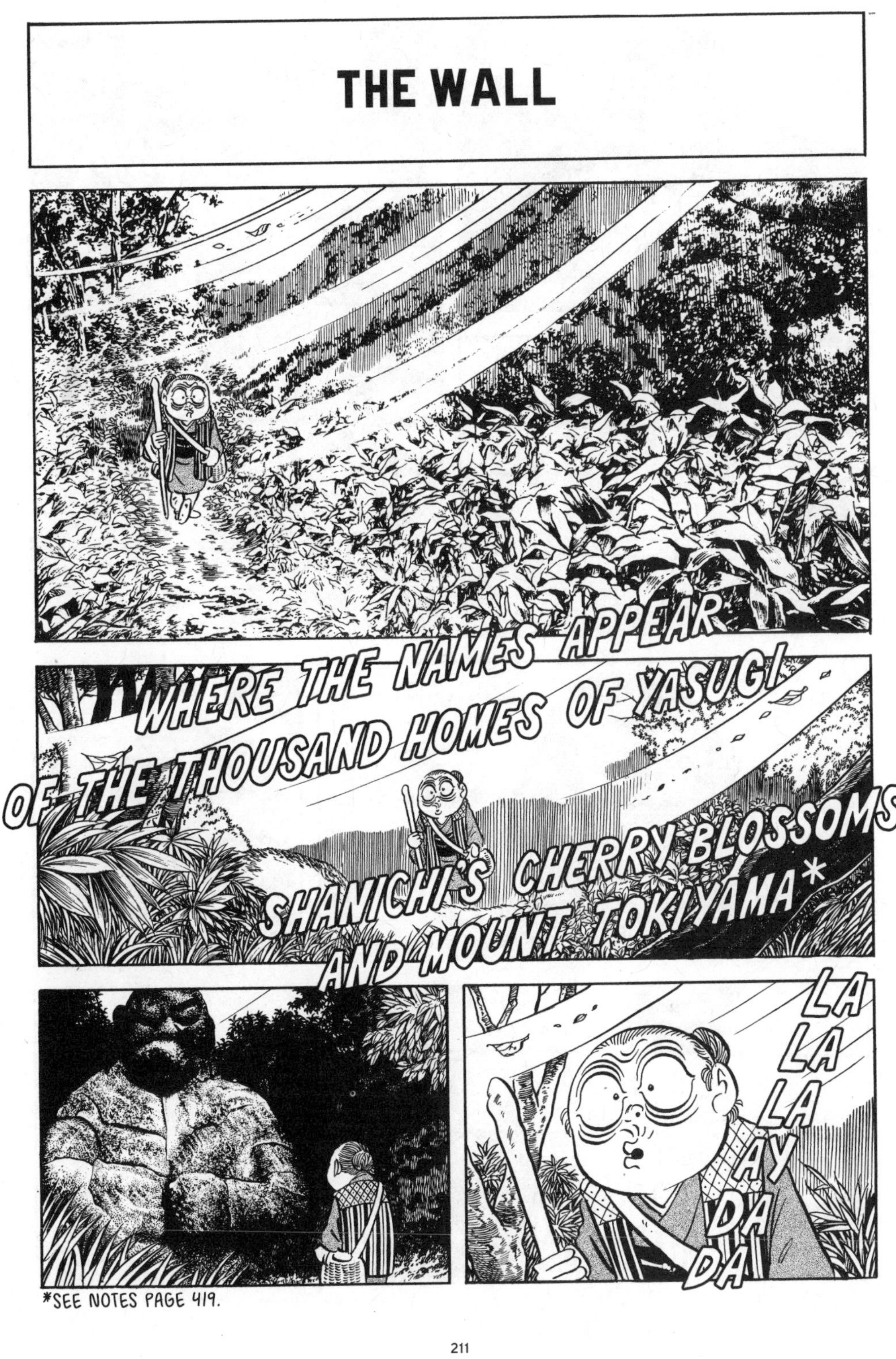
WHERE THE NAMES APPEAR
OF THE THOUSAND HOMES OF YASUGI
SHANICHI'S CHERRY BLOSSOMS
AND MOUNT TOKIYAMA*
LA LA LA LA AY DA DA DA

*SEE NOTES PAGE 419.

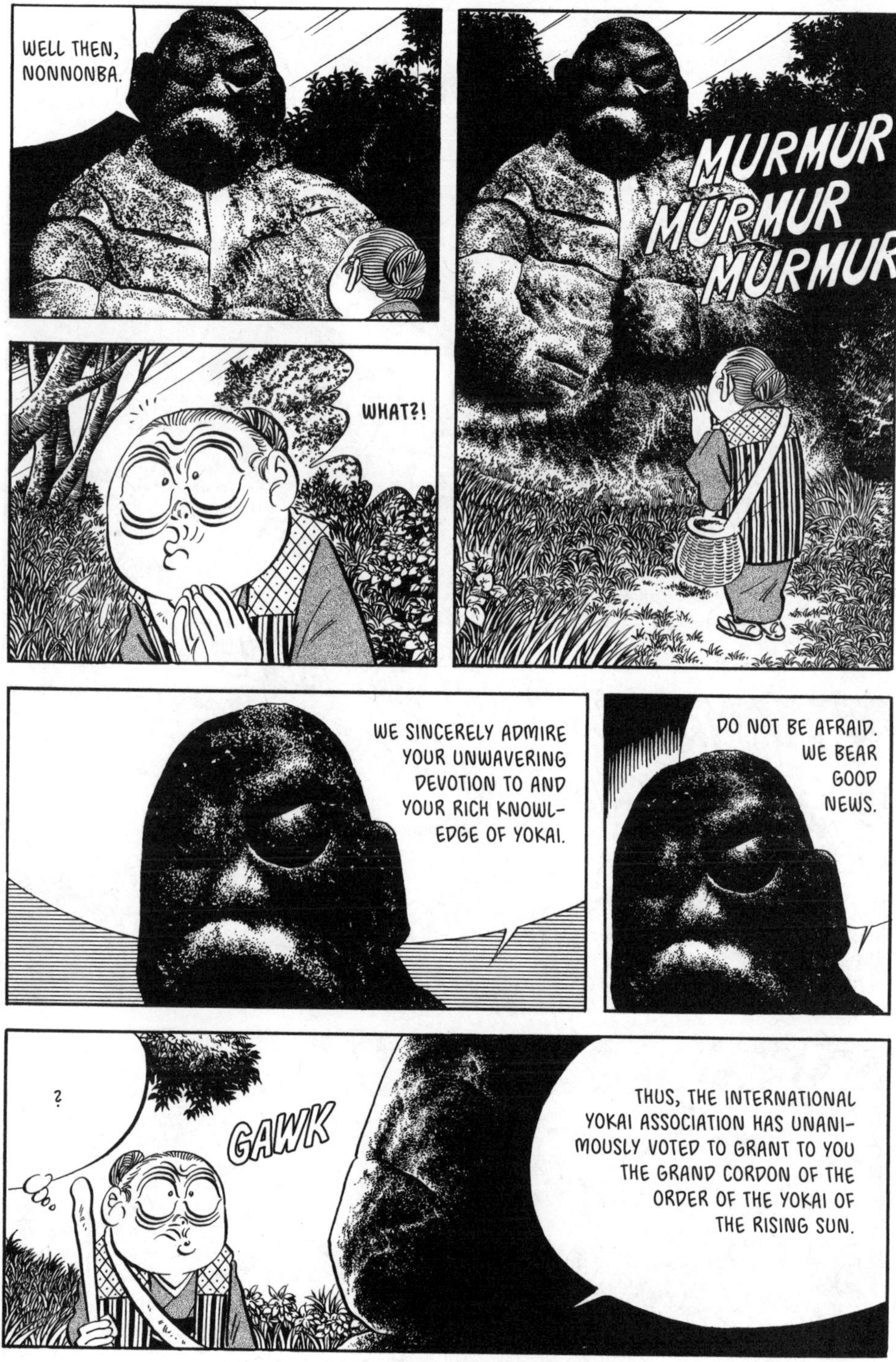
MURMUR
MURMUR
MURMUR
WELL THEN, NONNONBA.
WHAT?!
DO NOT BE AFRAID. WE BEAR GOOD NEWS.
WE SINCERELY ADMIRE YOUR UNWAVERING DEVOTION TO AND YOUR RICH KNOWL-EDGE OF YOKAI.
THUS, THE INTERNATIONAL YOKAI ASSOCIATION HAS UNANI-MOUSLY VOTED TO GRANT TO YOU THE GRAND CORDON OF THE ORDER OF THE YOKAI OF THE RISING SUN.
GAWK
?

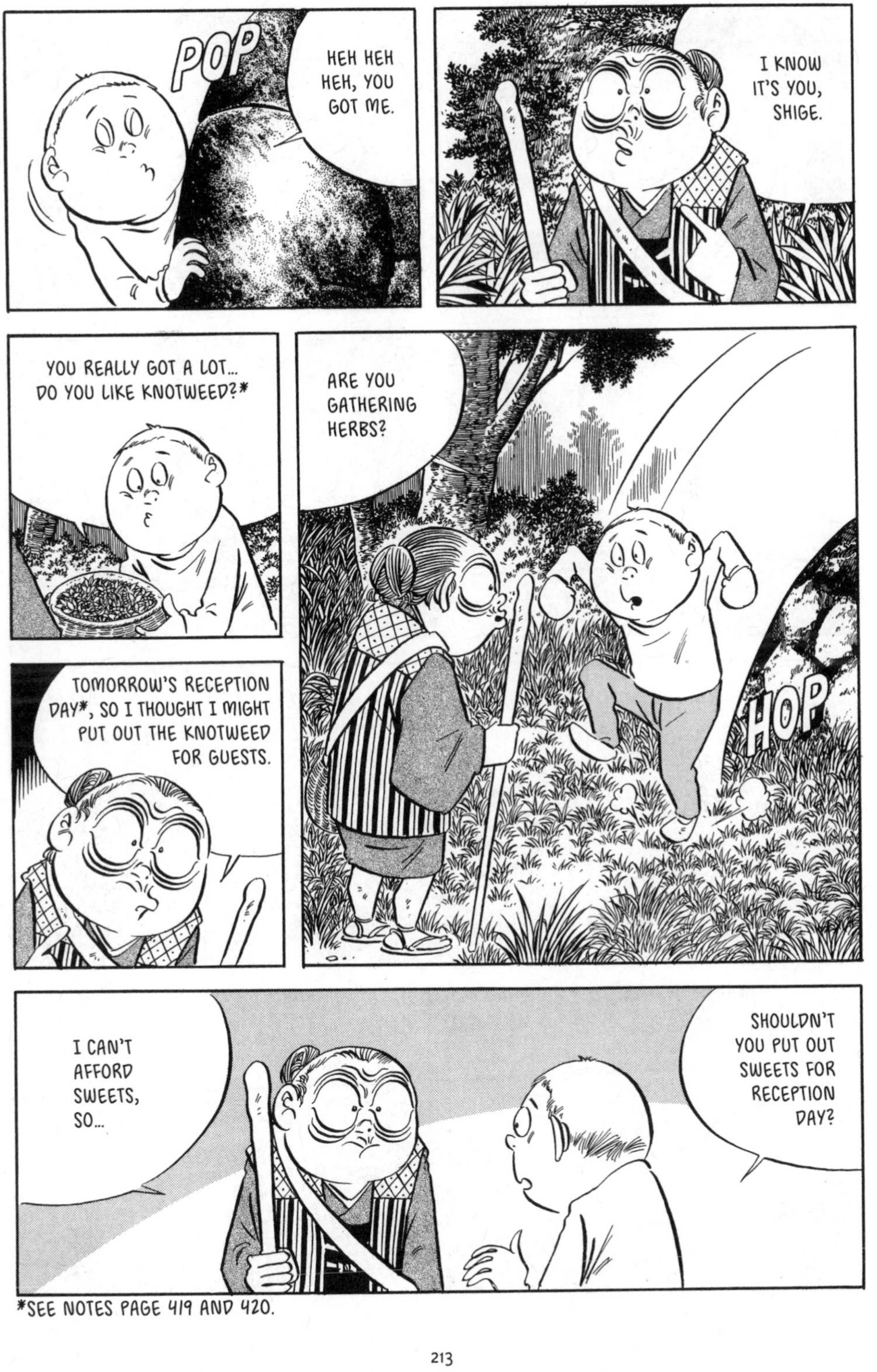
I KNOW IT'S YOU, SHIGE.
POP
HEH HEH HEH, YOU GOT ME.
ARE YOU GATHERING HERBS?
HOP
YOU REALLY GOT A LOT... DO YOU LIKE KNOTWEED?*
TOMORROW'S RECEPTION DAY*, SO I THOUGHT I MIGHT PUT OUT THE KNOTWEED FOR GUESTS.
SHOULDN'T YOU PUT OUT SWEETS FOR RECEPTION DAY?
I CAN'T AFFORD SWEETS, SO...

*SEE NOTES PAGE 419 AND 420.

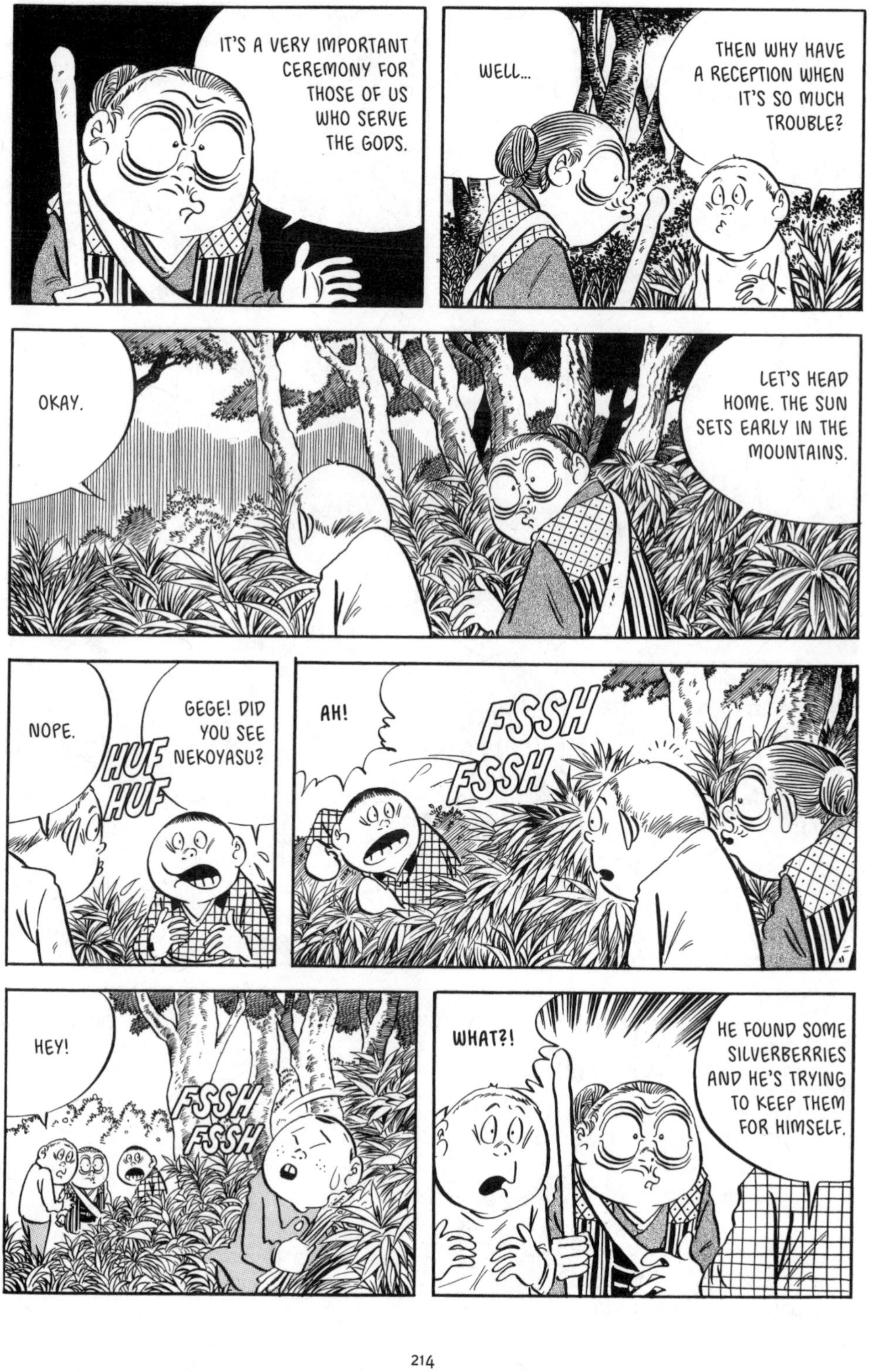
IT'S A VERY IMPORTANT CEREMONY FOR THOSE OF US WHO SERVE THE GODS.
THEN WHY HAVE A RECEPTION WHEN IT'S SO MUCH TROUBLE?
WELL...
LET'S HEAD HOME. THE SUN SETS EARLY IN THE MOUNTAINS.
OKAY.
GEGE! DID YOU SEE NEKOYASU?
HUF HUF
NOPE.
AH!
FSSH FSSH
HEY!
FSSH FSSH
HE FOUND SOME SILVERBERRIES AND HE'S TRYING TO KEEP THEM FOR HIMSELF.
WHAT?!

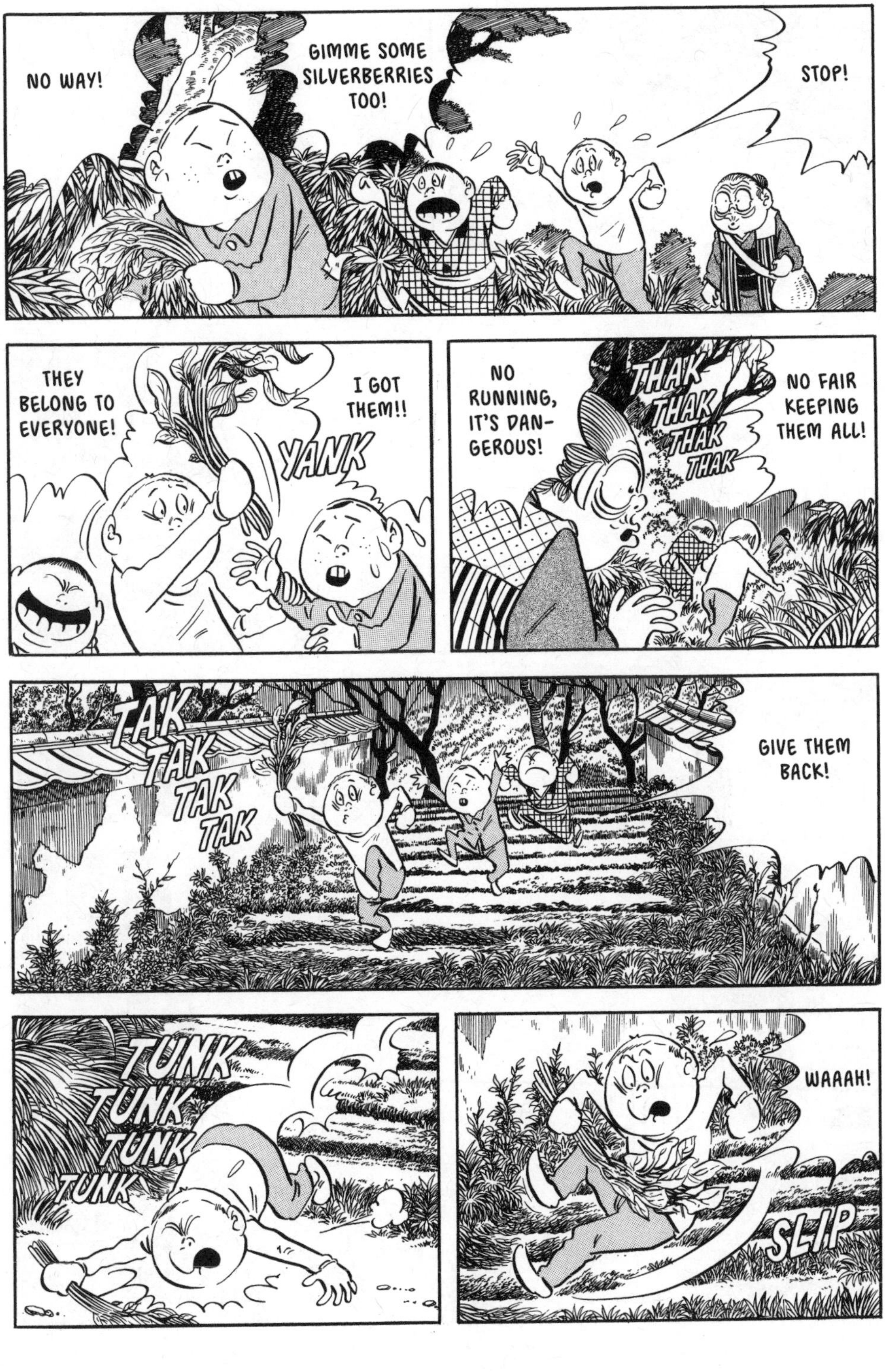
STOP!
GIMME SOME SILVERBERRIES TOO!
NO WAY!
NO FAIR KEEPING THEM ALL!
THAK THAK THAK THAK
NO RUNNING, IT'S DAN-GEROUS!
I GOT THEM!!
YANK
THEY BELONG TO EVERYONE!
GIVE THEM BACK!
TAK TAK TAK TAK
WAAAH!
SLIP
TUNK TUNK TUNK TUNK

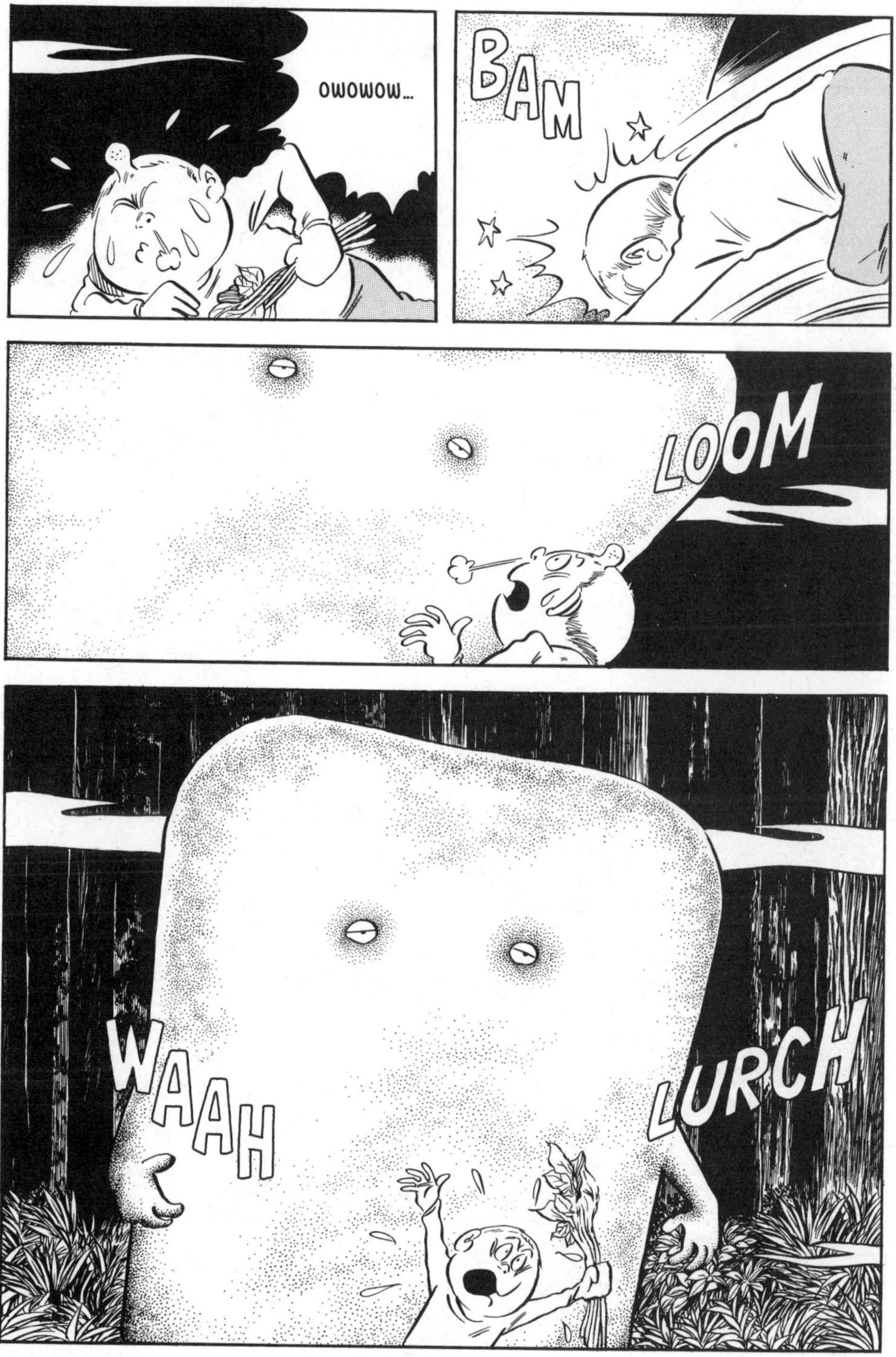
BAM
OWOWOW...
LOOM
LURCH
WAAH

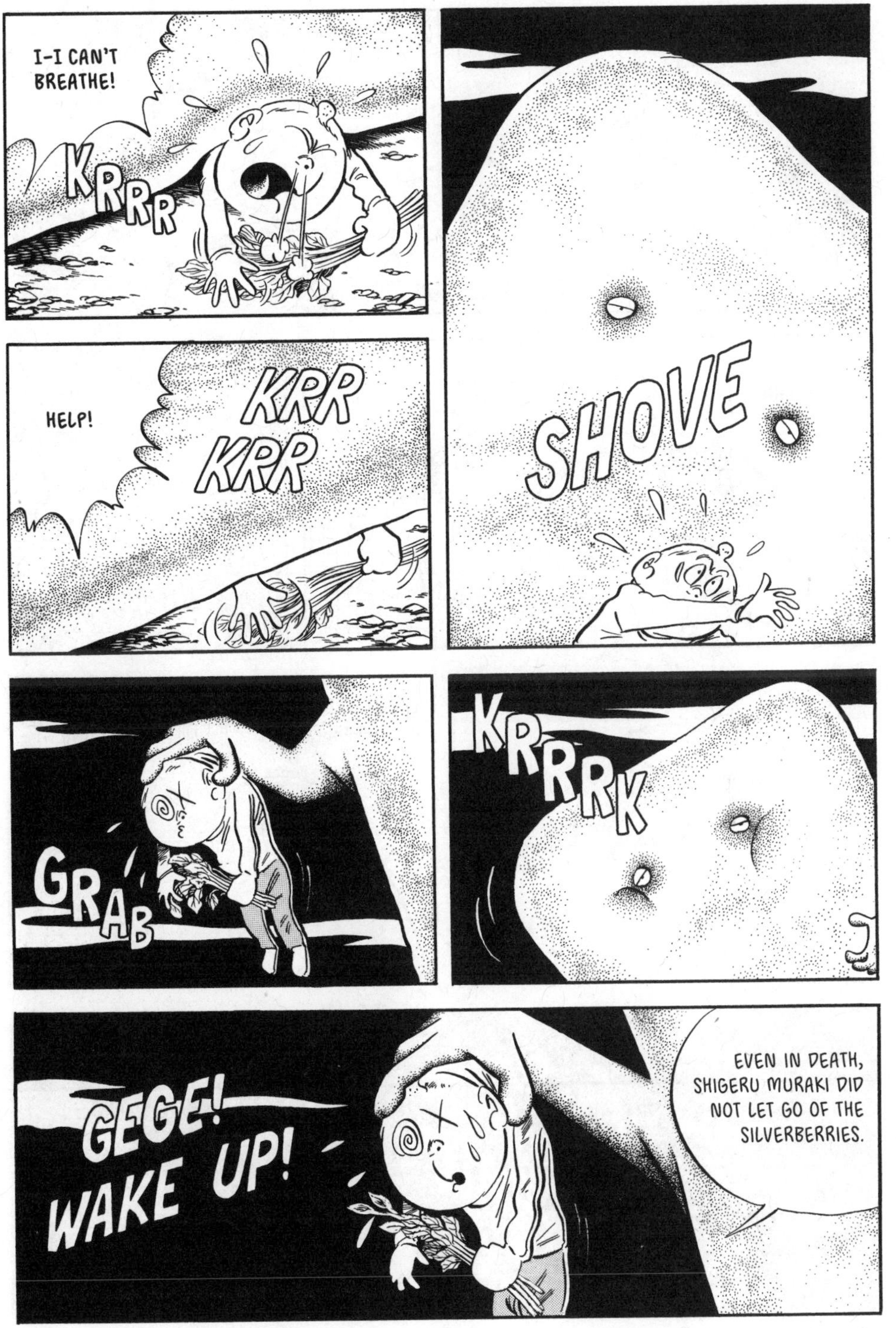
SHOVE
I-I CAN'T BREATHE!
KRRRR
HELP!
KRR KRR
KRRRRK
GRAB
EVEN IN DEATH, SHIGERU MURAKI DID NOT LET GO OF THE SILVERBERRIES.
GEGE! WAKE UP!

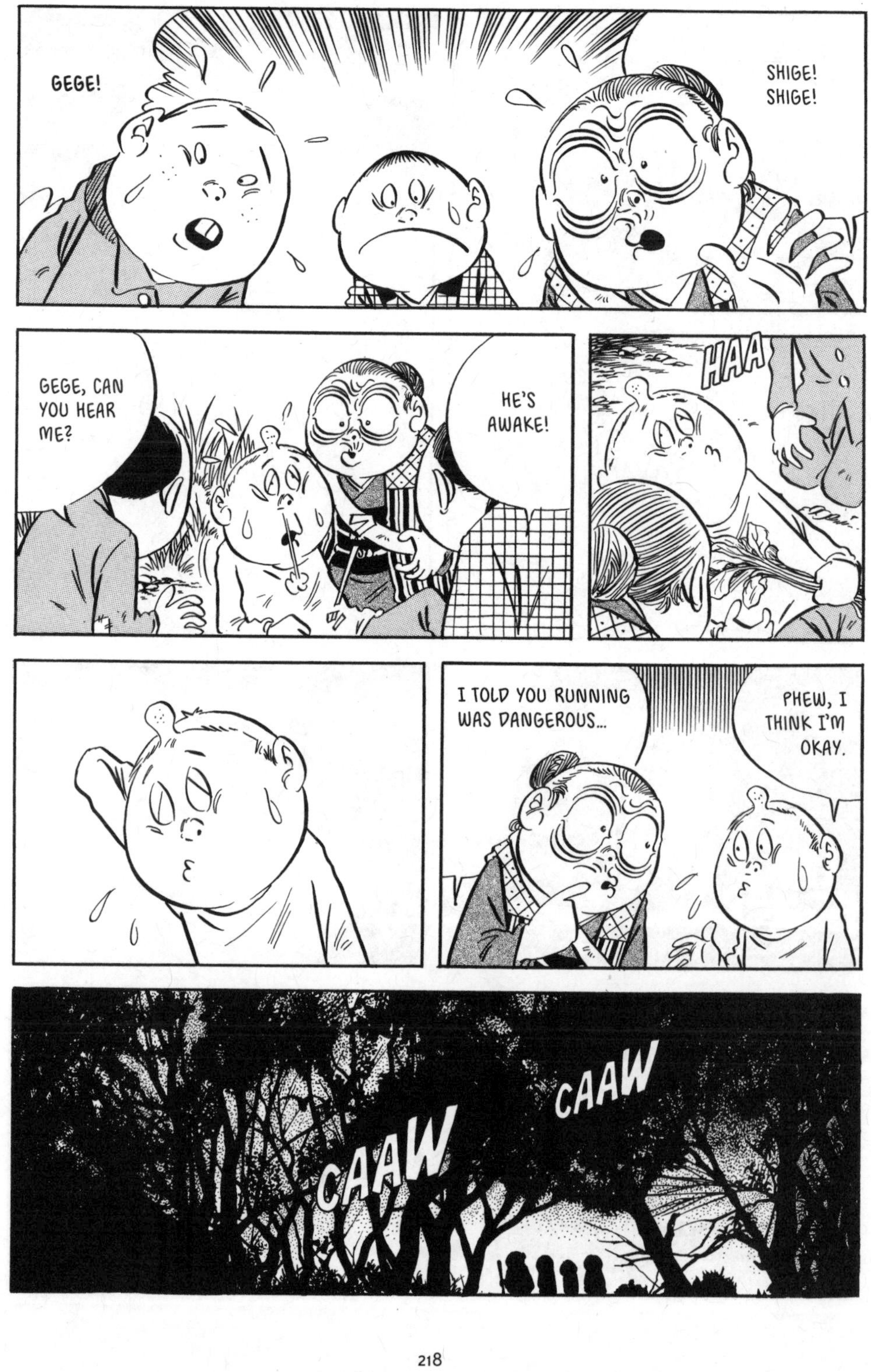
SHIGE! SHIGE!
GEGE!
HAA
HE'S AWAKE!
GEGE, CAN YOU HEAR ME?
PHEW, I THINK I'M OKAY.
I TOLD YOU RUNNING WAS DANGEROUS...
CAAW
CAAW

RECEPTION

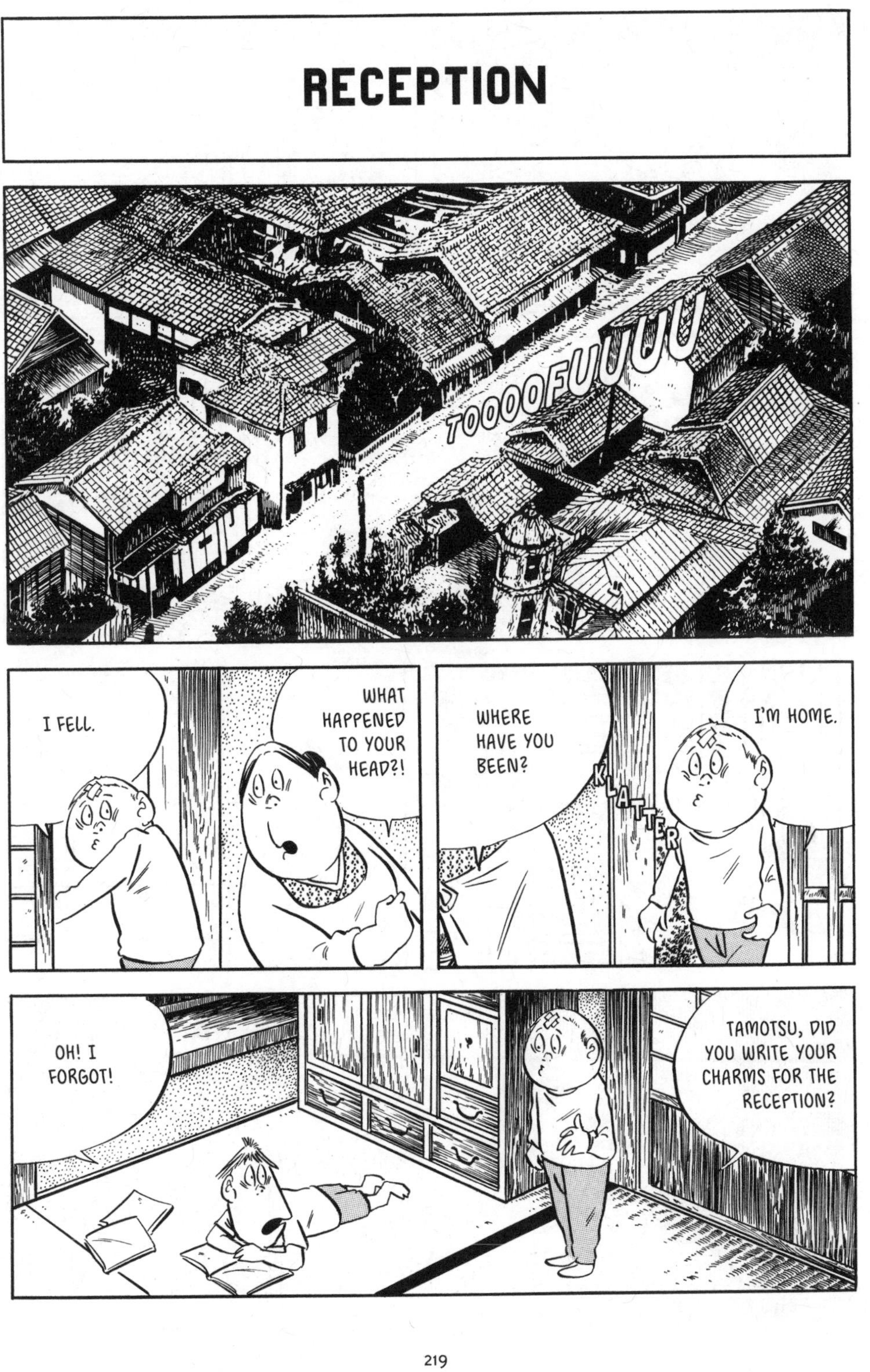
TOOOOFUUUU
I'M HOME.
WHERE HAVE YOU BEEN?
KLATTER
WHAT HAPPENED TO YOUR HEAD?!
I FELL.
TAMOTSU, DID YOU WRITE YOUR CHARMS FOR THE RECEPTION?
OH! I FORGOT!

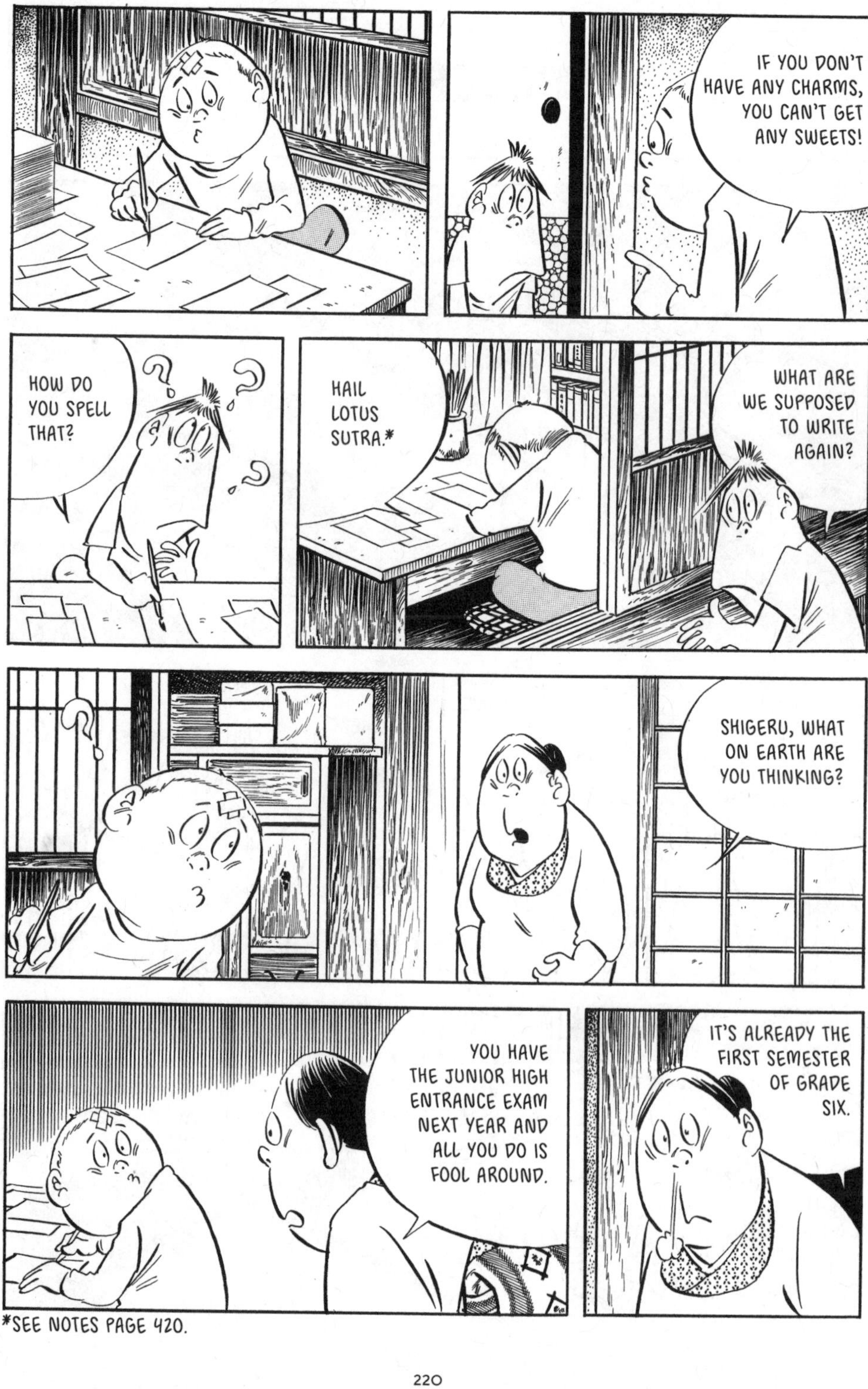
IF YOU DON'T HAVE ANY CHARMS, YOU CAN'T GET ANY SWEETS!
WHAT ARE WE SUPPOSED TO WRITE AGAIN?
HAIL LOTUS SUTRA.*
HOW DO YOU SPELL THAT?
SHIGERU, WHAT ON EARTH ARE YOU THINKING?
IT'S ALREADY THE FIRST SEMESTER OF GRADE SIX.
YOU HAVE THE JUNIOR HIGH ENTRANCE EXAM NEXT YEAR AND ALL YOU DO IS FOOL AROUND.

*SEE NOTES PAGE 420.

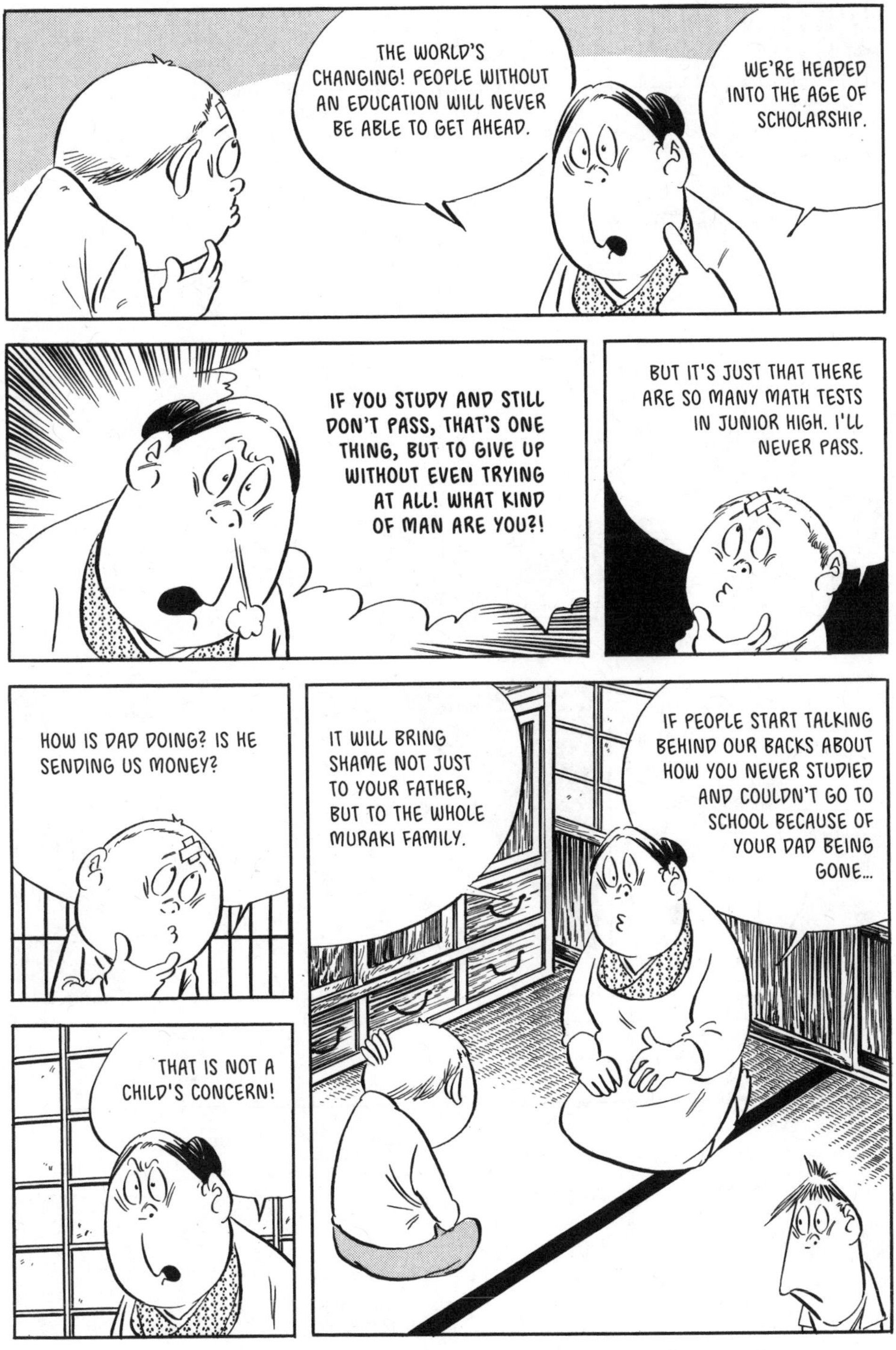
WE'RE HEADED INTO THE AGE OF SCHOLARSHIP.
THE WORLD'S CHANGING! PEOPLE WITHOUT AN EDUCATION WILL NEVER BE ABLE TO GET AHEAD.
BUT IT'S JUST THAT THERE ARE SO MANY MATH TESTS IN JUNIOR HIGH. I'LL NEVER PASS.
IF YOU STUDY AND STILL DON'T PASS, THAT'S ONE THING, BUT TO GIVE UP WITHOUT EVEN TRYING AT ALL! WHAT KIND OF MAN ARE YOU?!
IF PEOPLE START TALKING BEHIND OUR BACKS ABOUT HOW YOU NEVER STUDIED AND COULDN'T GO TO SCHOOL BECAUSE OF YOUR DAD BEING GONE...
IT WILL BRING SHAME NOT JUST TO YOUR FATHER, BUT TO THE WHOLE MURAKI FAMILY.
HOW IS DAD DOING? IS HE SENDING US MONEY?
THAT IS NOT A CHILD'S CONCERN!

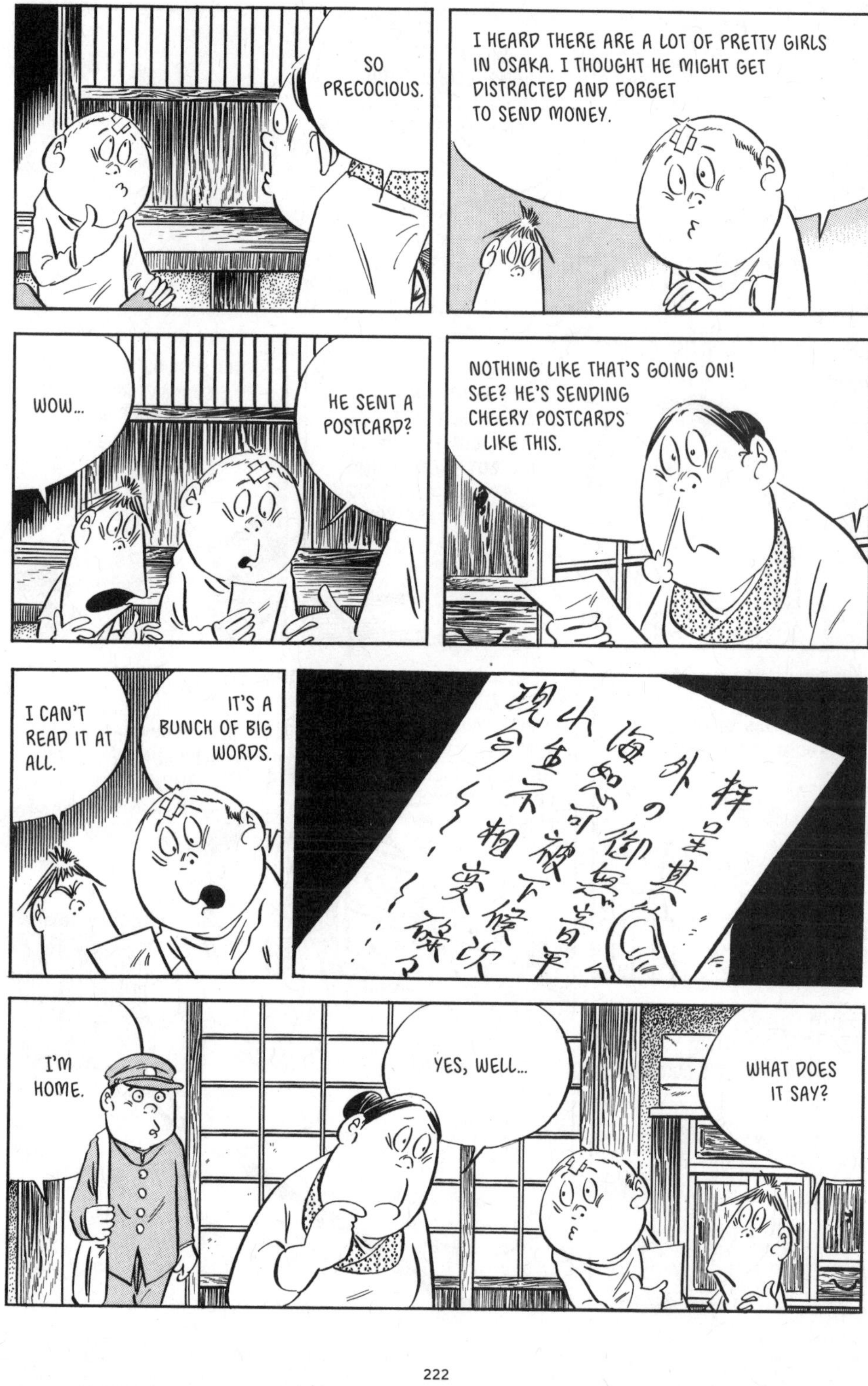
I HEARD THERE ARE A LOT OF PRETTY GIRLS IN OSAKA. I THOUGHT HE MIGHT GET DISTRACTED AND FORGET TO SEND MONEY.
SO PRECOCIOUS.
NOTHING LIKE THAT'S GOING ON! SEE? HE'S SENDING CHEERY POSTCARDS LIKE THIS.
HE SENT A POSTCARD?
WOW...
IT'S A BUNCH OF BIG WORDS.
I CAN'T READ IT AT ALL.
WHAT DOES IT SAY?
YES, WELL...
I'M HOME.

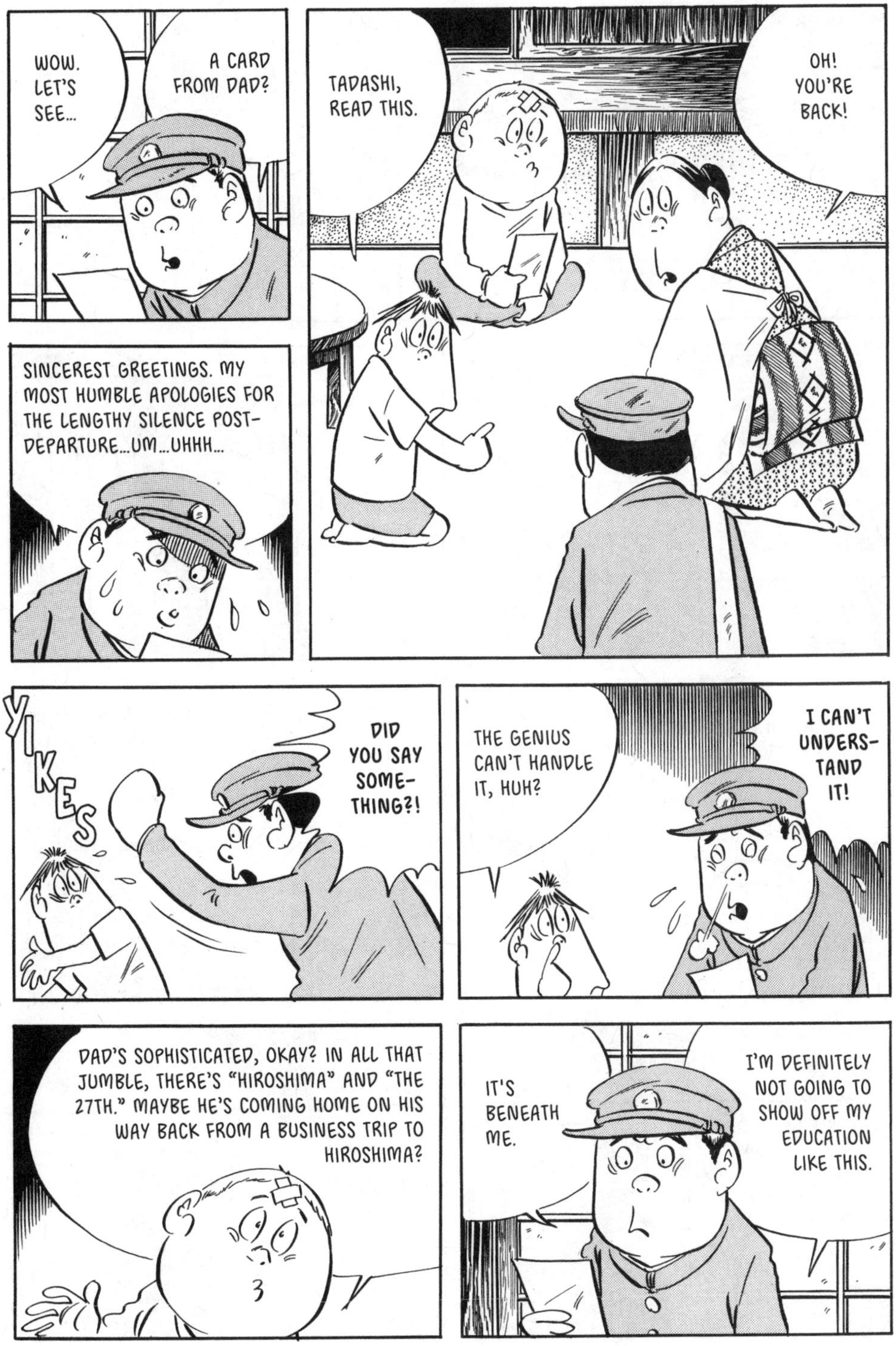
OH! YOU'RE BACK!
TADASHI, READ THIS.
A CARD FROM DAD?
WOW. LET'S SEE...
SINCEREST GREETINGS. MY MOST HUMBLE APOLOGIES FOR THE LENGTHY SILENCE POST-DEPARTURE...UM...UHHH...
I CAN'T UNDERS-TAND IT!
THE GENIUS CAN'T HANDLE IT, HUH?
DID YOU SAY SOME-THING?!
YIKES
I'M DEFINITELY NOT GOING TO SHOW OFF MY EDUCATION LIKE THIS.
IT'S BENEATH ME.
DAD'S SOPHISTICATED, OKAY? IN ALL THAT JUMBLE, THERE'S "HIROSHIMA" AND "THE 27TH." MAYBE HE'S COMING HOME ON HIS WAY BACK FROM A BUSINESS TRIP TO HIROSHIMA?

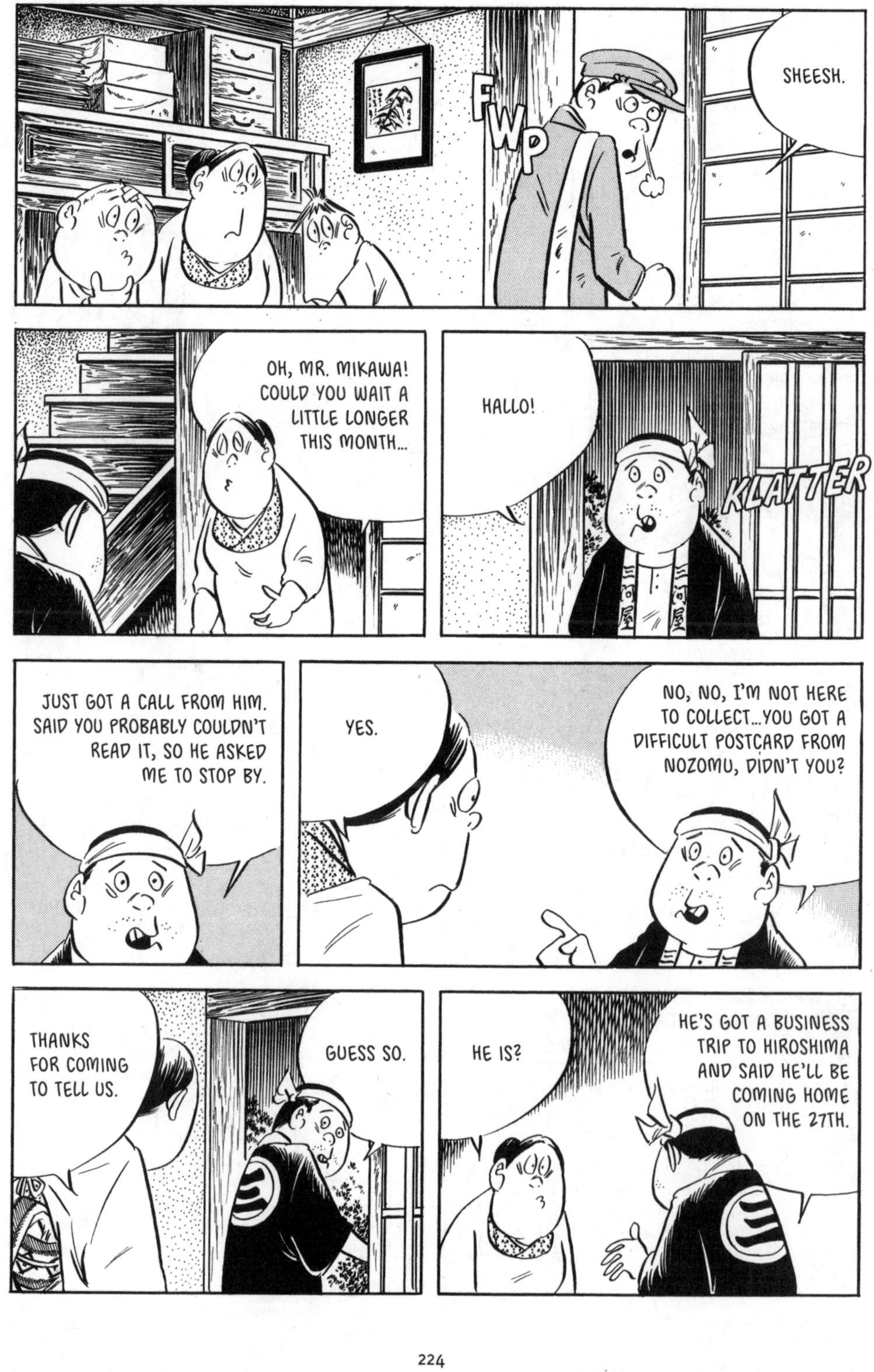
SHEESH.
FWP
HALLO!
KLATTER
OH, MR. MIKAWA! COULD YOU WAIT A LITTLE LONGER THIS MONTH...
NO, NO, I'M NOT HERE TO COLLECT...YOU GOT A DIFFICULT POSTCARD FROM NOZOMU, DIDN'T YOU?
YES.
JUST GOT A CALL FROM HIM. SAID YOU PROBABLY COULDN'T READ IT, SO HE ASKED ME TO STOP BY.
HE'S GOT A BUSINESS TRIP TO HIROSHIMA AND SAID HE'LL BE COMING HOME ON THE 27TH.
HE IS?
GUESS SO.
THANKS FOR COMING TO TELL US.

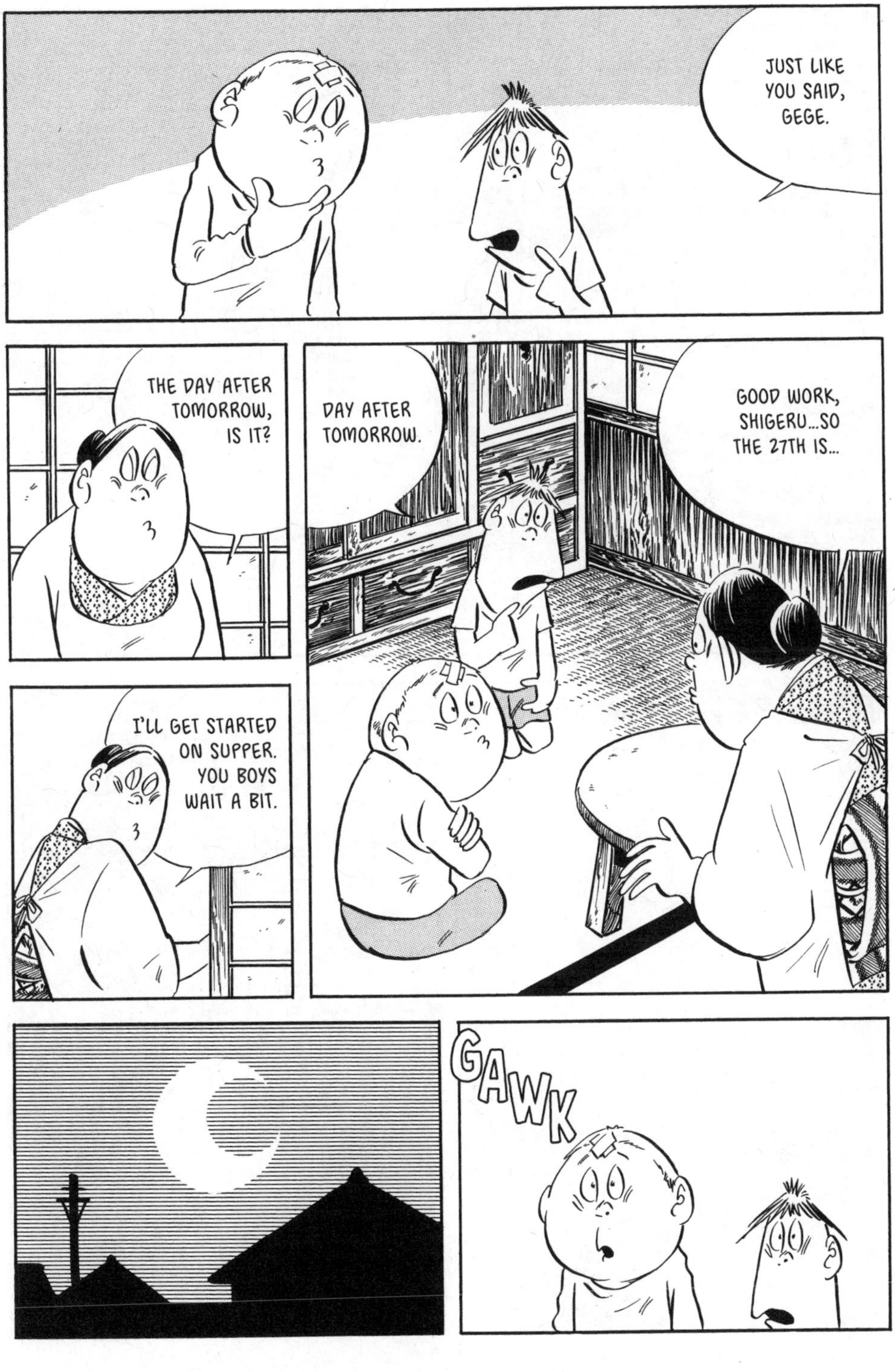
JUST LIKE YOU SAID, GEGE.
GOOD WORK, SHIGERU…SO THE 27TH IS…
DAY AFTER TOMORROW.
THE DAY AFTER TOMORROW, IS IT?
I'LL GET STARTED ON SUPPER. YOU BOYS WAIT A BIT.
GAWK

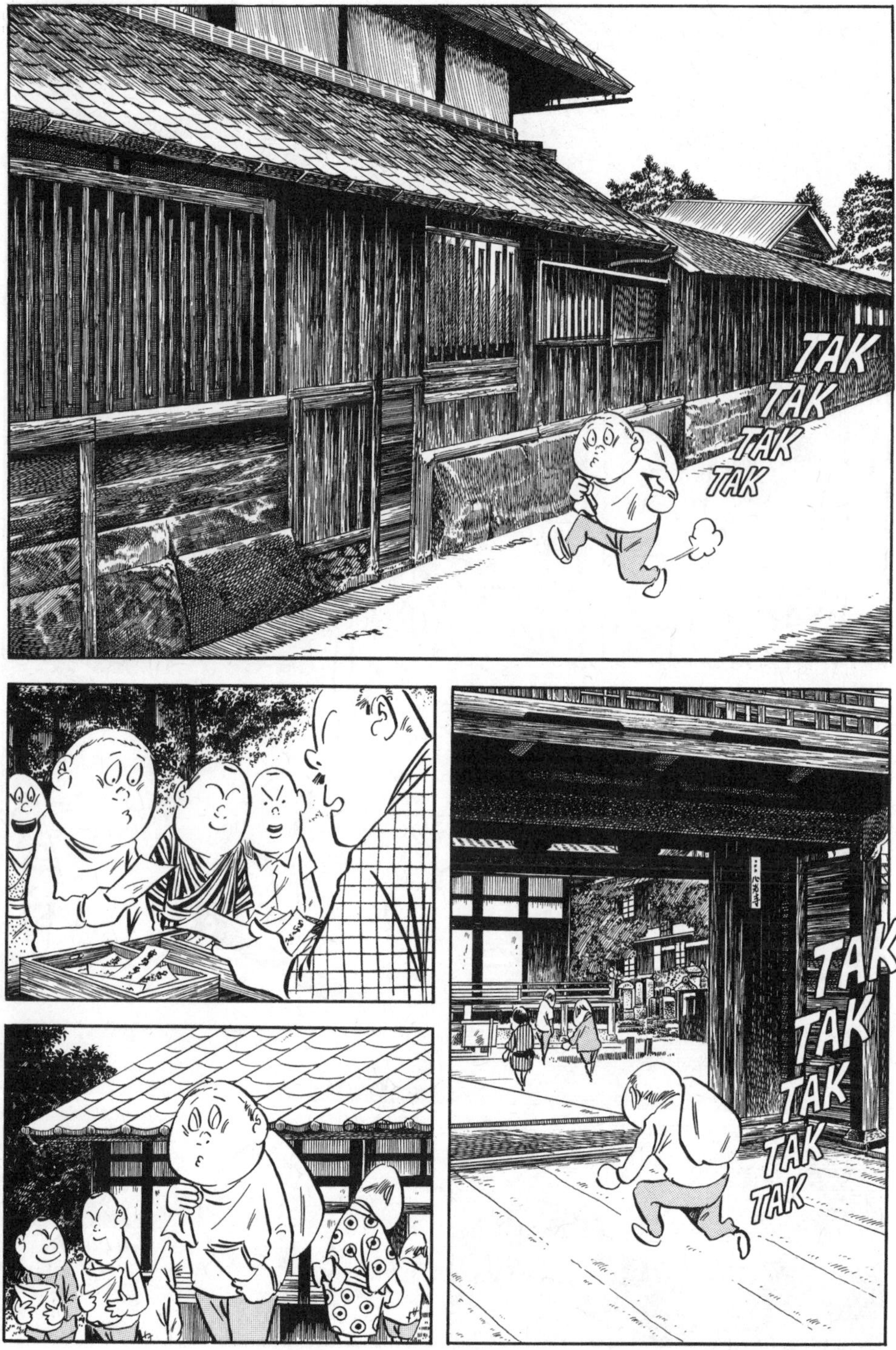
TAK
TAK
TAK
TAK
TAK
TAK
TAK
TAK
TAK

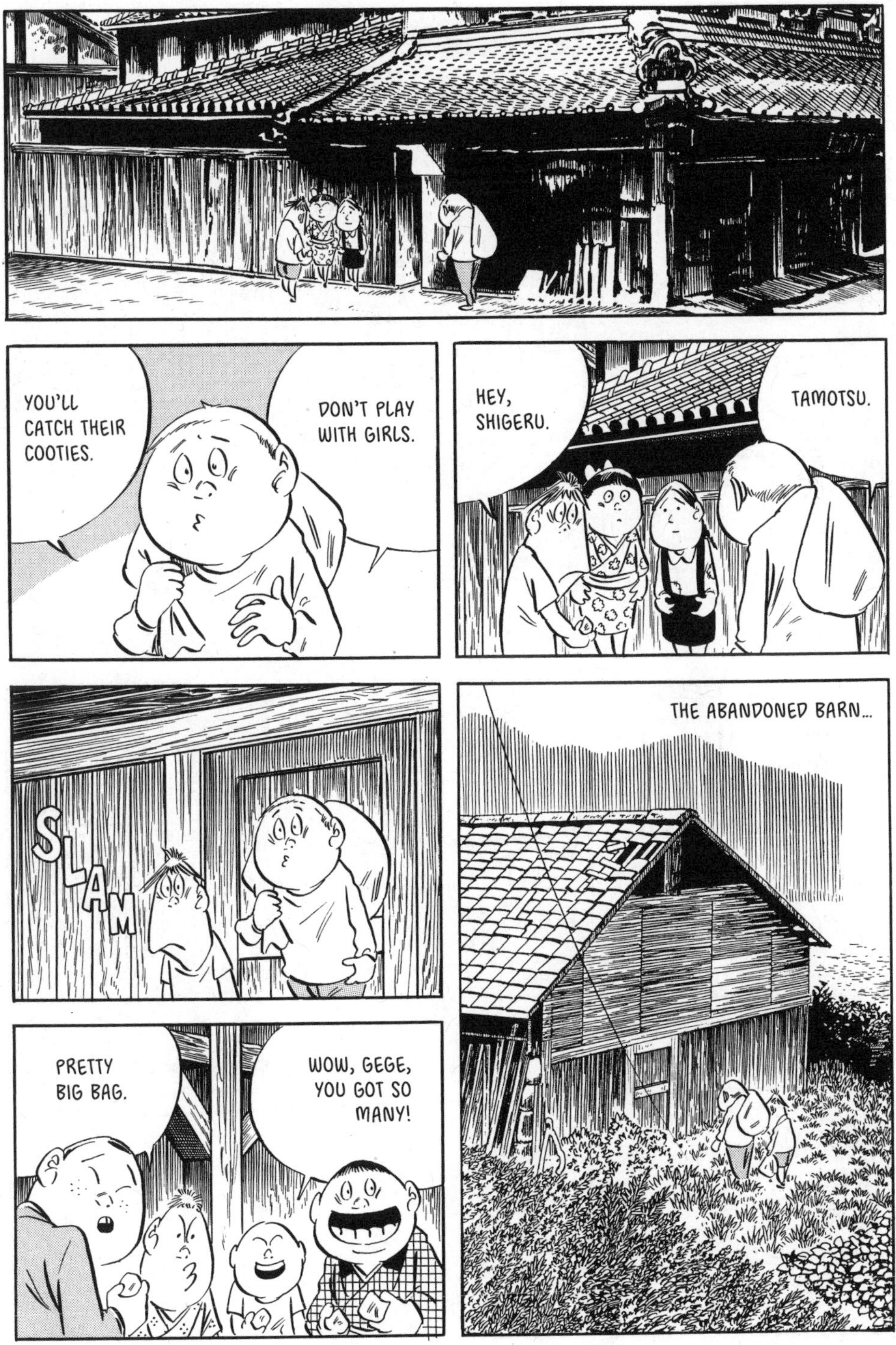
TAMOTSU.
HEY, SHIGERU.
DON'T PLAY WITH GIRLS.
YOU'LL CATCH THEIR COOTIES.
THE ABANDONED BARN...
SLAM
WOW, GEGE, YOU GOT SO MANY!
PRETTY BIG BAG.

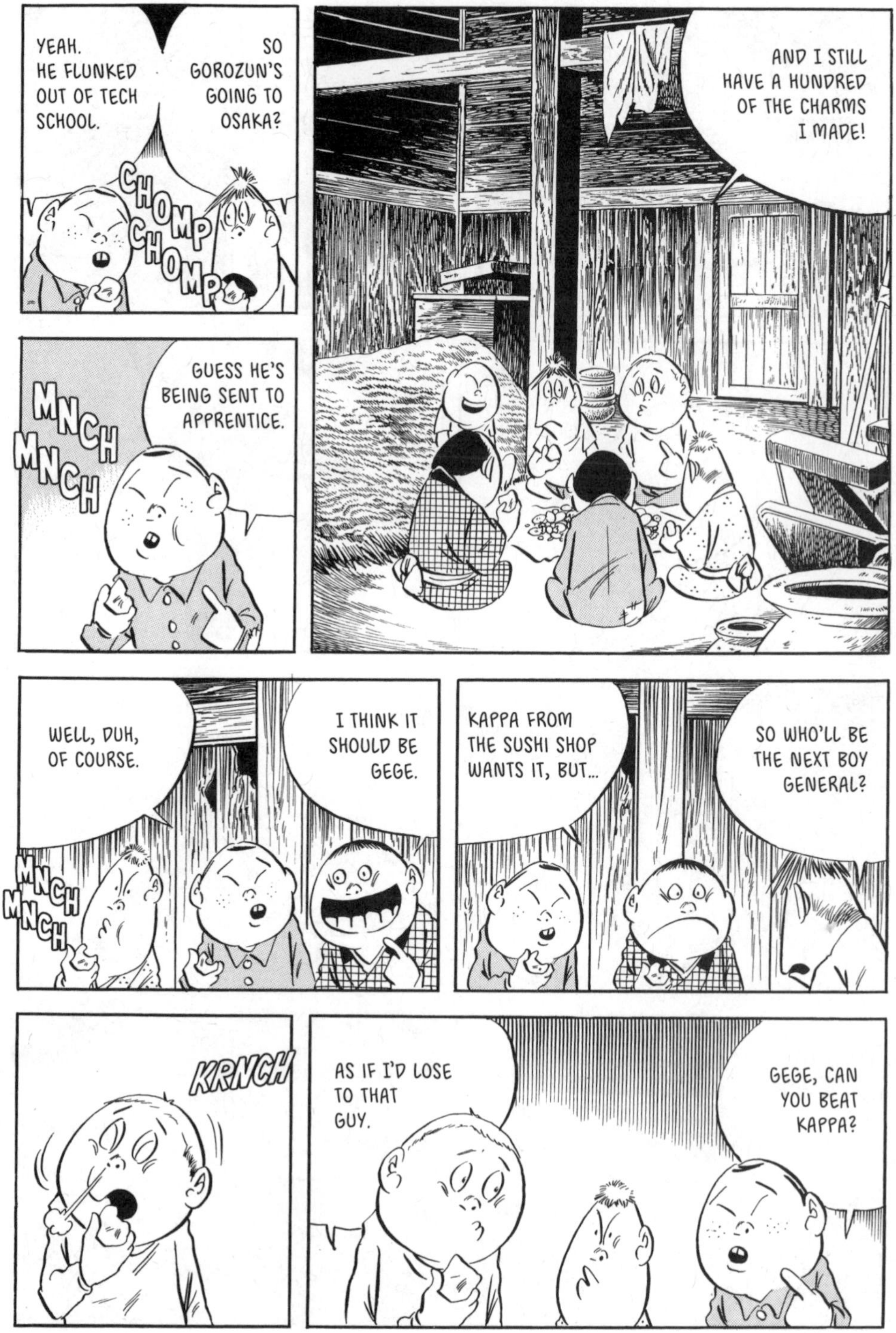
AND I STILL HAVE A HUNDRED OF THE CHARMS I MADE!
SO GOROZUN'S GOING TO OSAKA?
YEAH. HE FLUNKED OUT OF TECH SCHOOL.
CHOMP CHOMP
GUESS HE'S BEING SENT TO APPRENTICE.
MNCH MNCH
SO WHO'LL BE THE NEXT BOY GENERAL?
KAPPA FROM THE SUSHI SHOP WANTS IT, BUT...
I THINK IT SHOULD BE GEGE.
WELL, DUH, OF COURSE.
MNCH MNCH
GEGE, CAN YOU BEAT KAPPA?
AS IF I'D LOSE TO THAT GUY.
KRNCH

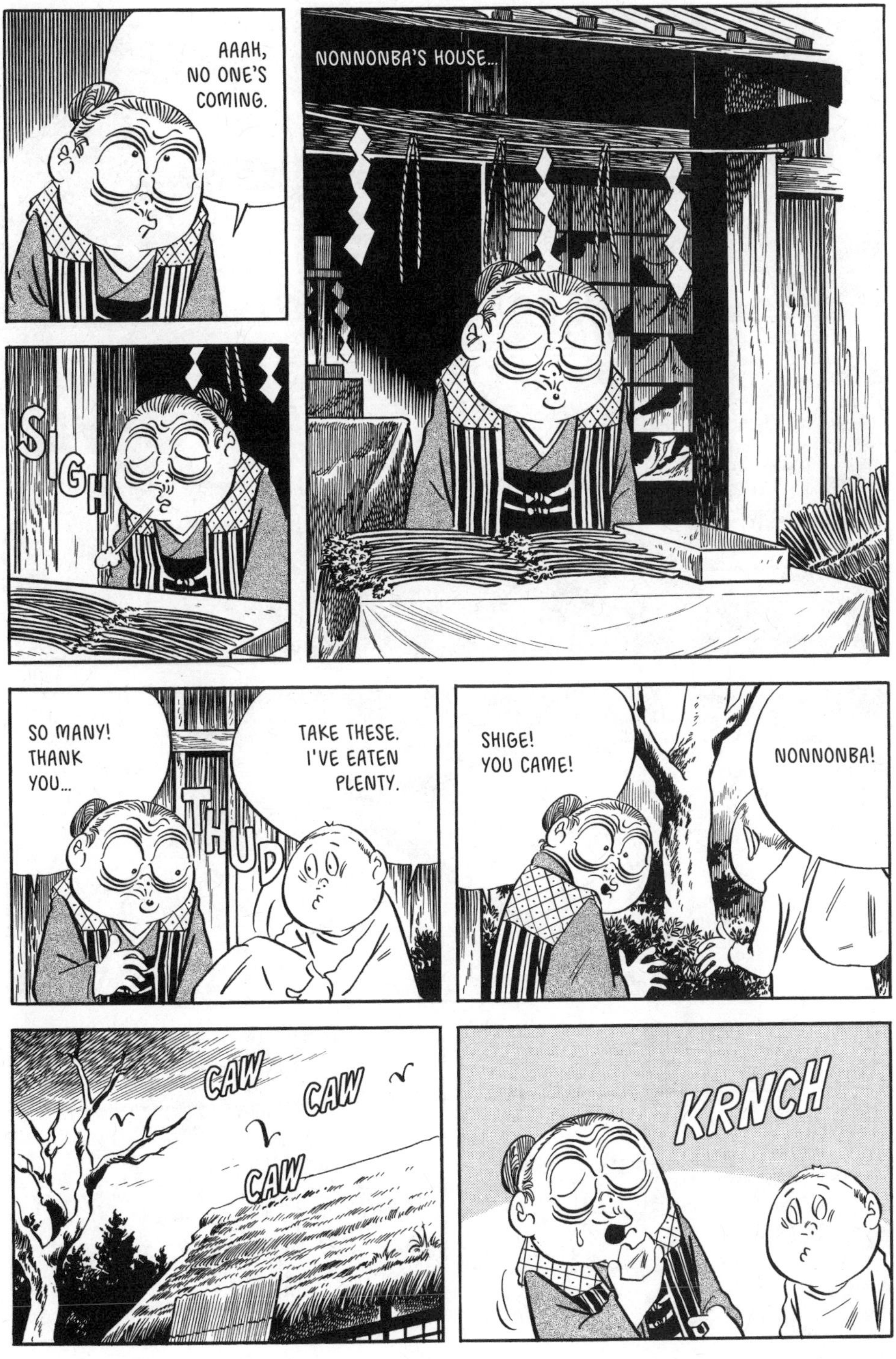
NONNONBA'S HOUSE...
AAAH, NO ONE'S COMING.
SIGH
NONNONBA!
SHIGE! YOU CAME!
TAKE THESE. I'VE EATEN PLENTY.
THUD
SO MANY! THANK YOU...
KRNCH
CAW
CAW
CAW

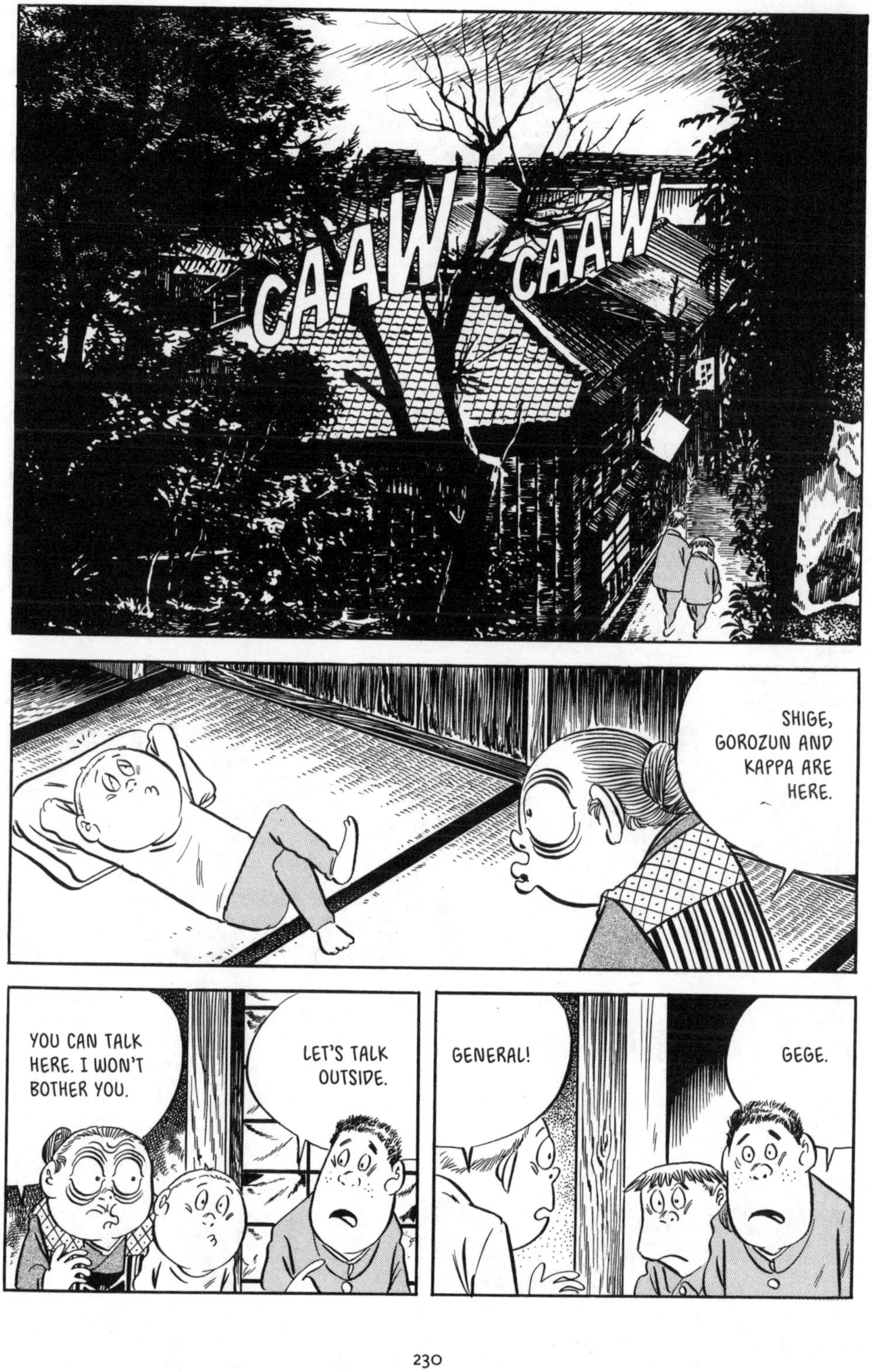
CAAW
CAAW
SHIGE, GOROZUN AND KAPPA ARE HERE.
GEGE.
GENERAL!
LET'S TALK OUTSIDE.
YOU CAN TALK HERE. I WON'T BOTHER YOU.

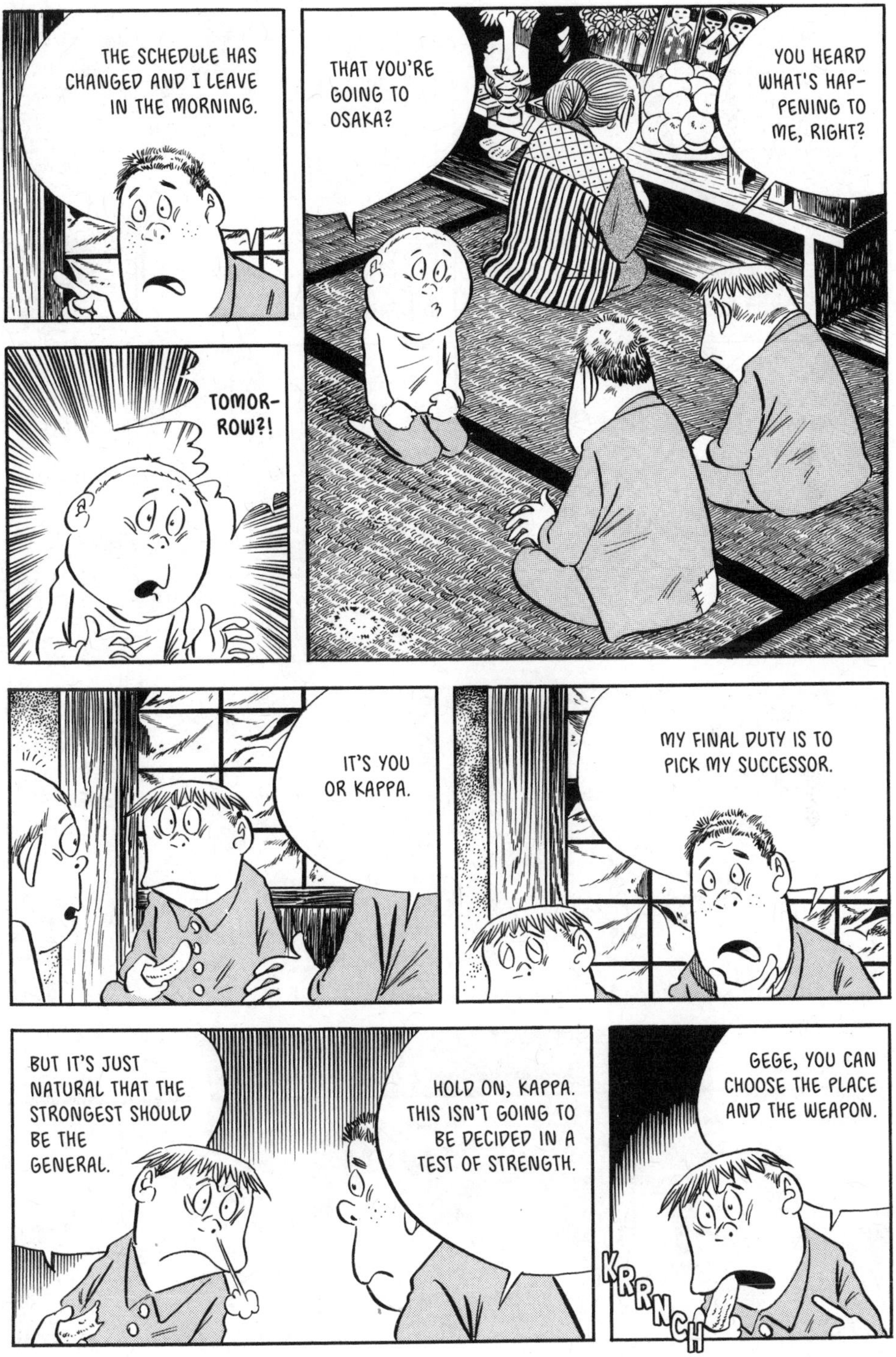
YOU HEARD WHAT'S HAP-PENING TO ME, RIGHT?
THAT YOU'RE GOING TO OSAKA?
THE SCHEDULE HAS CHANGED AND I LEAVE IN THE MORNING.
TOMOR-ROW?!
MY FINAL DUTY IS TO PICK MY SUCCESSOR.
IT'S YOU OR KAPPA.
GEGE, YOU CAN CHOOSE THE PLACE AND THE WEAPON.
KRRNCH
HOLD ON, KAPPA. THIS ISN'T GOING TO BE DECIDED IN A TEST OF STRENGTH.
BUT IT'S JUST NATURAL THAT THE STRONGEST SHOULD BE THE GENERAL.

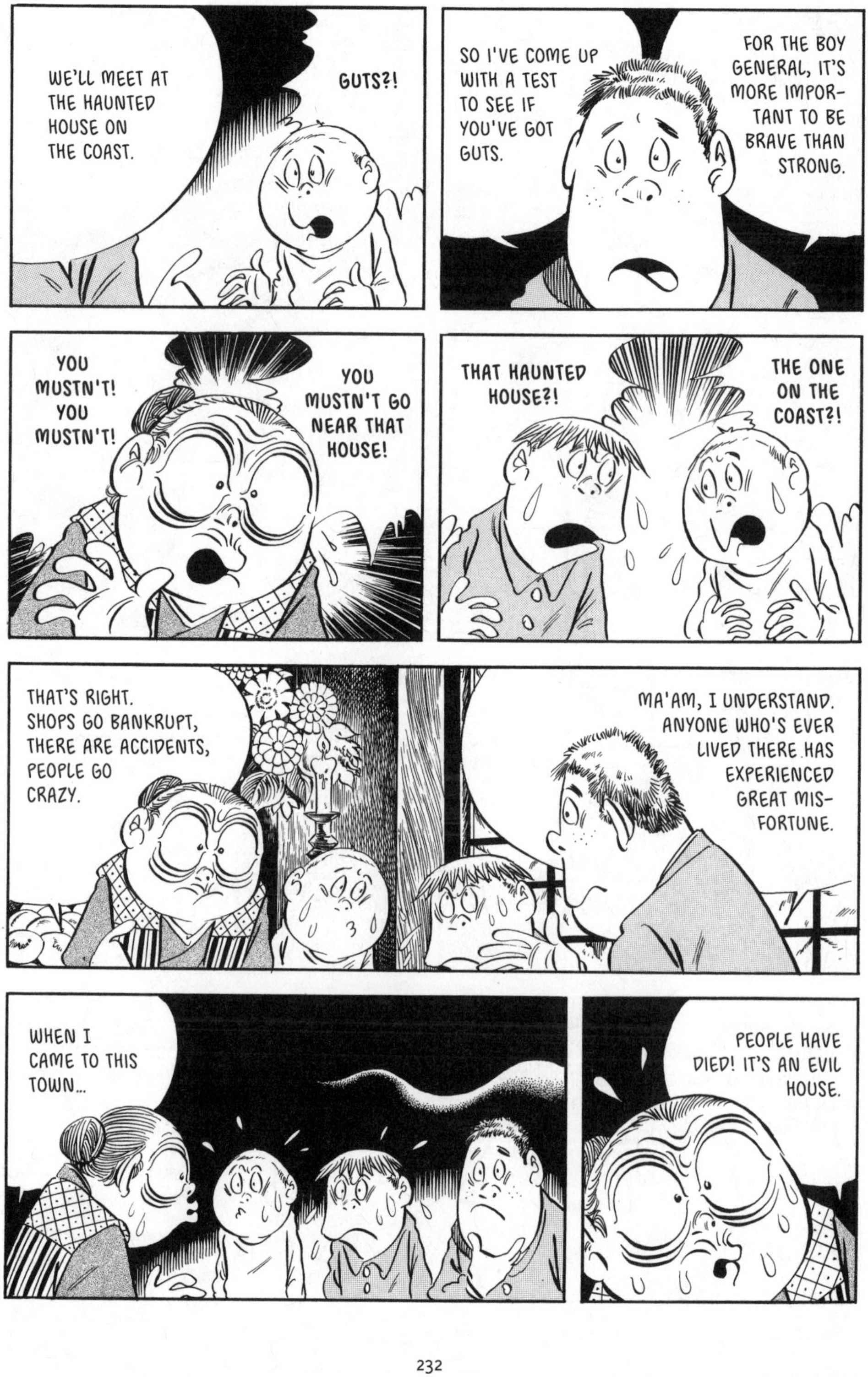
FOR THE BOY GENERAL, IT'S MORE IMPOR-TANT TO BE BRAVE THAN STRONG.
SO I'VE COME UP WITH A TEST TO SEE IF YOU'VE GOT GUTS.
GUTS?!
WE'LL MEET AT THE HAUNTED HOUSE ON THE COAST.
THE ONE ON THE COAST?!
THAT HAUNTED HOUSE?!
YOU MUSTN'T GO NEAR THAT HOUSE!
YOU MUSTN'T! YOU MUSTN'T!
MA'AM, I UNDERSTAND. ANYONE WHO'S EVER LIVED THERE HAS EXPERIENCED GREAT MIS-FORTUNE.
THAT'S RIGHT. SHOPS GO BANKRUPT, THERE ARE ACCIDENTS, PEOPLE GO CRAZY.
PEOPLE HAVE DIED! IT'S AN EVIL HOUSE.
WHEN I CAME TO THIS TOWN...

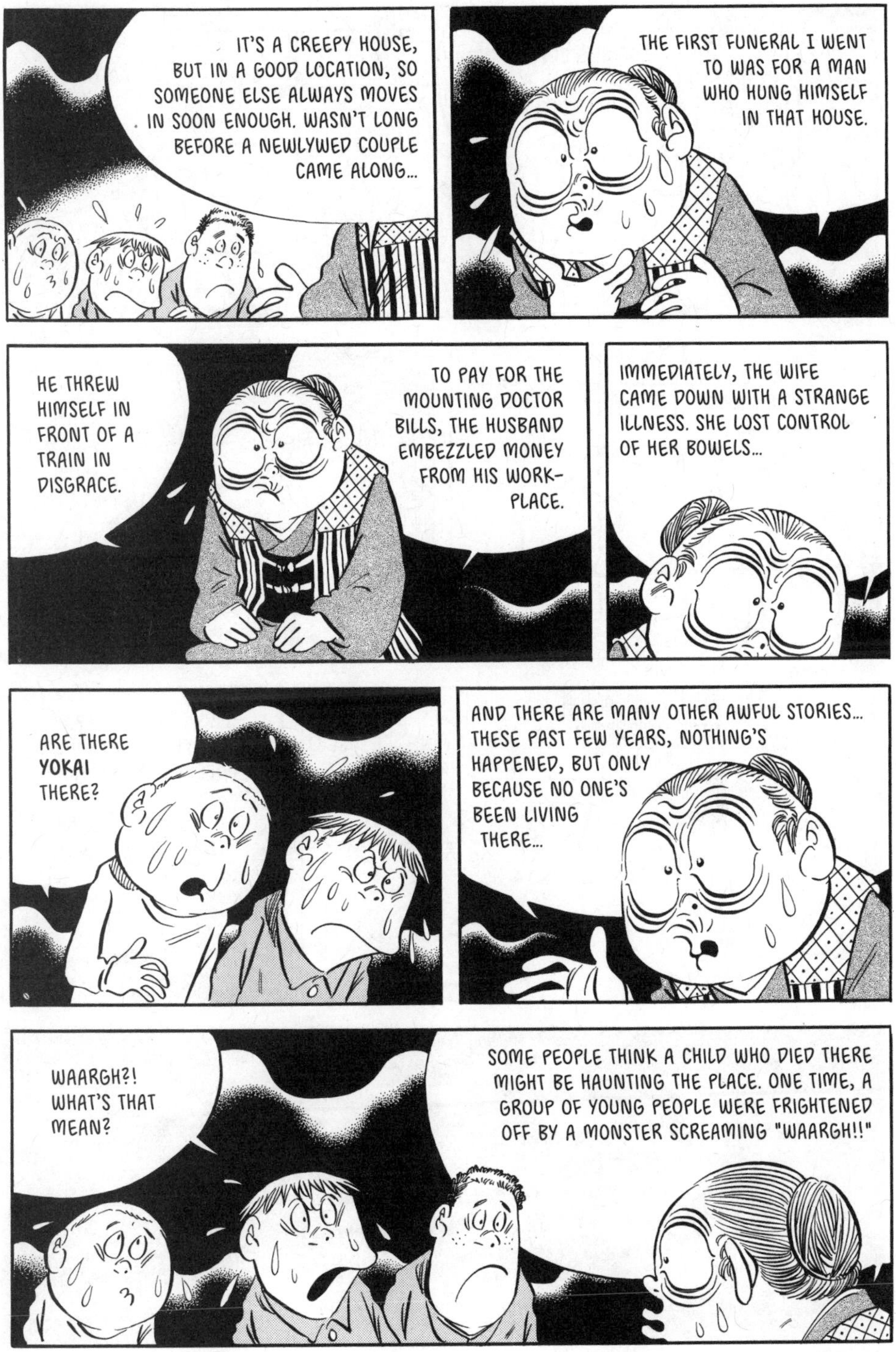
THE FIRST FUNERAL I WENT TO WAS FOR A MAN WHO HUNG HIMSELF IN THAT HOUSE.
IT'S A CREEPY HOUSE, BUT IN A GOOD LOCATION, SO SOMEONE ELSE ALWAYS MOVES IN SOON ENOUGH. WASN'T LONG BEFORE A NEWLYWED COUPLE CAME ALONG...
IMMEDIATELY, THE WIFE CAME DOWN WITH A STRANGE ILLNESS. SHE LOST CONTROL OF HER BOWELS...
TO PAY FOR THE MOUNTING DOCTOR BILLS, THE HUSBAND EMBEZZLED MONEY FROM HIS WORK-PLACE.
HE THREW HIMSELF IN FRONT OF A TRAIN IN DISGRACE.
AND THERE ARE MANY OTHER AWFUL STORIES... THESE PAST FEW YEARS, NOTHING'S HAPPENED, BUT ONLY BECAUSE NO ONE'S BEEN LIVING THERE...
ARE THERE **YOKAI** THERE?
SOME PEOPLE THINK A CHILD WHO DIED THERE MIGHT BE HAUNTING THE PLACE. ONE TIME, A GROUP OF YOUNG PEOPLE WERE FRIGHTENED OFF BY A MONSTER SCREAMING "WAARGH!!"
WAARGH?! WHAT'S THAT MEAN?

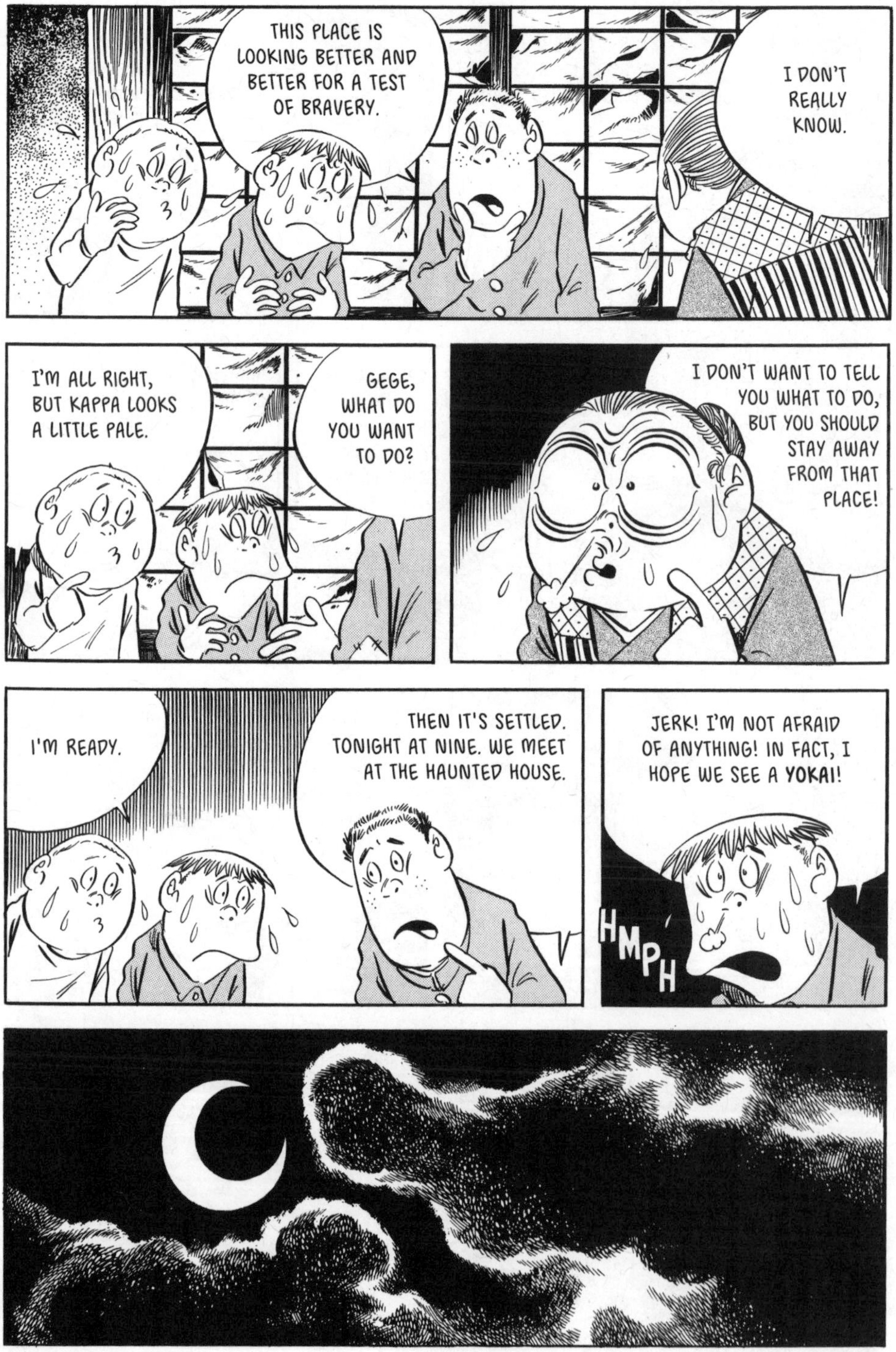
I DON'T REALLY KNOW.
THIS PLACE IS LOOKING BETTER AND BETTER FOR A TEST OF BRAVERY.
I DON'T WANT TO TELL YOU WHAT TO DO, BUT YOU SHOULD STAY AWAY FROM THAT PLACE!
GEGE, WHAT DO YOU WANT TO DO?
I'M ALL RIGHT, BUT KAPPA LOOKS A LITTLE PALE.
JERK! I'M NOT AFRAID OF ANYTHING! IN FACT, I HOPE WE SEE A **YOKAI**!
HMPH
THEN IT'S SETTLED. TONIGHT AT NINE. WE MEET AT THE HAUNTED HOUSE.
I'M READY.

THE HAUNTED HOUSE

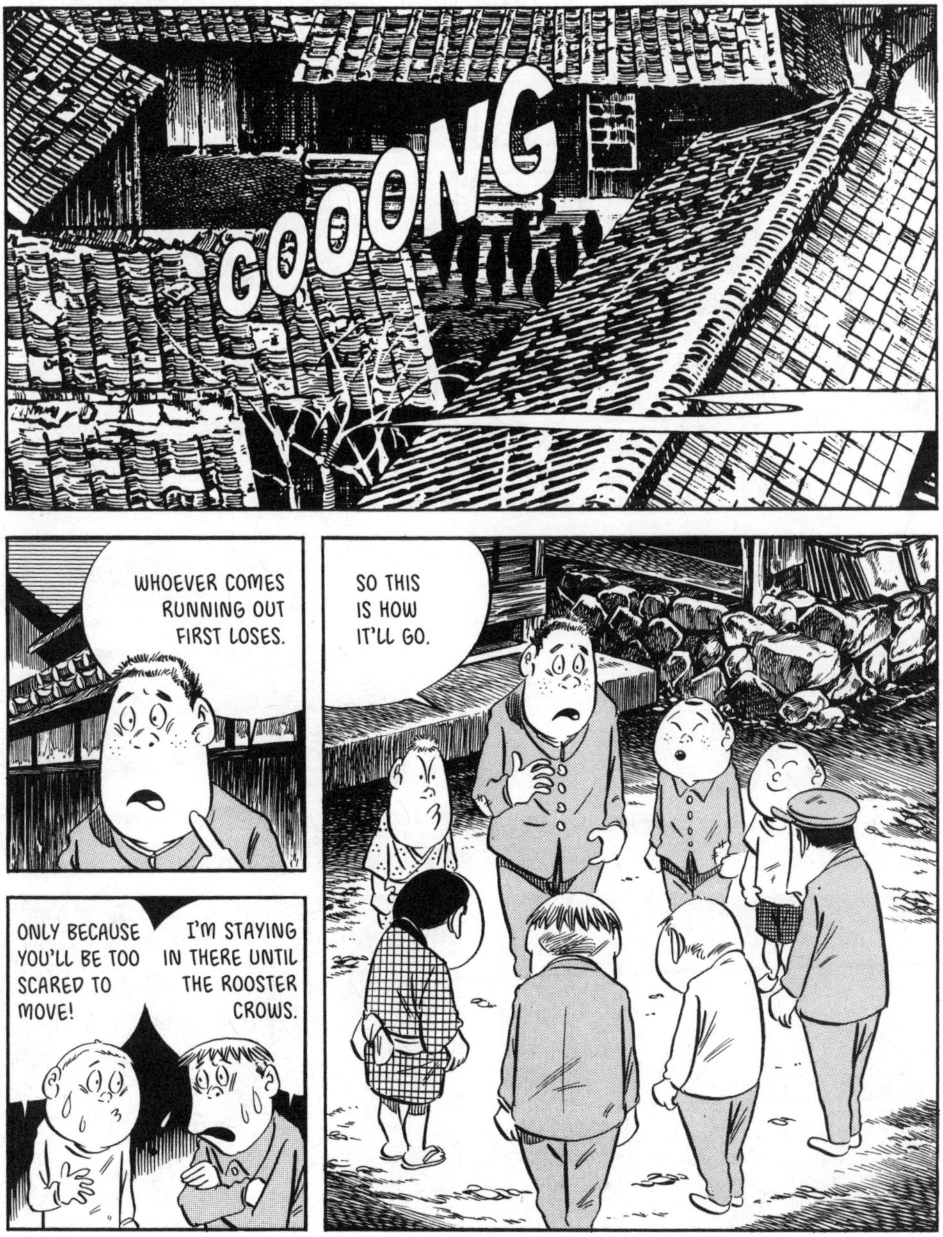
GOOONG
SO THIS IS HOW IT'LL GO.
WHOEVER COMES RUNNING OUT FIRST LOSES.
I'M STAYING IN THERE UNTIL THE ROOSTER CROWS.
ONLY BECAUSE YOU'LL BE TOO SCARED TO MOVE!

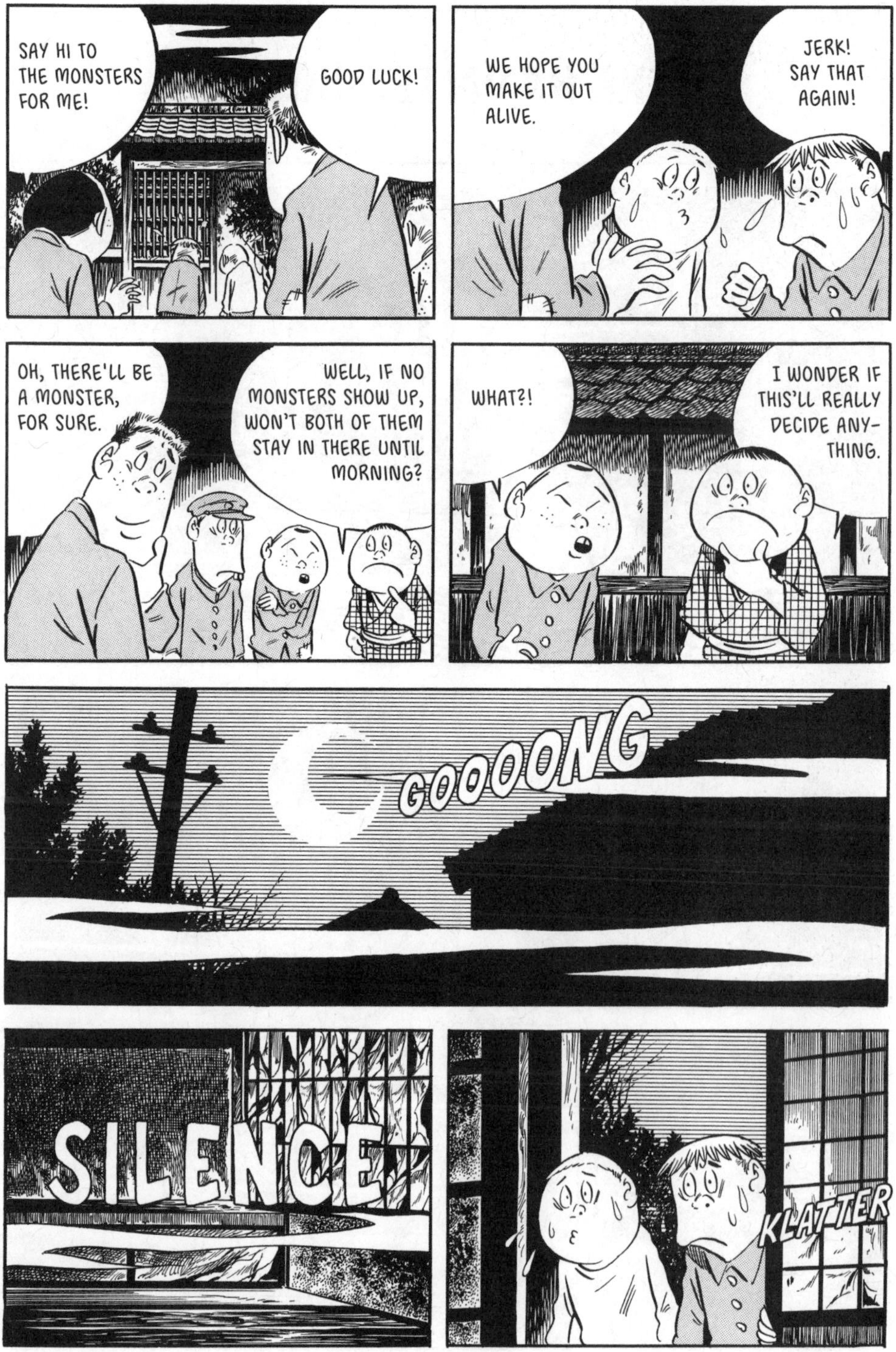
JERK! SAY THAT AGAIN!
WE HOPE YOU MAKE IT OUT ALIVE.
GOOD LUCK!
SAY HI TO THE MONSTERS FOR ME!
I WONDER IF THIS'LL REALLY DECIDE ANY-THING.
WHAT?!
WELL, IF NO MONSTERS SHOW UP, WON'T BOTH OF THEM STAY IN THERE UNTIL MORNING?
OH, THERE'LL BE A MONSTER, FOR SURE.
GOOOONG
KLATTER
SILENCE

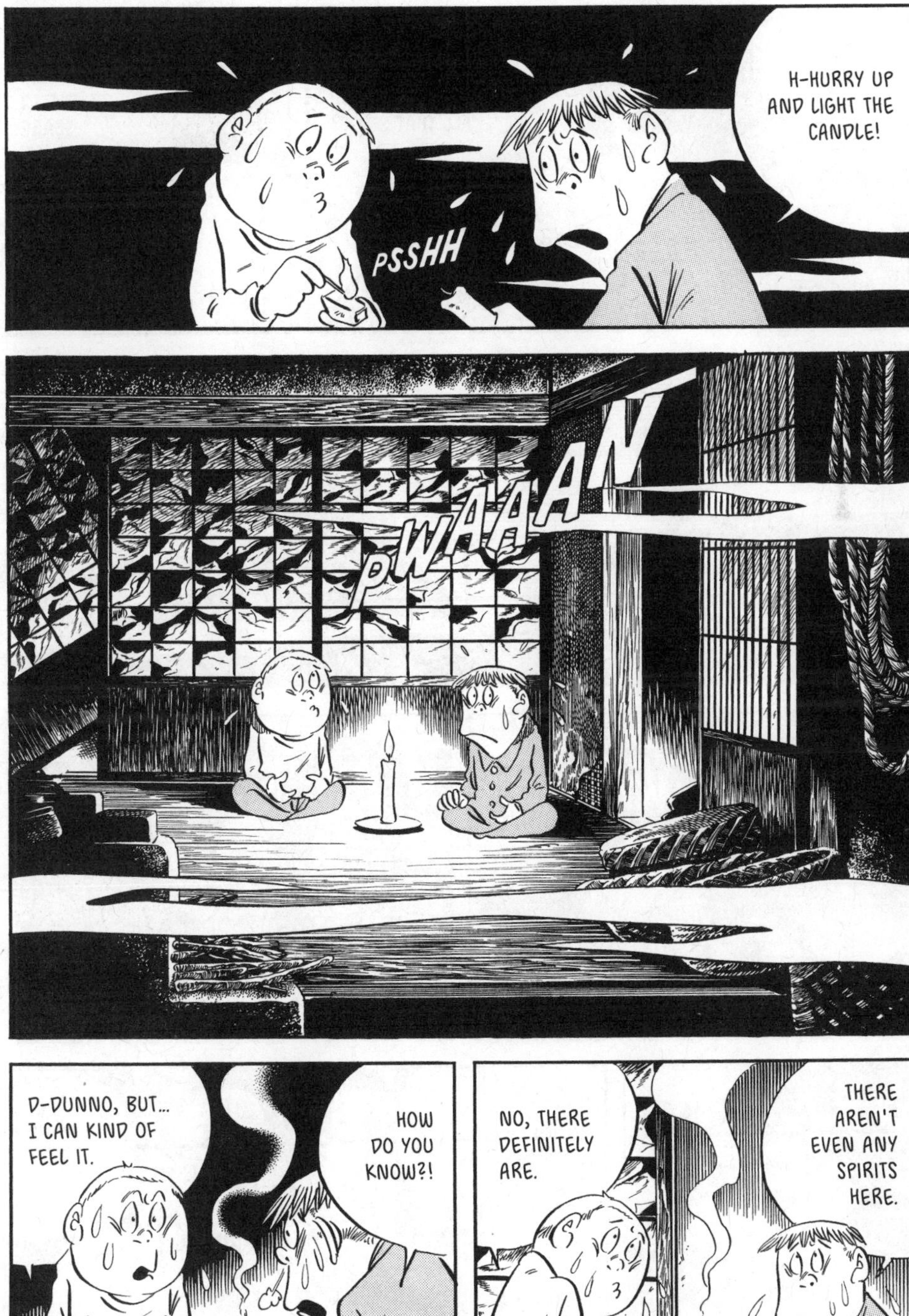
H-HURRY UP AND LIGHT THE CANDLE!
PSSHH
PWAAAAN
THERE AREN'T EVEN ANY SPIRITS HERE.
NO, THERE DEFINITELY ARE.
HOW DO YOU KNOW?!
D-DUNNO, BUT... I CAN KIND OF FEEL IT.

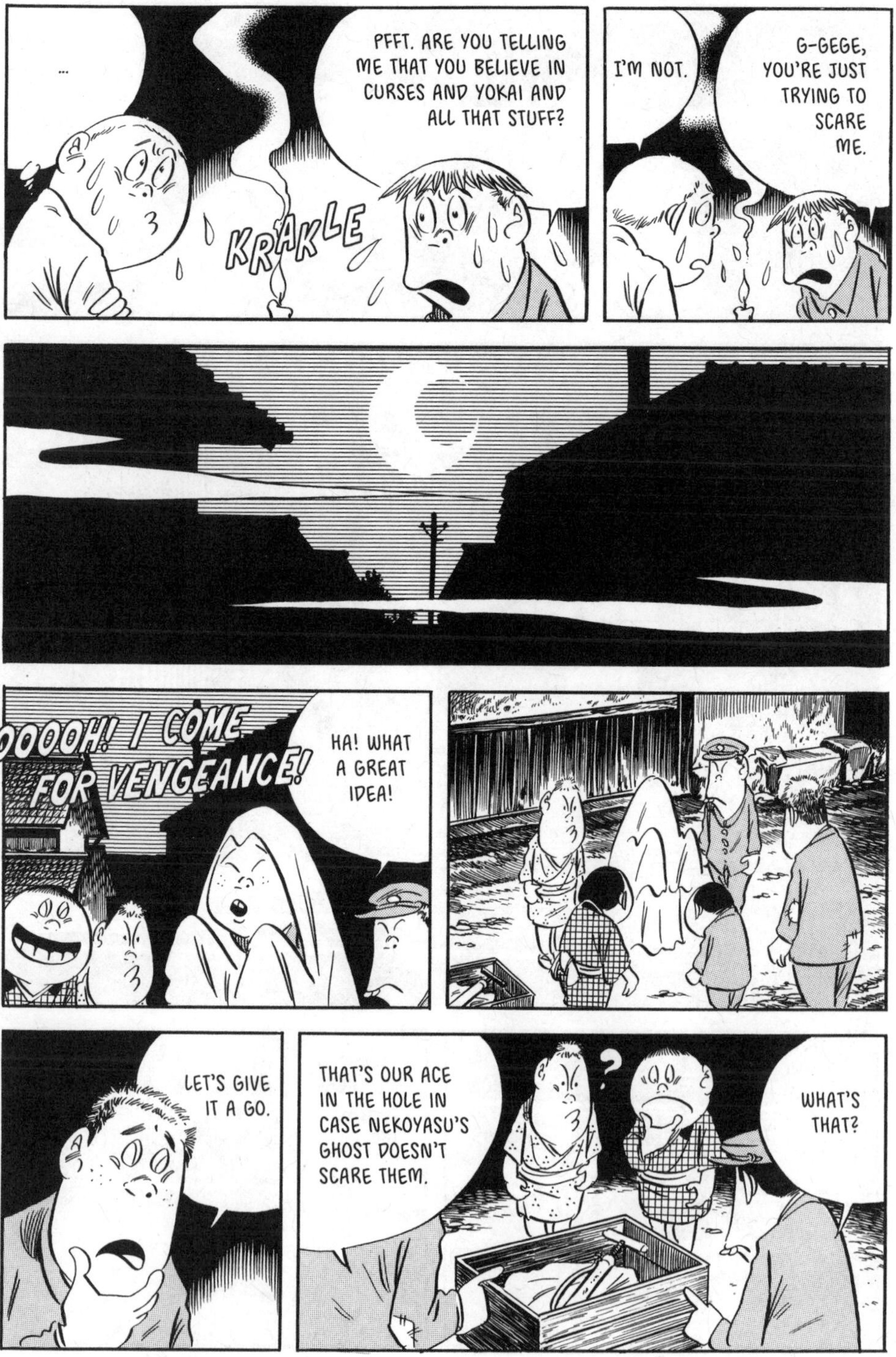
G-GEGE, YOU'RE JUST TRYING TO SCARE ME.
I'M NOT.
PFFT. ARE YOU TELLING ME THAT YOU BELIEVE IN CURSES AND YOKAI AND ALL THAT STUFF?
...
KRAKLE
HA! WHAT A GREAT IDEA!
OOOOH! I COME FOR VENGEANCE!
WHAT'S THAT?
THAT'S OUR ACE IN THE HOLE IN CASE NEKOYASU'S GHOST DOESN'T SCARE THEM.
LET'S GIVE IT A GO.

MY LITTLE MISSUS, MY MICHI
OH DEAR MICHI
IT'S BEEN SO LOOOONG
OKAY, NOW!
KSSH KSSH
BURBLE GURBLE

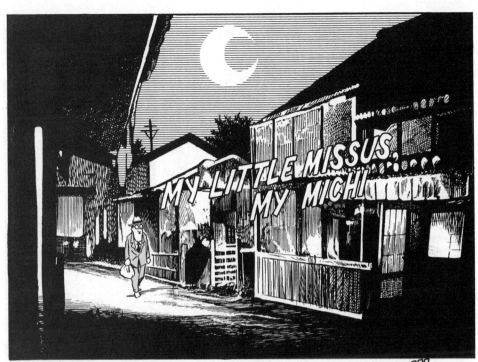

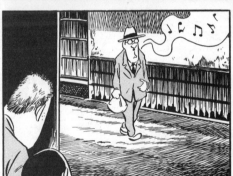

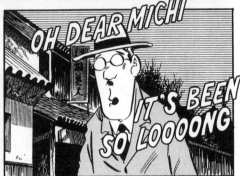

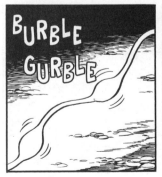

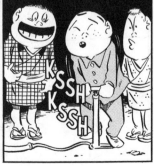

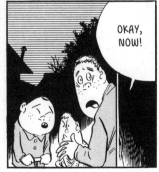

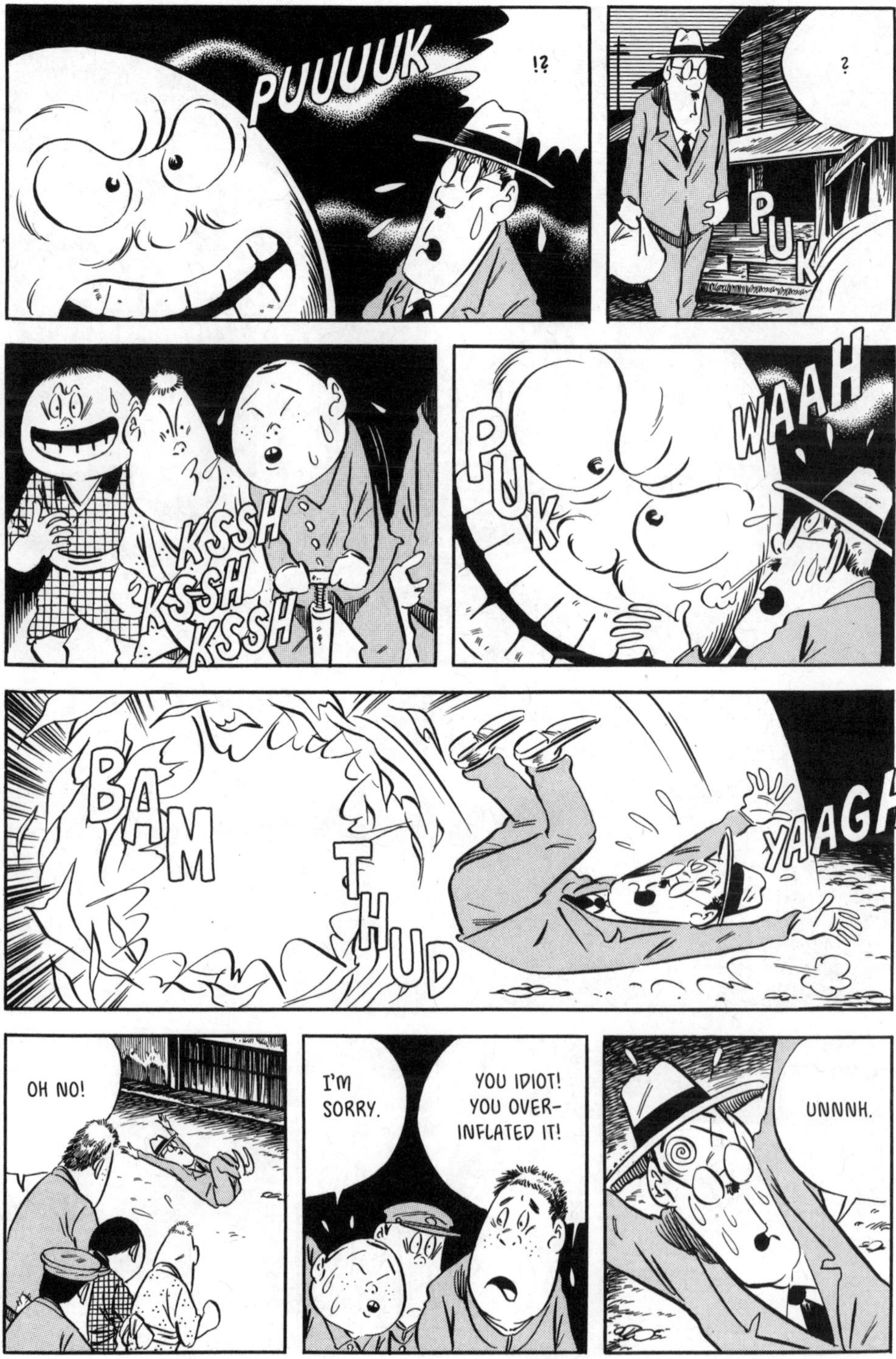
?
PUK
!?
PUUUUK
WAAH
PUK
KSSH
KSSH
KSSH
YAAGH
BAM
THUD
UNNNH.
YOU IDIOT! YOU OVER-INFLATED IT!
I'M SORRY.
OH NO!

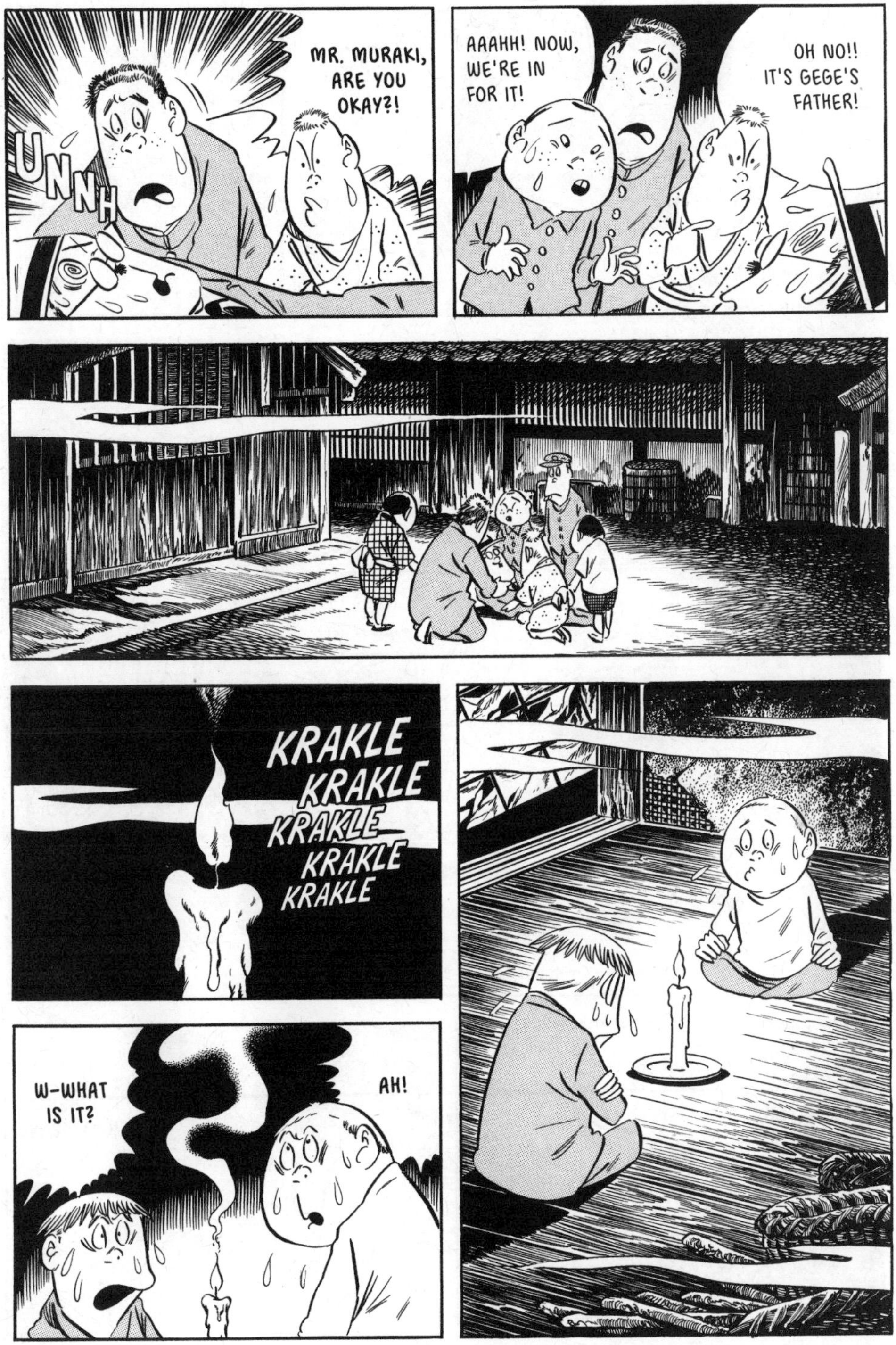
OH NO!! IT'S GEGE'S FATHER!
AAAHH! NOW, WE'RE IN FOR IT!
MR. MURAKI, ARE YOU OKAY?!
UNNH
KRAKLE KRAKLE KRAKLE KRAKLE KRAKLE
AH!
W-WHAT IS IT?

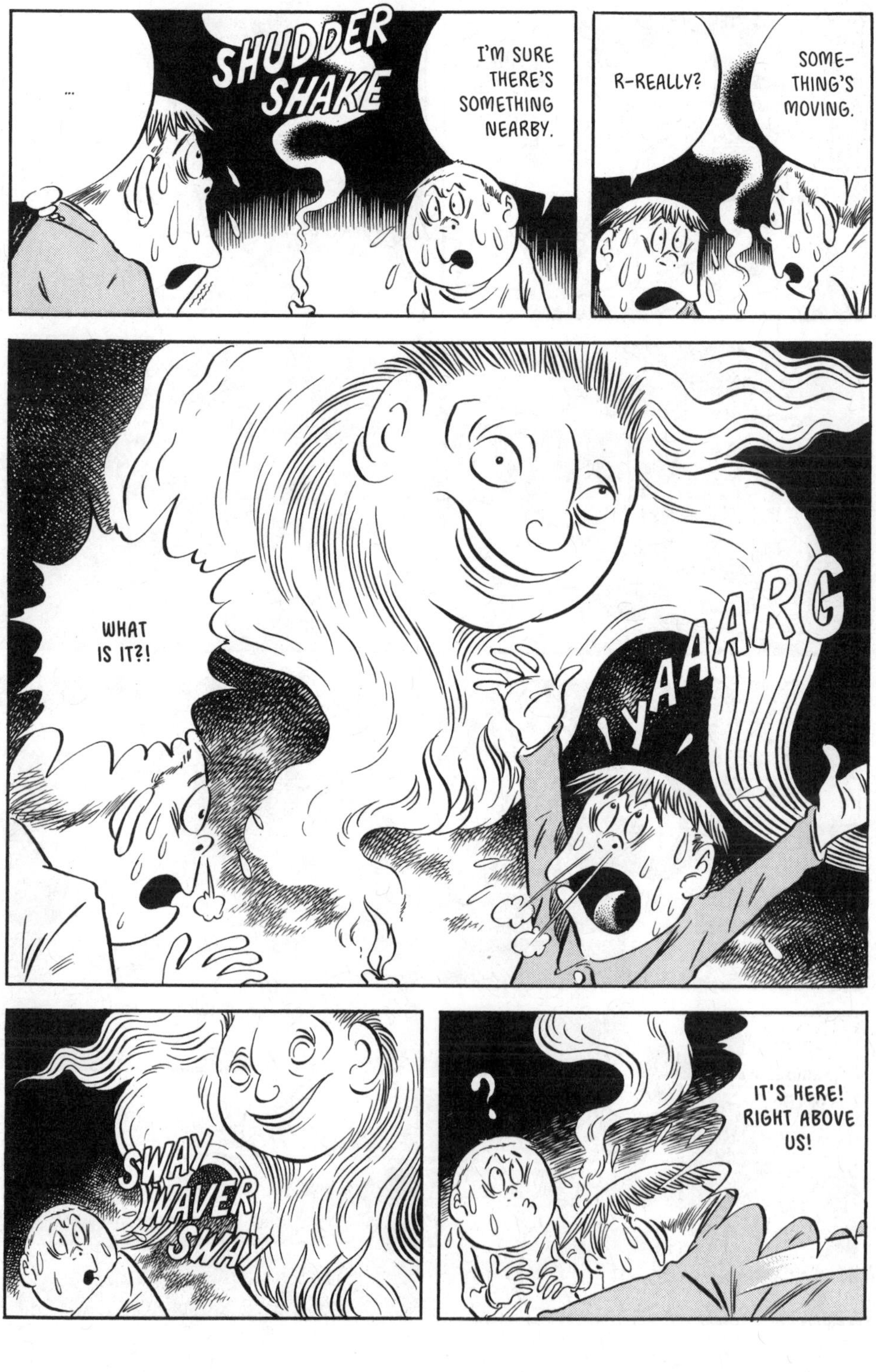
SOME-THING'S MOVING.
R-REALLY?
I'M SURE THERE'S SOMETHING NEARBY.
SHUDDER SHAKE
...
YAAAARG
WHAT IS IT?!
IT'S HERE! RIGHT ABOVE US!
?
SWAY WAVER SWAY

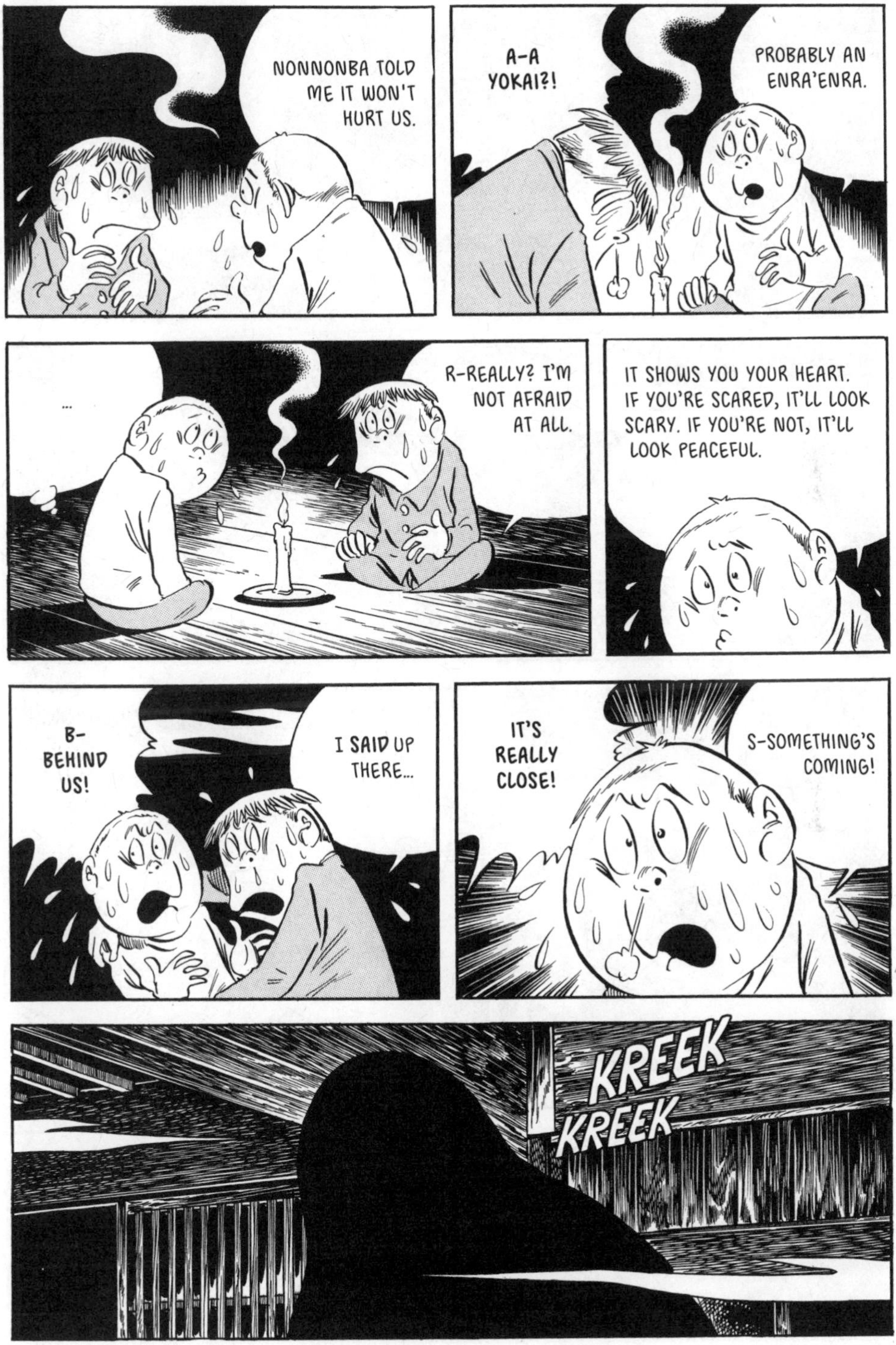
PROBABLY AN ENRA'ENRA.
A-A YOKAI?!
NONNONBA TOLD ME IT WON'T HURT US.
IT SHOWS YOU YOUR HEART. IF YOU'RE SCARED, IT'LL LOOK SCARY. IF YOU'RE NOT, IT'LL LOOK PEACEFUL.
R-REALLY? I'M NOT AFRAID AT ALL.
...
S-SOMETHING'S COMING!
IT'S REALLY CLOSE!
I SAID UP THERE...
B- BEHIND US!
KREEK
KREEK

SHAKE
SHAKE
SHAKE
HEH
HEH
HEH
HEH
FWWP
WAARGH
GEGE!
AAAH!

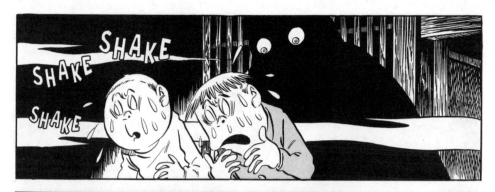

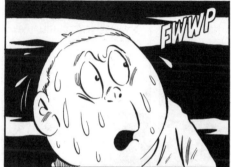

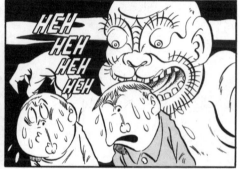

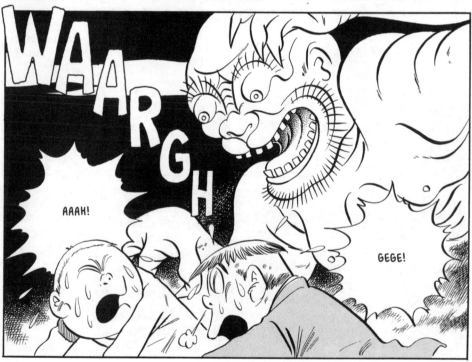

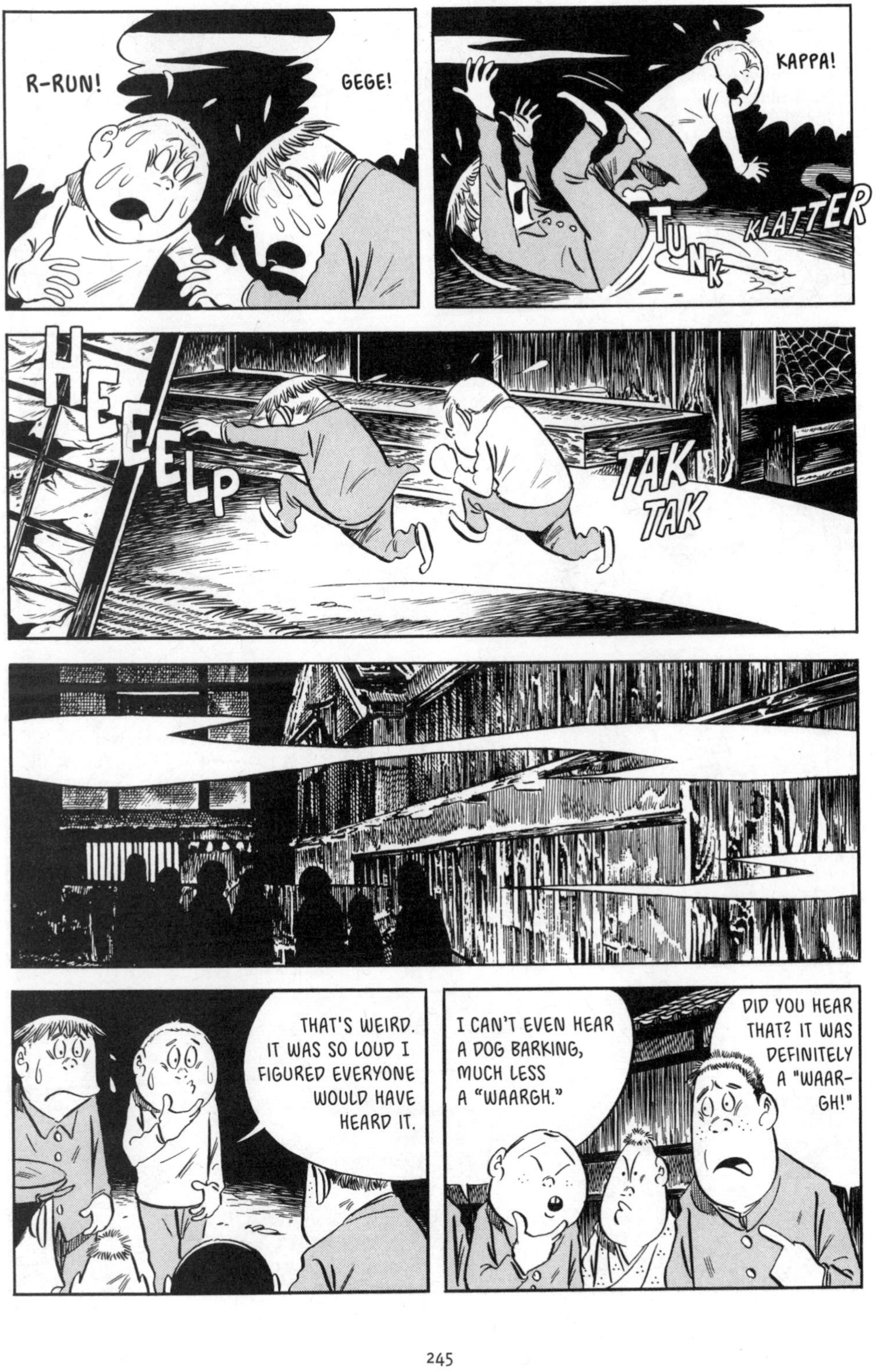
KAPPA!
TUNK
KLATTER
GEGE!
R-RUN!
TAK TAK
HEEELP
DID YOU HEAR THAT? IT WAS DEFINITELY A "WAARGH!"
I CAN'T EVEN HEAR A DOG BARKING, MUCH LESS A "WAARGH."
THAT'S WEIRD. IT WAS SO LOUD I FIGURED EVERYONE WOULD HAVE HEARD IT.

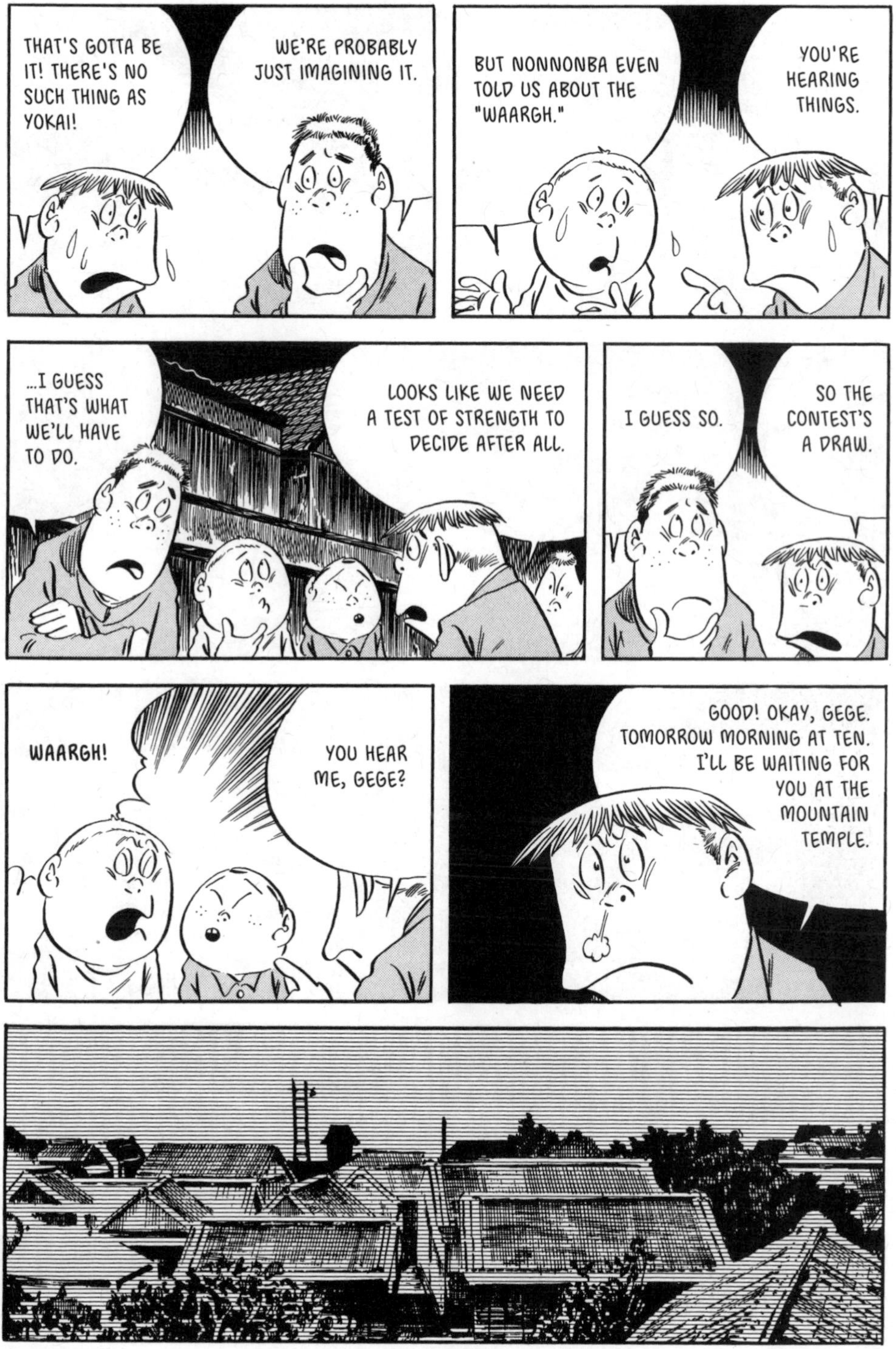
YOU'RE HEARING THINGS.
BUT NONNONBA EVEN TOLD US ABOUT THE "WAARGH."
WE'RE PROBABLY JUST IMAGINING IT.
THAT'S GOTTA BE IT! THERE'S NO SUCH THING AS YOKAI!
SO THE CONTEST'S A DRAW.
I GUESS SO.
LOOKS LIKE WE NEED A TEST OF STRENGTH TO DECIDE AFTER ALL.
...I GUESS THAT'S WHAT WE'LL HAVE TO DO.
GOOD! OKAY, GEGE. TOMORROW MORNING AT TEN. I'LL BE WAITING FOR YOU AT THE MOUNTAIN TEMPLE.
YOU HEAR ME, GEGE?
WAARGH!

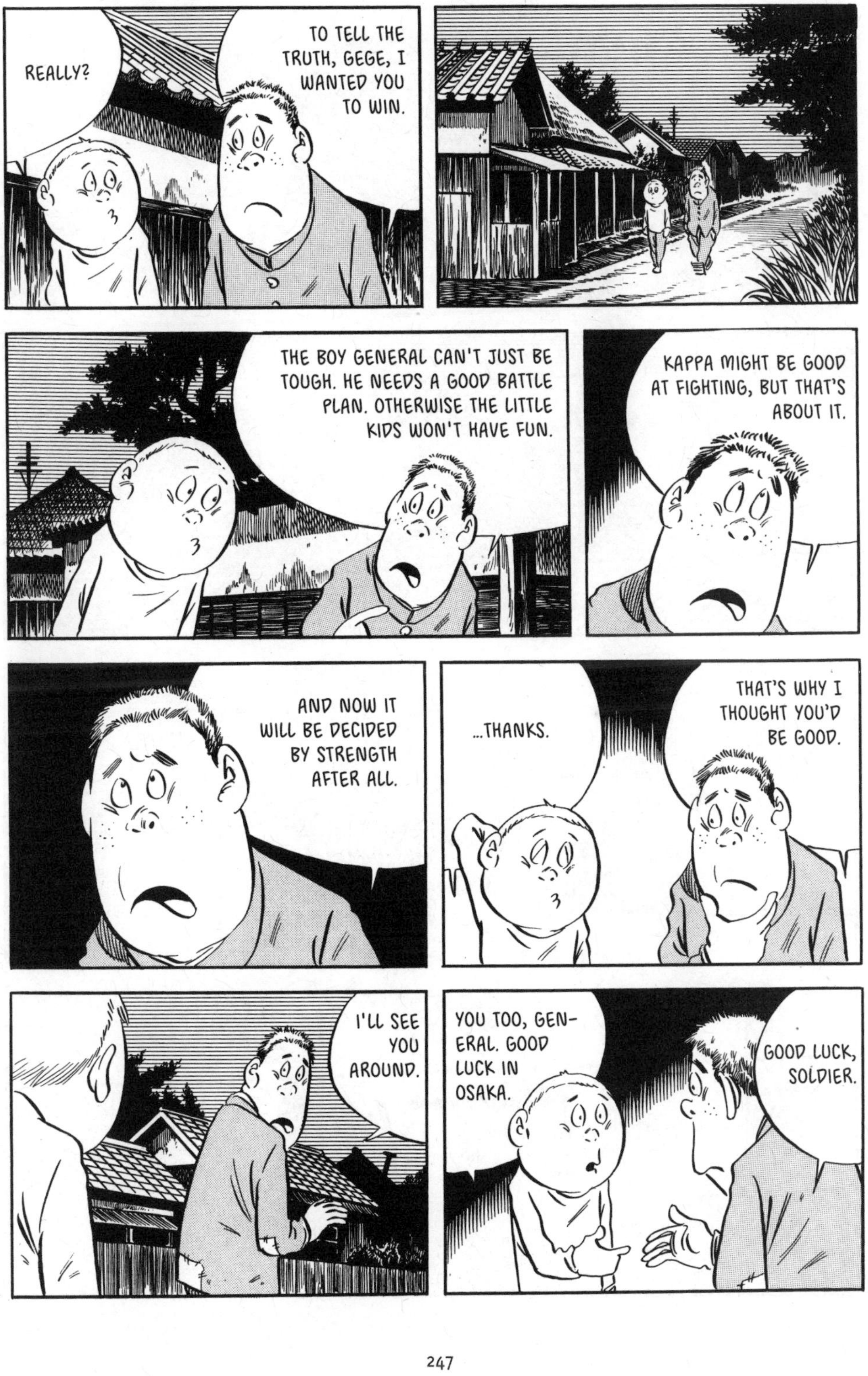
TO TELL THE TRUTH, GEGE, I WANTED YOU TO WIN.
REALLY?
KAPPA MIGHT BE GOOD AT FIGHTING, BUT THAT'S ABOUT IT.
THE BOY GENERAL CAN'T JUST BE TOUGH. HE NEEDS A GOOD BATTLE PLAN. OTHERWISE THE LITTLE KIDS WON'T HAVE FUN.
THAT'S WHY I THOUGHT YOU'D BE GOOD.
...THANKS.
AND NOW IT WILL BE DECIDED BY STRENGTH AFTER ALL.
GOOD LUCK, SOLDIER.
YOU TOO, GEN-ERAL. GOOD LUCK IN OSAKA.
I'LL SEE YOU AROUND.

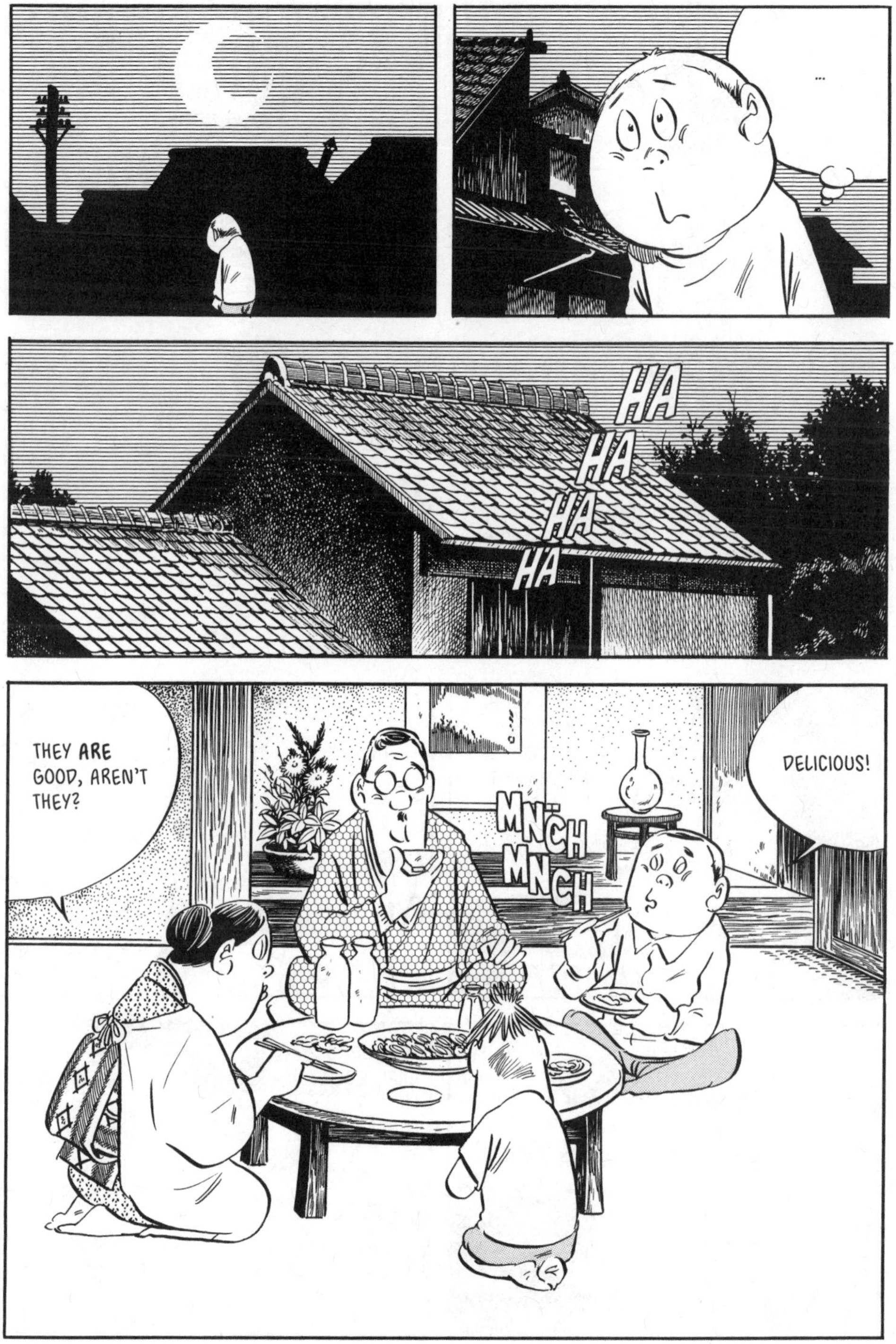
...
HA
HA
HA
HA
DELICIOUS!
MNCH MNCH
THEY ARE GOOD, AREN'T THEY?

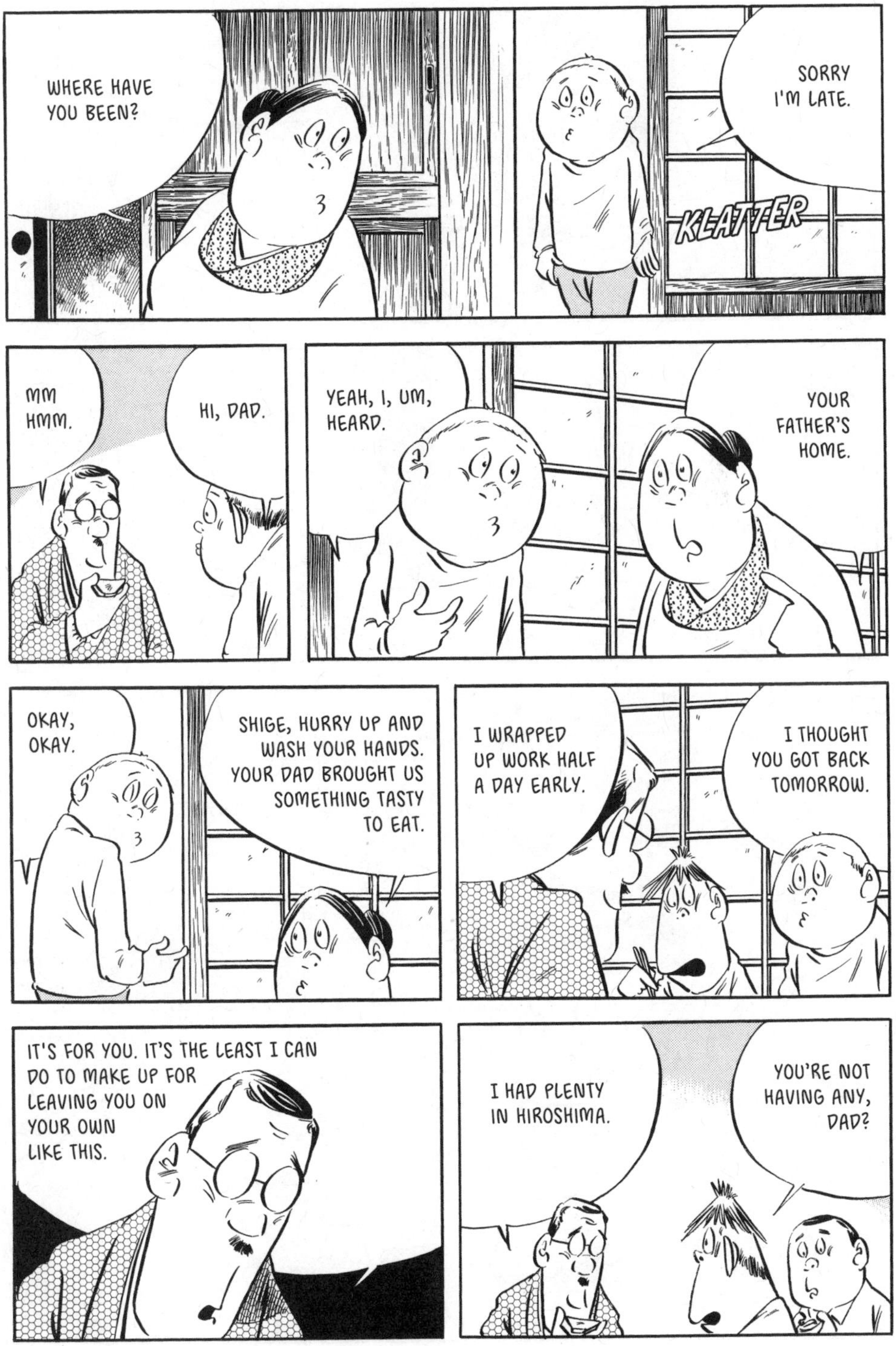
SORRY I'M LATE.
KLATTER
WHERE HAVE YOU BEEN?
YOUR FATHER'S HOME.
YEAH, I, UM, HEARD.
HI, DAD.
MM HMM.
I THOUGHT YOU GOT BACK TOMORROW.
I WRAPPED UP WORK HALF A DAY EARLY.
SHIGE, HURRY UP AND WASH YOUR HANDS. YOUR DAD BROUGHT US SOMETHING TASTY TO EAT.
OKAY, OKAY.
YOU'RE NOT HAVING ANY, DAD?
I HAD PLENTY IN HIROSHIMA.
IT'S FOR YOU. IT'S THE LEAST I CAN DO TO MAKE UP FOR LEAVING YOU ON YOUR OWN LIKE THIS.

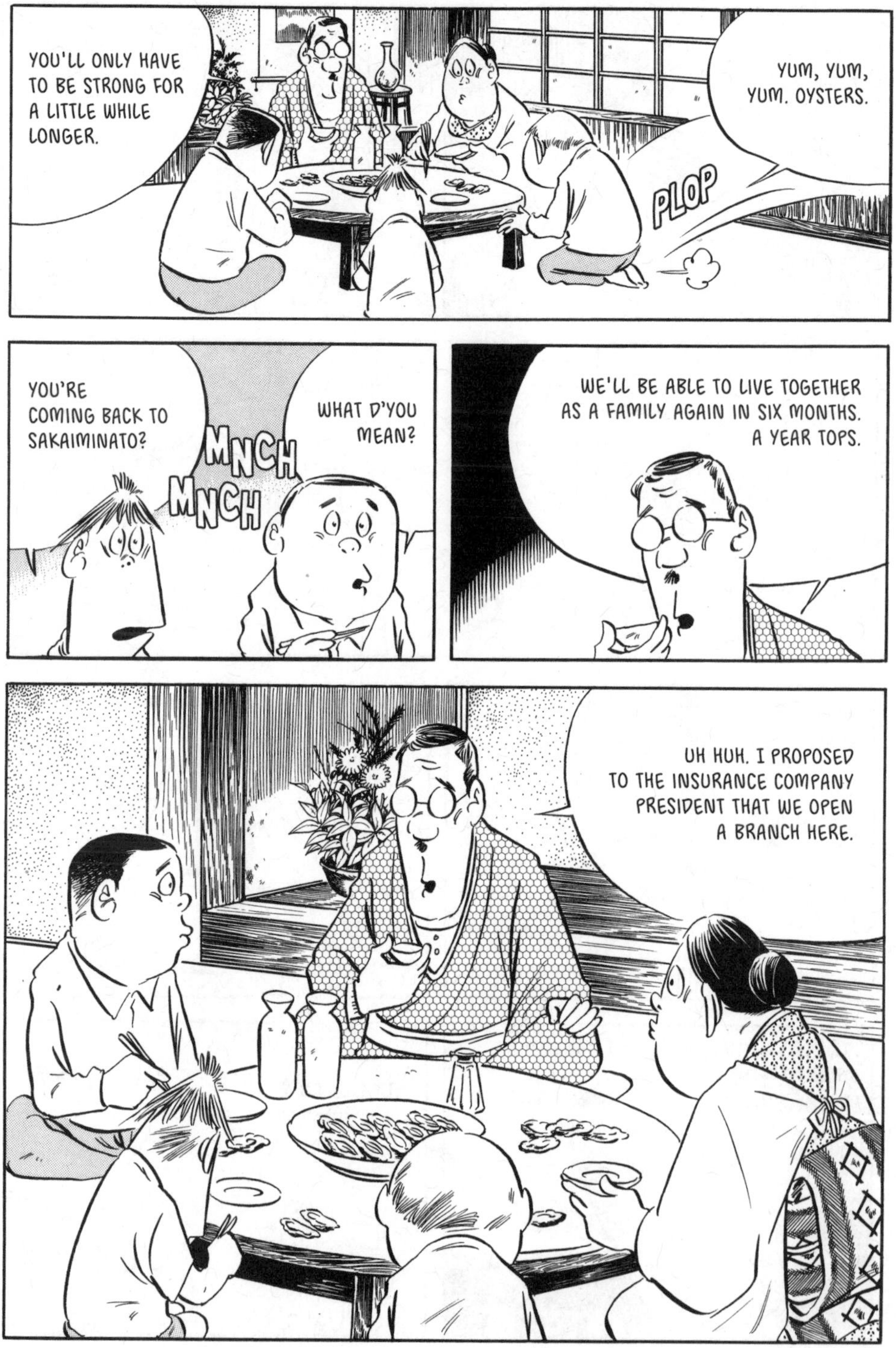
YUM, YUM, YUM. OYSTERS.
YOU'LL ONLY HAVE TO BE STRONG FOR A LITTLE WHILE LONGER.
PLOP
WE'LL BE ABLE TO LIVE TOGETHER AS A FAMILY AGAIN IN SIX MONTHS. A YEAR TOPS.
WHAT D'YOU MEAN?
YOU'RE COMING BACK TO SAKAIMINATO?
MNCH MNCH
UH HUH. I PROPOSED TO THE INSURANCE COMPANY PRESIDENT THAT WE OPEN A BRANCH HERE.

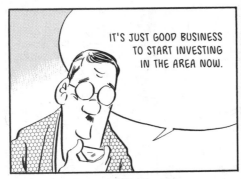

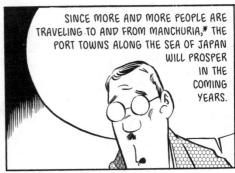

SINCE MORE AND MORE PEOPLE ARE TRAVELING TO AND FROM MANCHURIA,* THE PORT TOWNS ALONG THE SEA OF JAPAN WILL PROSPER IN THE COMING YEARS.
IT'S JUST GOOD BUSINESS TO START INVESTING IN THE AREA NOW.
THE PRESIDENT SEEMED TO AGREE WITH ME, SO I'LL PROBABLY BE BACK HERE AS THE LOCAL BRANCH MANAGER.
REALLY?
UH HUH, WHICH MEANS YOU'LL BE THE WIFE OF A BRANCH MANAGER.
OH MY!
BRANCH MANAGER, HUH?
NEEEAAT.
NOW, NOW, IT DOESN'T MUCH MATTER WHAT MY TITLE IS.
WHAT'S REALLY IMPORTANT IS WHO I AM INSIDE.

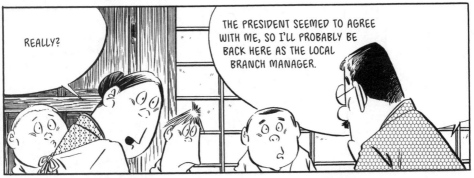

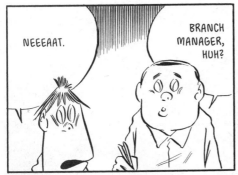

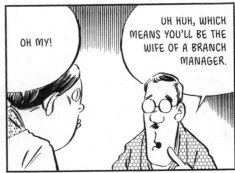

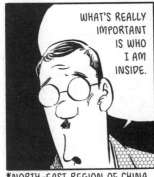

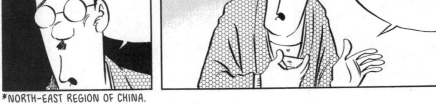

*NORTH-EAST REGION OF CHINA.

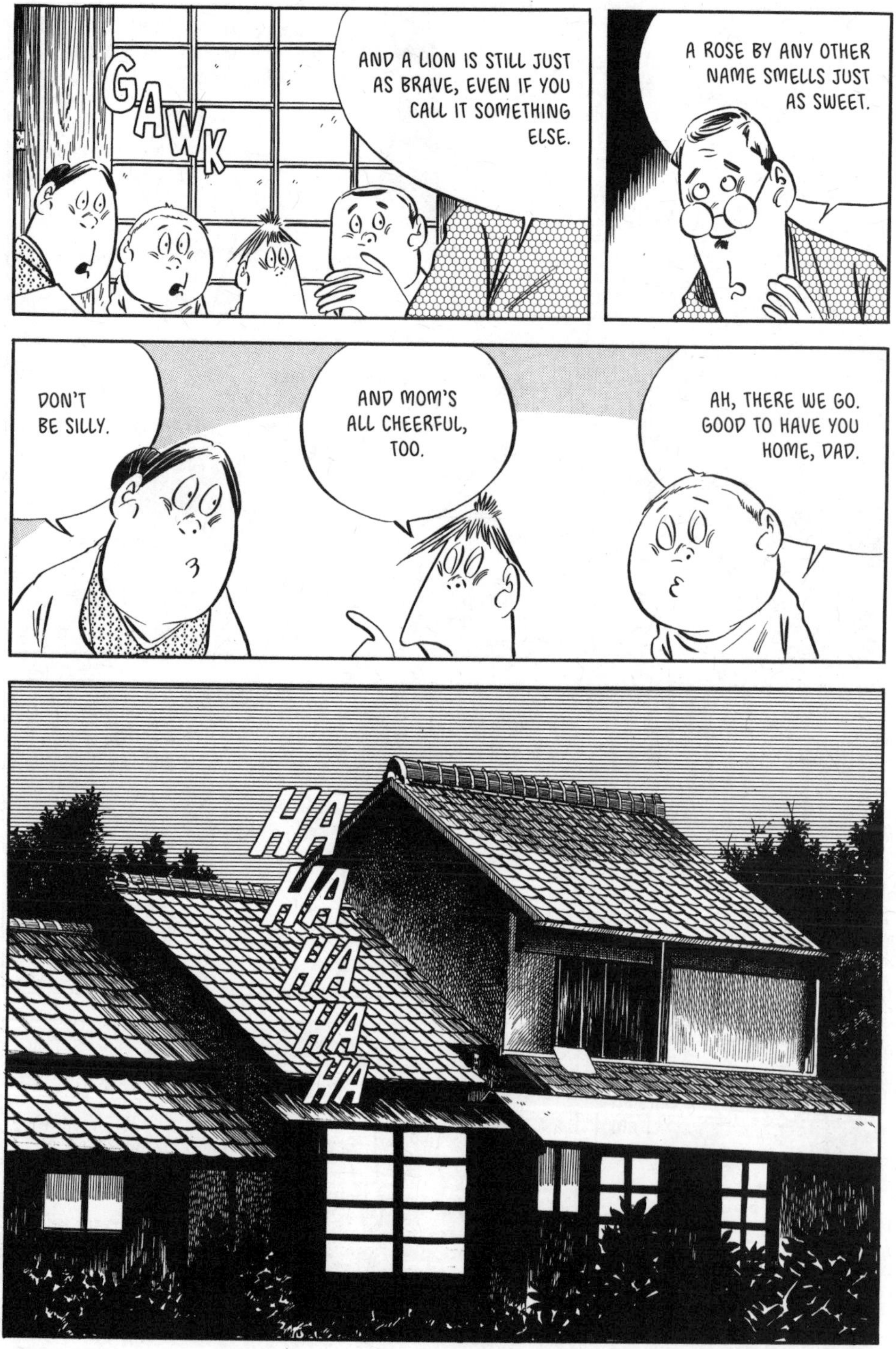
A ROSE BY ANY OTHER NAME SMELLS JUST AS SWEET.
AND A LION IS STILL JUST AS BRAVE, EVEN IF YOU CALL IT SOMETHING ELSE.
GAWK
AH, THERE WE GO. GOOD TO HAVE YOU HOME, DAD.
AND MOM'S ALL CHEERFUL, TOO.
DON'T BE SILLY.
HA HA HA HA HA

OUTCAST

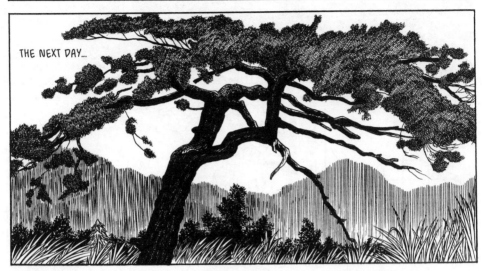

THE NEXT DAY...
HE'S LATE!
WHAT'S GOING ON WITH GEGE?
HE'S NOT COMING.
WHAT?
HIS WHOLE FAMILY HAS FOOD POISONING.
FOOD POISON-ING?
SMIRK

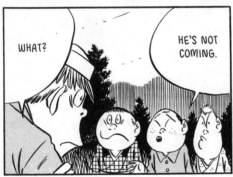

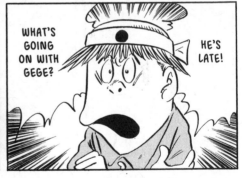

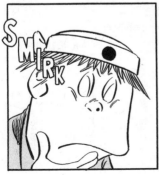

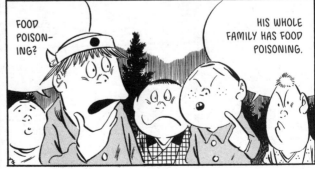

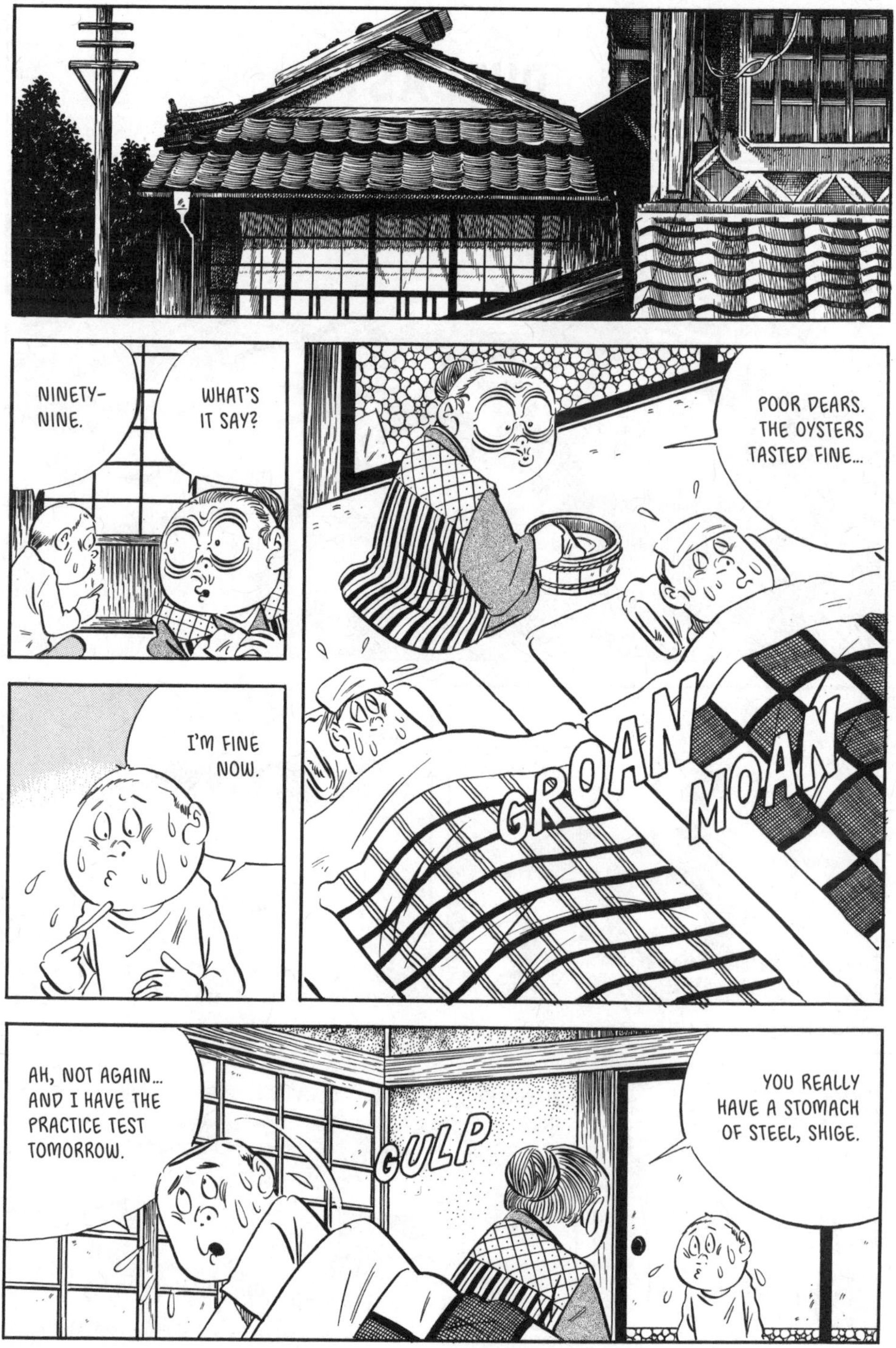
POOR DEARS. THE OYSTERS TASTED FINE...
MOAN
GROAN
WHAT'S IT SAY?
NINETY-NINE.
I'M FINE NOW.
YOU REALLY HAVE A STOMACH OF STEEL, SHIGE.
GULP
AH, NOT AGAIN... AND I HAVE THE PRACTICE TEST TOMORROW.

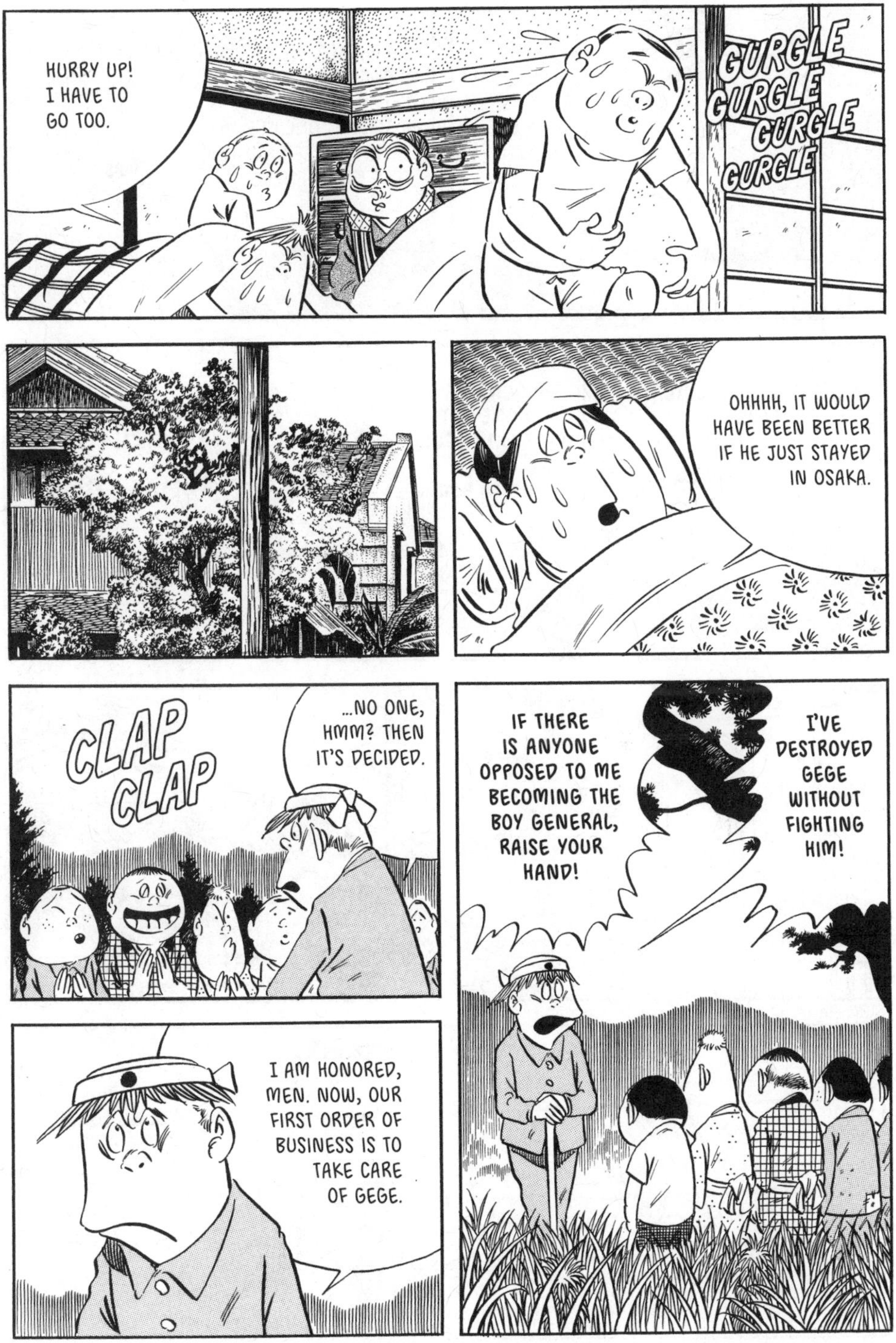
GURGLE GURGLE GURGLE GURGLE
HURRY UP! I HAVE TO GO TOO.
OHHHH, IT WOULD HAVE BEEN BETTER IF HE JUST STAYED IN OSAKA.
I'VE DESTROYED GEGE WITHOUT FIGHTING HIM!
IF THERE IS ANYONE OPPOSED TO ME BECOMING THE BOY GENERAL, RAISE YOUR HAND!
...NO ONE, HMM? THEN IT'S DECIDED.
CLAP CLAP
I AM HONORED, MEN. NOW, OUR FIRST ORDER OF BUSINESS IS TO TAKE CARE OF GEGE.

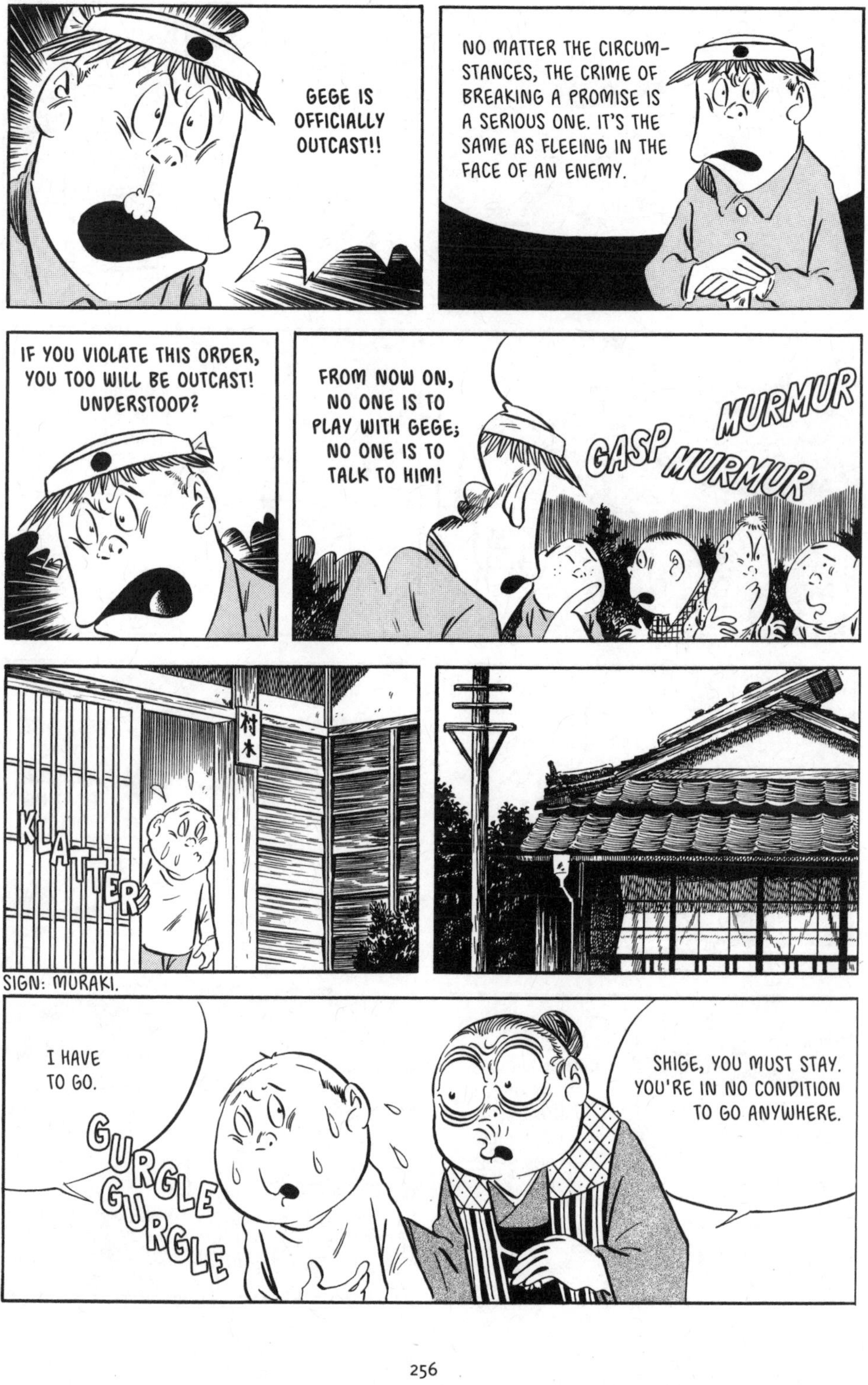
NO MATTER THE CIRCUMSTANCES, THE CRIME OF BREAKING A PROMISE IS A SERIOUS ONE. IT'S THE SAME AS FLEEING IN THE FACE OF AN ENEMY.
GEGE IS OFFICIALLY OUTCAST!!
FROM NOW ON, NO ONE IS TO PLAY WITH GEGE; NO ONE IS TO TALK TO HIM!
MURMUR
GASP
MURMUR
IF YOU VIOLATE THIS ORDER, YOU TOO WILL BE OUTCAST! UNDERSTOOD?
村木
KLATTER
SHIGE, YOU MUST STAY. YOU'RE IN NO CONDITION TO GO ANYWHERE.
I HAVE TO GO.
GURGLE GURGLE
SIGN: MURAKI.

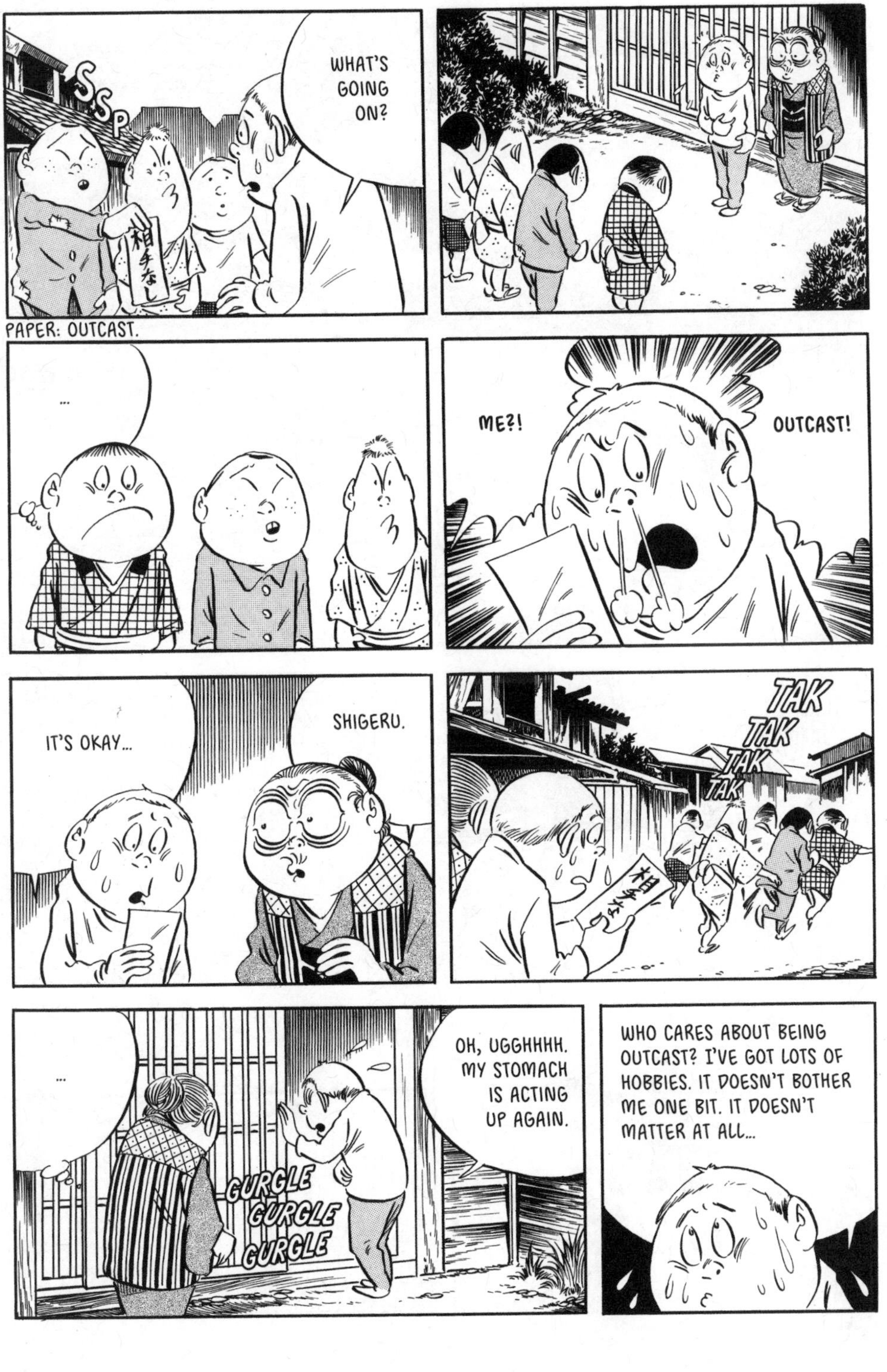

SSP
WHAT'S GOING ON?
PAPER: OUTCAST.
OUTCAST!
ME?!
...
TAK TAK TAK TAK
SHIGERU.
IT'S OKAY...
WHO CARES ABOUT BEING OUTCAST? I'VE GOT LOTS OF HOBBIES. IT DOESN'T BOTHER ME ONE BIT. IT DOESN'T MATTER AT ALL...
OH, UGGHHHH. MY STOMACH IS ACTING UP AGAIN.
...
GURGLE GURGLE GURGLE

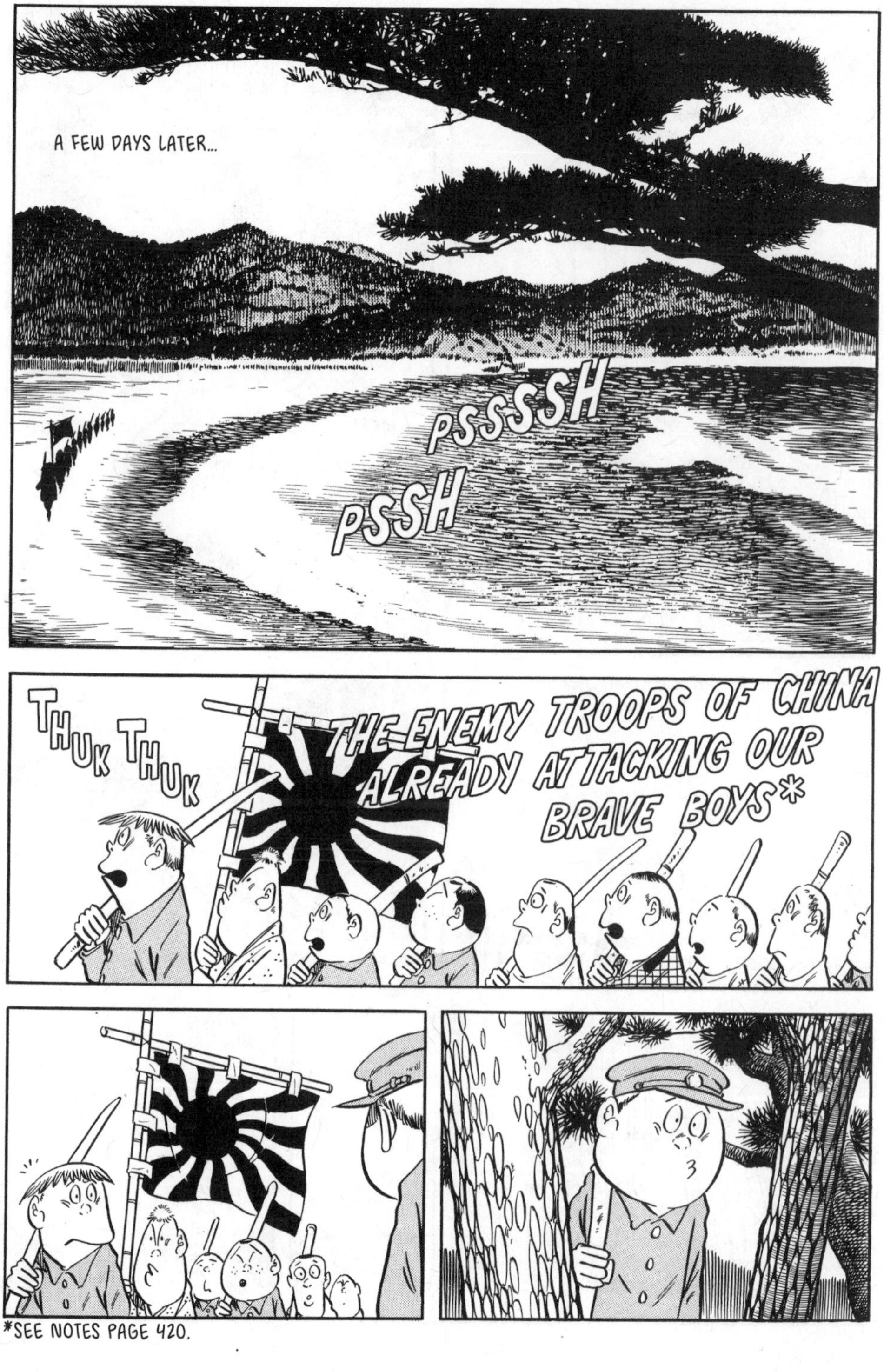
A FEW DAYS LATER...
PSSSSSH
PSSH
THE ENEMY TROOPS OF CHINA ALREADY ATTACKING OUR BRAVE BOYS*
THUK THUK

*SEE NOTES PAGE 420.

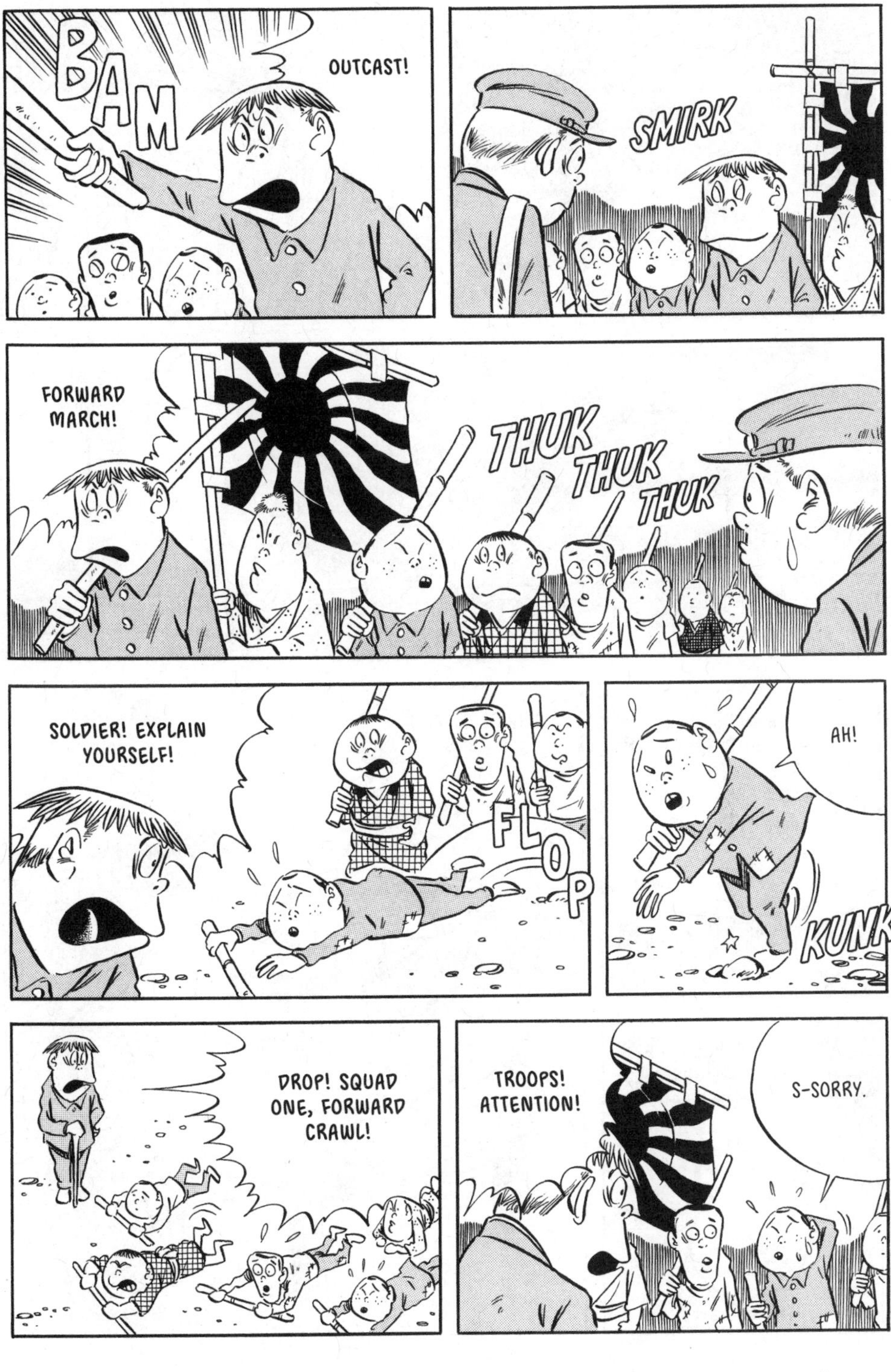
SMIRK
OUTCAST!
BAM
FORWARD MARCH!
THUK
THUK
THUK
AH!
KUNK
SOLDIER! EXPLAIN YOURSELF!
FLOP
S-SORRY.
TROOPS! ATTENTION!
DROP! SQUAD ONE, FORWARD CRAWL!

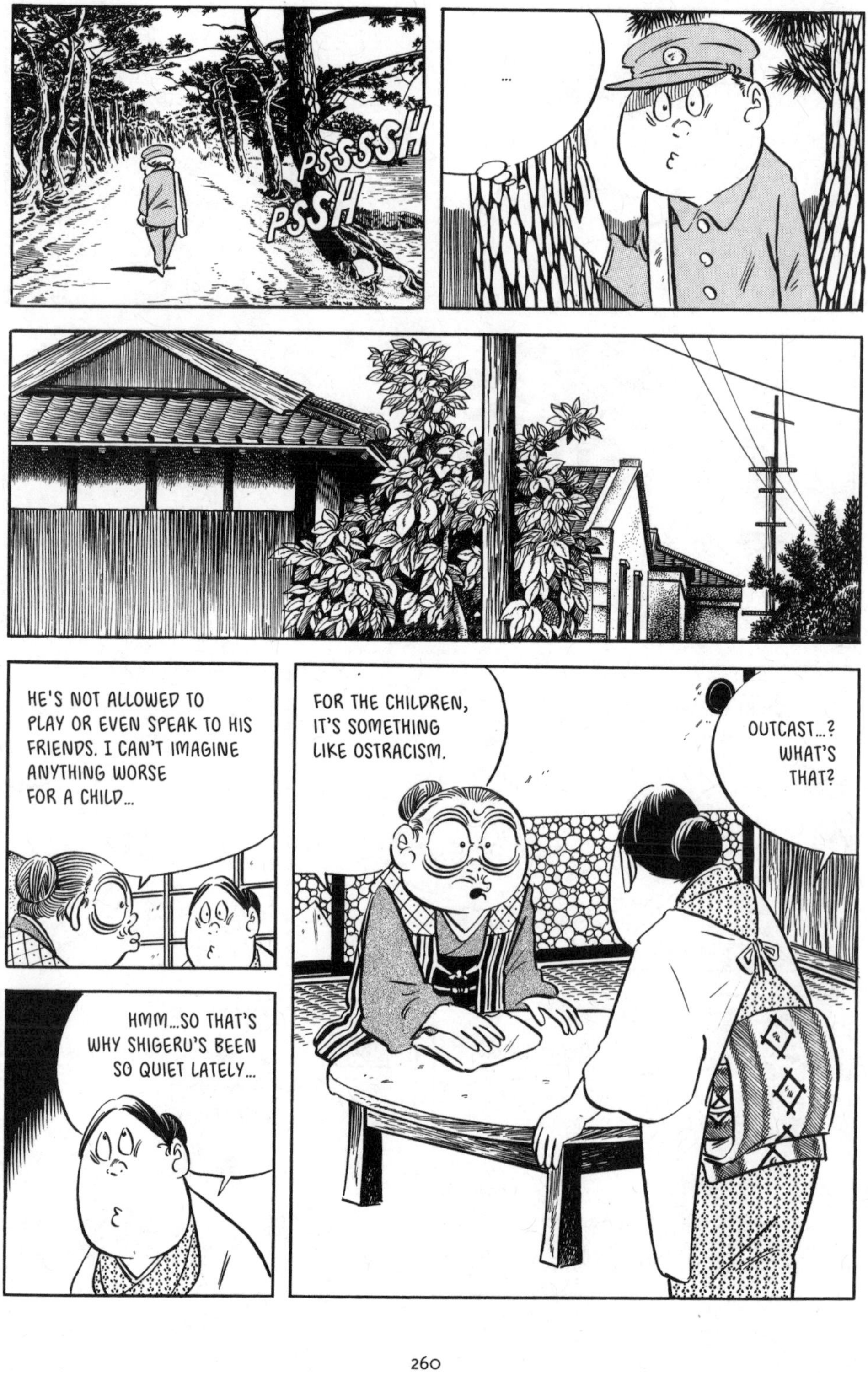
...
PSSSSH
PSSH
OUTCAST...? WHAT'S THAT?
FOR THE CHILDREN, IT'S SOMETHING LIKE OSTRACISM.
HE'S NOT ALLOWED TO PLAY OR EVEN SPEAK TO HIS FRIENDS. I CAN'T IMAGINE ANYTHING WORSE FOR A CHILD...
HMM...SO THAT'S WHY SHIGERU'S BEEN SO QUIET LATELY...

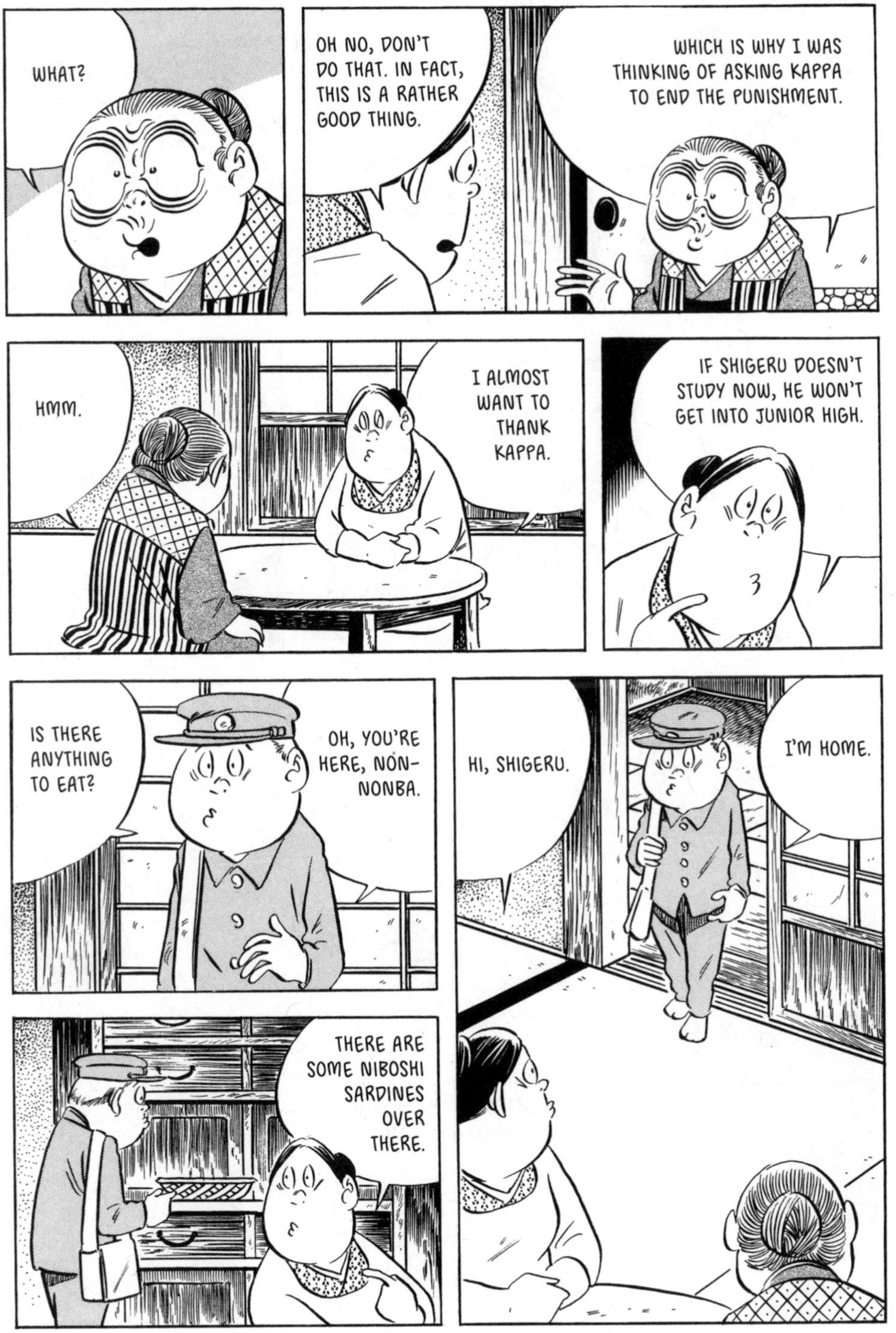
WHICH IS WHY I WAS THINKING OF ASKING KAPPA TO END THE PUNISHMENT.
OH NO, DON'T DO THAT. IN FACT, THIS IS A RATHER GOOD THING.
WHAT?
IF SHIGERU DOESN'T STUDY NOW, HE WON'T GET INTO JUNIOR HIGH.
I ALMOST WANT TO THANK KAPPA.
HMM.
I'M HOME.
HI, SHIGERU.
OH, YOU'RE HERE, NON-NONNONBA.
IS THERE ANYTHING TO EAT?
THERE ARE SOME NIBOSHI SARDINES OVER THERE.

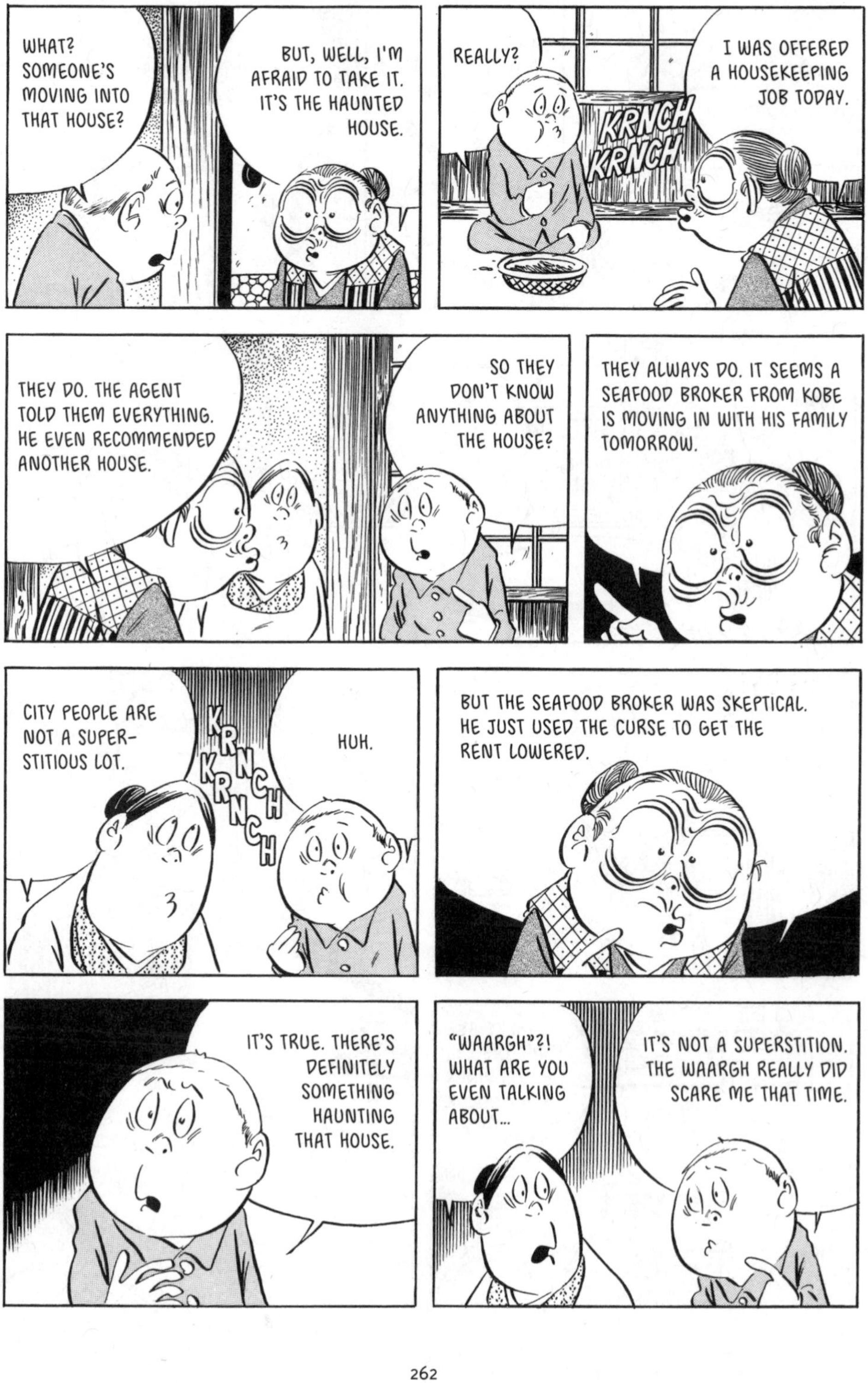
I WAS OFFERED A HOUSEKEEPING JOB TODAY.
REALLY?
KRNCH KRNCH
BUT, WELL, I'M AFRAID TO TAKE IT. IT'S THE HAUNTED HOUSE.
WHAT? SOMEONE'S MOVING INTO THAT HOUSE?
THEY ALWAYS DO. IT SEEMS A SEAFOOD BROKER FROM KOBE IS MOVING IN WITH HIS FAMILY TOMORROW.
SO THEY DON'T KNOW ANYTHING ABOUT THE HOUSE?
THEY DO. THE AGENT TOLD THEM EVERYTHING. HE EVEN RECOMMENDED ANOTHER HOUSE.
BUT THE SEAFOOD BROKER WAS SKEPTICAL. HE JUST USED THE CURSE TO GET THE RENT LOWERED.
HUH.
KRNCH KRNCH
CITY PEOPLE ARE NOT A SUPER-STITIOUS LOT.
IT'S NOT A SUPERSTITION. THE WAARGH REALLY DID SCARE ME THAT TIME.
"WAARGH"?! WHAT ARE YOU EVEN TALKING ABOUT...
IT'S TRUE. THERE'S DEFINITELY SOMETHING HAUNTING THAT HOUSE.

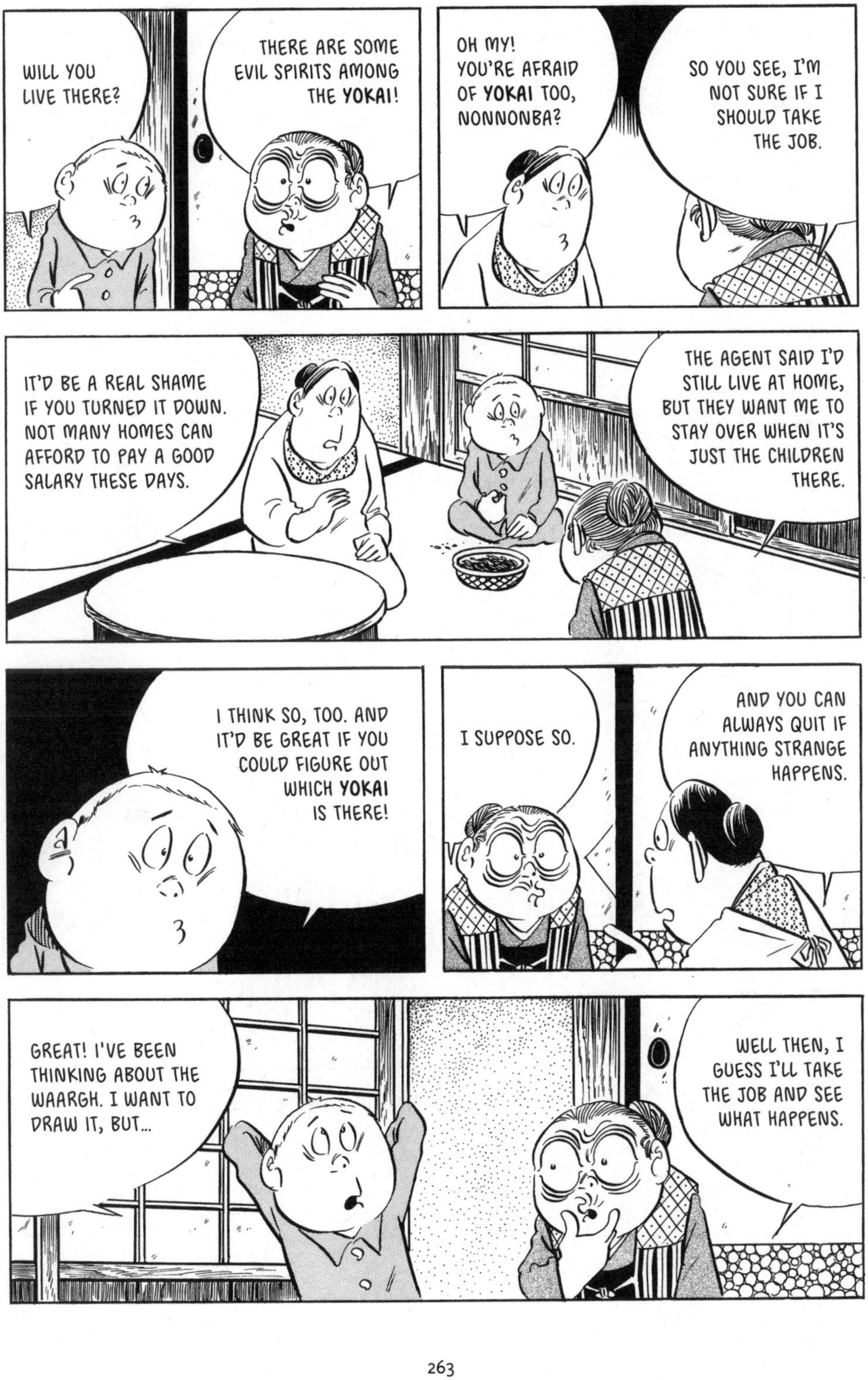
SO YOU SEE, I'M NOT SURE IF I SHOULD TAKE THE JOB.
OH MY! YOU'RE AFRAID OF YOKAI TOO, NONNONBA?
THERE ARE SOME EVIL SPIRITS AMONG THE YOKAI!
WILL YOU LIVE THERE?
THE AGENT SAID I'D STILL LIVE AT HOME, BUT THEY WANT ME TO STAY OVER WHEN IT'S JUST THE CHILDREN THERE.
IT'D BE A REAL SHAME IF YOU TURNED IT DOWN. NOT MANY HOMES CAN AFFORD TO PAY A GOOD SALARY THESE DAYS.
AND YOU CAN ALWAYS QUIT IF ANYTHING STRANGE HAPPENS.
I SUPPOSE SO.
I THINK SO, TOO. AND IT'D BE GREAT IF YOU COULD FIGURE OUT WHICH YOKAI IS THERE!
WELL THEN, I GUESS I'LL TAKE THE JOB AND SEE WHAT HAPPENS.
GREAT! I'VE BEEN THINKING ABOUT THE WAARGH. I WANT TO DRAW IT, BUT...

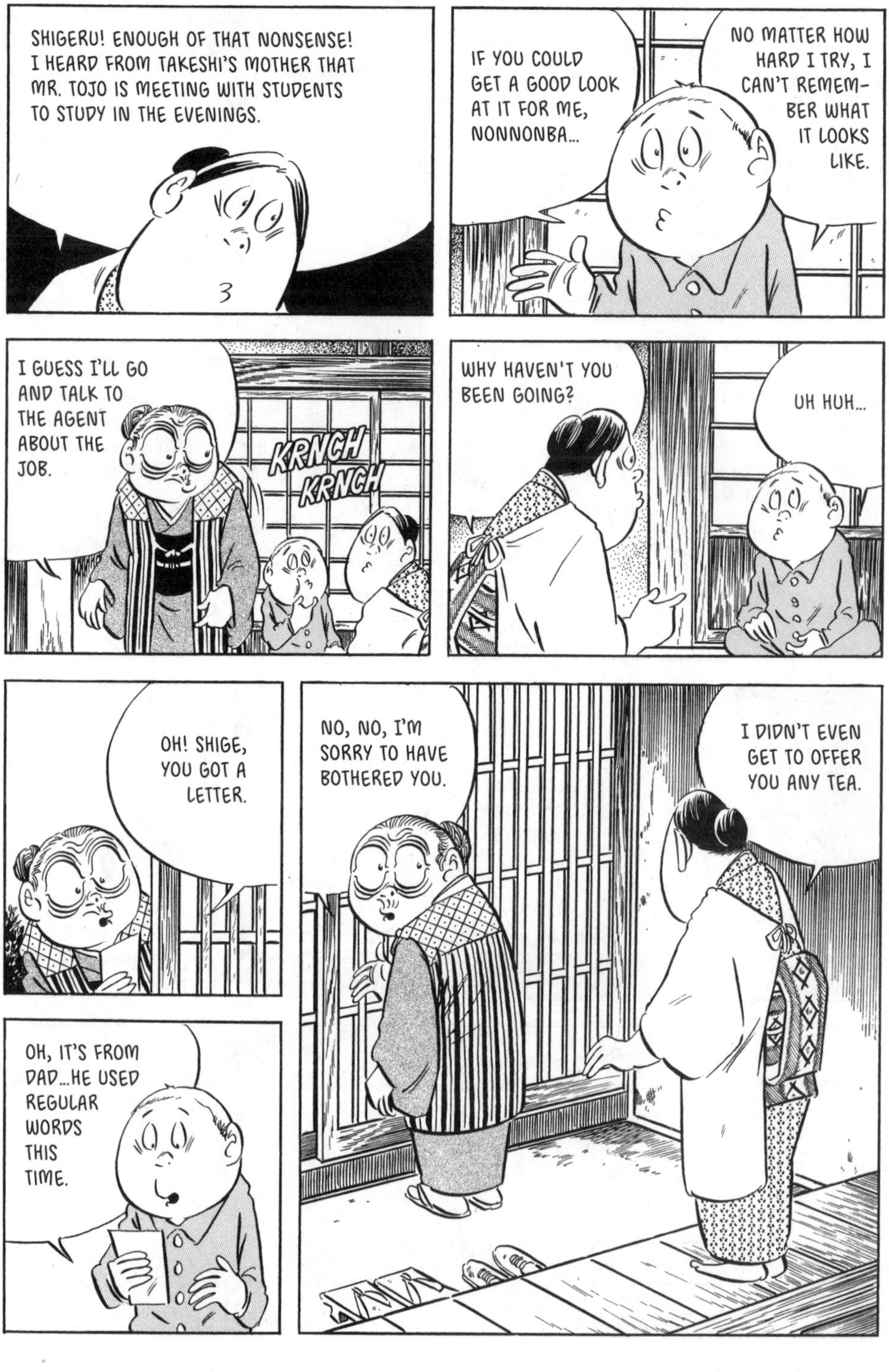
NO MATTER HOW HARD I TRY, I CAN'T REMEMBER WHAT IT LOOKS LIKE.
IF YOU COULD GET A GOOD LOOK AT IT FOR ME, NONNONBA...
SHIGERU! ENOUGH OF THAT NONSENSE! I HEARD FROM TAKESHI'S MOTHER THAT MR. TOJO IS MEETING WITH STUDENTS TO STUDY IN THE EVENINGS.
WHY HAVEN'T YOU BEEN GOING?
UH HUH...
KRNCH KRNCH
I GUESS I'LL GO AND TALK TO THE AGENT ABOUT THE JOB.
I DIDN'T EVEN GET TO OFFER YOU ANY TEA.
NO, NO, I'M SORRY TO HAVE BOTHERED YOU.
OH! SHIGE, YOU GOT A LETTER.
OH, IT'S FROM DAD...HE USED REGULAR WORDS THIS TIME.

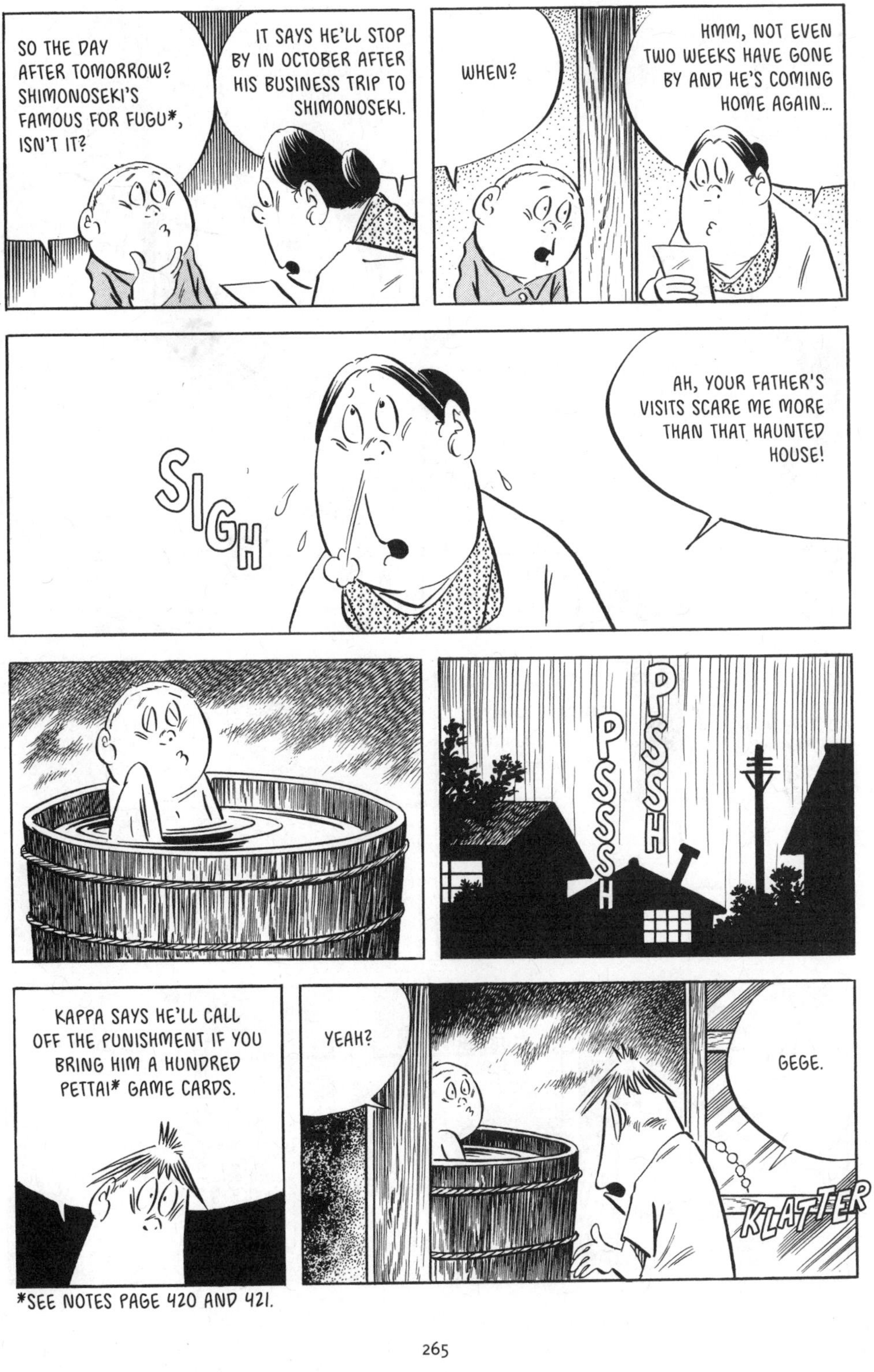
HMM, NOT EVEN TWO WEEKS HAVE GONE BY AND HE'S COMING HOME AGAIN...
WHEN?
IT SAYS HE'LL STOP BY IN OCTOBER AFTER HIS BUSINESS TRIP TO SHIMONOSEKI.
SO THE DAY AFTER TOMORROW? SHIMONOSEKI'S FAMOUS FOR FUGU*, ISN'T IT?
AH, YOUR FATHER'S VISITS SCARE ME MORE THAN THAT HAUNTED HOUSE!
SIGH
PSSH
PSSH
GEGE.
YEAH?
KLATTER
KAPPA SAYS HE'LL CALL OFF THE PUNISHMENT IF YOU BRING HIM A HUNDRED PETTAI* GAME CARDS.

*SEE NOTES PAGE 420 AND 421.

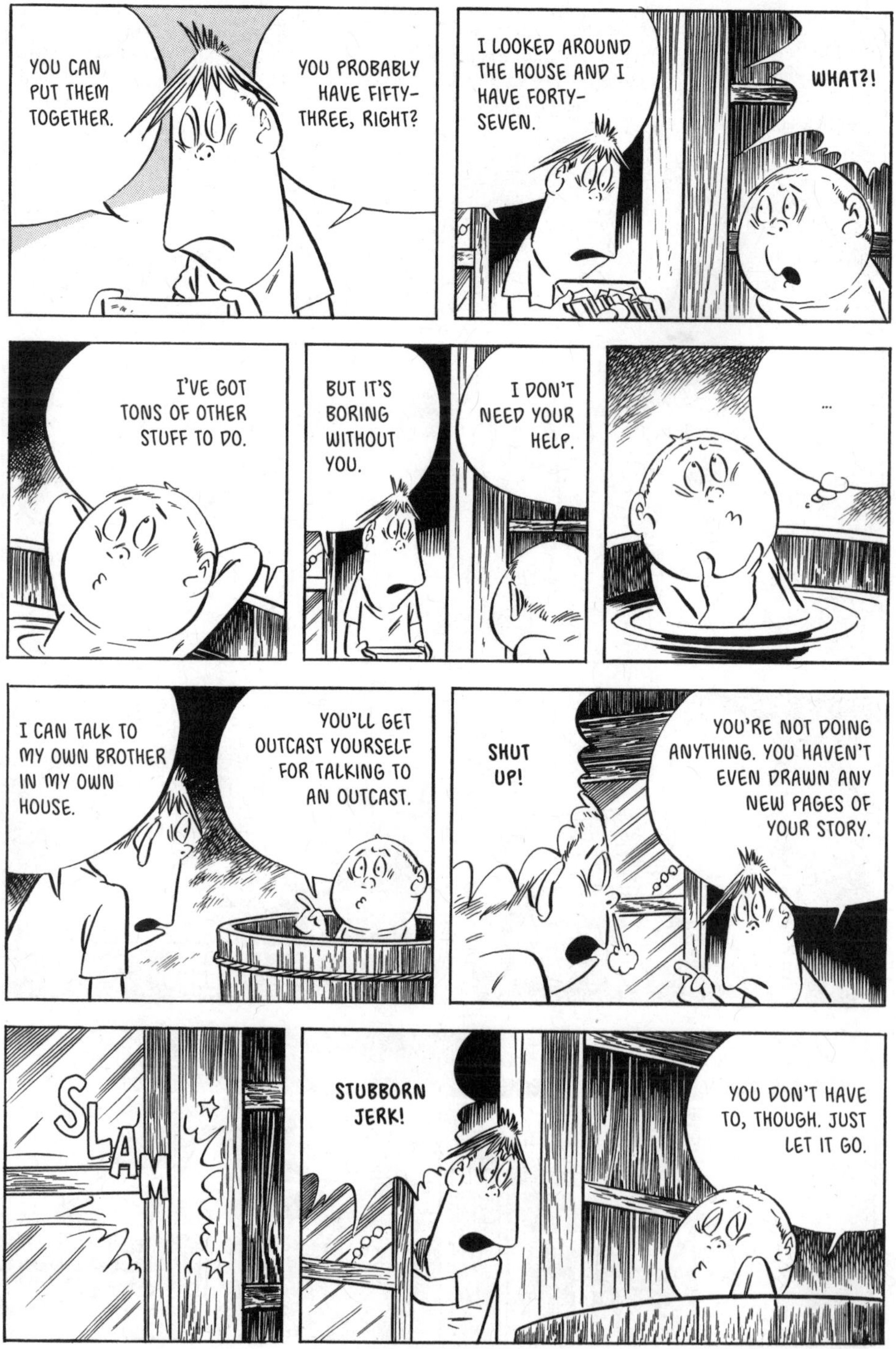
YOU CAN PUT THEM TOGETHER.
YOU PROBABLY HAVE FIFTY-THREE, RIGHT?
I LOOKED AROUND THE HOUSE AND I HAVE FORTY-SEVEN.
WHAT?!
I'VE GOT TONS OF OTHER STUFF TO DO.
BUT IT'S BORING WITHOUT YOU.
I DON'T NEED YOUR HELP.
...
I CAN TALK TO MY OWN BROTHER IN MY OWN HOUSE.
YOU'LL GET OUTCAST YOURSELF FOR TALKING TO AN OUTCAST.
SHUT UP!
YOU'RE NOT DOING ANYTHING. YOU HAVEN'T EVEN DRAWN ANY NEW PAGES OF YOUR STORY.
SLAM
STUBBORN JERK!
YOU DON'T HAVE TO, THOUGH. JUST LET IT GO.

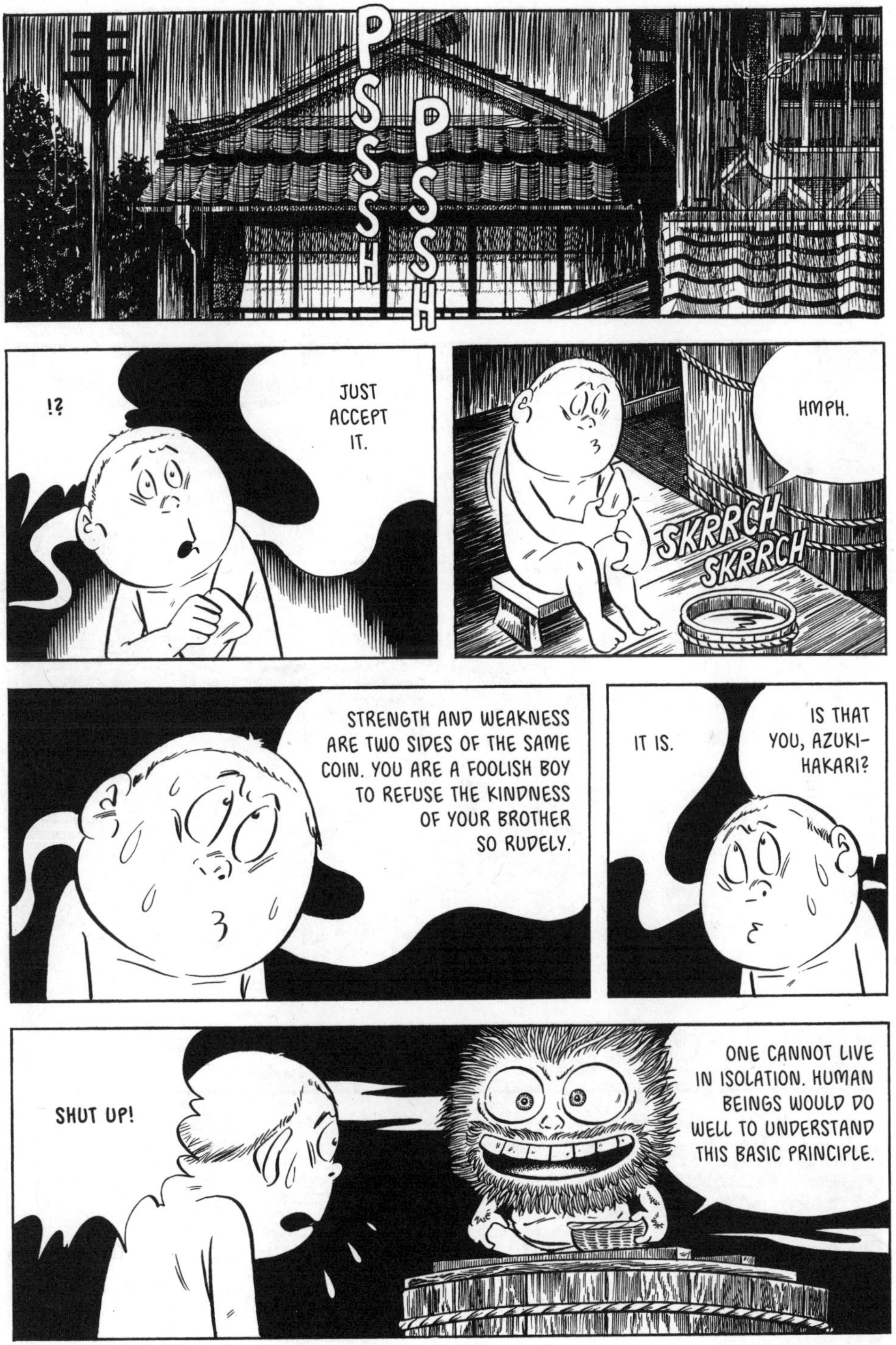
PSSSH
PSSH
HMPH.
SKRRCH
SKRRCH
JUST ACCEPT IT.
!?
IS THAT YOU, AZUKI-HAKARI?
IT IS.
STRENGTH AND WEAKNESS ARE TWO SIDES OF THE SAME COIN. YOU ARE A FOOLISH BOY TO REFUSE THE KINDNESS OF YOUR BROTHER SO RUDELY.
ONE CANNOT LIVE IN ISOLATION. HUMAN BEINGS WOULD DO WELL TO UNDERSTAND THIS BASIC PRINCIPLE.
SHUT UP!

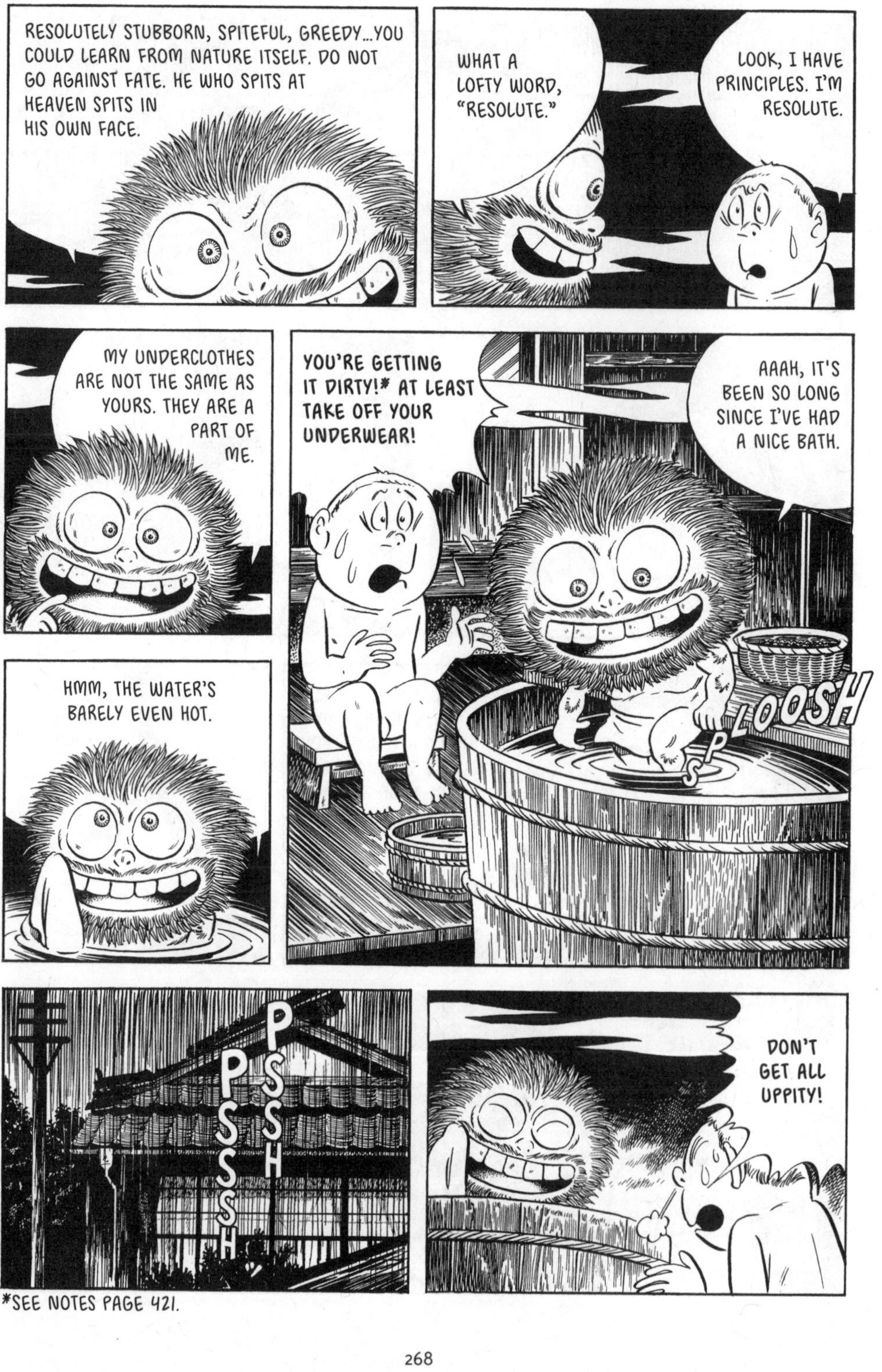
LOOK, I HAVE PRINCIPLES. I'M RESOLUTE.
WHAT A LOFTY WORD, "RESOLUTE."
RESOLUTELY STUBBORN, SPITEFUL, GREEDY...YOU COULD LEARN FROM NATURE ITSELF. DO NOT GO AGAINST FATE. HE WHO SPITS AT HEAVEN SPITS IN HIS OWN FACE.
AAAH, IT'S BEEN SO LONG SINCE I'VE HAD A NICE BATH.
YOU'RE GETTING IT DIRTY!* AT LEAST TAKE OFF YOUR UNDERWEAR!
SPLOOSH
MY UNDERCLOTHES ARE NOT THE SAME AS YOURS. THEY ARE A PART OF ME.
HMM, THE WATER'S BARELY EVEN HOT.
DON'T GET ALL UPPITY!
PSSH
PSSSH

*SEE NOTES PAGE 421.

HUNGRY GODS

THE NEXT DAY, THE TAKATORA INOKUMA FAMILY MOVED INTO THE HAUNTED HOUSE. A FAMILY OF FOUR.

TAK TAK*

*SEE NOTES PAGE 421.

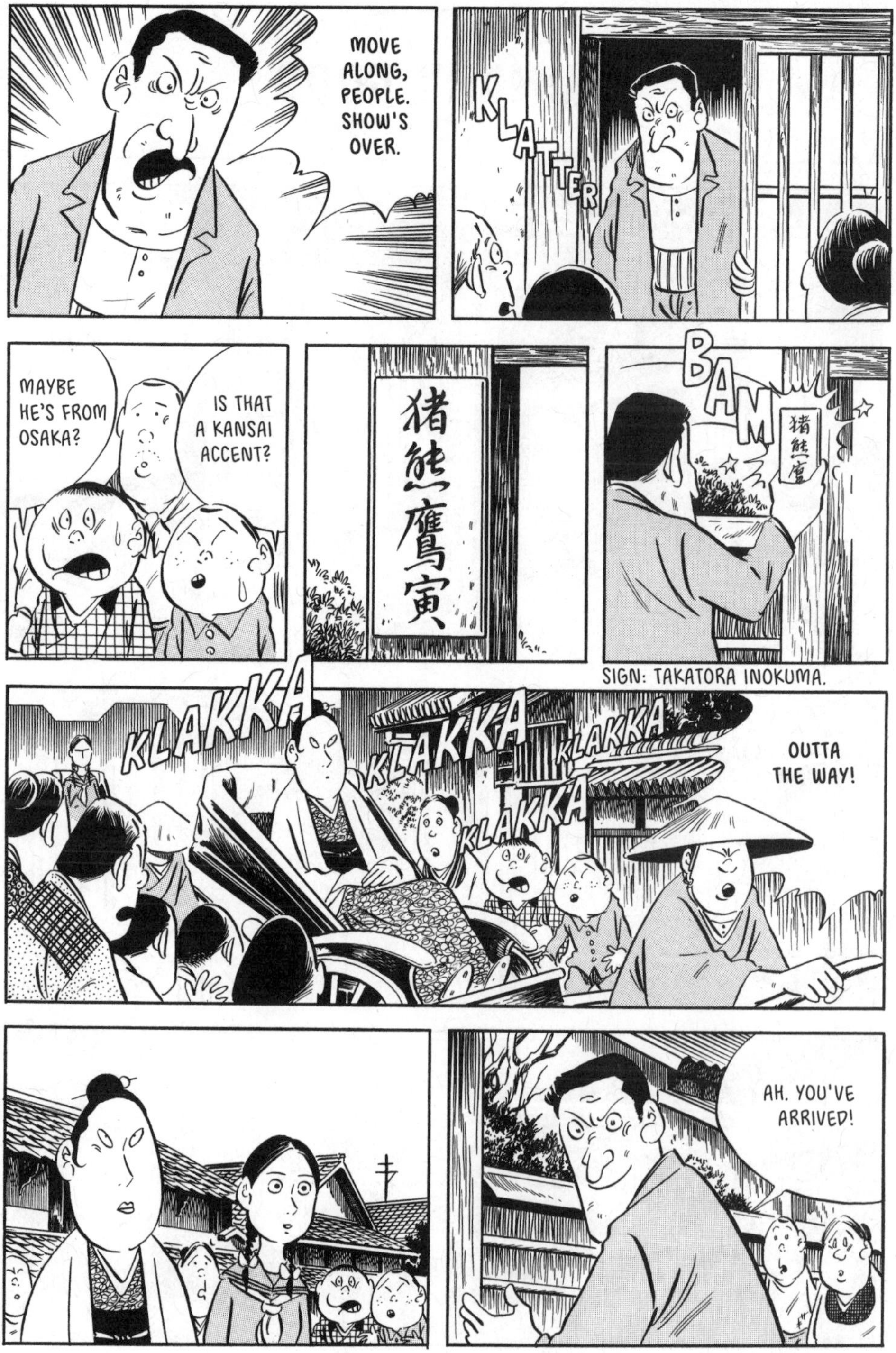
KLATTER
MOVE ALONG, PEOPLE. SHOW'S OVER.
BAM
猪熊鷹
猪熊鷹寅
IS THAT A KANSAI ACCENT?
MAYBE HE'S FROM OSAKA?
SIGN: TAKATORA INOKUMA.
OUTTA THE WAY!
KLAKKA
KLAKKA
KLAKKA
KLAKKA
KLAKKA
AH. YOU'VE ARRIVED!

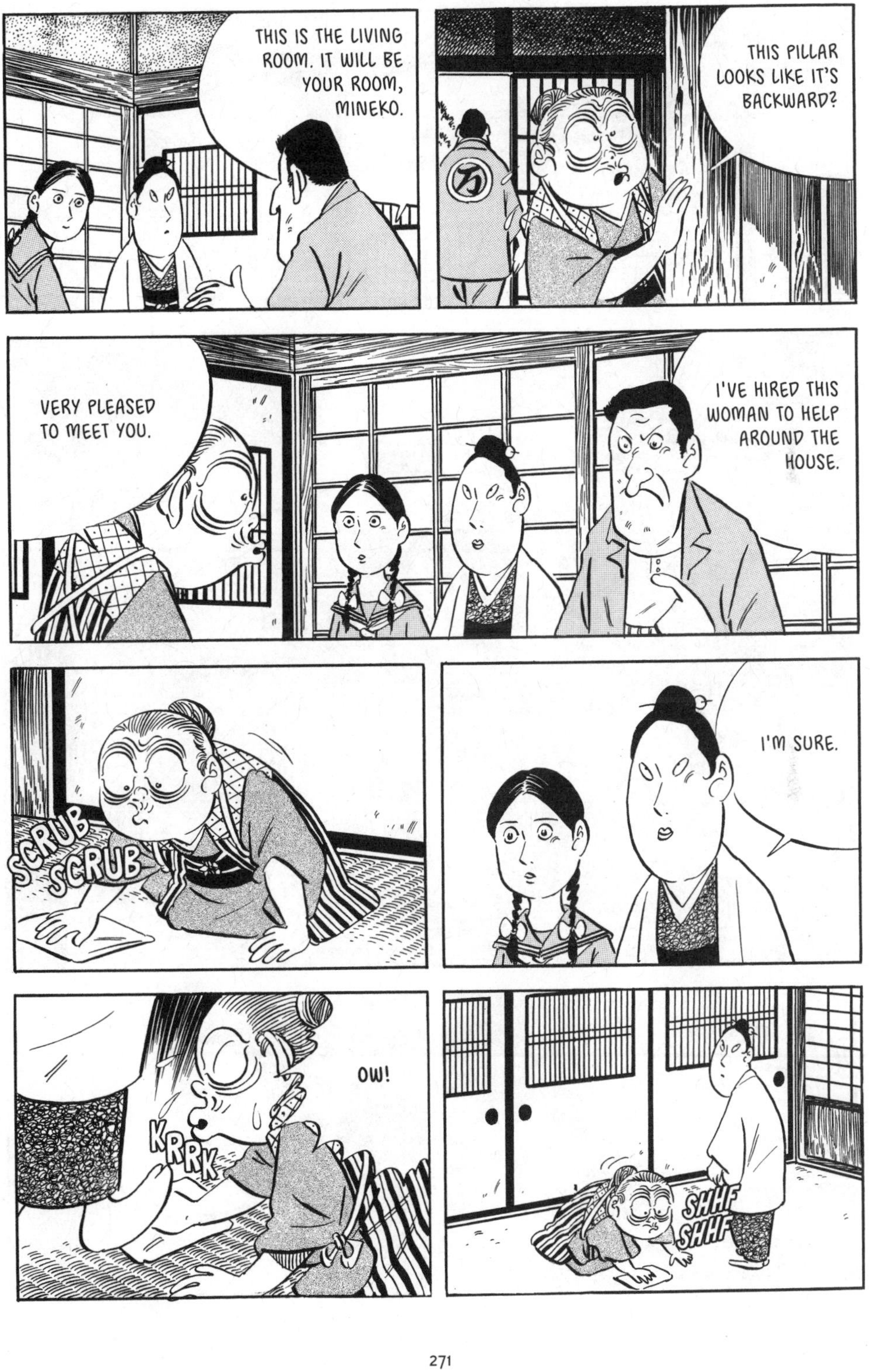
THIS PILLAR LOOKS LIKE IT'S BACKWARD?
THIS IS THE LIVING ROOM. IT WILL BE YOUR ROOM, MINEKO.
I'VE HIRED THIS WOMAN TO HELP AROUND THE HOUSE.
VERY PLEASED TO MEET YOU.
I'M SURE.
SCRUB SCRUB
SHHF SHHF
OW!
KRRK

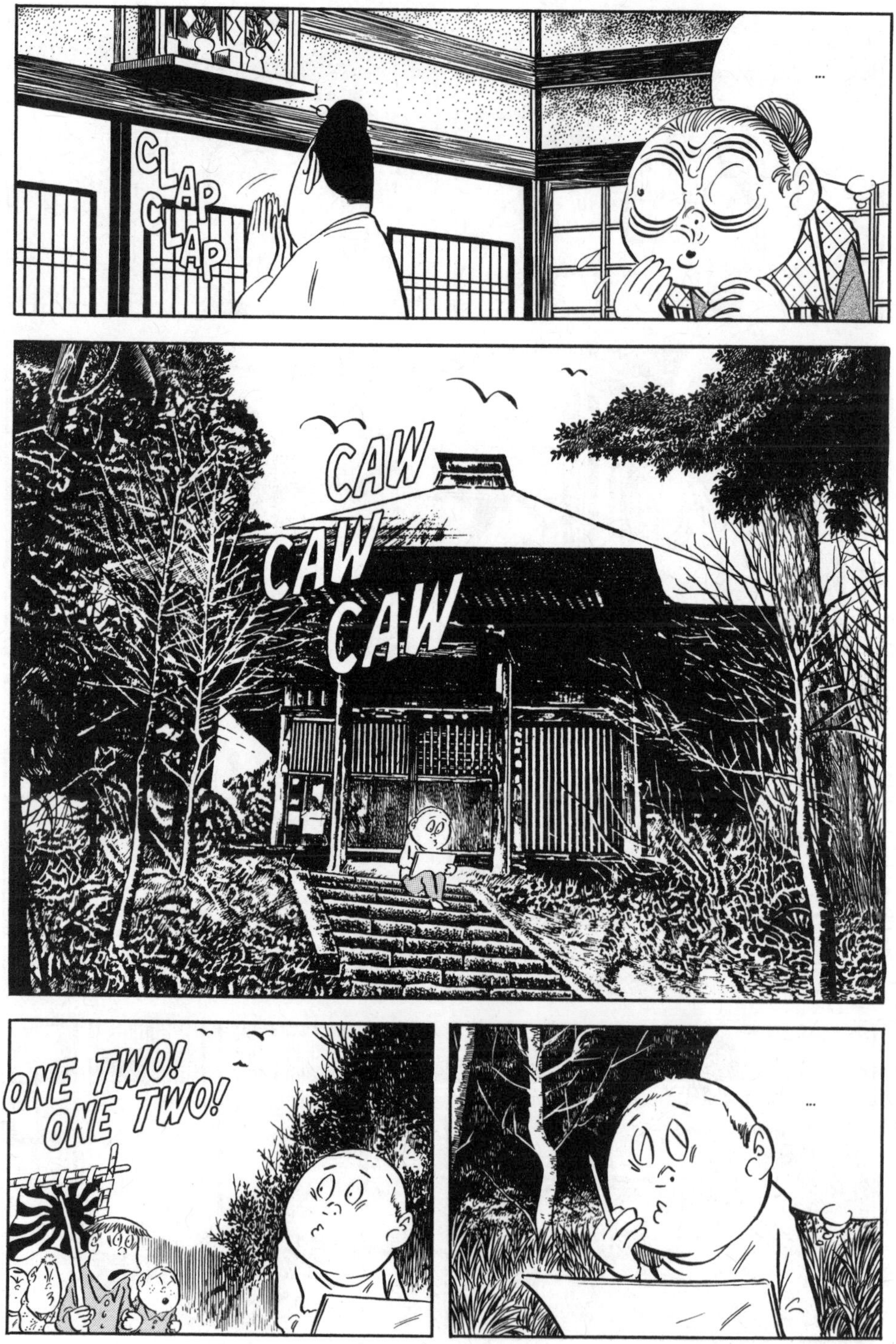
...
CLAP CLAP
CLAP CLAP
CAW
CAW
CAW
...
ONE TWO!
ONE TWO!

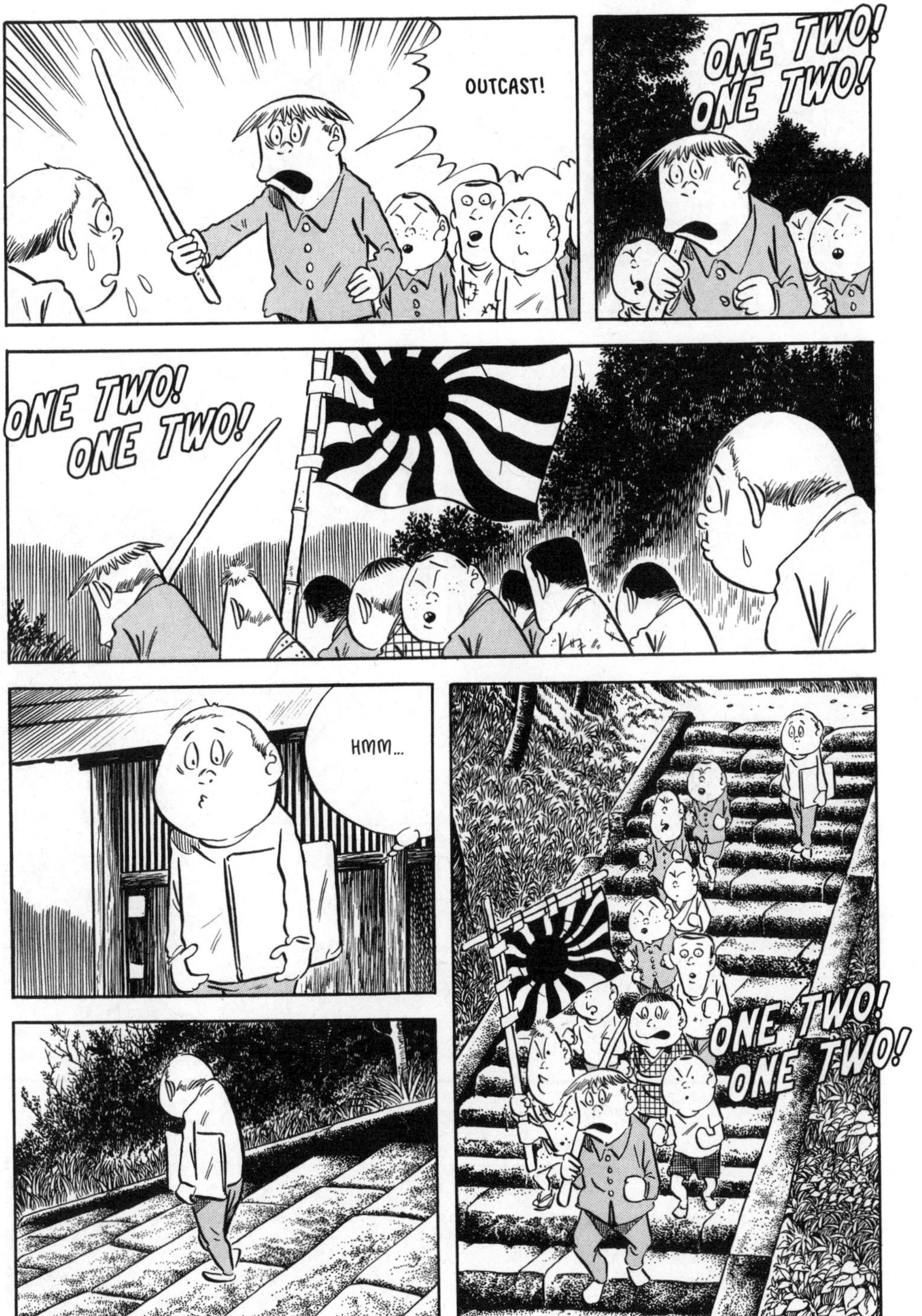
ONE TWO! ONE TWO!
OUTCAST!
ONE TWO! ONE TWO!
ONE TWO! ONE TWO!
HMM...

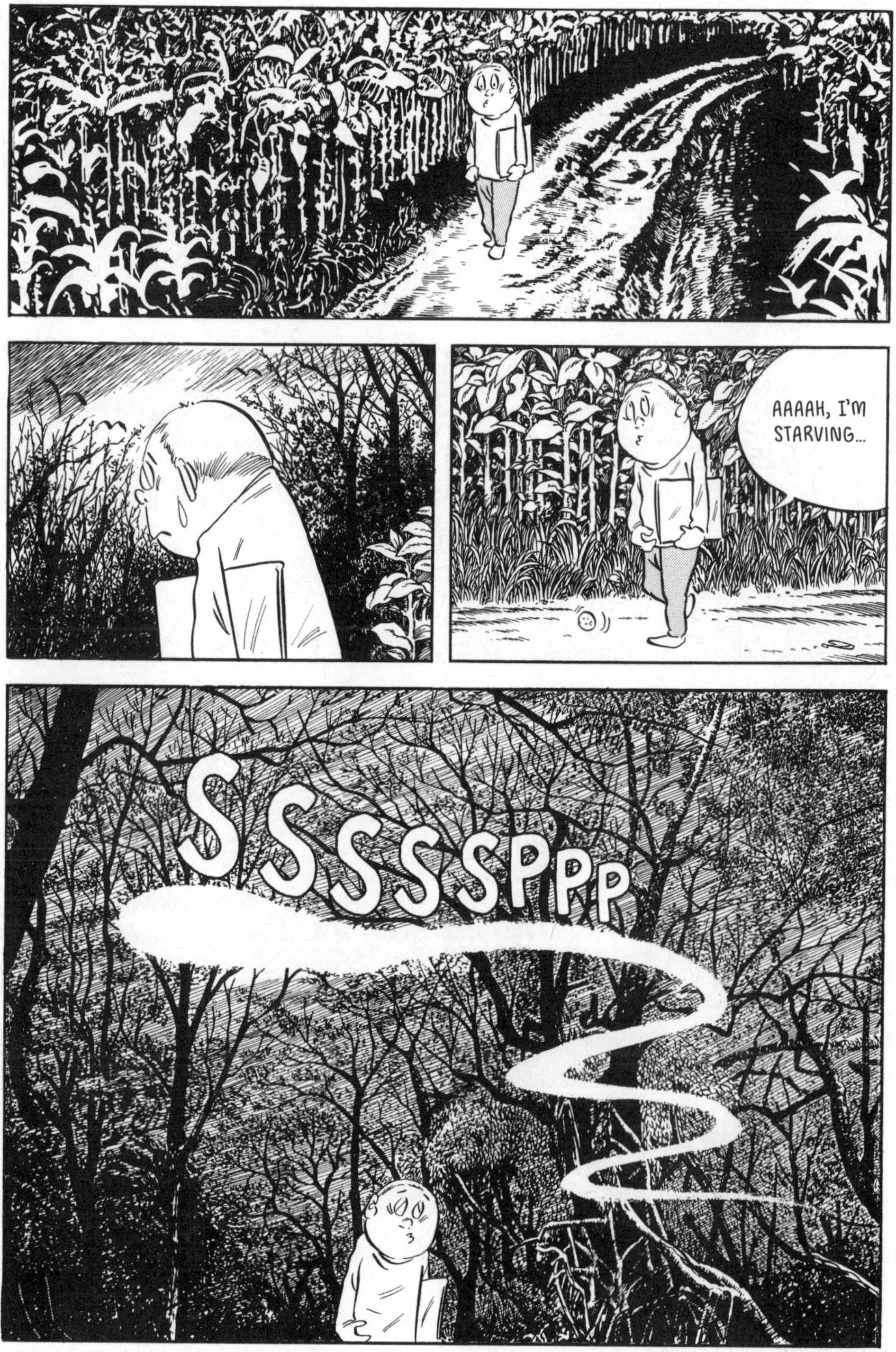
AAAAH, I'M STARVING...
SSSSSPPP

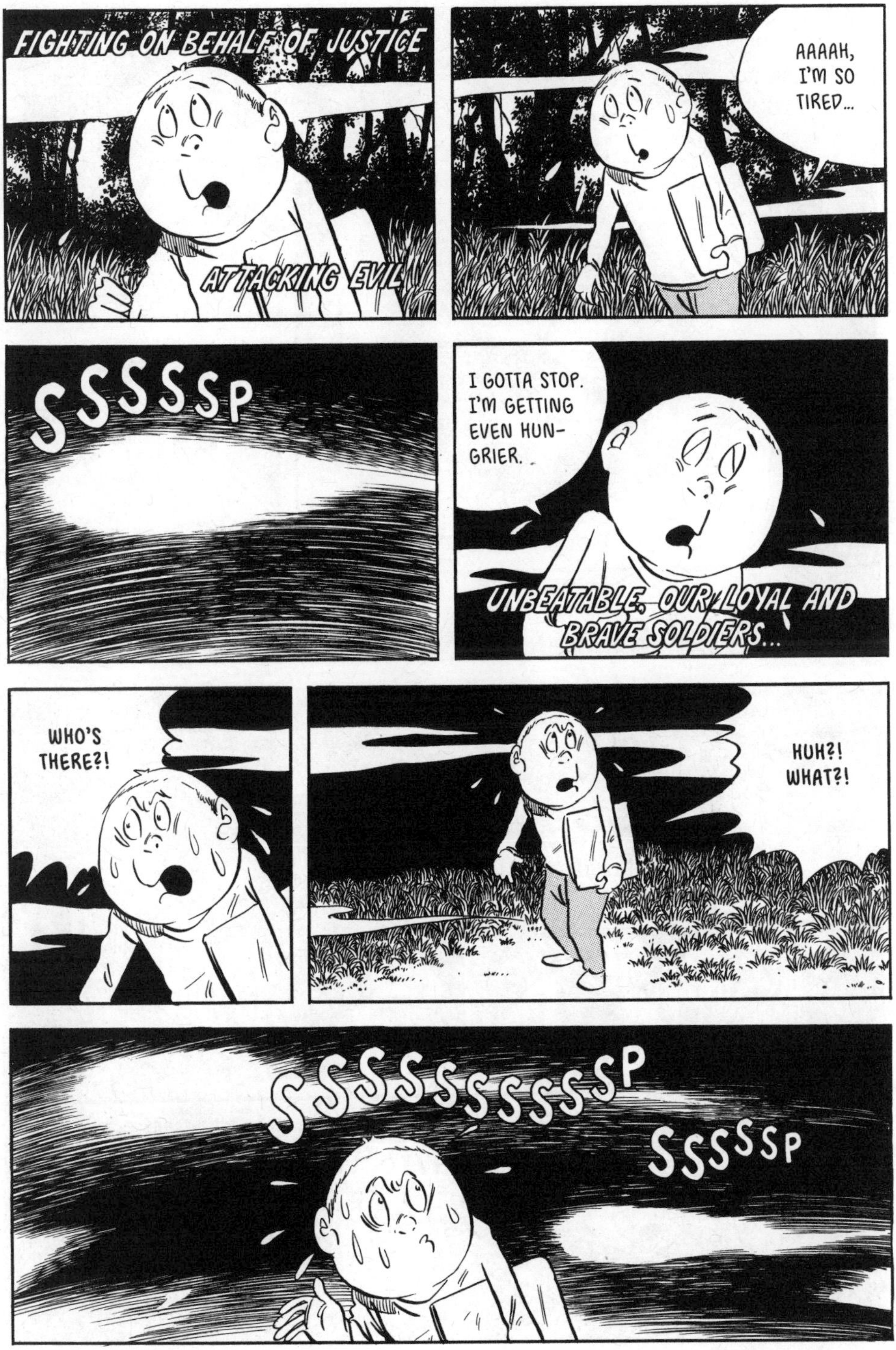
AAAAH, I'M SO TIRED...
FIGHTING ON BEHALF OF JUSTICE
ATTACKING EVIL
I GOTTA STOP. I'M GETTING EVEN HUN-GRIER.
UNBEATABLE, OUR LOYAL AND BRAVE SOLDIERS...
SSSSSP
HUH?! WHAT?!
WHO'S THERE?!
SSSSSSSSSSSP
SSSSSP

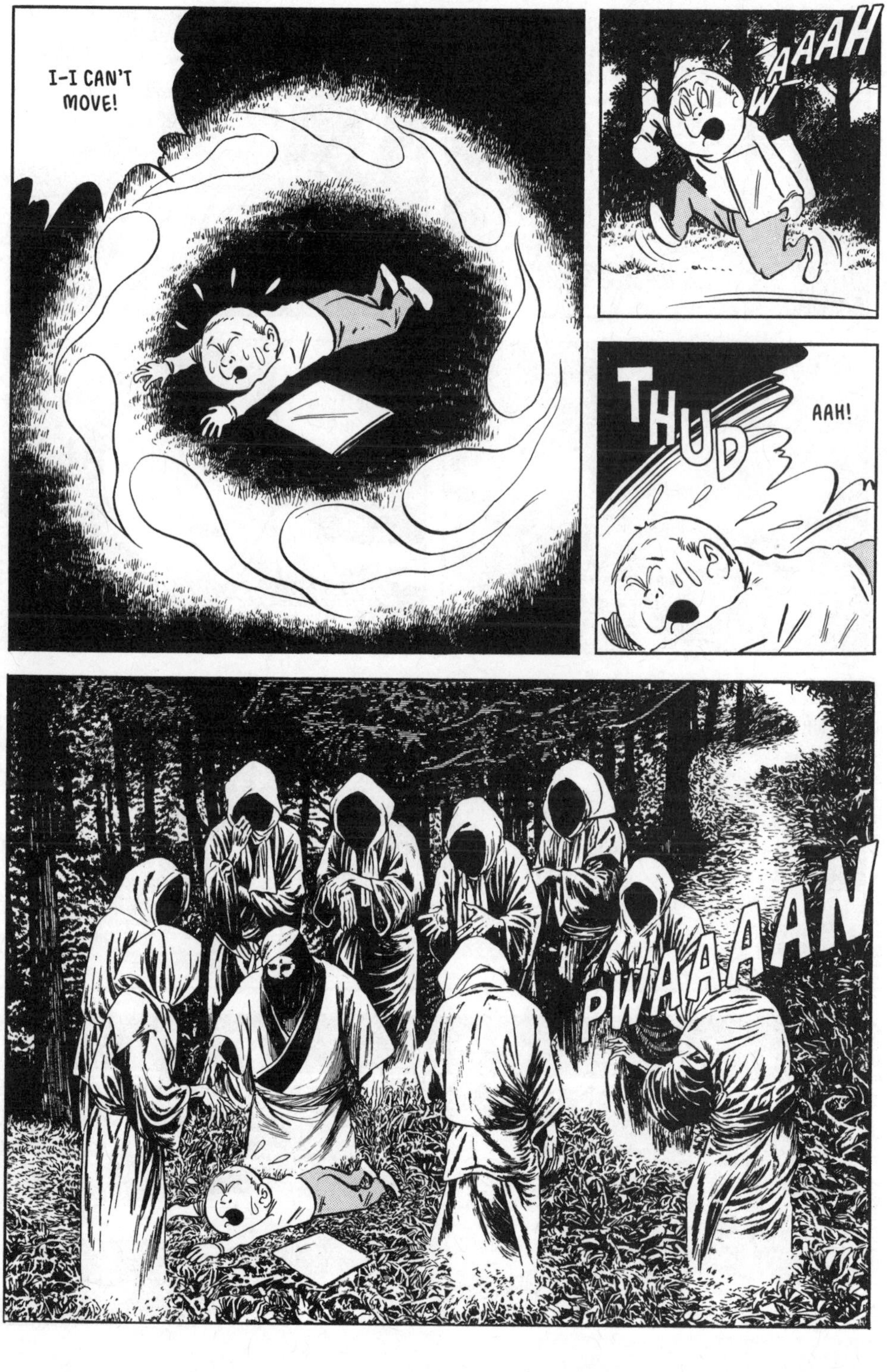
WAAAAH
THUD
AAH!
I-I CAN'T MOVE!
PWAAAAAN

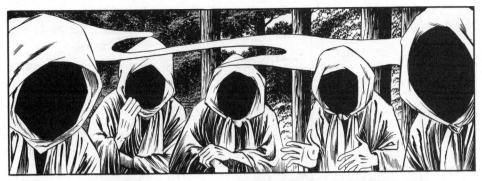

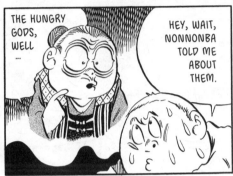

THE HUNGRY GODS!
HEY, WAIT, NONNONBA TOLD ME ABOUT THEM.
THE HUNGRY GODS, WELL ...
THEY'RE THE VENGEFUL GHOSTS OF TRAVELERS WHO STARVED TO DEATH. THE PEOPLE THEY POSSESS ARE PARALYZED FOR A WHILE AND THEN THEY DIE.
CAN THEY BE SAVED?
TO GET RID OF THE PARAL-YSIS, YOU HAVE TO EAT SOMETHING.
AND IF YOU HAVE NOTHING TO EAT, YOU CAN WRITE THE WORD "RICE" ON THE PALM OF YOUR HAND AND LICK IT THREE TIMES.

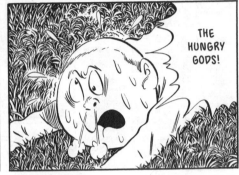

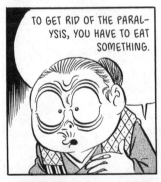

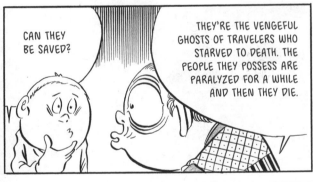

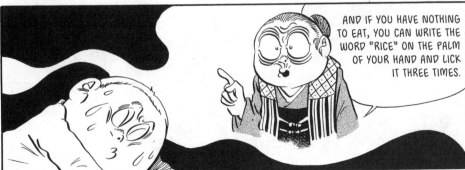

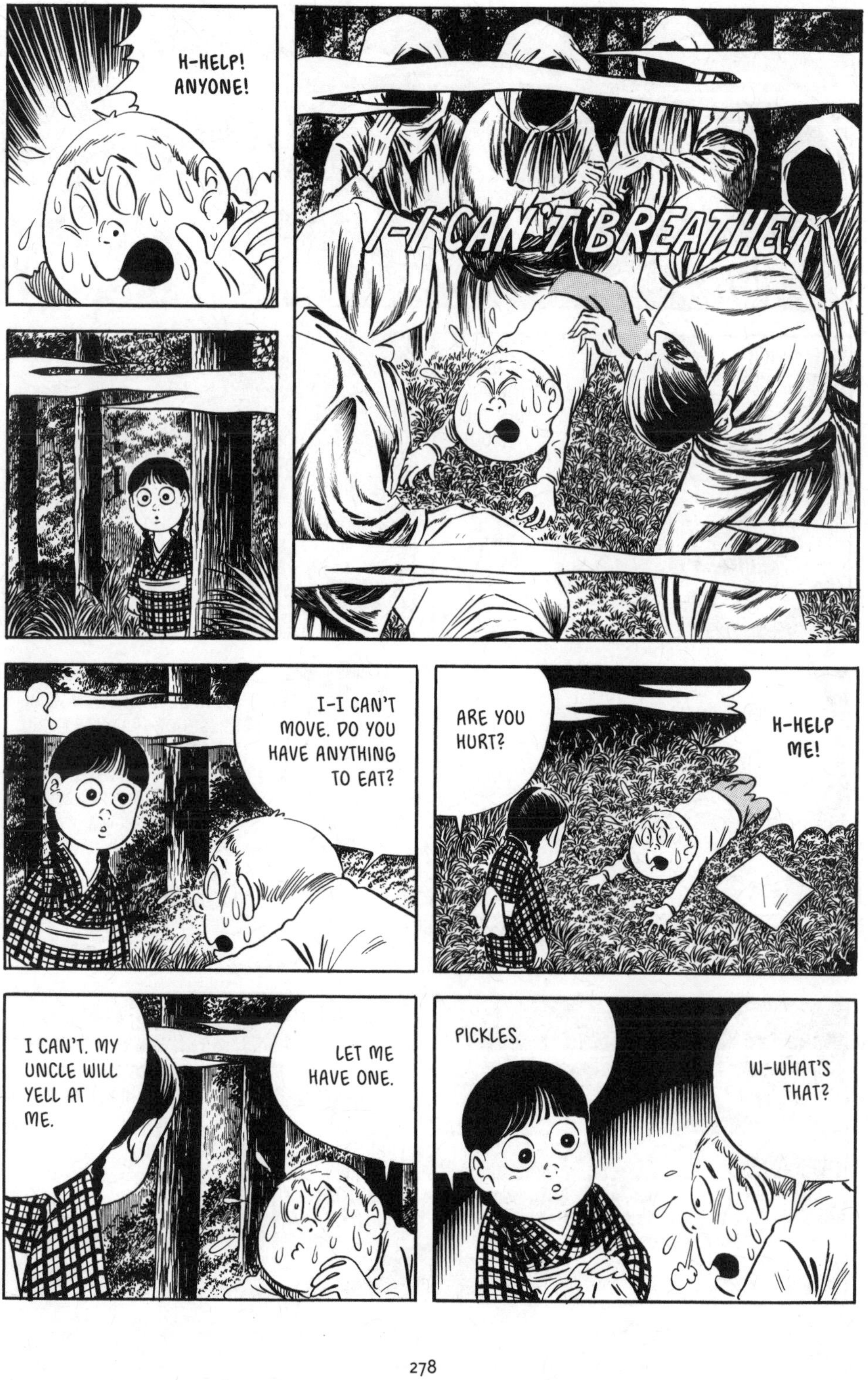
I-I CAN'T BREATHE!!
H-HELP! ANYONE!
H-HELP ME!
ARE YOU HURT?
I-I CAN'T MOVE. DO YOU HAVE ANYTHING TO EAT?
W-WHAT'S THAT?
PICKLES.
LET ME HAVE ONE.
I CAN'T. MY UNCLE WILL YELL AT ME.

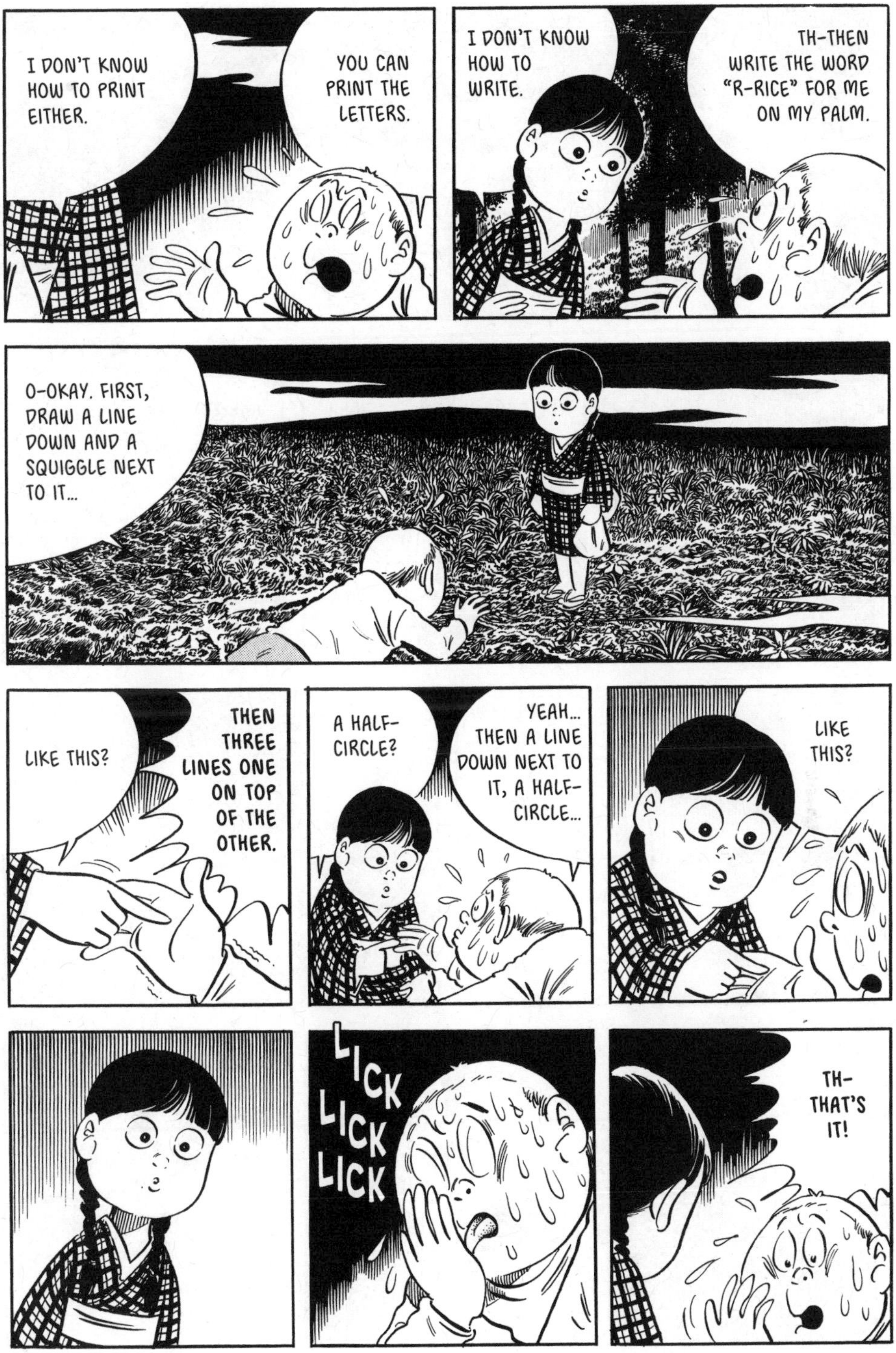
TH-THEN WRITE THE WORD "R-RICE" FOR ME ON MY PALM.
I DON'T KNOW HOW TO WRITE.
YOU CAN PRINT THE LETTERS.
I DON'T KNOW HOW TO PRINT EITHER.
O-OKAY. FIRST, DRAW A LINE DOWN AND A SQUIGGLE NEXT TO IT...
LIKE THIS?
YEAH... THEN A LINE DOWN NEXT TO IT, A HALF-CIRCLE...
A HALF-CIRCLE?
THEN THREE LINES ONE ON TOP OF THE OTHER.
LIKE THIS?
TH- THAT'S IT!
LICK LICK LICK

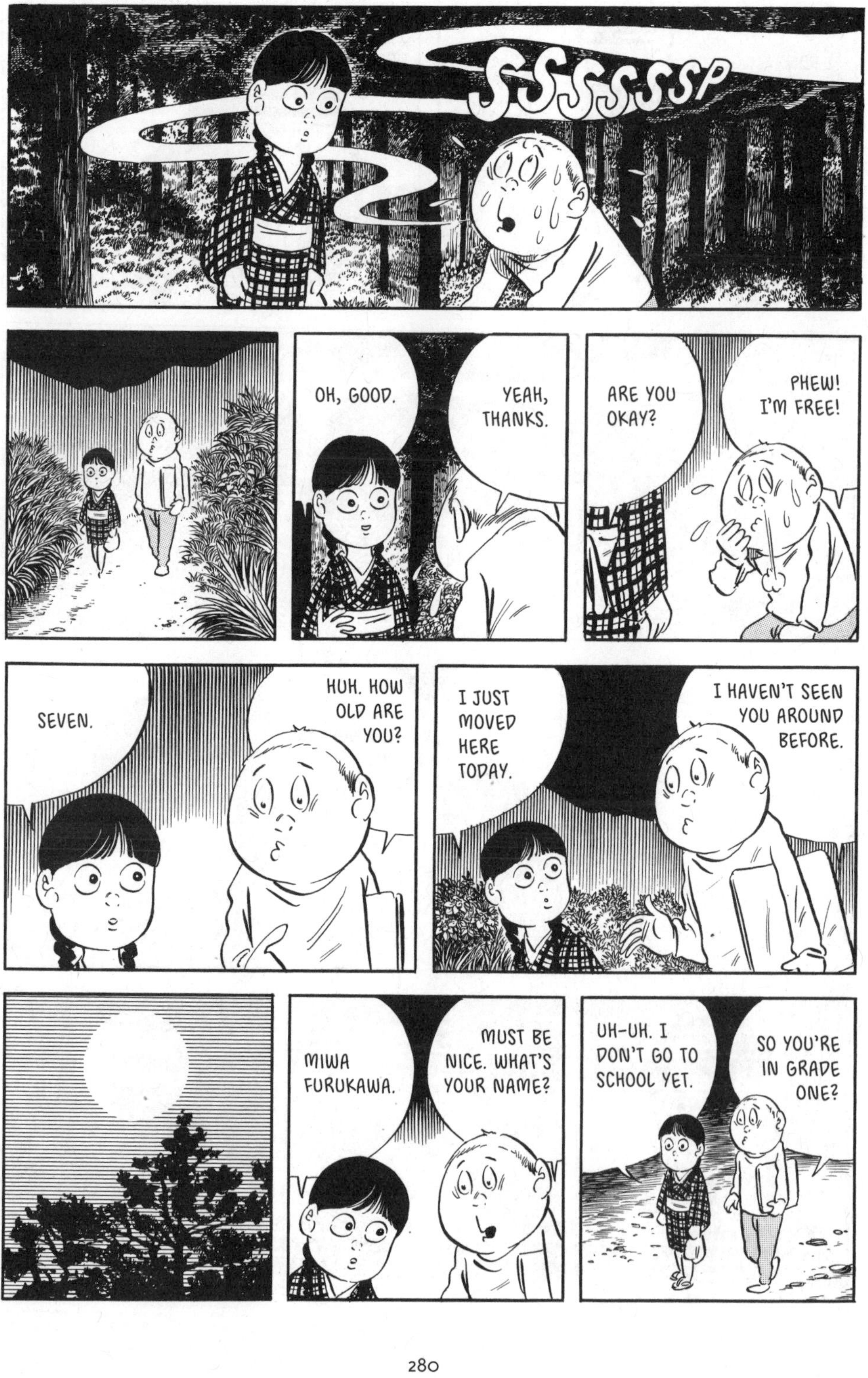
SSSSSSP
PHEW! I'M FREE!
ARE YOU OKAY?
YEAH, THANKS.
OH, GOOD.
I HAVEN'T SEEN YOU AROUND BEFORE.
I JUST MOVED HERE TODAY.
HUH. HOW OLD ARE YOU?
SEVEN.
SO YOU'RE IN GRADE ONE?
UH-UH. I DON'T GO TO SCHOOL YET.
MUST BE NICE. WHAT'S YOUR NAME?
MIWA FURUKAWA.

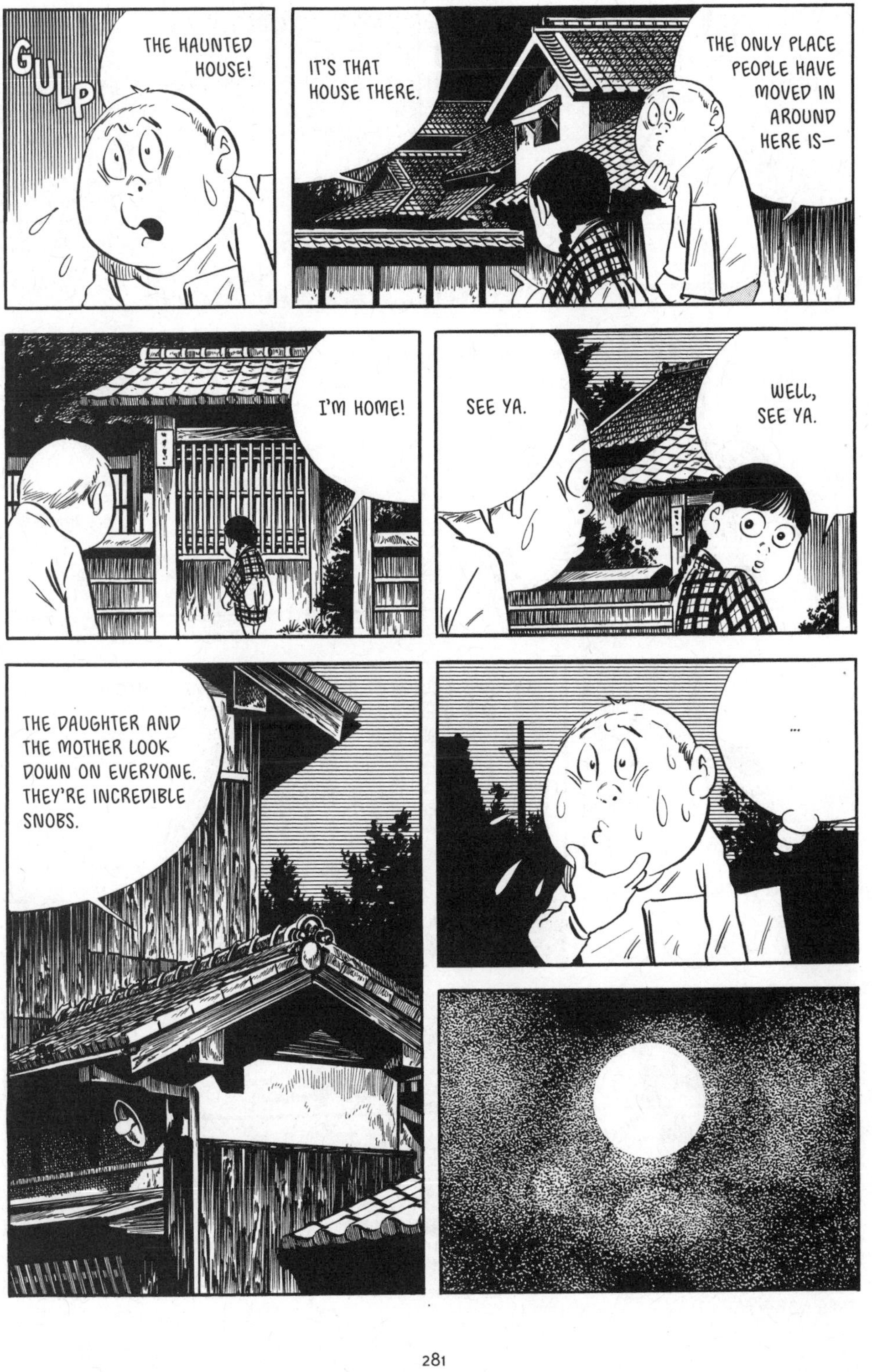
THE ONLY PLACE PEOPLE HAVE MOVED IN AROUND HERE IS—
IT'S THAT HOUSE THERE.
THE HAUNTED HOUSE!
GULP
WELL, SEE YA.
SEE YA.
I'M HOME!
...
THE DAUGHTER AND THE MOTHER LOOK DOWN ON EVERYONE. THEY'RE INCREDIBLE SNOBS.

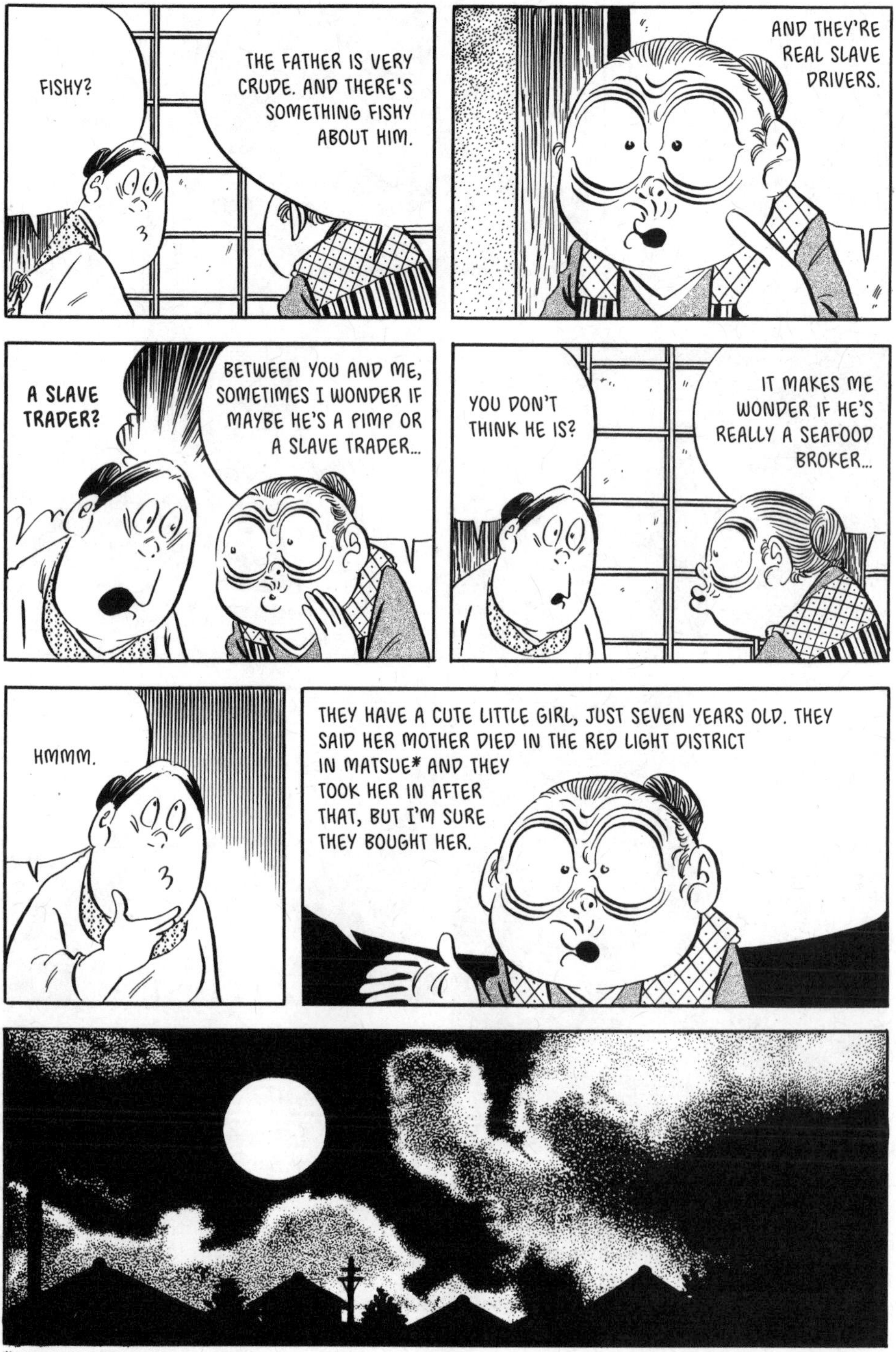
THE FATHER IS VERY CRUDE. AND THERE'S SOMETHING FISHY ABOUT HIM.
FISHY?
AND THEY'RE REAL SLAVE DRIVERS.
BETWEEN YOU AND ME, SOMETIMES I WONDER IF MAYBE HE'S A PIMP OR A SLAVE TRADER...
A SLAVE TRADER?
YOU DON'T THINK HE IS?
IT MAKES ME WONDER IF HE'S REALLY A SEAFOOD BROKER...
HMMM.
THEY HAVE A CUTE LITTLE GIRL, JUST SEVEN YEARS OLD. THEY SAID HER MOTHER DIED IN THE RED LIGHT DISTRICT IN MATSUE* AND THEY TOOK HER IN AFTER THAT, BUT I'M SURE THEY BOUGHT HER.

*SEE NOTE PAGE 421.

TADASHI IN LOVE

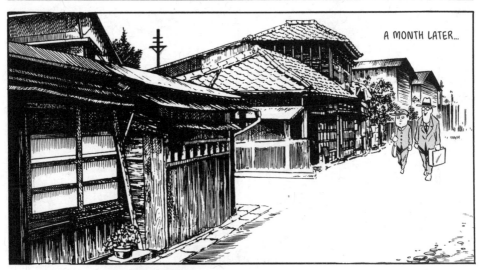

A MONTH LATER...
OH! DAD! YOU'RE HOME!
YES, I AM.
IT WAS A REAL SURPRISE! SOME KNUCKLEHEAD STEPPED ON MY FOOT ON THE TRAIN AND WHEN I LOOKED UP TO GLARE, IT WAS DAD.
SAY, DAD, SOME ANMITSU* SURE WOULD HIT THE SPOT!

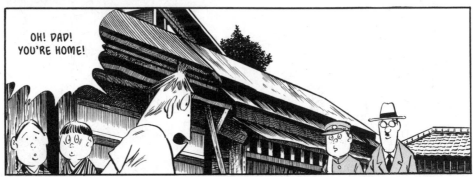

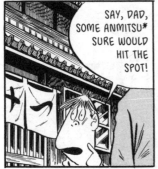

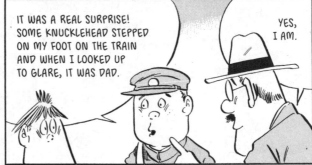

SIGN: ANMITSU. *ANMITSU IS A TREAT MADE UP OF AZUKI BEANS IN A SWEET SYRUP.

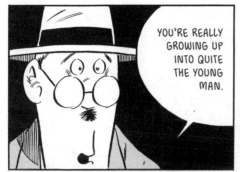

WE MEN DON'T EAT STUFF LIKE THAT!
WELL SAID, TADASHI.
YOU'RE REALLY GROWING UP INTO QUITE THE YOUNG MAN.
PFFT
MINEKO, SHALL WE HAVE SOME ANMITSU?
MMM! OKAY!
GAWK
HELLO!
あんみ
GAWK

SIGN: ANMITSU.

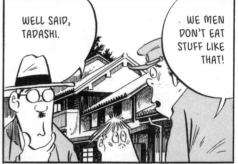

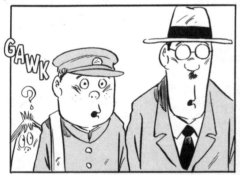

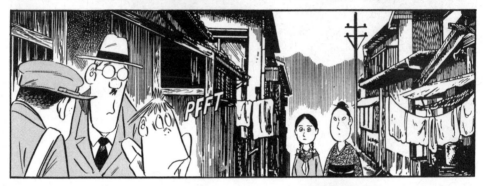

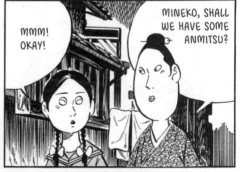

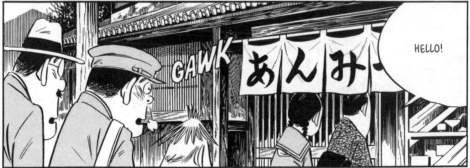

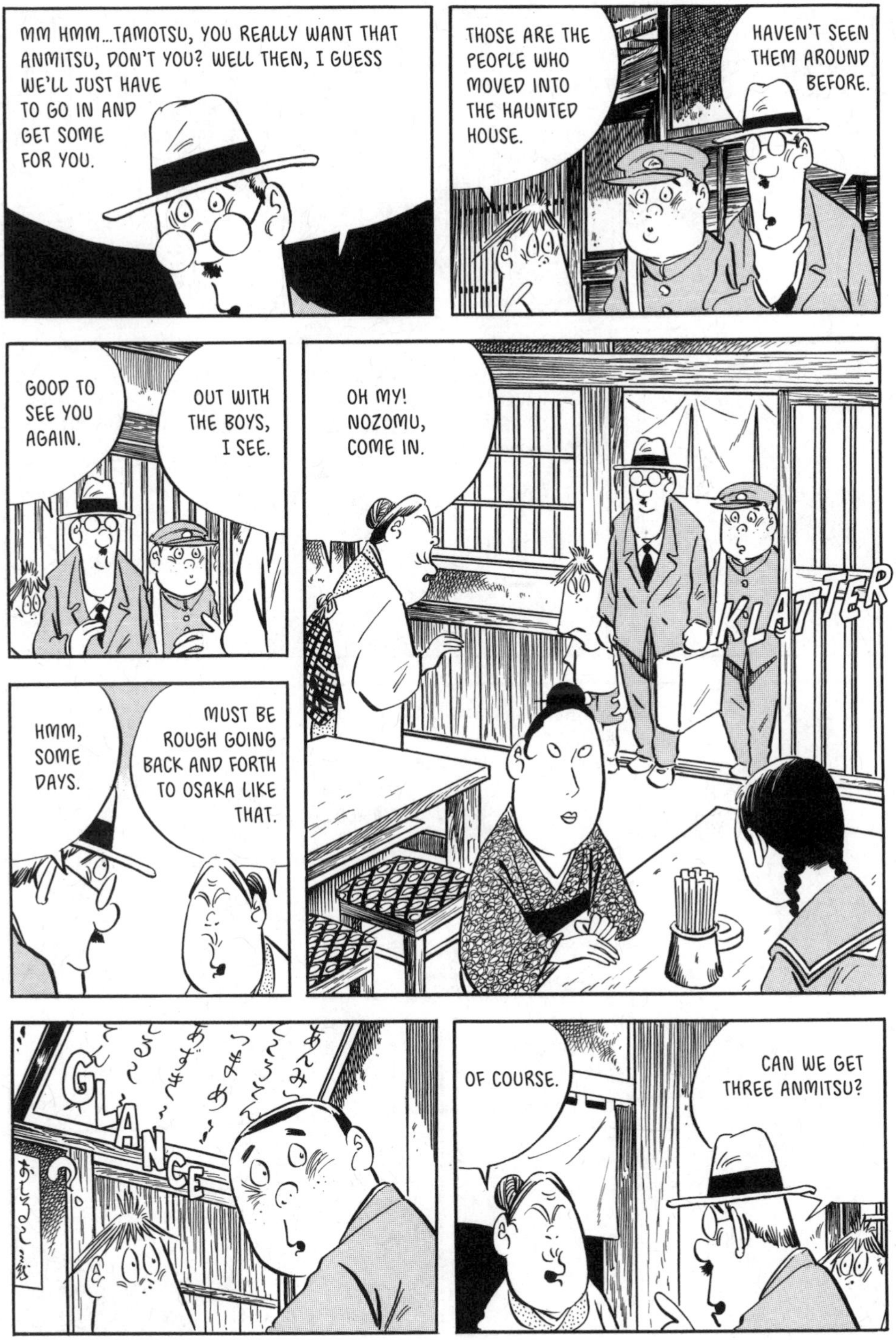
HAVEN'T SEEN THEM AROUND BEFORE.
THOSE ARE THE PEOPLE WHO MOVED INTO THE HAUNTED HOUSE.
MM HMM...TAMOTSU, YOU REALLY WANT THAT ANMITSU, DON'T YOU? WELL THEN, I GUESS WE'LL JUST HAVE TO GO IN AND GET SOME FOR YOU.
OH MY! NOZOMU, COME IN.
KLATTER
OUT WITH THE BOYS, I SEE.
GOOD TO SEE YOU AGAIN.
MUST BE ROUGH GOING BACK AND FORTH TO OSAKA LIKE THAT.
HMM, SOME DAYS.
CAN WE GET THREE ANMITSU?
OF COURSE.
GLANCE

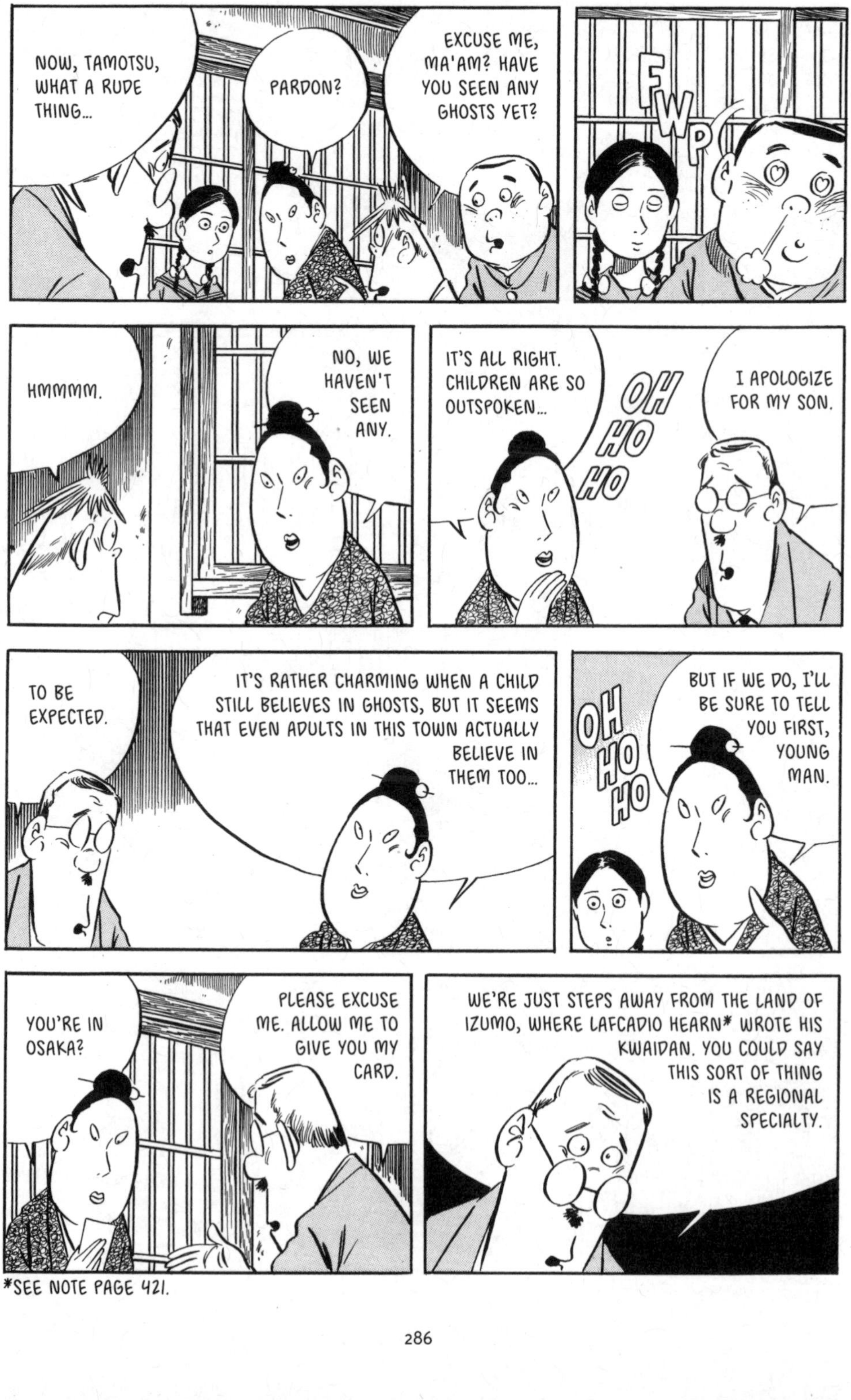
FWP
EXCUSE ME, MA'AM? HAVE YOU SEEN ANY GHOSTS YET?
PARDON?
NOW, TAMOTSU, WHAT A RUDE THING...
I APOLOGIZE FOR MY SON.
OH HO HO
IT'S ALL RIGHT. CHILDREN ARE SO OUTSPOKEN...
NO, WE HAVEN'T SEEN ANY.
HMMMM.
BUT IF WE DO, I'LL BE SURE TO TELL YOU FIRST, YOUNG MAN.
OH HO HO
IT'S RATHER CHARMING WHEN A CHILD STILL BELIEVES IN GHOSTS, BUT IT SEEMS THAT EVEN ADULTS IN THIS TOWN ACTUALLY BELIEVE IN THEM TOO...
TO BE EXPECTED.
WE'RE JUST STEPS AWAY FROM THE LAND OF IZUMO, WHERE LAFCADIO HEARN* WROTE HIS KWAIDAN. YOU COULD SAY THIS SORT OF THING IS A REGIONAL SPECIALTY.
PLEASE EXCUSE ME. ALLOW ME TO GIVE YOU MY CARD.
YOU'RE IN OSAKA?

*SEE NOTE PAGE 421.

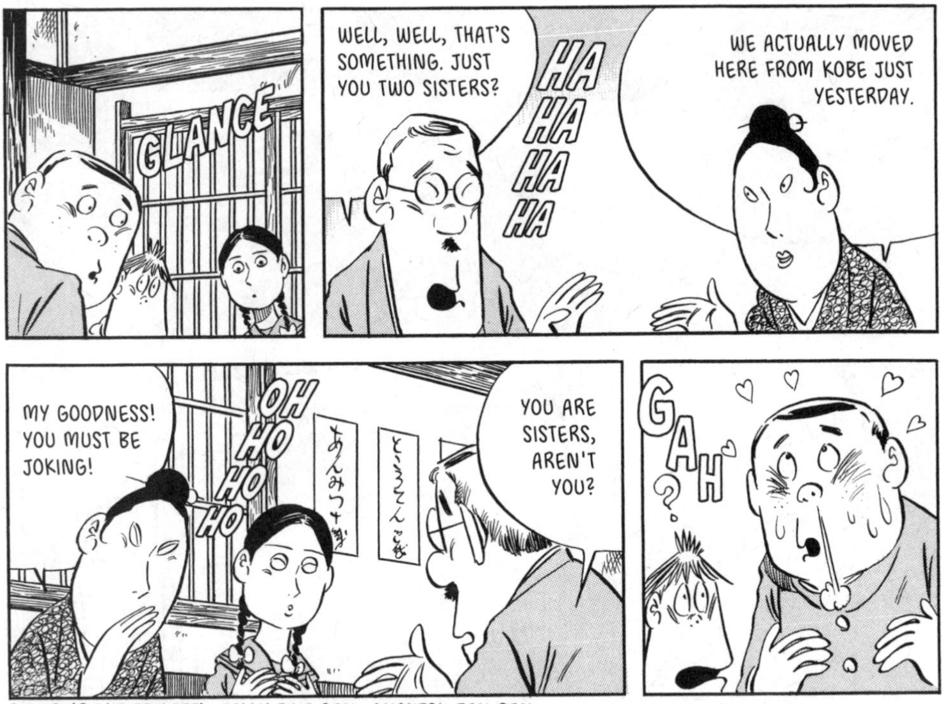
WE ACTUALLY MOVED HERE FROM KOBE JUST YESTERDAY.
HA HA HA HA
WELL, WELL, THAT'S SOMETHING. JUST YOU TWO SISTERS?
GLANCE
GAH
?
YOU ARE SISTERS, AREN'T YOU?
OH HO HO HO
MY GOODNESS! YOU MUST BE JOKING!

SIGNS (RIGHT TO LEFT): JELLY FIVE SEN; ANMITSU TEN SEN.

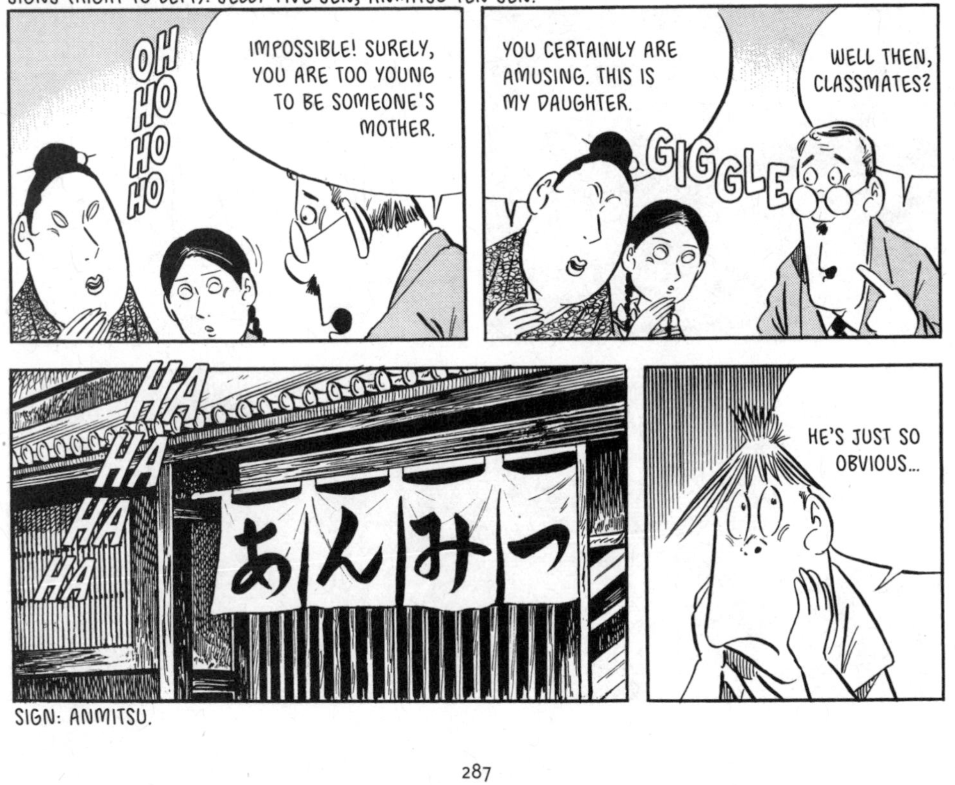
WELL THEN, CLASSMATES?
YOU CERTAINLY ARE AMUSING. THIS IS MY DAUGHTER.
GIGGLE
IMPOSSIBLE! SURELY, YOU ARE TOO YOUNG TO BE SOMEONE'S MOTHER.
OH HO HO HO HO
HE'S JUST SO OBVIOUS...
あんみつ
HA HA HA HA

SIGN: ANMITSU.

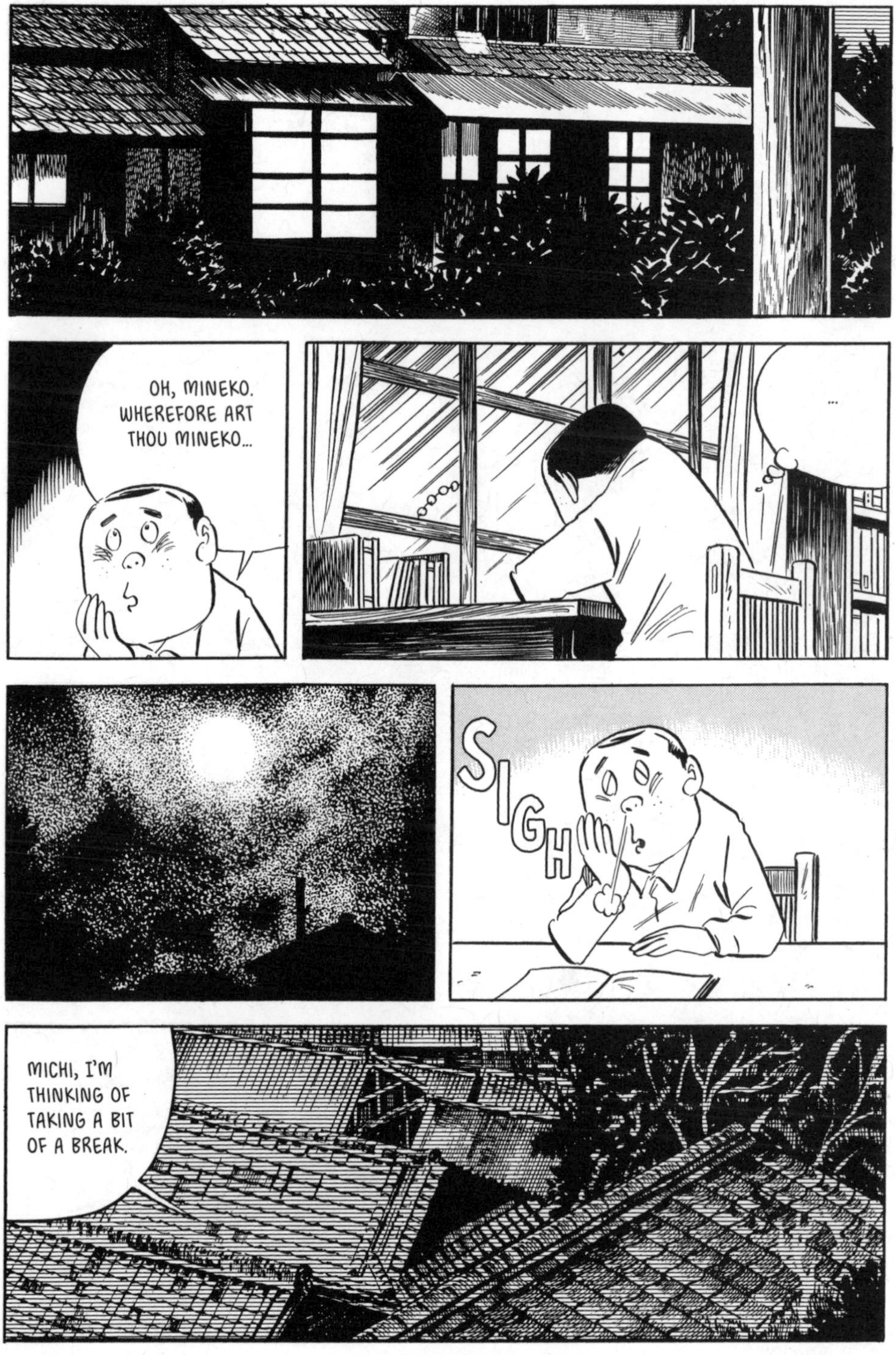
...
OH, MINEKO. WHEREFORE ART THOU MINEKO...
SIGH
MICHI, I'M THINKING OF TAKING A BIT OF A BREAK.

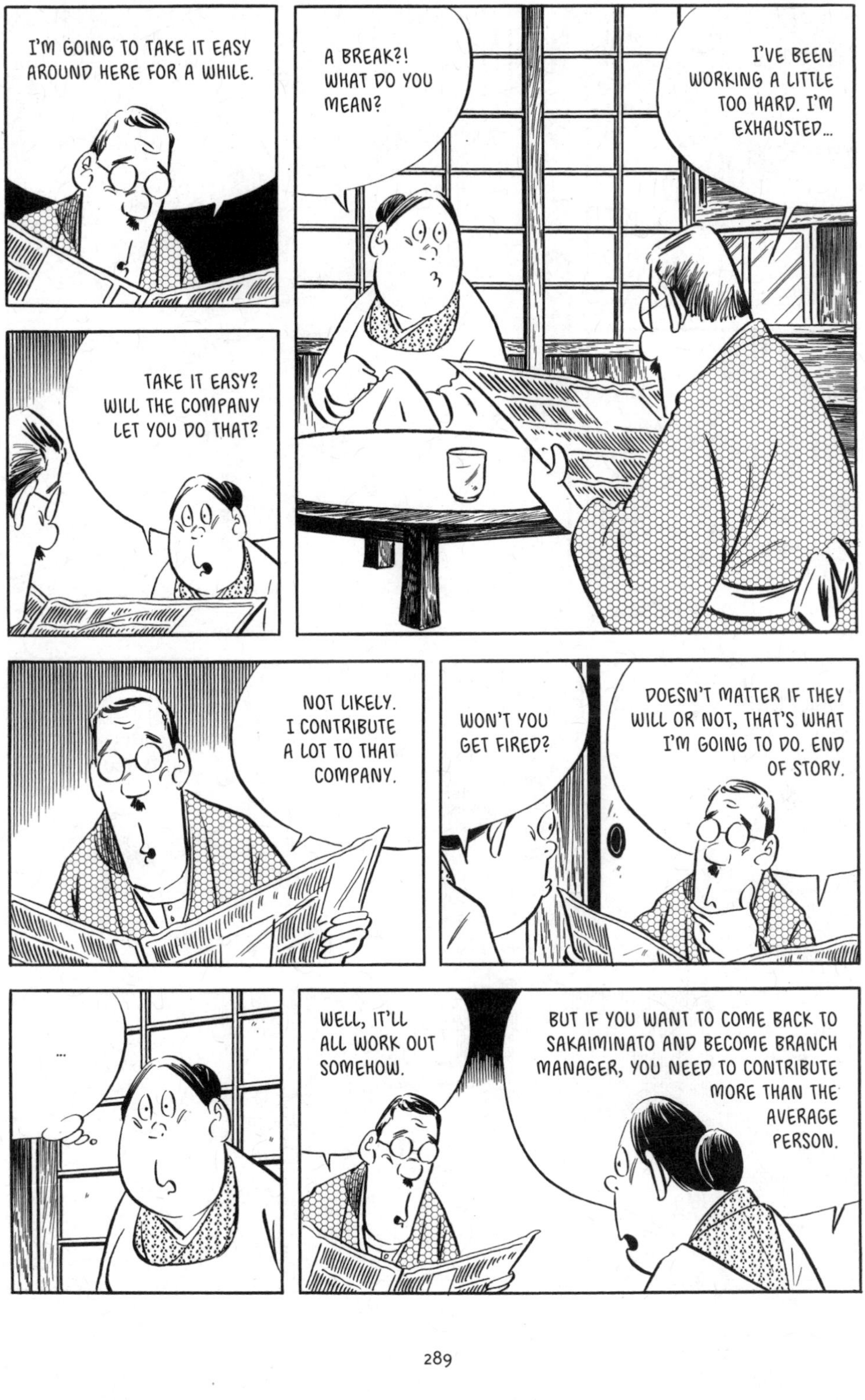
I'M GOING TO TAKE IT EASY AROUND HERE FOR A WHILE.
TAKE IT EASY? WILL THE COMPANY LET YOU DO THAT?
A BREAK?! WHAT DO YOU MEAN?
I'VE BEEN WORKING A LITTLE TOO HARD. I'M EXHAUSTED...
NOT LIKELY. I CONTRIBUTE A LOT TO THAT COMPANY.
WON'T YOU GET FIRED?
DOESN'T MATTER IF THEY WILL OR NOT, THAT'S WHAT I'M GOING TO DO. END OF STORY.
...
WELL, IT'LL ALL WORK OUT SOMEHOW.
BUT IF YOU WANT TO COME BACK TO SAKAIMINATO AND BECOME BRANCH MANAGER, YOU NEED TO CONTRIBUTE MORE THAN THE AVERAGE PERSON.

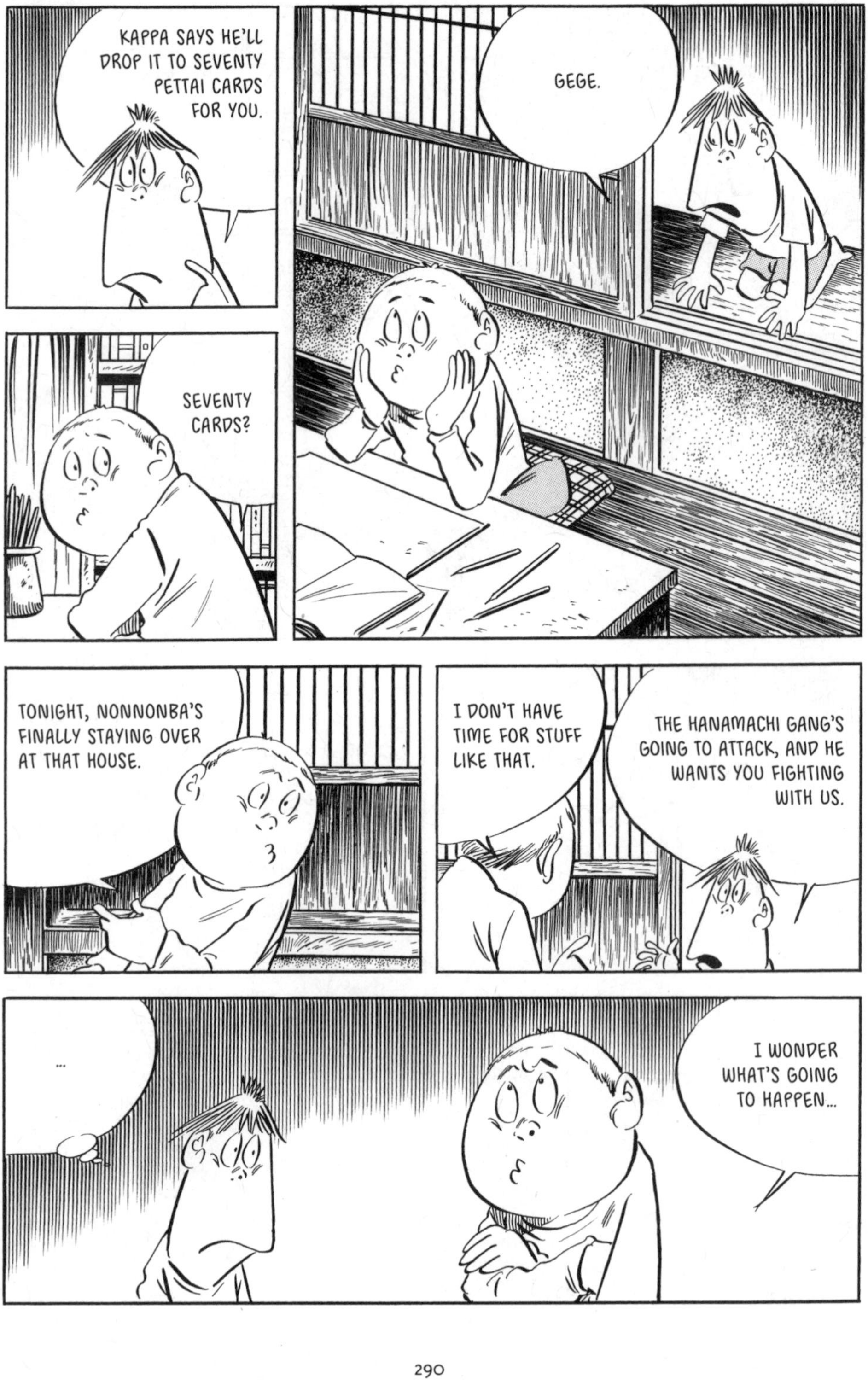
GEGE.
KAPPA SAYS HE'LL DROP IT TO SEVENTY PETTAI CARDS FOR YOU.
SEVENTY CARDS?
THE HANAMACHI GANG'S GOING TO ATTACK, AND HE WANTS YOU FIGHTING WITH US.
I DON'T HAVE TIME FOR STUFF LIKE THAT.
TONIGHT, NONNONBA'S FINALLY STAYING OVER AT THAT HOUSE.
I WONDER WHAT'S GOING TO HAPPEN...
...

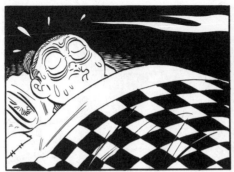

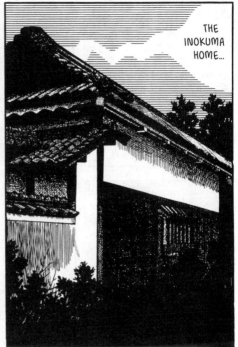

THE INOKUMA HOME...
AH, WHAT A STRANGE DREAM...
WHAT ARE YOU DOING THERE?
WHY ARE YOU IN THERE?
WHAT'S WRONG? DID SOMETHING BAD HAPPEN?

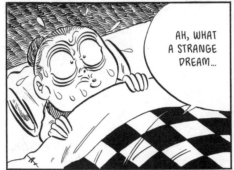

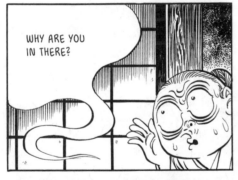

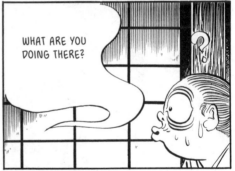

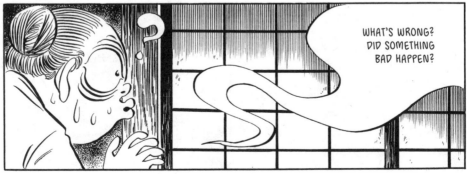

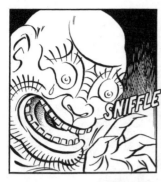

YOU CAN TALK TO ME.
HUH
SNIFFLE
IS SOMETHING MAKING YOU SAD?
WHAT'S GOING ON?
KLATTER
OH! GRAN!
THERE WAS A GHOST.
DID IT SCARE YOU?
NOPE. I FELT SORRY FOR IT.
THERE CERTAINLY IS A SPIRITUAL PRESENCE IN THE AIR.
YOU COULD ACTUALLY SEE IT?
I COULDN'T SEE IT TOTALLY CLEARLY, BUT IT WAS HERE.

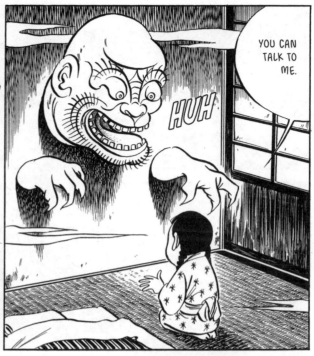

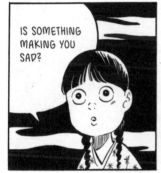

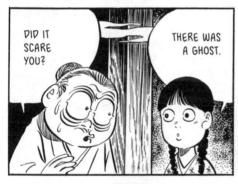

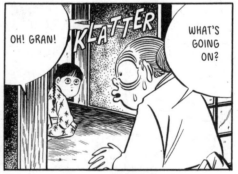

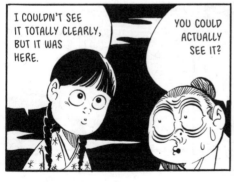

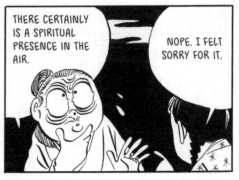

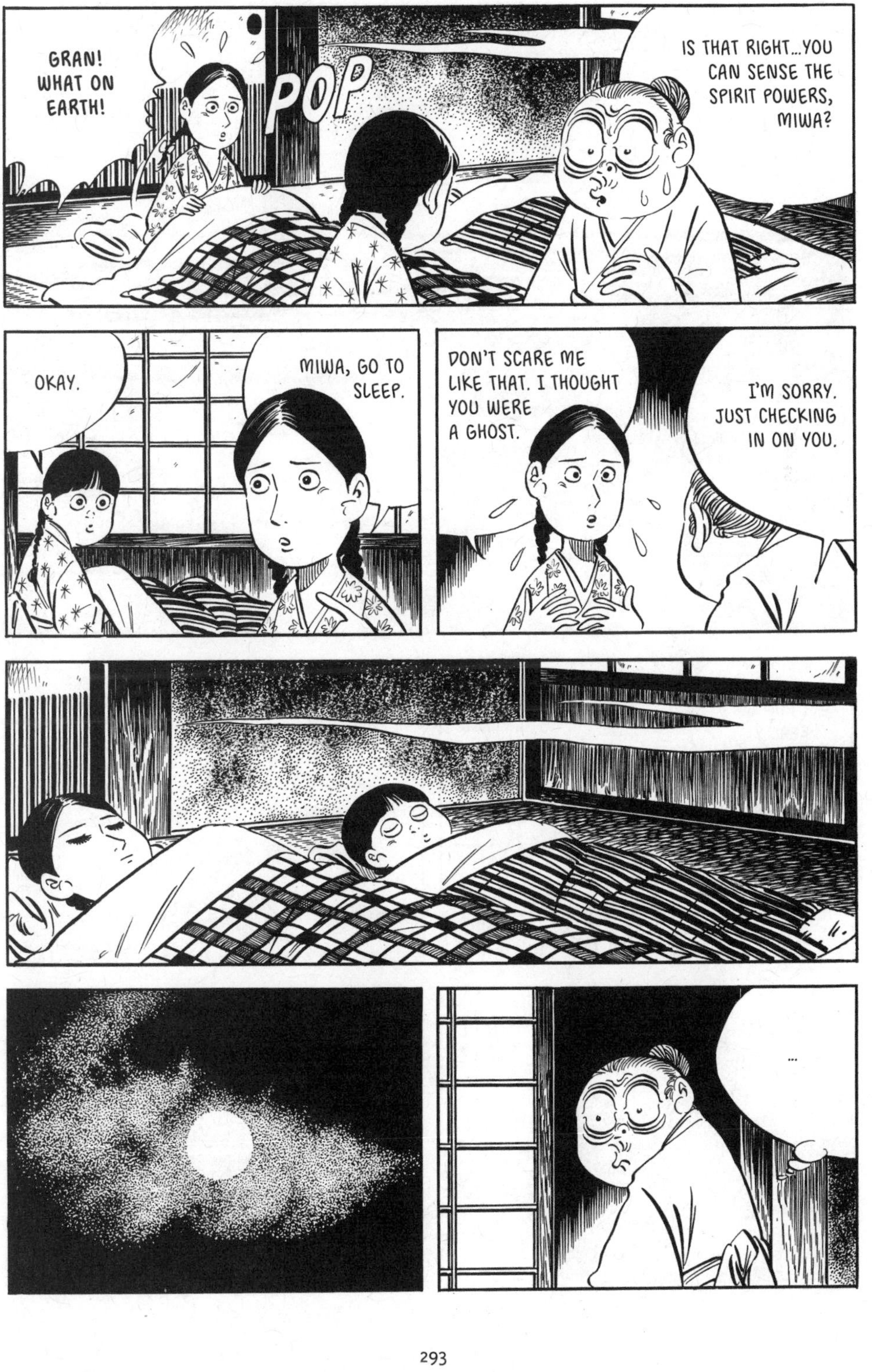
IS THAT RIGHT...YOU CAN SENSE THE SPIRIT POWERS, MIWA?
POP
GRAN! WHAT ON EARTH!
I'M SORRY. JUST CHECKING IN ON YOU.
DON'T SCARE ME LIKE THAT. I THOUGHT YOU WERE A GHOST.
MIWA, GO TO SLEEP.
OKAY.
...

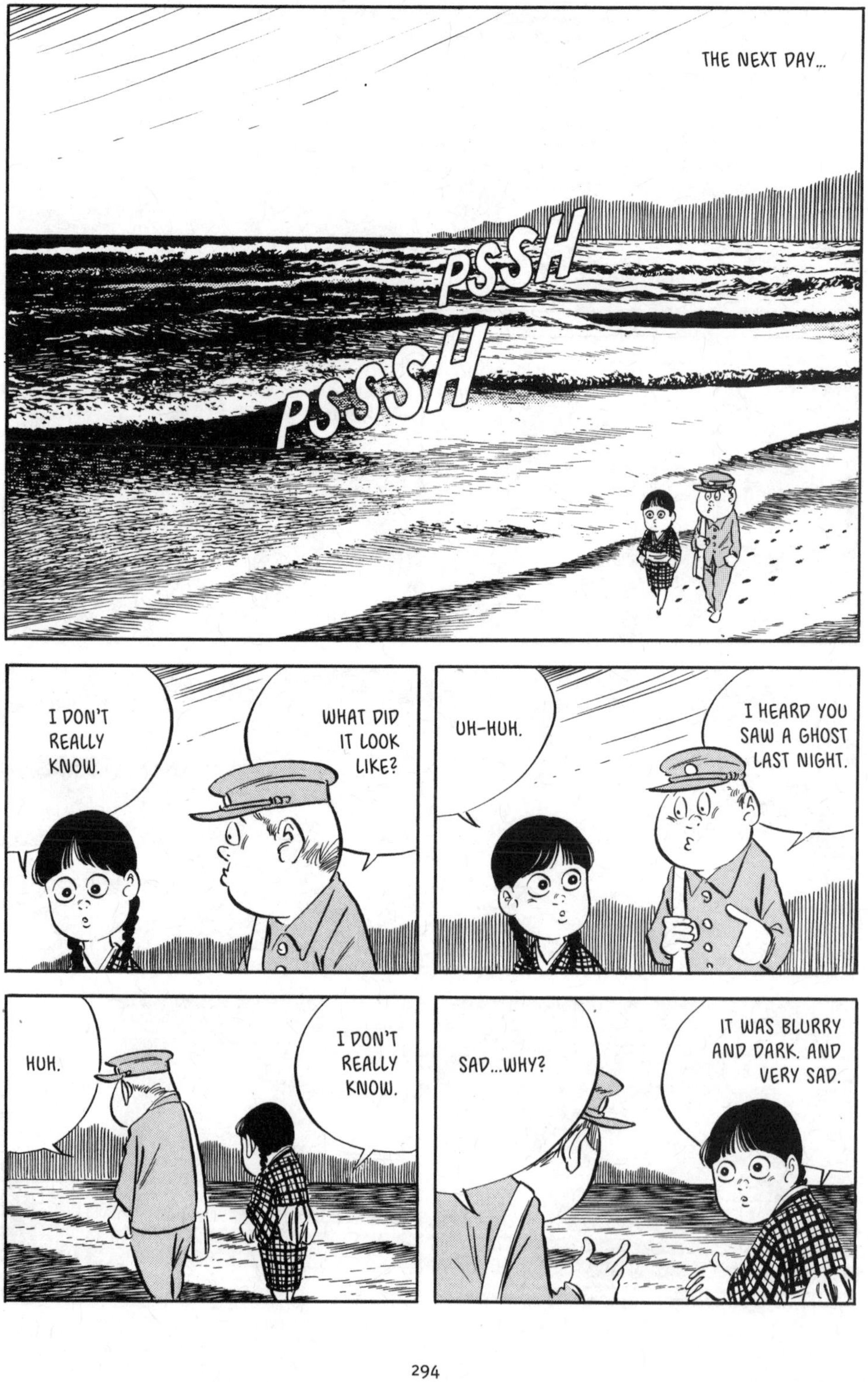
THE NEXT DAY...
PSSH
PSSSH
I HEARD YOU SAW A GHOST LAST NIGHT.
UH-HUH.
WHAT DID IT LOOK LIKE?
I DON'T REALLY KNOW.
IT WAS BLURRY AND DARK. AND VERY SAD.
SAD...WHY?
I DON'T REALLY KNOW.
HUH.

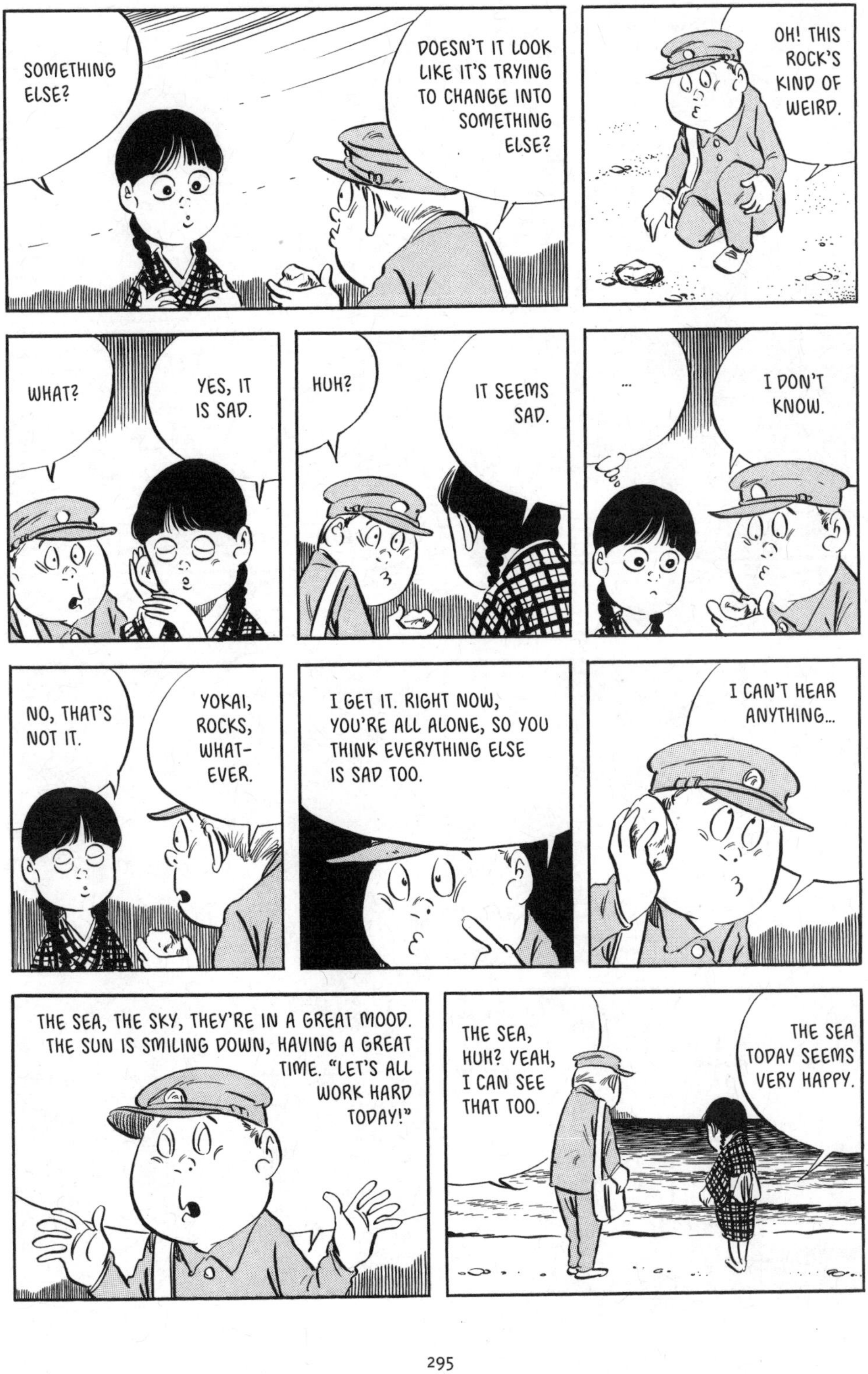
OH! THIS ROCK'S KIND OF WEIRD.
DOESN'T IT LOOK LIKE IT'S TRYING TO CHANGE INTO SOMETHING ELSE?
SOMETHING ELSE?
I DON'T KNOW.
...
IT SEEMS SAD.
HUH?
YES, IT IS SAD.
WHAT?
I CAN'T HEAR ANYTHING...
I GET IT. RIGHT NOW, YOU'RE ALL ALONE, SO YOU THINK EVERYTHING ELSE IS SAD TOO.
YOKAI, ROCKS, WHAT-EVER.
NO, THAT'S NOT IT.
THE SEA TODAY SEEMS VERY HAPPY.
THE SEA, HUH? YEAH, I CAN SEE THAT TOO.
THE SEA, THE SKY, THEY'RE IN A GREAT MOOD. THE SUN IS SMILING DOWN, HAVING A GREAT TIME. "LET'S ALL WORK HARD TODAY!"

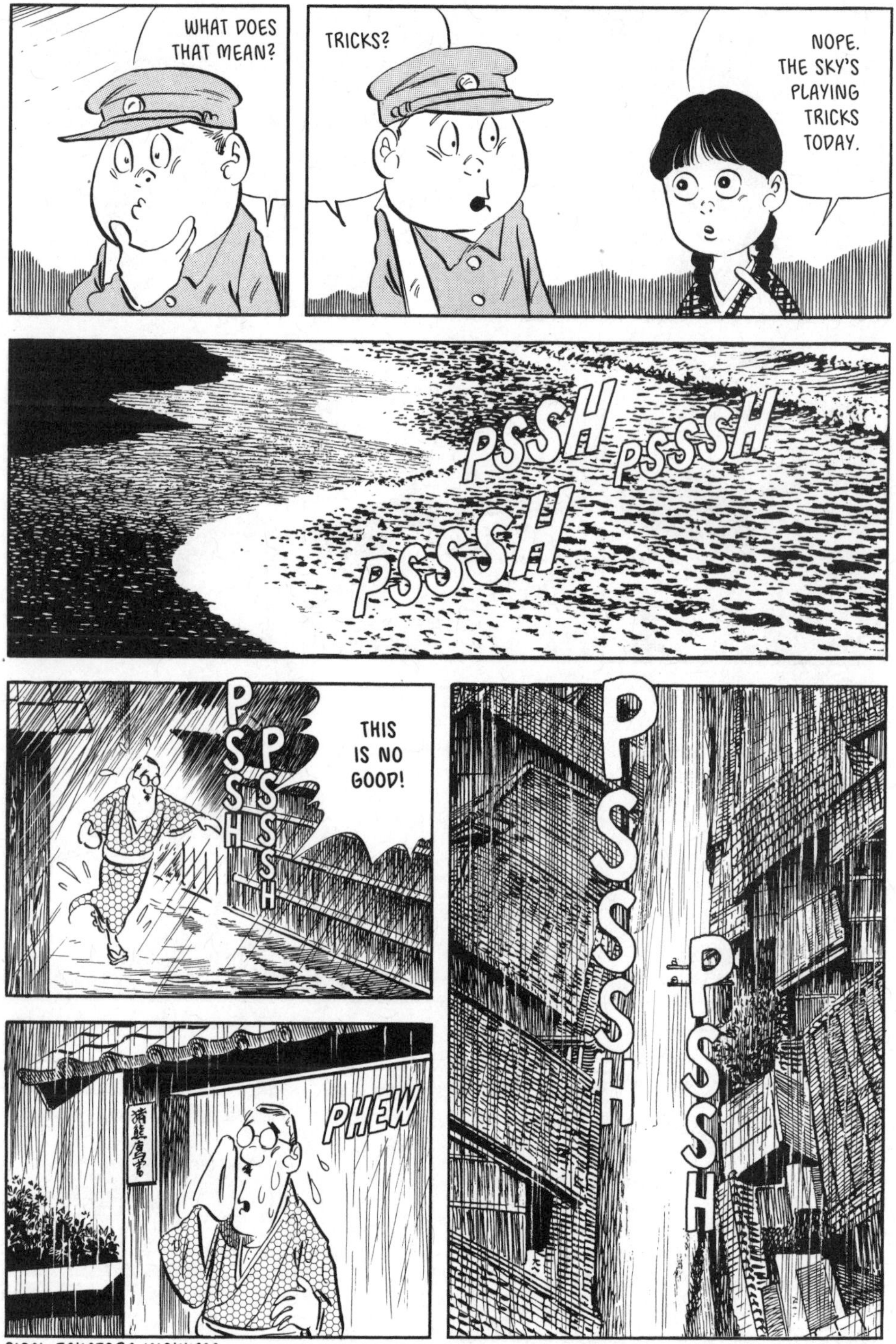

NOPE. THE SKY'S PLAYING TRICKS TODAY.
TRICKS?
WHAT DOES THAT MEAN?
PSSH
PSSSH
PSSSH
PSSSH
PSSSH
PSSH
PSSSH
THIS IS NO GOOD!
PHEW

SIGN: TAKATORA INOKUMA.

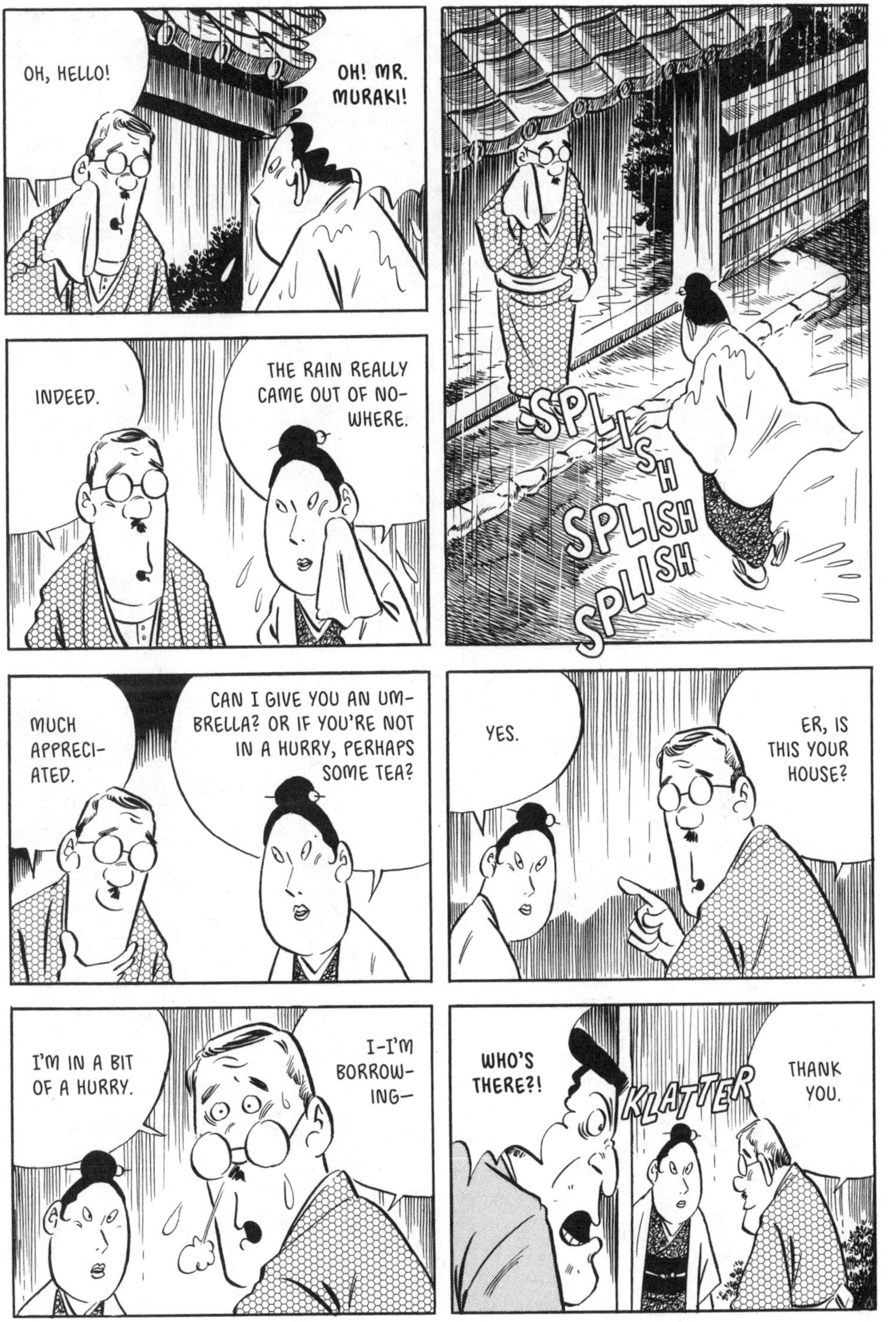
SPLISH
SPLISH
SPLISH
OH! MR. MURAKI!
OH, HELLO!
THE RAIN REALLY CAME OUT OF NO-WHERE.
INDEED.
ER, IS THIS YOUR HOUSE?
YES.
CAN I GIVE YOU AN UM-BRELLA? OR IF YOU'RE NOT IN A HURRY, PERHAPS SOME TEA?
MUCH APPRECI-ATED.
THANK YOU.
KLATTER
WHO'S THERE?!
I-I'M BORROW-ING—
I'M IN A BIT OF A HURRY.

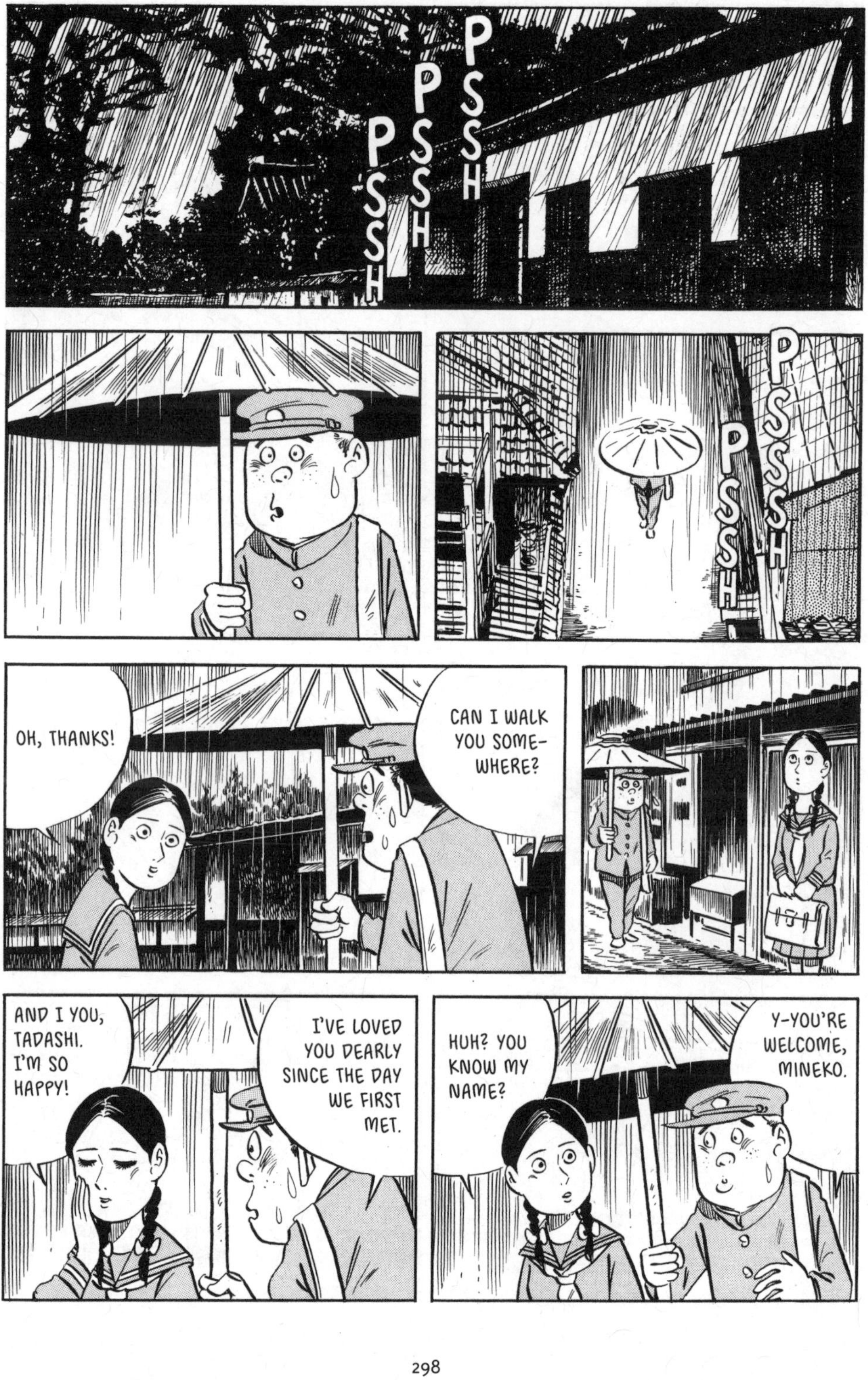
PSSH
PSSH
PSSH
PSSH
PSSH
CAN I WALK YOU SOME-WHERE?
OH, THANKS!
Y-YOU'RE WELCOME, MINEKO.
HUH? YOU KNOW MY NAME?
I'VE LOVED YOU DEARLY SINCE THE DAY WE FIRST MET.
AND I YOU, TADASHI. I'M SO HAPPY!

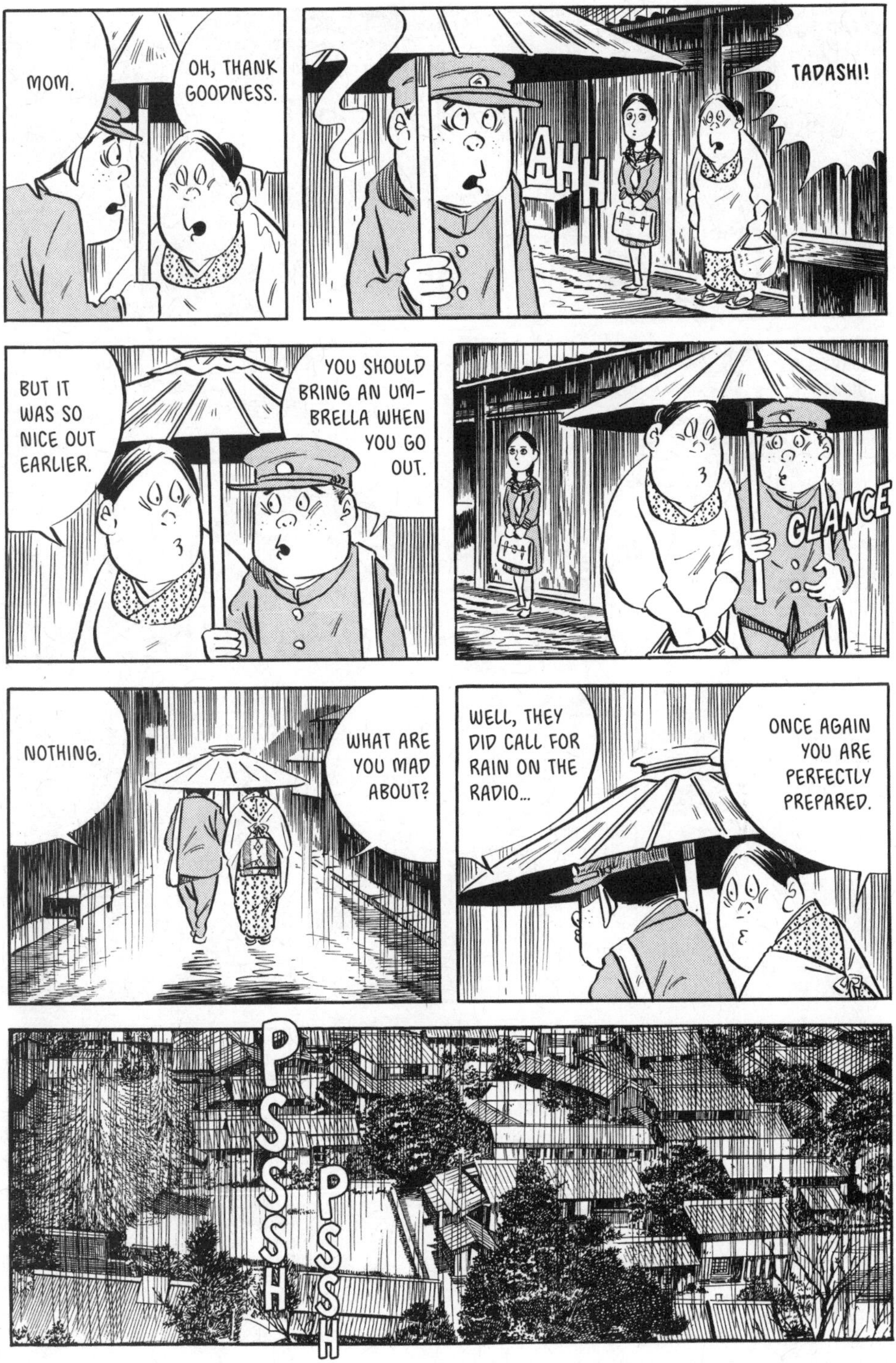
TADASHI!
AHH
OH, THANK GOODNESS.
MOM.
GLANCE
YOU SHOULD BRING AN UM-BRELLA WHEN YOU GO OUT.
BUT IT WAS SO NICE OUT EARLIER.
ONCE AGAIN YOU ARE PERFECTLY PREPARED.
WELL, THEY DID CALL FOR RAIN ON THE RADIO...
WHAT ARE YOU MAD ABOUT?
NOTHING.
PSSSH
PSSSH

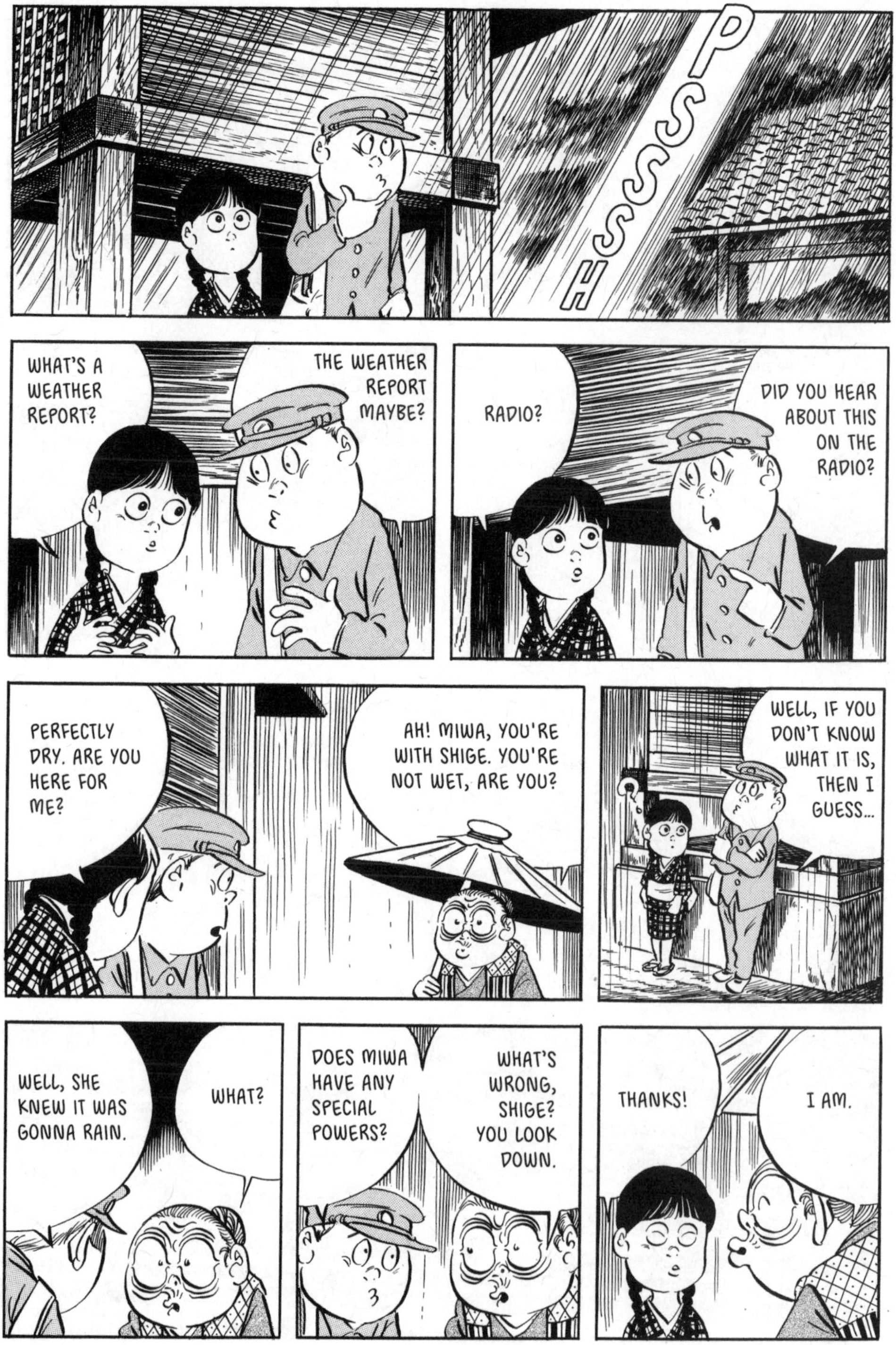
PSSSSH
DID YOU HEAR ABOUT THIS ON THE RADIO?
RADIO?
THE WEATHER REPORT MAYBE?
WHAT'S A WEATHER REPORT?
WELL, IF YOU DON'T KNOW WHAT IT IS, THEN I GUESS...
AH! MIWA, YOU'RE WITH SHIGE. YOU'RE NOT WET, ARE YOU?
PERFECTLY DRY. ARE YOU HERE FOR ME?
I AM.
THANKS!
WHAT'S WRONG, SHIGE? YOU LOOK DOWN.
DOES MIWA HAVE ANY SPECIAL POWERS?
WHAT?
WELL, SHE KNEW IT WAS GONNA RAIN.

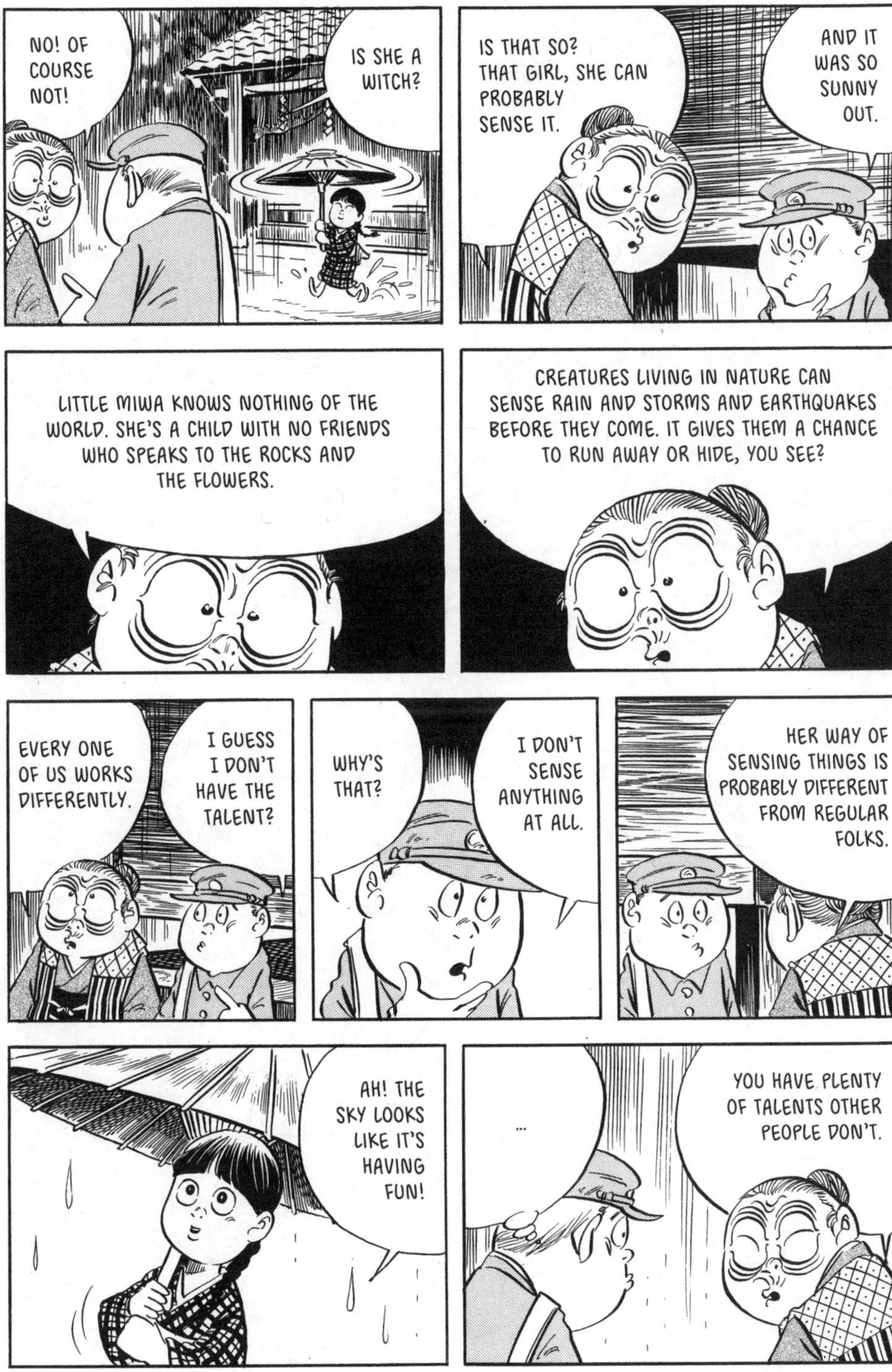
AND IT WAS SO SUNNY OUT.
IS THAT SO? THAT GIRL, SHE CAN PROBABLY SENSE IT.
IS SHE A WITCH?
NO! OF COURSE NOT!
CREATURES LIVING IN NATURE CAN SENSE RAIN AND STORMS AND EARTHQUAKES BEFORE THEY COME. IT GIVES THEM A CHANCE TO RUN AWAY OR HIDE, YOU SEE?
LITTLE MIWA KNOWS NOTHING OF THE WORLD. SHE'S A CHILD WITH NO FRIENDS WHO SPEAKS TO THE ROCKS AND THE FLOWERS.
HER WAY OF SENSING THINGS IS PROBABLY DIFFERENT FROM REGULAR FOLKS.
I DON'T SENSE ANYTHING AT ALL.
WHY'S THAT?
I GUESS I DON'T HAVE THE TALENT?
EVERY ONE OF US WORKS DIFFERENTLY.
YOU HAVE PLENTY OF TALENTS OTHER PEOPLE DON'T.
...
AH! THE SKY LOOKS LIKE IT'S HAVING FUN!

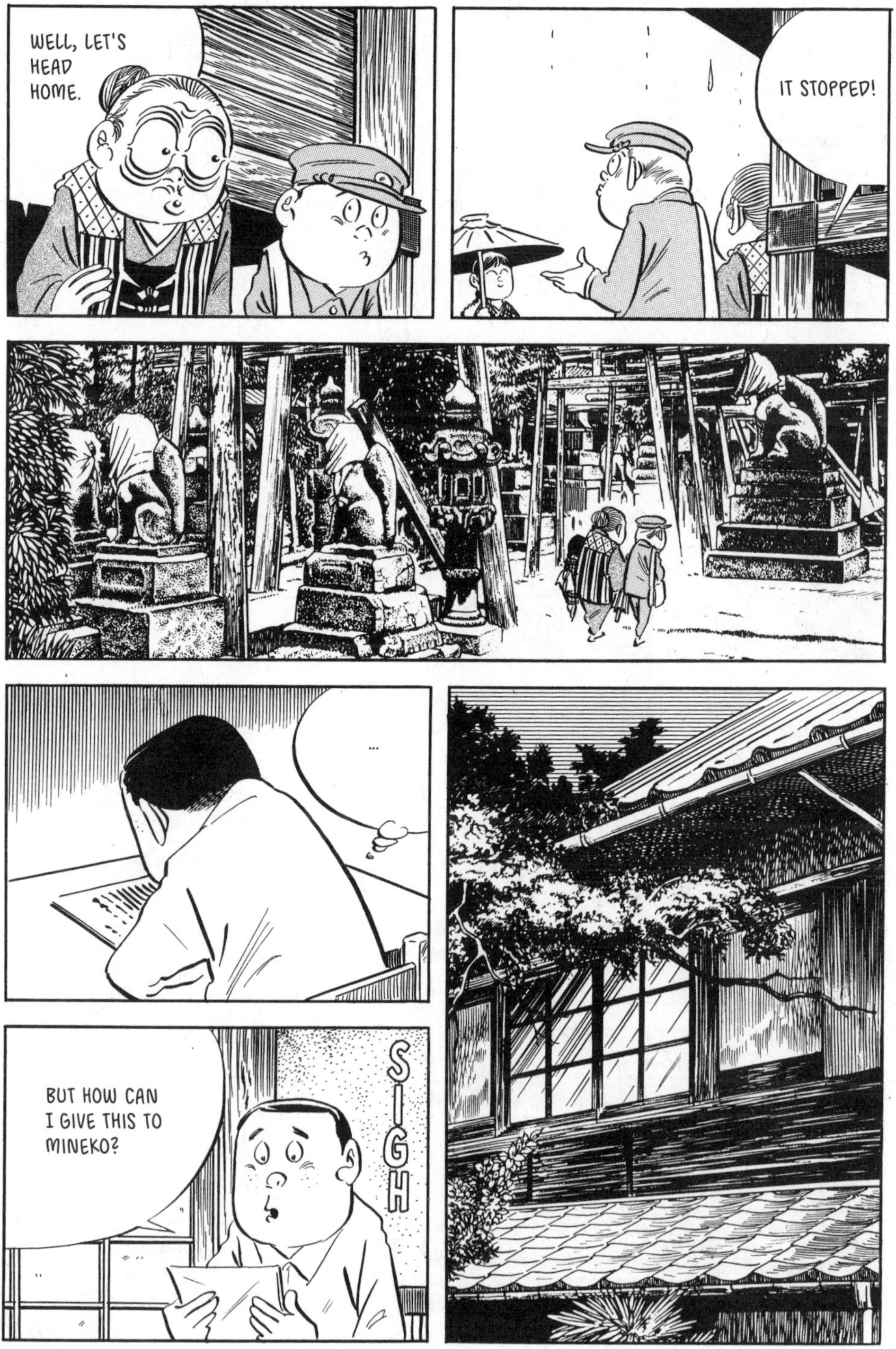
IT STOPPED!
WELL, LET'S HEAD HOME.
...
BUT HOW CAN I GIVE THIS TO MINEKO?
SIGH

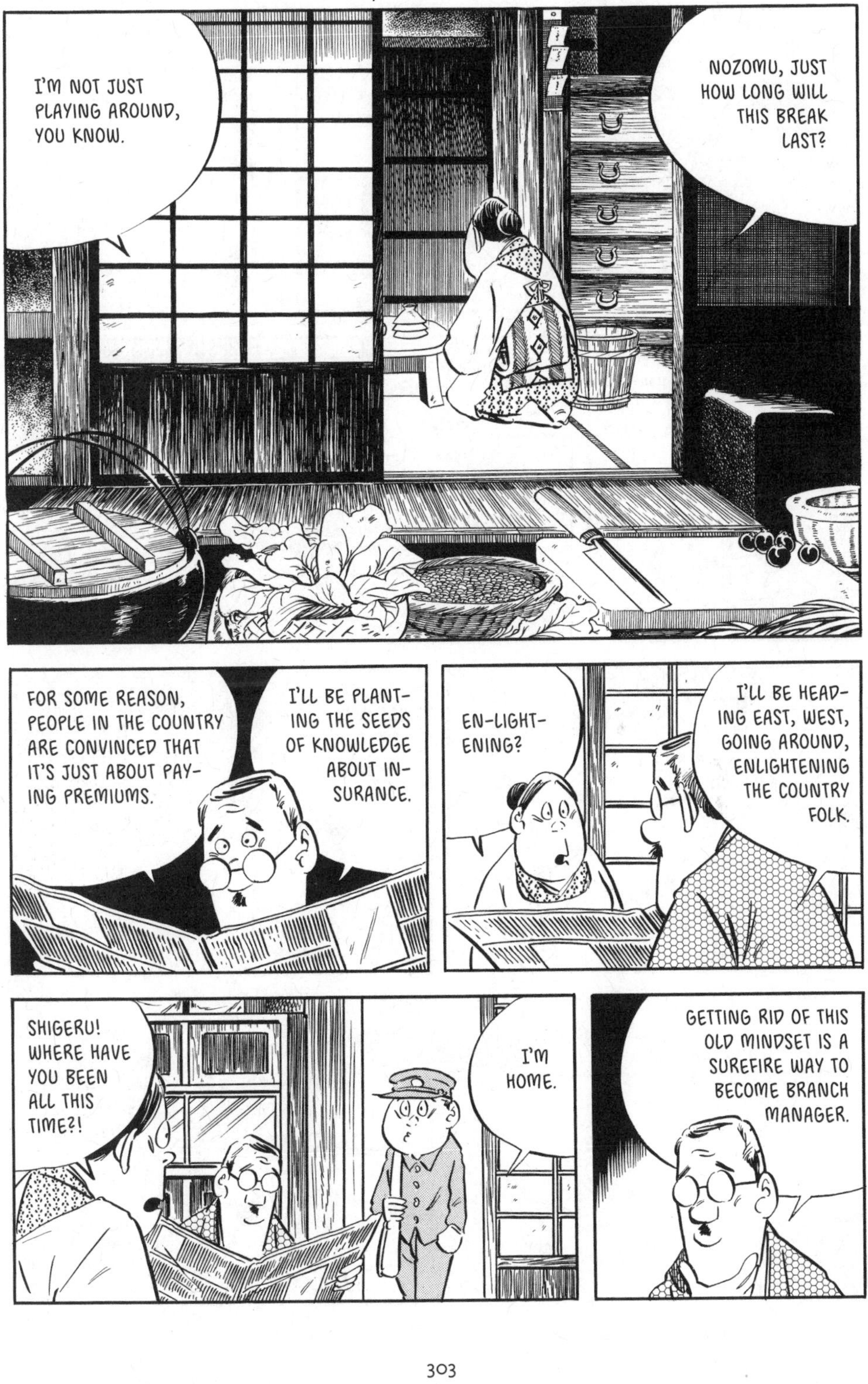
NOZOMU, JUST HOW LONG WILL THIS BREAK LAST?
I'M NOT JUST PLAYING AROUND, YOU KNOW.
I'LL BE HEADING EAST, WEST, GOING AROUND, ENLIGHTENING THE COUNTRY FOLK.
EN-LIGHTENING?
I'LL BE PLANTING THE SEEDS OF KNOWLEDGE ABOUT INSURANCE.
FOR SOME REASON, PEOPLE IN THE COUNTRY ARE CONVINCED THAT IT'S JUST ABOUT PAYING PREMIUMS.
GETTING RID OF THIS OLD MINDSET IS A SUREFIRE WAY TO BECOME BRANCH MANAGER.
I'M HOME.
SHIGERU! WHERE HAVE YOU BEEN ALL THIS TIME?!

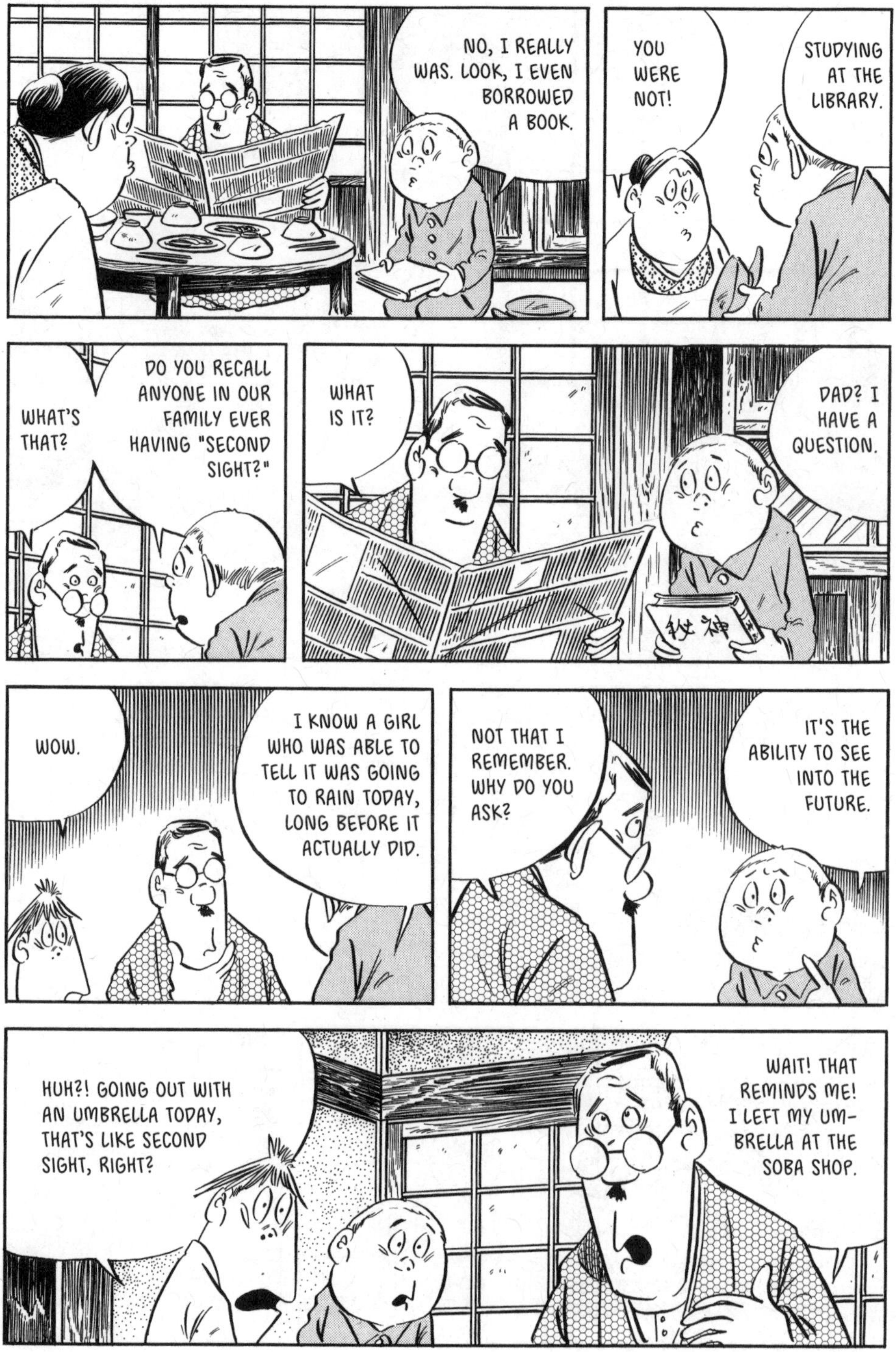
STUDYING AT THE LIBRARY.
YOU WERE NOT!
NO, I REALLY WAS. LOOK, I EVEN BORROWED A BOOK.
DAD? I HAVE A QUESTION.
WHAT IS IT?
DO YOU RECALL ANYONE IN OUR FAMILY EVER HAVING "SECOND SIGHT?"
WHAT'S THAT?
IT'S THE ABILITY TO SEE INTO THE FUTURE.
NOT THAT I REMEMBER. WHY DO YOU ASK?
I KNOW A GIRL WHO WAS ABLE TO TELL IT WAS GOING TO RAIN TODAY, LONG BEFORE IT ACTUALLY DID.
WOW.
WAIT! THAT REMINDS ME! I LEFT MY UM-BRELLA AT THE SOBA SHOP.
HUH?! GOING OUT WITH AN UMBRELLA TODAY, THAT'S LIKE SECOND SIGHT, RIGHT?

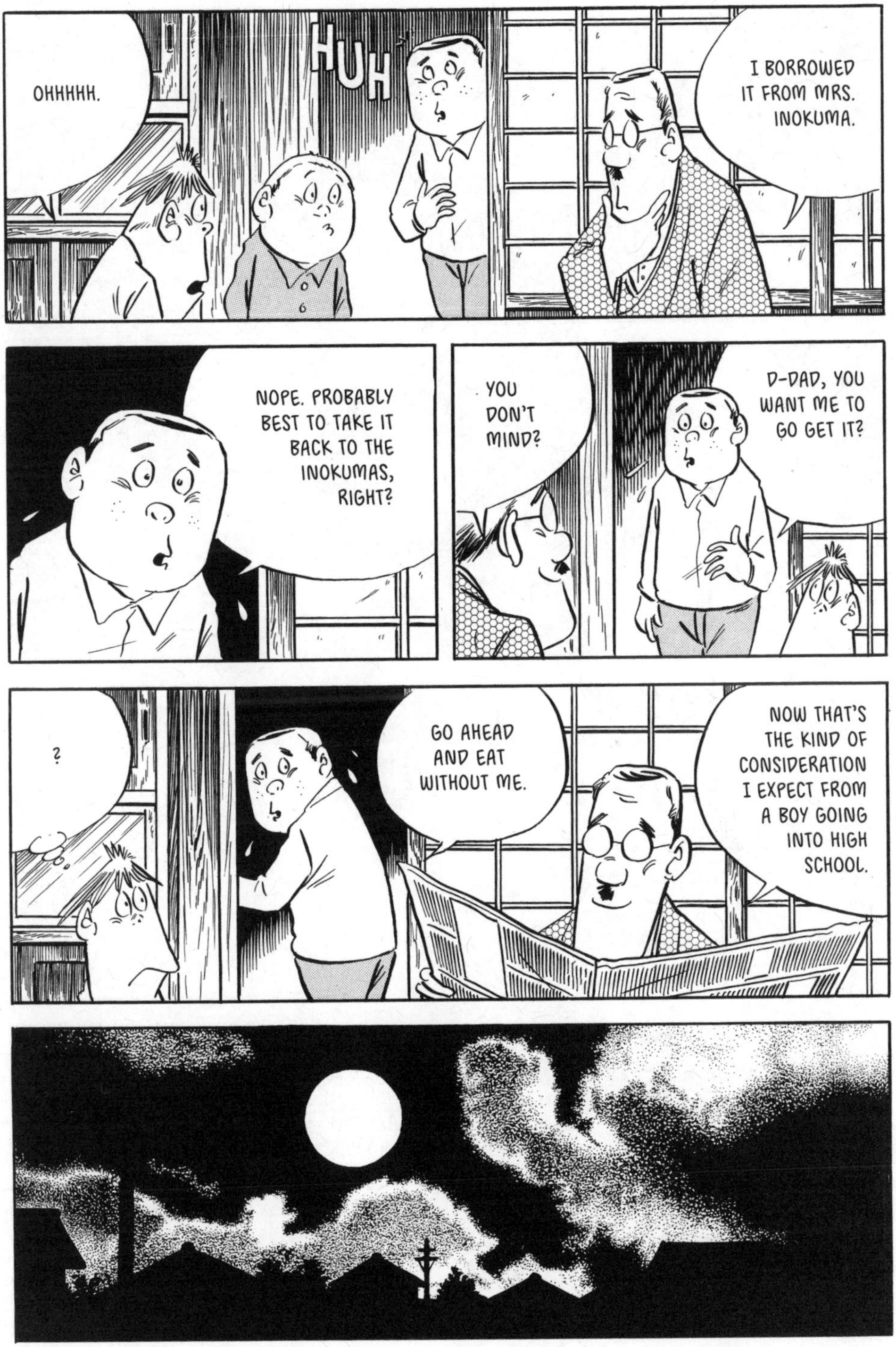
I BORROWED IT FROM MRS. INOKUMA.
HUH
OHHHHH.
D-DAD, YOU WANT ME TO GO GET IT?
YOU DON'T MIND?
NOPE. PROBABLY BEST TO TAKE IT BACK TO THE INOKUMAS, RIGHT?
NOW THAT'S THE KIND OF CONSIDERATION I EXPECT FROM A BOY GOING INTO HIGH SCHOOL.
GO AHEAD AND EAT WITHOUT ME.
?

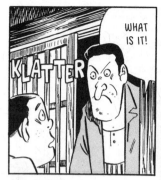

G-GOOD EVENING.
KLATTER
WHAT IS IT!
U-UM, MY NAME IS MURAKI.
I CAME BY TO RETURN THE UMBRELLA MY FATHER BORROWED EARLIER.
OH. WELL, IN THAT CASE, THANKS.
UH, UM, IS MINEKO HOME?
SHE'S IN THE BATH RIGHT NOW.
THE BATH...
GO AROUND BACK. YOU CAN AT LEAST TALK TO HER.
GAH
N-NO, THAT'S ALL RIGHT. THANKS.

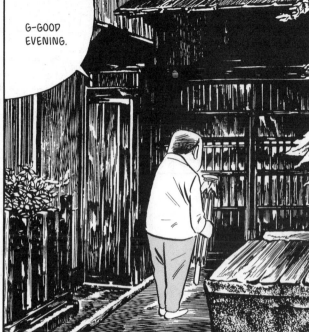

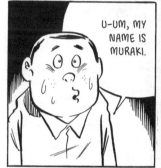

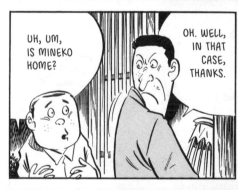

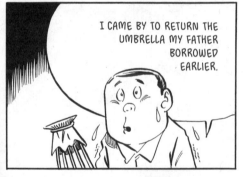

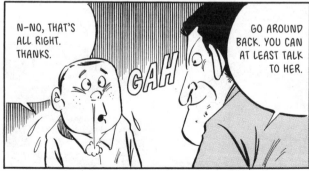

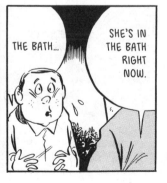

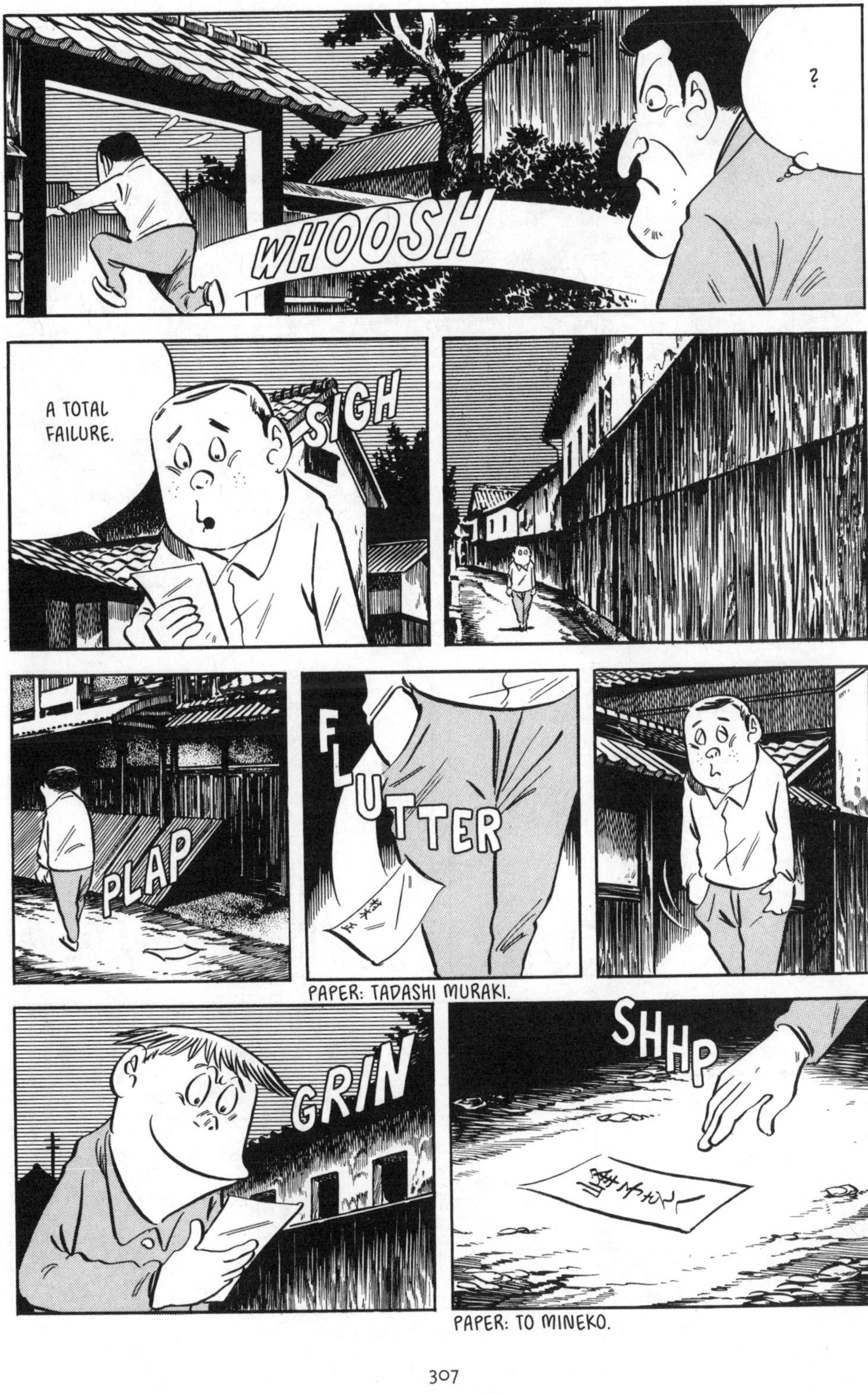
?
WHOOSH
A TOTAL FAILURE.
SIGH
FLUTTER
PAPER: TADASHI MURAKI.
PLAP
SHHP
PAPER: TO MINEKO.
GRIN

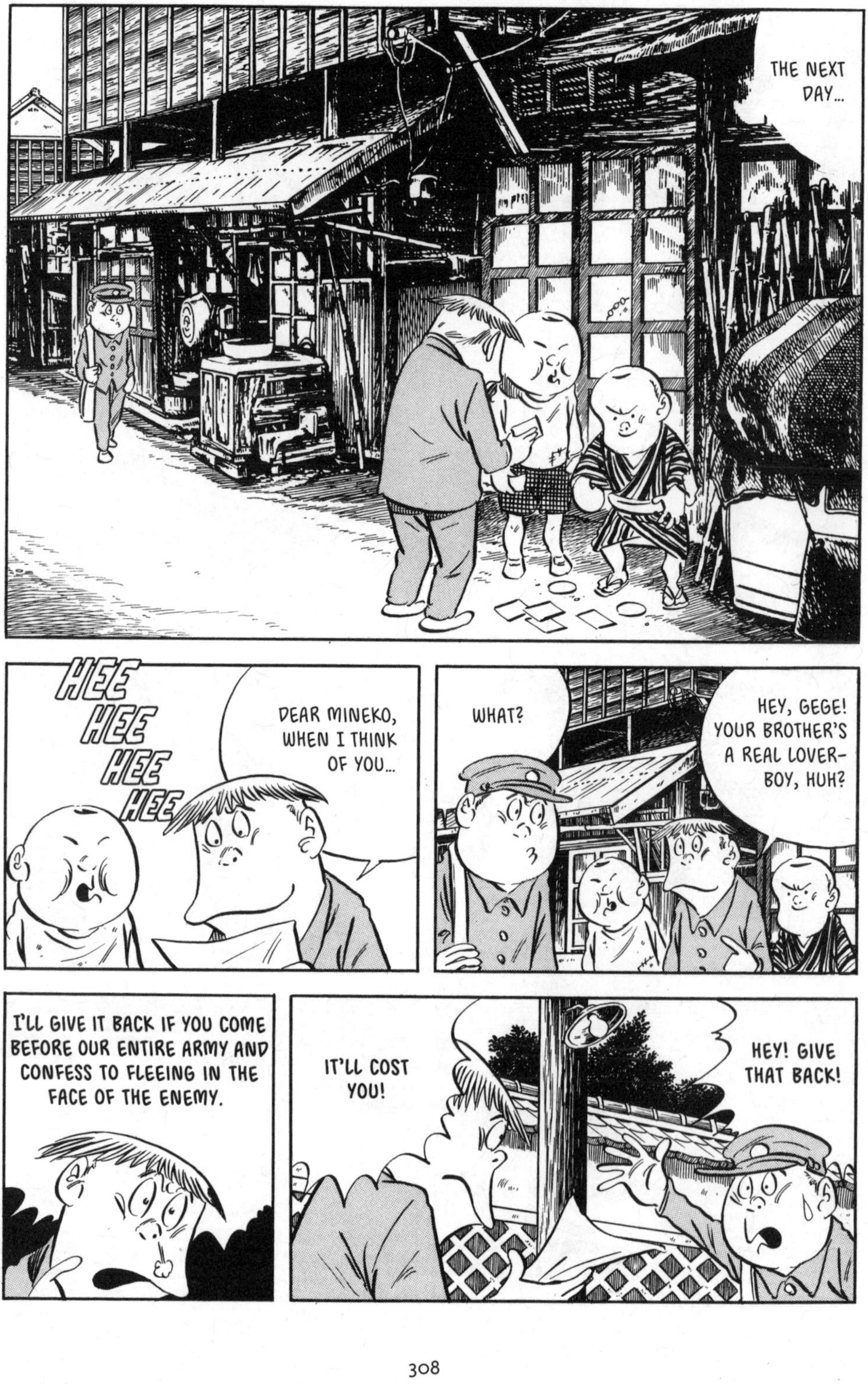
THE NEXT DAY...
HEY, GEGE! YOUR BROTHER'S A REAL LOVER-BOY, HUH?
WHAT?
DEAR MINEKO, WHEN I THINK OF YOU...
HEE HEE HEE HEE
HEY! GIVE THAT BACK!
IT'LL COST YOU!
I'LL GIVE IT BACK IF YOU COME BEFORE OUR ENTIRE ARMY AND CONFESS TO FLEEING IN THE FACE OF THE ENEMY.

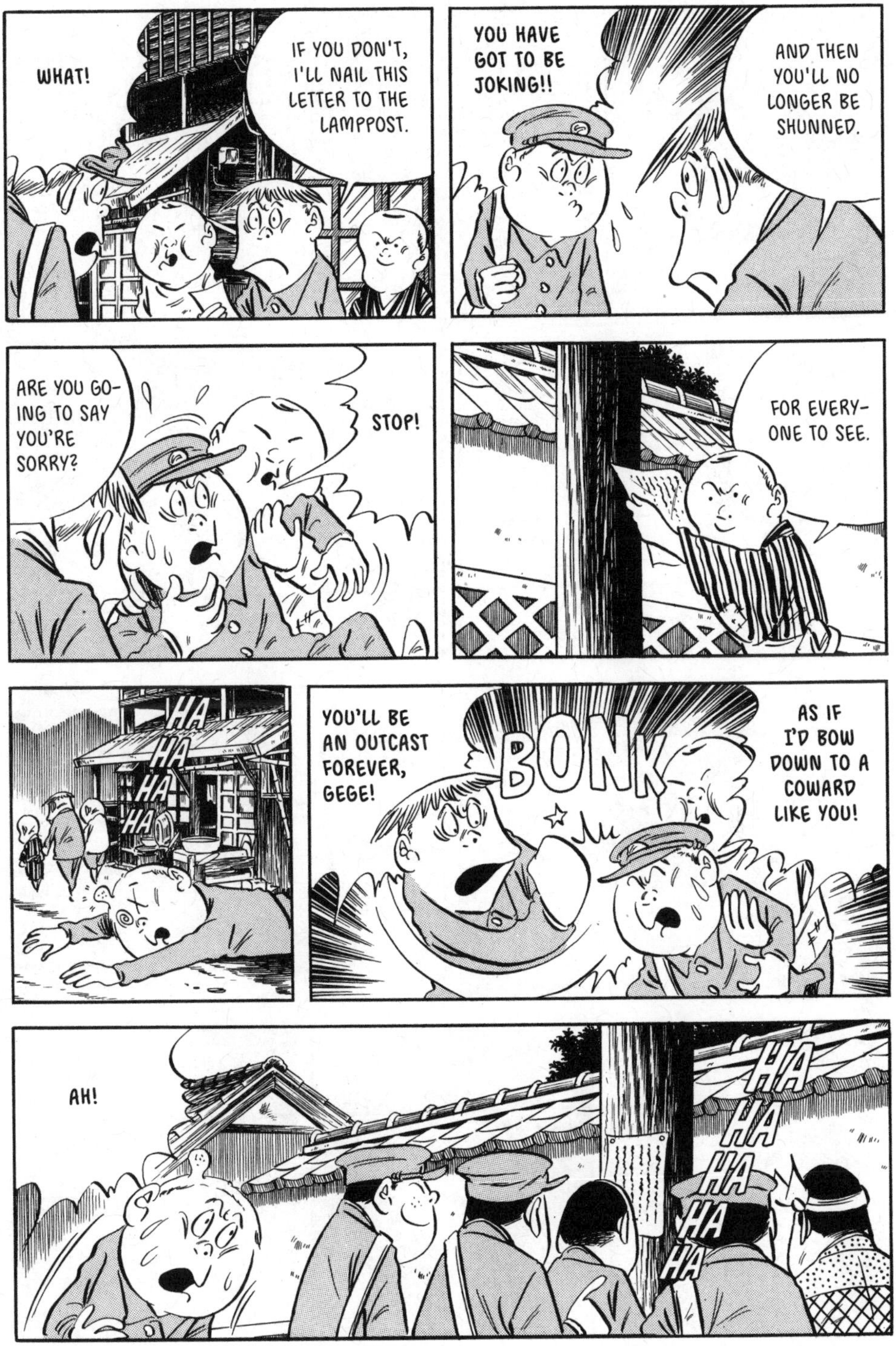
AND THEN YOU'LL NO LONGER BE SHUNNED.
YOU HAVE GOT TO BE JOKING!!
IF YOU DON'T, I'LL NAIL THIS LETTER TO THE LAMPPOST.
WHAT!
FOR EVERY-ONE TO SEE.
STOP!
ARE YOU GO-ING TO SAY YOU'RE SORRY?
AS IF I'D BOW DOWN TO A COWARD LIKE YOU!
BONK
YOU'LL BE AN OUTCAST FOREVER, GEGE!
HA HA HA HA
HA HA HA HA HA
AH!

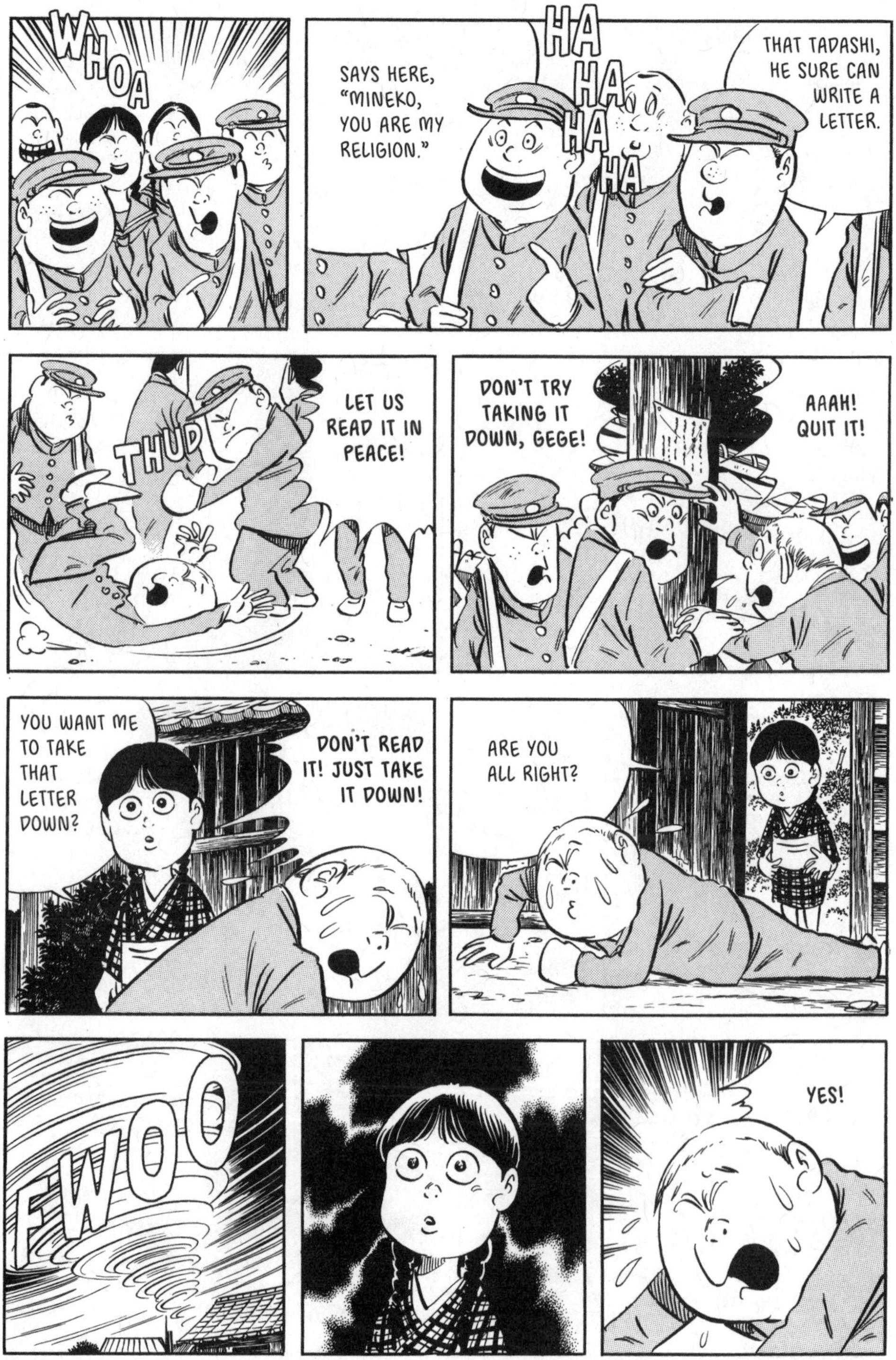
THAT TADASHI, HE SURE CAN WRITE A LETTER.
HA HA HA HA
SAYS HERE, "MINEKO, YOU ARE MY RELIGION."
WHOA
AAAH! QUIT IT!
DON'T TRY TAKING IT DOWN, GEGE!
LET US READ IT IN PEACE!
THUD
ARE YOU ALL RIGHT?
DON'T READ IT! JUST TAKE IT DOWN!
YOU WANT ME TO TAKE THAT LETTER DOWN?
YES!
FWOO

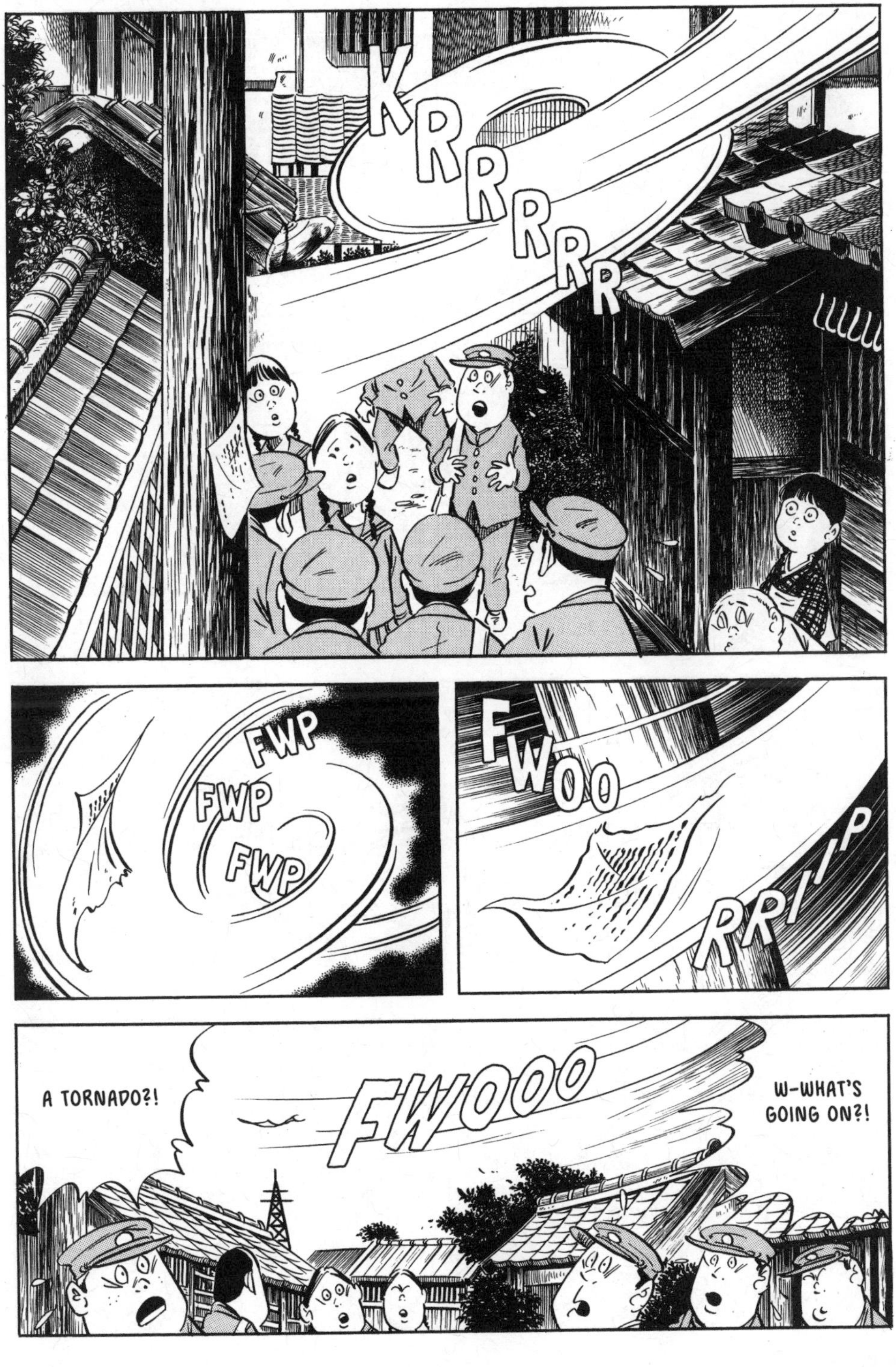
KRRRRR
FWOO
RRIIIP
FWP
FWP
FWP
W-WHAT'S GOING ON?!
FWOOO
A TORNADO?!

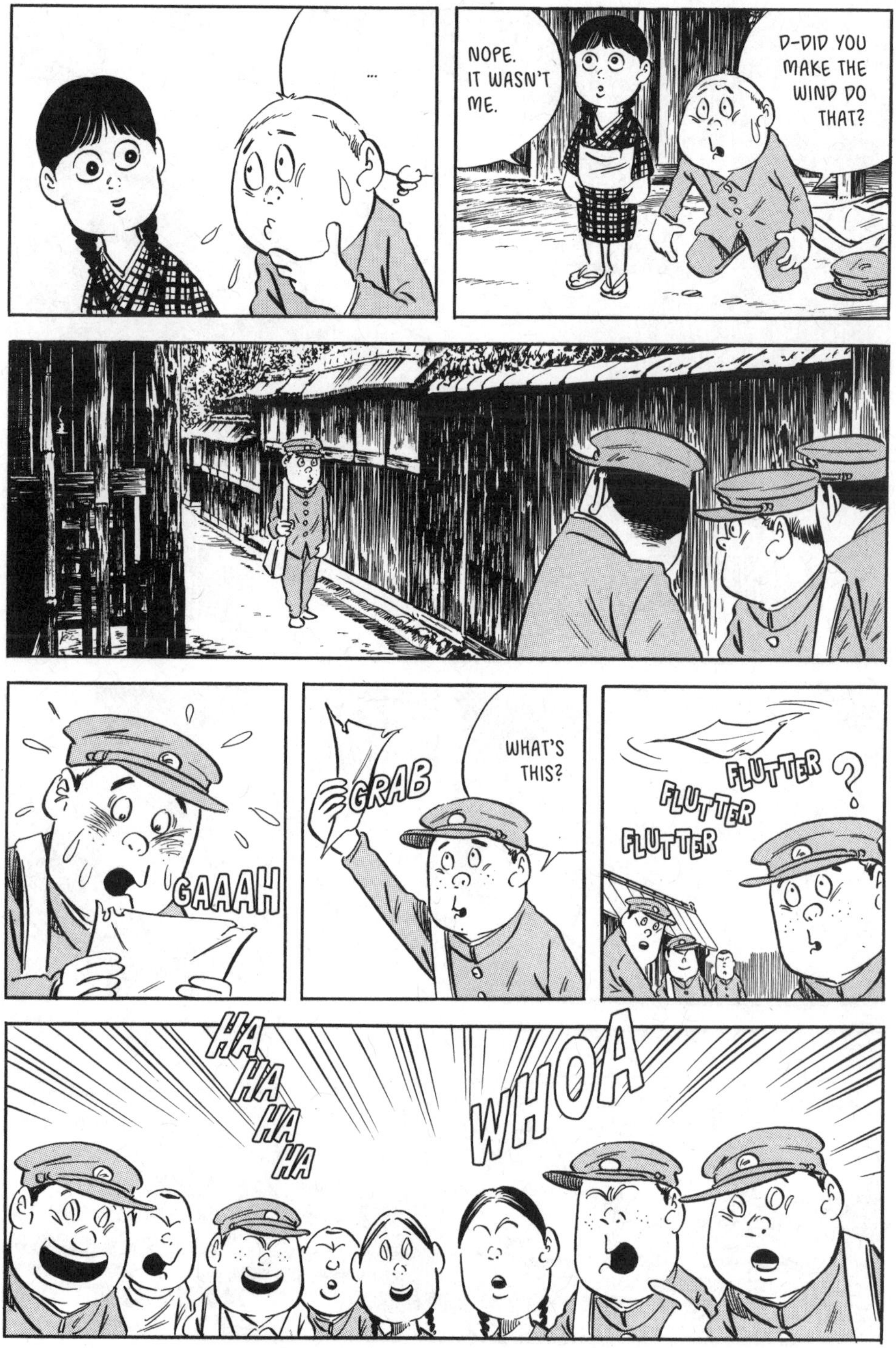
D-DID YOU MAKE THE WIND DO THAT?
NOPE. IT WASN'T ME.
...
?
FLUTTER
FLUTTER
FLUTTER
WHAT'S THIS?
GRAB
GAAAH
WHOA
HA HA HA HA

YOKAI THEATRE

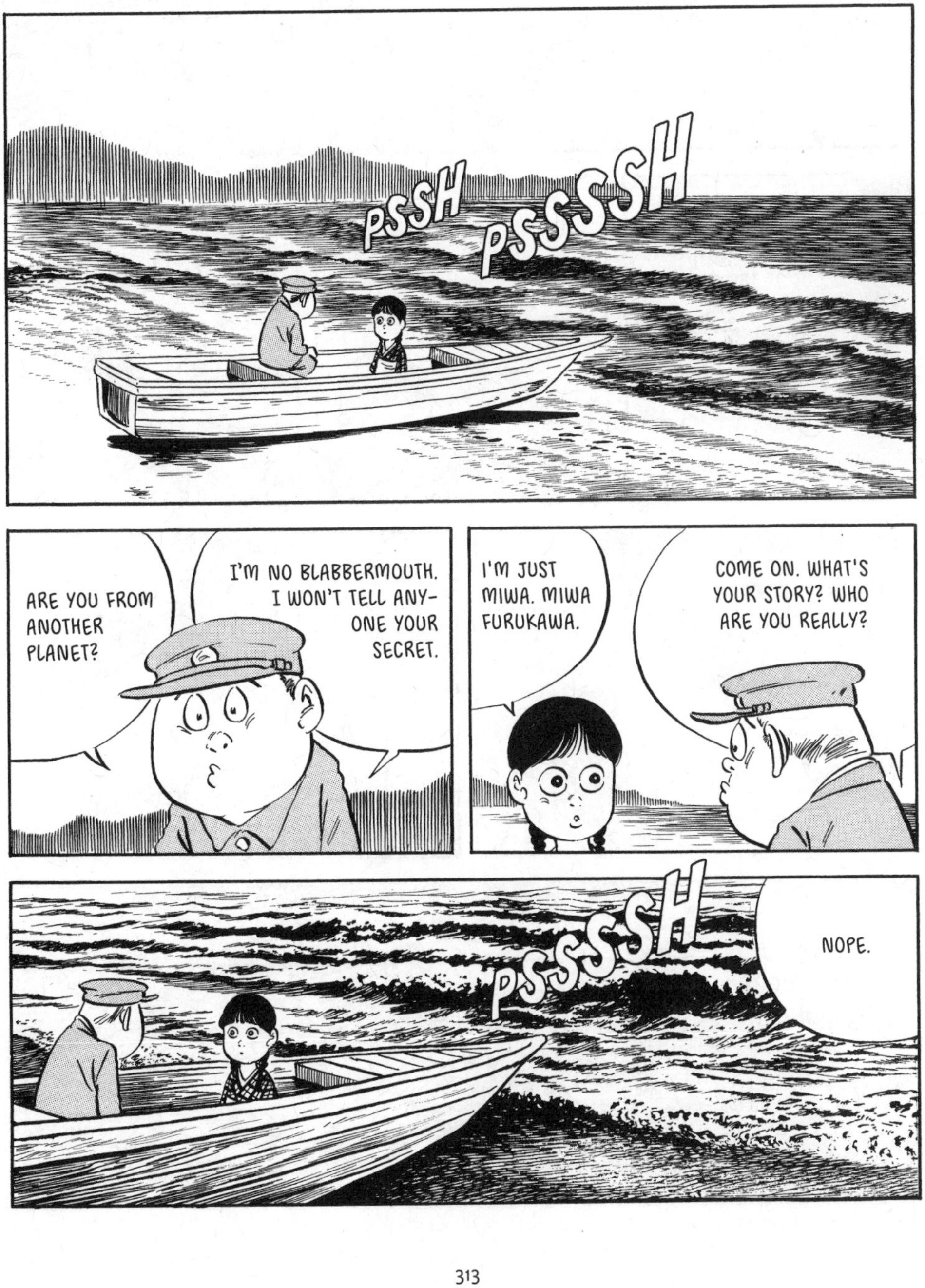
PSSSSH
PSSH
COME ON. WHAT'S YOUR STORY? WHO ARE YOU REALLY?
I'M JUST MIWA. MIWA FURUKAWA.
I'M NO BLABBERMOUTH. I WON'T TELL ANYONE YOUR SECRET.
ARE YOU FROM ANOTHER PLANET?
NOPE.
PSSSSH

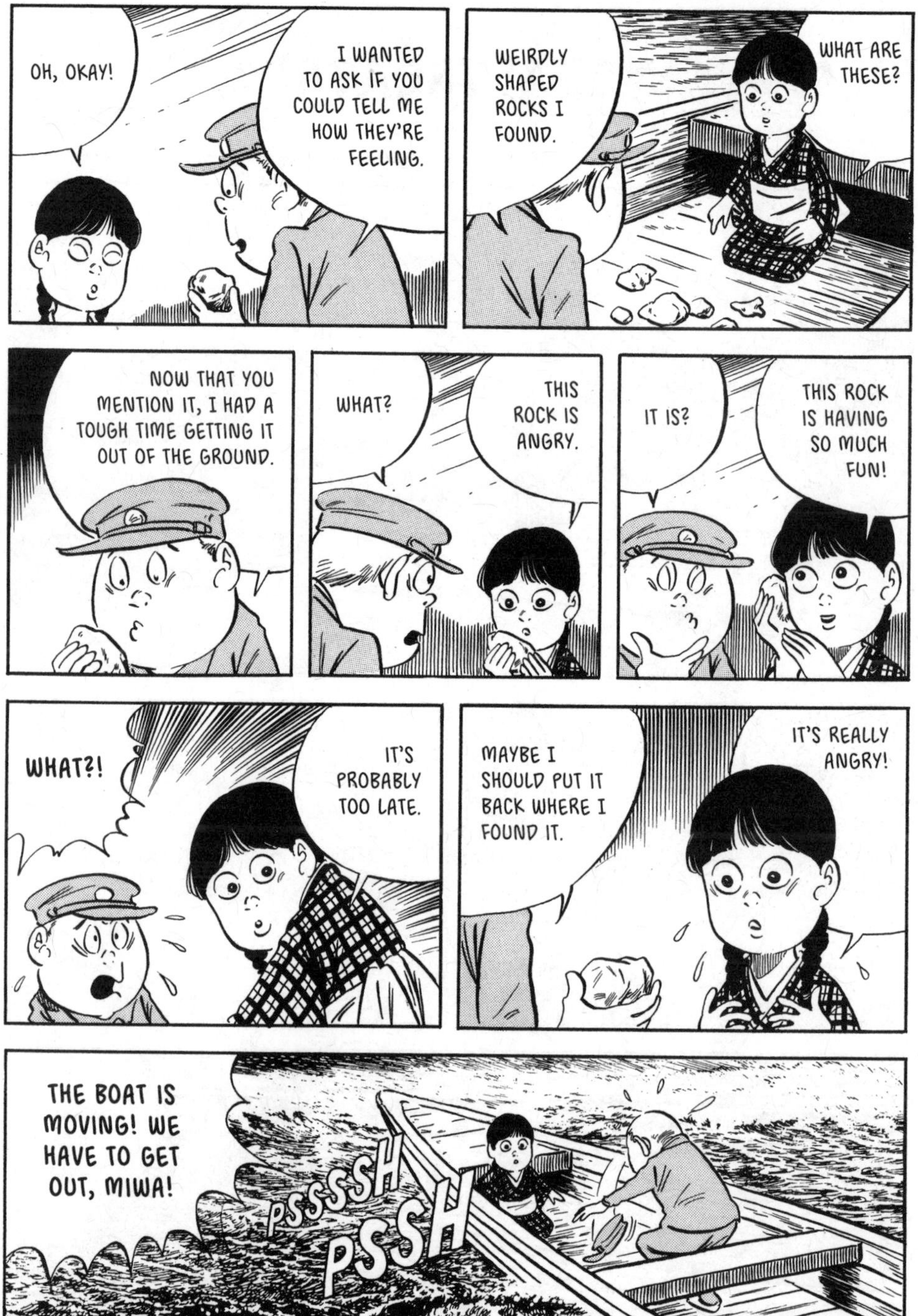
WHAT ARE THESE?
WEIRDLY SHAPED ROCKS I FOUND.
I WANTED TO ASK IF YOU COULD TELL ME HOW THEY'RE FEELING.
OH, OKAY!
THIS ROCK IS HAVING SO MUCH FUN!
IT IS?
THIS ROCK IS ANGRY.
WHAT?
NOW THAT YOU MENTION IT, I HAD A TOUGH TIME GETTING IT OUT OF THE GROUND.
IT'S REALLY ANGRY!
MAYBE I SHOULD PUT IT BACK WHERE I FOUND IT.
IT'S PROBABLY TOO LATE.
WHAT?!
THE BOAT IS MOVING! WE HAVE TO GET OUT, MIWA!
PSSSSH
PSSH

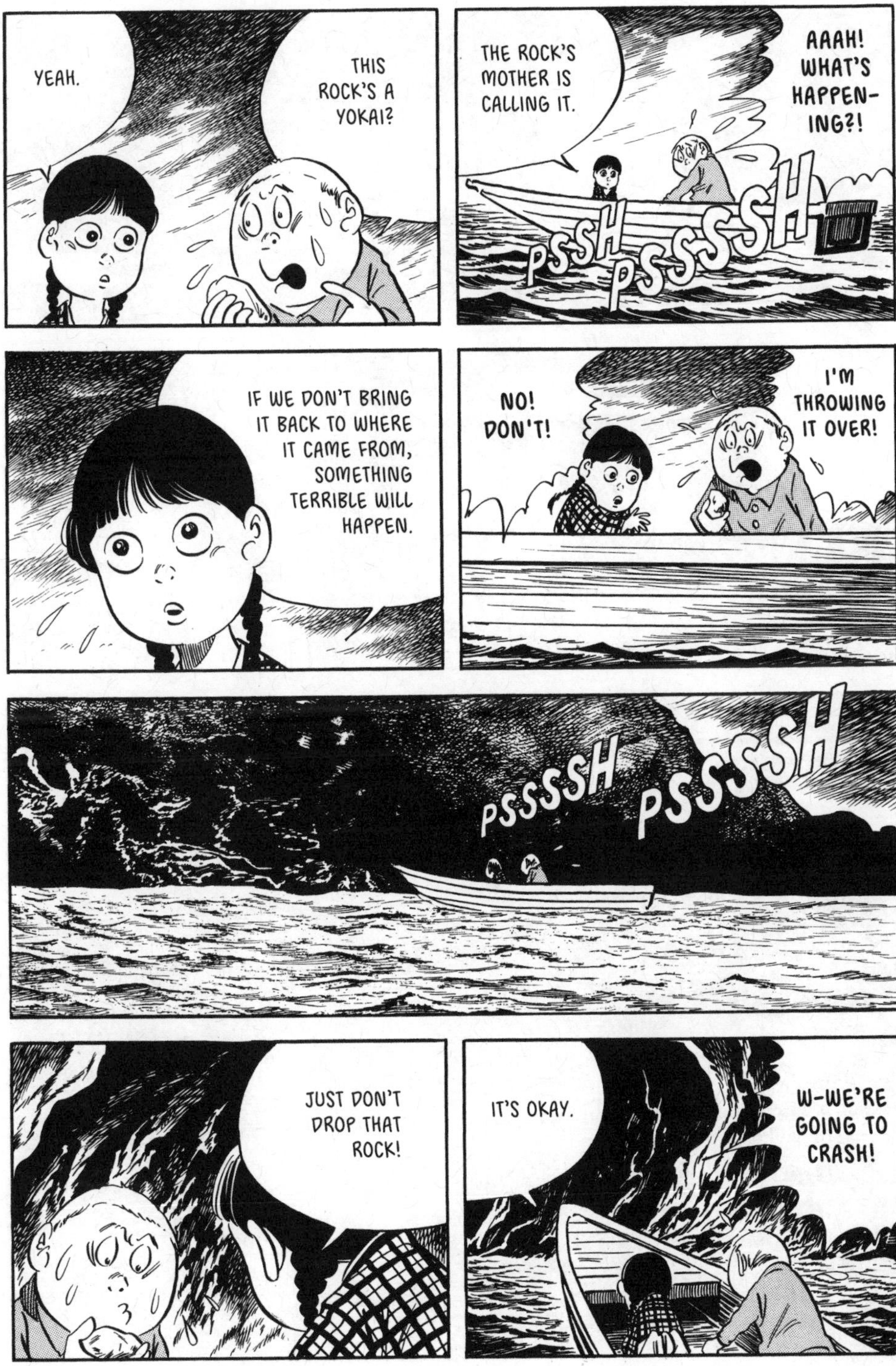
AAAH! WHAT'S HAPPEN-ING?!
THE ROCK'S MOTHER IS CALLING IT.
PSSH
PSSSSSH
THIS ROCK'S A YOKAI?
YEAH.
I'M THROWING IT OVER!
NO! DON'T!
IF WE DON'T BRING IT BACK TO WHERE IT CAME FROM, SOMETHING TERRIBLE WILL HAPPEN.
PSSSSSH
PSSSSH
W-WE'RE GOING TO CRASH!
IT'S OKAY.
JUST DON'T DROP THAT ROCK!

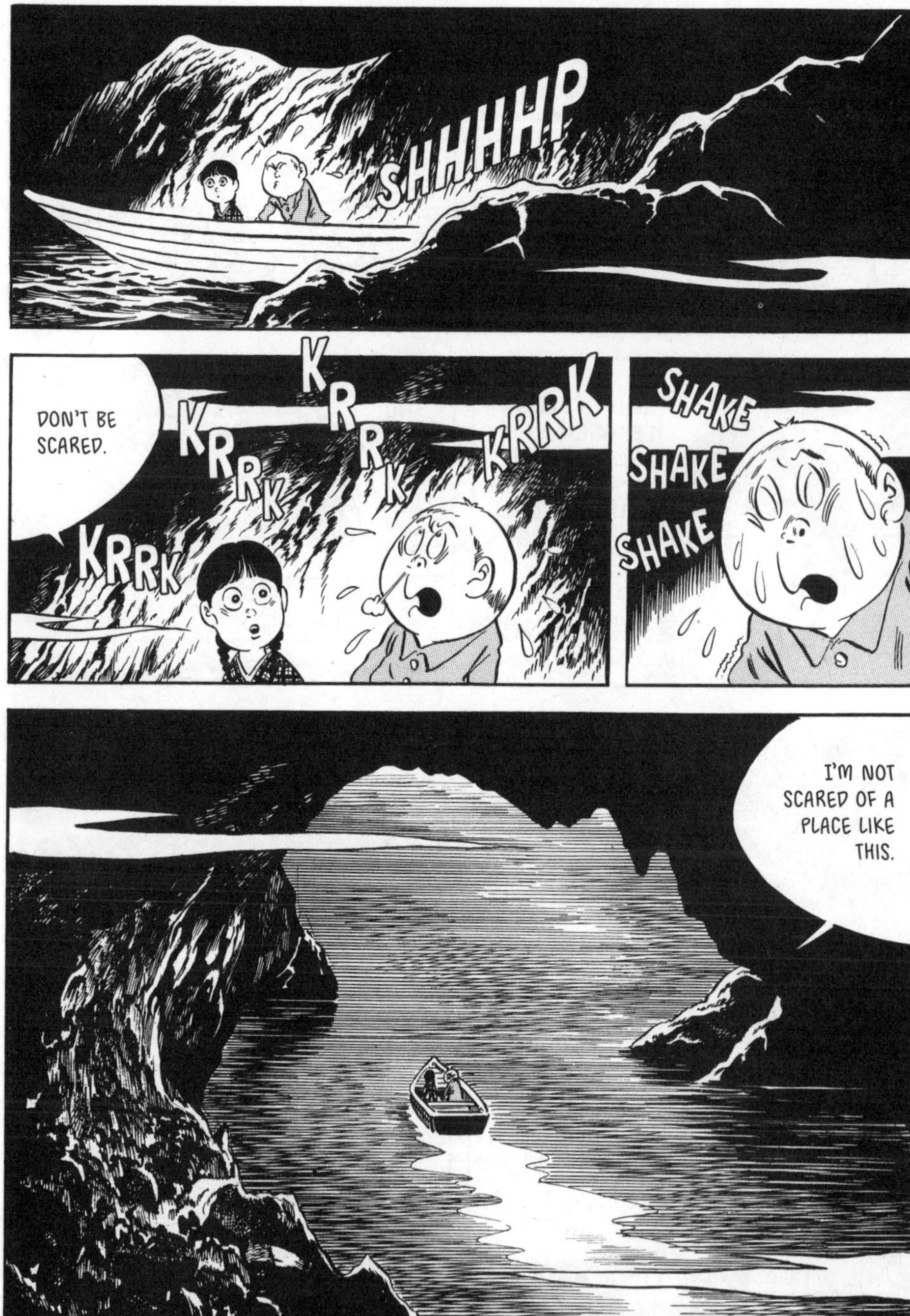
SHHHHP
SHAKE
SHAKE
SHAKE
KRRRK
KRRK
KRRK
DON'T BE SCARED.
KRRK
I'M NOT SCARED OF A PLACE LIKE THIS.

AAAH!

PSSSSH

PSSSSH

NO, IT'S A WATER TIGER, A SUIKO* IT GUARDS THIS CAVE.

A-A KAPPA!

SHHHHHP

*SEE NOTES PAGE 421.

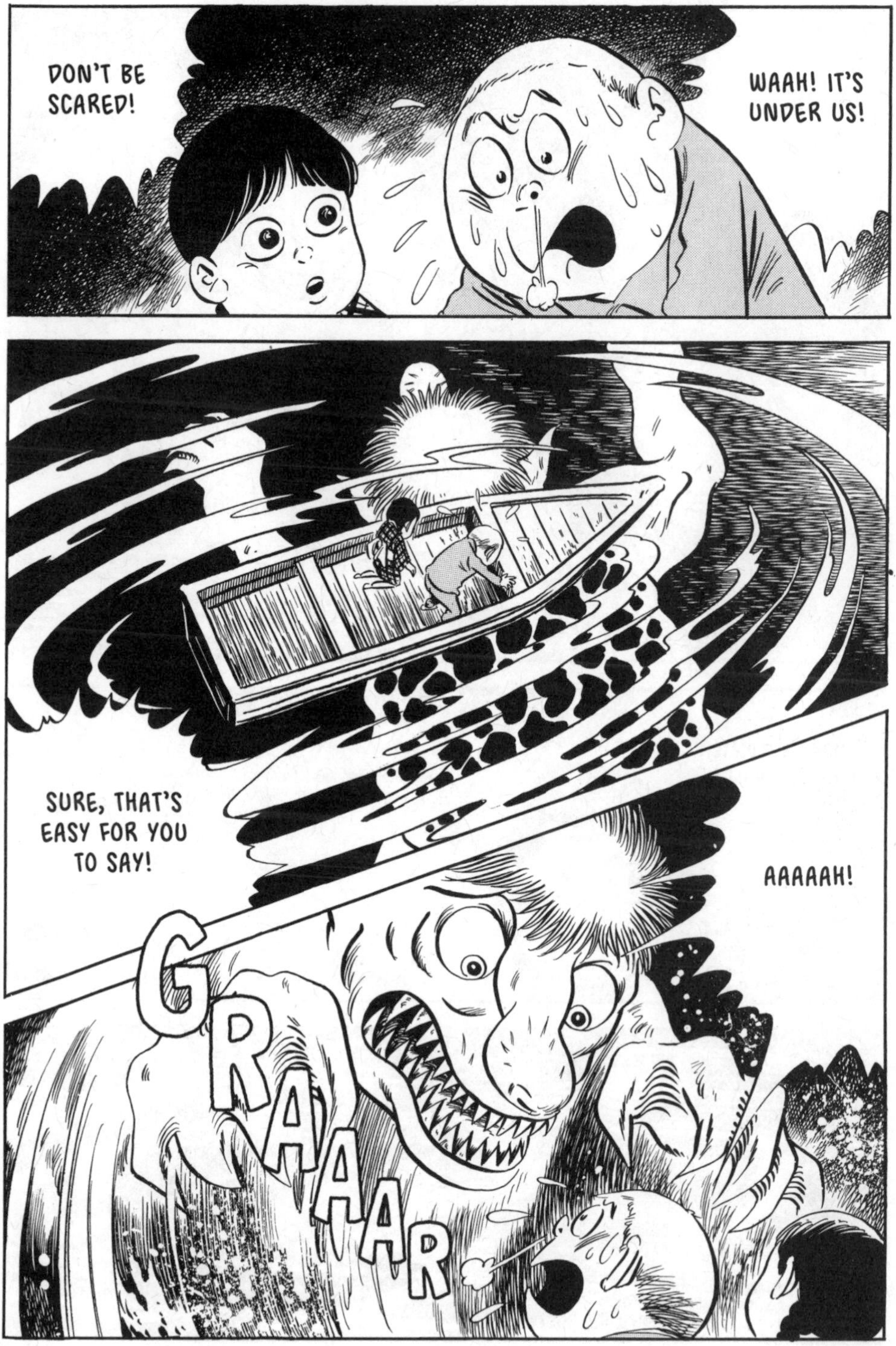
WAAH! IT'S UNDER US!
DON'T BE SCARED!
SURE, THAT'S EASY FOR YOU TO SAY!
AAAAAH!
GRAAAAR

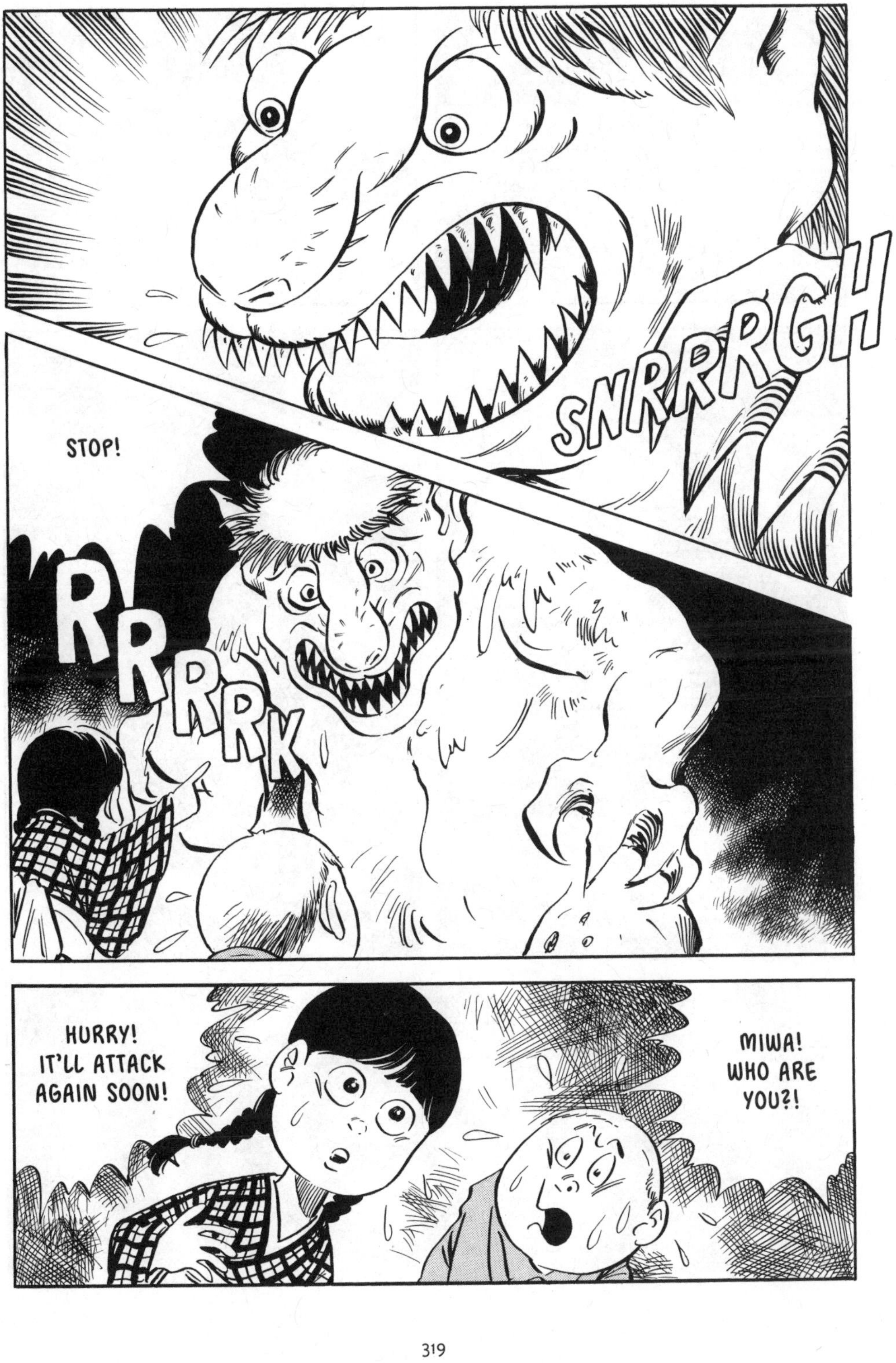
SNRRRGH
RRRRRK
STOP!
MIWA! WHO ARE YOU?!
HURRY! IT'LL ATTACK AGAIN SOON!

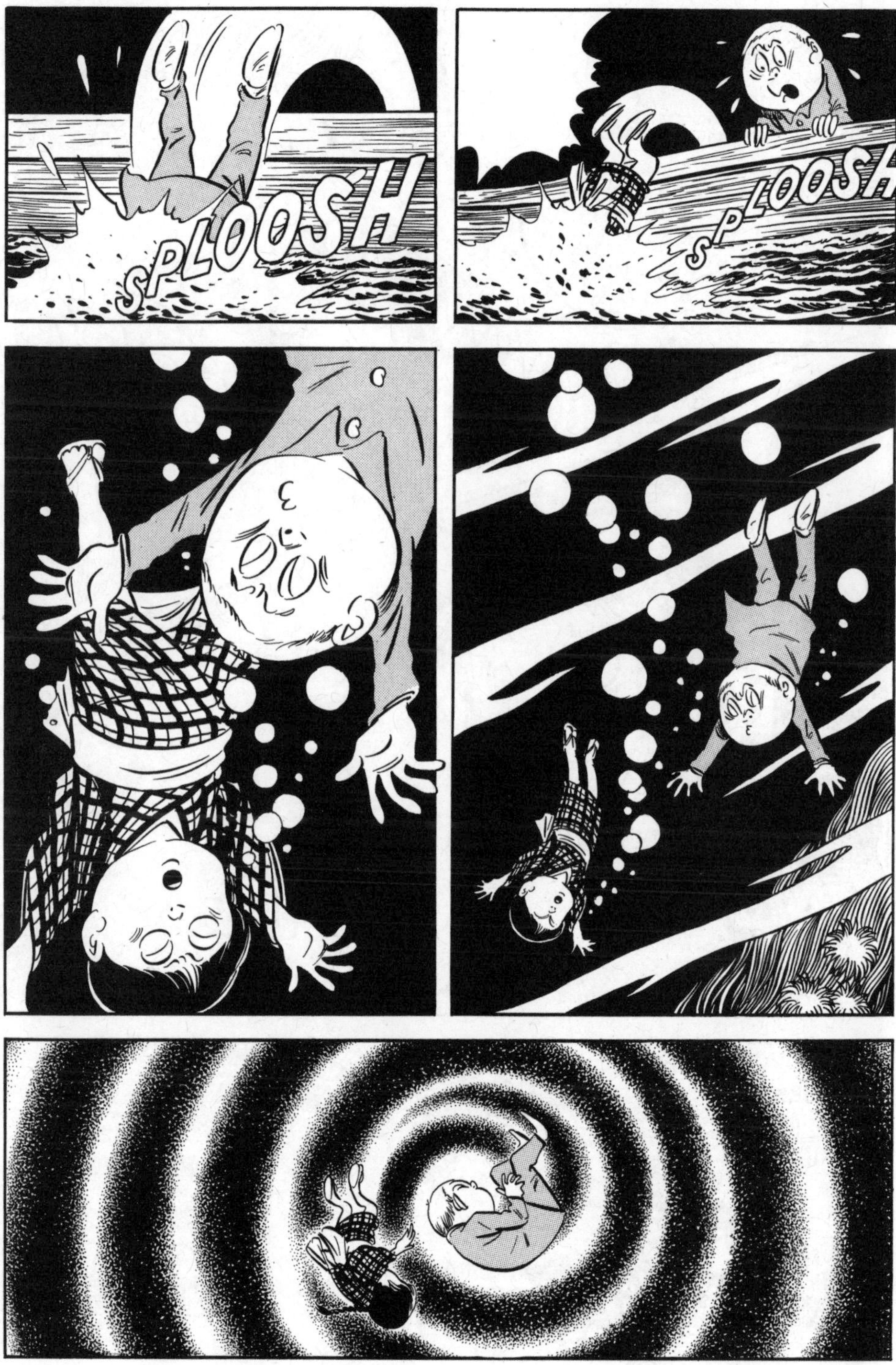
SPLOOSH
SPLOOSH

THUMP
THUMP
OWOWOW... ARE YOU OKAY, MIWA?
I'M FINE.
DO YOU STILL HAVE THE ROCK?
IT'S RIGHT HERE.
WHERE ARE WE?

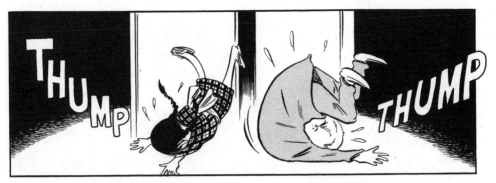

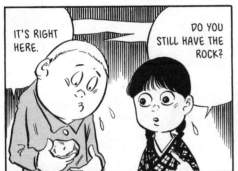

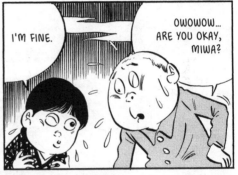

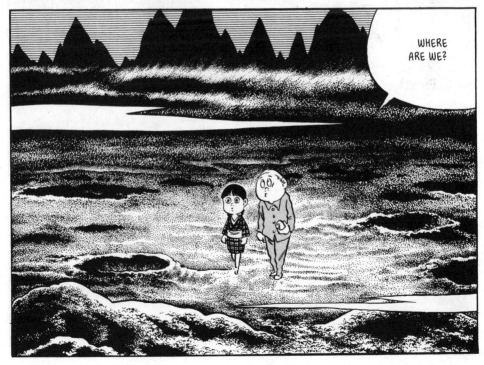

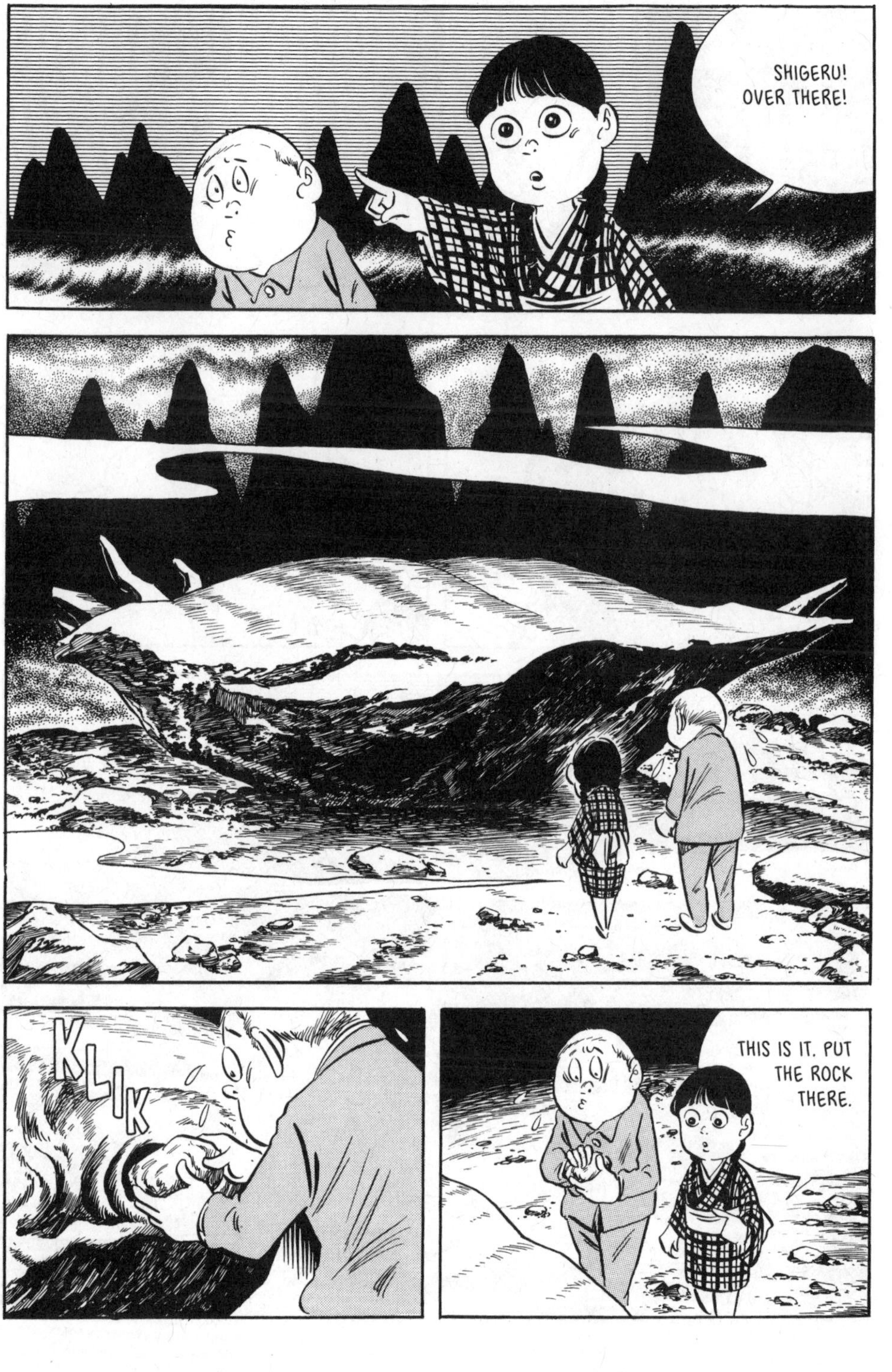
SHIGERU! OVER THERE!
THIS IS IT. PUT THE ROCK THERE.
KLIK

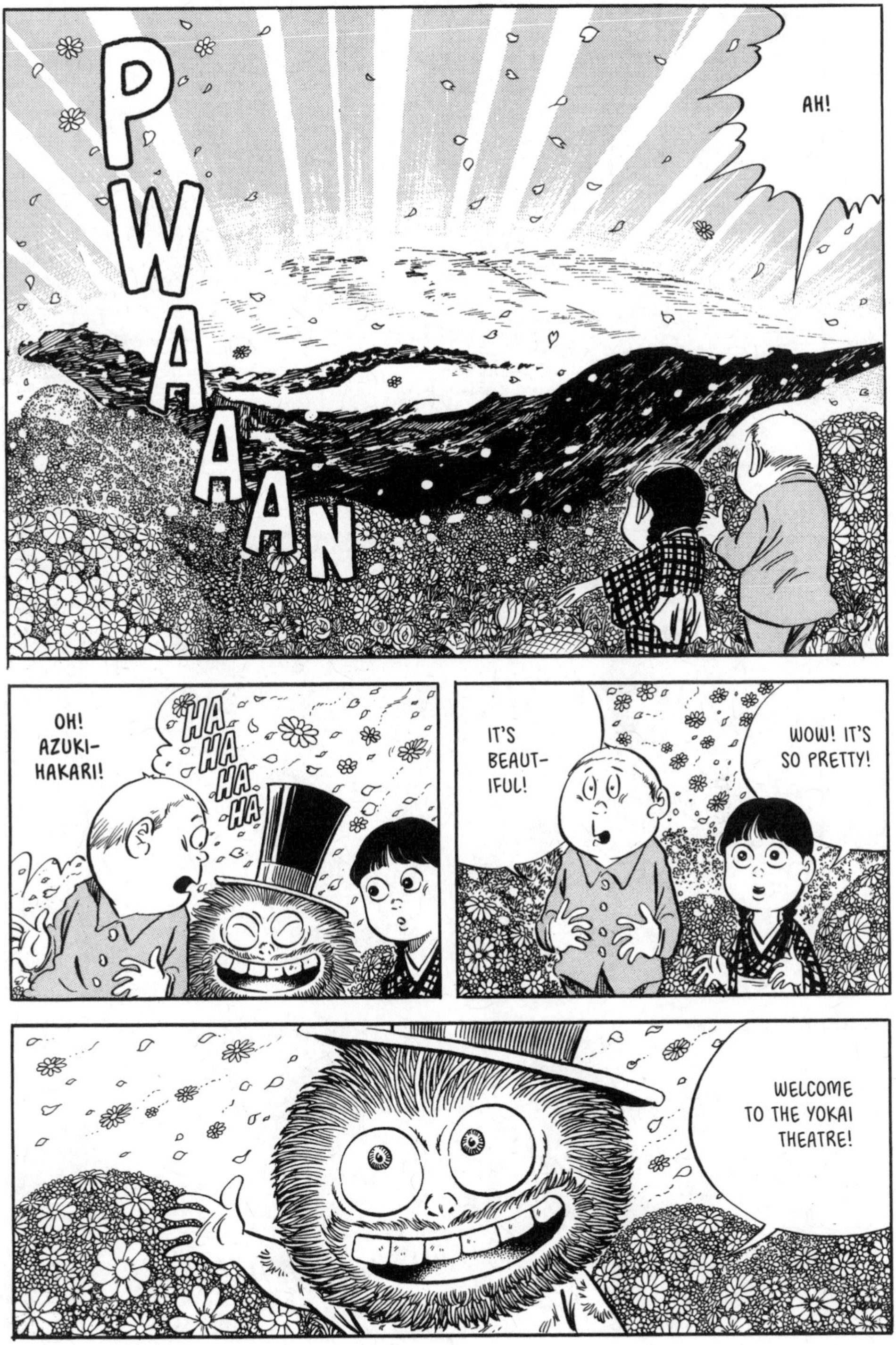
AH!
PWAAAAN
WOW! IT'S SO PRETTY!
IT'S BEAUT-IFUL!
HA HA HA HA HA
OH! AZUKI-HAKARI!
WELCOME TO THE YOKAI THEATRE!

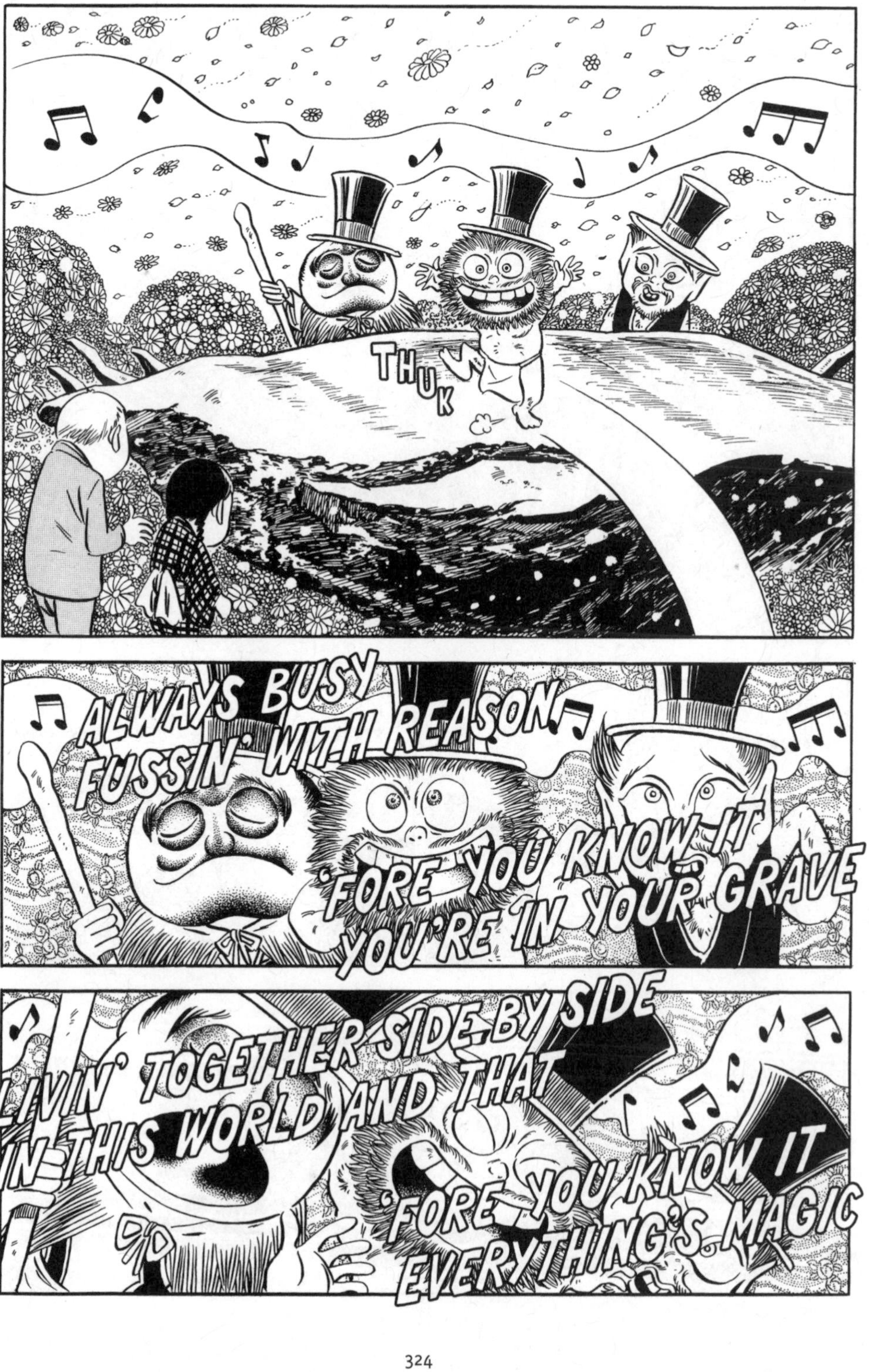
THUK
ALWAYS BUSY FUSSIN' WITH REASON
'FORE YOU KNOW IT YOU'RE IN YOUR GRAVE
LIVIN' TOGETHER SIDE BY SIDE IN THIS WORLD AND THAT
'FORE YOU KNOW IT EVERYTHING'S MAGIC

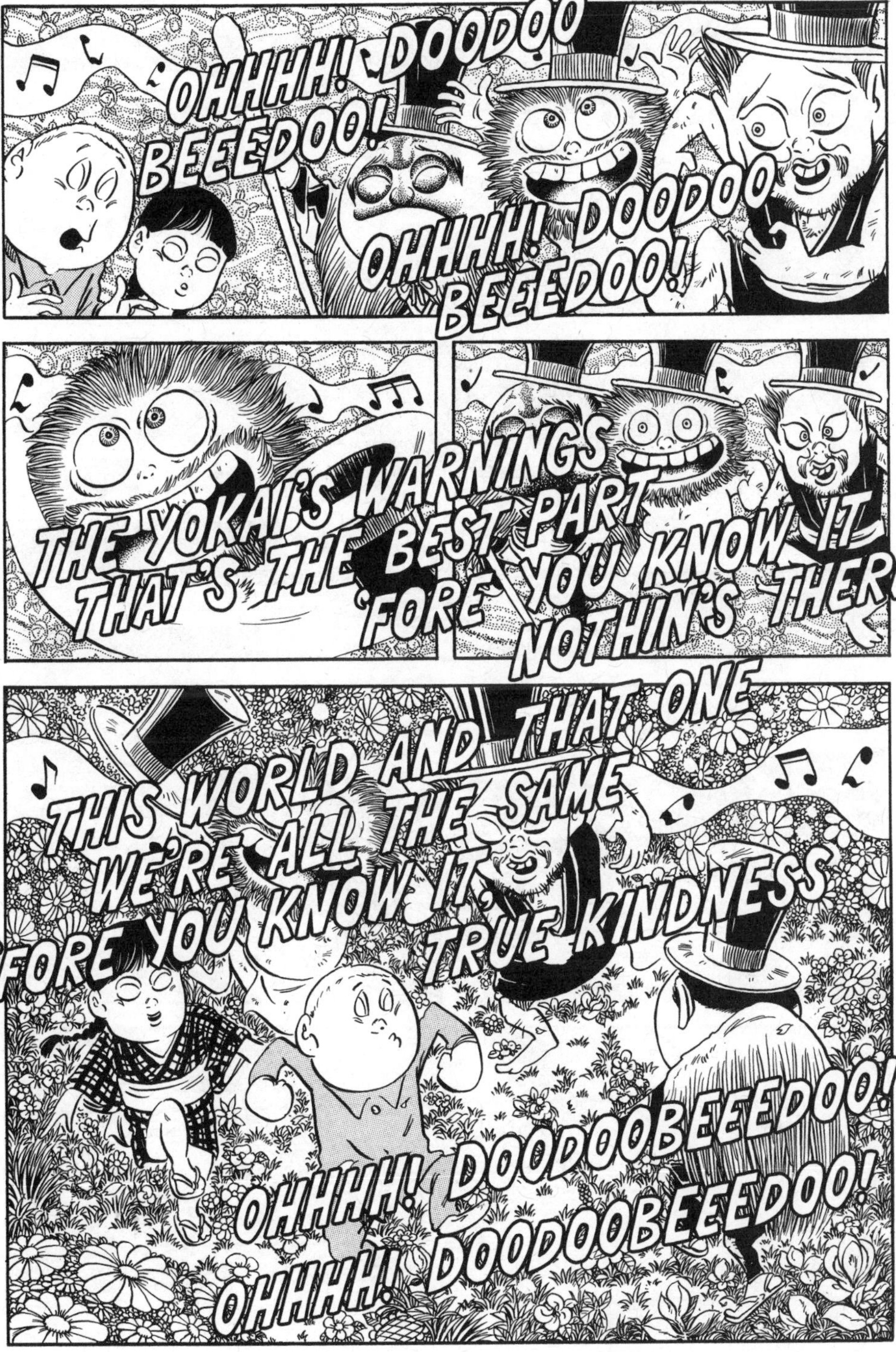
OHHHH! DOODOO BEEEDOO!
OHHHH! DOODOO BEEEDOO!
THE YOKAI'S WARNINGS
THAT'S THE BEST PART
'FORE YOU KNOW IT
NOTHIN'S THERE
THIS WORLD AND THAT ONE
WE'RE ALL THE SAME
'FORE YOU KNOW IT,
TRUE KINDNESS
OHHHH! DOODOOBEEEDOO!
OHHHH! DOODOOBEEEDOO!

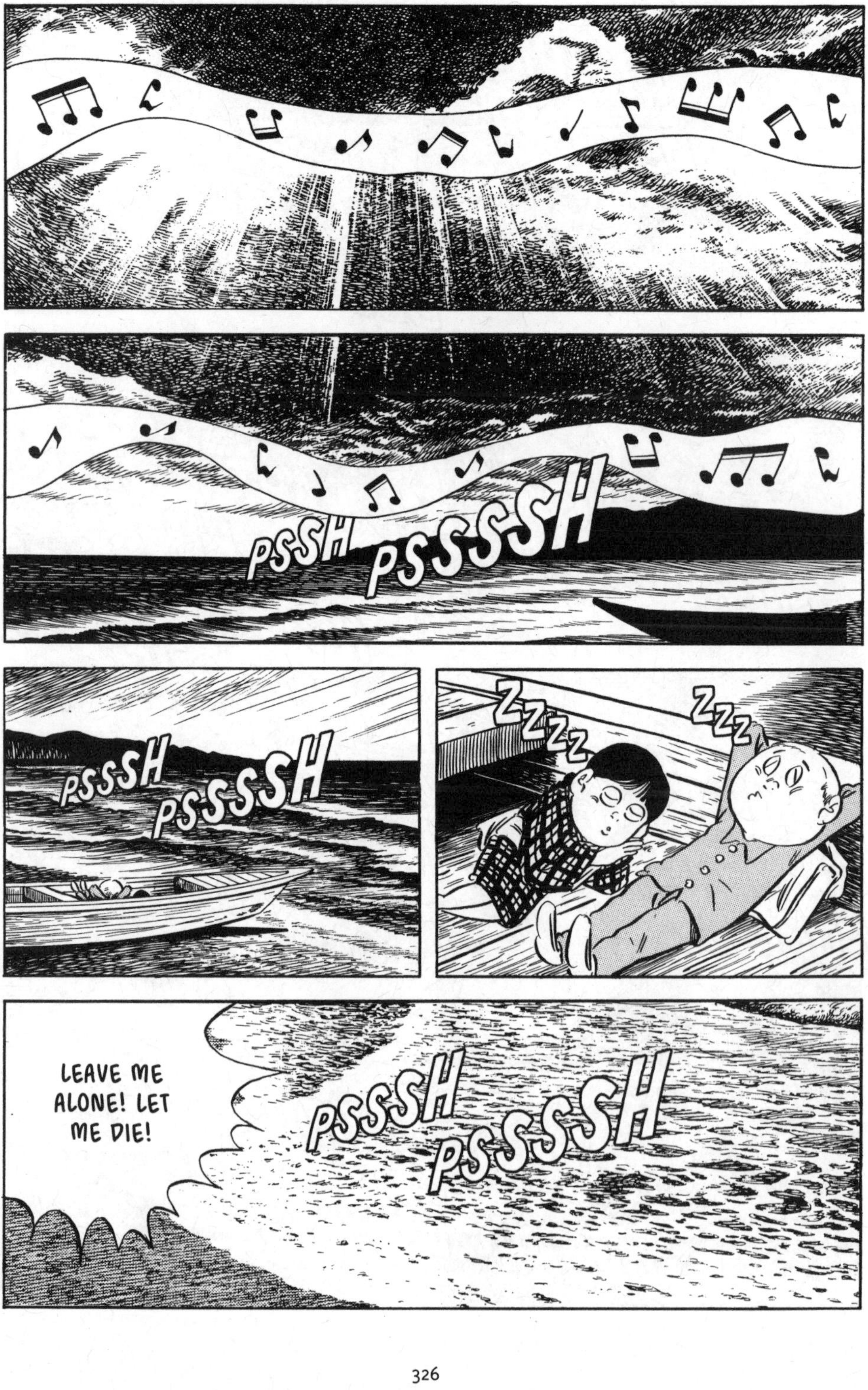
PSSH
PSSSSH
ZZZZ
ZZZ
PSSSH
PSSSSH
LEAVE ME ALONE! LET ME DIE!
PSSSH
PSSSSH

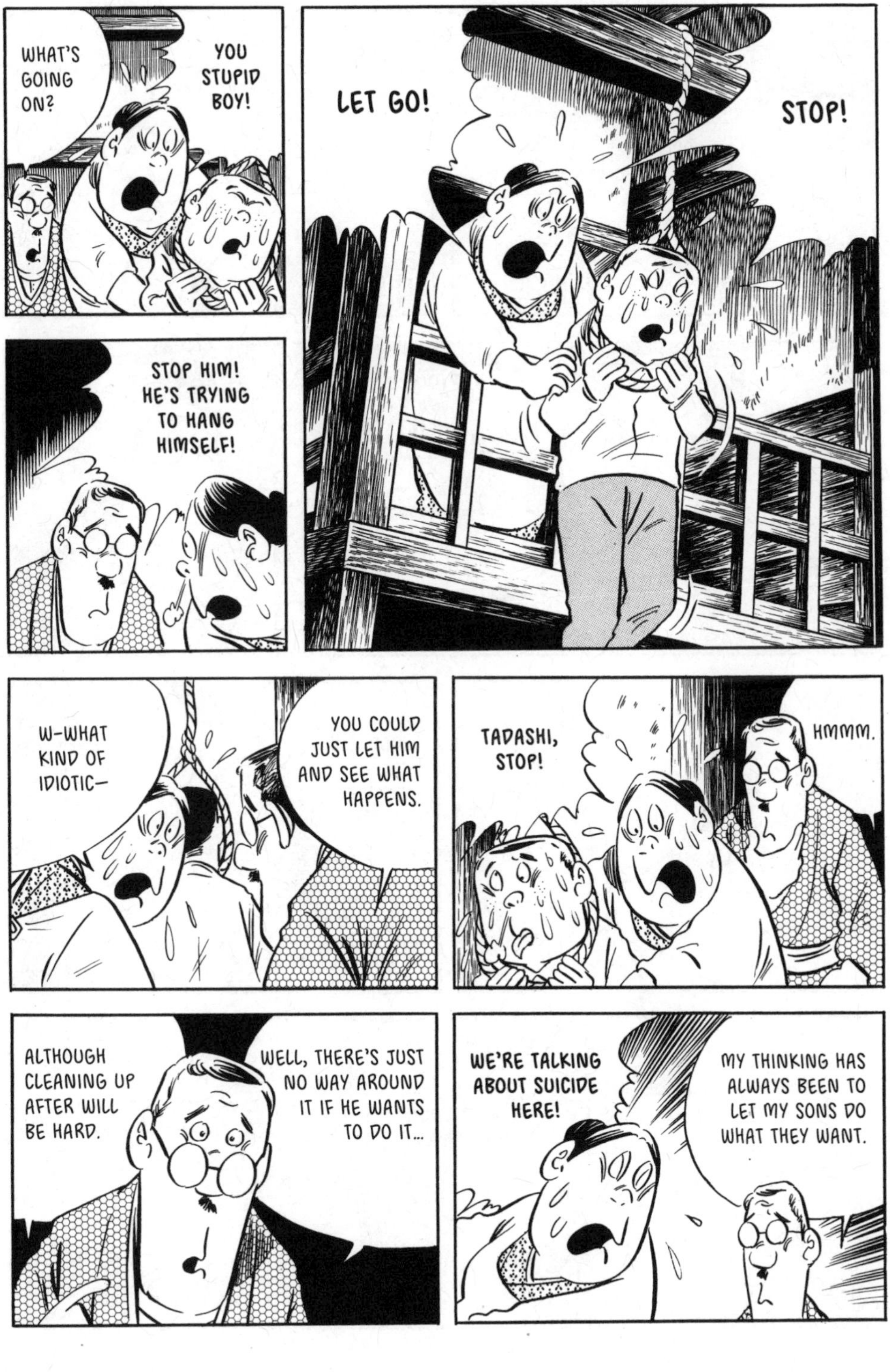
STOP!
LET GO!
YOU STUPID BOY!
WHAT'S GOING ON?
STOP HIM! HE'S TRYING TO HANG HIMSELF!
HMMM.
TADASHI, STOP!
YOU COULD JUST LET HIM AND SEE WHAT HAPPENS.
W-WHAT KIND OF IDIOTIC—
MY THINKING HAS ALWAYS BEEN TO LET MY SONS DO WHAT THEY WANT.
WE'RE TALKING ABOUT SUICIDE HERE!
WELL, THERE'S JUST NO WAY AROUND IT IF HE WANTS TO DO IT...
ALTHOUGH CLEANING UP AFTER WILL BE HARD.

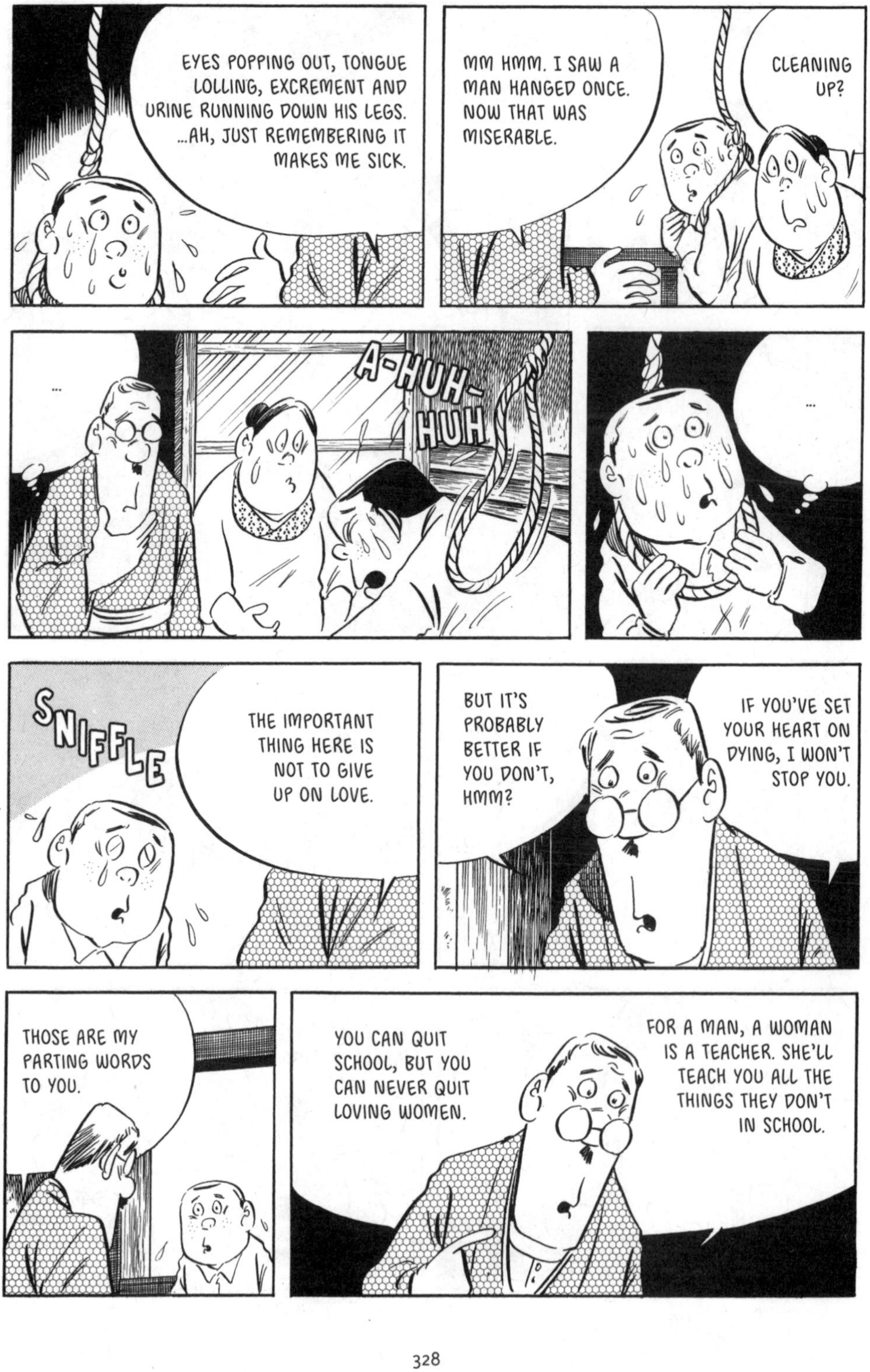
CLEANING UP?
MM HMM. I SAW A MAN HANGED ONCE. NOW THAT WAS MISERABLE.
EYES POPPING OUT, TONGUE LOLLING, EXCREMENT AND URINE RUNNING DOWN HIS LEGS. ...AH, JUST REMEMBERING IT MAKES ME SICK.
...
A-HUH-HUH
...
IF YOU'VE SET YOUR HEART ON DYING, I WON'T STOP YOU.
BUT IT'S PROBABLY BETTER IF YOU DON'T, HMM?
SNIFFLE
THE IMPORTANT THING HERE IS NOT TO GIVE UP ON LOVE.
FOR A MAN, A WOMAN IS A TEACHER. SHE'LL TEACH YOU ALL THE THINGS THEY DON'T IN SCHOOL.
YOU CAN QUIT SCHOOL, BUT YOU CAN NEVER QUIT LOVING WOMEN.
THOSE ARE MY PARTING WORDS TO YOU.

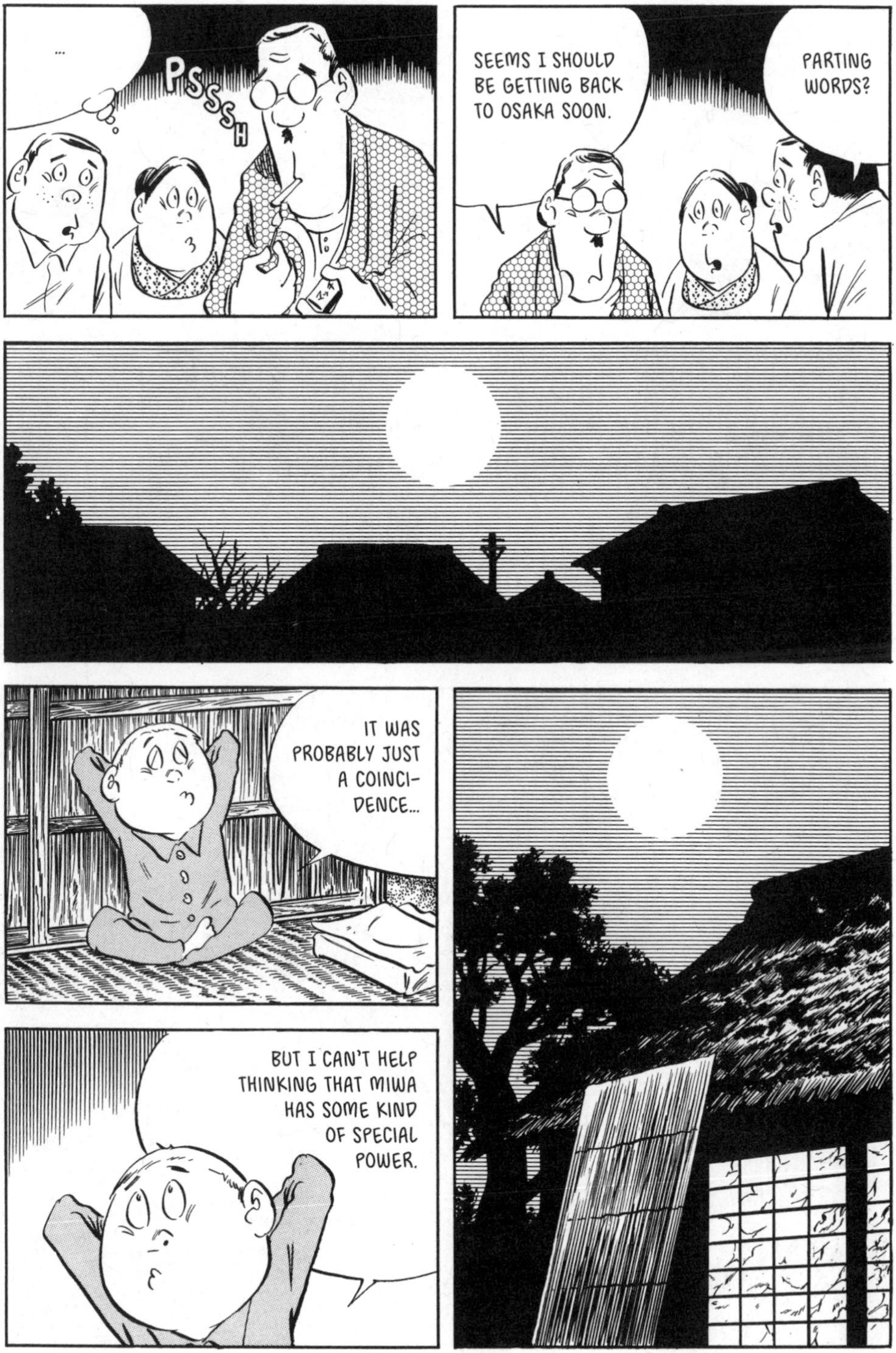
PARTING WORDS?
SEEMS I SHOULD BE GETTING BACK TO OSAKA SOON.
...
PSSSH
IT WAS PROBABLY JUST A COINCI- DENCE...
BUT I CAN'T HELP THINKING THAT MIWA HAS SOME KIND OF SPECIAL POWER.

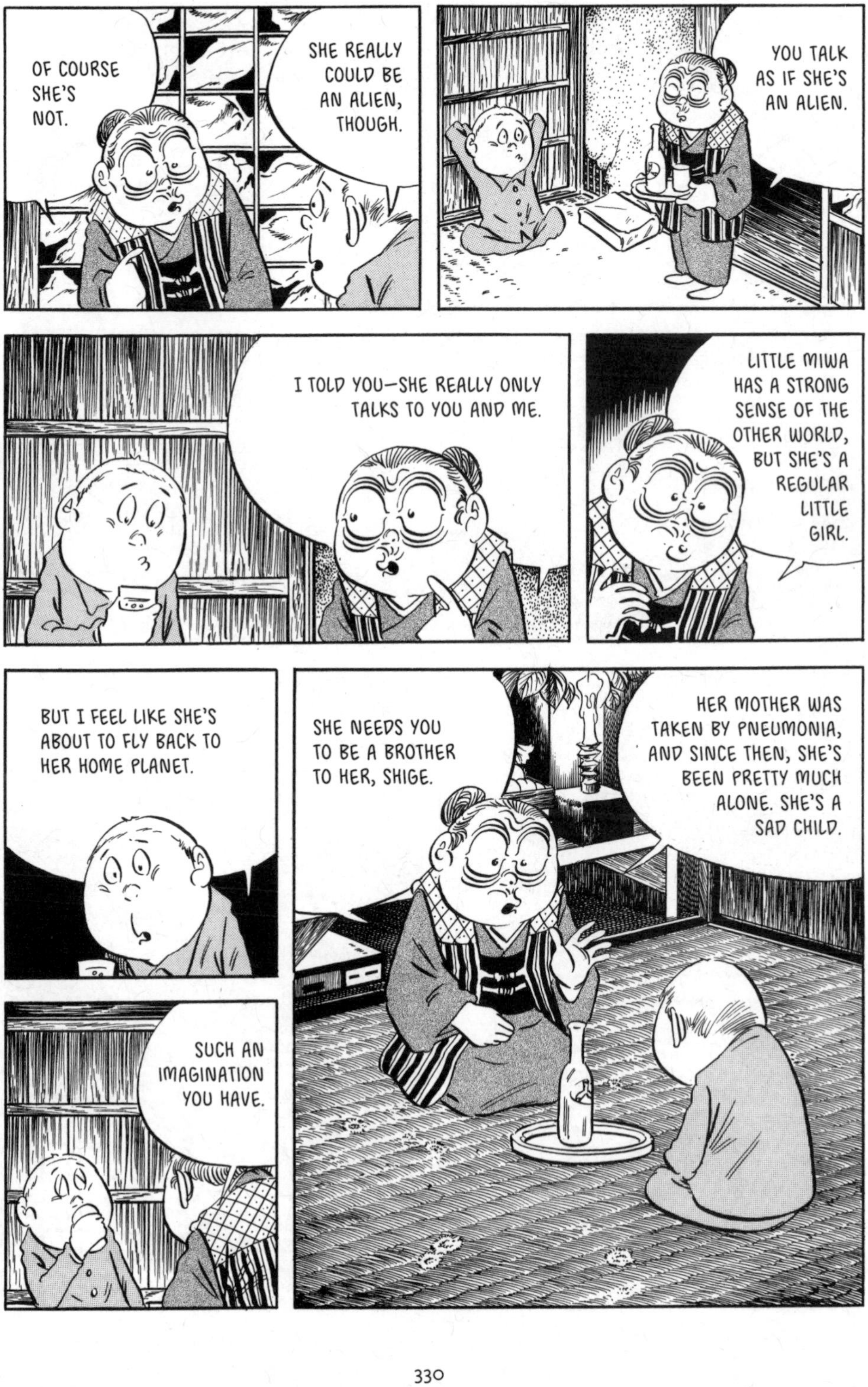
YOU TALK AS IF SHE'S AN ALIEN.
SHE REALLY COULD BE AN ALIEN, THOUGH.
OF COURSE SHE'S NOT.
LITTLE MIWA HAS A STRONG SENSE OF THE OTHER WORLD, BUT SHE'S A REGULAR LITTLE GIRL.
I TOLD YOU—SHE REALLY ONLY TALKS TO YOU AND ME.
HER MOTHER WAS TAKEN BY PNEUMONIA, AND SINCE THEN, SHE'S BEEN PRETTY MUCH ALONE. SHE'S A SAD CHILD.
SHE NEEDS YOU TO BE A BROTHER TO HER, SHIGE.
BUT I FEEL LIKE SHE'S ABOUT TO FLY BACK TO HER HOME PLANET.
SUCH AN IMAGINATION YOU HAVE.

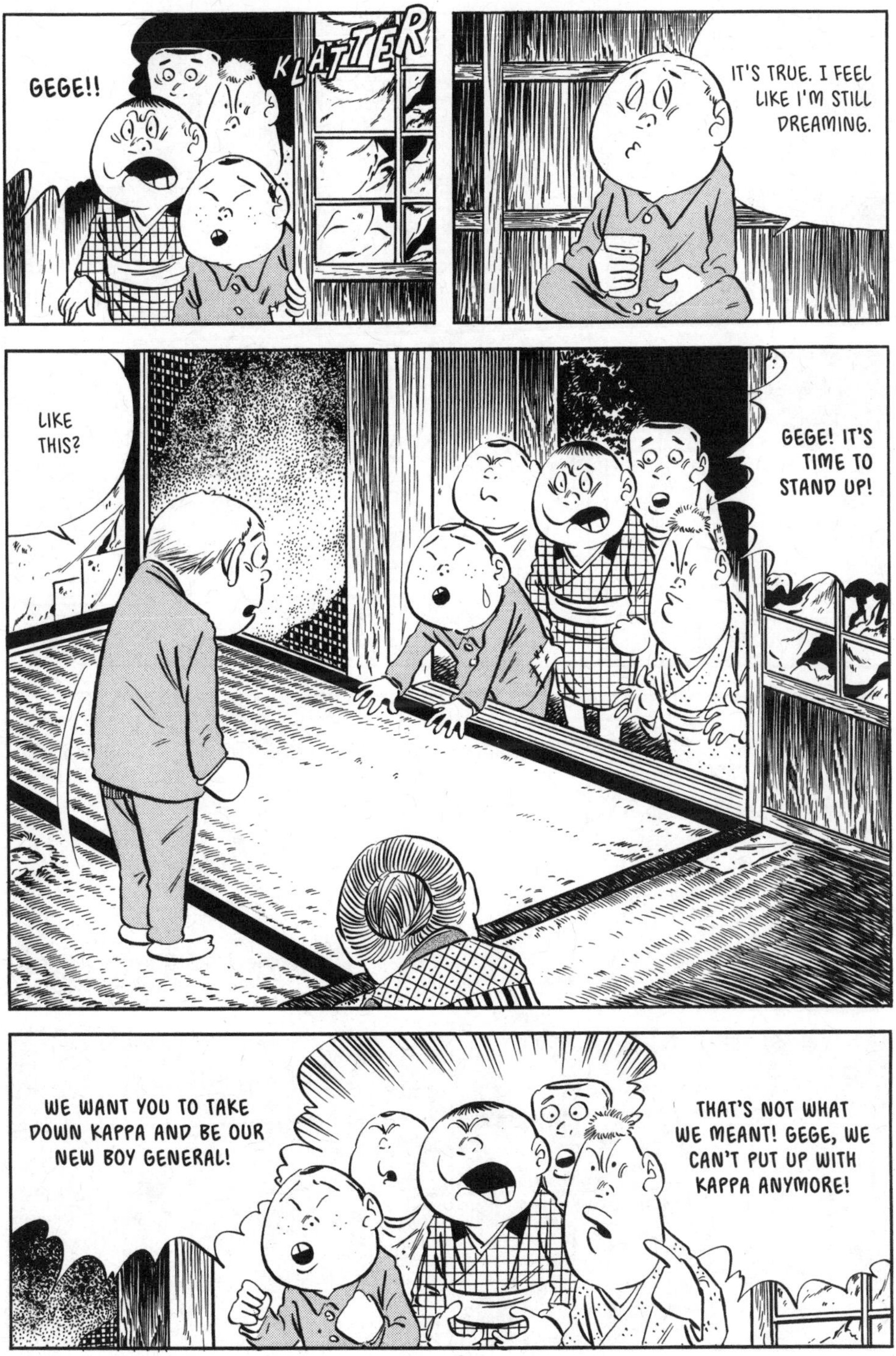
IT'S TRUE. I FEEL LIKE I'M STILL DREAMING.
GEGE!!
KLATTER
GEGE! IT'S TIME TO STAND UP!
LIKE THIS?
THAT'S NOT WHAT WE MEANT! GEGE, WE CAN'T PUT UP WITH KAPPA ANYMORE!
WE WANT YOU TO TAKE DOWN KAPPA AND BE OUR NEW BOY GENERAL!

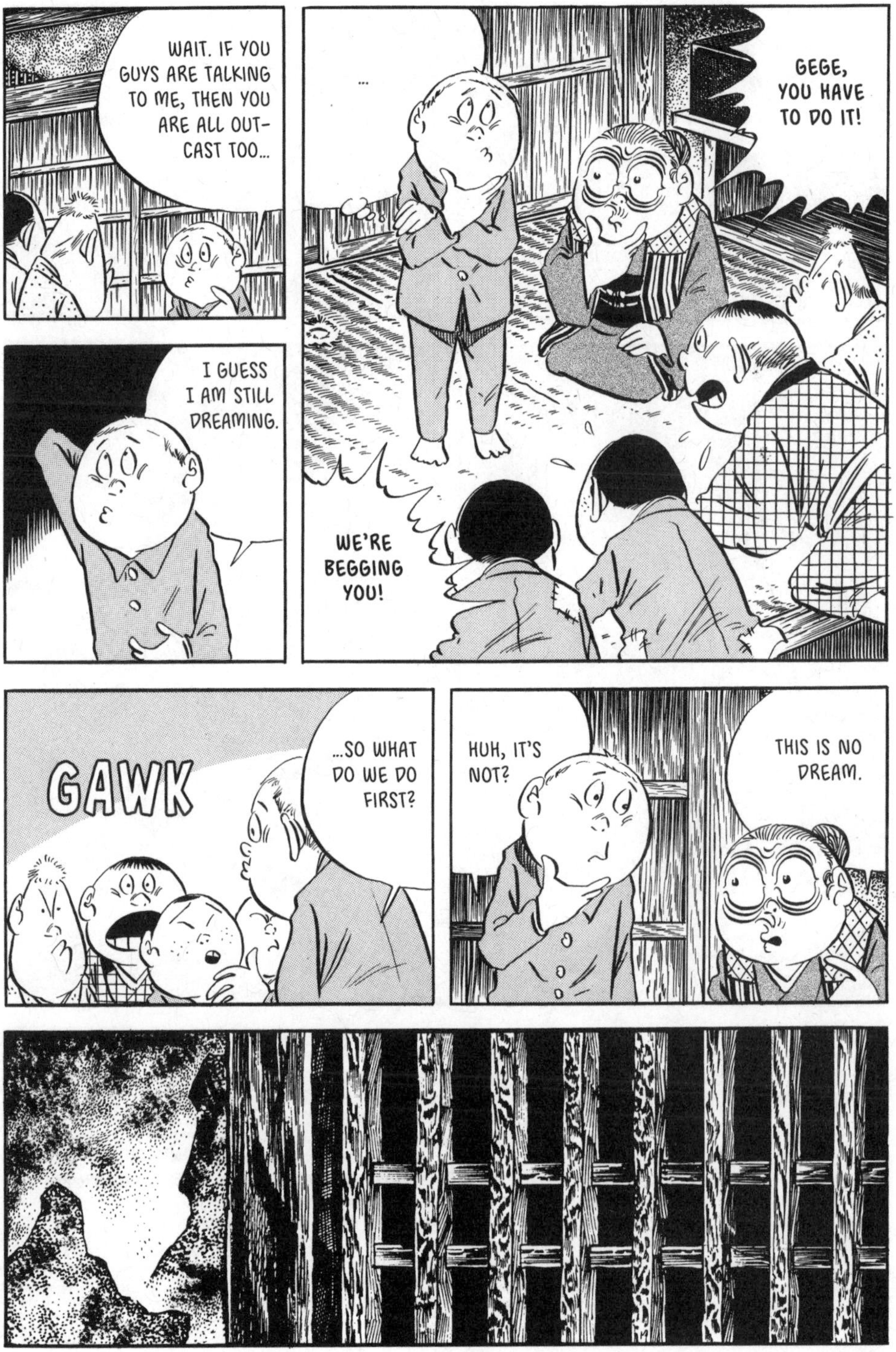
GEGE, YOU HAVE TO DO IT!
...
WE'RE BEGGING YOU!
WAIT. IF YOU GUYS ARE TALKING TO ME, THEN YOU ARE ALL OUT-CAST TOO...
I GUESS I AM STILL DREAMING.
THIS IS NO DREAM.
HUH, IT'S NOT?
...SO WHAT DO WE DO FIRST?
GAWK

SLAVE DEALER

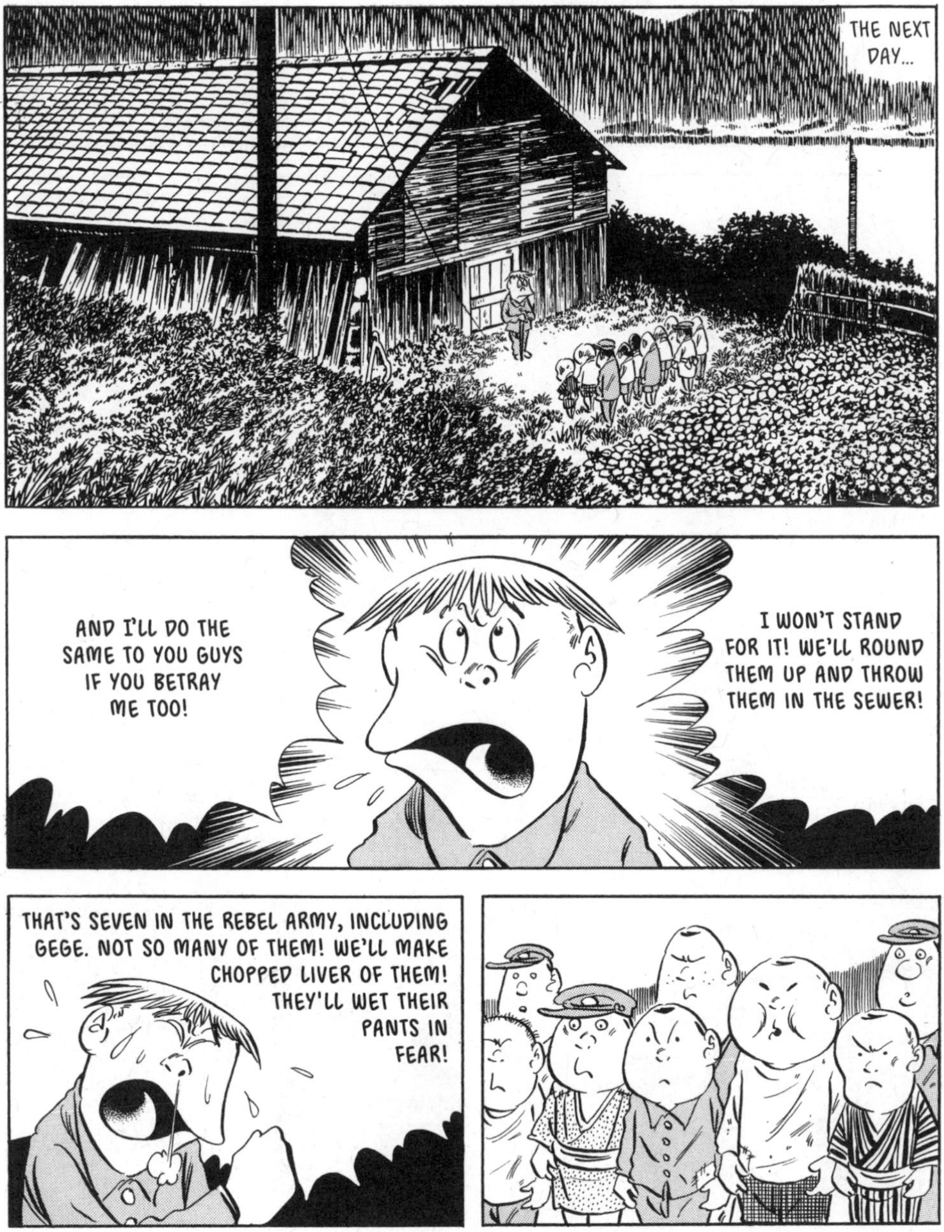
THE NEXT DAY...
I WON'T STAND FOR IT! WE'LL ROUND THEM UP AND THROW THEM IN THE SEWER!
AND I'LL DO THE SAME TO YOU GUYS IF YOU BETRAY ME TOO!
THAT'S SEVEN IN THE REBEL ARMY, INCLUDING GEGE. NOT SO MANY OF THEM! WE'LL MAKE CHOPPED LIVER OF THEM! THEY'LL WET THEIR PANTS IN FEAR!

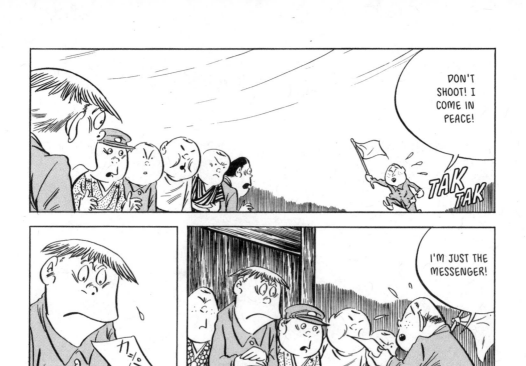

DON'T SHOOT! I COME IN PEACE!
TAK TAK
I'M JUST THE MESSENGER!
カッパへ
LETTER: TO KAPPA.
KAPPA, IT'S STUPID FOR FRIENDS TO FIGHT FRIENDS...
IF YOU MUST HAVE A FIGHT, THEN LET'S DECIDE THIS JUST THE TWO OF US, YOU AND ME.
じゃないか
場所はまかせ
以上
平和主義者
LETTER:...A FIGHT / YOU AND ME / THE PLACE IS UP TO YOU. / YOURS TRULY, / A PACIFIST, / SHIGERU MURAKI.

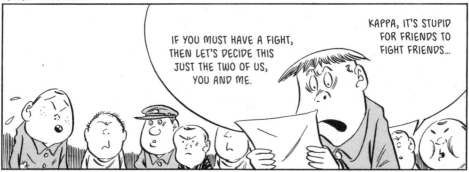

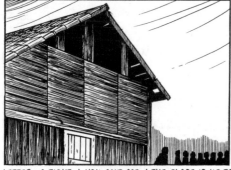

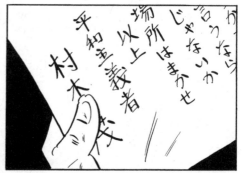

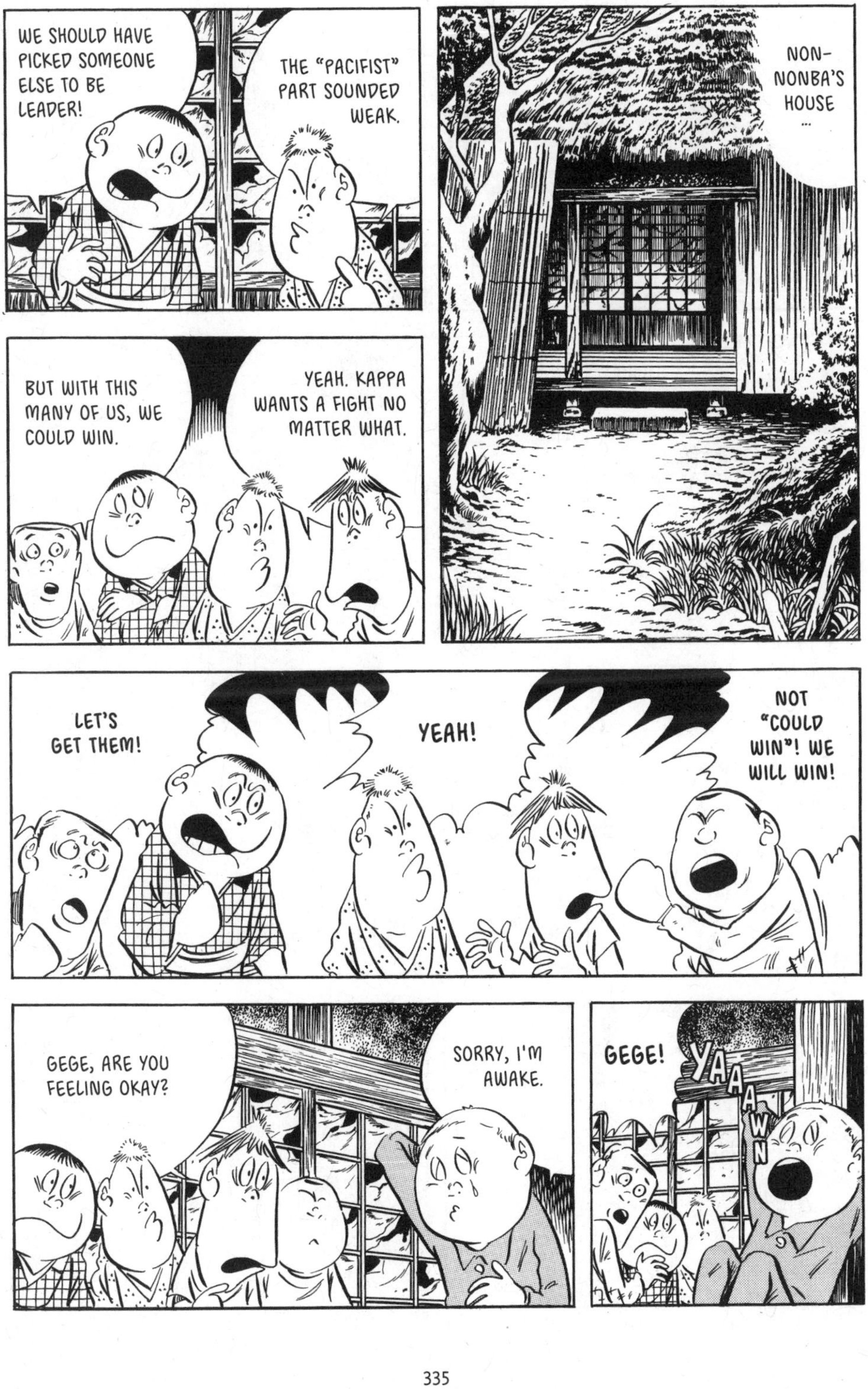
NON-NONBA'S HOUSE ...
THE "PACIFIST" PART SOUNDED WEAK.
WE SHOULD HAVE PICKED SOMEONE ELSE TO BE LEADER!
YEAH. KAPPA WANTS A FIGHT NO MATTER WHAT.
BUT WITH THIS MANY OF US, WE COULD WIN.
NOT "COULD WIN"! WE WILL WIN!
YEAH!
LET'S GET THEM!
GEGE!
YAAAAWN
SORRY, I'M AWAKE.
GEGE, ARE YOU FEELING OKAY?

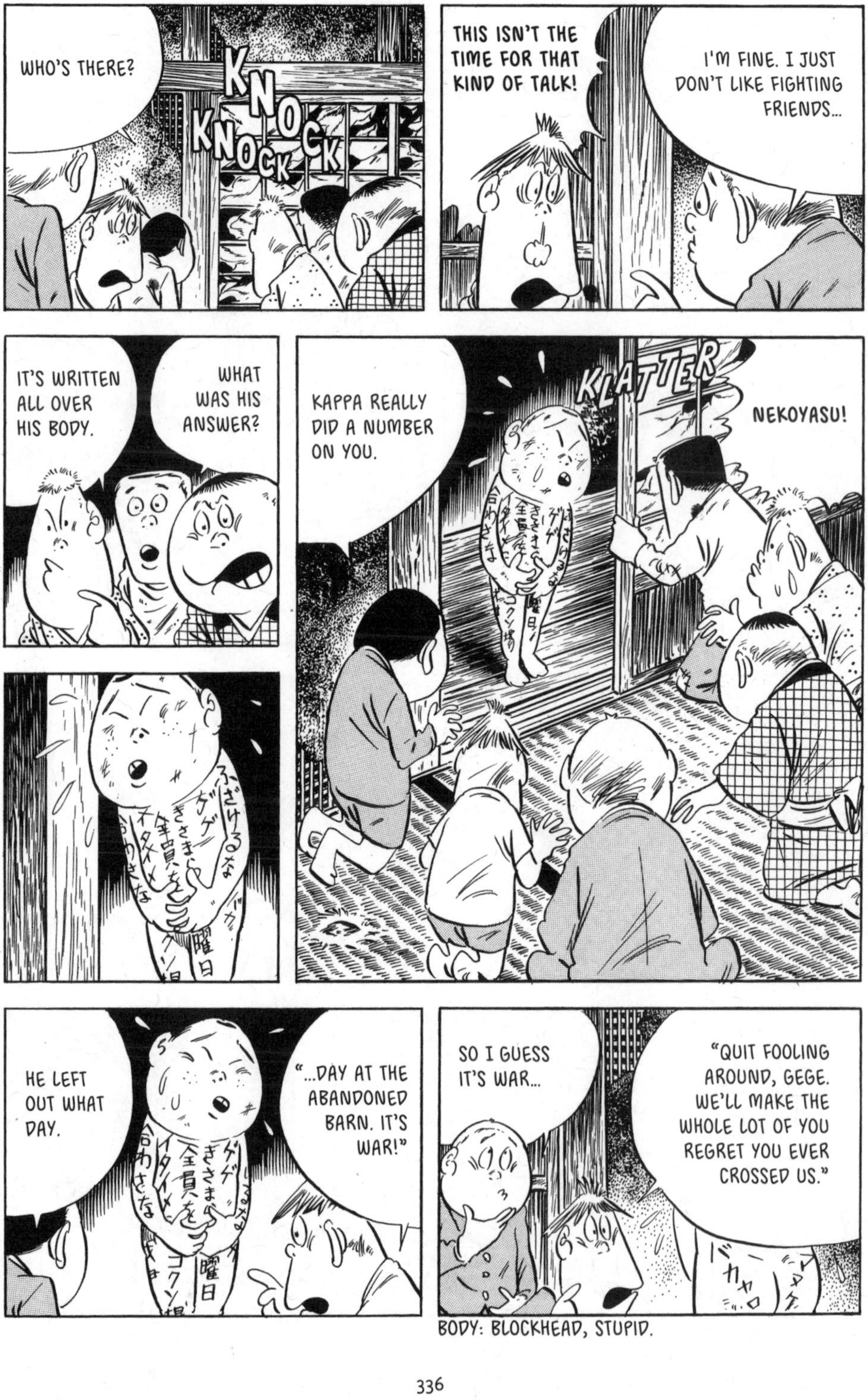
I'M FINE. I JUST DON'T LIKE FIGHTING FRIENDS...
THIS ISN'T THE TIME FOR THAT KIND OF TALK!
WHO'S THERE?
KNOCK KNOCK KNOCK KNOCK
NEKOYASU!
KLATTER
KAPPA REALLY DID A NUMBER ON YOU.
WHAT WAS HIS ANSWER?
IT'S WRITTEN ALL OVER HIS BODY.
"QUIT FOOLING AROUND, GEGE. WE'LL MAKE THE WHOLE LOT OF YOU REGRET YOU EVER CROSSED US."
SO I GUESS IT'S WAR...
"...DAY AT THE ABANDONED BARN. IT'S WAR!"
HE LEFT OUT WHAT DAY.
BODY: BLOCKHEAD, STUPID.

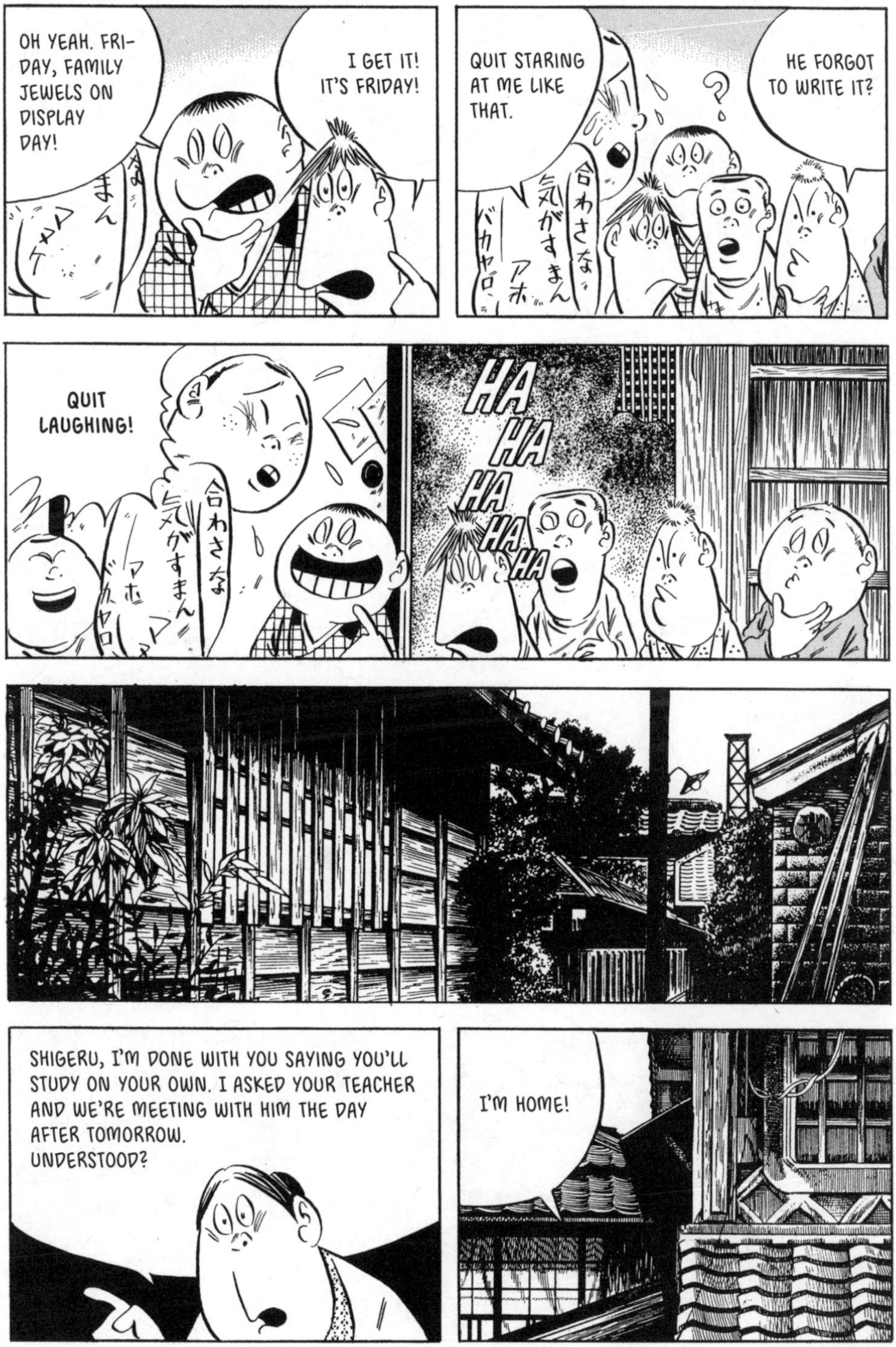
HE FORGOT TO WRITE IT?
QUIT STARING AT ME LIKE THAT.
合わさな
気がすまん
アホ
バカヤロ
I GET IT! IT'S FRIDAY!
OH YEAH. FRI-DAY, FAMILY JEWELS ON DISPLAY DAY!
HA HA HA HA HA
QUIT LAUGHING!
合わさな
気がすまん
アホ
バカヤロ
I'M HOME!
SHIGERU, I'M DONE WITH YOU SAYING YOU'LL STUDY ON YOUR OWN. I ASKED YOUR TEACHER AND WE'RE MEETING WITH HIM THE DAY AFTER TOMORROW. UNDERSTOOD?

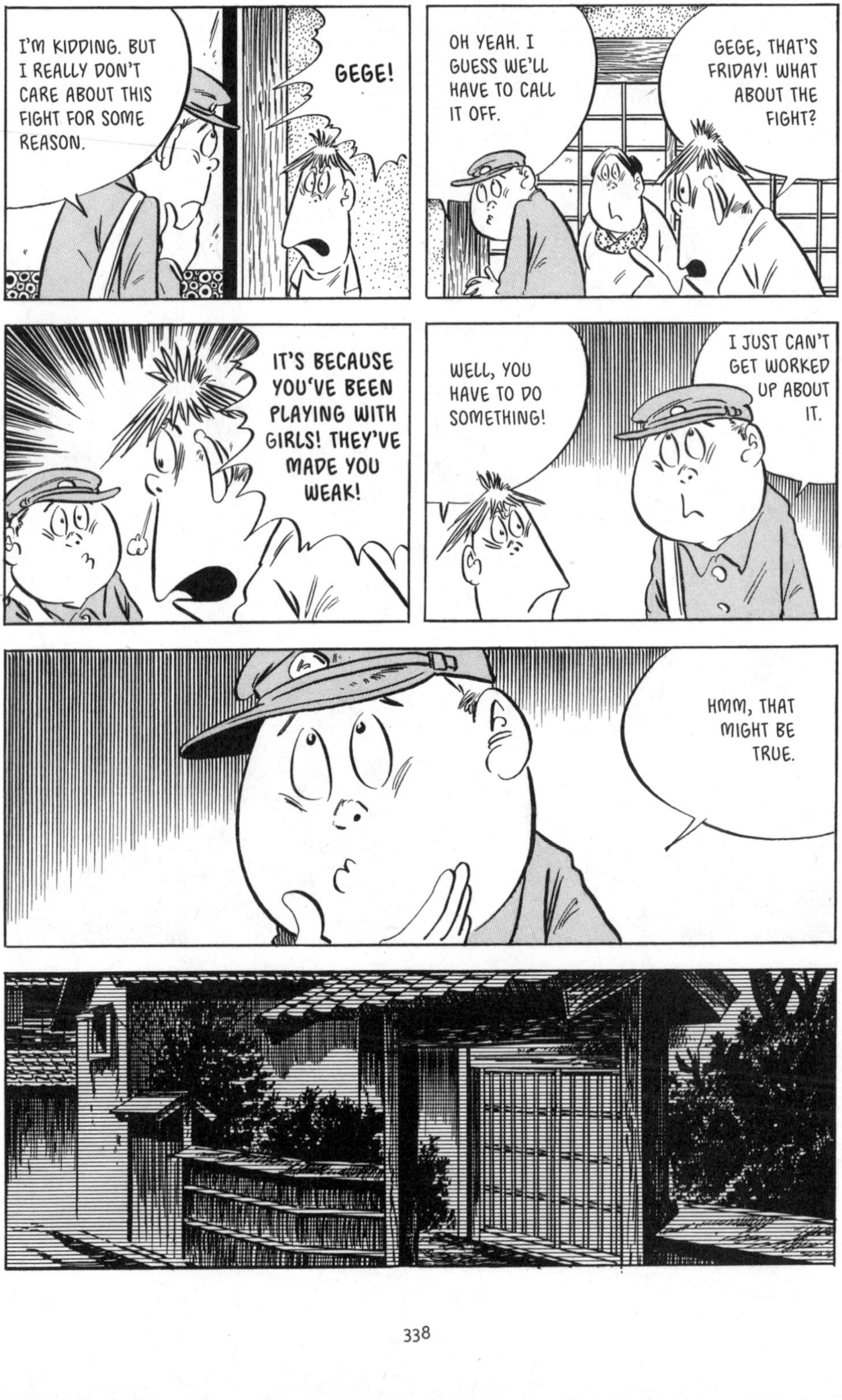
GEGE, THAT'S FRIDAY! WHAT ABOUT THE FIGHT?
OH YEAH. I GUESS WE'LL HAVE TO CALL IT OFF.
GEGE!
I'M KIDDING. BUT I REALLY DON'T CARE ABOUT THIS FIGHT FOR SOME REASON.
I JUST CAN'T GET WORKED UP ABOUT IT.
WELL, YOU HAVE TO DO SOMETHING!
IT'S BECAUSE YOU'VE BEEN PLAYING WITH GIRLS! THEY'VE MADE YOU WEAK!
HMM, THAT MIGHT BE TRUE.

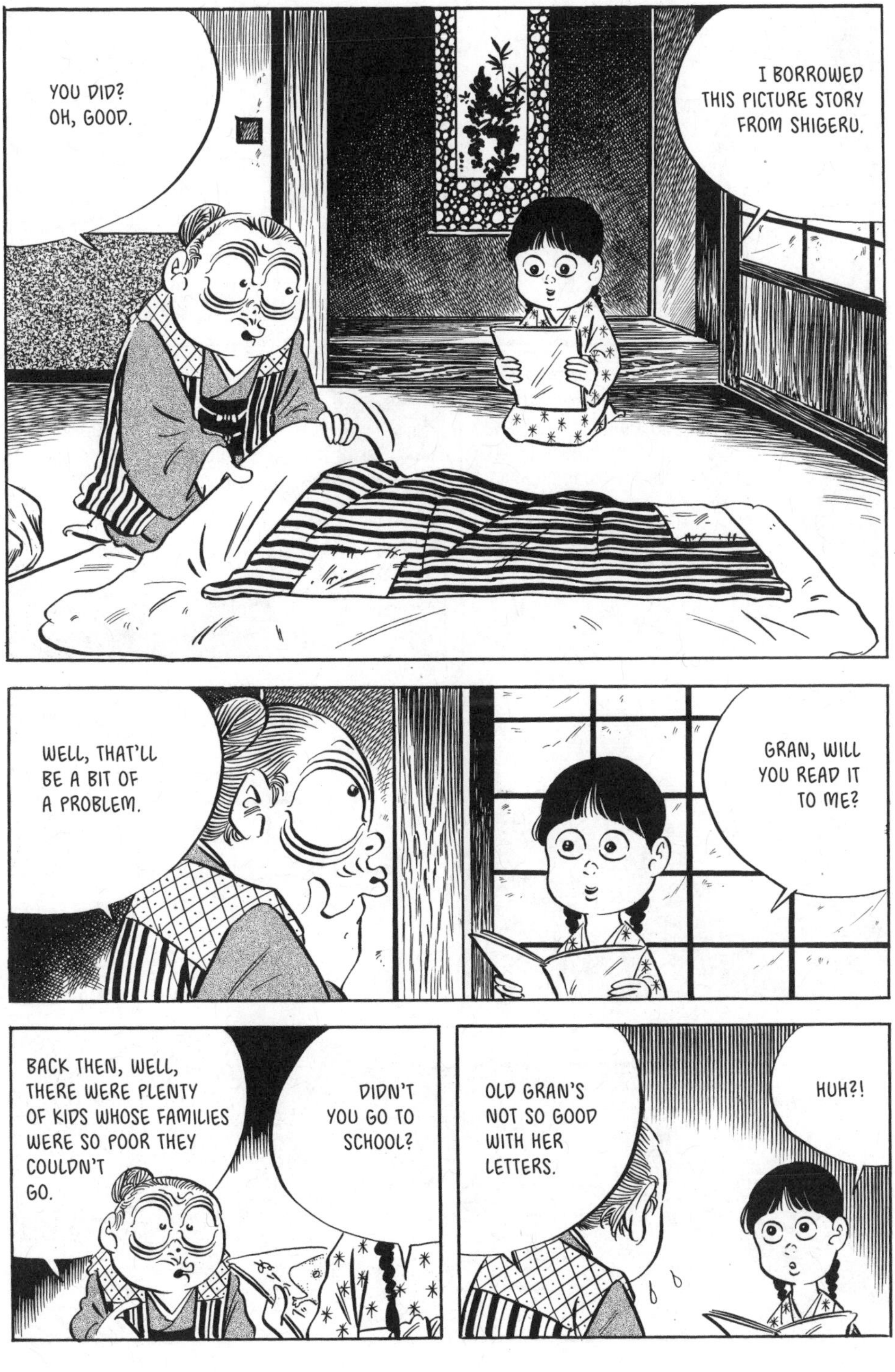
I BORROWED THIS PICTURE STORY FROM SHIGERU.
YOU DID? OH, GOOD.
GRAN, WILL YOU READ IT TO ME?
WELL, THAT'LL BE A BIT OF A PROBLEM.
HUH?!
OLD GRAN'S NOT SO GOOD WITH HER LETTERS.
DIDN'T YOU GO TO SCHOOL?
BACK THEN, WELL, THERE WERE PLENTY OF KIDS WHOSE FAMILIES WERE SO POOR THEY COULDN'T GO.

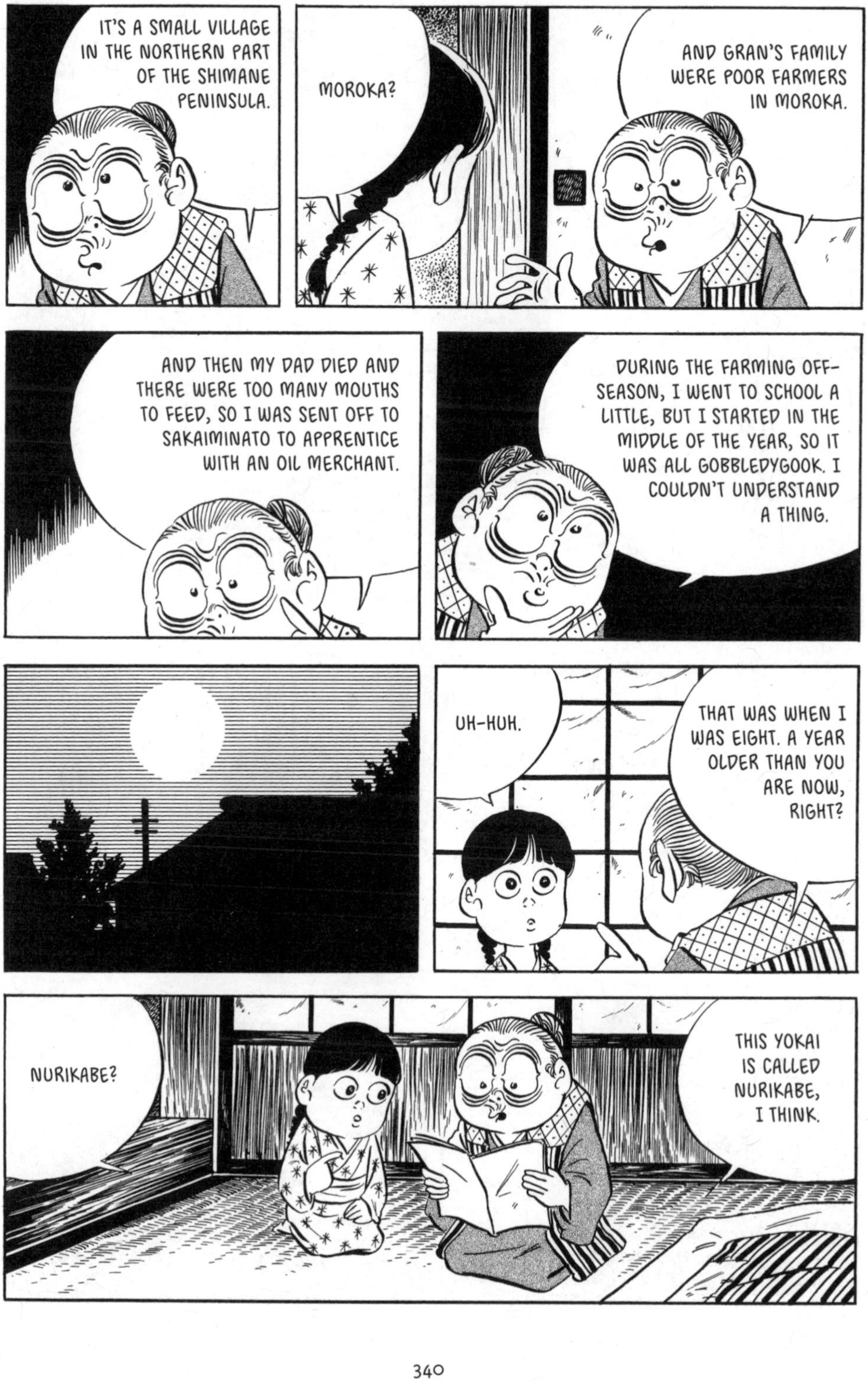
AND GRAN'S FAMILY WERE POOR FARMERS IN MOROKA.
MOROKA?
IT'S A SMALL VILLAGE IN THE NORTHERN PART OF THE SHIMANE PENINSULA.
DURING THE FARMING OFF-SEASON, I WENT TO SCHOOL A LITTLE, BUT I STARTED IN THE MIDDLE OF THE YEAR, SO IT WAS ALL GOBBLEDYGOOK. I COULDN'T UNDERSTAND A THING.
AND THEN MY DAD DIED AND THERE WERE TOO MANY MOUTHS TO FEED, SO I WAS SENT OFF TO SAKAIMINATO TO APPRENTICE WITH AN OIL MERCHANT.
THAT WAS WHEN I WAS EIGHT. A YEAR OLDER THAN YOU ARE NOW, RIGHT?
UH-HUH.
THIS YOKAI IS CALLED NURIKABE, I THINK.
NURIKABE?

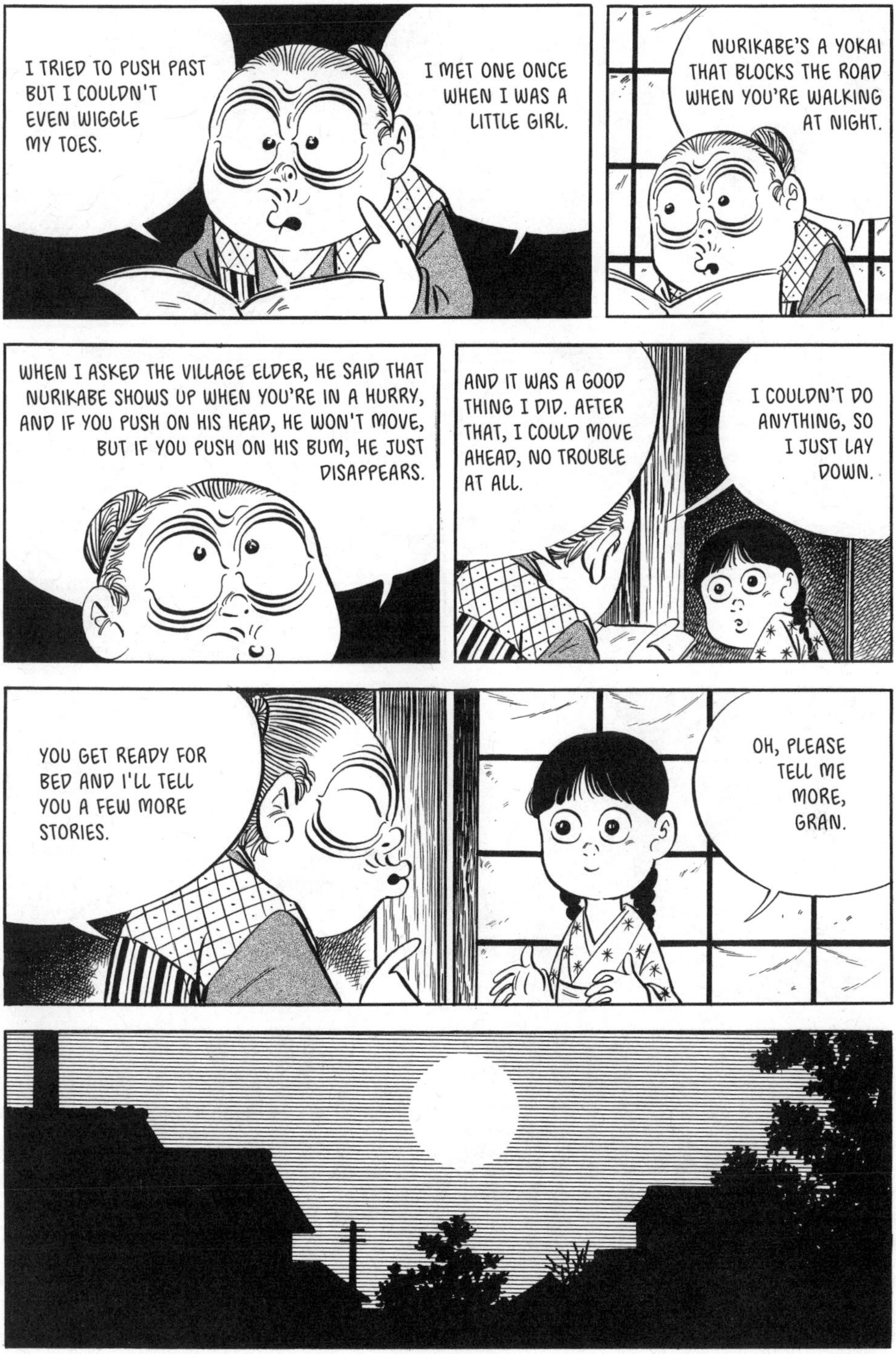
NURIKABE'S A YOKAI THAT BLOCKS THE ROAD WHEN YOU'RE WALKING AT NIGHT.
I MET ONE ONCE WHEN I WAS A LITTLE GIRL.
I TRIED TO PUSH PAST BUT I COULDN'T EVEN WIGGLE MY TOES.
I COULDN'T DO ANYTHING, SO I JUST LAY DOWN.
AND IT WAS A GOOD THING I DID. AFTER THAT, I COULD MOVE AHEAD, NO TROUBLE AT ALL.
WHEN I ASKED THE VILLAGE ELDER, HE SAID THAT NURIKABE SHOWS UP WHEN YOU'RE IN A HURRY, AND IF YOU PUSH ON HIS HEAD, HE WON'T MOVE, BUT IF YOU PUSH ON HIS BUM, HE JUST DISAPPEARS.
OH, PLEASE TELL ME MORE, GRAN.
YOU GET READY FOR BED AND I'LL TELL YOU A FEW MORE STORIES.

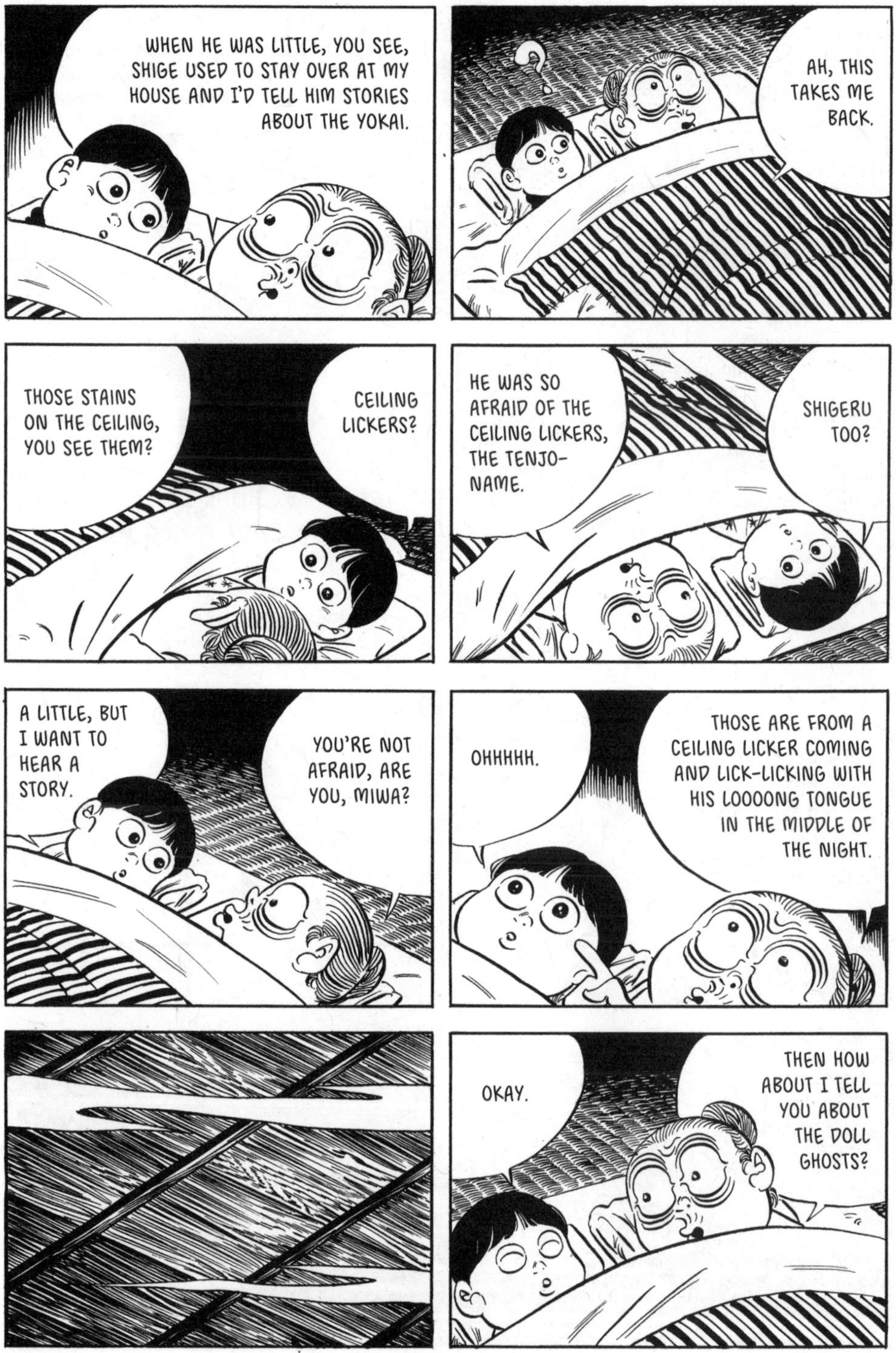
AH, THIS TAKES ME BACK.
WHEN HE WAS LITTLE, YOU SEE, SHIGE USED TO STAY OVER AT MY HOUSE AND I'D TELL HIM STORIES ABOUT THE YOKAI.
SHIGERU TOO?
HE WAS SO AFRAID OF THE CEILING LICKERS, THE TENJO-NAME.
CEILING LICKERS?
THOSE STAINS ON THE CEILING, YOU SEE THEM?
THOSE ARE FROM A CEILING LICKER COMING AND LICK-LICKING WITH HIS LOOOONG TONGUE IN THE MIDDLE OF THE NIGHT.
OHHHHH.
YOU'RE NOT AFRAID, ARE YOU, MIWA?
A LITTLE, BUT I WANT TO HEAR A STORY.
THEN HOW ABOUT I TELL YOU ABOUT THE DOLL GHOSTS?
OKAY.

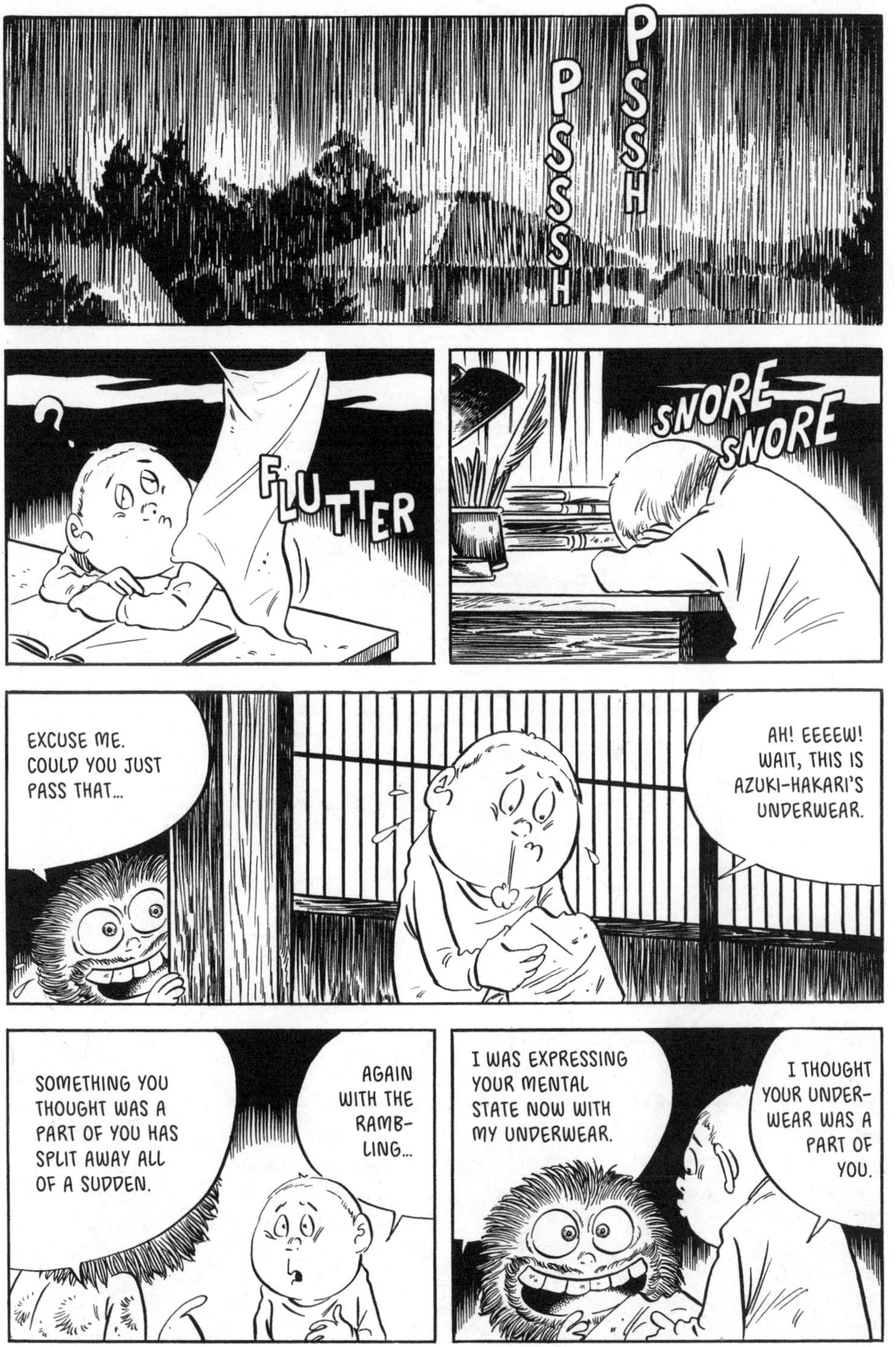
PSSH
PSSSH
SNORE SNORE
?
FLUTTER
AH! EEEEW! WAIT, THIS IS AZUKI-HAKARI'S UNDERWEAR.
EXCUSE ME. COULD YOU JUST PASS THAT...
I THOUGHT YOUR UNDER-WEAR WAS A PART OF YOU.
I WAS EXPRESSING YOUR MENTAL STATE NOW WITH MY UNDERWEAR.
AGAIN WITH THE RAMB-LING...
SOMETHING YOU THOUGHT WAS A PART OF YOU HAS SPLIT AWAY ALL OF A SUDDEN.

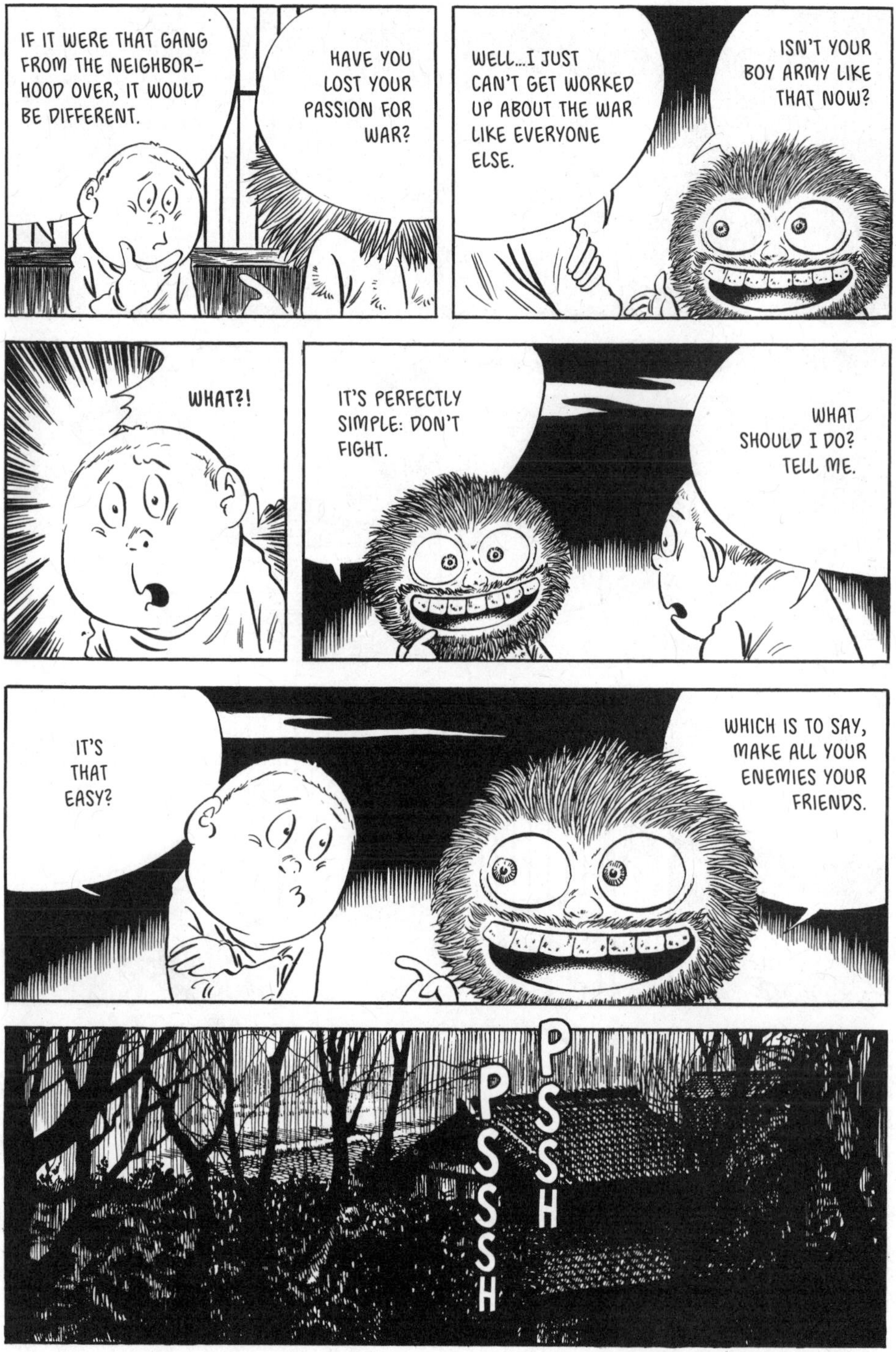
ISN'T YOUR BOY ARMY LIKE THAT NOW?
WELL...I JUST CAN'T GET WORKED UP ABOUT THE WAR LIKE EVERYONE ELSE.
HAVE YOU LOST YOUR PASSION FOR WAR?
IF IT WERE THAT GANG FROM THE NEIGHBOR-HOOD OVER, IT WOULD BE DIFFERENT.
WHAT SHOULD I DO? TELL ME.
IT'S PERFECTLY SIMPLE: DON'T FIGHT.
WHAT?!
WHICH IS TO SAY, MAKE ALL YOUR ENEMIES YOUR FRIENDS.
IT'S THAT EASY?
PSSH
PSSSH

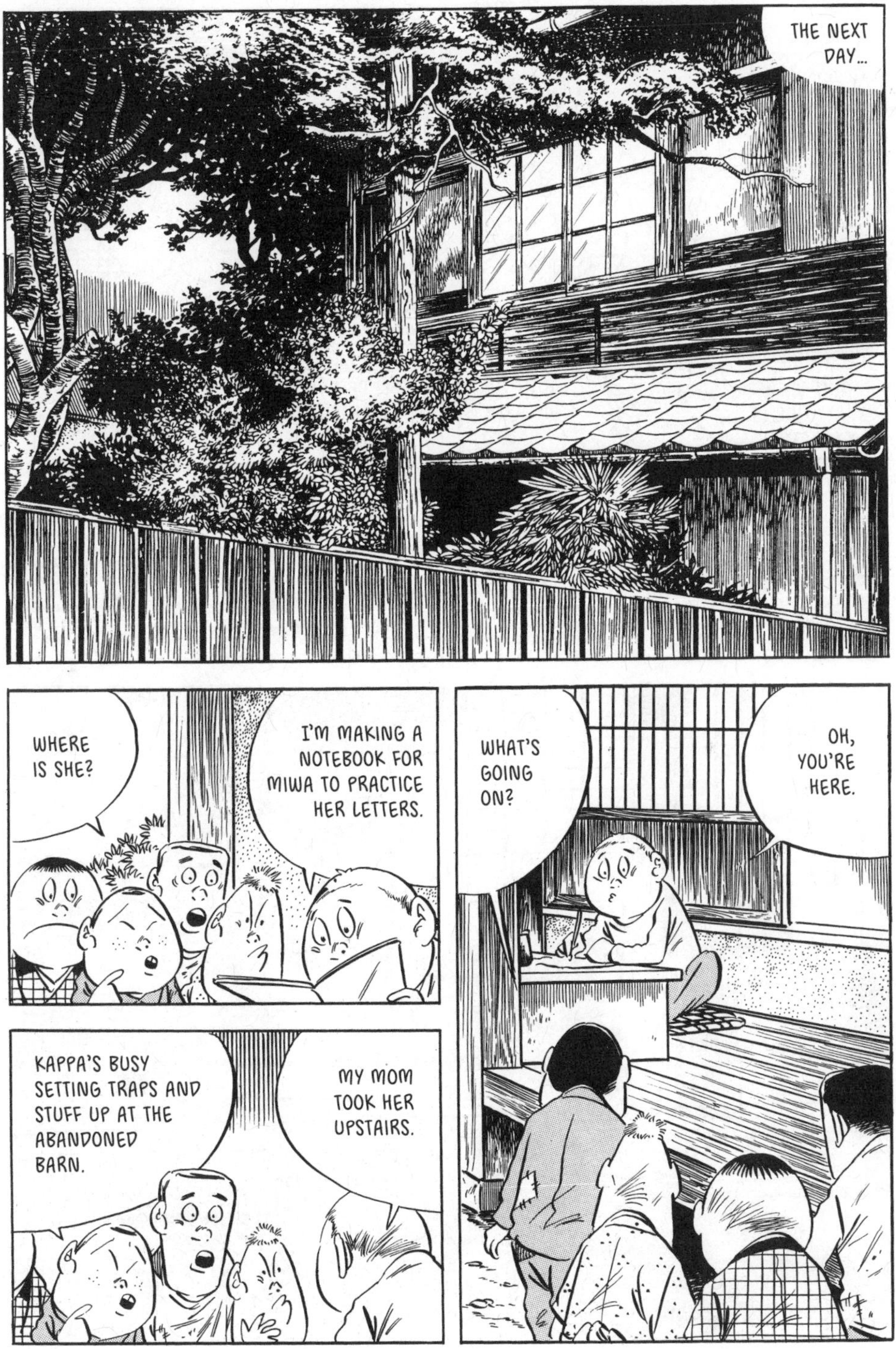
THE NEXT DAY...
OH, YOU'RE HERE.
WHAT'S GOING ON?
I'M MAKING A NOTEBOOK FOR MIWA TO PRACTICE HER LETTERS.
WHERE IS SHE?
MY MOM TOOK HER UPSTAIRS.
KAPPA'S BUSY SETTING TRAPS AND STUFF UP AT THE ABANDONED BARN.

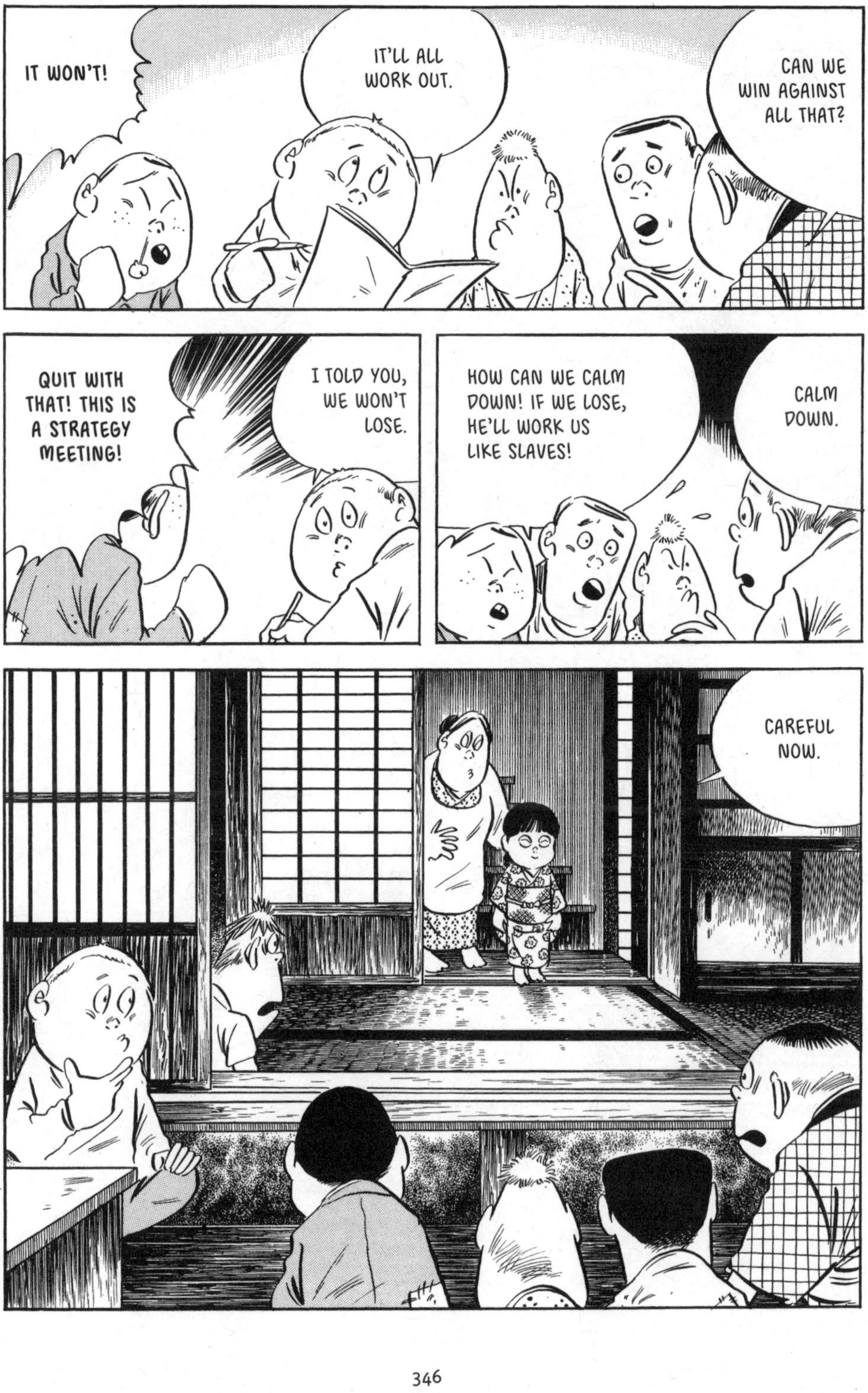
CAN WE WIN AGAINST ALL THAT?
IT'LL ALL WORK OUT.
IT WON'T!
CALM DOWN.
HOW CAN WE CALM DOWN! IF WE LOSE, HE'LL WORK US LIKE SLAVES!
I TOLD YOU, WE WON'T LOSE.
QUIT WITH THAT! THIS IS A STRATEGY MEETING!
CAREFUL NOW.

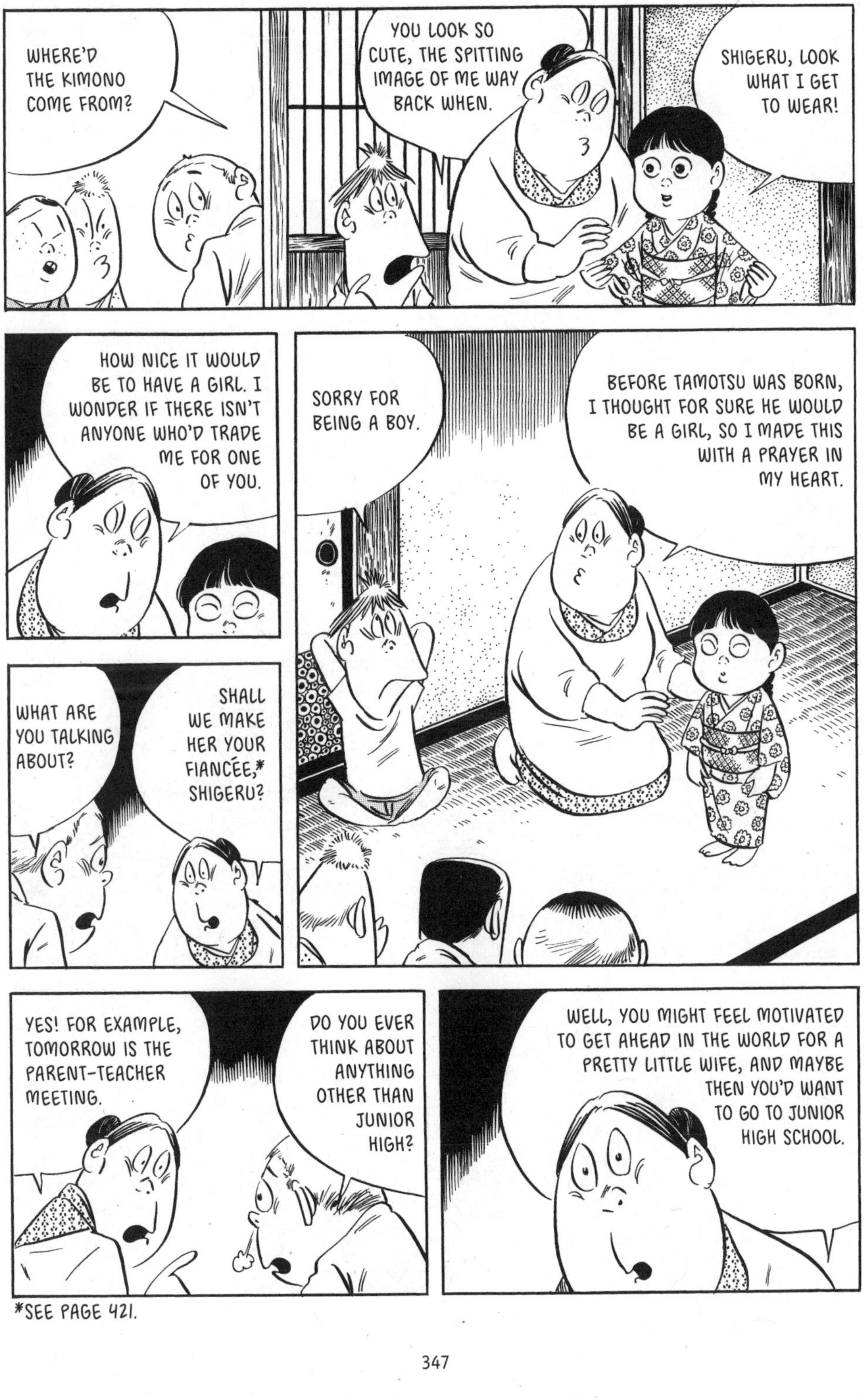
SHIGERU, LOOK WHAT I GET TO WEAR!
YOU LOOK SO CUTE, THE SPITTING IMAGE OF ME WAY BACK WHEN.
WHERE'D THE KIMONO COME FROM?
BEFORE TAMOTSU WAS BORN, I THOUGHT FOR SURE HE WOULD BE A GIRL, SO I MADE THIS WITH A PRAYER IN MY HEART.
SORRY FOR BEING A BOY.
HOW NICE IT WOULD BE TO HAVE A GIRL. I WONDER IF THERE ISN'T ANYONE WHO'D TRADE ME FOR ONE OF YOU.
SHALL WE MAKE HER YOUR FIANCÉE,* SHIGERU?
WHAT ARE YOU TALKING ABOUT?
WELL, YOU MIGHT FEEL MOTIVATED TO GET AHEAD IN THE WORLD FOR A PRETTY LITTLE WIFE, AND MAYBE THEN YOU'D WANT TO GO TO JUNIOR HIGH SCHOOL.
DO YOU EVER THINK ABOUT ANYTHING OTHER THAN JUNIOR HIGH?
YES! FOR EXAMPLE, TOMORROW IS THE PARENT-TEACHER MEETING.

*SEE PAGE 421.

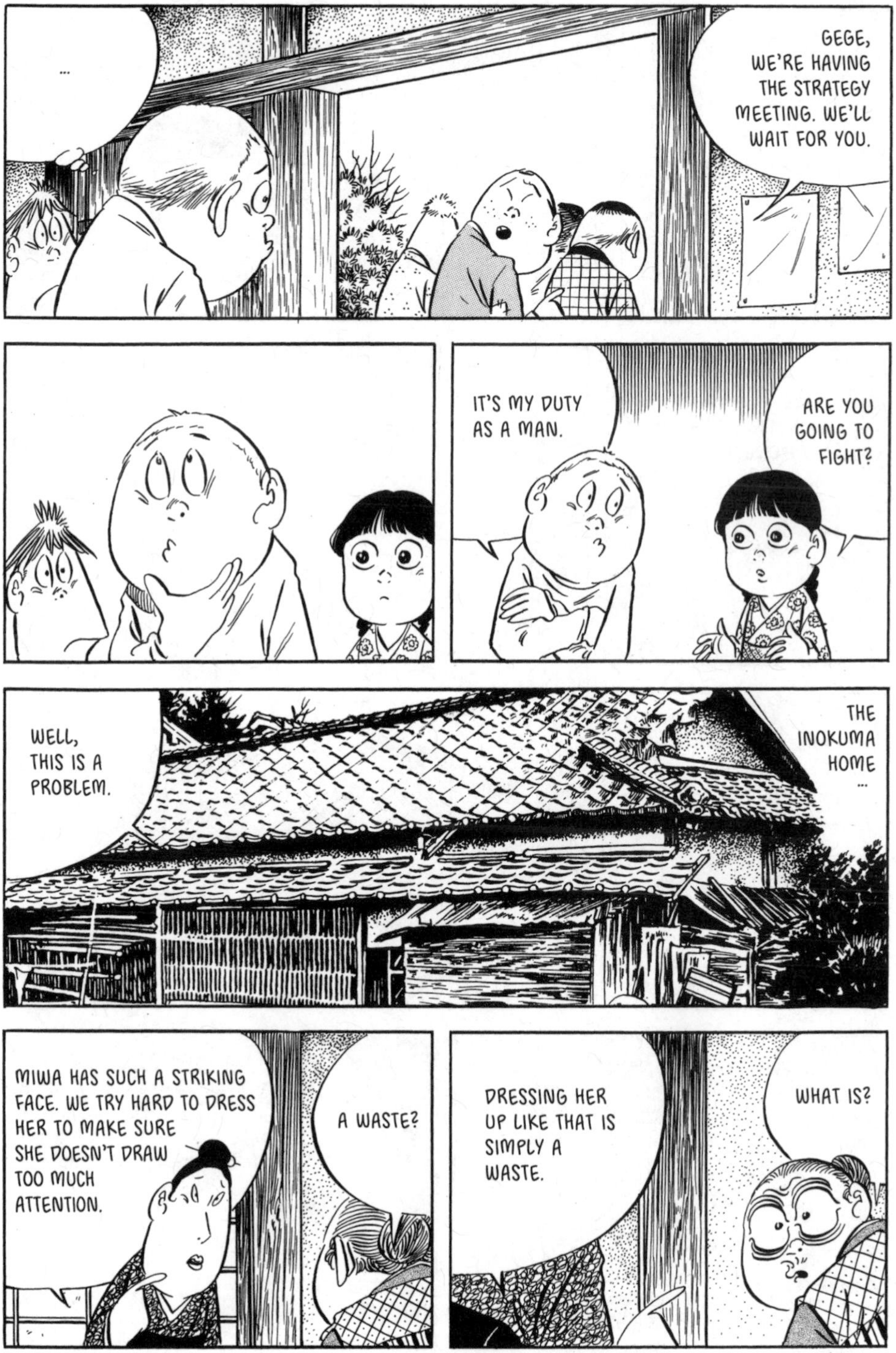
GEGE, WE'RE HAVING THE STRATEGY MEETING. WE'LL WAIT FOR YOU.
...
ARE YOU GOING TO FIGHT?
IT'S MY DUTY AS A MAN.
THE INOKUMA HOME ...
WELL, THIS IS A PROBLEM.
WHAT IS?
DRESSING HER UP LIKE THAT IS SIMPLY A WASTE.
A WASTE?
MIWA HAS SUCH A STRIKING FACE. WE TRY HARD TO DRESS HER TO MAKE SURE SHE DOESN'T DRAW TOO MUCH ATTENTION.

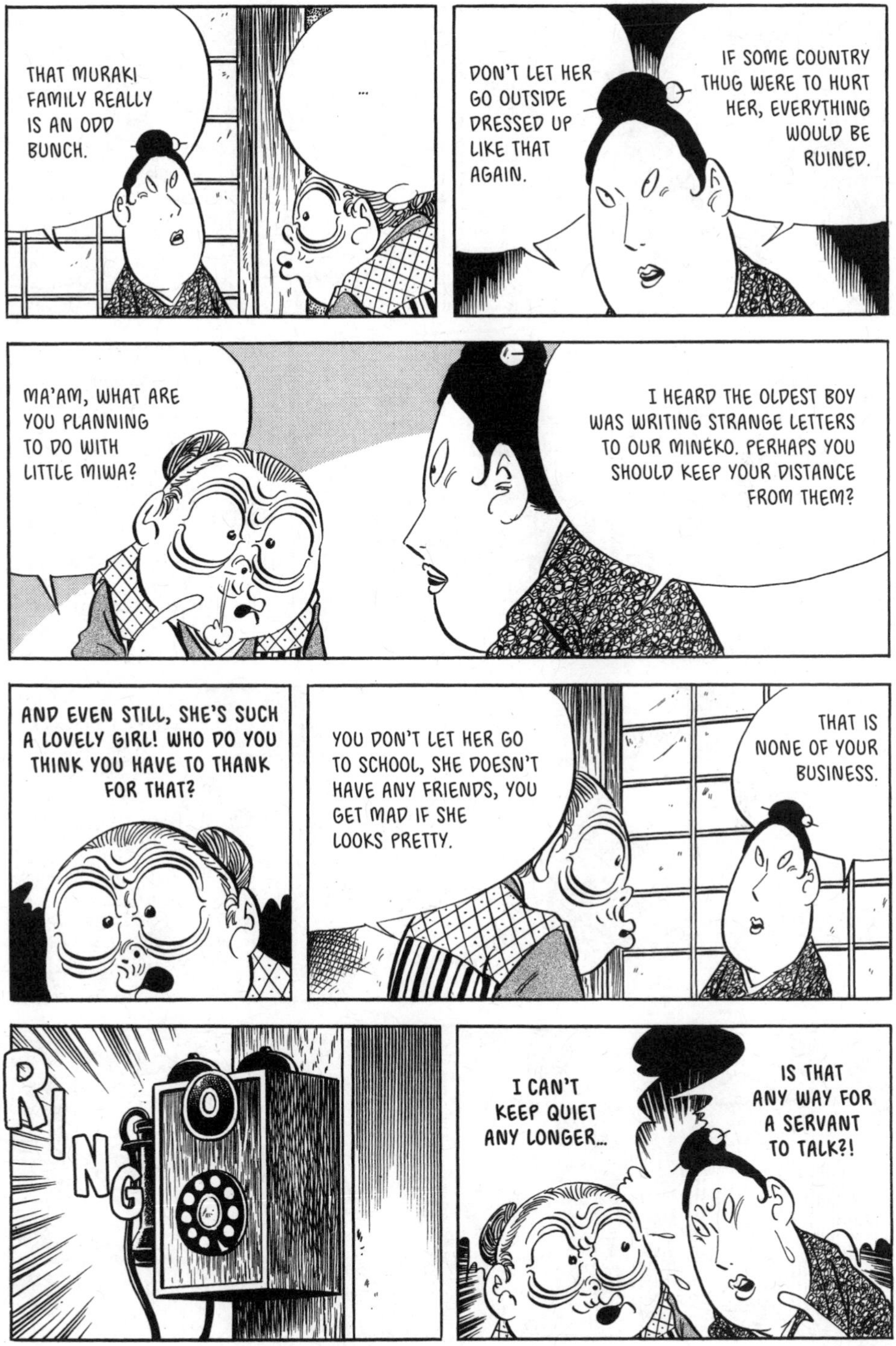
IF SOME COUNTRY THUG WERE TO HURT HER, EVERYTHING WOULD BE RUINED.
DON'T LET HER GO OUTSIDE DRESSED UP LIKE THAT AGAIN.
...
THAT MURAKI FAMILY REALLY IS AN ODD BUNCH.
I HEARD THE OLDEST BOY WAS WRITING STRANGE LETTERS TO OUR MINEKO. PERHAPS YOU SHOULD KEEP YOUR DISTANCE FROM THEM?
MA'AM, WHAT ARE YOU PLANNING TO DO WITH LITTLE MIWA?
THAT IS NONE OF YOUR BUSINESS.
YOU DON'T LET HER GO TO SCHOOL, SHE DOESN'T HAVE ANY FRIENDS, YOU GET MAD IF SHE LOOKS PRETTY.
AND EVEN STILL, SHE'S SUCH A LOVELY GIRL! WHO DO YOU THINK YOU HAVE TO THANK FOR THAT?
IS THAT ANY WAY FOR A SERVANT TO TALK?!
I CAN'T KEEP QUIET ANY LONGER...
RING

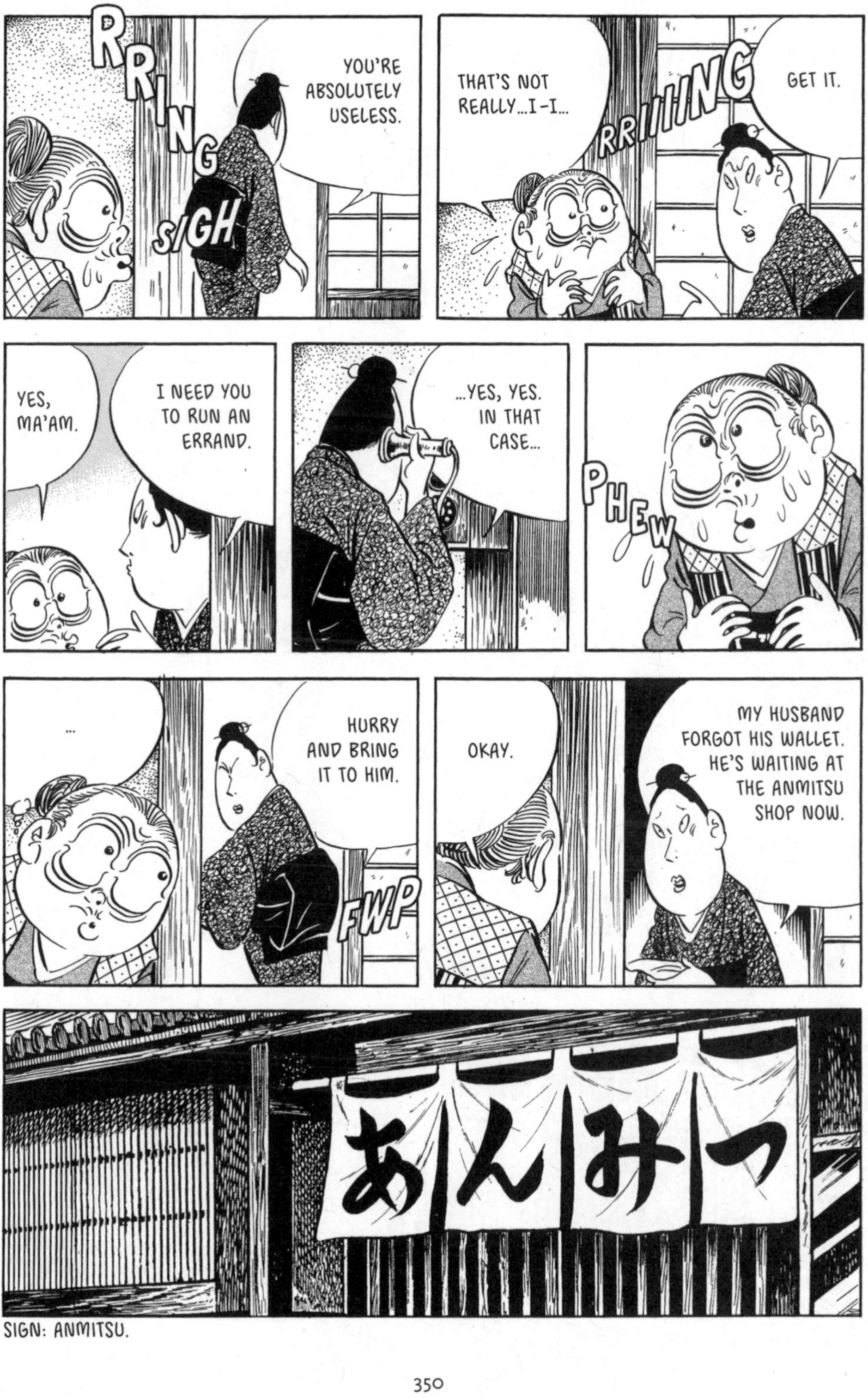
GET IT.
RRIIIIING
THAT'S NOT REALLY...I-I...
YOU'RE ABSOLUTELY USELESS.
RRING
SIGH
PHEW
...YES, YES. IN THAT CASE...
I NEED YOU TO RUN AN ERRAND.
YES, MA'AM.
MY HUSBAND FORGOT HIS WALLET. HE'S WAITING AT THE ANMITSU SHOP NOW.
OKAY.
HURRY AND BRING IT TO HIM.
FWP
...
あんみつ
SIGN: ANMITSU.

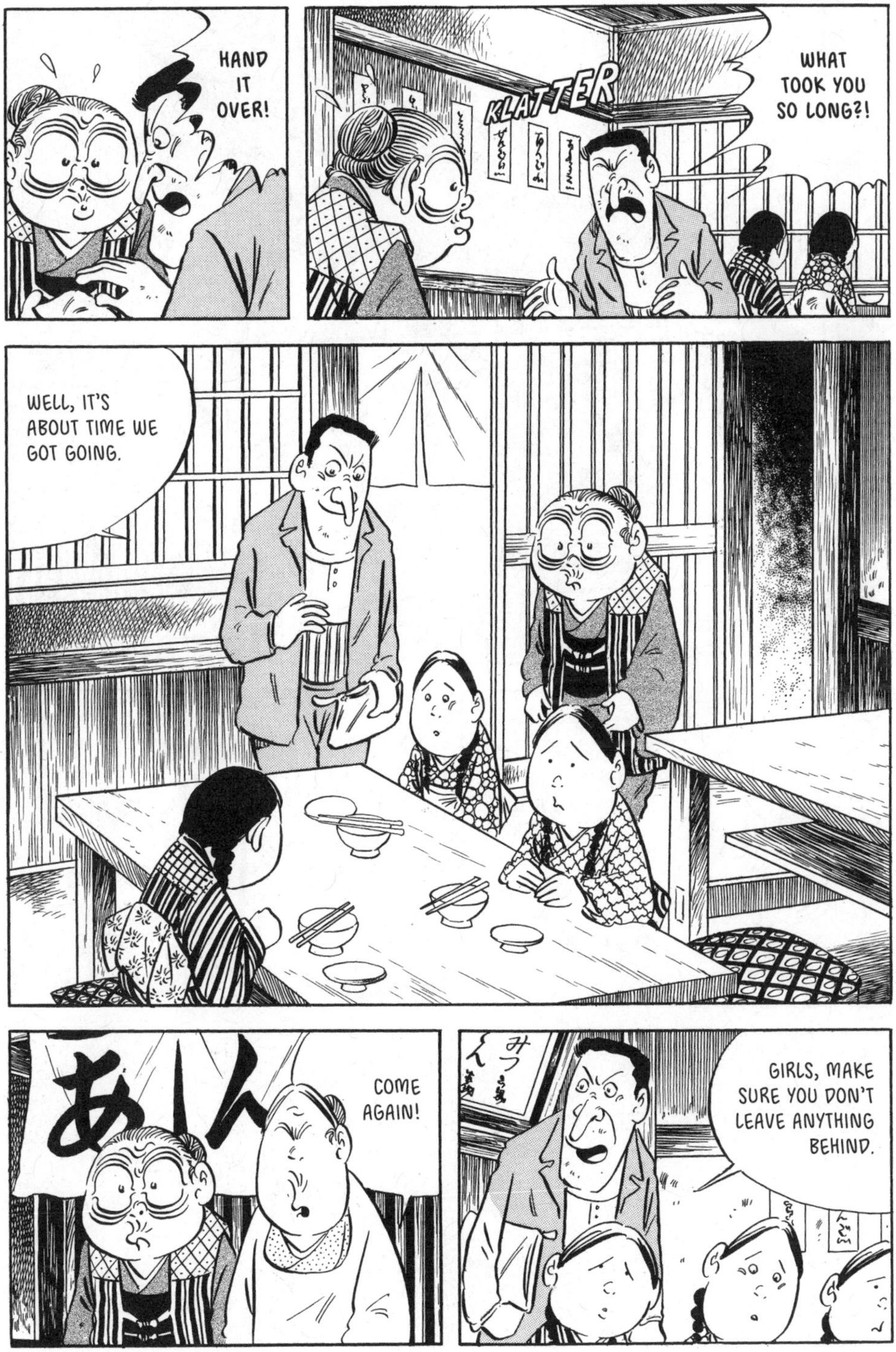
KLATTER
WHAT TOOK YOU SO LONG?!
HAND IT OVER!
WELL, IT'S ABOUT TIME WE GOT GOING.
GIRLS, MAKE SURE YOU DON'T LEAVE ANYTHING BEHIND.
あん
COME AGAIN!

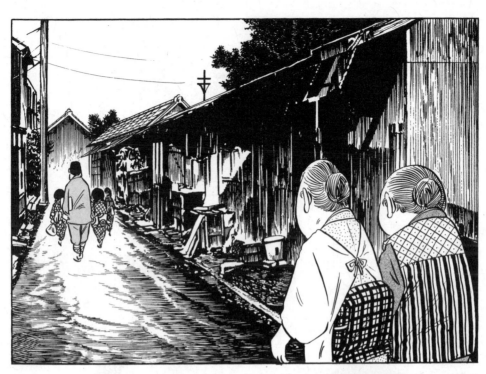

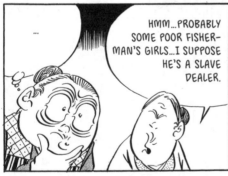

HE SAID THEY'RE HEADED FOR KOBE.
WHERE ARE THE GIRLS FROM?
HMM...PROBABLY SOME POOR FISHER-MAN'S GIRLS...I SUPPOSE HE'S A SLAVE DEALER.
...

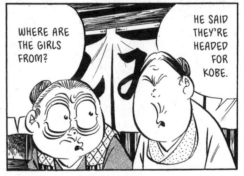

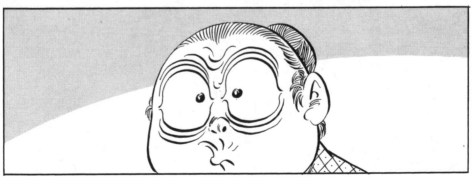

DUEL

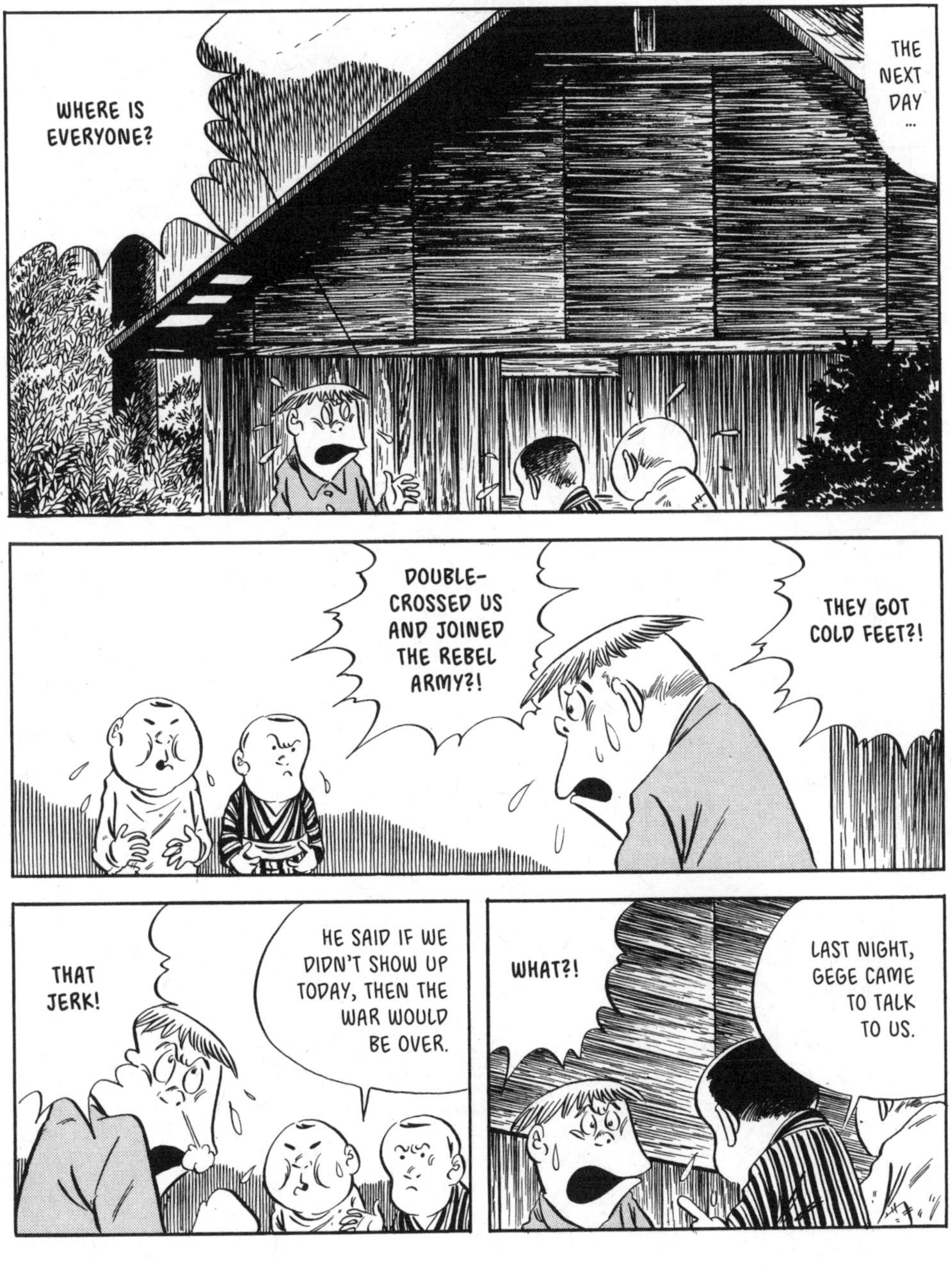
THE NEXT DAY ...
WHERE IS EVERYONE?
THEY GOT COLD FEET?!
DOUBLE-CROSSED US AND JOINED THE REBEL ARMY?!
LAST NIGHT, GEGE CAME TO TALK TO US.
WHAT?!
HE SAID IF WE DIDN'T SHOW UP TODAY, THEN THE WAR WOULD BE OVER.
THAT JERK!

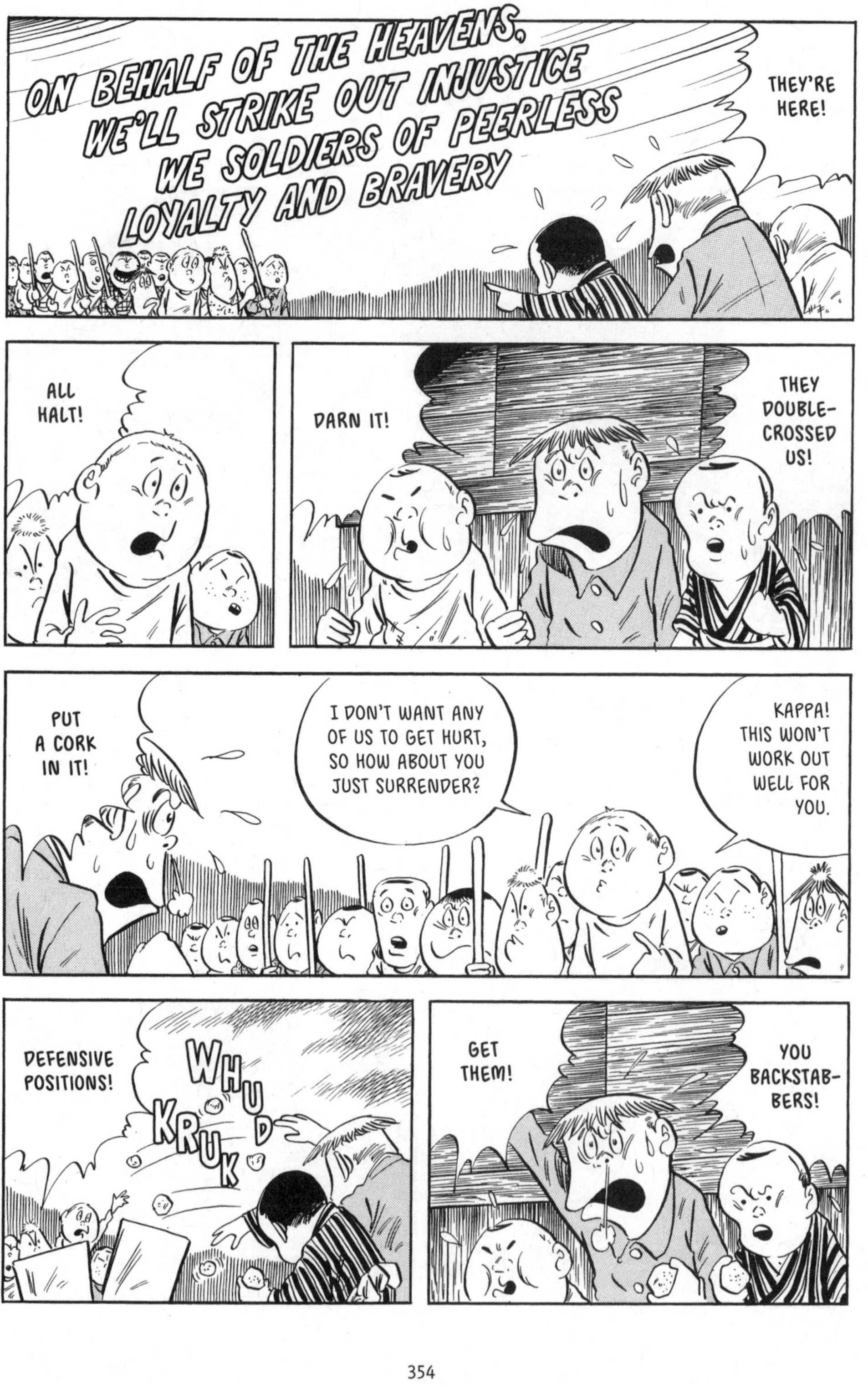
ON BEHALF OF THE HEAVENS, WE'LL STRIKE OUT INJUSTICE WE SOLDIERS OF PEERLESS LOYALTY AND BRAVERY
THEY'RE HERE!
THEY DOUBLE-CROSSED US!
DARN IT!
ALL HALT!
KAPPA! THIS WON'T WORK OUT WELL FOR YOU.
I DON'T WANT ANY OF US TO GET HURT, SO HOW ABOUT YOU JUST SURRENDER?
PUT A CORK IN IT!
YOU BACKSTAB-BERS!
GET THEM!
DEFENSIVE POSITIONS!
WHUD
KRUK

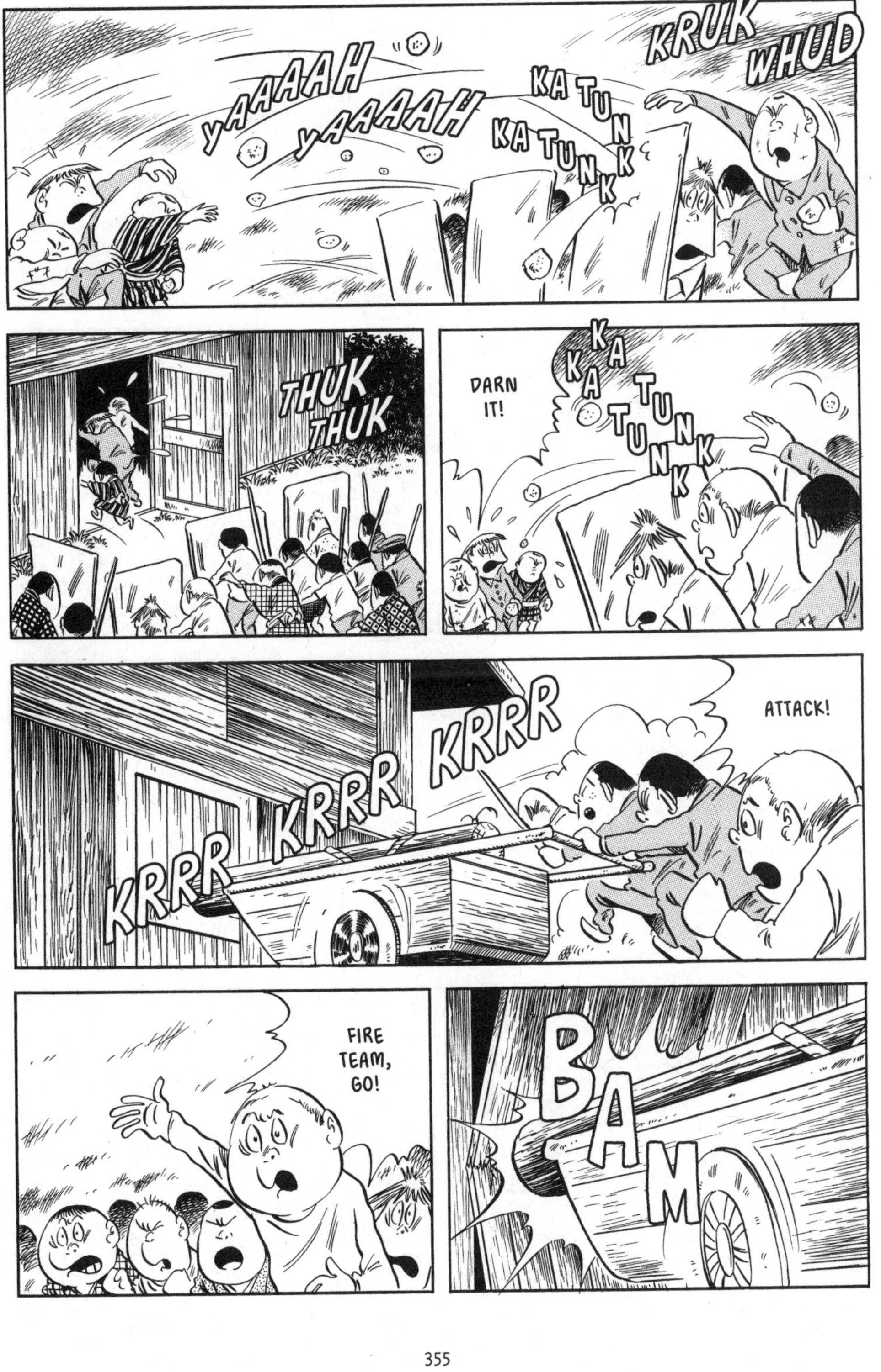
KRUK
WHUD
KA TUNK
KA TUNK
YAAAAAH
YAAAAH
DARN IT!
KA TUNK
KA TUNK
THUK THUK
ATTACK!
KRRR
KRRR
KRRR
BAM
FIRE TEAM, GO!

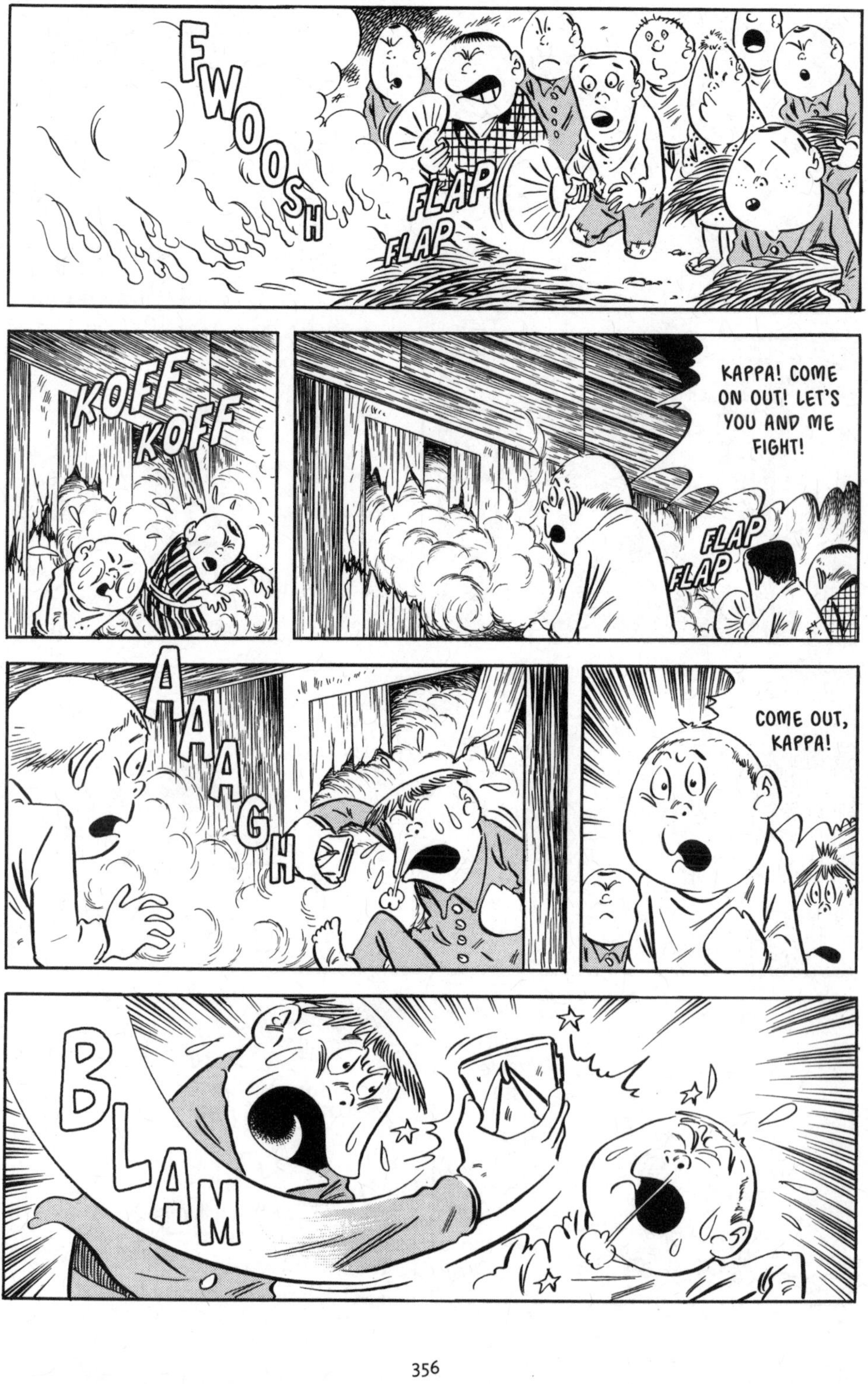
FWOOSH
FLAP
FLAP
KAPPA! COME ON OUT! LET'S YOU AND ME FIGHT!
FLAP
FLAP
KOFF
KOFF
COME OUT, KAPPA!
AAAAGH
BLAM

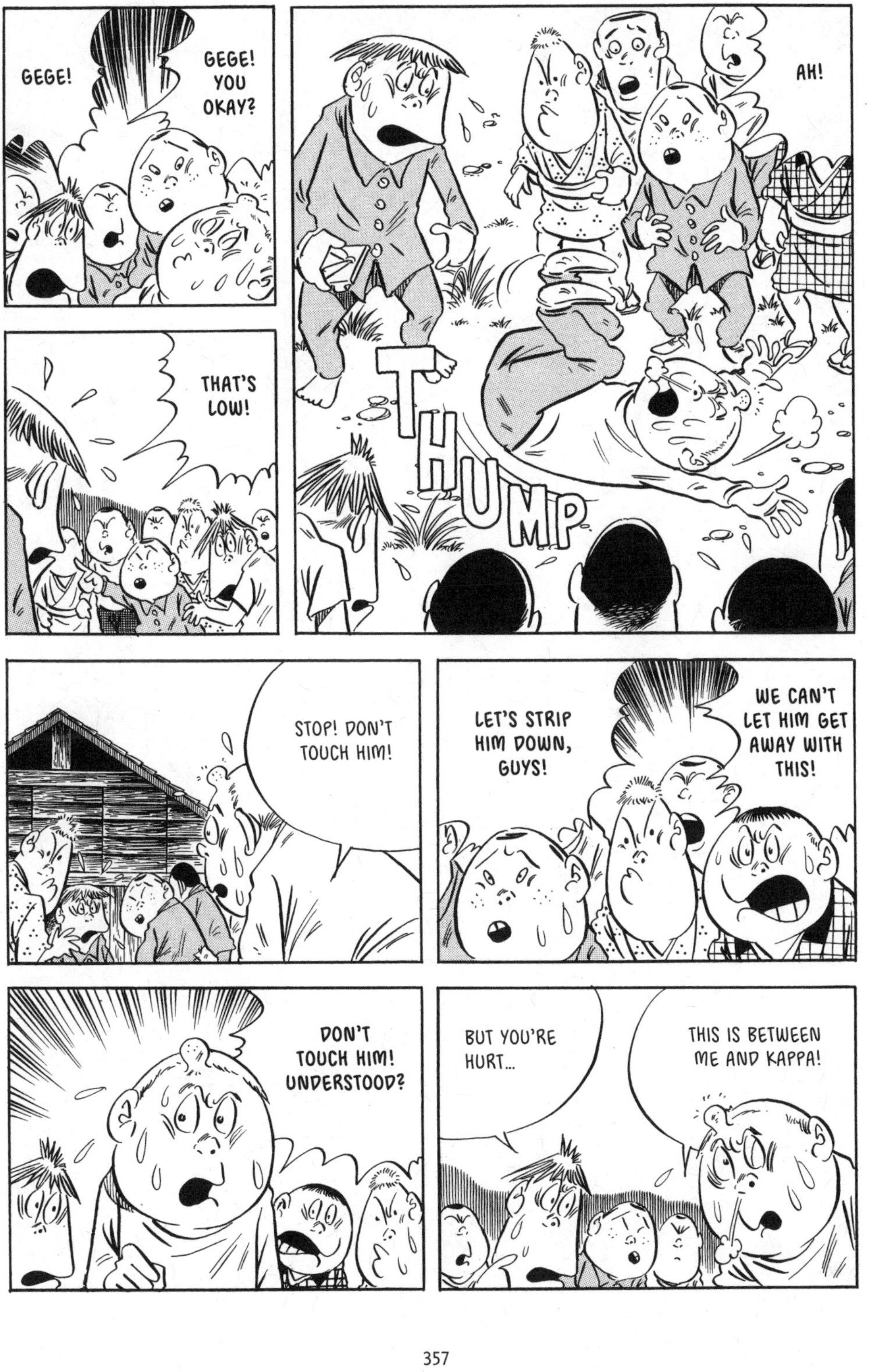
AH!
THUMP
GEGE! YOU OKAY?
GEGE!
THAT'S LOW!
WE CAN'T LET HIM GET AWAY WITH THIS!
LET'S STRIP HIM DOWN, GUYS!
STOP! DON'T TOUCH HIM!
THIS IS BETWEEN ME AND KAPPA!
BUT YOU'RE HURT...
DON'T TOUCH HIM! UNDERSTOOD?

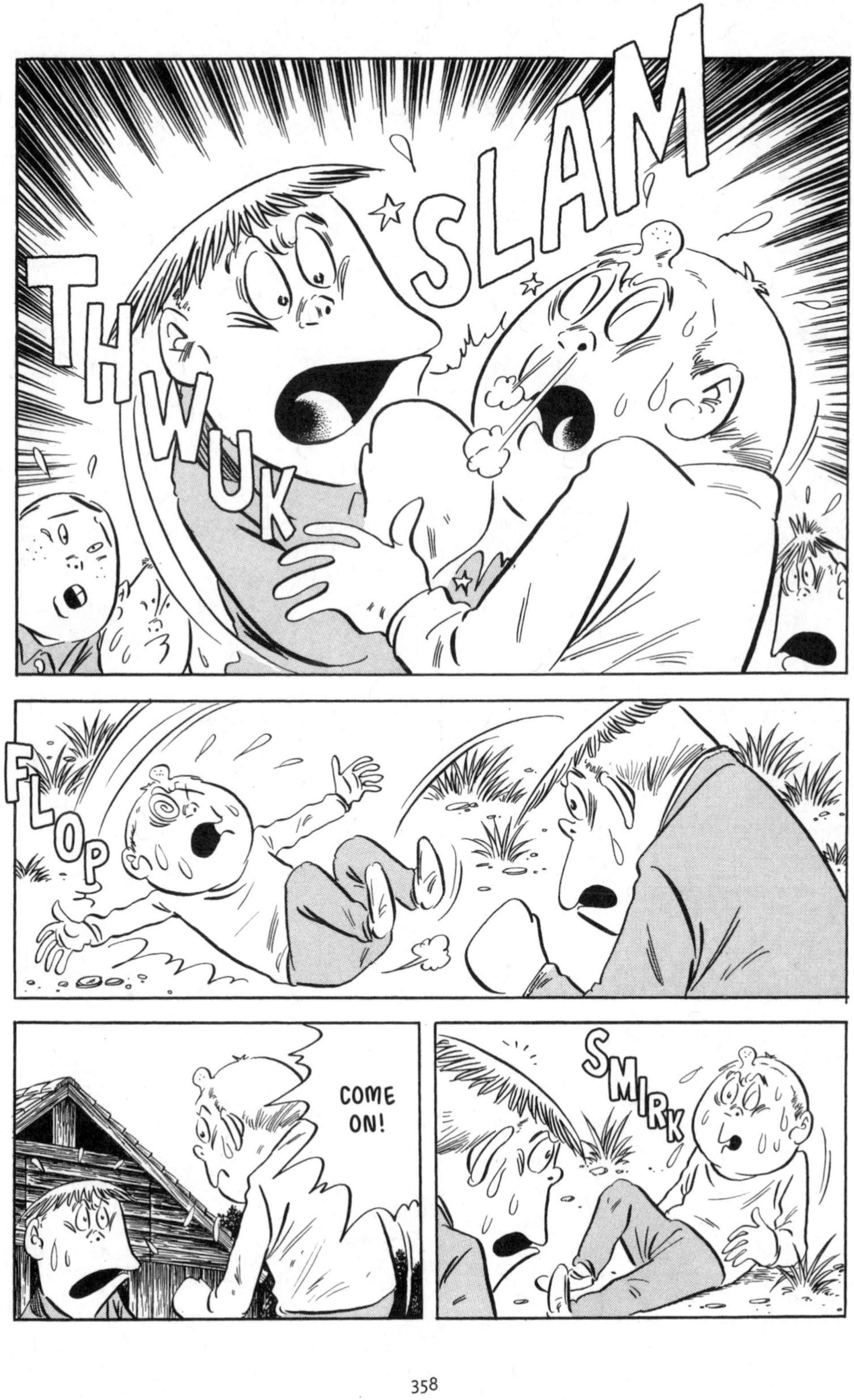
SLAM
THWUK
FLOP
SMIRK
COME ON!

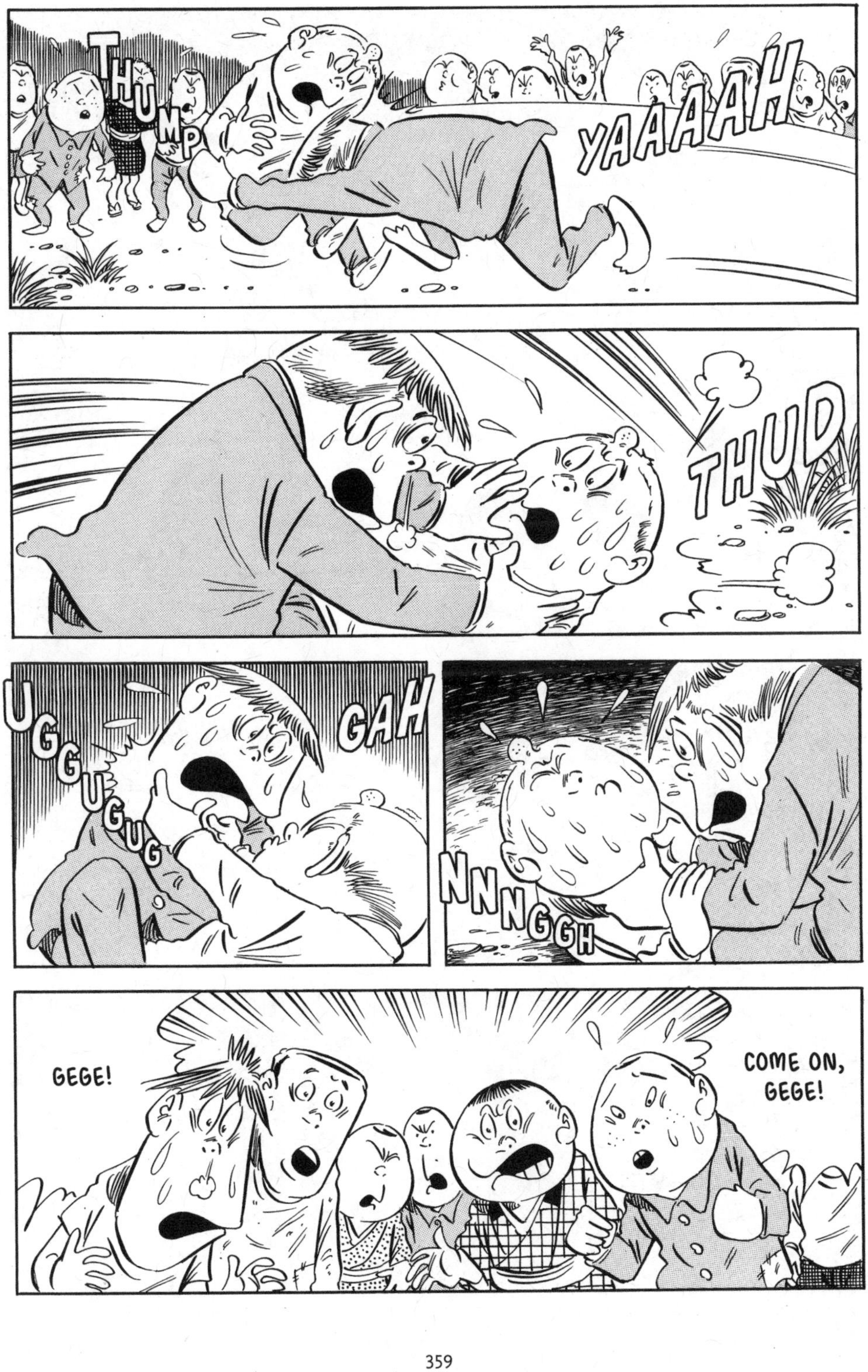
YAAAAAH
THUMP
THUD
NNNGGH
GAH
UGGUGUG
COME ON, GEGE!
GEGE!

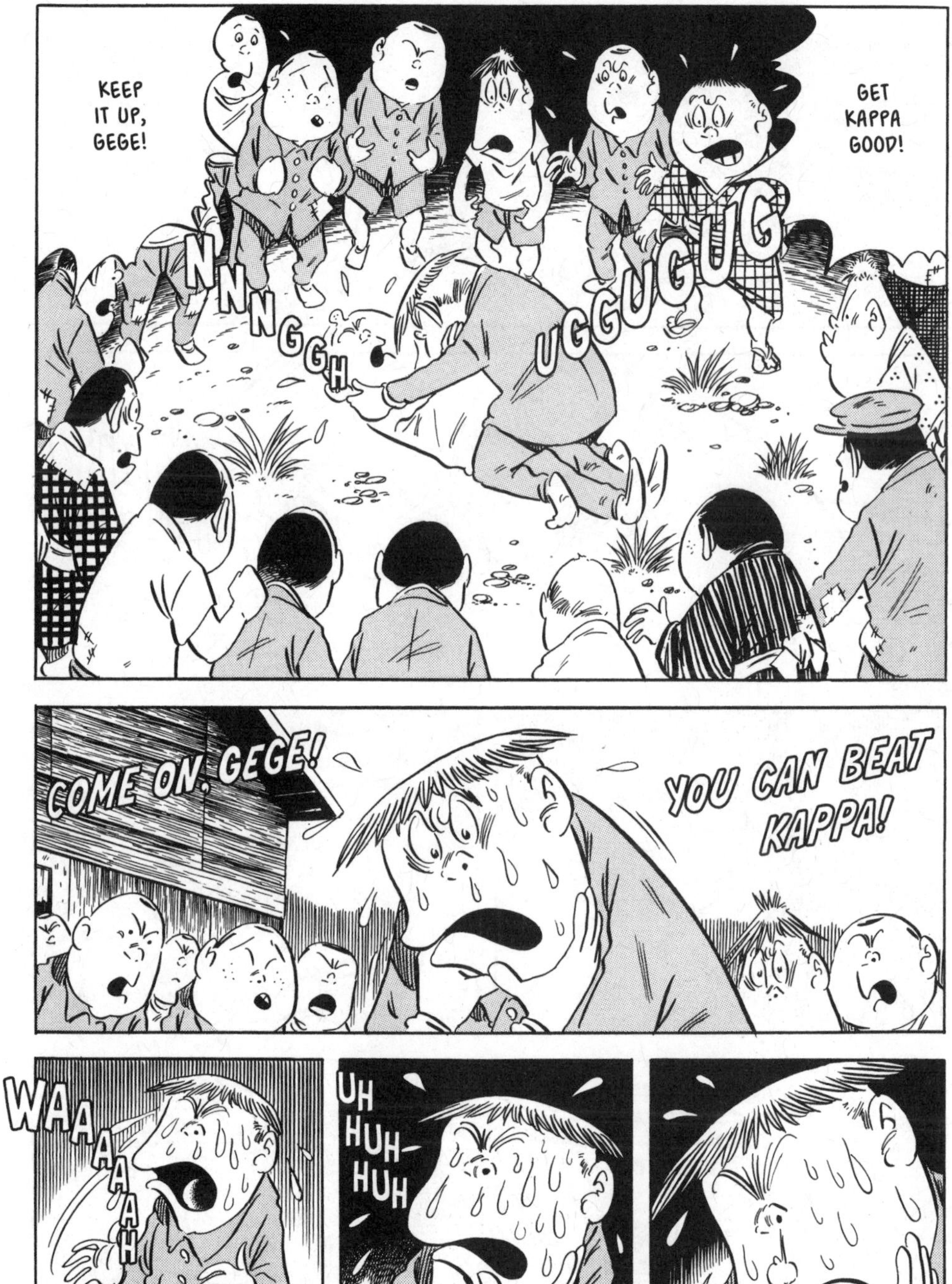
GET KAPPA GOOD!
KEEP IT UP, GEGE!
UGGUGUG
NNNGGH
YOU CAN BEAT KAPPA!
COME ON, GEGE!
UH HUH-HUH
WAAAAAH

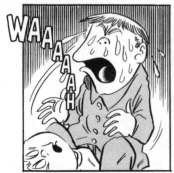

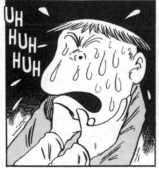

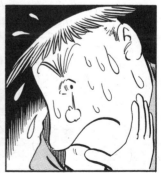

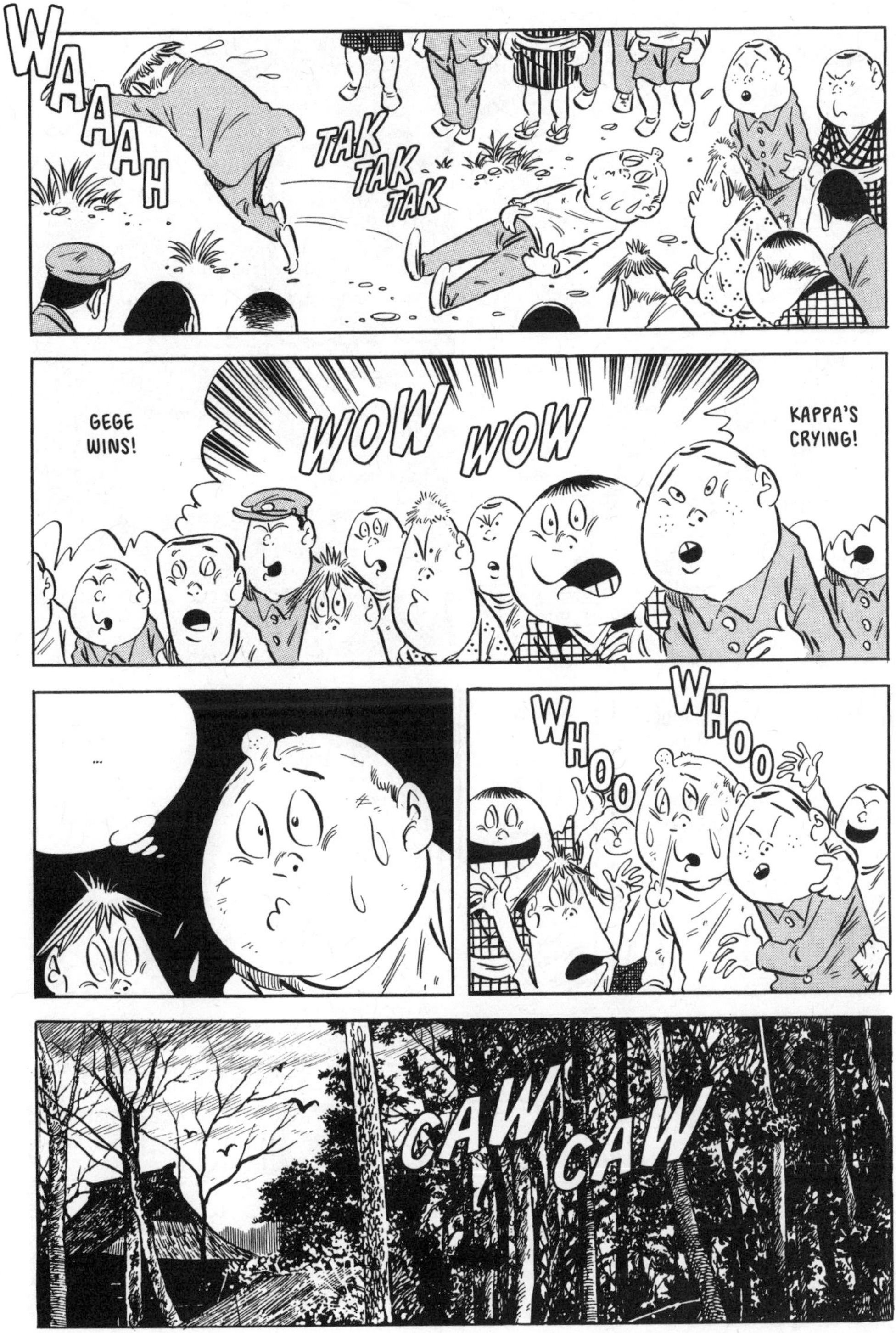
WAAAAH
TAK TAK TAK
KAPPA'S CRYING!
WOW WOW
GEGE WINS!
WHOO
WHOO
...
CAW CAW

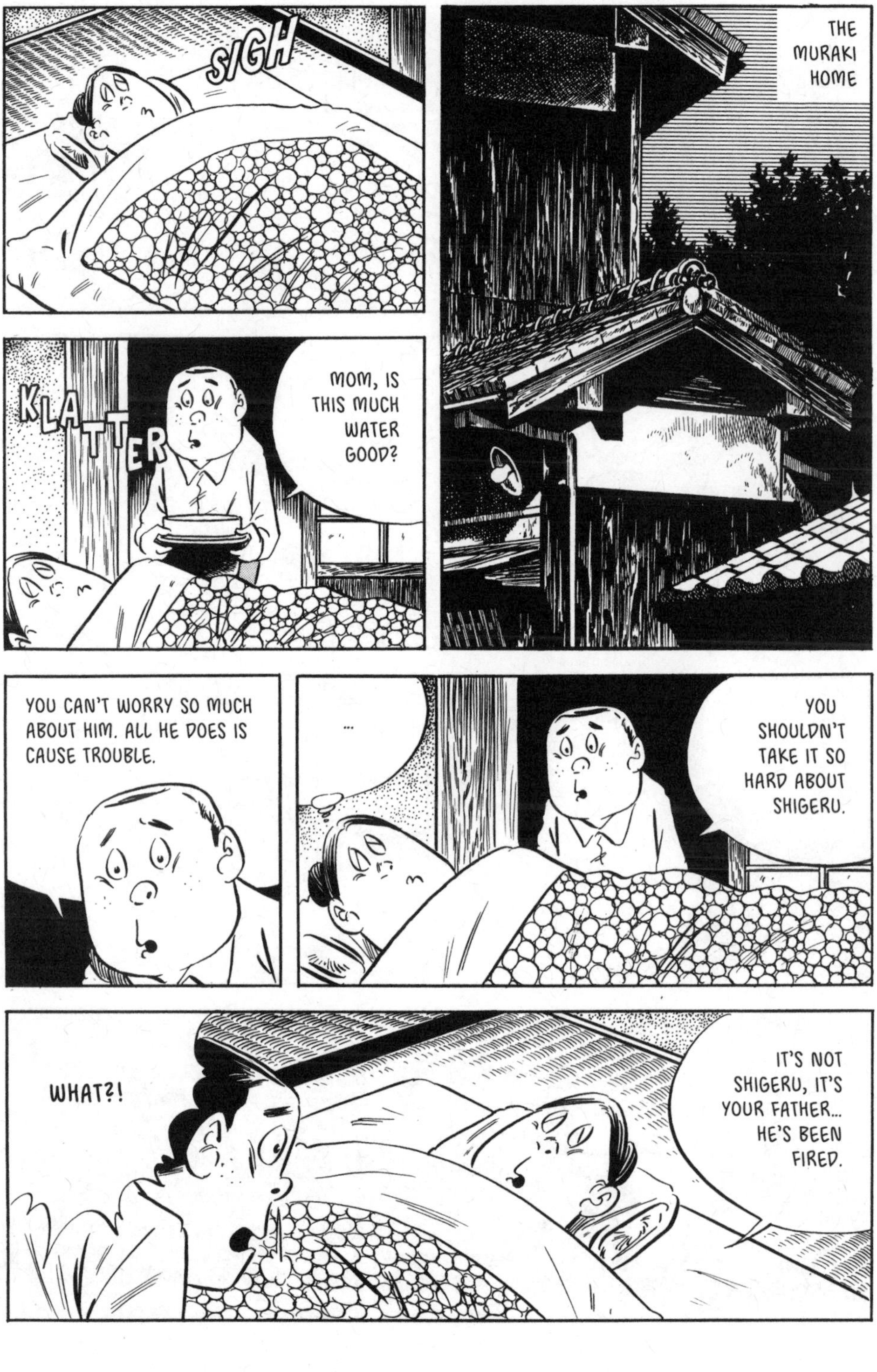
THE MURAKI HOME
SIGH
KLATTER
MOM, IS THIS MUCH WATER GOOD?
YOU SHOULDN'T TAKE IT SO HARD ABOUT SHIGERU.
...
YOU CAN'T WORRY SO MUCH ABOUT HIM. ALL HE DOES IS CAUSE TROUBLE.
IT'S NOT SHIGERU, IT'S YOUR FATHER... HE'S BEEN FIRED.
WHAT?!

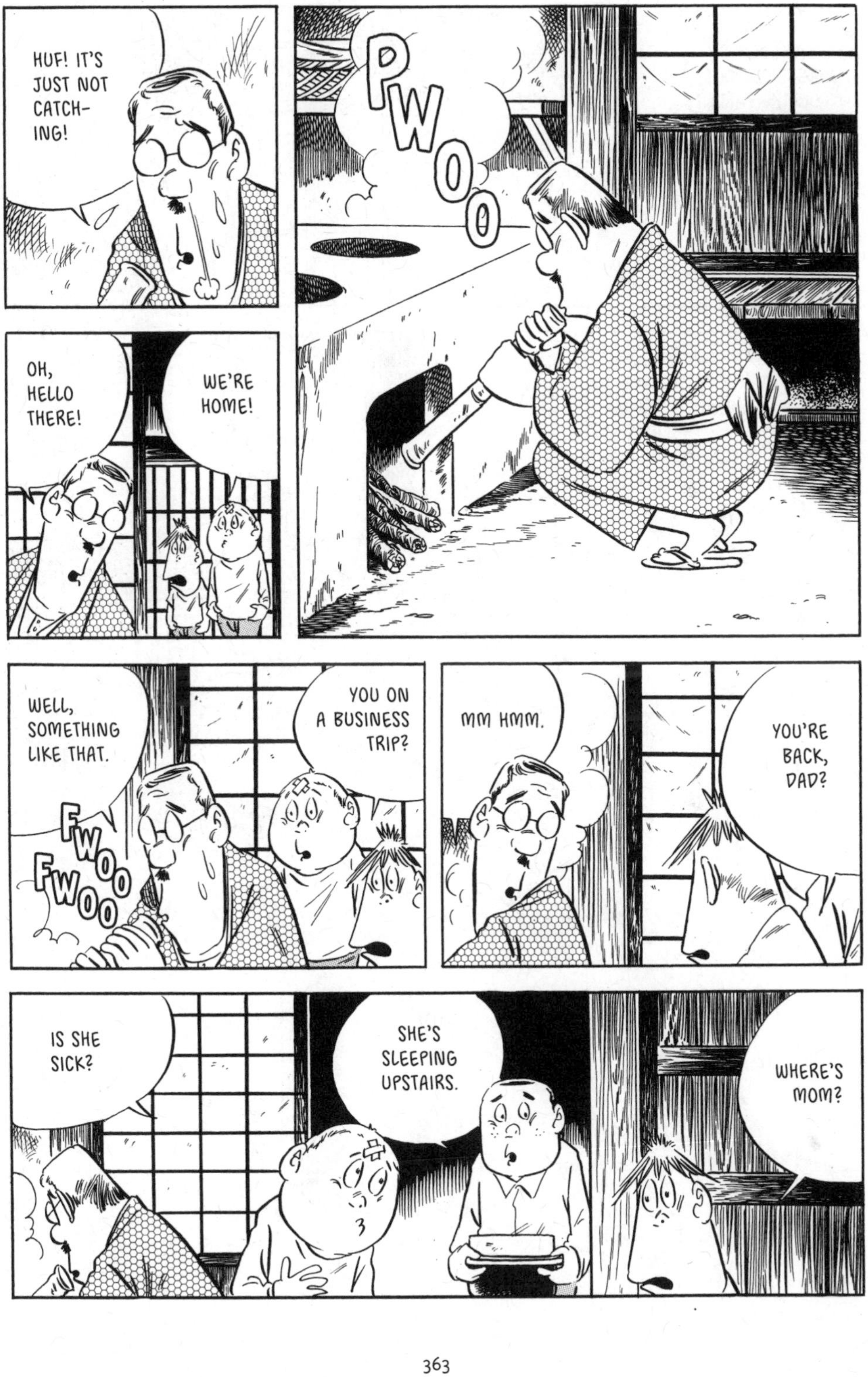
PWOOO
HUF! IT'S JUST NOT CATCHING!
WE'RE HOME!
OH, HELLO THERE!
YOU'RE BACK, DAD?
MM HMM.
YOU ON A BUSINESS TRIP?
WELL, SOMETHING LIKE THAT.
FWOO FWOO
WHERE'S MOM?
SHE'S SLEEPING UPSTAIRS.
IS SHE SICK?

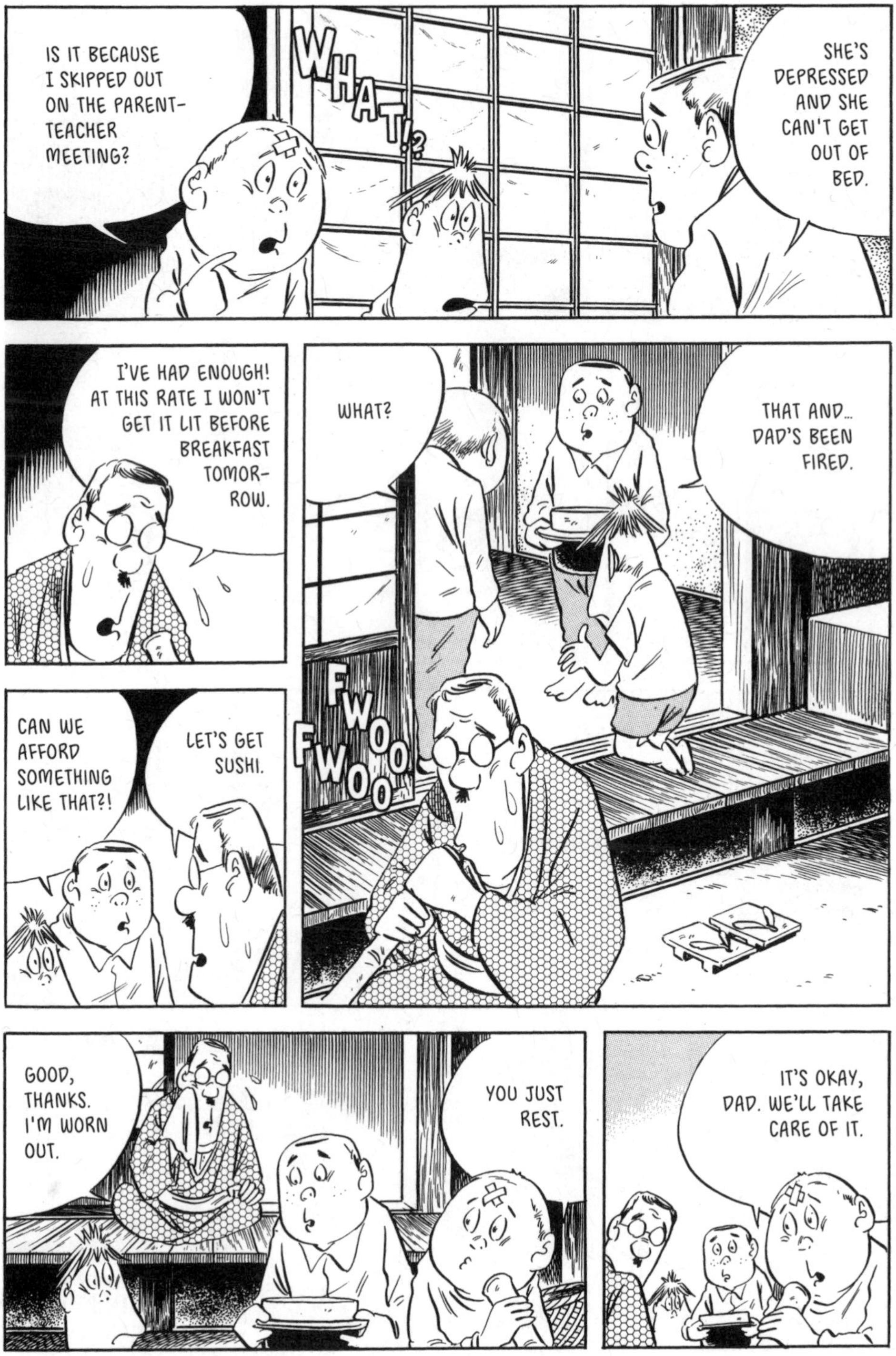
SHE'S DEPRESSED AND SHE CAN'T GET OUT OF BED.
WHAT!?
IS IT BECAUSE I SKIPPED OUT ON THE PARENT-TEACHER MEETING?
THAT AND... DAD'S BEEN FIRED.
WHAT?
FWOO FWOO
I'VE HAD ENOUGH! AT THIS RATE I WON'T GET IT LIT BEFORE BREAKFAST TOMOR-ROW.
LET'S GET SUSHI.
CAN WE AFFORD SOMETHING LIKE THAT?!
IT'S OKAY, DAD. WE'LL TAKE CARE OF IT.
YOU JUST REST.
GOOD, THANKS. I'M WORN OUT.

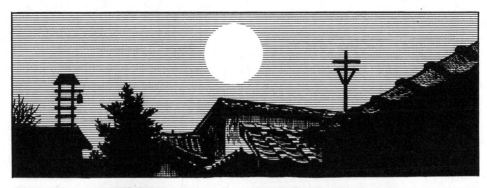

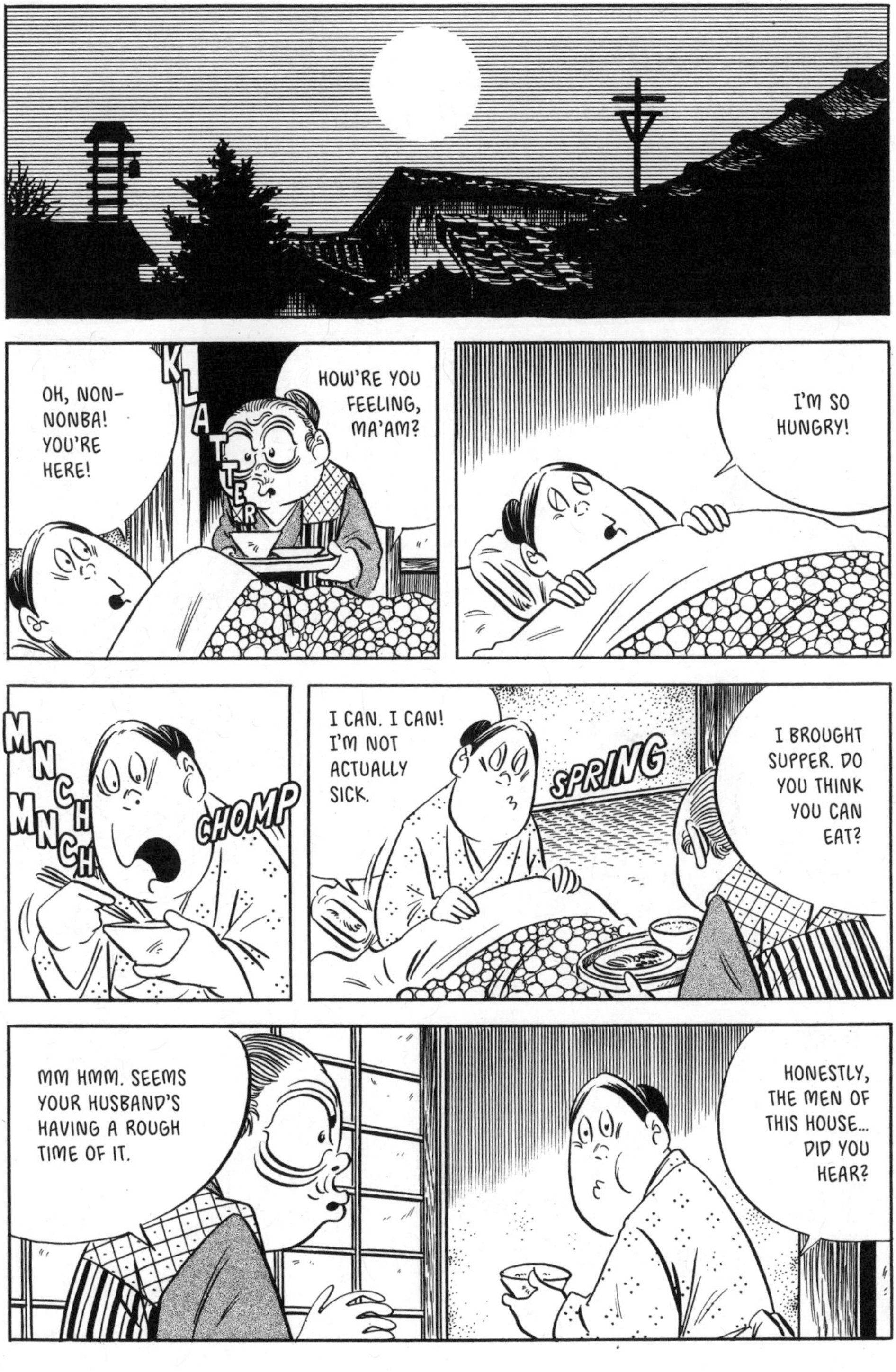
I'M SO HUNGRY!
HOW'RE YOU FEELING, MA'AM?
KLATTER
OH, NON-NONBA! YOU'RE HERE!
I BROUGHT SUPPER. DO YOU THINK YOU CAN EAT?
SPRING
I CAN. I CAN! I'M NOT ACTUALLY SICK.
CHOMP
MNCH MNCH
HONESTLY, THE MEN OF THIS HOUSE... DID YOU HEAR?
MM HMM. SEEMS YOUR HUSBAND'S HAVING A ROUGH TIME OF IT.

I HEARD THE MISSUS TALKING ON THE PHONE, AND, WELL, SHE'S GOING TO BE SOLD TO A GEISHA HOUSE IN KOBE.

WHAT?!

AND HE'S NOT THE ONLY ONE. LITTLE MIWA'S GOING TO BE SOLD.

REALLY?

TRUTH IS, THEY WERE SUPPOSED TO SEND HER SOONER, BUT THEY COULDN'T DECIDE ON A PRICE, SO THINGS GOT DRAWN OUT.

AND THAT'S WHY THEY WEREN'T SENDING HER TO SCHOOL.

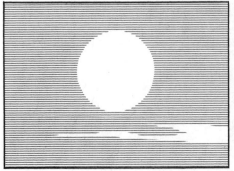

I BROUGHT YOU SOME TEA.

SORRY ABOUT EARLIER, MOM.

...

WHAT SHOULD I TELL SHIGE?

POOR LITTLE MIWA

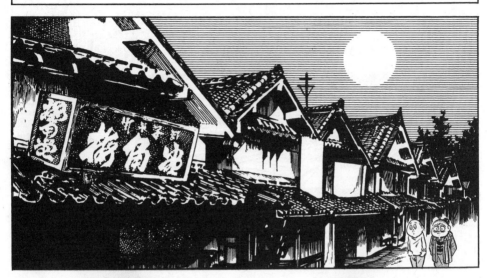

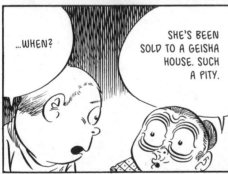

SHIGE, ABOUT MIWA, SHE'S BEING SENT TO KOBE.
KOBE?! WHY?
SHE'S BEEN SOLD TO A GEISHA HOUSE. SUCH A PITY.
...WHEN?
I DON'T KNOW. SEEMS LIKE THEY'LL TAKE HER ANY DAY NOW.
...

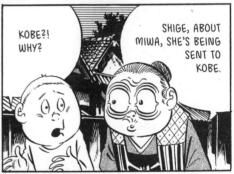

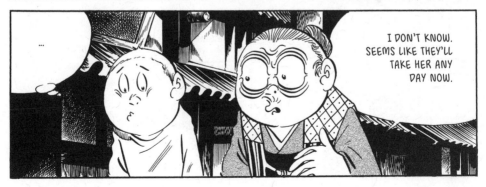

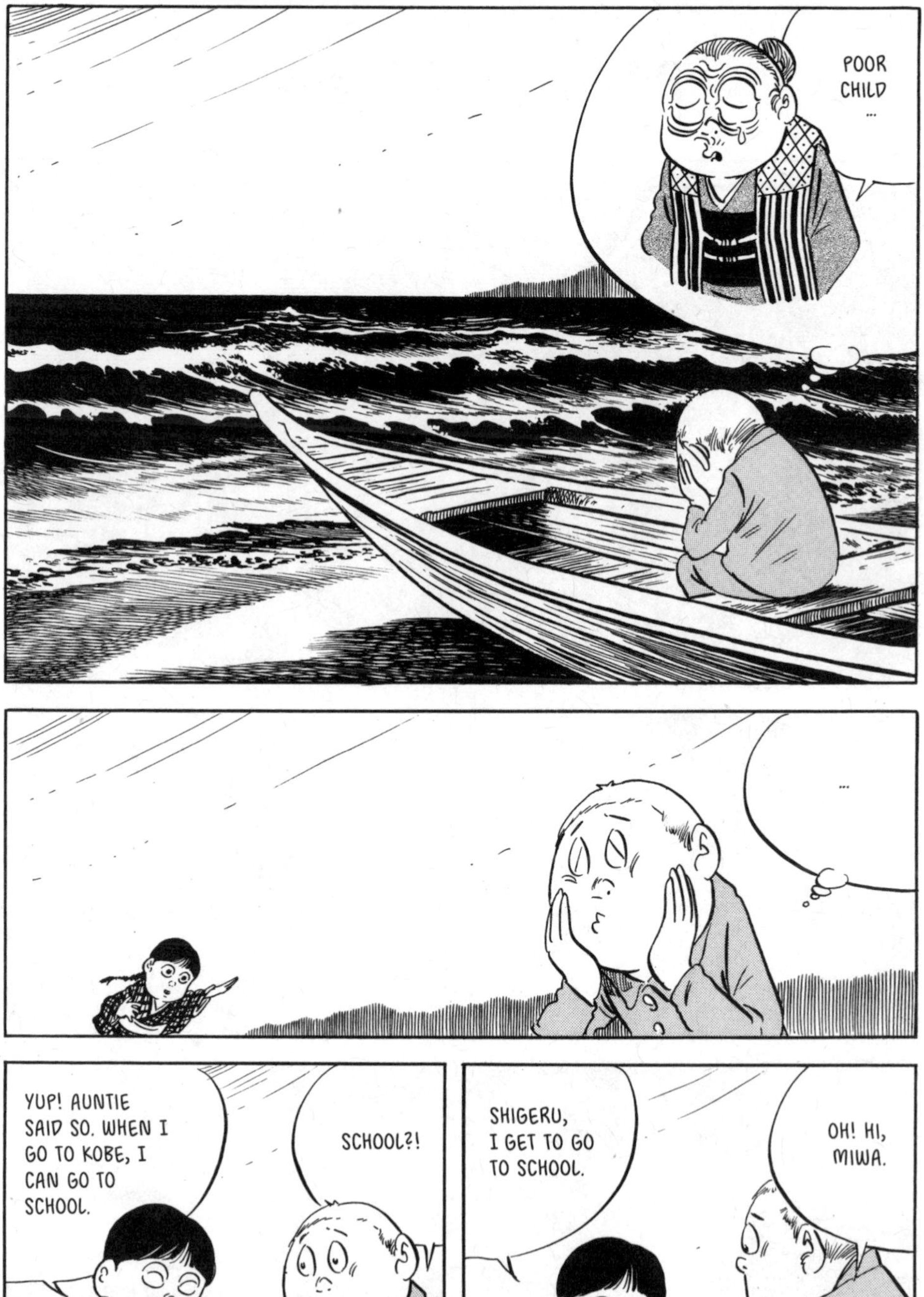
POOR CHILD ...
...
OH! HI, MIWA.
SHIGERU, I GET TO GO TO SCHOOL.
SCHOOL?!
YUP! AUNTIE SAID SO. WHEN I GO TO KOBE, I CAN GO TO SCHOOL.

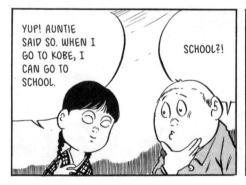

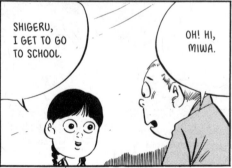

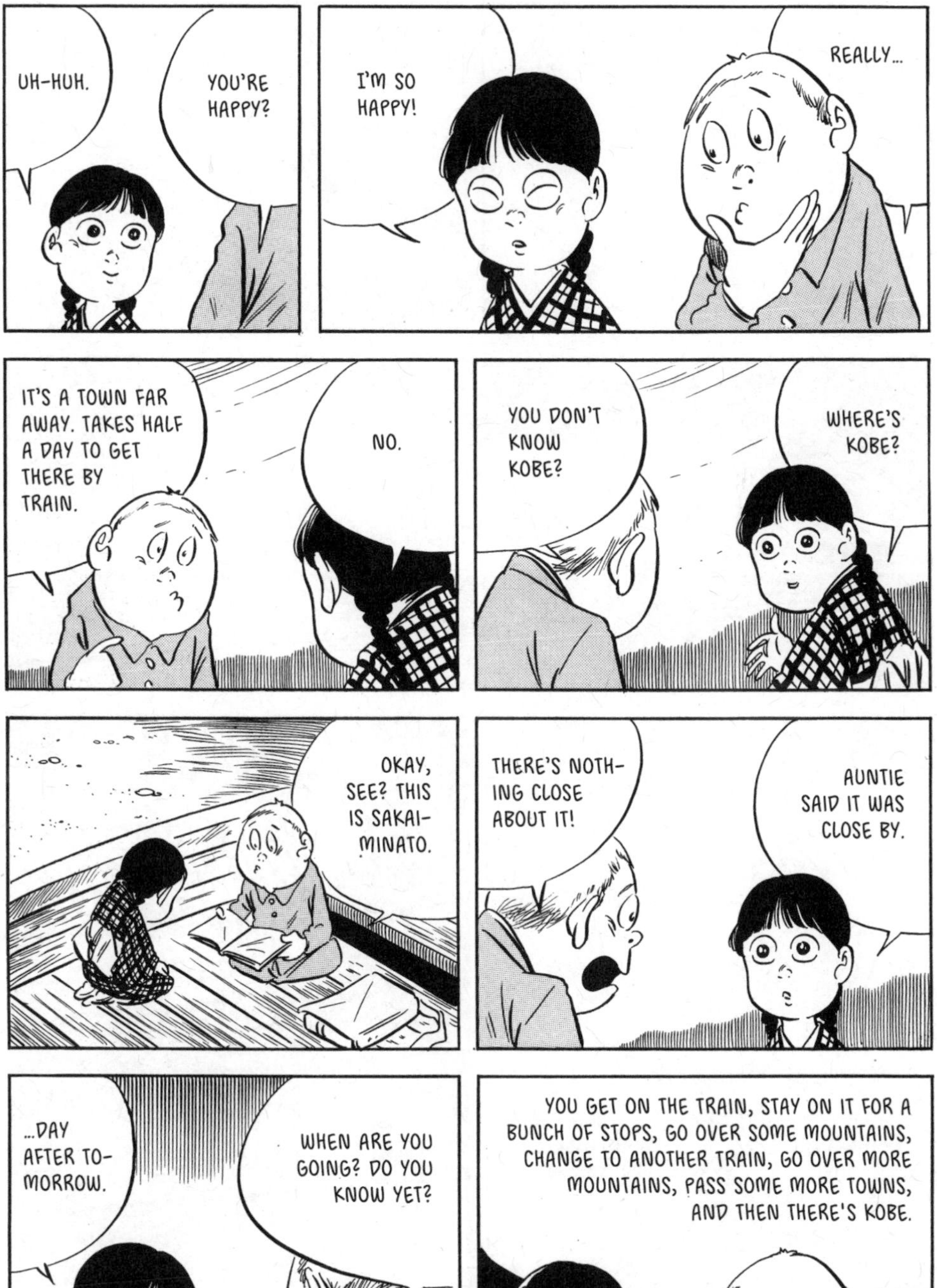
REALLY...
I'M SO HAPPY!
YOU'RE HAPPY?
UH-HUH.
WHERE'S KOBE?
YOU DON'T KNOW KOBE?
NO.
IT'S A TOWN FAR AWAY. TAKES HALF A DAY TO GET THERE BY TRAIN.
AUNTIE SAID IT WAS CLOSE BY.
THERE'S NOTHING CLOSE ABOUT IT!
OKAY, SEE? THIS IS SAKAIMINATO.
YOU GET ON THE TRAIN, STAY ON IT FOR A BUNCH OF STOPS, GO OVER SOME MOUNTAINS, CHANGE TO ANOTHER TRAIN, GO OVER MORE MOUNTAINS, PASS SOME MORE TOWNS, AND THEN THERE'S KOBE.
WHEN ARE YOU GOING? DO YOU KNOW YET?
...DAY AFTER TOMORROW.

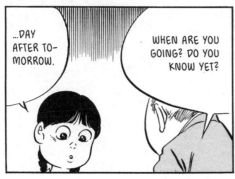

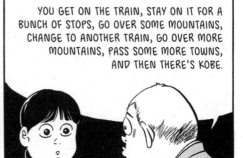

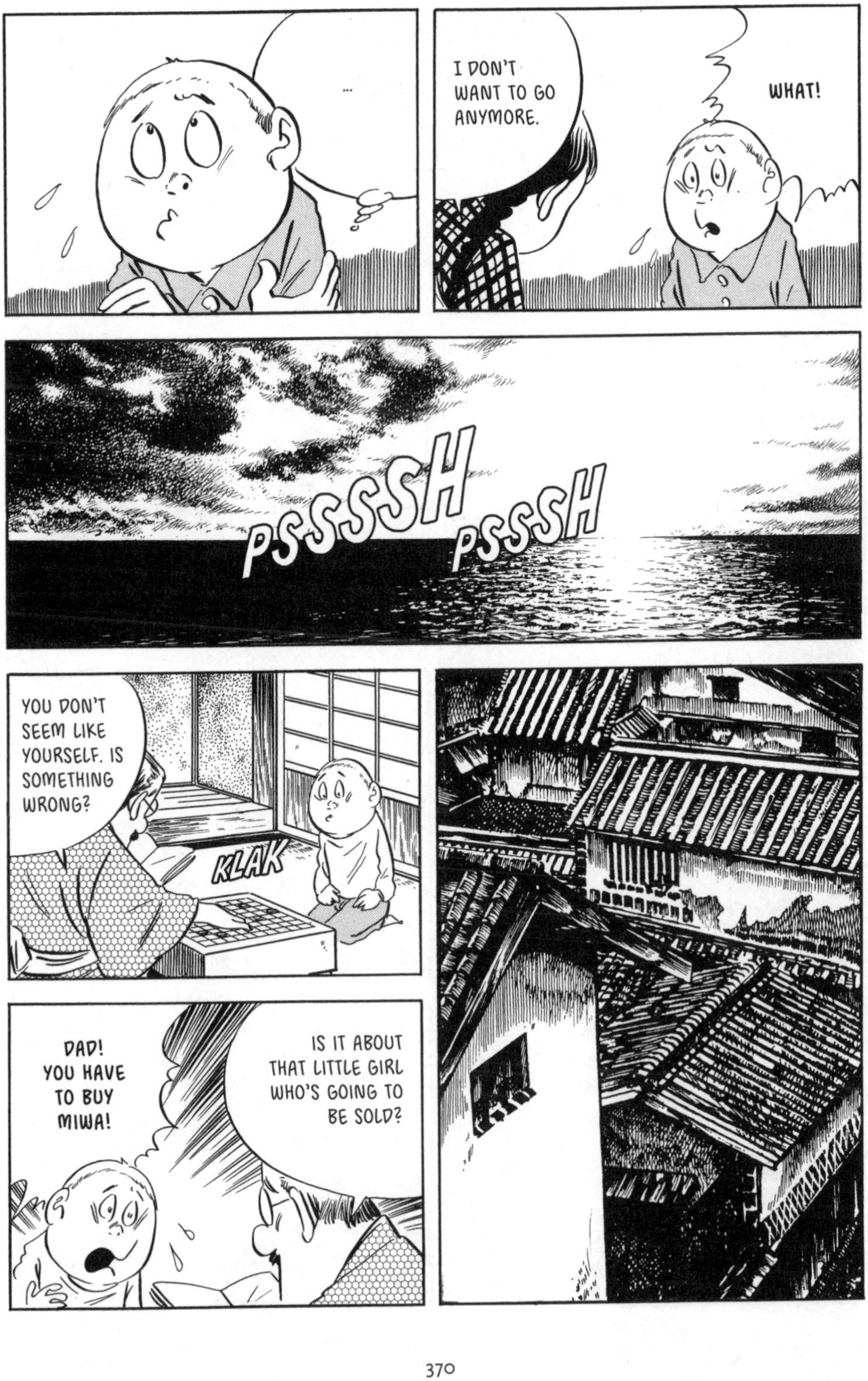
I DON'T WANT TO GO ANYMORE.
WHAT!
...
PSSSSH
PSSSH
YOU DON'T SEEM LIKE YOURSELF. IS SOMETHING WRONG?
KLAK
IS IT ABOUT THAT LITTLE GIRL WHO'S GOING TO BE SOLD?
DAD! YOU HAVE TO BUY MIWA!

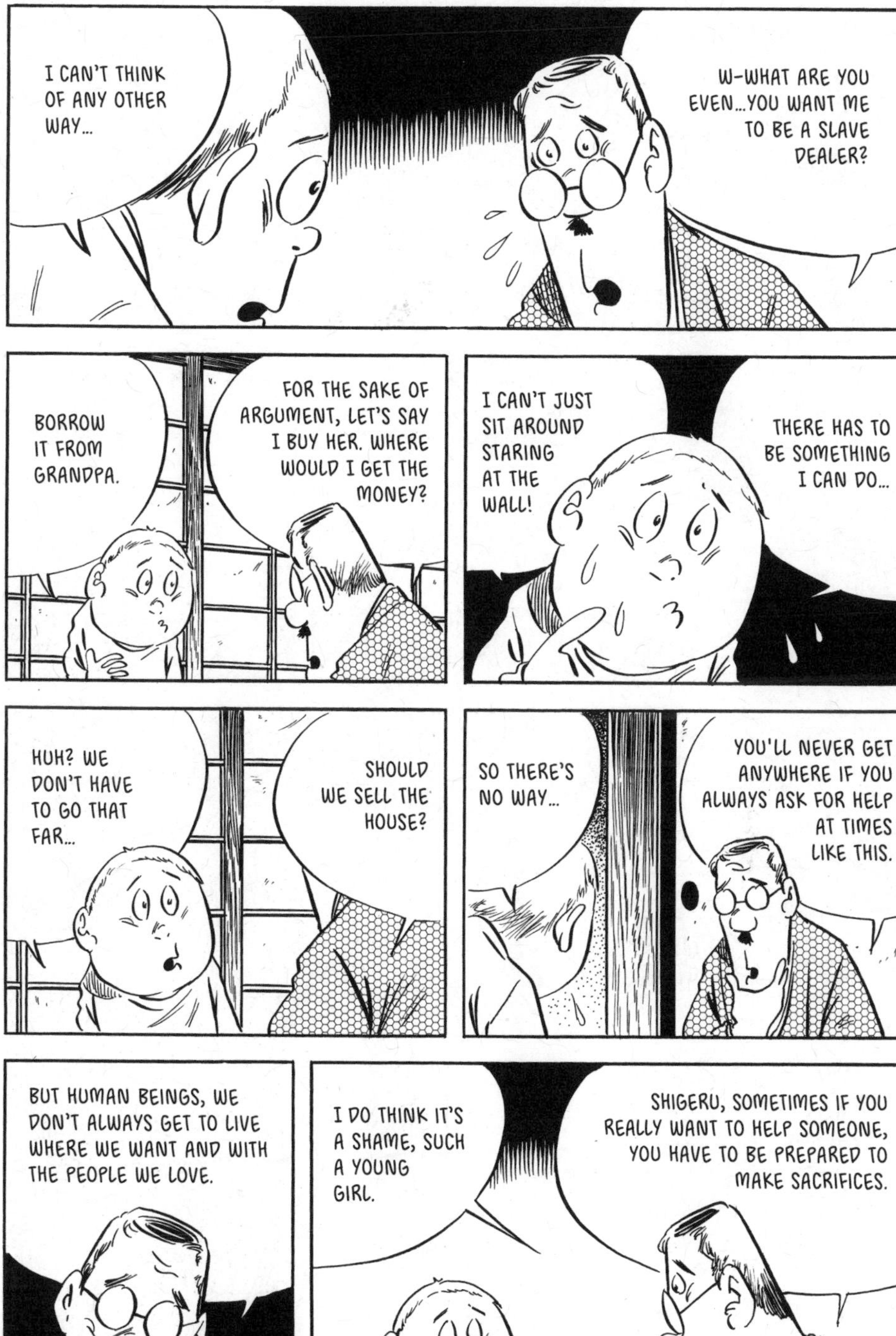
W-WHAT ARE YOU EVEN...YOU WANT ME TO BE A SLAVE DEALER?
I CAN'T THINK OF ANY OTHER WAY...
THERE HAS TO BE SOMETHING I CAN DO...
I CAN'T JUST SIT AROUND STARING AT THE WALL!
FOR THE SAKE OF ARGUMENT, LET'S SAY I BUY HER. WHERE WOULD I GET THE MONEY?
BORROW IT FROM GRANDPA.
YOU'LL NEVER GET ANYWHERE IF YOU ALWAYS ASK FOR HELP AT TIMES LIKE THIS.
SO THERE'S NO WAY...
SHOULD WE SELL THE HOUSE?
HUH? WE DON'T HAVE TO GO THAT FAR...
SHIGERU, SOMETIMES IF YOU REALLY WANT TO HELP SOMEONE, YOU HAVE TO BE PREPARED TO MAKE SACRIFICES.
I DO THINK IT'S A SHAME, SUCH A YOUNG GIRL.
BUT HUMAN BEINGS, WE DON'T ALWAYS GET TO LIVE WHERE WE WANT AND WITH THE PEOPLE WE LOVE.

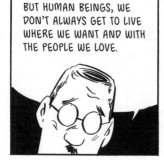

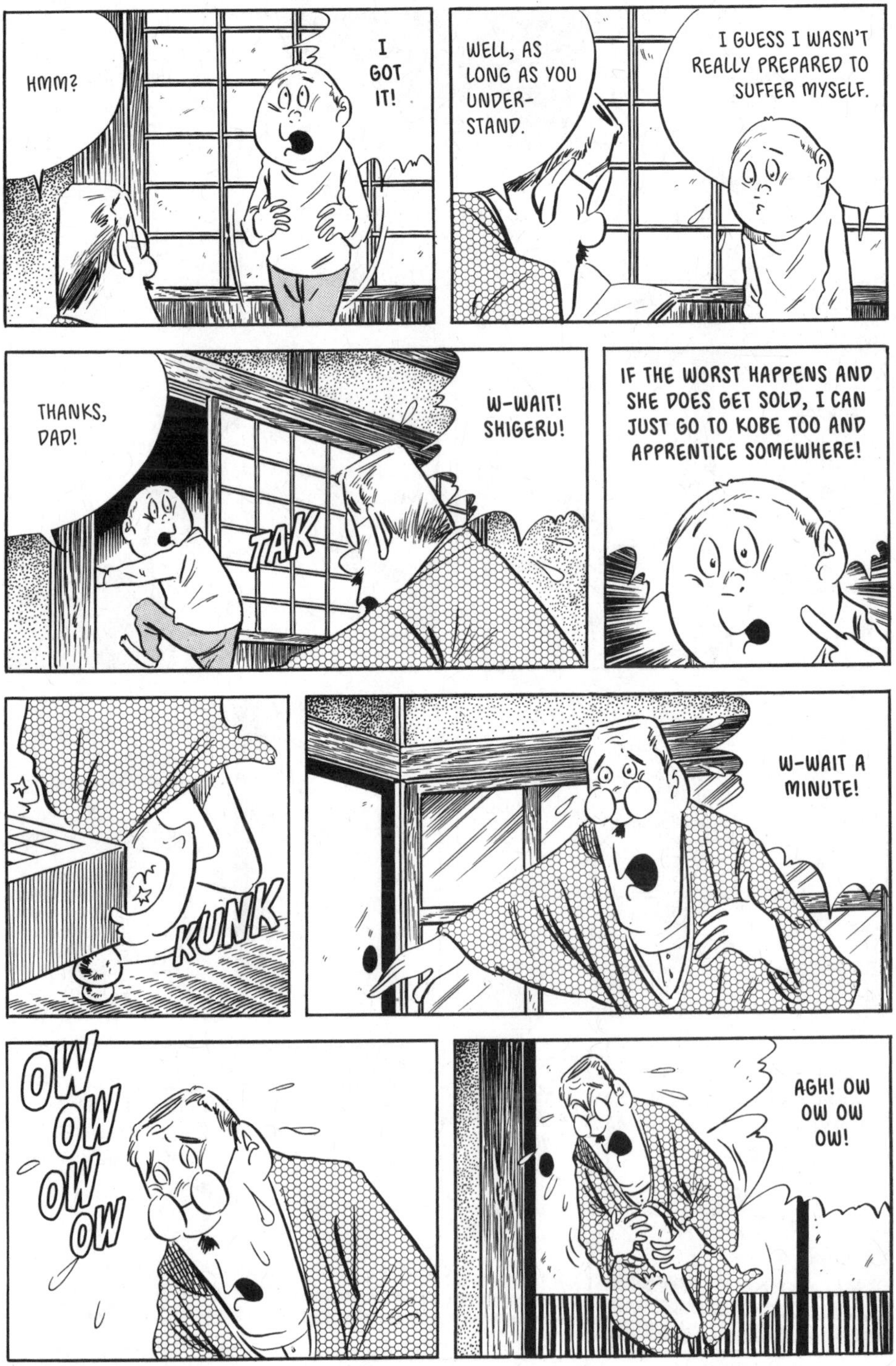
I GUESS I WASN'T REALLY PREPARED TO SUFFER MYSELF.
WELL, AS LONG AS YOU UNDER-STAND.
I GOT IT!
HMM?
IF THE WORST HAPPENS AND SHE DOES GET SOLD, I CAN JUST GO TO KOBE TOO AND APPRENTICE SOMEWHERE!
W-WAIT! SHIGERU!
THANKS, DAD!
TAK
W-WAIT A MINUTE!
KUNK
AGH! OW OW OW OW!
OW OW OW OW OW

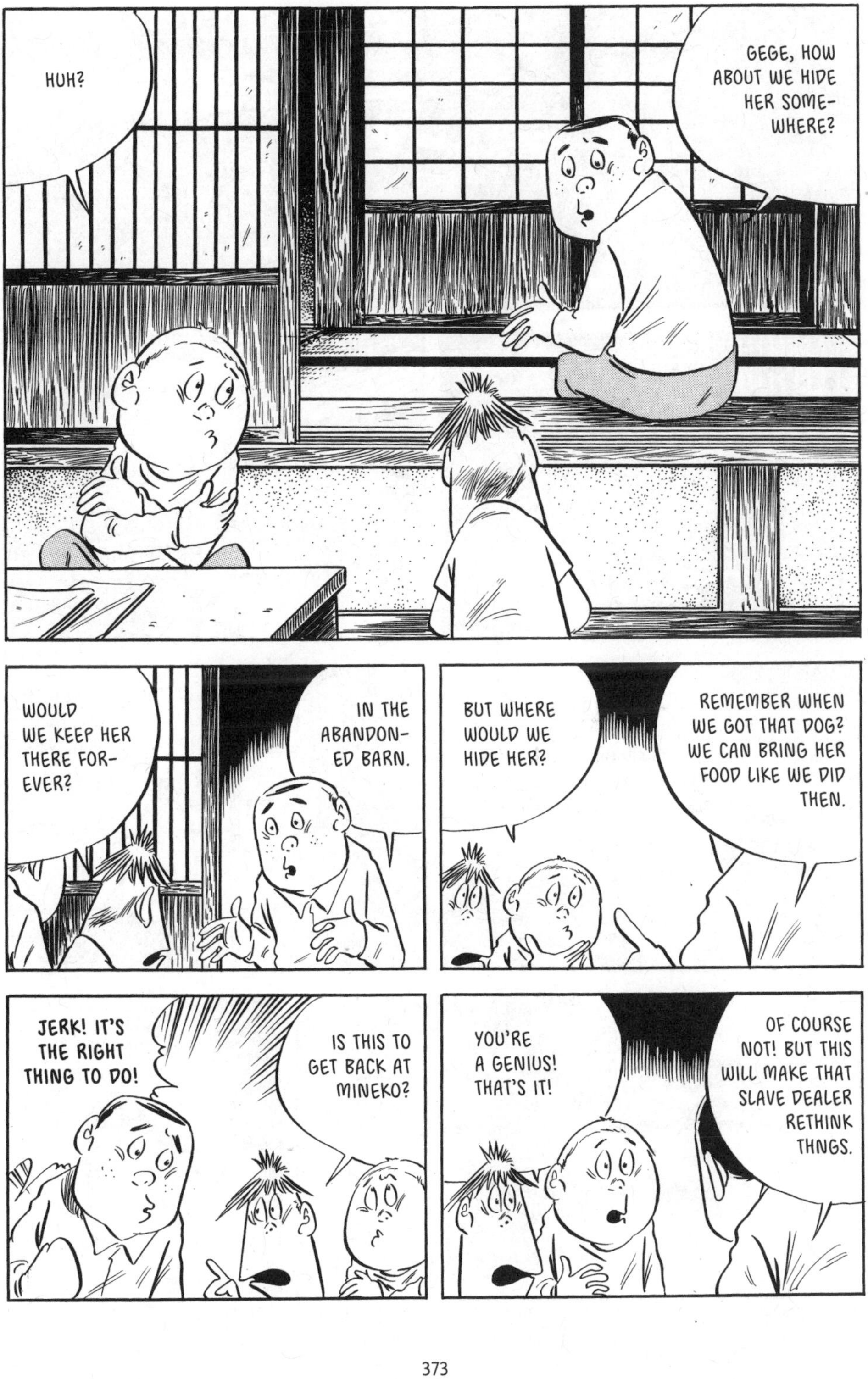
GEGE, HOW ABOUT WE HIDE HER SOME-WHERE?
HUH?
REMEMBER WHEN WE GOT THAT DOG? WE CAN BRING HER FOOD LIKE WE DID THEN.
BUT WHERE WOULD WE HIDE HER?
IN THE ABANDON-ED BARN.
WOULD WE KEEP HER THERE FOR-EVER?
OF COURSE NOT! BUT THIS WILL MAKE THAT SLAVE DEALER RETHINK THNGS.
YOU'RE A GENIUS! THAT'S IT!
IS THIS TO GET BACK AT MINEKO?
JERK! IT'S THE RIGHT THING TO DO!

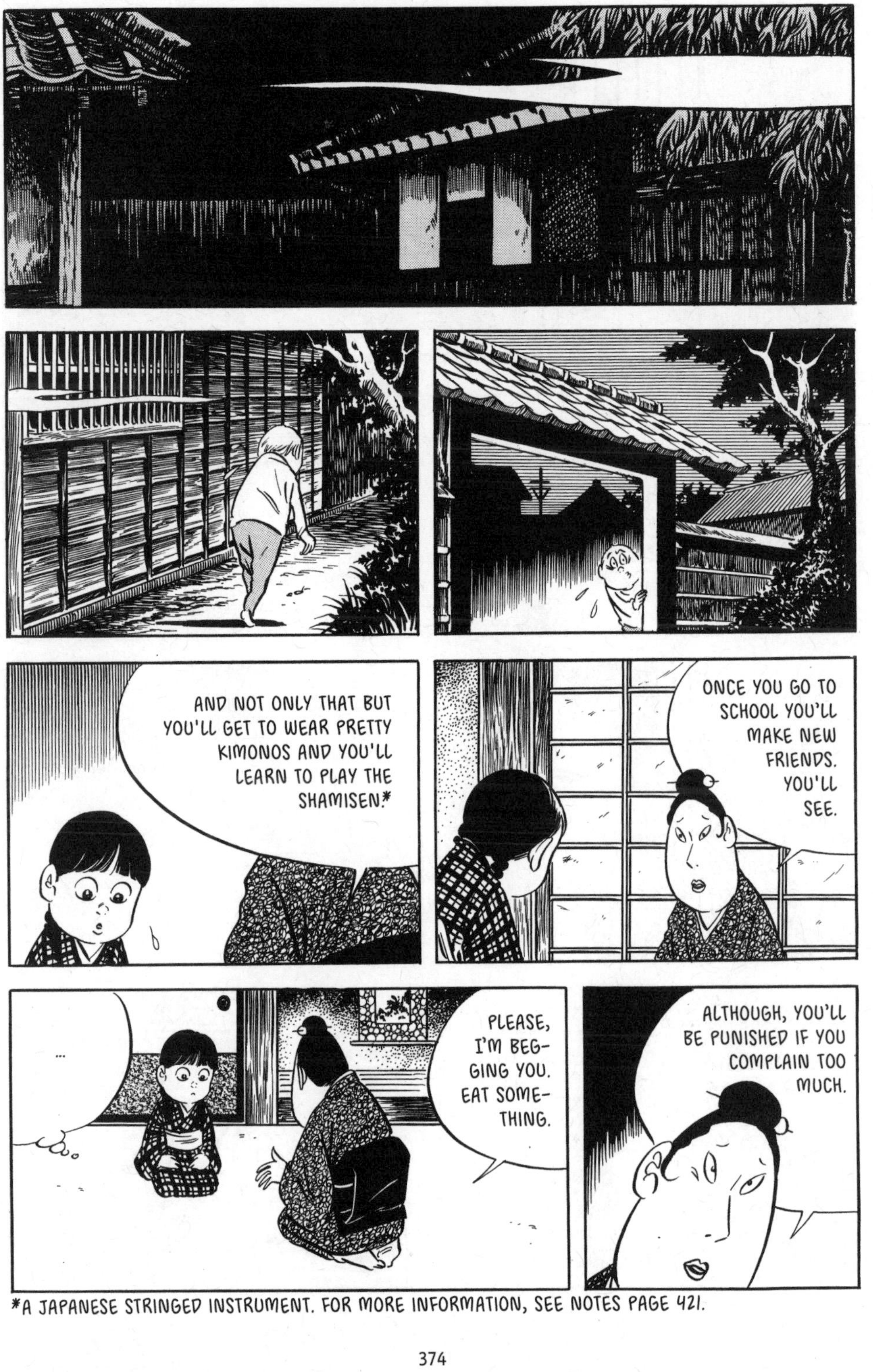
ONCE YOU GO TO SCHOOL YOU'LL MAKE NEW FRIENDS. YOU'LL SEE.
AND NOT ONLY THAT BUT YOU'LL GET TO WEAR PRETTY KIMONOS AND YOU'LL LEARN TO PLAY THE SHAMISEN!*
ALTHOUGH, YOU'LL BE PUNISHED IF YOU COMPLAIN TOO MUCH.
PLEASE, I'M BEGGING YOU. EAT SOMETHING.
...

*A JAPANESE STRINGED INSTRUMENT. FOR MORE INFORMATION, SEE NOTES PAGE 421.

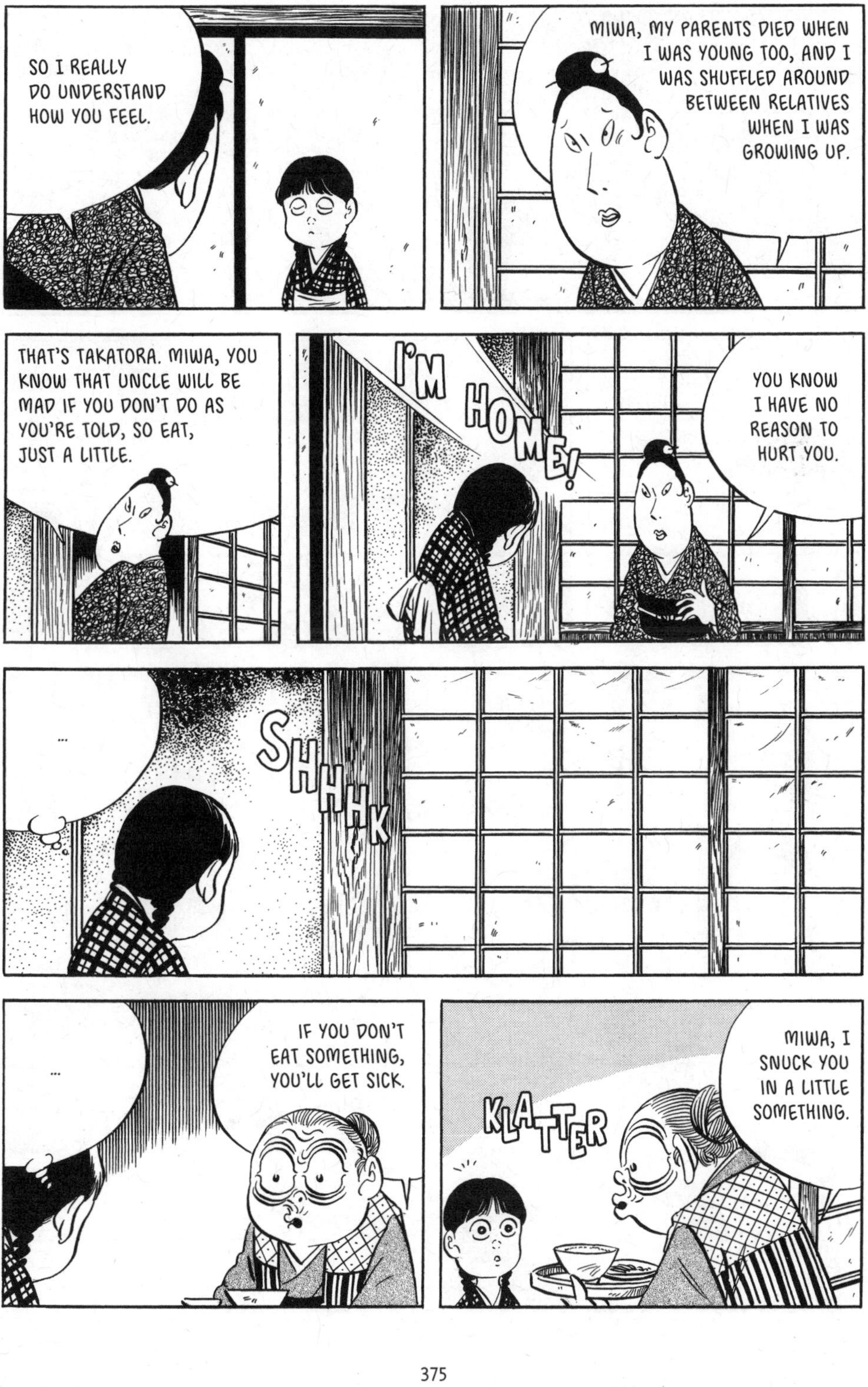
MIWA, MY PARENTS DIED WHEN I WAS YOUNG TOO, AND I WAS SHUFFLED AROUND BETWEEN RELATIVES WHEN I WAS GROWING UP.
SO I REALLY DO UNDERSTAND HOW YOU FEEL.
YOU KNOW I HAVE NO REASON TO HURT YOU.
I'M HOME!
THAT'S TAKATORA. MIWA, YOU KNOW THAT UNCLE WILL BE MAD IF YOU DON'T DO AS YOU'RE TOLD, SO EAT, JUST A LITTLE.
SHHHK
...
MIWA, I SNUCK YOU IN A LITTLE SOMETHING.
KLATTER
IF YOU DON'T EAT SOMETHING, YOU'LL GET SICK.
...

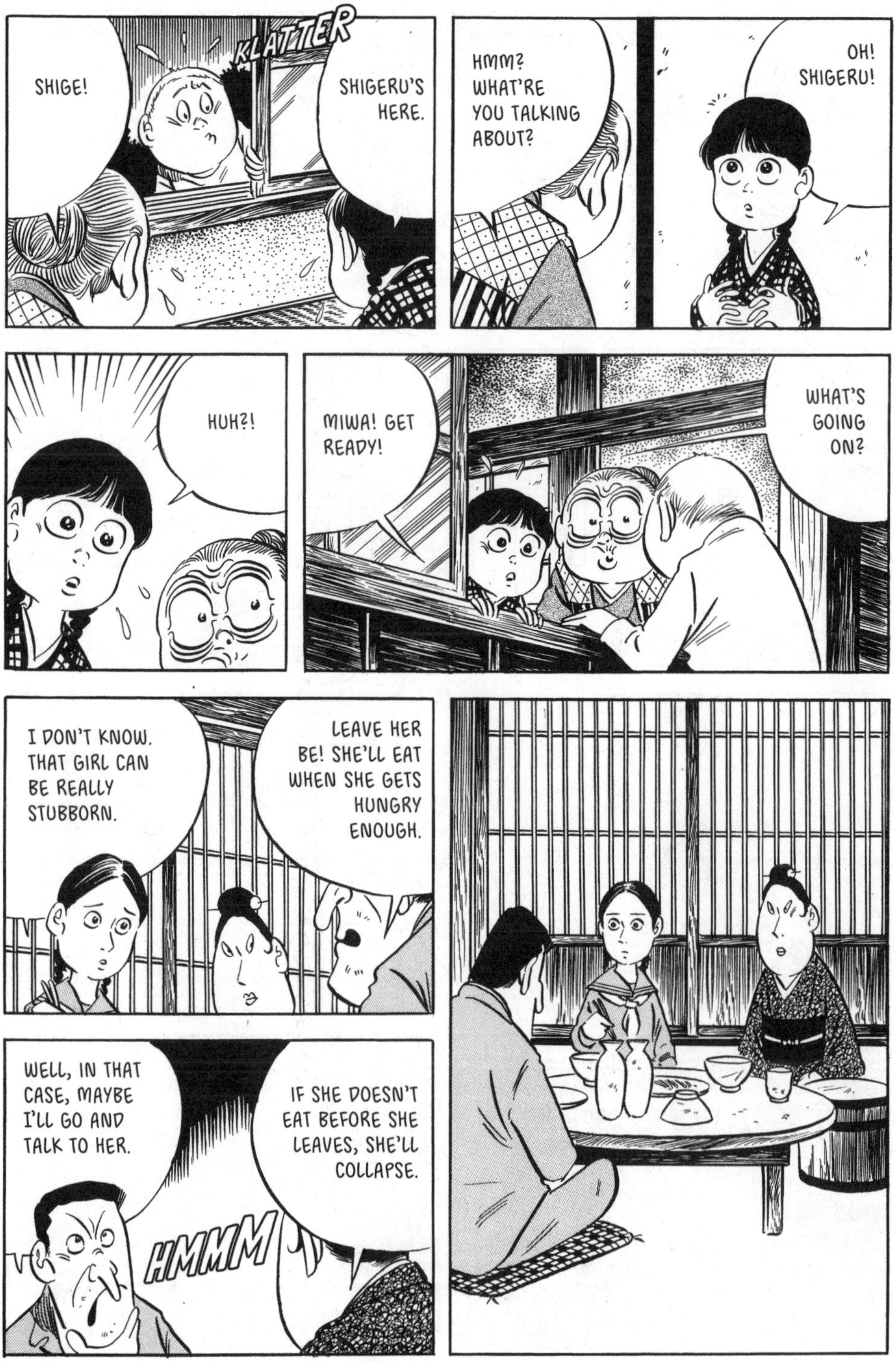
OH! SHIGERU!
HMM? WHAT'RE YOU TALKING ABOUT?
KLATTER
SHIGERU'S HERE.
SHIGE!
WHAT'S GOING ON?
MIWA! GET READY!
HUH?!
LEAVE HER BE! SHE'LL EAT WHEN SHE GETS HUNGRY ENOUGH.
I DON'T KNOW. THAT GIRL CAN BE REALLY STUBBORN.
IF SHE DOESN'T EAT BEFORE SHE LEAVES, SHE'LL COLLAPSE.
WELL, IN THAT CASE, MAYBE I'LL GO AND TALK TO HER.
HMMM

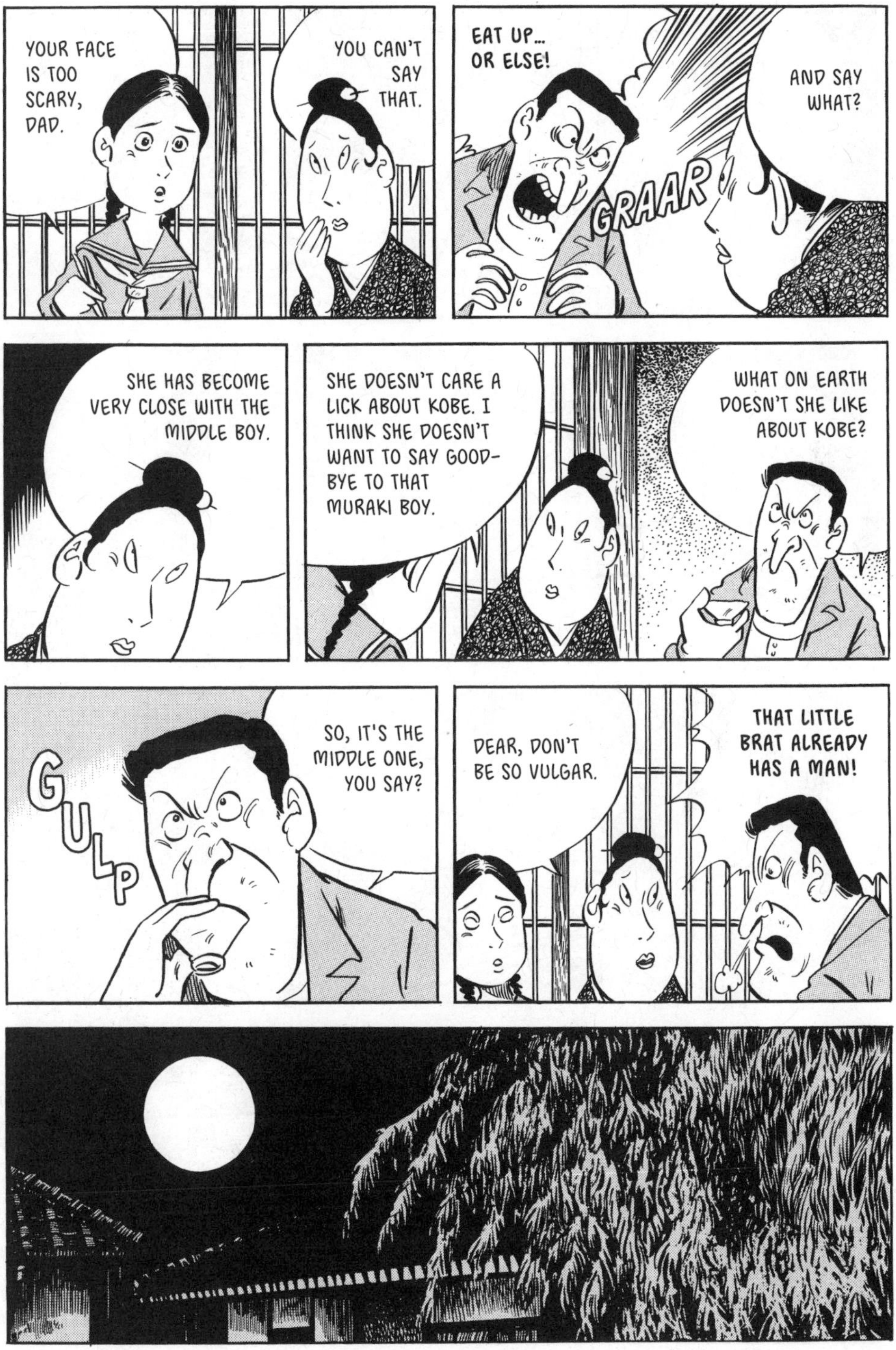
AND SAY WHAT?
GRAAR
EAT UP... OR ELSE!
YOU CAN'T SAY THAT.
YOUR FACE IS TOO SCARY, DAD.
WHAT ON EARTH DOESN'T SHE LIKE ABOUT KOBE?
SHE DOESN'T CARE A LICK ABOUT KOBE. I THINK SHE DOESN'T WANT TO SAY GOOD-BYE TO THAT MURAKI BOY.
SHE HAS BECOME VERY CLOSE WITH THE MIDDLE BOY.
THAT LITTLE BRAT ALREADY HAS A MAN!
DEAR, DON'T BE SO VULGAR.
SO, IT'S THE MIDDLE ONE, YOU SAY?
GULP

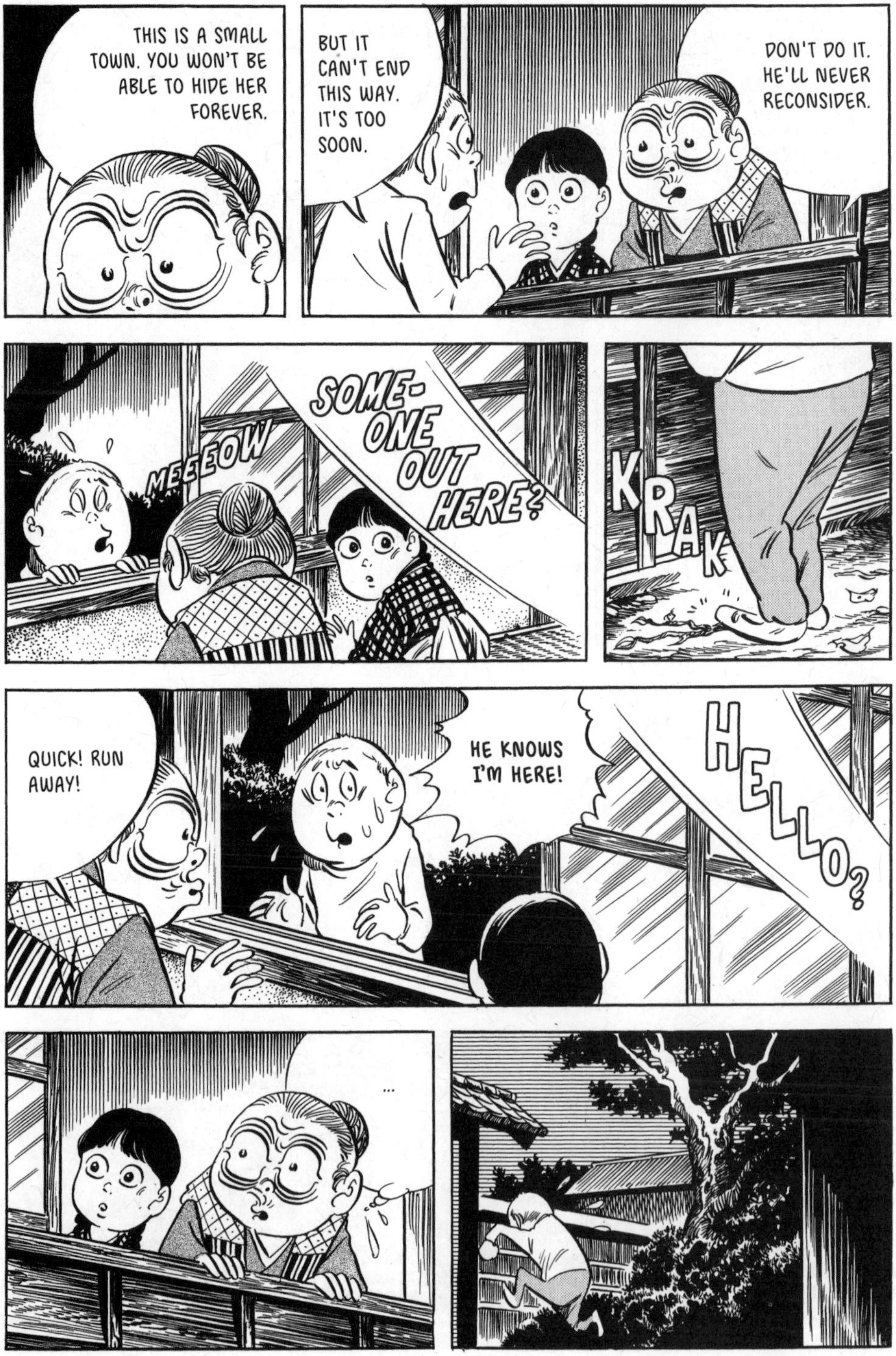
DON'T DO IT. HE'LL NEVER RECONSIDER.
BUT IT CAN'T END THIS WAY. IT'S TOO SOON.
THIS IS A SMALL TOWN. YOU WON'T BE ABLE TO HIDE HER FOREVER.
KRAK
SOME-ONE OUT HERE?
MEEEOW
HELLO?
HE KNOWS I'M HERE!
QUICK! RUN AWAY!
...

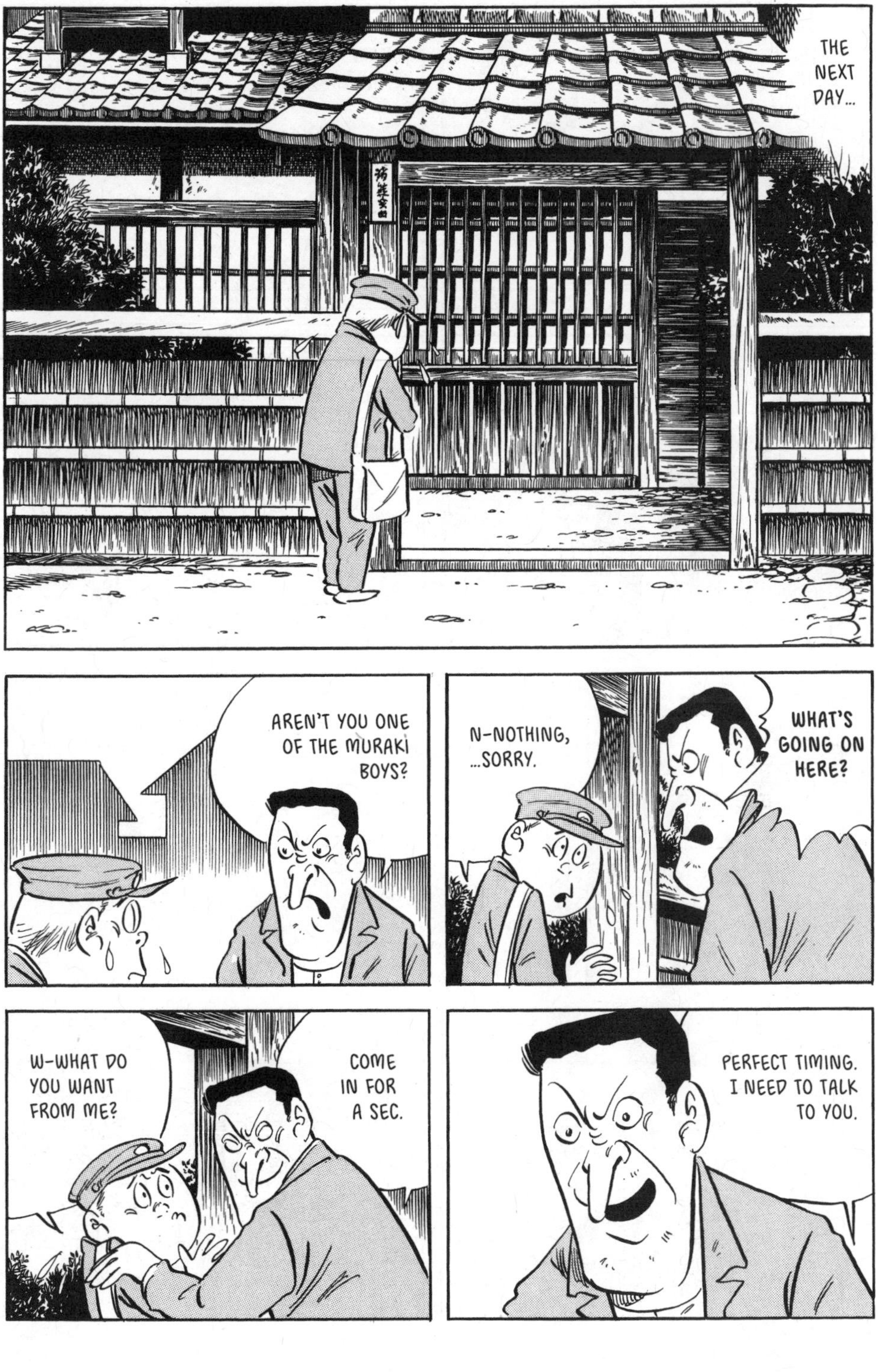
THE NEXT DAY...
WHAT'S GOING ON HERE?
N-NOTHING, ...SORRY.
AREN'T YOU ONE OF THE MURAKI BOYS?
PERFECT TIMING. I NEED TO TALK TO YOU.
COME IN FOR A SEC.
W-WHAT DO YOU WANT FROM ME?

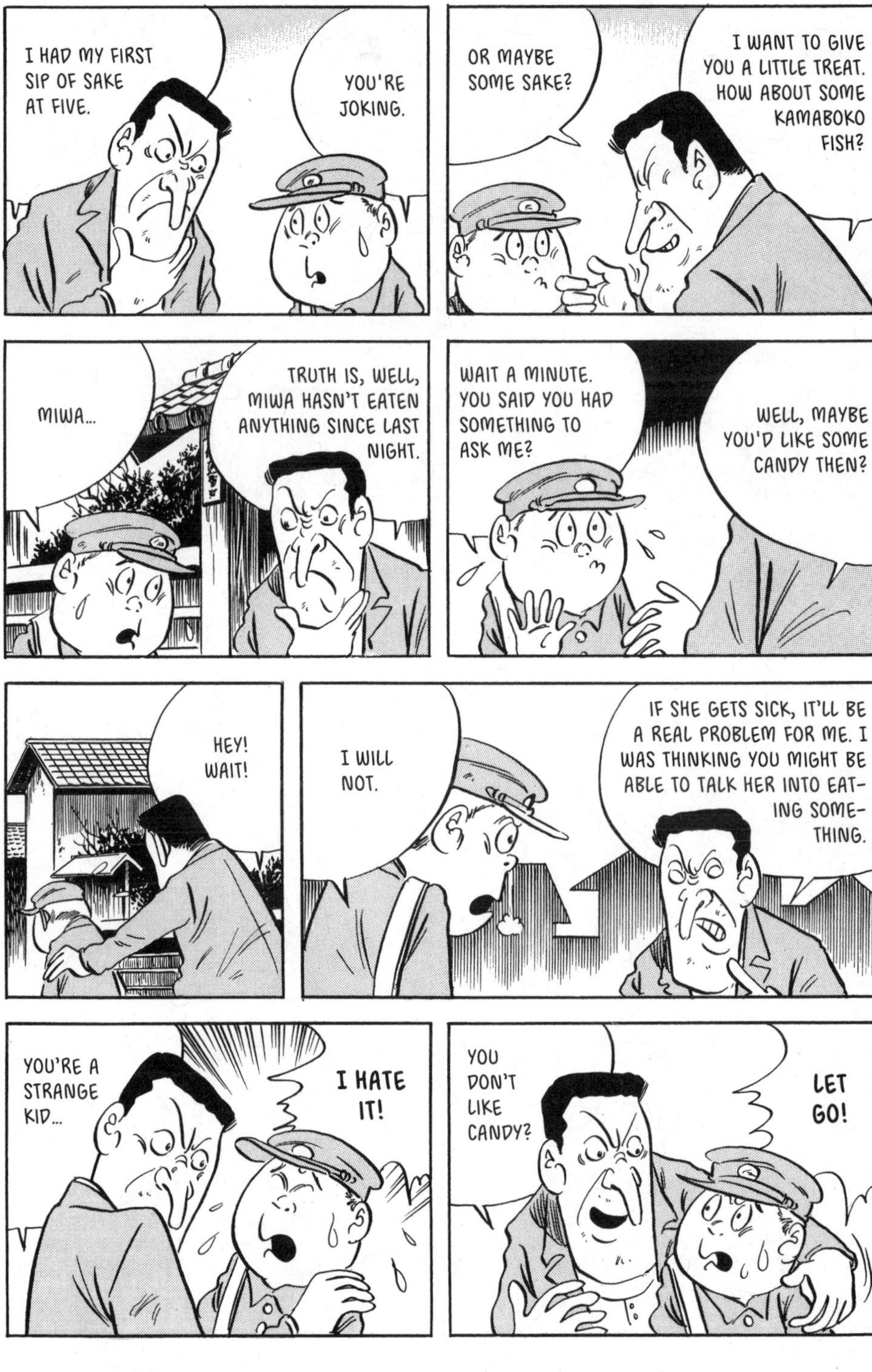

I WANT TO GIVE YOU A LITTLE TREAT. HOW ABOUT SOME KAMABOKO FISH?
OR MAYBE SOME SAKE?
YOU'RE JOKING.
I HAD MY FIRST SIP OF SAKE AT FIVE.
WELL, MAYBE YOU'D LIKE SOME CANDY THEN?
WAIT A MINUTE. YOU SAID YOU HAD SOMETHING TO ASK ME?
TRUTH IS, WELL, MIWA HASN'T EATEN ANYTHING SINCE LAST NIGHT.
MIWA...
IF SHE GETS SICK, IT'LL BE A REAL PROBLEM FOR ME. I WAS THINKING YOU MIGHT BE ABLE TO TALK HER INTO EAT-ING SOME-THING.
I WILL NOT.
HEY! WAIT!
LET GO!
YOU DON'T LIKE CANDY?
I HATE IT!
YOU'RE A STRANGE KID...

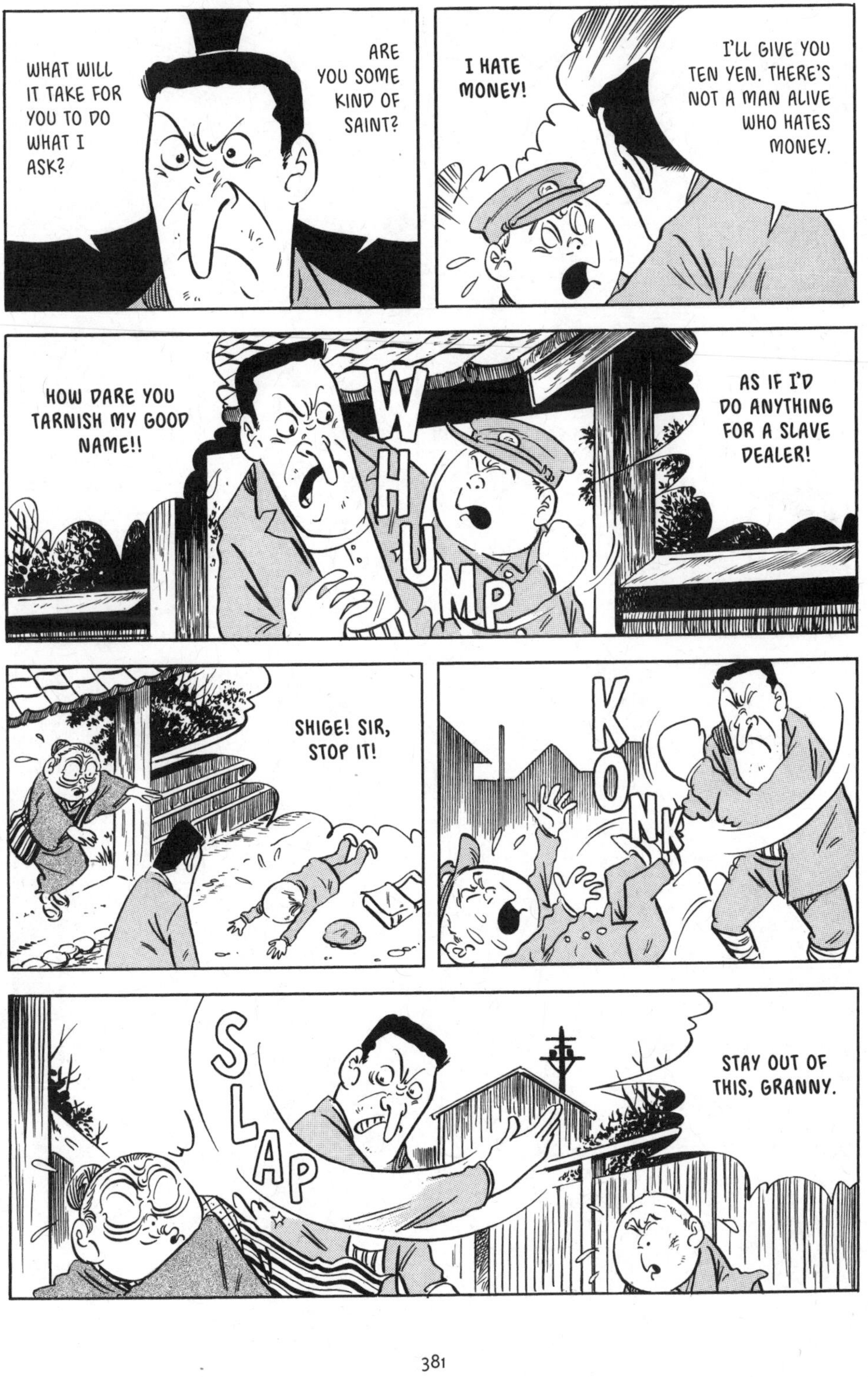
I'LL GIVE YOU TEN YEN. THERE'S NOT A MAN ALIVE WHO HATES MONEY.
I HATE MONEY!
ARE YOU SOME KIND OF SAINT?
WHAT WILL IT TAKE FOR YOU TO DO WHAT I ASK?
AS IF I'D DO ANYTHING FOR A SLAVE DEALER!
WHUMP
HOW DARE YOU TARNISH MY GOOD NAME!!
KONK
SHIGE! SIR, STOP IT!
STAY OUT OF THIS, GRANNY.
SLAP

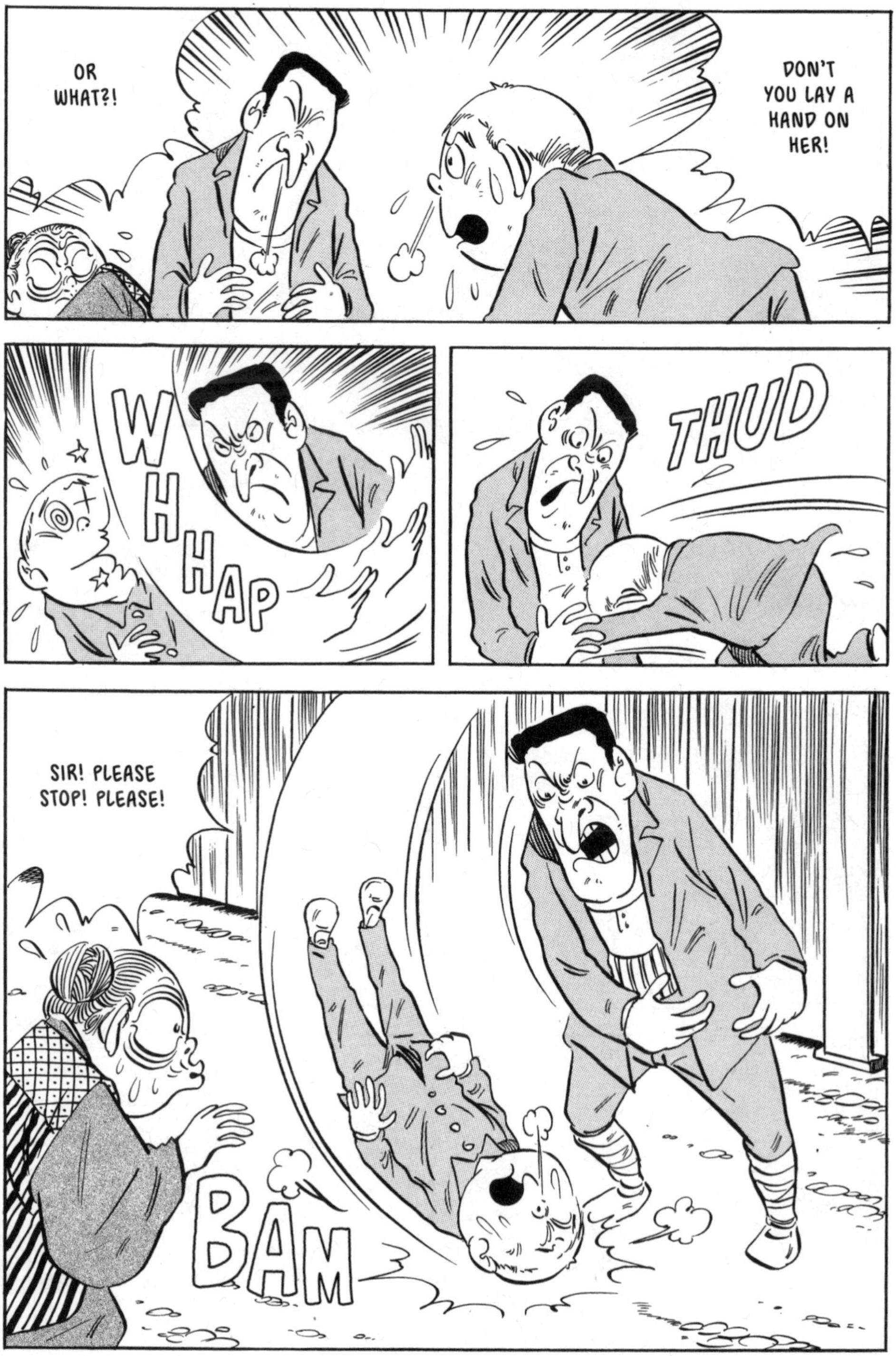
DON'T YOU LAY A HAND ON HER!
OR WHAT?!
THUD
WHHAP
SIR! PLEASE STOP! PLEASE!
BAM

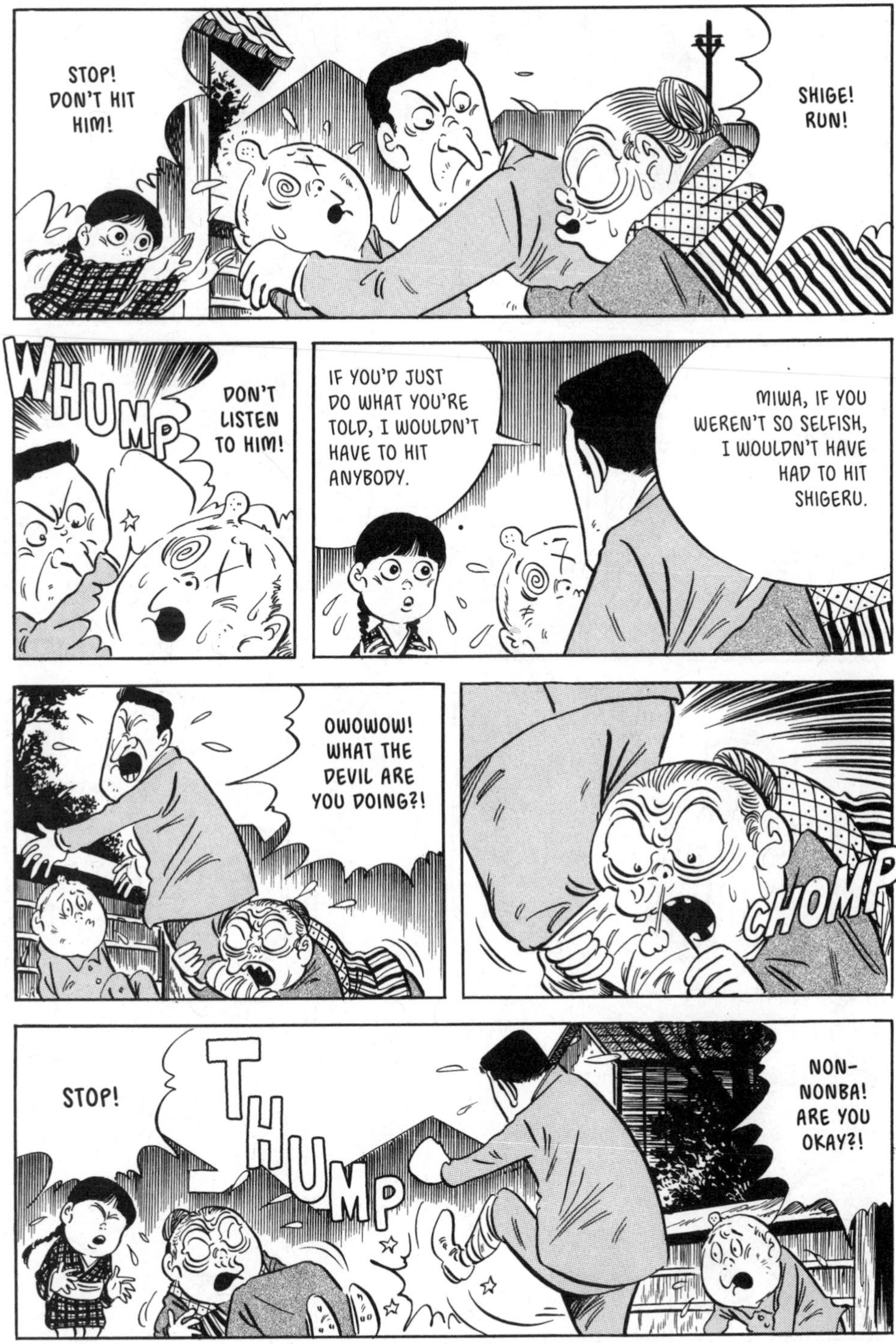
SHIGE! RUN!
STOP! DON'T HIT HIM!
MIWA, IF YOU WEREN'T SO SELFISH, I WOULDN'T HAVE HAD TO HIT SHIGERU.
IF YOU'D JUST DO WHAT YOU'RE TOLD, I WOULDN'T HAVE TO HIT ANYBODY.
DON'T LISTEN TO HIM!
WHUMP
CHOMP
OWOWOW! WHAT THE DEVIL ARE YOU DOING?!
NON-NONBA! ARE YOU OKAY?!
THUMP
STOP!

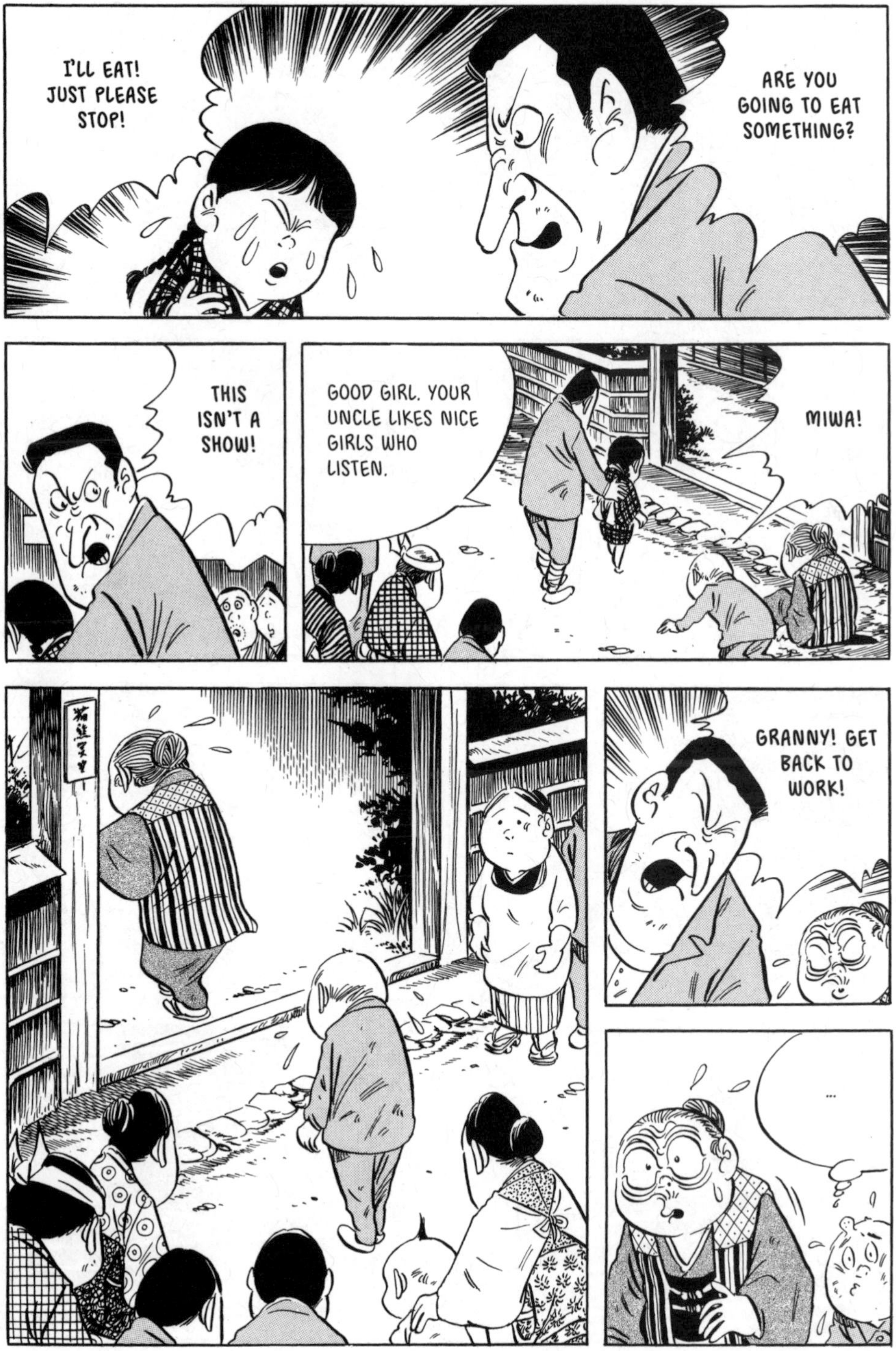
ARE YOU GOING TO EAT SOMETHING?
I'LL EAT! JUST PLEASE STOP!
MIWA!
GOOD GIRL. YOUR UNCLE LIKES NICE GIRLS WHO LISTEN.
THIS ISN'T A SHOW!
GRANNY! GET BACK TO WORK!
...

FAREWELL

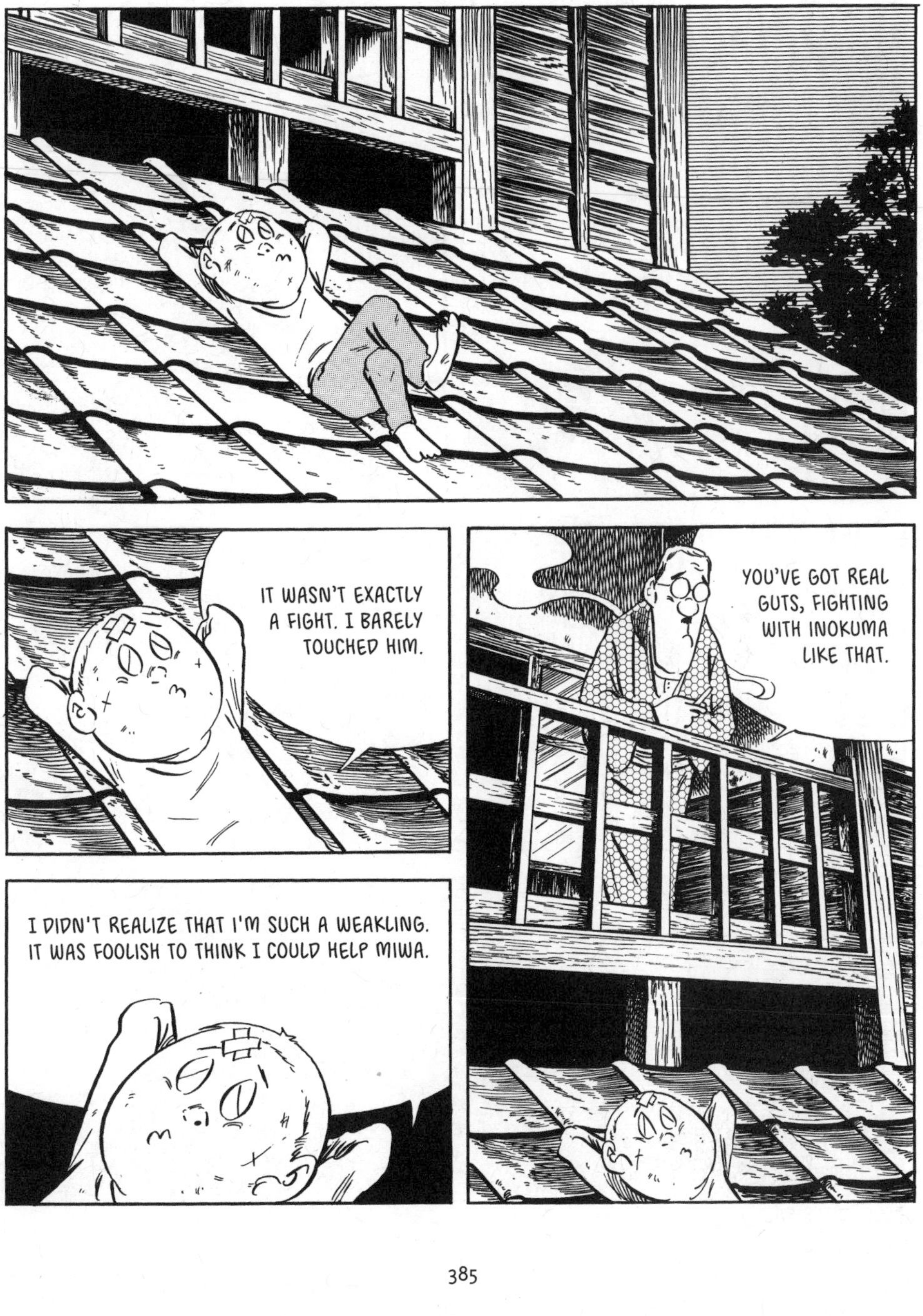
YOU'VE GOT REAL GUTS, FIGHTING WITH INOKUMA LIKE THAT.
IT WASN'T EXACTLY A FIGHT. I BARELY TOUCHED HIM.
I DIDN'T REALIZE THAT I'M SUCH A WEAKLING. IT WAS FOOLISH TO THINK I COULD HELP MIWA.

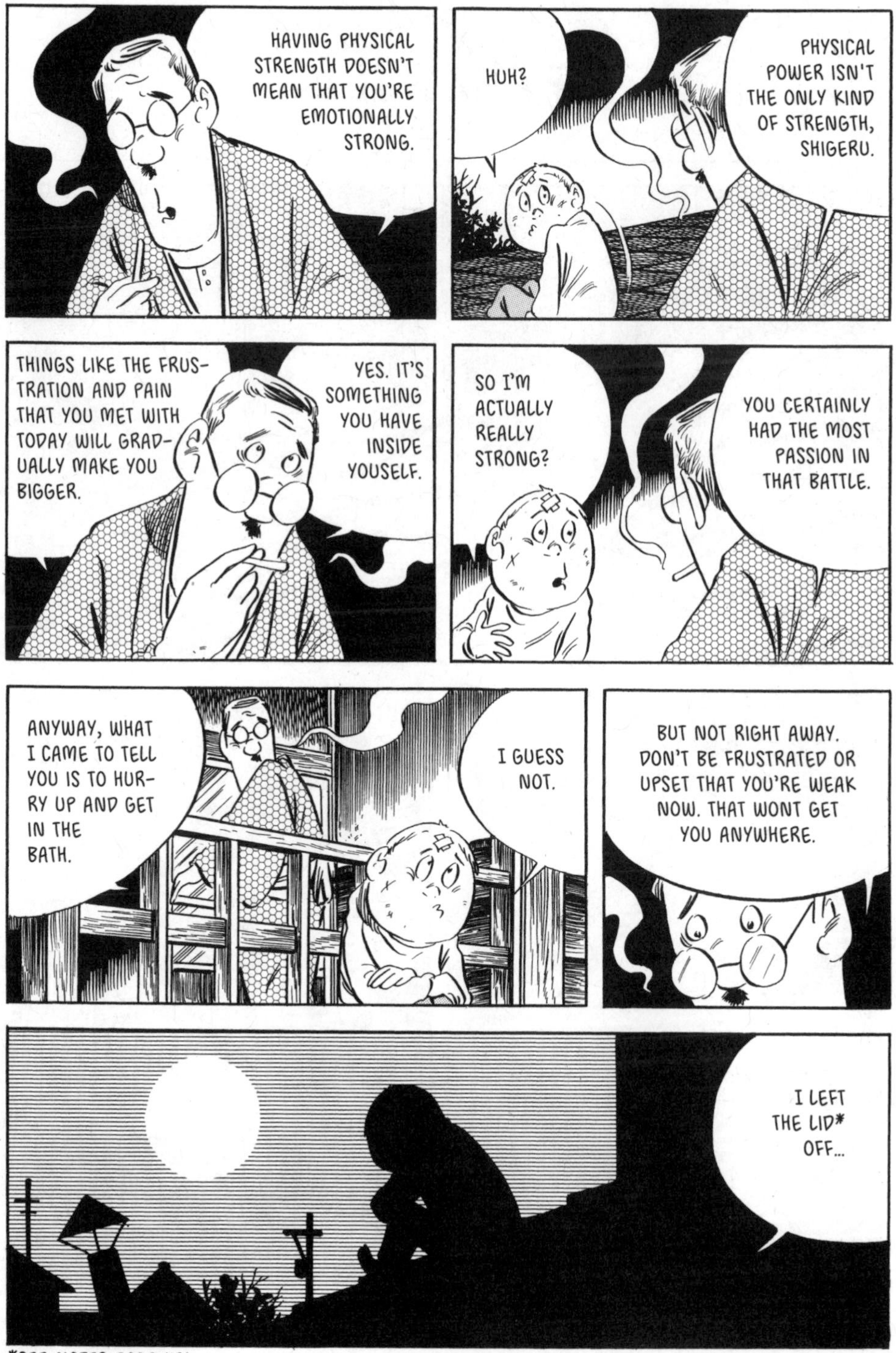
PHYSICAL POWER ISN'T THE ONLY KIND OF STRENGTH, SHIGERU.
HUH?
HAVING PHYSICAL STRENGTH DOESN'T MEAN THAT YOU'RE EMOTIONALLY STRONG.
YOU CERTAINLY HAD THE MOST PASSION IN THAT BATTLE.
SO I'M ACTUALLY REALLY STRONG?
YES. IT'S SOMETHING YOU HAVE INSIDE YOUSELF.
THINGS LIKE THE FRUS-TRATION AND PAIN THAT YOU MET WITH TODAY WILL GRAD-UALLY MAKE YOU BIGGER.
BUT NOT RIGHT AWAY. DON'T BE FRUSTRATED OR UPSET THAT YOU'RE WEAK NOW. THAT WONT GET YOU ANYWHERE.
I GUESS NOT.
ANYWAY, WHAT I CAME TO TELL YOU IS TO HUR-RY UP AND GET IN THE BATH.
I LEFT THE LID* OFF...

*SEE NOTES PAGE 421.

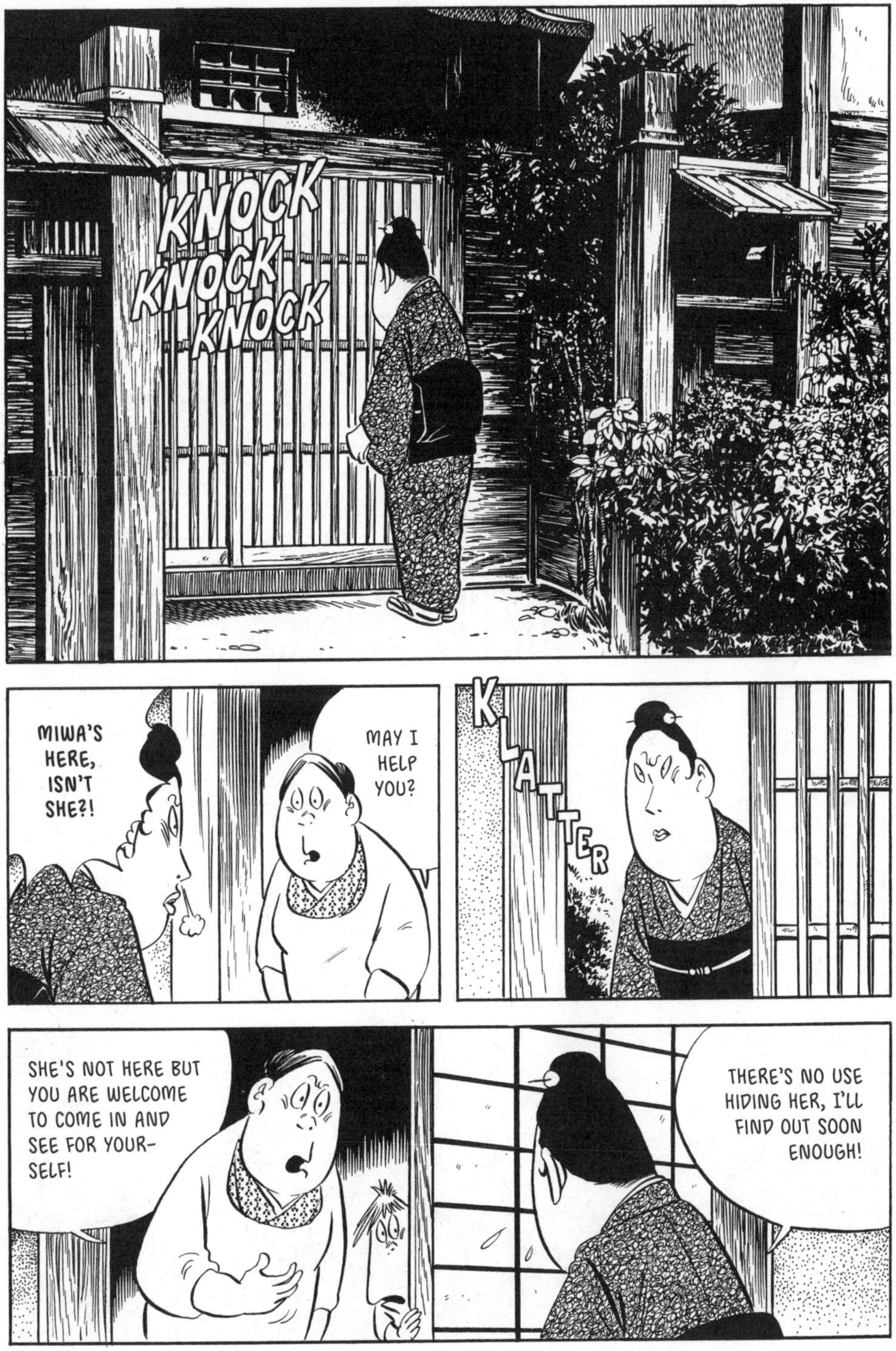
KNOCK KNOCK KNOCK
KLATTER
MAY I HELP YOU?
MIWA'S HERE, ISN'T SHE?!
THERE'S NO USE HIDING HER, I'LL FIND OUT SOON ENOUGH!
SHE'S NOT HERE BUT YOU ARE WELCOME TO COME IN AND SEE FOR YOUR-SELF!

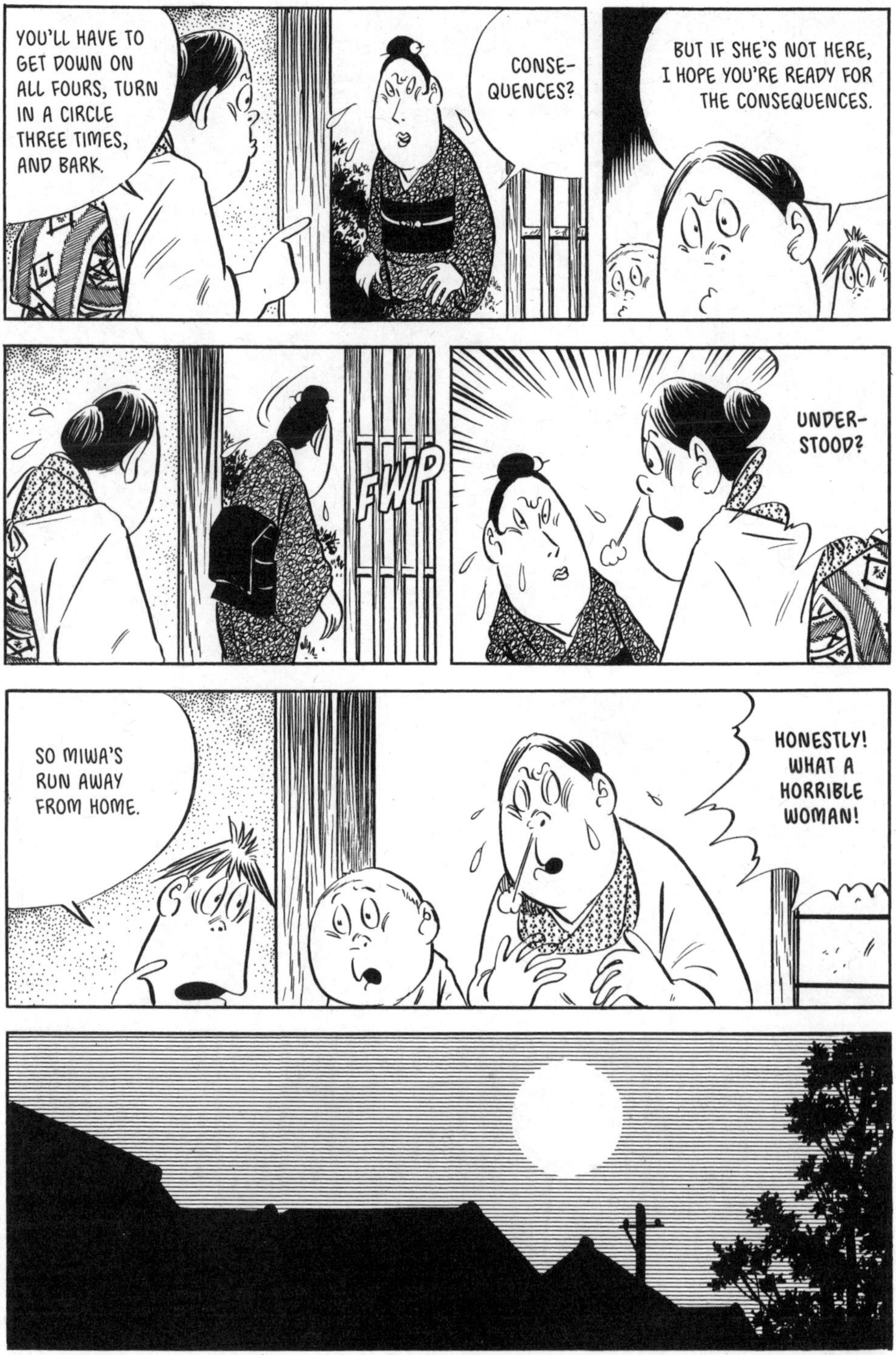
BUT IF SHE'S NOT HERE, I HOPE YOU'RE READY FOR THE CONSEQUENCES.
CONSE-QUENCES?
YOU'LL HAVE TO GET DOWN ON ALL FOURS, TURN IN A CIRCLE THREE TIMES, AND BARK.
UNDER-STOOD?
FWP
HONESTLY! WHAT A HORRIBLE WOMAN!
SO MIWA'S RUN AWAY FROM HOME.

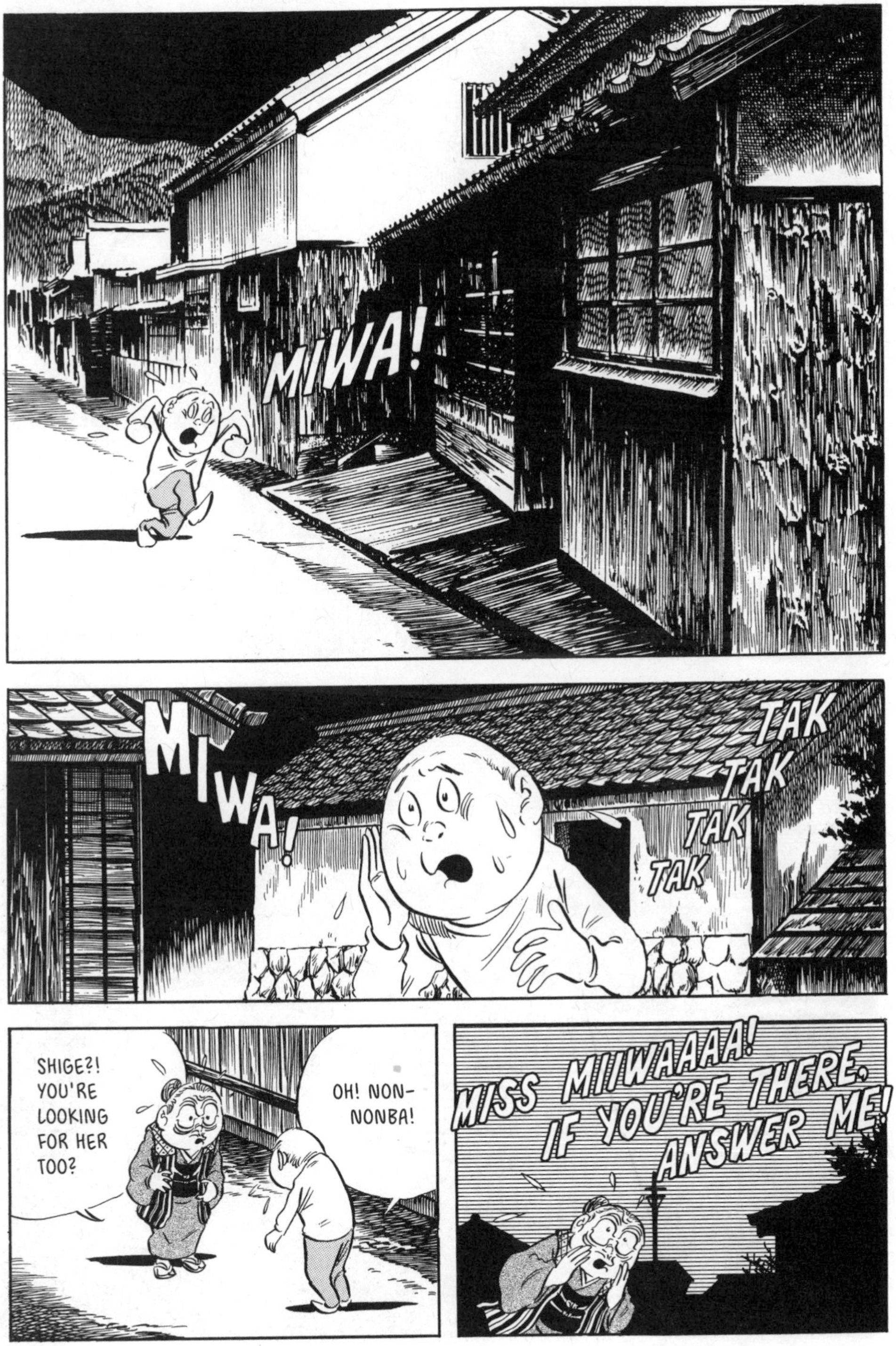
MIWA!
TAK
TAK
TAK
TAK
MIWA!
MISS MIIWAAAA! IF YOU'RE THERE, ANSWER ME!
OH! NON-NONBA!
SHIGE?! YOU'RE LOOKING FOR HER TOO?

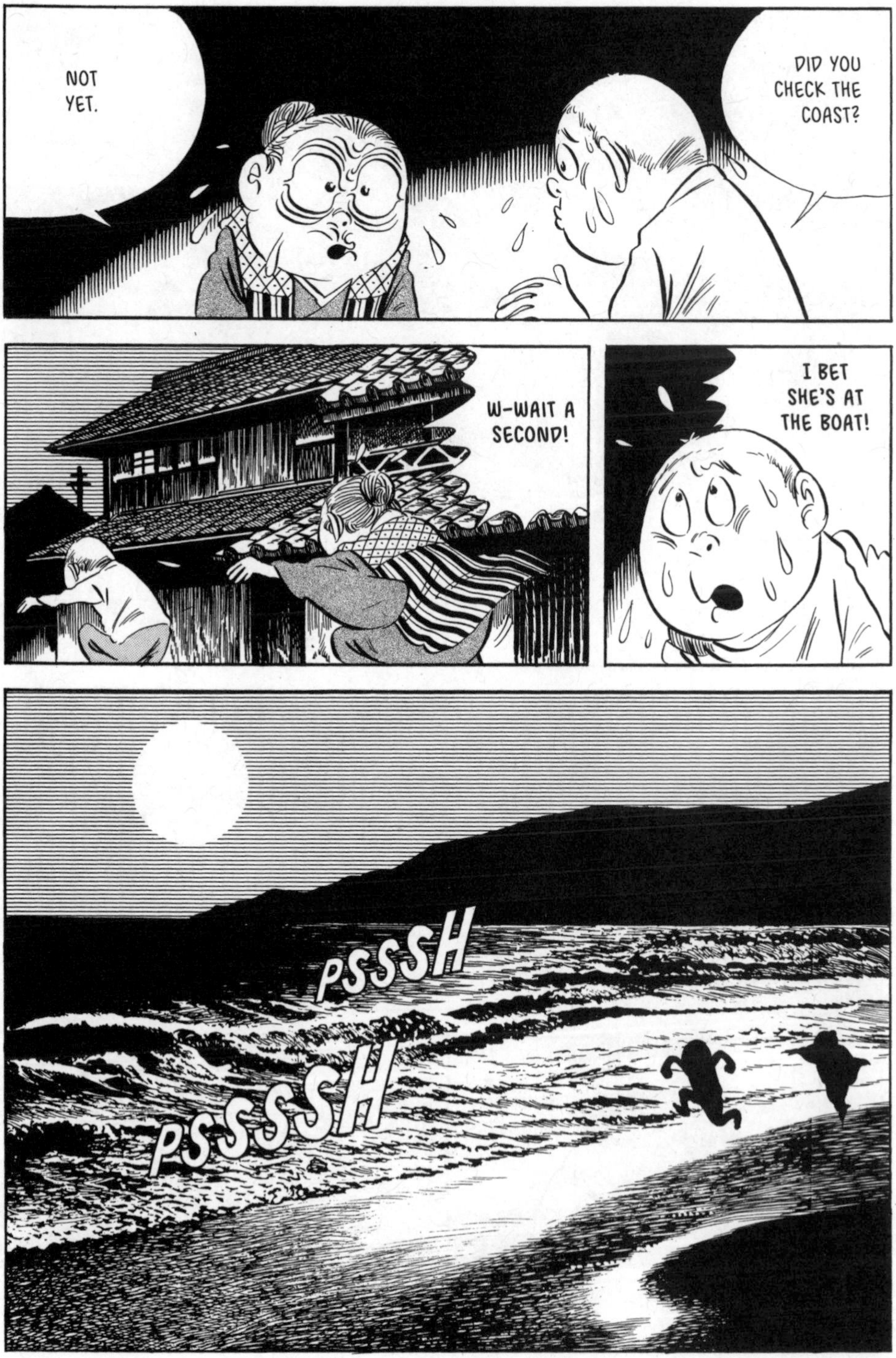
DID YOU CHECK THE COAST?
NOT YET.
I BET SHE'S AT THE BOAT!
W-WAIT A SECOND!
PSSSH
PSSSSH

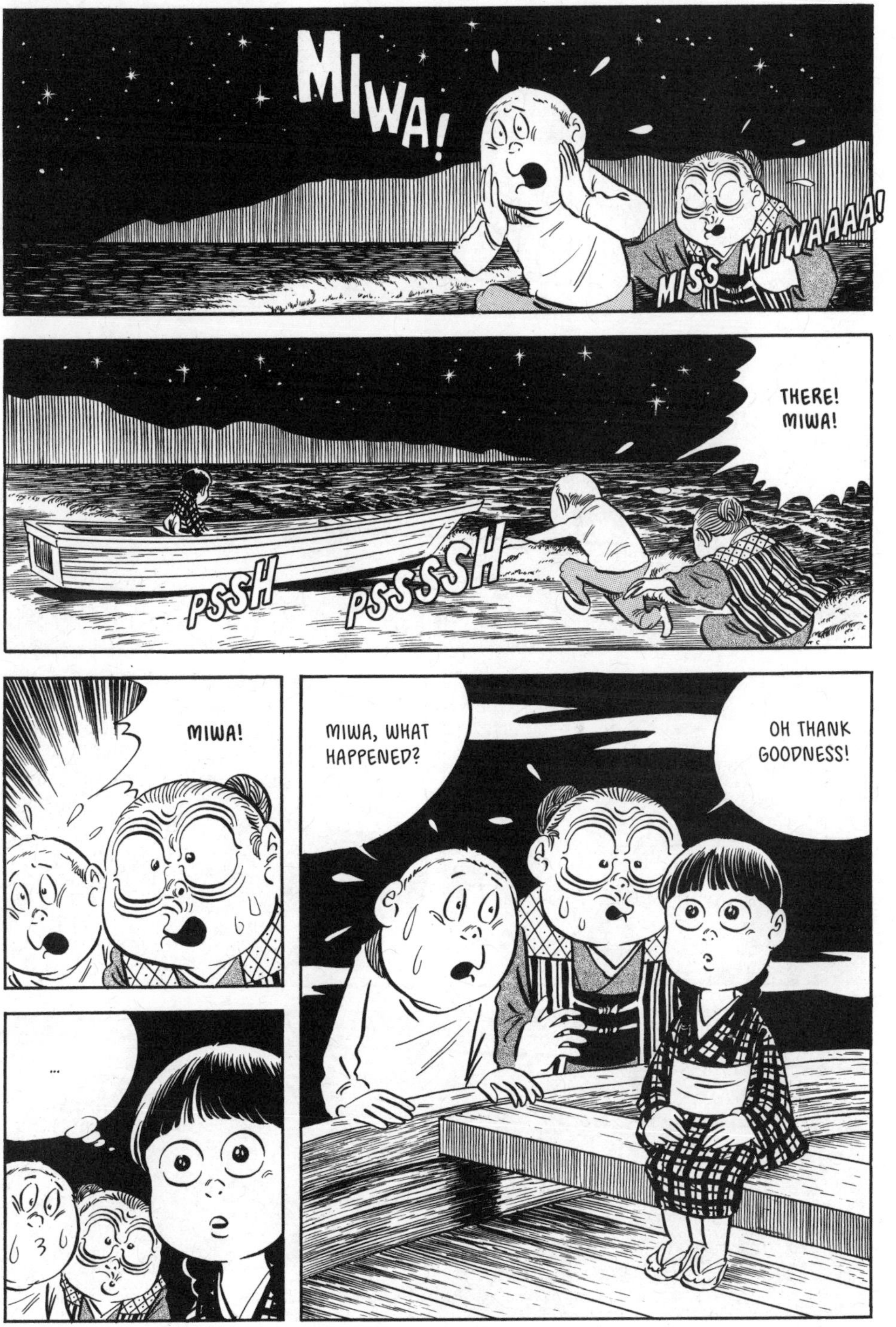
MIWA!
MISS MIIWAAAA!
THERE! MIWA!
PSSSSH
PSSH
OH THANK GOODNESS!
MIWA, WHAT HAPPENED?
MIWA!
...

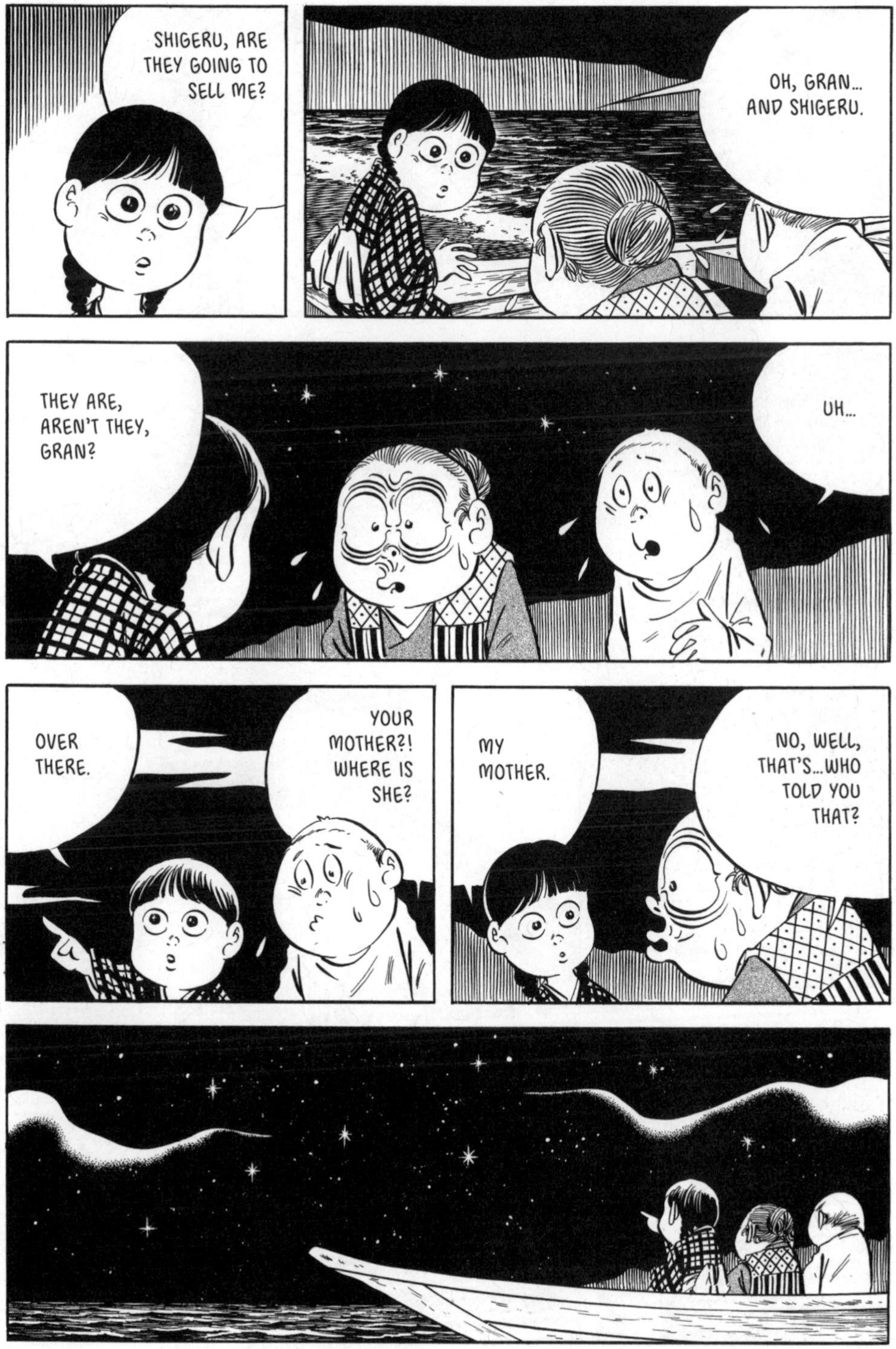
OH, GRAN... AND SHIGERU.
SHIGERU, ARE THEY GOING TO SELL ME?
UH...
THEY ARE, AREN'T THEY, GRAN?
NO, WELL, THAT'S...WHO TOLD YOU THAT?
MY MOTHER.
YOUR MOTHER?! WHERE IS SHE?
OVER THERE.

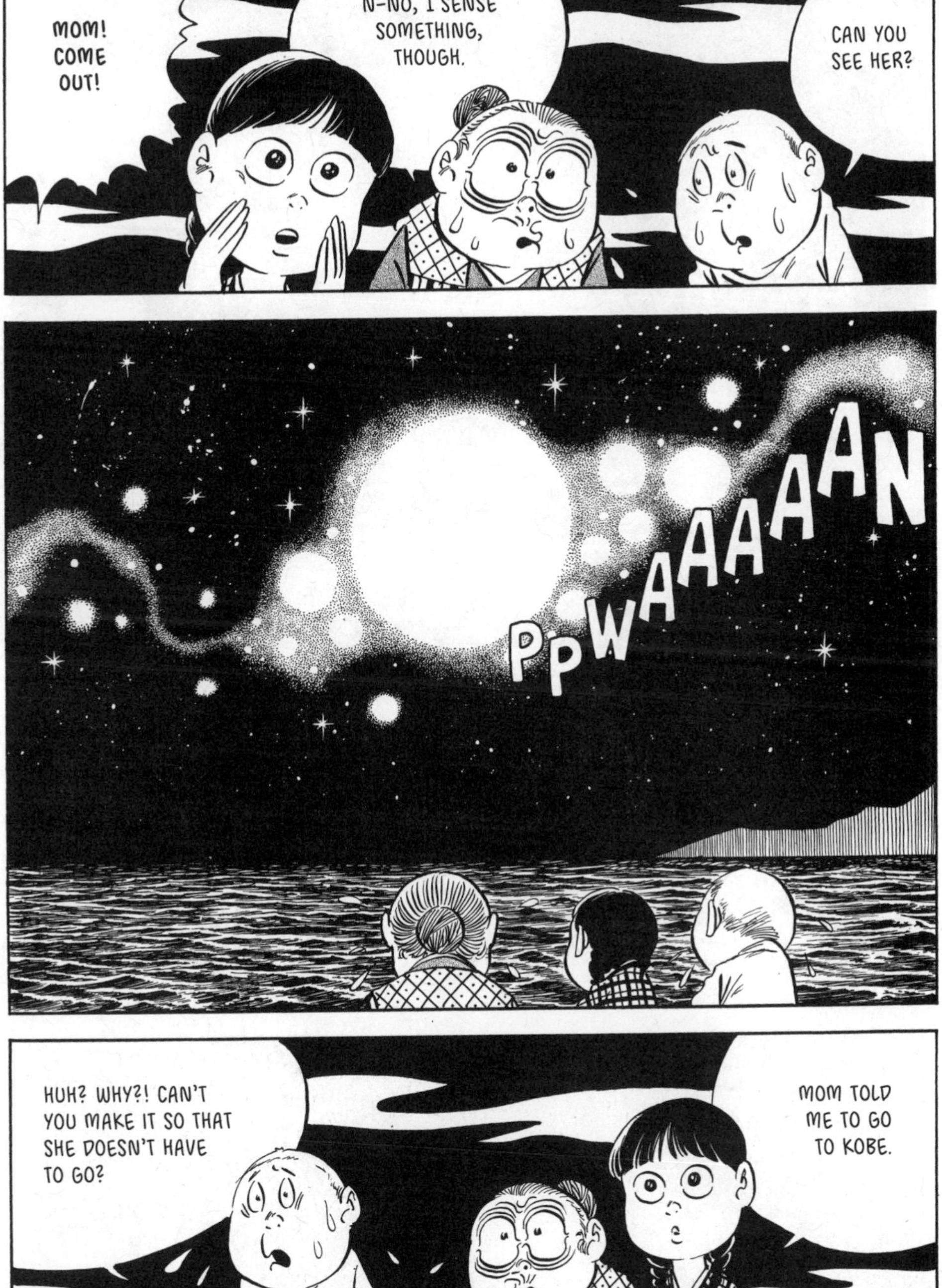

CAN YOU SEE HER?
N-NO, I SENSE SOMETHING, THOUGH.
MOM! COME OUT!
PPWAAAAAN
MOM TOLD ME TO GO TO KOBE.
HUH? WHY?! CAN'T YOU MAKE IT SO THAT SHE DOESN'T HAVE TO GO?

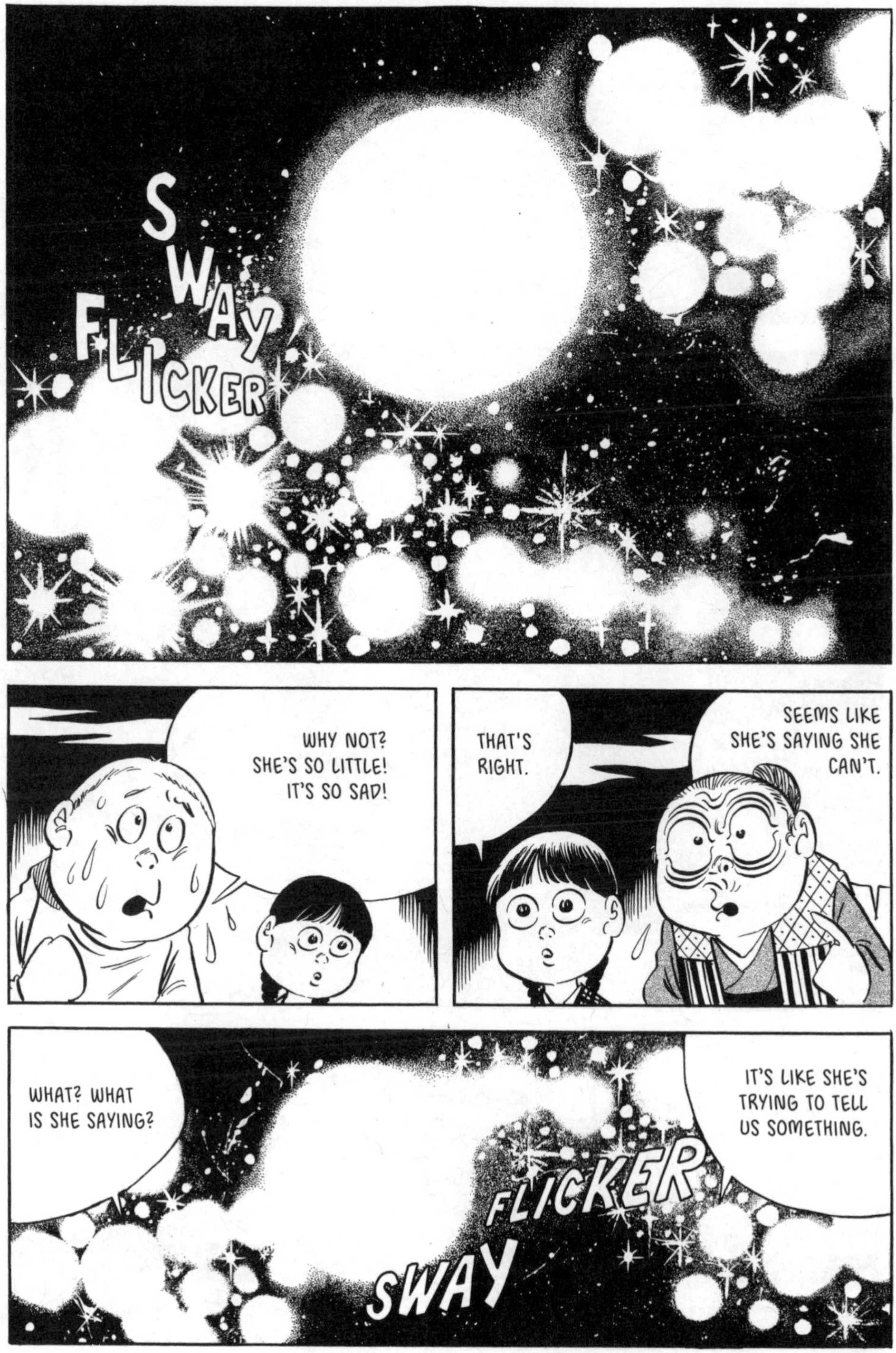
SWAY
FLICKER
SEEMS LIKE SHE'S SAYING SHE CAN'T.
THAT'S RIGHT.
WHY NOT? SHE'S SO LITTLE! IT'S SO SAD!
IT'S LIKE SHE'S TRYING TO TELL US SOMETHING.
WHAT? WHAT IS SHE SAYING?
FLICKER
SWAY

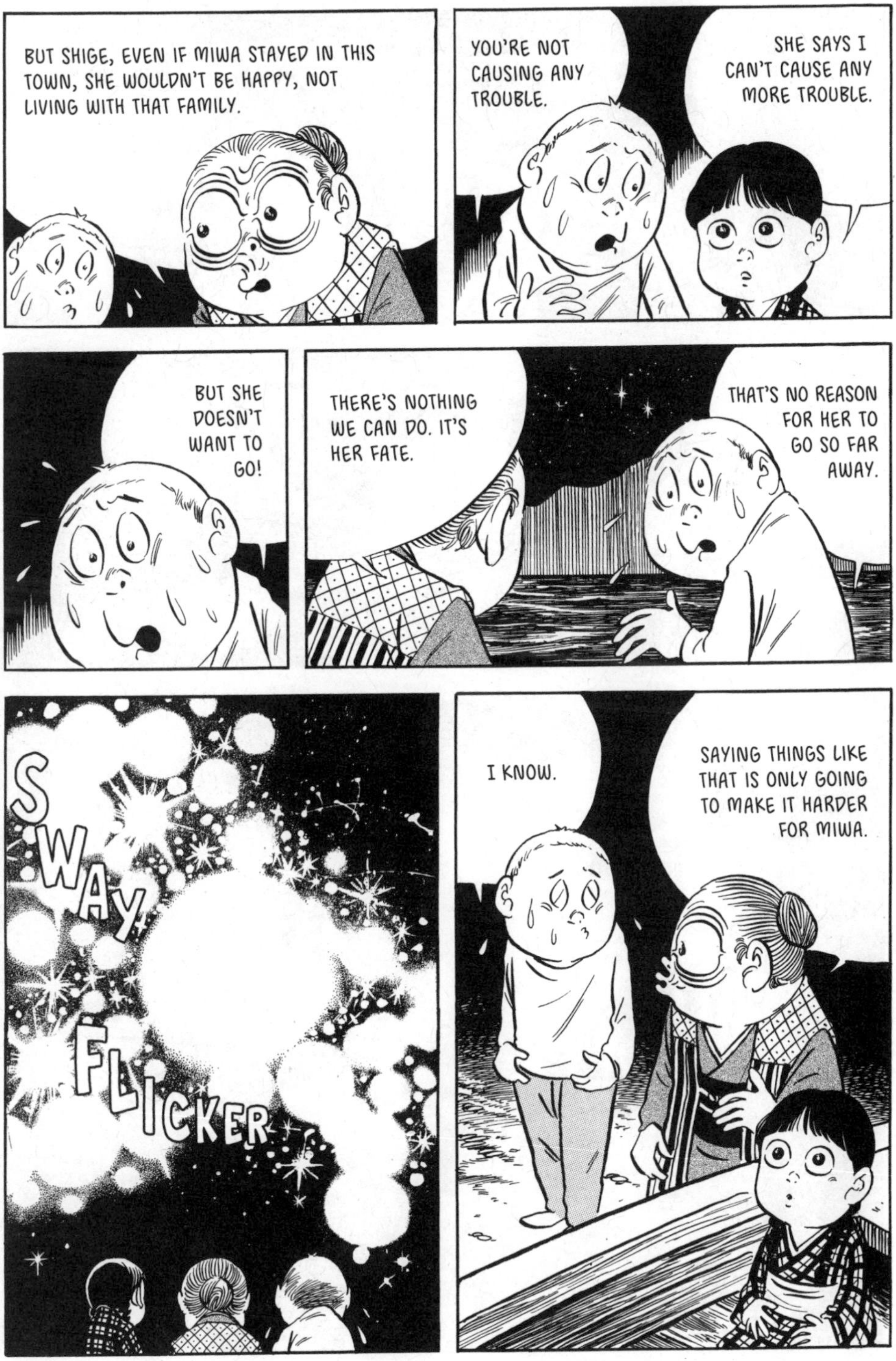
SHE SAYS I CAN'T CAUSE ANY MORE TROUBLE.
YOU'RE NOT CAUSING ANY TROUBLE.
BUT SHIGE, EVEN IF MIWA STAYED IN THIS TOWN, SHE WOULDN'T BE HAPPY, NOT LIVING WITH THAT FAMILY.
THAT'S NO REASON FOR HER TO GO SO FAR AWAY.
THERE'S NOTHING WE CAN DO. IT'S HER FATE.
BUT SHE DOESN'T WANT TO GO!
SAYING THINGS LIKE THAT IS ONLY GOING TO MAKE IT HARDER FOR MIWA.
I KNOW.
SWAY
FLICKER

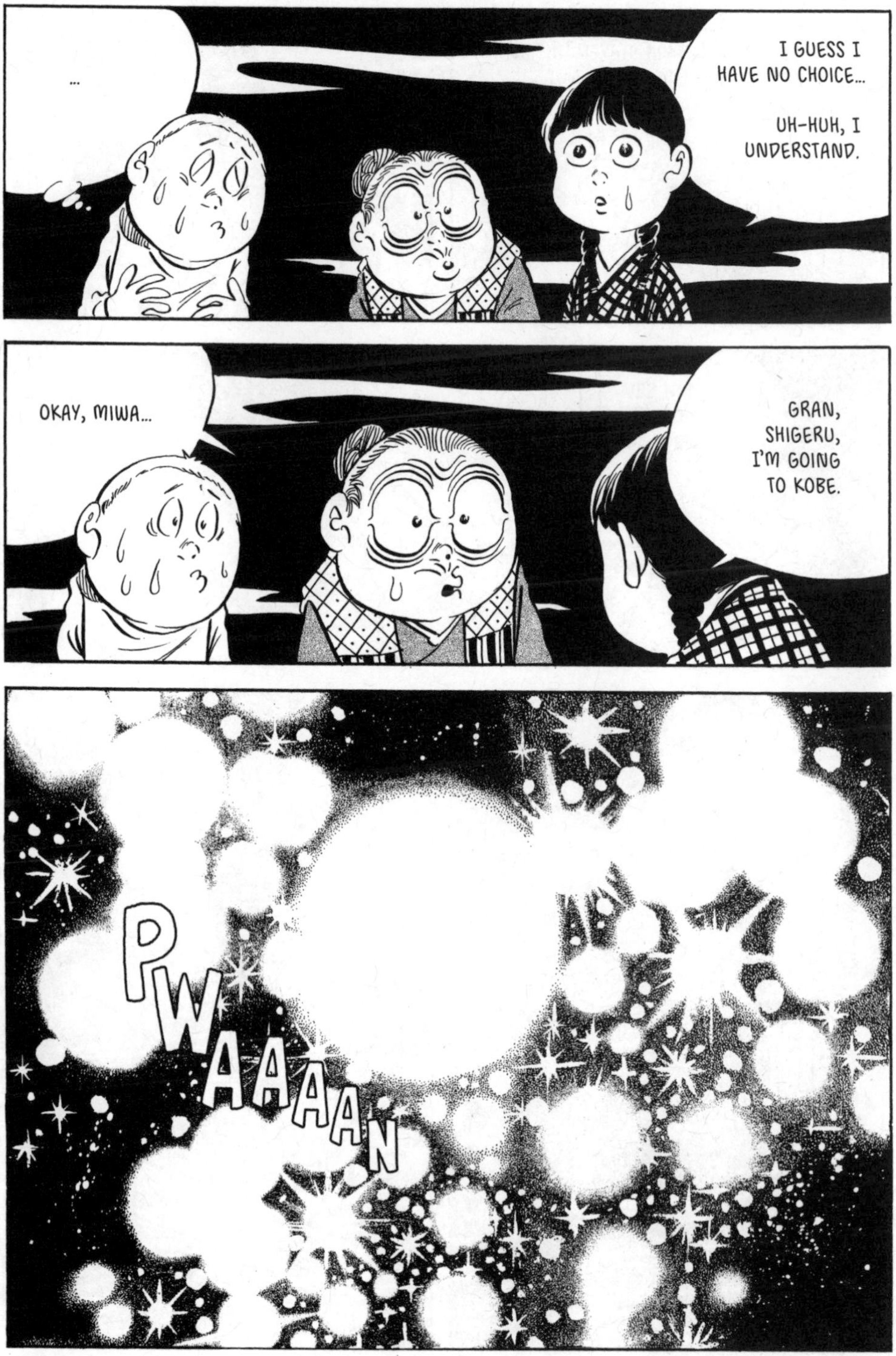
I GUESS I HAVE NO CHOICE...
UH-HUH, I UNDERSTAND.
...
GRAN, SHIGERU, I'M GOING TO KOBE.
OKAY, MIWA...
PWAAAAAN

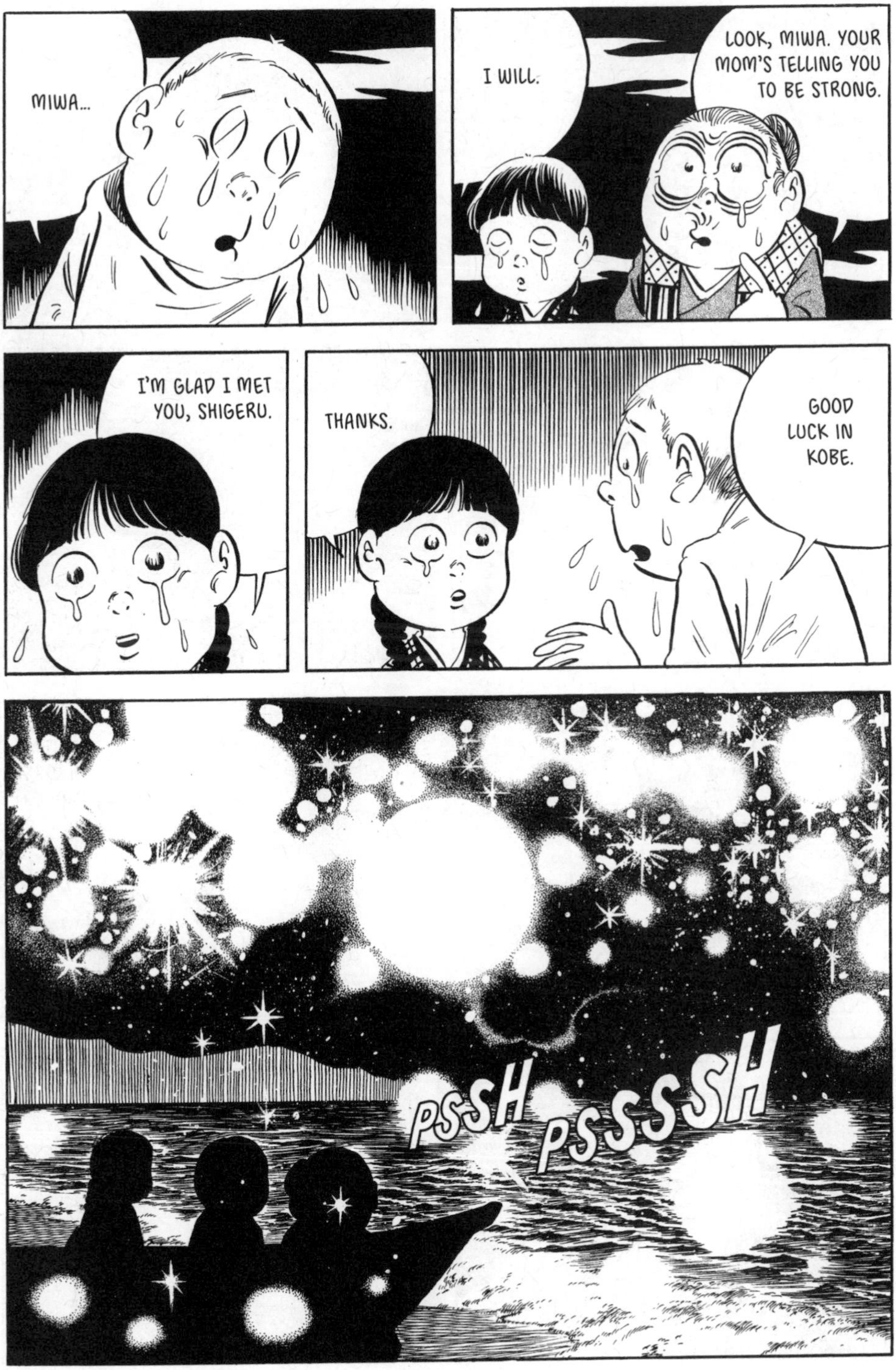
LOOK, MIWA. YOUR MOM'S TELLING YOU TO BE STRONG.
I WILL.
MIWA...
GOOD LUCK IN KOBE.
THANKS.
I'M GLAD I MET YOU, SHIGERU.
PSSH
PSSSSH

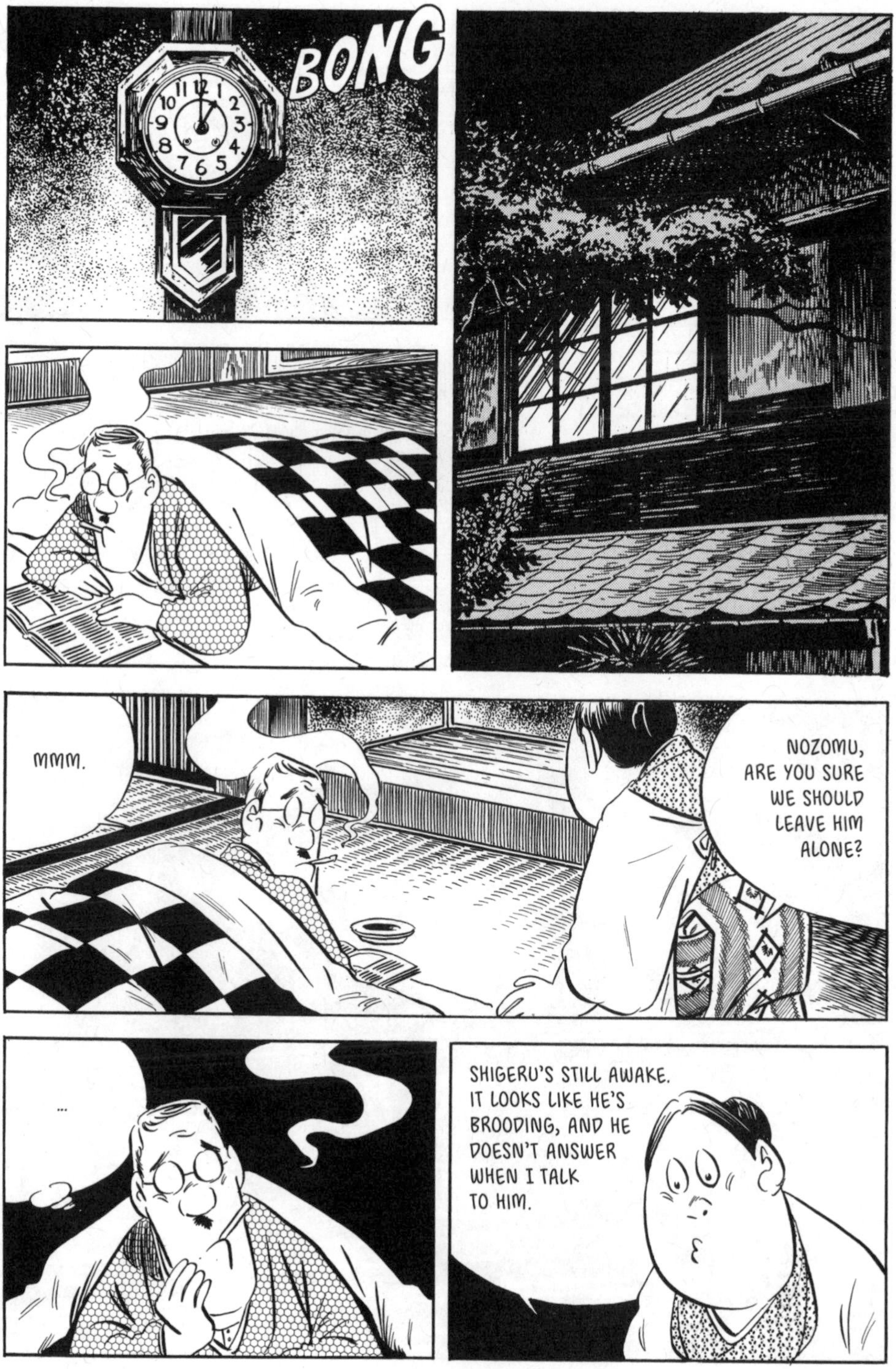
BONG
NOZOMU, ARE YOU SURE WE SHOULD LEAVE HIM ALONE?
MMM.
SHIGERU'S STILL AWAKE. IT LOOKS LIKE HE'S BROODING, AND HE DOESN'T ANSWER WHEN I TALK TO HIM.
...

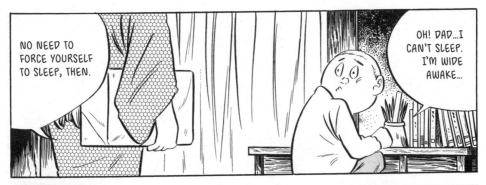

OH! DAD...I CAN'T SLEEP. I'M WIDE AWAKE...
NO NEED TO FORCE YOURSELF TO SLEEP, THEN.
OKAY.
I KNOW HOW YOU'RE FEEL-ING.
NOTHING'S HARDER THAN NOT BEING ABLE TO HELP A GOOD FRIEND.
YOUR OWN TROUBLES ARE ONE THING, BUT IT'S MUCH HARDER WHEN IT'S OUT OF YOUR HANDS.
THAT'S TRUE.
BUT YOU SEE, SHIGERU, THERE'S ALWAYS A LITTLE BUD OF HAPPINESS IN TIMES OF DESPAIR.
YOU THINK SO?
YOU'LL LEARN FROM THIS. FIGURING OUT NOW WHAT MATTERS TO YOU WILL HELP YOU FIND HAPPINESS LATER ON IN LIFE.
MOST PEOPLE SPEND THEIR DAYS IN VAIN, WITHOUT HOPE, DAY AFTER DAY.

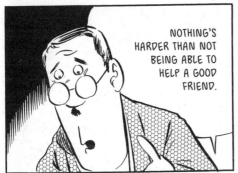

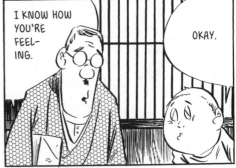

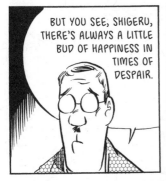

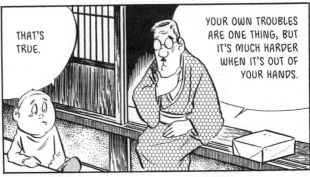

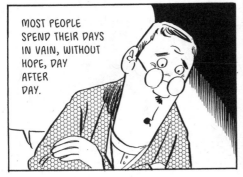

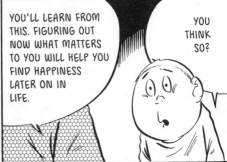

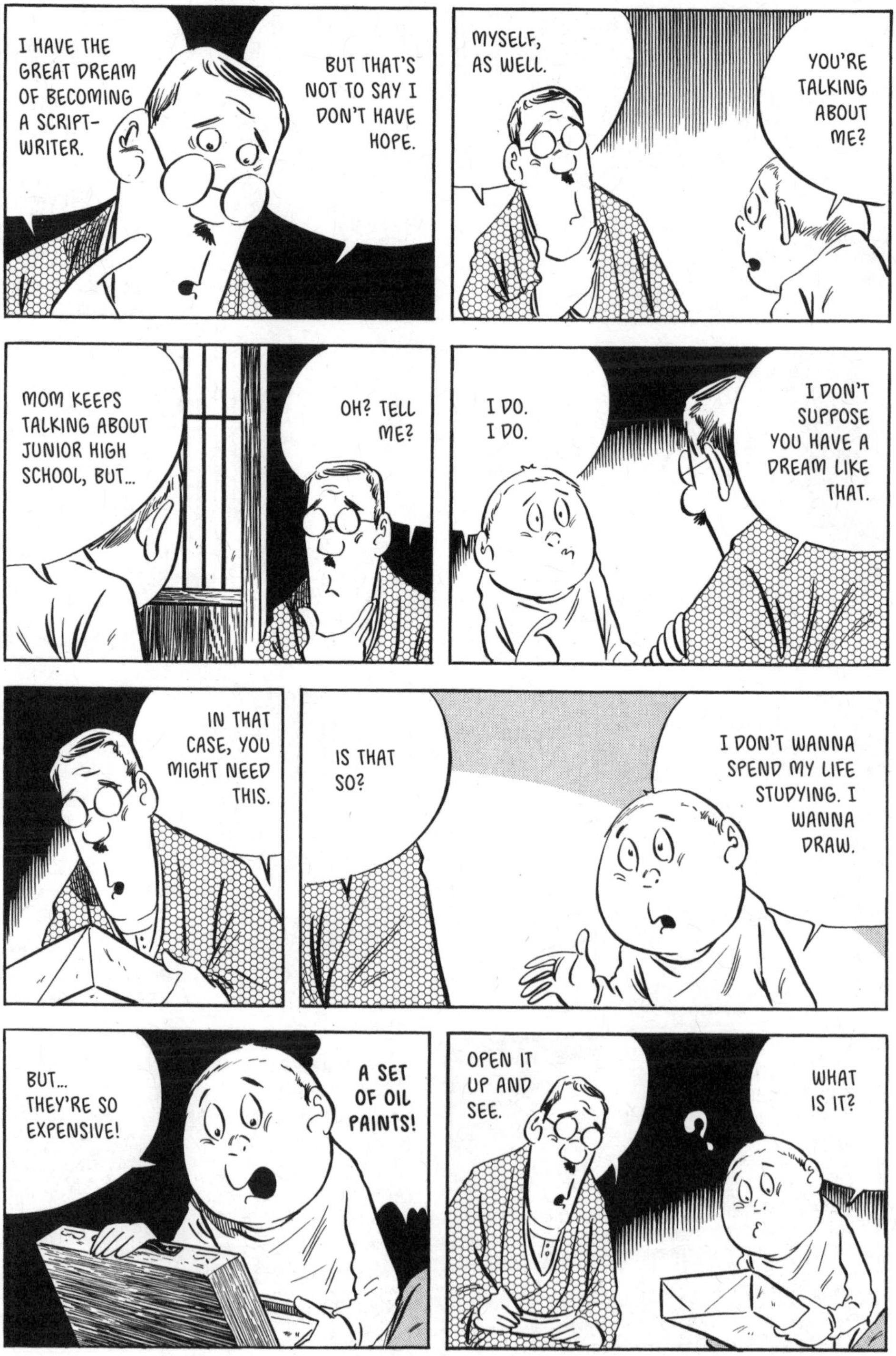
YOU'RE TALKING ABOUT ME?
MYSELF, AS WELL.
BUT THAT'S NOT TO SAY I DON'T HAVE HOPE.
I HAVE THE GREAT DREAM OF BECOMING A SCRIPT-WRITER.
I DON'T SUPPOSE YOU HAVE A DREAM LIKE THAT.
I DO. I DO.
OH? TELL ME?
MOM KEEPS TALKING ABOUT JUNIOR HIGH SCHOOL, BUT...
I DON'T WANNA SPEND MY LIFE STUDYING. I WANNA DRAW.
IS THAT SO?
IN THAT CASE, YOU MIGHT NEED THIS.
WHAT IS IT?
OPEN IT UP AND SEE.
A SET OF OIL PAINTS!
BUT... THEY'RE SO EXPENSIVE!

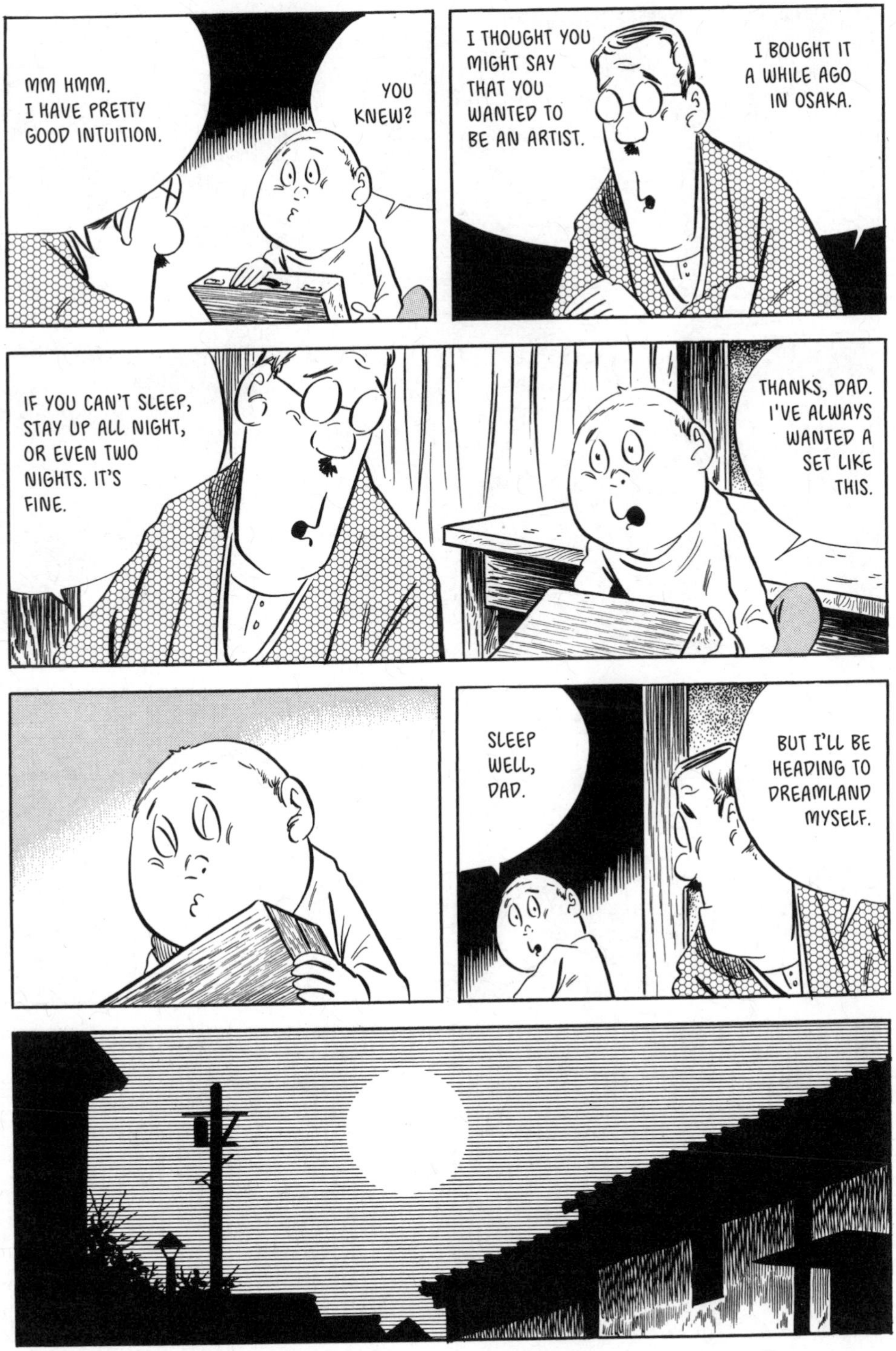
I BOUGHT IT A WHILE AGO IN OSAKA.
I THOUGHT YOU MIGHT SAY THAT YOU WANTED TO BE AN ARTIST.
YOU KNEW?
MM HMM. I HAVE PRETTY GOOD INTUITION.
THANKS, DAD. I'VE ALWAYS WANTED A SET LIKE THIS.
IF YOU CAN'T SLEEP, STAY UP ALL NIGHT, OR EVEN TWO NIGHTS. IT'S FINE.
BUT I'LL BE HEADING TO DREAMLAND MYSELF.
SLEEP WELL, DAD.

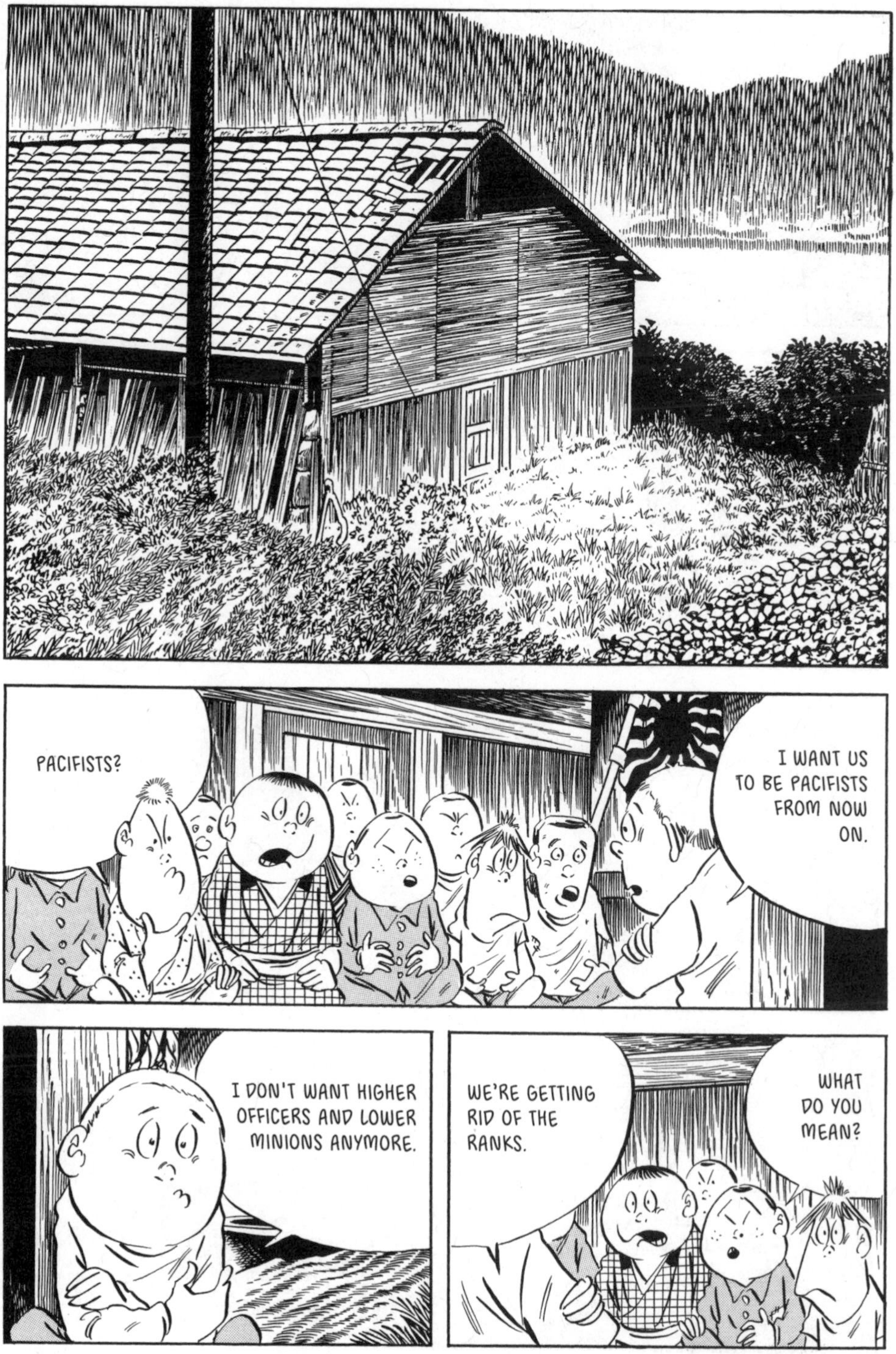
I WANT US TO BE PACIFISTS FROM NOW ON.
PACIFISTS?
WHAT DO YOU MEAN?
WE'RE GETTING RID OF THE RANKS.
I DON'T WANT HIGHER OFFICERS AND LOWER MINIONS ANYMORE.

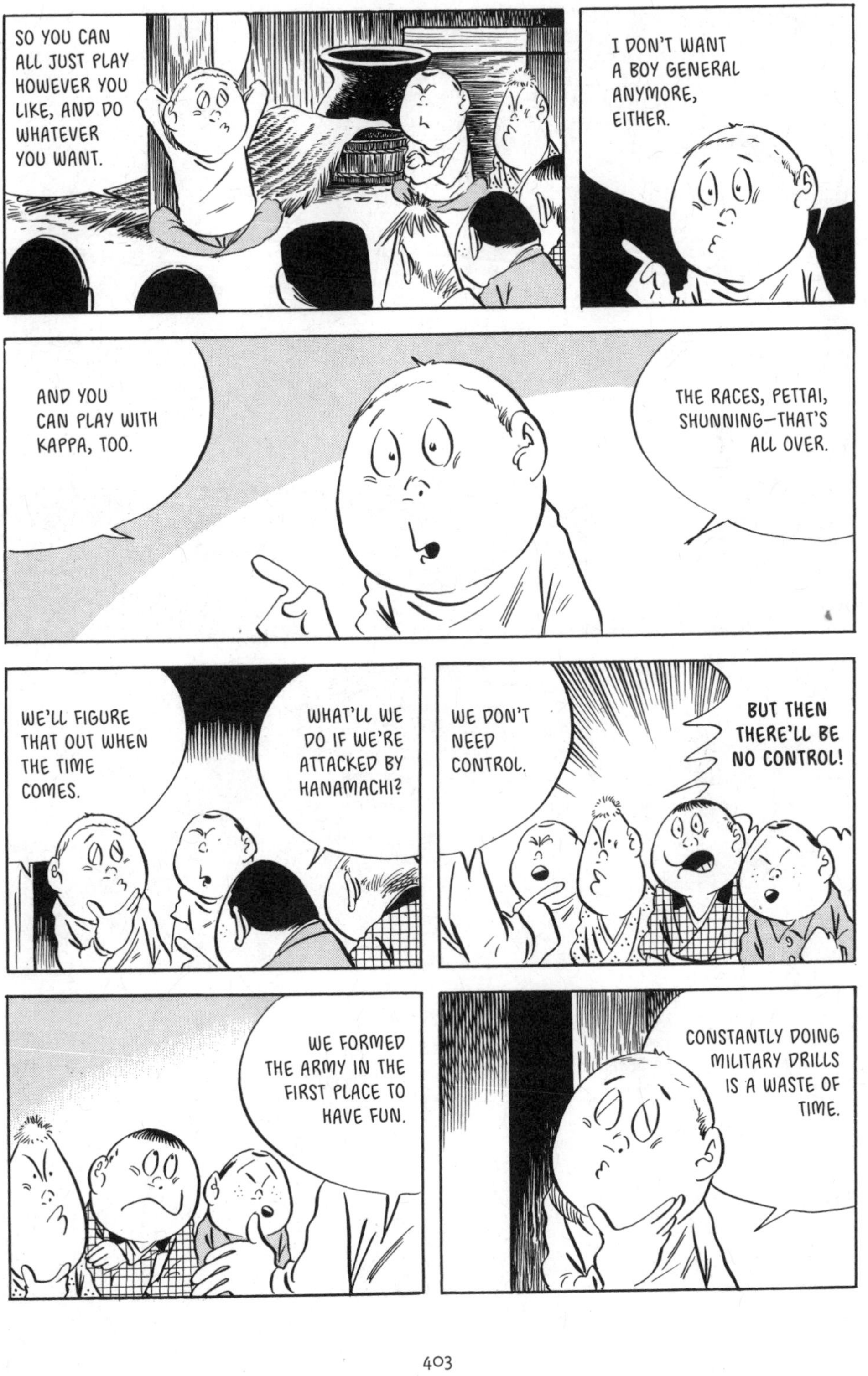
I DON'T WANT A BOY GENERAL ANYMORE, EITHER.
SO YOU CAN ALL JUST PLAY HOWEVER YOU LIKE, AND DO WHATEVER YOU WANT.
THE RACES, PETTAI, SHUNNING—THAT'S ALL OVER.
AND YOU CAN PLAY WITH KAPPA, TOO.
BUT THEN THERE'LL BE NO CONTROL!
WE DON'T NEED CONTROL.
WHAT'LL WE DO IF WE'RE ATTACKED BY HANAMACHI?
WE'LL FIGURE THAT OUT WHEN THE TIME COMES.
CONSTANTLY DOING MILITARY DRILLS IS A WASTE OF TIME.
WE FORMED THE ARMY IN THE FIRST PLACE TO HAVE FUN.

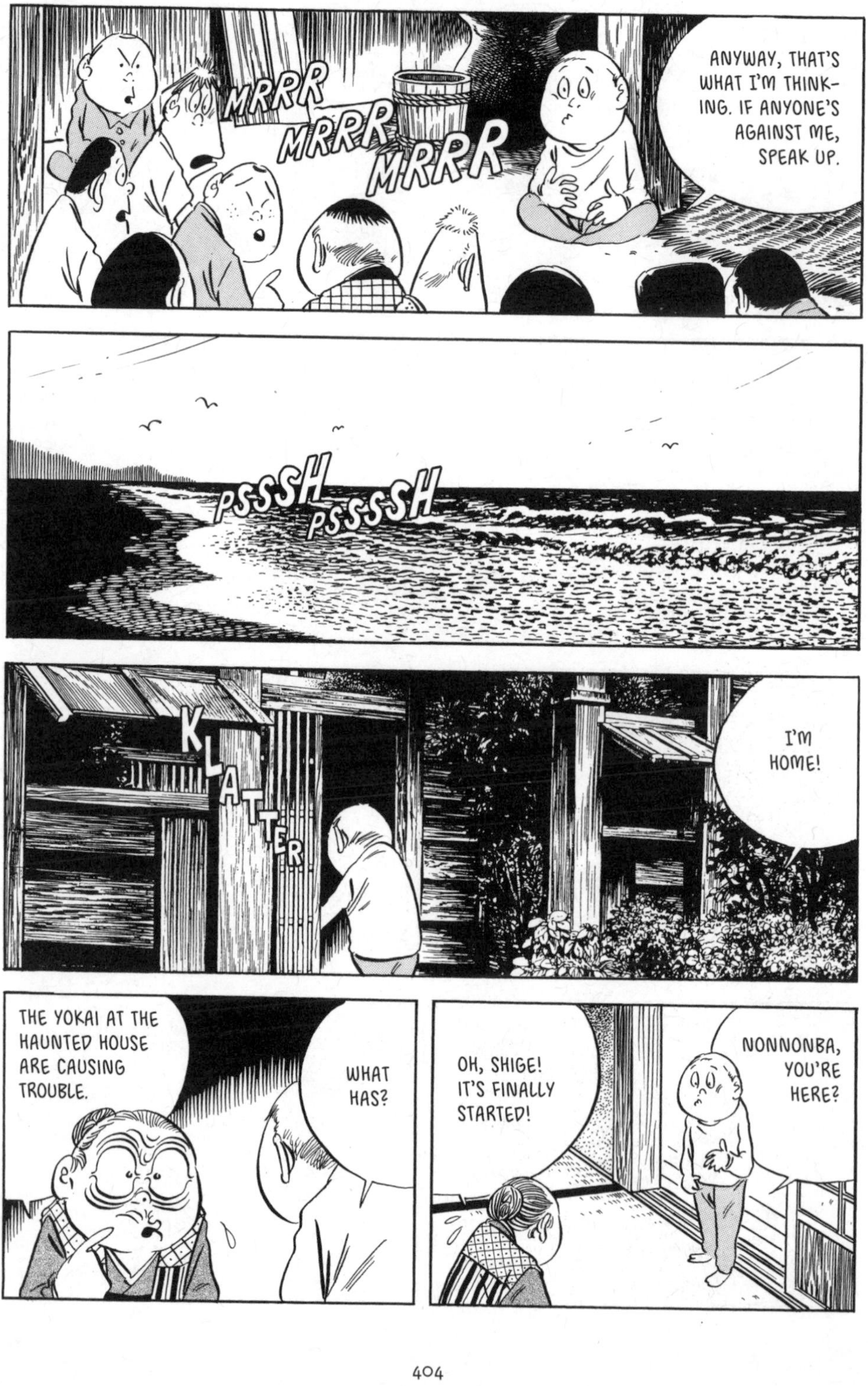
ANYWAY, THAT'S WHAT I'M THINK-ING. IF ANYONE'S AGAINST ME, SPEAK UP.
MRRR MRRR MRRR
PSSSH PSSSSH
I'M HOME!
KLATTER
NONNONBA, YOU'RE HERE?
OH, SHIGE! IT'S FINALLY STARTED!
WHAT HAS?
THE YOKAI AT THE HAUNTED HOUSE ARE CAUSING TROUBLE.

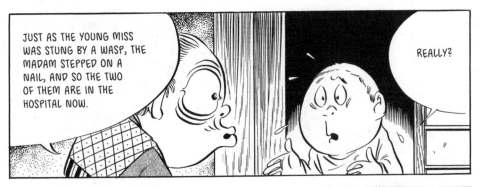

REALLY?
JUST AS THE YOUNG MISS WAS STUNG BY A WASP, THE MADAM STEPPED ON A NAIL, AND SO THE TWO OF THEM ARE IN THE HOSPITAL NOW.
MAYBE IT'S JUST A COINCIDENCE?
IT MOST CERTAINLY IS NOT. LAST NIGHT, WHEN I WENT BACK TO THE HOUSE TO GET SOMETHING I FORGOT, THE MASTER HAD JUST RETURNED FROM KOBE, AND...
AAAAAH!
WAARGH

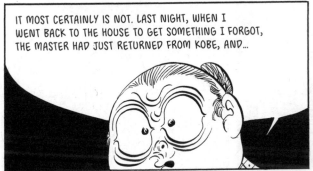

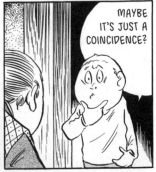

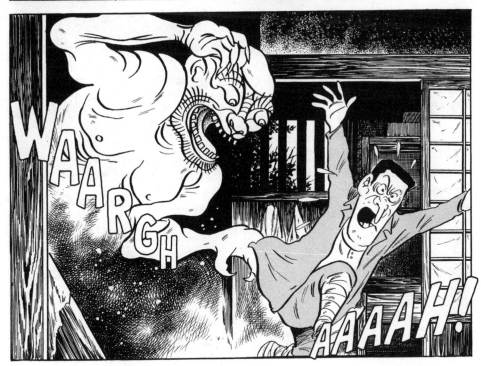

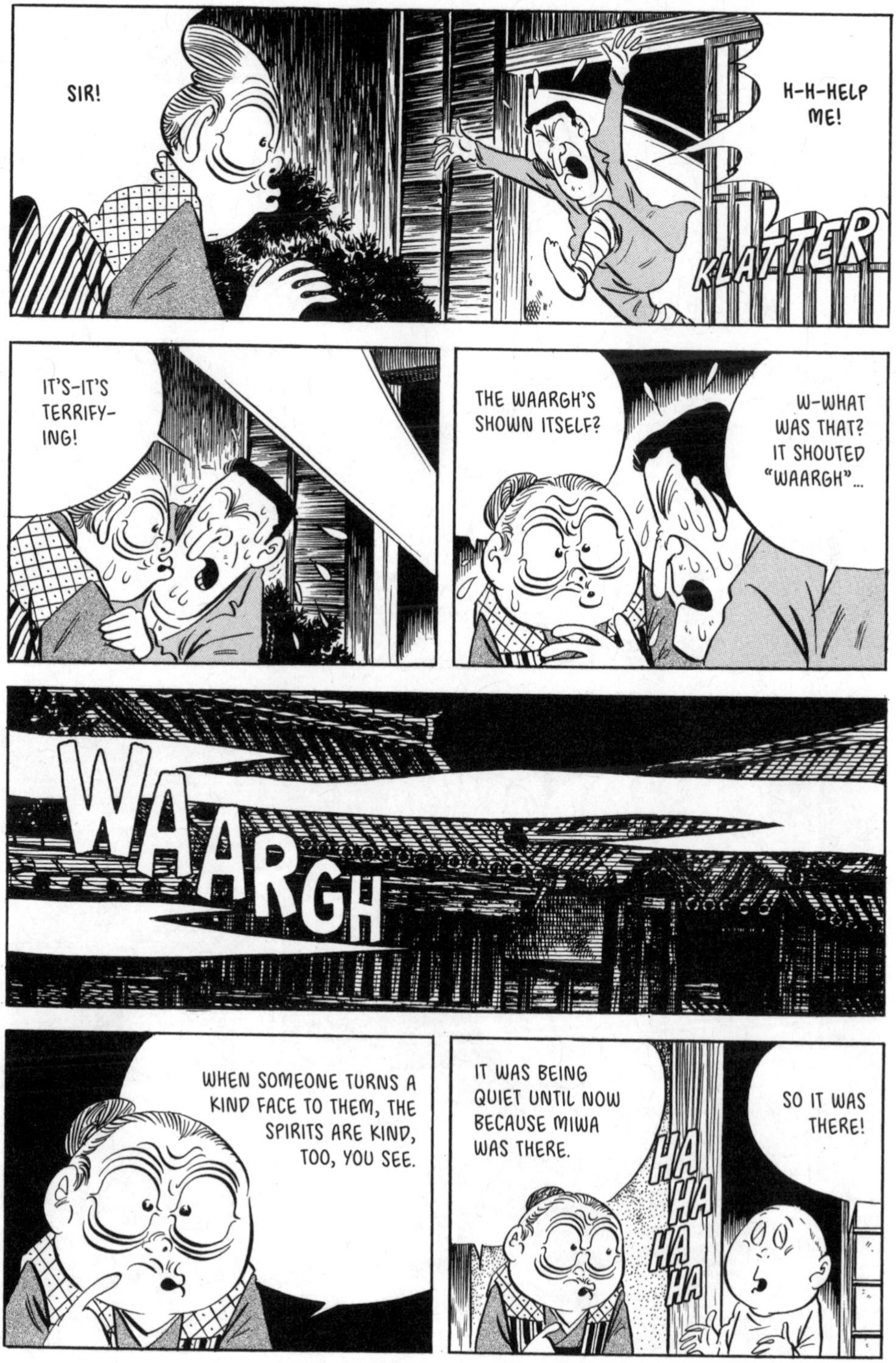
H-H-HELP ME!
SIR!
KLATTER
W-WHAT WAS THAT? IT SHOUTED "WAARGH"...
THE WAARGH'S SHOWN ITSELF?
IT'S-IT'S TERRIFY-ING!
WAARGH
SO IT WAS THERE!
IT WAS BEING QUIET UNTIL NOW BECAUSE MIWA WAS THERE.
HA HA HA HA HA
WHEN SOMEONE TURNS A KIND FACE TO THEM, THE SPIRITS ARE KIND, TOO, YOU SEE.

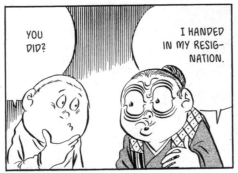

SEEMS LIKE THINGS WILL BE PRETTY BAD AROUND THERE FOR A WHILE.
WILL YOU BE ALL RIGHT, NONNONBA?
I HANDED IN MY RESIG-NATION.
YOU DID?
YUP! OH, THAT'S RIGHT! MISS MIWA ASKED ME TO GIVE YOU THIS LETTER.
WHAT?
TAKE A LOOK.
ありがとお
みわ
SHE WROTE IT SO WELL.
THE BIG CITY'S CLAMORING WITH TERRIBLE PEOPLE—PEOPLE WHO'D EVEN STEAL FROM YOKAI.
LETTER: THANK YOU. / MIWA.

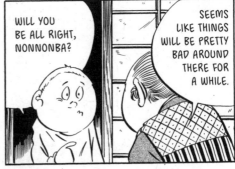

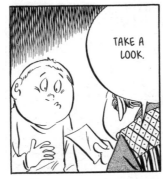

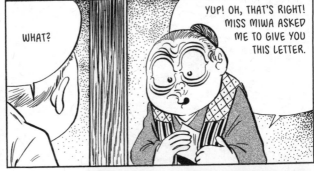

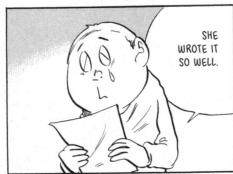

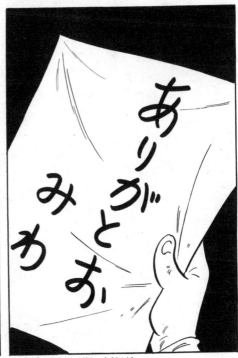

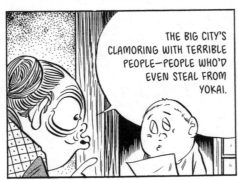

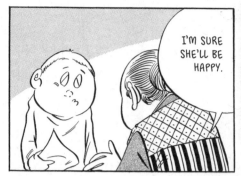

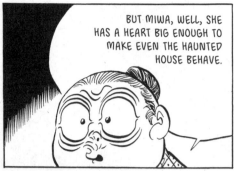

BUT MIWA, WELL, SHE HAS A HEART BIG ENOUGH TO MAKE EVEN THE HAUNTED HOUSE BEHAVE.
I'M SURE SHE'LL BE HAPPY.
YEAH. SHE HAS TO BE.

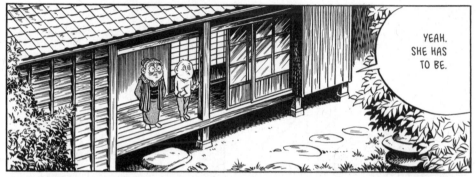

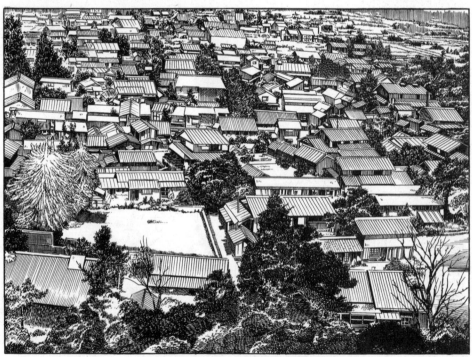

A JAPANESE YOKAI EXPERT IN SEARCH OF BRITISH FAIRIES

KIMIE IMURA

Reading *NonNonBa*, I laughed long and hard like a child, my heart often full of a bittersweet nostalgia. These boys—imperial boy general Tadashi, future boy general Gege—together in the abandoned barn in Sakaiminato, with their free, mischievous, and above all, intense play, consumed me. This nostalgia remains sharp in my heart no matter how many times I read their story; I feel it could even pierce my chest. But it is a good feeling, as if I have been given a glimpse into a world of courageous men through the strict laws of the boy army: the severity of absolute obedience; the fist, a lesson to those who do not submit; the fight, or rather the battle, with the neighboring army; the earnest tests of strength.

The boy generals of my own childhood who joined me in my exploring of unknown spaces—the pine forest, the garden behind the hospital—all died young. I've often wondered if this wasn't because they were, in the end, too courageous—as if they never grew out of the recklessness of their youth, beginning as boy generals and ending as war generals. But Gege, *NonNonBa*'s boy general, has taken his experiences from that time and made them bear fruit, giving us so many wonderful works based on these precious moments that I find myself filled with surprise and a deep respect. This book is a valuable record of an enviably happy boyhood, a time without after-school cram school, when playing was studying.

Mizuki credits an elderly neighbor, whom his family called "NonNonBa," with inspiring him to draw pictures and manga of *yokai*. In the Sakaiminato area, people who served Buddha were referred to as "NonNon-san," and so the nickname was an abbreviation of "NonNon Obaasan" (Grandmother NonNon). Although she lived with her elderly husband, a "prayer hand" whose job was to pray for the sick to get well, NonNonBa was for one reason or another always at Shigeru's house, telling him about the Tanabata Star Festival, or the O-bon festival of the dead, about the origins of various holidays, or the nature of yokai. Doted on by this grandmother figure, the young boy gradually became fascinated by the yokai. The more of NonNonBa's stories that he

listened to, the more keenly aware he became of the supernatural world, until eventually collecting yokai became the focus of his life.

When NonNonBa told the story of Tenjoname, the ceiling licker, while Mizuki was lying in bed at night staring up at the stains on the ceiling, he must have really feared—and really felt the presence of—the long-tongued monster. Standing in a grassy field at twilight, after realizing that the seagull cries all around him were actually the cries of Kawa-akago[1], it was understandable that he began to notice monsters everywhere. The stories of yokai and their individual idiosyncrasies—the dirt-licking Akaname; the abandoned cleaning rag, Shiro-uneri; the split-tailed cat spirit, Nekomata; the ocean-dwelling Umibozu; the child-snatching Kotori-bozu; the per-

sistent BetoBeto-san—passed through the mouth of NonNonBa into the ears of the boy general. And Mizuki, with his ability to sense yokai, captured their spirits deftly, giving them shape and recreating them on the page. When meditating on the nature of yokai, he has said, his thoughts come straight from his heart and, in the end, always return to these times with NonNonBa; he feels that her spirit is inside of him and continues to live on.

The San-in region of Honshu (which includes Mizuki's childhood home of Tottori and the neighboring Shimane prefecture) was rich in folklore about the "eight million gods." Many of these local stories were collected by the scholar Lafcadio Hearn in the now-classic Kwaidan, but Mizuki did not learn about yokai from books. Instead, he became part of the oral story-telling tradition of the region, and learned to recognize the role of yokai in everyday life. His early im-

---

I   Kawa-akago is a yokai that lives by rivers and lakes. It is believed to be the spirit of a child who drowned.

YOU CAN
TALK TO
ME.

mersion in this supernatural world through the teachings of NonNonBa allowed him to see beyond the visible world. Because Mizuki had this kind of background, with this kind of boyhood, the yokai in his work are not ephemeral, made-up creatures, but solid, legitimate existences with real weight.

Our hero, with his many interests, tried a succession of different things: collecting newspaper mastheads, building model battleships. He still has the collection of drawings he called the "Tenkondo Gashu" (meaning a collection of pictures of the insect kingdom), the pages of which are filled with his imaginings and drawings of insects and the natural world. Amongst these are several drawings of nature spirits, little people who are more like fairies than yokai. One of these drawings was of a rice sprite. It was accompanied by a poem that made a deep impression on me: "This is inside the rice. Inside that hard shell lives a little person. You can split the rice in half, you can look at it with a microscope, but you will never be able to see the little person." Ever since his childhood, Mizuki has been powerfully aware of a world that exists beyond the visible; he has given expression to that world through his work.

I was able to get close to the boy general, Shigeru Mizuki, thanks to an NHK radio program on Japanese and Western yokai in 1990. When I talked about my trip to study island fairies, and my plan to spend two weeks over the spring holiday travelling to Cornwall, the Isles of Scilly, the Isle of Man, the Isle of Arran, and various places in Ireland, Mizuki mentioned that he would like to come along, and he ended up joining me on the trip. When he called me, announcing, "I'm in London now," I couldn't help but be surprised by how quickly he sprang into action, even though I had been expecting him. I was truly excited to go looking for fairies with the world leader in yokai research.

The trip was a wonderful experience. With my husband, our son, and a photographer, there were five of us. We searched far and wide, looking in places featured in Arthurian legends and Yeats's writing, as well as in holes left by large rocks, where pixies and leprechauns are particularly likely to be found. Mizuki clambered over prehistoric megaliths, crossed streams flowing among the rocks of Dartmoor, descended into the basin of the Glencar waterfall, all the while insisting, "They're here, I can feel them." In the blink of an eye he became once more Sakaiminato's boy general Gege, nimble and brave. Camera in hand, he deftly captured the mysterious natural world of gnarled trees and mossy rocks, and just when you thought he was here, he was over there. I too felt my old excitement at exploring unknown spaces, and I followed Mizuki in my boots, tramping through ferns and thickets. A rolling fog soon wrapped itself around us, and we stopped, having lost sight of where we were going. We were on a hilltop with a wilderness of stones as far as the eye could see and megaliths in the distance, notably Cornwall's ancient quoit in Zennor. I vividly recall feeling a presence about to appear, and the sensation that the Western fairies had come out to greet the doctor of Japanese yokai.

The sensitivity of this Japanese yokai expert's antennae, effortlessly sensing the invisible world, allowed Mizuki to detect fairies all over the UK. They say that fairies live in a seed in the heart of a person who believes, that they particularly favor the pure and innocent. The appearance or essence of yokai and fairies may differ according to local folk histories and customs, but those characteristics derived from the supernatural nature of their presence are always the same.

"The magnetic field for yokai and fairies is really intense in the UK, isn't it? And the population of yokai is quite large." Having spent my life introducing the fairies of the British Isles to Japan, I am delighted and grateful to Mizuki for these words. Coming from this celebrated artist, who even now has the heart of the boy general from Sakaiminato, these words were like a seal of approval for British fairy studies.

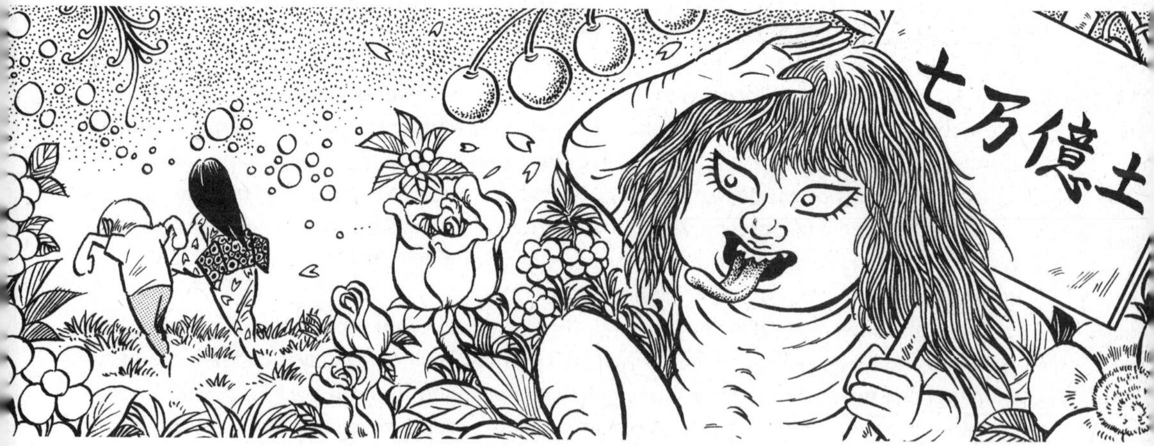
七万億土

Kimie Imura is the author of numerous books on fairies and the supernatural, with the majority of her work focusing on Celtic and British fairies. She is also the chairperson of the Fairy Association founded by Shigeru Mizuki, the honorary president of the Utsunomiya Fairy Museum, and the president of the Fairy Art Museum.

"A Japanese Yokai Expert in Search of British Fairies" was originally published in Chikuma Shonen Toshokan *37 in 1977. The version appearing here is an edited version of the original.*

9: 'A hundred thousand worlds' is from the Buddhist term *juumanokudo*, meaning the countless Buddhist worlds between this world and *Sukhavati*, or paradise. The term is also used to indicate paradise itself.

15: *Okayu* is a rice porridge, often eaten as a comfort food when one has a cold or the flu.

34: The Japanese here is *obake*, which refers to monsters, ghosts, goblins, and other supernatural creatures. It is nearly synonymous with yokai.

48: Umibozu is a yokai that lives in the ocean. It rises up at night during calm seas and tries to destroy ships sailing nearby. It is thought to be quite large, the tallest being the size of a redwood. The yokai Umizato appears in several Edo period paintings, as a giant towering over the ocean and carrying a *biwa* lute. Tomokazuki is a female ocean-dwelling yokai seen by female shell divers. She takes on the form of the person who sees her. Mizuchi refers to a variety of yokai snakes living in bodies of water.

49: Mr. Sticky, or BetoBeto-san, is a yokai that follows people walking along at night. Although he does not cause harm, the sound of his *geta* sandals behind the walker is unnerving.

54: Denjiro Okouchi (1898–1962) was a Japanese film and theatre star who made his debut in 1925. He worked with many of Japan's most famous directors, including Akira Kurosawa.

54: Tange Sazen is the name of the character played by Denjiro Okouchi in a series of popular *jidaigeki* period films. The most widely appreciated of these films now is 1935's *Tange Sazen Yowa: Hyakuman Ryo no Tsubo*, or *The Million Ryo Pot*.

54: Ofuji Kushimaki is the name of Tange Sazen's lover in *Shinpan O-oka Seitan*, a three-part movie from 1928 starring Denjiro Okouchi.

56: The teacher is likely referring to the fact that Japan was censured by the League of Nations after Japan's invasion of Manchuria, leading to the country leaving the organization in 1933. This period also saw a considerable push toward economic growth and the rise of nationalistic attitudes that ultimately led to Japan's participation in WWII.

71: In Japanese mythology, Hoichi the Earless was a very gifted blind minstrel who, despite his great talent, remained very poor. At one point, Hoichi is tricked into playing his biwa lute for a ghostly court, and his friend, a priest, painted his body with the *kanji* characters of the Heart Sutra for protection. The priest neglected to paint the characters on Hoichi's ears, however,

TREMBLE
SHUDDER
TREMBLE

I–IT'S HERE!
HURRY!!

and when the samurai from the ghost court came to fetch him, all that he could see were Hoichi's ears, which he ripped off to bring back to his lord as proof that he could find no other trace of Hoichi. Yakumo Koizumi, better known as Lafcadio Hearn (see note for page 286) in English, produced the first English translation of this story.

72: *Chuji-tabi Nikk*i is a silent jidaigeki period film starring Denjiro Okouchi, produced in 1927.

86: This is a Japanese Imperial Army war song written by Takeki Owada and Toyokichi Fukazawa in 1904.

93: The flag here is the one flown by fishermen returning with a large catch of fish. Presumably, the children would have easy access to such flags since they live on the coast in Sakaiminato where many of the citizens would have been fishermen.

99: A *jizo* is a bodhisattva believed to lead dead children to the land of the dead, and is thought to protect travellers as well. Finding one in the ground would be seen as a fortuitous event. Stone jizo statues can be seen throughout Japan, often wearing red caps and bibs.

104: Asakusa is a neighborhood in Tokyo, most famous for the large Senso-ji temple there. It was once one of the major entertainment districts of Tokyo, particularly famous for its theatres before World War II, but is now seen as a traditional Tokyo neighborhood preserving the atmosphere of old Tokyo.

109: Natsume Soseki (1867–1916) is considered to be one of Japan's preeminent authors. He is best known for his novels *I Am a Cat*, *Kokoro*, and *Botchan*. His portrait was on the 1000 yen note from 1984 until 2004.

120: Isami Kondo was the commander of the famed *Shinsengumi*, a special police force from the late Edo period. The men of the Shinsengumi were known for their bravery and strength in the face of any danger, and have been a staple of Japanese pop culture, the subject of many films, TV shows, anime and manga, and were even made into a series of collectible figures in 2004 and 2005.

126: See note for page 48.

134: A sen was one-hundredth of a yen and was removed from circulation at the end of 1953.

134: *O-chugen* is an annual custom when gifts are given to people who have helped the giver in some way. Most often, these people are work-related, but neighbors and other acquaintances may also receive O-chugen gifts. Depending on the region, the date for O-chugen falls on July 15 or August 15. Similarly, *O-bon* is the ancestor festival celebrated on July 15 or August 15, and is a time for people to return to their hometowns to visit their ancestors' graves and join in festivities. The spirits of ancestors are said to return for the festival, and at the end of the three-day festival, the living see them off to the spirit world by lighting lanterns and setting them off in the river or ocean.

158: This stems from the Japanese myth of the trickster fox. They are well known for playing tricks on people, and often shape-shift, much to the bafflement of onlookers.

158: *Manju* is a bun-like sweet generally made from rice flour filled with a sweet bean paste.

161: *Sekihan*, literally 'red rice,' is rice steamed with *azuki* beans, which give the rice a pinkish color, and is served on special occasions and in times of celebration.

207: NonNonBa chants an appeal to Yakushi Nyorai, the Buddha of healing in Shingon Buddhism. Candâli and Mâtàngi are the Sanskrit names that are generally used for Yakushi Nyorai in English.

211: The song sung here is 'Yasugi Bushi' (Song of Yasugi), a famous and notoriously difficult folk song from the Shimane region.

213: Japanese knotweed is used as a healing herb in traditional medicine.

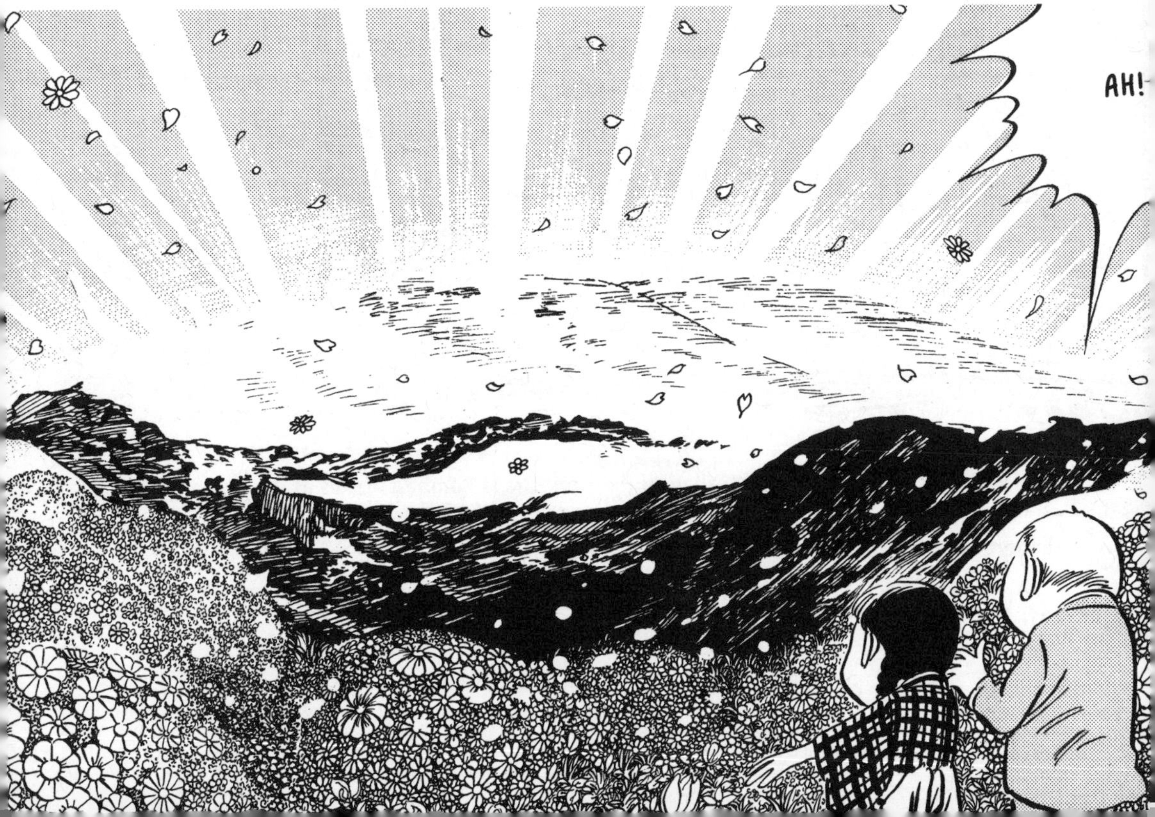
AH!

213: Reception day comes from the custom of *settai*, the practice of giving gifts, usually of food or money, to pilgrims to aid them in their pilgrimage. The pilgrim is obligated to accept the gift and usually responds by giving the settai giver one of the pilgrim's prayer slips. In many rural areas, a day is devoted to this custom of giving to pilgrims, and laypeople make prayer slips and bring them to neighboring temples or shrines in exchange for some kind of gift, usually food.

220: 'Hail Lotus Sutra', or *Nanmyouhougekkyo*, is the first line of the Lotus Sutra, one of the foundations of Nichiren Buddhism.

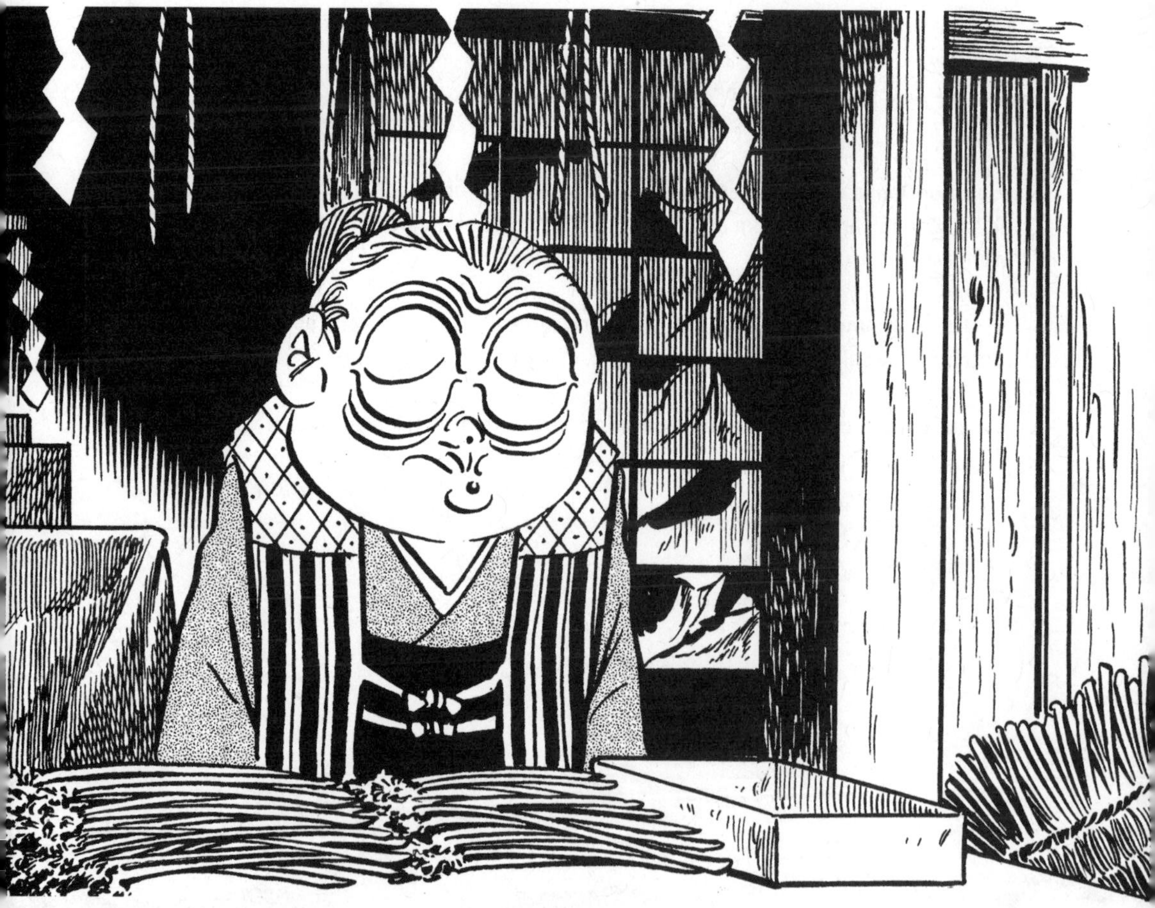

258: Released in 1932, this song, 'Ballad of the Three Brave Bombers,' takes as its theme three soldiers who sacrificed themselves to open up a path of attack for the Japanese forces in the Shanghai Incident, a short war between Chinese and Japanese forces in 1932.

265: The Japanese word for pufferfish.

265: *Pettai* (better known as *menko*) is a card game very similar to the game pogs, played in Japan since the seventeenth century. Players place their cards on the ground and then try to flip them by throwing other cards at them.

268: In Japan, the bath is used for soaking after washing. Before entering the bathtub, the bather washes very thoroughly, usually sitting on a small stool used for that purpose and rinsing with buckets of water from the tap.

269: Mrs. Inokuma is clapping her hands in prayer in front of the household altar (the shelf above her head), where photos of ancestors are generally placed so that members of the household can pay their respects.

282: Matsue is the capital of Shimane prefecture, about thirty kilometres from Sakaiminato.

286: Also known as Koizumi Yakumo, Lafcadio Hearn (1850–1904) was a Greek-born writer who eventually became a Japanese citizen. He wrote extensively about Japan, in particular its myths and monsters, and spent a good deal of time in Matsue, the capital of Shimane prefecture, not far from Sakaiminato.

317: The *suiko* is often confused with the *kappa* due to their similar appearances, but the *suiko* is larger, fiercer, and much more likely to take a person's life.

347: The word for fiancée used here, *iinazuke*, generally denotes someone promised in marriage by the parents when both partners are still children.

374: The *shamisen* is a Japanese stringed instrument played with a large plectrum, traditionally played by geisha.

386: Because the bath in Japan is used to soak and relax after first washing outside the bathtub, the entire family uses the same bath water. Covering it with a lid when no one is in it helps to keep the water hot for the next user.

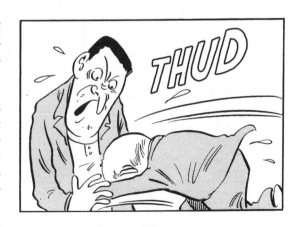

This book is presented in the traditional Japanese manner and is meant to be read from right to left. The cover at the opposite end is considered the front of the book.

To begin reading, please flip over and start at the other end, making your way "backward" through the book, starting at the top right corner and reading the panels (and the word balloons) from right to left. Continue on to the next row and repeat.

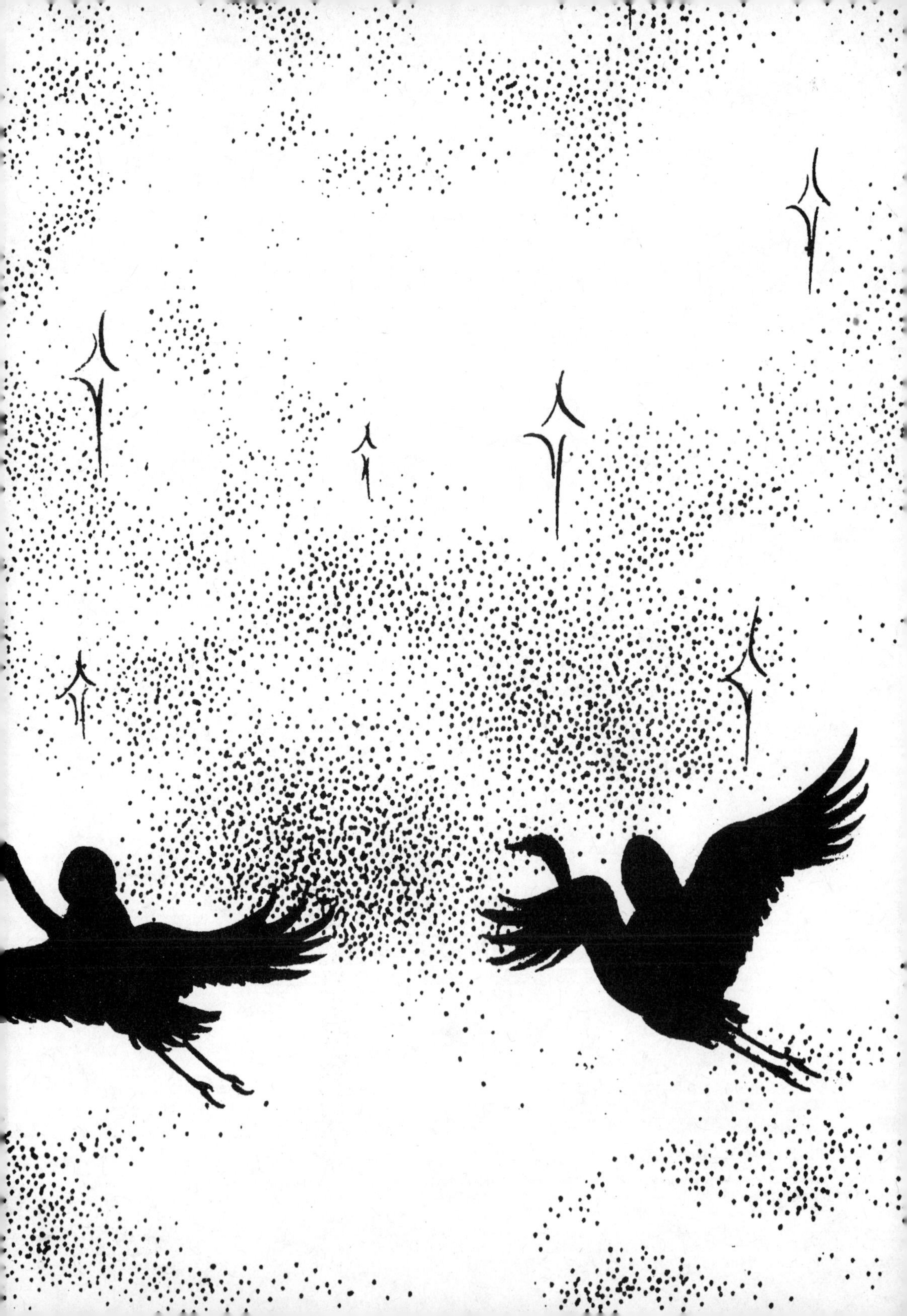